A contract is an agreement under which two parties make reciprocal commitments in terms of their behavior to coordinate. As this concept has become essential to economics in the last thirty years, three main theoretical frameworks have emerged: "incentive theory," "incomplete-contract theory," and "transaction-costs theory." These frameworks have enabled scholars to renew both the microeconomics of coordination (with implications for industrial organization, labor economics, law and economics, and organization design) and the macroeconomics of "market" (decentralized) economies and of the institutional framework. These developments have resulted in new analyses of firms' strategy and State intervention (regulation of public utilities, anti-trust, public procurement, institutional design, liberalization policies, etc.). Based on contributions by the leading scholars in the field, this book provides an overview of the past and recent developments in these analytical currents, presents their various aspects, and proposes expanding horizons for theoreticians and practitioners.

Eric Brousseau is Professor of Economics at the University of Paris X and member of the Institut Universitaire de France. He is the director of the department GIFT of FORUM (University of Paris X and Centre National de la Recherche Scientifique), and associate researcher at ATOM (University of Paris I). He coordinates a CNRS research consortium on Information Technologies and the Society, and organizes the European School on New Institutional Economics. He is member of the Boards of the International Society for New Institutional Economics and of the Schumpeter Society.

Jean-Michel Glachant is Head of the Department of Economics at the University of Paris XI. He is a member of the International Society for New Institutional Economics, the International Association for Energy Economics, and the Association Française de Science Economique, as well as head of the Electricity Reforms Group at the ADIS research centre.

The Economics of Contracts

Theories and applications

edited by

Eric Brousseau and Jean-Michel Glachant

CAMBRIDGE UNIVERSITY PRESS

PUBLISHED BY THE PRESS SYNDICATE OF THE UNIVERSITY OF CAMBRIDGE
The Pitt Building, Trumpington Street, Cambridge, United Kingdom

CAMBRIDGE UNIVERSITY PRESS
The Edinburgh Building, Cambridge CB2 2RU, UK
40 West 20th Street, New York, NY 10011-4211, USA
477 Williamstown Road, Port Melbourne, VIC 3207, Australia
Ruiz de Alarcón 13, 28014 Madrid, Spain
Dock House, The Waterfront, Cape Town 8001, South Africa

http://www.cambridge.org

First published 2002

Printed in the United Kingdom at the University Press, Cambridge

Typeface Plantin 10/12 pt   *System* LaTeX 2_ε [TB]

A catalogue record for this book is available from the British Library

Library of Congress Cataloguing in Publication data
The economics of contracts : theories and applications/edited by Eric Brousseau
and Jean-Michel Glachant.
    p.   cm.
Includes revised and translated versions of chapters which appeared in a special
issue of Revue d'économie industrielle (2002, 92)
Includes bibliographical references and index.
ISBN 0 521 81490 1–ISBN 0 521 89313 5 (pb.)
1. Contracts–Economic aspects. I. Brousseau, Eric. II. Glachant, Jean-Michel.
K840 .E28 2002
338–dc21   2002019300

ISBN 0 521 81490 1 hardback
ISBN 0 521 89313 5 paperback

Contents

List of figures   *page* viii
List of tables   ix
List of contributors   x
Acknowledgments   xvi

Part I Introduction

1 The economics of contracts and the renewal of economics   3
   ERIC BROUSSEAU AND JEAN-MICHEL GLACHANT
   Appendix: Canonical models of theories of contract   31
   M'HAND FARES

Part II Contracts, organizations, and institutions

2 The New Institutional Economics   45
   RONALD COASE

3 Contract and economic organization   49
   OLIVER E. WILLIAMSON

4 The role of incomplete contracts in self-enforcing
   relationships   59
   BENJAMIN KLEIN

5 Entrepreneurship, transaction-cost economics, and the
   design of contracts   72
   EIRIK G. FURUBOTN

Part III Law and economics

6 The contract as economic trade   99
   JACQUES GHESTIN

7 Contract theory and theories of contract regulation   116
   ALAN SCHWARTZ

8   Economic reasoning and the framing of contract law:
     sale of an asset of uncertain value   126
     VICTOR P. GOLDBERG

9   A transactions-cost approach to the analysis of property
     rights   140
     GARY D. LIBECAP

Part IV Theoretical developments: where do we stand?

10   Transaction costs and incentive theory   159
     ERIC MALIN AND DAVID MARTIMORT

11   Norms and the theory of the firm   180
     OLIVER HART

12   Allocating decision rights under liquidity constraints   193
     PHILIPPE AGHION AND PATRICK REY

13   Complexity and contract   213
     W. BENTLEY MACLEOD

14   Authority, as flexibility, is at the core of labor contracts   241
     OLIVIER FAVEREAU AND BERNARD WALLISER

15   Positive agency theory: place and contributions   251
     GÉRARD CHARREAUX

Part V Testing contract theories

16   Econometrics of contracts: an assessment of
     developments in the empirical literature on contracting   273
     SCOTT E. MASTEN AND STÉPHANE SAUSSIER

17   Experiments on moral hazard and incentives: reciprocity
     and surplus-sharing   293
     CLAUDIA KESER AND MARC WILLINGER

**Part VI Applied issues: contributions to industrial
organization**

18   Residual claims and self-enforcement as incentive
     mechanisms in franchise contracts: substitutes or
     complements?   315
     FRANCINE LAFONTAINE AND
     EMMANUEL RAYNAUD

19 The quasi-judicial role of large retailers: an efficiency
    hypothesis of their relation with suppliers   337
    BENITO ARRUÑADA

20 Interconnection agreements in telecommunications
    networks: from strategic behaviors to property rights   358
    GODEFROY DANG-NGUYEN AND THIERRY PÉNARD

21 Licensing in the chemical industry   373
    ASHISH ARORA AND ANDREA FOSFURI

**Part VII Policy issues: anti-trust and regulation
of public utilities**

22 Inter-company agreements and EC competition law   395
    MICHEL GLAIS

23 Incentive contracts in utility regulation   416
    MATTHEW BENNETT AND CATHERINE
    WADDAMS PRICE

24 Contractual choice and performance: the case of water
    supply in France   440
    CLAUDE MÉNARD AND STÉPHANE SAUSSIER

25 Institutional or structural: lessons from international
    electricity sector reforms   463
    GUY L.F. HOLBURN AND PABLO T. SPILLER

26 Electricity sector restructuring and competition: a
    transactions-cost perspective   503
    PAUL L. JOSKOW

Bibliography   531
Index of names   570
Subject index   579

Figures

1A.1	Comparative efficiency of the three governance structures	*page* 41
3.1	Incentive intensity and administrative controls	55
13.1	Time line for agency relationship	218
13.2	Time line for hold-up problem	220
13.3	Time line for authority relationship	222
13.4	Time line for *ex post* hold-up	224
14.1	Highway construction	243
14.2	Simon's model	247
15.1	The building blocks of PAT	254
21.1	Who was licensing chemical technologies, 1980s	380
21.2	Market for chemical technology as a function of investor's type	381
21.3	Share of SEFs licensing, by size of product market	382
21.4	Market share of SEFs and licensing, by chemical producers	387
21.5	Product differentiation and licensing	388
25.1	US retail electricity rates, 1990–1999	471
25.2	Unit spot price, California wholesale market, January 1999–November 2000	484
25.3	Unit spot price, El Salvador wholesale market, January 1998–May 2000	490
26.1	Competitive wholesale and retail markets	513

Tables

1.1	Schematic representation of the different approaches	*page*	15
1A.1	Efficiency under different property-rights allocations		37
5.1	A comparison of models		78
13.1	Cost of a complete state-contingent contract		226
13.2	Contract payoffs		233
15.1	PAT versus TCT: a revised comparative assessment		266
17.1	Parameters of the experiment by Keser and Willinger (2000)		301
17.2	Activity costs in the experiment by Keser and Willinger (2001)		303
19.1	Average profit margin as a function of credit and payment periods in EU countries		343
19.2	Correlation coefficients between country averages of credit and payment periods and causes of late payment in domestic transactions		348
19.3	Average payment periods, average delays, and economic developments		348
21.1	Licensing strategies, selected chemical producers		385
24.1	Permanent average population, by type of arrangement		443
24.2	Distribution of contractual arrangements, by regional agencies		444
24.3	Variables and their meaning		452
24.4	Determinants of contractual choice		454
24.5	Modes of organization and performance		458
25.1	Organizational and ownership structure of competitive wholesale electricity markets		474

Contributors

PHILIPPE AGHION is Professor of Economics at Harvard University, His main fields of interest are the theory of contracts and the theory of growth. Together, both theories allow a better understanding of the links between technical change and institutional evolutions. His most recent research focuses on the relationship between competition and growth, and he is currently starting a project on contracts and growth.

ASHISH ARORA is Associate Professor of Economics at Heinz School, and Research Director at the Carnegie Mellon Software Center, both at Carnegie Mellon University. Arora's research focuses on the economics of technological change, intellectual property rights, and technology licensing. He has published extensively on the growth and development of biotechnology and the chemical industry. His most recent book is *Markets for Technology* (MIT Press).

BENITO ARRUÑADA is Professor of Business Organization at Universitat Pompeu Fabra, Barcelona, Spain. In addition to retailing, his research deals with contractual practices in the franchising, auditing, healthcare, public administration, construction, trucking, fishing, and conveyancing industries, as well as the impact of different legal rules, such as those on payment delays, multidisciplinary professional firms, corporate governance, and land registration.

MATTHEW BENNETT received his PhD from the department of economics at the University of Warwick. His dissertation centered around competition and regulation policy. He is currently working in the University of Toulouse under a Marie Curie training grant, on the interaction of license auctions and optimal regulatory contracts.

ERIC BROUSSEAU is Professor of Economics at the University of Paris X. He works with two research centers: FORUM (University of Paris X), where he is the director of the department of industrial organization, and ATOM at the University of Paris (Panthéon-Sorbonne). His area of interest is the economics of coordination, mainly contractual and institutional economics. His applied fields of research include the economics of intellectual property rights and the economics of the digital economy.

GÉRARD CHARREAUX is Professor in Management Science at the Université de Bourgogne. He is presently coordinator of the research program in finance, governance, and organizational architecture for the Laboratoire d'Analyse et de Techniques Economiques (Latec-Cnrs) and editor of the review *Finance Contrôle Strategie*. His main fields of research are corporate governance and corporate finance.

RONALD COASE is Clifton R. Musser Professor Emeritus of Economics at the University of Chicago Law School. He was editor of the *Journal of Law and Economics* 1964–82. In 1991, he was awarded the Alfred Nobel Memorial Prize in Economic Sciences.

GODEFROY DANG-NGUYEN is Professor and Head of the Economics and Human Sciences Department, ENST Bretagne. He is currently doing research on the impact of information technology on corporations, institutions, and public policy. He is invited Professor at the College of Europe in Bruges.

M'HAND FARES is a research fellow at INRA, ESR-Montpellier (UMR MOISA) and member of the research center ATOM-GENI (University of Paris I). His major fields of interest are contracting and organization, law and economics, and organization of the agro-food industry.

OLIVIER FAVEREAU is Professor of Economics at the University of Paris X. He is also the head of FORUM, a research unit which develops an institutionalist program of research, in four fields: money and macroeconomics, industrial economics, employment systems, and transition and development studies. His own work deals with conventions and institutions on the labor market.

ANDREA FOSFURI is Assistant Professor at the Business Department of the University Carlos III, Madrid, and research affiliate at CEPR, London. He has published in several leading economics and management journals, and co-authored with Ashish Arora and Alfonso Gambardella the book *Markets for Technology: Economics of Innovation and Corporate Strategy* (MIT Press).

EIRIK G. FURUBOTN is Research Fellow at the Private Enterprise Research Center, Texas A&M University, College Station, Texas, USA. He is also Honorary Professor of Economics at the University of Saarland, Saarbrucken, Germany, and member of the Advisory Board of the *Journal of Institutional and Theoretical Economics*.

JACQUES GHESTIN is Professor Emeritus of Law at the University de Paris I (Panthéon-Sorbonne). He is the main author of several treatises dedicated to civil law and contractual law. He is also a lawyer, and practices international contracting and arbitration.

JEAN-MICHEL GLACHANT is Professor of Economics at the University of Paris Sud. He was formerly the director of the research center ATOM at the University of Paris Panthéon-Sorbonne, and currently heads the economics department of the research center ADIS at the University of Paris XI. He is also member of the Economic Advisory Council of the French electricity regulation commission (CRE).

MICHEL GLAIS is a Professor of Economics at the University of Rennes. He specializes in anti-trust and competition law, business strategy, and corporate finance and assessment. He lectures for several Universities in Europe and America: Herriot-Wyatt (Edinburgh); Boston College; University of New Hampshire; La Sapienza (Roma); Baltic Business School (Sweden). He is also a chartered expert at Court, and involved in private consultancy for several major corporations.

VICTOR P. GOLDBERG is the Thomas Macioce Professor of Law and the Co-Director of the Center for Law & Economic Studies at Columbia University. His current research focus is an application of economic reasoning to contract law cases and doctrine.

OLIVER HART is the Andrew E. Furer Professor of Economics at Harvard University, and a Research Associate of the National Bureau of Economic Research (NBER). He is also Centennial Visiting Professor at the London School of Economics. He works on the theory of the firm and financial contracting.

GUY L.F. HOLBURN is an Assistant Professor at the University of Western Ontario, Richard Ivey School of Business. Prior to joining Ivey, he completed his MA in Economics and PhD at the University of California, Berkeley. His research focuses on utility and regulation issues, particularly as applied to the electricity industry. He has also worked as a consultant for Bain and Co. and for the California Public Utilities Commission.

PAUL L. JOSKOW is the Elizabeth and James Killian Professor of Economics and Management at the Massachusetts Institute of Technology (MIT), Director of the MIT Center for Energy and Environmental Policy Research, and a Research Associate of the National Bureau of Economic Research.

CLAUDIA KESER is research staff member at the IBM T. J. Watson Research Center, Yorktown Heights, New York and associated fellow of the Centre Interuniversitaire de Recherche en Analyse des Organisations (CIRANO), Montreal.

BENJAMIN KLEIN is Professor of Economics at UCLA and President of Economic Analysis at LLC, an economic consulting firm based in Los Angeles. His research interests focus on the law and economics of contractual arrangements and anti-trust policy, including vertical distribution arrangements, vertical integration, and competitive marketing policies.

FRANCINE LAFONTAINE is Professor of Business Economics and Public Policy at the University of Michigan Business School. She is also a Faculty Research Fellow at the National Bureau of Economic Research (NBER). Her research focuses on incentives issues and contracting practices, with special emphasis on the franchise and trucking industries.

GARY D. LIBECAP is Anheuser Busch Professor and Professor of Economics and Law at the University of Arizona in Tucson. He also is Director of the Karl Eller Center and Research Associate in the National Bureau of Economic Research. His research interests focus on the issues of property rights, economic behavior, and resource use.

W. BENTLEY MACLEOD is Professor of Economics and Law at the University of Southern California, a Director of the Center for Law, Economics and Organization, and is currently visiting Professor of Economics and Law at the California Institute of Technology. His recent research concerns the theoretical and empirical implications of bounded rationality for contract form.

ERIC MALIN is Professor of Economics at the University of La Réunion. He is member of GREMAQ (Toulouse) and CERESUR (La Réunion). His main research interests include network economics, price discrimination, and health economics.

DAVID MARTIMORT is Professor at the University of Toulouse. He is also member of the Institut d'Economie Industrielle (IDEI) in Toulouse and CEPR, London. His work concerns collusion in organizations and mechanism design in multiprincipals' environment. He has authored a textbook with Jean-Jacques Laffont on incentives, *The Theory of Incentives: The Principal–Agent Model*. He has been invited to teach contract theory at Harvard, Pompeu Fabra, and Université de Montreal.

SCOTT E. MASTEN is Professor of Business Economics and Public Policy at the University of Michigan Business School. His research interests include contracting practices, contract law, and their relation to economic organization.

CLAUDE MÉNARD is Full Professor of Economics at the University of Paris Panthéon-Sorbonne and director of the Center for Analytical Theory of Organizations and Markets (ATOM). He is President (2001–02) of the International Society for New Institutional Economics (ISNIE). His fields of interest are mainly the economics of organization and the economics of regulation/deregulation.

THIERRY PÉNARD is Professor of Economics at the University of Rennes I and affiliated to CREREG. His fields of specialization include the economics of networks, game theory, and anti-trust policy. His current research focuses on the economics of telecommunications and the Internet.

EMMANUEL RAYNAUD is a researcher at INRA-SADAPT (National Institute of Agronomical Research) and a member of the Center for Analytical Theory of Organizations and Markets (ATOM) (University of Paris Panthéon-Sorbonne). His field of specialization includes the economics of contracts and organization. His current research focuses on product quality and vertical coordination in European agro-food industries and on franchising (design of contracts and dual distribution in franchise chains).

PATRICK REY is Professor of Economics at the University of Toulouse and Research Director at the Institut d'Economie Industrielle (IDEI). He has also been Associate Professor at the Ecole Polytechnique since 1991. His fields of interest cover industrial organization, public economics, competition law and policy, regulation of natural monopolies, corporate finance, banking and financial intermediation, contract theory, and theory of the firm and of organizations.

STÉPHANE SAUSSIER is Professor of Economics at the University of Nancy II. He is also Deputy Director of the Center for Analytical Theory of Organizations and Markets (ATOM) (University of Paris Panthéon-Sorbonne). Specializing in the economics of organizations and contracts, he has been working on several fields of application such as technology licensing agreements, water supply, coal contracts, and franchise contracts, focusing on contractual choices and make-or-buy decision.

ALAN SCHWARTZ is Sterling Professor of Law and Professor of Management, Yale University. He has been Editor of the *Journal of*

Law, Economics and Organization, President of the American Law and Economics Association, and Chair of the Section on Contracts of the Association of American Law Schools. He currently is Director of the Yale Law School Center for the Study of Corporate Law and serves on the boards of two publicly traded companies.

PABLO T. SPILLER is the Joe Shoong Professor of International Business and Public Policy, and chairs the Business and Public Policy Group, at the Haas School of Business of the University of California, Berkeley. Prior to joining Berkeley, he was on the faculties of the University of Pennsylvania, the University of Illinois, and the Hoover Institution at Stanford University. He has published more than eighty articles and five books, and has received numerous awards from the National Science Foundation, the Olin Foundation, the Bradley Foundation, the Ameritech Foundation, and the National Center for Supercomputer Applications.

CATHERINE WADDAMS PRICE is Professor of Regulation and Director of the Centre for Competition and Regulation, University of East Anglia, Norwich, United Kingdom. Her main research interests are in economic regulation of markets, the introduction of competition, and the distributional consequences. She formerly acted as an economic expert for the UK energy regulator, and is now a member of the UK Competition Commission.

BERNARD WALLISER is Professor of Economics at Ecole Nationale des Ponts et Chaussées and Director of Studies at the Ecole des Hautes Etudes en Sciences Sociales (Paris). Involved in economic methodology, he is now leading a program in "Cognitive Economics," concerned with the study of agents' beliefs, reasoning methods, and learning processes when these agents are involved in social networks.

OLIVER E. WILLIAMSON is the Edgar F. Kaiser Professor of Business, Professor of Economics, and Professor of Law at the University of California, Berkeley. He is the founding co-editor of the *Journal of Law, Economics and Organization* and a member of the National Academy of Science.

MARC WILLINGER is Professor of Economics at the University Louis Pasteur (Strasbourg, France). His current research activities contribute to the development of experimental economics, with applications to contract design, efficiency of environmental policy instruments, decision-making under uncertainty, and the dynamics of cooperation.

Acknowledgments

This book draws partially from a special issue of the *Revue d'Economie Industrielle* entitled "The Economics of Contracts in Prospect and Retrospect," (92, 2000) in which Eric Brousseau and Jean-Michel Glachant edited earlier versions of some of the chapters of that book.

The publishers and editors would like to thank Les Editions Techniques et Economiques for permission to publish revised or translated versions of the chapters 1–4, 6–8, 10, 13–22, and 24, which appeared in the special issue of *Revue d'Economie Industrielle* (2000, 92).

The editors are also grateful to the board of the *Revue d'Economie Industrielle*, and especially to its Editor in Chief Jacques de Bandt for having facilitated the publication of these chapters in that book.

The editors are also indebted to Marie-Line Priot (FORUM, University of Paris X) for secretarial support and to Paul Klassen for translation.

Part I

Introduction

1 The economics of contracts and the renewal of economics

Eric Brousseau and Jean-Michel Glachant

1 Introduction

To an economist, a contract is an agreement under which two parties make reciprocal commitments in terms of their behavior – a *bilateral coordination arrangement*. Of course, this formulation touches on the legal concept of the contract (a meeting of minds creating effects in law), but also transcends it. Over the course of the past thirty years, the "contract" has become a central notion in economic analysis (section 2), giving rise to three principal fields of study: "incentives," "incomplete contracts," and "transaction costs" (section 3). This opened the door to a revitalization of our understanding of the operation of market economies ... and of the practitioner's "toolbox" (section 4).

The goal of this chapter is to provide an overview of recent developments in these analytical currents, to present their various aspects (section 5), and to propose expanding horizons (section 6). The potential of these approaches, which have fundamentally impacted on many areas of economic analysis in recent decades, is far from exhausted. This is evinced by the contributions in this book, which draw on a variety of methodological camps and disciplines.

2 The central role of the notion of the contract in economic analysis

Even though the notion of the contract has long been central to our understanding of the operation of decentralized social systems, especially in the tradition of the *philosophie des lumières*, only recently have economists begun to render it justice. Following in the footsteps of Smith and Walras, they long based their analyses of the functioning of decentralized economies on the notions of market and price system. This application of Walrasian analysis, in which supply meets demand around a posted price, does not satisfactorily account for the characteristics of a decentralized economy (cf. Ronald Coase's chapter 2 in

3

this volume). First, and paradoxically for a model of economic analysis, it does not account for the costs of operating the market. Next, it assumes the pre-existence of collective coordination (implicitly institutional) – the properties of the traded merchandise are fixed in advance, all market actors effectively participate in the tâtonnement process, etc. – in contradiction with the idea that the market is truly decentralized. Finally, this model is unrealistic because, in practice, agents exchange goods and services outside of equilibrium and in a bilateral context, i.e. without knowledge of the levels and prices at which other agents are trading, and without knowledge of whether these prices clear the market.

Contract economics was born in the 1970s from a twofold movement of dissatisfaction *vis-à-vis* Walrasian market theory:

- On a *theoretical* level, new analytical tools were sought to explain how economic agents determine the properties, quantities, and prices of the resources they trade in face-to-face encounters. If these agents are subject to transaction costs, if they can benefit from informational advantages, or if there are situations in which irreversible investments must be made, then it is reasonable to expect that one will not see the same goods traded at the same price and under the same rules as on a Walrasian market. Price theory and, by extension, the analysis of the formation of economic aggregates (prices, traded quantities and qualities, etc.), were fundamentally affected by the work of Akerlof (1970), Arrow (1971), and Stiglitz (1977), among others.

- On an *empirical* level, problems associated with the regulation of competition drove a renewal of economic thinking. The analysis of certain types of inter-firm contracts, such as selective distributorship agreements, long-term cooperation agreements, etc., was revamped. Previously considered anti-competitive, the beneficial welfare effects of these arrangements had been ignored. The devices available to public authorities for creating incentives and controlling producers of services of public interest were also subjected to a reexamination. Economic theory had not considered the possibility that either party could appropriate the rent from monopolistic operation of such services. Demsetz and Williamson, Baron and Laffont, to name only a few, renewed the approach to these issues of "regulation."

This twofold origin explains the remarkable development of contract theory and its key contribution to a fundamental redesign of all areas of economic analysis, from the study of microeconomic interactions to that of macroeconomic aggregates (such as the labor market), passing on the way the various domains of applied economics, finance, international trade, industrial organization, etc.

This success is essentially attributable to the analytical power of the notion of contract. On the one hand, the idea of contract focuses attention on elementary social structures, those that regulate coordination at a bilateral level. On the other hand, despite its simplicity as a concept, the contract allows us to examine a number of key issues. We can point to at least four:

- First, the analysis of contracts allows us to reexamine the exact nature of *difficulties associated with economic coordination*, while deepening our understanding of the functioning and the basis of coordination mechanisms.
- Second, this approach illuminates the details of *various provisions for coordination*: routines, incentives, the authority principle, means of coercion, conflict resolution, etc.
- Third, analysis of the origins of contracts sheds light on how agents *conceptualize the rules and decision-making structures* that frame their behavior.
- Finally, studying the *evolution of contractual mechanisms* helps us understand changes in the structures that frame economic activity.

The contractual approach thus allows us to analyze coordination mechanisms within a simplified but rigorous framework. It not only illuminates the properties of contracts, but also those of other harmonization instruments, such as markets, organizations, and institutions (cf. Oliver Williamson's chapter 3 in this volume). These collective arrangements reveal mechanisms comparable to those typical of contracts (participation incentives, allocation of decision rights, provisions to give credibility to commitments, etc.).

It should be noted that the analysis of contracts must also be clear on the limits of this approach to economic activity. Specifically, this is true for organizations and institutions that are not reducible to the notion of the contract. On the one hand, organizations and institutions have a fundamentally collective character: an individual will join them without negotiating each rule governing the relations between members. Moreover, the evolution of this relational framework cannot be controlled by any individual acting alone. On the other hand, the properties of organizations' and institutions' collective arrangements do not derive uniquely from the content of the bilateral relationships linking each of their elements, but also from the communal articulation of these arrangements – in other words, the topology of the interaction networks.

The contractual approach is also relevant because of the exchanges it makes possible with other disciplines. These include law, of course, but also management, sociology, anthropology, political and administrative sciences, and philosophy. The notion of the contract is simultaneously broader in scope and more general than the notion of the market. This has allowed the economic analysis of the contract to export some of its results, notably the difficulty of creating perfect incentive mechanisms, the incentive–insurance dilemma, or the impossibility, under many conditions, of drafting complete contracts (cf. Alt and Shepsle 1990). But the contractual approach has also provided a gateway for imports that have proven indispensable to advances in economic analysis (cf. section 6). Other intellectual and methodological traditions have allowed us to extend the economics of contractual coordination. Legal analysis, for example, specifies the role of various mechanisms that ultimately guarantee the performance of contracts and brings to light their "embedding" into the general rules that give them meaning and complete them. Management sciences emphasize that economic agents concretely act on the complementary relationship between contracts and imperfect incentive provisions to resolve coordination problems (e.g. Koenig 1999).

3   Three principal currents

3.1   Origins

While we can speak of "contract economics" in general, it is worthwhile to distinguish between several branches of contract theory, into which various analytical traditions have converged that were themselves renewed in the process. While these currents all sprang from dissatisfaction with the standard analytical model of the market, different methodologies gave rise to them.

One of the new models derives from the lineage of the standard model. Arrow's work on the functioning of insurance markets (Arrow 1971), and that of Akerlof (1970) on the market for used automobiles, led to the theory of incomplete information. Challenging the assumption that all actors on a market have access to symmetrical, or identical, information, the authors drew attention to the consequences of one individual having an informational advantage. They emphasized the importance of implementing disclosure mechanisms to limit the ability of the "informed" to take advantage of the "under-informed." This line of research dates from the 1960s.

As early as the 1930s, however, other foundations of modern contract analysis were laid. Coase was the first to enunciate the idea that the existence of coordination costs on the market justifies resorting to various coordination mechanisms in a decentralized economy, especially hierarchical coordination within firms (cf. Coase 1937, 1988). Some forty years later this analysis was taken up and expanded by Williamson.

But Coase was not the only influence on Williamson. The latter's early work in the 1960s represented the Carnegie behaviorist school, along with Cyert and March (Cyert and March 1963). Here we find the lineage of theories of the firm whose formulation began in the 1930s, but whose full development occurred primarily in the 1950s. Managerial and behaviorist approaches to the firm (from Berle and Means 1932 to Simon 1947, passing over Hall and Hitch 1939), as well as the controversies surrounding their development (cf. Machlup 1967), permitted considerable advances in the understanding of non-price coordination. Starting in the 1970s, many of these advances were revisited by economists interested in the properties of contractual, organizational, and institutional means of coordination.

Another "school" had a profound influence on contemporary contract theory: property rights (Alchian 1961, Demsetz 1967, Furubotn and Pejovich 1974). In a certain sense, Coase also laid the foundations for this approach with his analysis of the problem of externalities (Coase 1960), which brought to light the implications of property-rights definitions for the issue of efficiency. This contribution then merged with further developments from the Chicago school. Comparative analysis of alternate property-rights systems revealed that the allocation of residual rights (the right to determine the use of resources and to appropriate the ensuing income) may, or may not, motivate an efficient use of resources. This approach yielded essential elements of theories of the firm and of contracts (Alchian and Demsetz 1972, Klein, Crawford and Alchian 1978). Under certain types of relational arrangements, only a reallocation of property rights can overcome economic agents' propensity to be opportunistic. This school also focused economists' attention on the specific consequences of the manipulation of incentive systems.

Finally, it would be impossible to ignore the contributions of other disciplines. Economic analysis of the law has concentrated on certain aspects of contractual relationships. It is also noteworthy that one of the primary concepts in the economic analysis of contracts, the notion of the "hybrid form" proposed by Williamson (1985), drew directly on Macneil's (1974) socio-legal analysis. On another level, economic views of non-market coordination were profoundly influenced by developments in management sciences, by sociology and psycho-sociology, by administrative sciences, and by the history of organizations, as is evinced by the frequency of references to Barnard, Simon, and Chandler (Barnard 1938, Simon 1947, Chandler 1962). As to the economics of institutions, which develops an analysis more concerned with the role of the institutional environment on the design and the performance of contracts, it traces its roots to history, to political science, and to ethnology (cf. Eggertsson 1990, North 1990).

Arising from these precursors, three schools dominate the field of contract economics today: incentive theory (IT), incomplete-contract theory (ICT), and transaction-costs theory (TCT). These are distinguished by differences in their underlying assumptions, leading them to emphasize different problems. The standard models of these three theories are described in the appendix to this chapter by M'hand Fares.

3.2   *Incentive theory*

Incentive theory (IT) draws on several of the traditional hypotheses of Walrasian economic theory. Notably, it assumes that economic agents are endowed with substantial, or Savage, rationality (Savage 1954), that they possess complete information concerning the structure of the issues they confront along with unlimited computational abilities, and that they have a complete and ordered preference set.

The information available to these agents is "complete" in the sense that, even though they cannot precisely anticipate a future that remains stochastic, they do know the structure of all the problems that may occur. What they cannot know, where applicable, is what issues will in fact arise, nor in what sequence. Thus, they envision the future on the basis of probabilities (objective or subjective). This links to the notion of risk, as described by Knight (1921) (even though Knight did not account for subjective probabilities). Given this theoretical framework, agents imagine the most efficient solutions as functions of the different possible states of nature and compute their expected values. These calculations are possible since agents are endowed with unlimited abilities in this area. In other words: calculating costs them nothing in terms of time or resources. Finally, since agents' preference functions are complete and stable over time, they effectively choose optimal solutions.

The assumption that diverges from the Walrasian universe is that the two contracting parties do not have access to the same information on certain variables. This is an evolution toward a more realistic conception. In a decentralized economy, there is no reason why one party should know, *ex ante*, the private information of the other (such as her preferences, the quality of her resources, her willingness to pay, or her reservation price). Depending on whether the variable on which there is asymmetric information is exogenous – i.e. not subject to manipulation during the exchange by the party possessing it – or endogenous – i.e. vulnerable to such manipulation – we speak of models of adverse selection or moral hazard, respectively. Adverse selection, for example, is exemplified by a potential employer's uncertainty concerning a job seeker's level of competence, while moral hazard refers to uncertainty about the level of effort the latter will supply.

Incentive theory (IT) starts from a canonical situation in which an under-informed party – called the "principal" – puts into place an incentive scheme to induce the informed party – the "agent" – to either disclose information (adverse-selection model) or to adopt behavior compatible with the interests of the principal (moral-hazard model). The incentive scheme consists of remuneration being conditional on signals that result from the agent's behavior (such as the choice of an option from a list of propositions considered a "menu" of contracts or as the visible result of the effort supplied when the effort itself is not observable).

The existence of such an incentive scheme relies on two key assumptions:

- While the principal is under-informed, not knowing the true value of the hidden variable, she does know both the *probability distribution* of this variable and the agent's *preference structure*. The principal can thus put herself "in the place" of the agent to anticipate the latter's reactions to the set of conceivable remuneration schemes, and then select the one she prefers from those acceptable to the agent.
- There is an *institutional framework*, hidden but competent and benevolent, which ensures that the principal respects her commitments. Thus, any proposition made by the principal is credible to the agent. Moreover, the proposed remuneration scheme is based upon "verifiable" information, i.e. observable by a third party.

The solution to adverse selection problems relies on the design of a "menu of contracts" that will induce self-revelation by the agent of her private information. The principal designs a set of optional contracts – i.e. a set of payment formulae linked to various counterparts by the agent. While he does not know the agent's private information, he knows the set of possible values it may take. Since he also knows her preferences, she is able to design a contract that maximizes the agent's utility for each possible value of that private information. When the agent faces the resulting set of possible options, she spontaneously chooses the contract that maximizes her utility, allowing the principal to infer private information. Of course, the principal's interest is to obtain this revelation in exchange for the lowest possible payment.

The canonical moral-hazard problem occurs when one relevant dimension of the agent's input is not observable by the principal – one dimension is costly to the agent, and that affects the principal's welfare. For instance, an employer cares about an employee's productivity. However, he cannot deduce the efforts she actually supplied from the observed productivity, because the productivity of a single agent depends on many other variables that are not under her control and not observable to the principal (coworkers' efforts, the productivity of capital, randomness in the production process, etc.). To incite the agent, the apparent optimal remuneration mechanism would be to linearly index her wage on her observed productivity. However, if the agent is risk averse, she will not accept such a payment scheme, as it could provide her with negative or very low remuneration, even when the poor outcome would not be attributable to her own level of effort. Because of risk aversion, the agent would prefer to be paid a fixed wage. However, in that case she would not be motivated to provide her best effort. To solve this "incentive versus insurance" dilemma, the optimal payment scheme combines a fixed base pay and a variable bonus indexed on the observed result; yielding a non-linear payment scheme.

Into this analytical framework, which was formulated during the first half of the 1980s, many refinements were subsequently incorporated that considerably extended its reach (cf., for example, Salanié 1997). First, the theories of adverse selection and moral hazard were combined. Subsequent extensions included teaming one principal with several agents, letting informational asymmetry apply to several variables, repeating interactions over time, etc. Chapter 10 in this volume by Eric Malin and David Martimort provides a good overview of the analytical strength of this theoretical framework.

3.3   Incomplete contract theory

Incomplete contract theory (ICT) is the most recent. Its initial purpose was to model some of Williamson's propositions about vertical integration (Grossman and Hart 1986), but subsequent developments led it in different directions. ICT thus came to examine the impacts of the institutional framework on contract design, though its roots lay in the study of the effects of property-rights allocations on the distribution of the residual surplus between agents and on their incentives to invest.

In terms of its assumptions, ICT is also close to "standard" neoclassical theory. In particular, agents are deemed to possess Savage rationality. However, it is distinguished from both Walrasian theory and incentive theory by a key hypothesis. ICT postulates that complete contracting of agents' future actions is impossible when no third party can "verify," *ex post*, the real value of some of the variables central to the interaction between the agents. Here the institutional framework is no longer implicit. On the contrary, the issue here is that the "judge," symbolizing the authority that ultimately ensures the performance of the contract, is incapable of observing or evaluating some relevant variables – such as the level of effort or of some investments. It follows that contracting on unverifiable variables is useless, and other means must be found to ensure efficient coordination.

To focus on the issues arising from non-verifiability (failure of the institutional framework), ICT assumes that there is no asymmetry in the parties' information. Both observe all the available information during each period of trade, while the "judge" cannot verify some of it, which is therefore non-contractible. Uncertainty arises because each agent has to act on the non-contractible variable in the absence of complete information on the outcome of his behavior since he cannot anticipate with certainty what the other will do. Formally, this is represented by contracting over two periods. During the first period the agents realize non-verifiable investments. The second period is devoted to trade, the characteristics of which, in terms of price and quantity, are the only verifiable variables. This generates a dilemma: since it is possible to contract only on verifiable variables, agents can commit only on the characteristics of their trade in the second period. Now, the level of investment realized by the parties in the first period depends upon this contracted level of trade. However, once the actual level of the investments is known by the end of the first period, along with the state of nature in which the trade will take place, the *ex ante* contracted level of trade is no longer optimal. *Ex post*, it would thus be optimal to renegotiate the amount of the trade. But, if the agents anticipate this renegotiation, they will no longer have an incentive to efficiently invest *ex ante* (since the contracted amount of trade is no longer credible).

The solution to this coordination dilemma consists of signing a commitment constraining the scope of the *ex post* negotiations in order to provide an incentive to each party to invest optimally *ex ante*. This arrangement assigns a unilateral decision right to one of the parties to determine the effective level of trade *ex post*, while a default option protects the interests of the second party by establishing a minimal level of trade. Two families of models have been created deriving from this framework. The first is represented by the work of Hart and Moore (1988). An efficient level of investment is not obtained from the beneficiary of the default option, since this option is insufficiently sophisticated to motivate him to invest at the optimal level under all conditions. The *ex ante* inefficiency follows from the fact that the default option is contingent on the state of nature that materializes. The second family is an extension to the work of Aghion, Dewatripont and Rey (1994), who postulate that the default option may provide an incentive for the beneficiary to invest optimally. They assume that the judge will be capable of verifying, and of rendering enforceable, default options of great complexity and that he will oppose any renegotiation of these provisions.

ICT thus establishes a direct link between the ability of judicial institutions to observe or evaluate the nature of implementable contracts and their efficiency. When some variables are unobservable, contracts are incomplete. Thus, the capabilities of judicial institutions determine the level of sophistication of the default clause, which motivates efficient behavior on behalf of the party that does not benefit from renegotiation rights (i.e. the right to decide and to the residual surplus).

Though ICT has been the subject of a vast literature it remains less well developed than IT. This is partly attributable to the dispute between its proponents (especially Oliver Hart) and those of IT (especially Jean Tirole) and TCT. Tirole (1999) points out a logical inconsistency between the assumption of agents' perfect rationality and their inability to implement a revelation mechanism, *ex ante*, that will force them to reveal to the judge the true level of their investments, *ex post* (thus *de facto* eliminating non-verifiability). Hart, and other advocates of ICT, reject this criticism. For such a revelation mechanism to work, it should not be renegotiable *ex post*. They maintain further that if it were, this would be tantamount to imputing verification abilities to the judge that he generally lacks. As to transactions-costs economists, they acknowledge the usefulness of the analytical framework suggested by IT, but emphasize that it does not draw all the conclusions implied by the rationality constraints imputed to the judge. If the judge's rationality is irremediably bounded, as ICT *de facto* assumes in postulating that he is unable to verify certain variables, why assume that the contracting parties' rationality escapes similar limitations? It would be more consistent to resort to a hypothesis of bounded rationality for all the actors – the parties and the judge – as is the case in the TCT (Brousseau and Fares 2000).

Chapter 11 by Oliver Hart in this volume nicely points out how ICT considerably enriches the economic analysis of the firm and provides stimulating insights into law and economics since it is able to account for the impact of the institutional framework upon the economics contractual practices. Chapter 12 in this volume by Philippe Aghion and Patrick Rey focuses on the allocation of control rights under various circumstances among parties facing wealth constraints. It points out how participation constraints interact with efficiency considerations in designing optimal incomplete contracts.

3.4   *The new institutional transaction costs theory*

TCT is based on the assumption of non-Savage rationality. This rationality is "bounded" in the sense of Simon (1947, 1976). This means that agents have limited abilities to calculate, but also that they operate in a universe in which they do not know, *a priori*, the structure of the set of problems that may arise. These agents are confronted with "radical" uncertainty (in the sense of Knight 1921 or Shackle 1955), rendering them unable to compose complete contracts.

Contractual incompleteness in TCT can be considered "strong," since it has another source: institutional failure (Williamson 1985, 1996). As is the case in ICT, institutions that are ultimately responsible for ensuring the performance of contracts cannot enforce those clauses that pertain to unverifiable variables. Moreover, judges are also prisoners of their bounded rationality. They may take a long time before pronouncing judgment, refuse to rule, make mistakes, etc. Thus, the performance of contracts is not guaranteed by external mechanisms.

Consequently, the bounded rationality of agents and judges combine to explain the acceptance of contracts that remain incomplete. To ensure coordination despite the incompleteness of their contracts, agents must, on the one hand, make provision for procedures to dictate the actions of each, *ex post*, and, on the other hand, implement means to ensure the *ex post* performance of their commitments. In this case the contract allocates decision rights to: (a) one, or (b) both of the parties (negotiation procedures), or (c) to a third party (distinct from the judge). It also puts into place a series of supervisory and coercion mechanisms to ensure that the parties respect their mutual commitments. The contract thus creates a "private order," by virtue of which the parties will be able to ensure each other's cooperation *ex post*.

TCT facilitates analysis of how economic agents combine commitment constraints – designed to guarantee the realization of specific investments – with flexibility constraints – needed because of the impossibility of perfectly foreseeing the coordination modes that would be optimal *ex post*. Olivier Favereau and Bernard Walliser in chapter 14 in this volume draw on an analysis formulated in terms of option values to propose an innovative rereading of the "commitment–flexibility" dilemma originally presented by Simon (1951). TCT, however, assumes a broader approach, in that it simultaneously deals with the efficiency of adjustments *ex post* and constraints on the performance of contracts:

- TCT insists on safeguards to protect each party from the potential for opportunistic behavior on behalf of the other and to provide incentives to commit to the transaction. In this regard, it emphasizes the *manipulation of the costs of breaking the agreement* – using security deposits ("hostages") or irreversible investments – and the *length of the commitment*.
- The longer this duration, the more difficult it becomes to predict efficient future adjustments. It thus becomes necessary to *redefine the parties' obligations* over the course of the performance of the contract. We here observe a paradoxical aspect to contractual incompleteness with

respect to the credibility of the commitment: since the parties know that revisions are possible in the future, they are less inclined to violate their commitments when the contract does not provide them with an efficient (or satisfactory) outcome.

- Finally, TCT insists on *private conflict resolution mechanisms*. Since commitments are open-ended and specific, conflict resolution cannot be efficiently ensured by outside authorities. Under these conditions, the contracting parties must agree beforehand on bilateral procedures for resolving disagreements.

However, owing to the bounded rationality of the agents who design and implement them, all these bilateral coordination devices remain imperfect. They are also costly to devise and manage, so the contracting parties will, as much as possible, fall back on collective provisions emanating from the institutional framework. This latter plays two essential roles:

- First, it provides a *basic set of coordination rules*, freeing agents from the need to invent, or reinvent, all of them within their contractual relationships. For example, external technical standards eliminate the need to compose a voluminous specification manual, while "common knowledge" specific to a profession dispenses with the requirement to formally describe the criteria defining certain characteristics, or behavior, as "standard" or "fair."
- Second, the institutional framework lends credibility to *sanctions guaranteeing the performance of contractual obligations*. Reputation, the self-regulating systems of some professions, and public authorities' power to regulate and coerce, all provide further support for the contracting parties.

This has important consequences for the analysis of contracts. On the one hand, the nature of implementable contractual arrangements is highly dependent on the real characteristics of the institutional framework, particularly on the makeup of its failings. On the other hand, the institutional framework cannot be reduced to its public components, such as the legal environment and the judiciary. Formal collective institutions (such as professional codes of conduct or "self-regulations" enforced by corporations or professional associations) join with their "informal" analogs (including behavioral rules imposed by relational networks such as professions, social and ethnic groups, etc.) to flesh out the full complement of relevant properties of the institutional framework (North 1990).

3.5   *The three base models and their ramifications*

The three base models (IT, ICT, TCT) can be represented schematically and juxtaposed with the Walrasian model (WT is Walrasian Theory) (table 1.1).

Table 1.1. *Schematic representation of the different approaches*

Theory	Rationality	Contracting parties' information	External institutions	Principal issue
WT	Savage	Complete and symmetric	Perfect (precluding deviations from the announced plans)	Centralized and simultaneous establishment of all equilibrium prices and traded quantities
IT	Savage	Complete and asymmetric	Perfect (guaranteeing the performance of commitments)	Disclosure and incentives ensured by payment schemes
ICT	Savage	Complete and symmetric	Imperfect (unable to verify some variables)	Allocation of decision rights and residual surplus to motivate non-contractible investments
TCT	Simon	Incomplete and asymmetric	Very imperfect (unable to verify some variables and subject to bounded rationality)	Creation of procedures for decision making *ex post* and of mechanisms to render the commitments enforceable

The three alternatives to the Walrasian approach shown in table 1.1 have given rise to various offshoots or hybrids. In applied economics, in particular, the nature of the issues dealt with have often made it necessary to move away from the canonical forms of the three theories. While these theories are somewhat competitive, they should also be viewed as complementary to the extent that they do not emphasize the same dimensions of contracts. To simplify, IT focuses on remuneration schemes, ICT relates to renegotiation provisions that are framed by default clauses, and TCT deals with how rights to decide, control, and coerce are allocated between the parties. Sometimes a combination of several approaches is called for to explain a real phenomenon, as was demonstrated by the work of Holmström and Milgrom (1994) on the internal governance of firms.

Positive agency theory (Jensen and Meckling 1976, Fama 1980) constitutes one of the archetypes of these hybridizations. As Gérard Charreaux points out in chapter 15 in this volume, this theory aims to analyze relationships within organizations on the basis of assumptions that are quite realistic. Thus, it shares with TCT the notion that efficient (rather than optimal) coordination results from the combination of several imperfect contractual and institutional mechanisms. However, positive agency theory emphasizes the coordination of the allocation of decision rights and the mechanisms governing remuneration and the assignment of residual incomes (in the tradition of the analysis of Alchian and Demsetz 1972) and thus also draws on incentive theory.

4   Many fields of application

The application of contract theory to various branches of economic analysis has generated a multiplicity of results: on the microeconomic level for the analysis of different types of contractual practices (sub-section 4.1); in macroeconomic reexaminations of the properties of a truly decentralized economy (sub-section 4.2); and, finally, for the regulation of interdependence in relationships between individuals within a given institutional environment (sub-section 4.3).

4.1   A rereading of microeconomic interactions

Recognition of the contract as an object of economic analysis was expanded by the study of different categories of contractual relations. These studies allowed the theory to be extended so as to better characterize the coordination regimes effective in certain industries and to clarify the choices of some economic decision-makers. In management, for example, studies on efficient methods of coordination with suppliers, partners, or distributors are legion (cf., for example, in the *Strategic Management Journal*). In economics, this research has accompanied the redesign of public policy, especially related to competition and the regulation of services of general interest (also known as "public services" or "utilities").

Issues relating to industrial organization have motivated the greatest number of such studies. In a break with traditional approaches, which focused on anti-competitive consequences of bilateral relationships, systematic investigation of inter-firm contracting practices has sought to illuminate their contributions to economic efficiency.

One of the most-studied practices has undoubtedly been contracting between firms and their suppliers. Subsequent to the landmark case of the relationship between General Motors and Fisher Body – one of its suppliers in the 1920s (Klein, Crawford and Alchian 1978; cf. also Benjamin

Klein's chapter 4 in this volume and the *Journal of Law and Economics* (43 (1), April 2000) that dedicates several papers to this case) – contemporary industries, especially automobile manufacturing, have seen their contractual practices repeatedly scrutinized (e.g. Aoki 1988). These analyses have differentiated between various categories of sub-contracting and partnership relationships and have examined their impact on firm and industry competitiveness. During the 1990s comparative analysis of the vertical-integration decision and partnership contracts provided the frame of reference for tracing the evolution of corporate practices: be they outsourcing policies resulting from a refocusing on the core business, or the development of industrial partnerships to increase flexibility in production and follow the acceleration of the pace of innovation (e.g. Deakin and Michie 1997).

The determinants and consequences of long-term contracts have been researched in other industries, notably those belonging to the energy sector. They have provided a better understanding of the economics of negotiation mechanisms and of private conflict resolution, as well as of the comparative efficiency of contractual adjustment mechanisms in various contexts. Moreover, the analysis of long-term contracts – often associated with the initial phase of the deployment of transportation networks and the exploitation of new mineral deposits – has yielded a better understanding of the feasibility of liberalizing network industries once the initial investment has been recuperated or the interconnections have multiplied (Joskow and Schmalensee 1983). Three important results have been obtained in this area. First, contrary to intuition, many long-term contracts are relatively flexible (Goldberg and Erickson 1987, Crocker and Masten 1991). Second, these contracts are central to the provision of those utilities that are indispensable to modern economies – water, gas, electricity, etc. Third, to some extent these contracts have proven compatible with other modes of coordination (such as spot markets), allowing flexibility, security, and freedom of choice to coexist.

Distribution agreements linking manufacturers, wholesalers or the creators of commercial concepts with distributors have also stimulated a large body of work, especially on franchising. The franchisor, having created a business model distinguished by a brand, delegates the actual implementation of this model to others (the franchisees). Horizontal externalities are generated between the distributors (since the behavior of each impacts on the shared brand image) as well as vertical externalities between the franchisor and the franchisees (either of whose actions affect the level of sales). The franchise system is designed to internalize these externalities as much as possible. This results both from the specific form of each contract, as well as from the general architecture of the contractual network, as is underlined in chapter 18 in this volume by Francine Lafontaine and Emmanuel Raynaud.

Distribution agreements also encompass looser relationships between manufacturers or wholesalers and distributors – comprising the wide array of "vertical restrictions." They are so designated to the extent that these vertical contracts do not limit themselves to an agreement on the unit price of the goods traded, but also impose *de facto* behavioral constraints on the buyer, i.e. the distributor. Price constraints (regressive pricing, systems of rebates and volume discounts, binding retail prices, etc.) or "non-price" restrictions (service requirements) implemented in vertical contracts allow various pricing issues to be resolved (the double-marginalization problem): provision of services related to sales (consulting, after-sales service), management of competition between points of sale and between networks. Klein and Saft (1985) and OECD (1994) provide interesting summaries underlining the complex impact of these practices on social welfare and on the division of surpluses between distributors and their partners. Benito Arruñada in chapter 19 in this volume provides an opportune reminder that the distributor himself may impose constraints upstream, which may be designed to increase economic efficiency and not necessarily reveal a desire for more market power.

Another very interesting family of contracts deals with trade in technology and, more generally, intangibles. In an economy increasingly based on knowledge and information, arrangements for immaterial transactions become essential. The specific interest of the case of technology licensing agreements is that it applies to resources that are complex and imperfectly protected by the body of laws governing intellectual and industrial property rights. The implementation of efficient contractual mechanisms requires recourse to specialized collective devices that simplify and secure such transactions (cf. Bessy and Brousseau 1998). The analysis of the dynamics of trade in technology allows us to understand how these market infrastructures are progressively assembled. Chapter 21 in this volume by Ashish Arora and Andrea Fosfuri provides an account of such a dynamic in the chemical industry. The experience acquired by the contracting parties, the appearance of intermediaries, and the standardization of practices explain the fall in transaction costs and the multiplication of agreements that foster the dissemination of information over time.

Agreements governing interconnections between network operators also merit attention because of their implications for the organization of markets and for competition. As Godefroy Dang-Nguyen and Thierry Pénard emphasize in chapter 20 in this volume, these agreements raise issues pertaining to the financial management of externalities (interconnection tariffs) arising, and from the allocation of property rights to operators.

These questions are now being asked in all networked industries, but they have a wider relevance since they apply to interdependence between producers of complex product-services. Production organized as the assembly of elementary components is gaining ground in many industrial sectors (e.g. computers, automobile) and services (tourism, banking and insurance).

Finally, a great deal of attention has been paid to the delegation, or concession – interpreted as contractual (Goldberg 1976) – by public authorities to private operators of the production of certain goods or services in a non-competitive environment (armaments, infrastructure, public goods). Baron and Myerson (1982), Baron and Besanko (1984), and especially Laffont and Tirole (1993) bolstered the study of regulation by emphasizing the informational asymmetries between public trusteeship and regulated firms, galvanizing a search for new regulatory practices. Confronted with the difficulty of implementing efficient regulations (cf. chapter 23 in this volume by Matthew Bennett and Catherine Waddams Price), there has been a movement toward opening the provision of these services to competition. In some cases, however, establishing competition between operators has proven a difficult task, owing to either the degree of specialization of the required investment (degree of "specificity", Williamson 1976) or to the necessity of maintaining a direct, centralized coordination between the supply of, and the demand for, these services (Glachant 1998, 2002). Public authorities must then contract efficiently with service providers in a monopoly position. In chapter 24 in this volume on urban water supply systems, Claude Ménard and Stéphane Saussier analyze the profusion and complexity of choices that arise.

All in all, given that contracts are tools of coordination whose flexibility and adaptability allow them to be tailored to the exact conditions of their use, contract analysts have been able to raise doubts about the applicability of traditional theoretical approaches and the policies they support. The relevant level of analysis is more sub-microeconomic than traditional microeconomics, because it examines in detail the management of transactions. The unit of analysis is no longer the market or the industry, but the transaction. This change in perspective has enriched industrial economics and, more recently, inspired a renewal in law and economics:

• In industrial economics, we are freed from a conception of behavior exclusively dictated by the *structure of the market or of the industry*. Conceptualizations of the nature of the limits of the firm have been overthrown, and traditional assumptions about the primacy of technological determinants vigorously contested. A new type of organizational arrangement has been identified: the "hybrid form." Relationships between firms are no longer exclusively market based, but may also draw on a private order, which is relatively stable and organized in networks (e.g. Ménard 1996).

• Studies in the area of law and economics were energized as traditional beliefs about the efficiency of seeking redress in court, and by extension in the legislature, in legal rulings and in judges, were called into question in light of the concepts of *bounded rationality and transaction costs*. Several alternative systems of law are now recognized for the implementation of and enforcement of contracts. The efficiency of recourse to the law and the judge is now challenged by that of recourse to "private orders" and private conflict-resolution mechanisms.

This renewal of theoretical analysis has extended even into the domains of economic decision-making and of public policy design. For example, Victor Goldberg in chapter 8 in this volume emphasizes how legal principles must draw on economic reasoning to evaluate the legitimacy of some contract clauses that may appear unorthodox at first glance. But not only contract law is impacted – similar changes have swept competition policy. Chapter 22 in this volume by Michel Glais provides an opportune reminder that the definition of pertinent regulatory exemptions remains open in European Community (EC) law. We could enumerate other areas of law and public policy, such as insurance, health, and environmental protection, etc., to which the economic analysis of contracts can be applied . . . not to mention many dimensions of management.

4.2   The analysis of the functioning of a decentralized market economy

The contractual approach to coordination has had repercussions far beyond the analysis of bilateral interactions. It is at the root of a renewed analysis of the functioning of a decentralized economy. Efforts have been made to comprehend the consequences of substituting the concept of a Walrasian market model with one in which agents meet and contract in a truly decentralized manner. The economics of labor and employment constitute the preferred field of application of these new approaches, which are particularly suited to explaining the rather paradoxical operation of the labor "market" (e.g. Shapiro and Stiglitz 1984). The theory of implicit contracts prepared the way, followed by several other approaches – notably the efficiency wage and labor market segmentation – explaining the disequilibria in labor markets on the basis of incentive contracts.

The theory of implicit contracts (Azariadis 1975) signaled the abandonment of the idea that economic agents could design a complete system of contingent markets to cover all eventualities in future states of nature. The wage relationship is understood as a risk-sharing contract between employees and employers. This implicit contract establishes wage and employment levels that do not correspond to those of competition market equilibrium. Despite its flaws, this theory deserves credit for opening a breach in the preceding orthodoxy.

The theory of efficiency wages represented a second wave beginning in the early 1980s (Akerlof 1984, Yellen 1984), which ultimately provided new foundations for labor economics and modern macroeconomics. In the presence of informational asymmetries between employers and workers, firms cannot rely exclusively on competition or on internal controls to attract the best professionals and guarantee the required levels of effort and quality. Incentive contracts fulfill this role by paying an informational rent to the employee to resolve issues of adverse selection and moral risk. It follows that the price of labor is higher than its Walrasian value (equal to the marginal productivity of labor) and that, consequently, labor demand is below supply. This generates an endogenous disequilibrium in the market on the basis of microeconomic behavior that is perfectly rational. These results were reinforced by theories of labor market segmentation.

Not only the labor market experiences spontaneous disequilibria, but also markets for goods and services. This is reinforced when they are characterized by imperfect competition owing to a concentration of industries, to differentiation strategies, or to price discrimination. The New Keynesian Economics (Mankiw 1990, Romer 1991) traces from inter-individual interactions to the formation of global equilibria and macroeconomic aggregates in order to analyze the properties of market economies and to generate consequences for economic policy. In general terms, since markets do not spontaneously move to equilibrium, they appear to have Keynesian properties that, under certain circumstances, may justify public intervention in order to alleviate the shortfall in global demand. The great contribution of contract economics is to underline that price formation at a bilateral level may prevent spontaneous market adjustment. This failure to adjust is not attributable to external constraints (of a regulatory nature), but rather to the decentralization of decisions. This is not to suggest, of course, that regulations and public intervention are exempt from any distortionary effects.

4.3   The analysis of institutions and of the institutional environment

Another field stimulated by the economic approach to contracts has been the analysis of institutions. Contractual relationships develop in the presence of ground rules that facilitate their appearance and stability and determine the modalities and the conditions of their efficiency. These institutions, which define the "rules of the game" and its frame, constitute what the New Institutional Economics calls the "institutional environment."

Agents enter into contracts on the assumption of the upstream existence of laws that establish their ability to contract. Consequently, a favorite extension of contract analysis is the study of the nature and diversity of property-rights regimes. The study of these regimes' attributes extends well beyond simple legal or administrative rules. It covers all provisions contributing to the definition of the characteristics of rights of use (measure) or responsible for limiting access to resources to authorized economic agents (enforcement) (cf. Barzel 1989). As pointed out and illustrated in chapter 9 in this volume by Gary Libecap, contract analysis and property-rights analysis can be matched according to two different approaches. On the one hand, the delineation and distribution of property rights provide an explanation for why contracting sometimes does, and sometimes does not, lead to an efficient outcome under various circumstances. On the other hand, contract analysis sheds light on the circumstances under which a decentralized process can enable economic agents to establish an efficient allocation and delineation of property rights. Such analyses are essential for a better understanding of how to manage economic reforms (e.g. agrarian reforms) and design property-rights regimes for new economic resources (e.g. information in the digital world).

The study of contractual relationships also relies on the analysis of institutions designed to assist in their enforcement, be they formal (administration, legal system, but also professional associations), or informal (culture, traditions and customs). Here economic analysis joins with other disciplines, especially law, sociology, administrative and political sciences.

One of the great empirical questions revolves around the viability and efficiency of transposing contractual arrangements into institutional environments of a fundamentally different nature. These transpositions may result from expansion of industrial or financial operators beyond the boundaries of their home countries, or from a transformation of the institutional environment (i.e. the implementation of the single-market regulatory framework in the European Union (EU), or the institutional reconstruction of the countries of the former Communist Bloc). One of the fields that has been most subject to empirical examination is that of regulated activities (telecommunications, water, electricity, etc.) (e.g. World Bank 1995, Levy and Spiller 1996, Glachant and Finon 2000). Based on the analysis of reforms to the electricity sector in various countries, two chapters in this volume nicely review the issues at stake in the design of so-called "deregulation" processes (that should more precisely be qualified as "liberalization" processes). Paul Joskow in chapter 26 emphasizes the idea that the efficient outcome of such processes relies mostly on the design of an institutional framework able to limit contractual hazards. Indeed, self-regulation by competitive pressure cannot be sufficient in these industries characterized by huge fixed costs (and therefore concentration) and interoperability constraints (resulting in interdependencies and coordination needs among operators). Guy Holburn and Pablo Spiller in chapter 25 address the problems raised by the need to design such an efficient institutional frame. Since the instances in charge of regulating industries are part of a broader institutional set that comprises formal and informal institutions, the design of devices aimed at monitoring and supervising an industry (or the competitive process) has to be consistent with the institutional framework within which it is embedded. Optimal "deregulation" can therefore vary widely across countries, and at the same time may require broad political or social reforms.

This backdrop to contracts is important because institutions determine the rules of the game for each relationship. It is also important, however, because contractual coordination is incomplete by construction. Neither the formation of agents' capacity to contract, nor their provisions for negotiating, formalizing, or implementing contracts could exist without the support of other coordination modes. Contractual relationships rest on informal and incalculable arrangements, such as convention (Orléan 1994), as well as on rules or norms controlled by formal institutions. On the whole, contracts do not constitute a closed universe, and an essential element of the interplay in contractual relationships comes from their institutional environment (e.g. Ménard 2000).

This broadening of perspective lends some legitimacy to a rehabilitation of public intervention in the management of relationships between economic agents. It is not a matter of substituting for them, as was sometimes the case in the past, but rather of developing efficient infrastructures to promote these interactions. In these matters conceptions of the role of the public authority have also evolved, since contractual approaches have contributed to underline the capacity of actors to adapt and organize themselves. The government should not treat all the structures emanating from agents' actions as arrangements to be subverted or nationalized, but rather as provisions with efficiency aspects that should be promoted and deleterious aspects to be curbed (e.g. collusion). Chapter 7 in this volume by Alan Schwartz outlines the vast research program opened up by that perspective.

5   Different theories, different methods

Extensions to these various approaches to the field of contract economics have followed diverging paths. Essentially more hypothetical and deductive, IT and ICT primarily strive to develop a formal view of the relationships between contracting parties using the most generic models possible. TCT was developed more from empirical work. However, there have been several formalizations of TCT, and some tests of IT. Developments in modeling (sub-section 5.1), on the one hand, and in empirical work (sub-section 5.2), on the other, thus raise issues addressing all economic approaches to contracts.

5.1   Differences in methodological perspective

Given their foothold in perfect rationality, IT and ICT have not presented any significant obstacles to the construction of formal models representing the interactions between agents and the manner in which they conceptualize payments or renegotiation schemes to resolve issues of asymmetric information or incomplete contracting.

Progress in modeling IT has primarily consisted of refining tools that are increasingly generic (moving from discrete to continuous cases, moving from models separating adverse selection and moral hazard to models associating them, moving from models in which asymmetries pertain to a single variable to multitask models with asymmetries on several variables, moving from two-party models to models of a principal, an agent, and an intermediary-supervisor, etc.). In general terms, the evolution of these models has revealed that the more complex the problem to be solved, the more complicated the optimal incentive scheme, leading to second-best solutions very distant from the first-best (i.e. the amount of the informational rent abandoned to the agent increases). As Arrow pointed out (Arrow 1985), this result is surprising since, in practice, incentive schemes that are actually used are relatively "rustic" compared to those in the theory. Moreover, from a normative perspective, these complex schemes are not easily implementable in the real world. Thus, assumptions have been explored that generate theoretical contracts closer to observed incentive schemes and that generate simpler recommendations. This is the goal, for example, of the article by Holmström and Milgrom (1991) on the fixed wage.

ICT followed a different path. In an effort to replicate the predictions of Coase and Williamson concerning the vertical-integration decision on the basis of Savage rationality, it was initially constructed on a collection of purely ad hoc hypotheses. It later evolved around the search for more generic assumptions that could generate the results of contractual incompleteness and optimality. This process gave rise to a theory very different from Williamson's.

TCT was built on a different methodology, being more inductive. It proceeded by categorization, identifying different classes of solutions to coordination problems. Thus, three generic categories came into being: "markets," "hierarchies," and "hybrid forms," but also a multitude of sub-categories of contract classes (see pp. 16–20 above). The value of this method is well known, and it underlies the "empirical success story" that is TCT, according to Williamson. The theoretical propositions of TCT are constructed on the basis of empirical observations, facilitating the subsequent elaboration of propositions that are testable on observable variables. However, it also harbors concealed flaws. On one hand, there is a proliferation of categorizations and typologies unique to each author, sometimes creating a certain conceptual ambiguity. On the other hand, TCT must assume that observed contracts are subject to selection processes that obey the theory's conjecture – the minimization of transaction costs. This underlies the claim that the contract types observed most frequently under given circumstances are those that are relatively most efficient. Now, to be rigorous, it would be necessary to substantiate the contention that the selection process is capable of eliminating forms of coordination that generate excessive transaction costs.

Two principal reasons can be given for the methodological features of TCT. First, it does not rest on a definition of bounded rationality that would allow the decisions of the contracting parties to be axiomatized. Rationality in TCT is defined only as an absence of Savage rationality. In this matter the theory remains inductive. Also, TCT does not derive from a detailed analysis of selection processes that could compensate for the absence of a specific decision-making model while accounting for the behavior of a representative agent subject to a selection process, as is the case with evolutionary economics.

5.2 Empirical verification: case studies, econometrics, and experiments

While Hart and Holmström (1987) expressed regret at the absence of empirical verification of the economics of contracts, such studies have in the meanwhile proliferated to the point of making an exact count impossible. A survey by Shelanski and Klein (1995) counted over 150 papers dealing exclusively with the field of transaction costs (cf. also Coeurderoy and Quélin 1997). The two principal characteristics of these empirical verifications are the coexistence of econometric tests and case studies, and the large proportion dedicated to the issue of transaction costs.

Questions that have been tested econometrically can be grouped into three families (cf. chapter 16 in this volume by Scott Masten and Stéphane Saussier, as well as Crocker and Masten 1996). First is the issue of contracts other than those defining a "pure" commercial transaction. A variant on this approach isolates the duration of the contract as the relevant variable: Why contract for a non-null duration? For several successive transactions rather than for only one? Second, the "make or buy" issue is examined: Why have a good or service supplied internally rather than from an external source? Finally, econometric tests are also applied to the determinants of the variety of clauses in contracts: price formulas, guarantees, attribution of decision or supervision powers, conception of arbitrage mechanisms, etc. Overall, TCT has presented the largest number of testable propositions for these three types of empirical verification. For the aforementioned methodological reasons, it is sometimes the only theory with anything to say on the subject. Moreover, so far its propositions have successfully withstood many attempts at econometric refutation. IT, however, has yielded explanations of the incentive effects of different forms of land rental (i.e. farming versus sharecropping; Stiglitz 1974) or remuneration provisions in franchise contracts (while at the same time finding its propositions pertaining to the risk-aversion hypothesis discredited). Salanié (1999) presents the econometric literature, of which there is still a dearth, on IT. These differences between the treatment of TCT and IT are attributable to the restrictive assumptions of the latter, which make it difficult to formulate testable assumptions on empirical data. As to ICT, so far it has been the object of only a handful of tests, limited exclusively to the issue of vertical integration. There, again, very strict assumptions render econometric testing delicate.

The difficulty of formulating testable propositions is only one of the problems encountered when testing theories of contracts. Gathering data is also a significant obstacle. First, obtaining information on in-force, or recently ended, contracts is hampered by issues of confidentiality. Next, constructing the databases presents methodological difficulties specific to the coding and normalization of the descriptions of the contents of contract documents. Finally, econometric tests are stymied by the poor quality of available data, be it on the contracts themselves or their explanatory variables. Such are the reasons why case studies continue to play a role, universally recognized as irreplaceable, in empirical verification. Given this context, legal scholars and managers, being anchored in the practice of case studies both in their academic training and in the day-to-day functioning of their professions, have occupied a prominent position with their work.

It should be noted that econometrics is not the only discipline capable of subjecting theoretical propositions to rigorous protocols of empirical verification. The controlled nature of investigations conducted by the practitioners of experimental economics lends itself to testing conjectures arising from very strict hypotheses like those of IT. Thus, Claudia Keser and Marc Willinger in chapter 17 in this volume demonstrate that most contracts presented in experimental tests do not respect the incentive constraint as conjectured by IT, either in single-period or repeated principal–agent interaction simulations. These results do not contradict the optimization assumption, but rather reveal the presence of other motives in the contract relationship, such as equity and reciprocity (suggesting the principles of contract law evoked in Jacques Ghestin's chapter 6 in this volume).

6   Perspectives

The future of the economic analysis of contracts is contingent on progress in four areas: the measurement and collection of data (sub-section 6.1); modeling bounded rationality (sub-section 6.2); analysis of the institutional framework (sub-section 6.3); and, finally, collaboration with professionals and scholars in other disciplines (sub-section 6.4).

6.1   Measurement and data collection

Significant improvements are expected in the availability of empirical data. One key limitation that has hampered the evolution of the economic analysis of contracts to date is that of collecting data appropriate to the issues it raises. Official statistical agencies are focused on measuring phenomena whose scope are macroeconomic or pertain to the microeconomics of markets or industries. The sub-microeconomic level, that of the contract and the transaction, is not recognized and will not readily be recognized because of confidentiality issues (trade secrets). A further issue of "measurement" is that dimensions useful for the analysis of contracts are not part of the available accounting or statistical standards. Until now, gathering the appropriate data has largely relied on individual investigations and the voluntary participation of a few firms. The cost of these collections and their near cottage-industry character explains the small size of the available databases as well as their heterogeneity. In the future a more efficient compilation could come from: first, recovering individual series already identified in official statistical data-sheets of a microeconomic nature; second, gaining access to databases used for voluntary inter-firm benchmarking or anti-trust purposes; third, developing and using trade-specific databases maintained by private or public foundations or professional associations. These types of advances can already be seen when a scientific evaluation of professional practices is required in response to challenges under evolving regulations.

6.2   Modeling bounded rationality

The formalization of different elements of the economic analysis of contracts and, consequently, the generation of testable propositions, is still deficient. A major shortcoming in this field is the modeling of bounded rationality. In the absence of models adapted to the specification of the rationality of the contracting parties, formalized analytical constructs rely on assumptions of hyper-rationality to deal with behavior originating from semi-strong rationality. In this process, however, the observed behavior and the stylized facts that should be explained are largely eliminated. An important aspect of the future of the economic analysis of contracts thus depends on the possible development of models of bounded rationality. Two possible avenues present themselves. One begins with the standard model of rationality and proceeds to explore various aspects of the degeneration of rationality. The work by Bentley MacLeod, in chapter 13 in this volume, provides a good example of this type of approach. The other approach explores the way in which actors' rationality is formed and how deductive reasoning ties into collective and social patterns of behavior to model their choices, values, and routines. Here, the contributions of psychology, sociology, and anthropology are mobilized along with the more traditional methods of economists. Simon's work constitutes an essential reference.

Reverting to current models of rationality will provide for a better understanding of how contracts are conceived and evolve over time under the influence of learning and selection processes. Special focus should be placed on the coordination difficulties that are solved by contracts, as this will facilitate a rigorous analysis of the design and consistency of the various contractual mechanisms. These are, indeed, "systems" that we have not yet been able to consider with sufficient rigor (for a first attempt at this, see Brickley 1999).

6.3   Selection processes

As pointed out by North (1990), and earlier by Alchian (1950), the processes according to which viable contractual or institutional forms are selected is of importance as well. While the design of contracts and institutions depends upon agents' behavior, the competitive process validates or invalidates agents' choices. IT, ICT and TCT implicitly (for the two former) or explicitly (for the latter) assume that selection is perfect and eliminates less efficient (or more costly in terms of transaction costs) co-ordination devices. As demonstrated by advances in evolutionary theory, both in economics and in biology, evolution and selection processes lead neither to a unique and final equilibrium, nor to an optimum. Economics in general, and contractual economics in particular, lacks a satisfactory approach to selection processes, though such a theory of selection would be essential to the definition of some efficiency criteria that would be more realistic than the standards "maximizing revenues, minimizing costs." Indeed, "efficient" could also mean "flexible," "favorable to innovation," "remediable," etc. In a sense, the contribution by Eirik Furubotn, in chapter 5 in this volume, is a good example of the broadening of perspective needed to build a more satisfactory analytical framework for the study of the properties of a truly decentralized economy and for identifying strategies that are both sustainable and preferable in terms of individual or collective welfare. There are, however, other research directions to be explored. The analysis of competition among alternative contractual and organizational forms, innovation in contract design, learning by govern-ing, and learning about governance mechanisms (etc.) thus open quite a wide research agenda. This is pointed out by Ronald Coase in chapter 2 in this volume.

6.4 *Institutional framework and enforcement*

Significant progress is also expected from a better understanding of the effects of the institutional framework on contract choices. A program of work along those lines has already been initiated (cf. sub-section 4.3, but also Aoki 2001). More generally, a multiplication of comparative studies conducted on the variety of contracts governing the same pro-fessions within the same industry in different institutional environments can be expected. These will doubtlessly allow a better identification of those characteristics of the environment relevant to the conception of contractual arrangements, as well as an analysis of factors influencing the relative performance of these arrangements. In exchange, such analyses will open the door to the design of institutional frameworks that are more efficient... while respectful of current practices.

6.5 *Cross-disciplinary fertilizations*

Finally, theoretical developments remain highly dependent on a better understanding and grasp of empirical reality. The economic analysis of contracts should benefit from closer and more promising collaborations with professionals and scholars in other disciplines. Many professionals, in business as well as consulting, but also working in national and international institutions, seek such exchanges ("will perform analysis in exchange for access to data"). An entire sector, that of the legal professions – representing an operational rather than an academic discipline, Law – is expressing a growing demand for economic analysis of legal cases and offering the basis for a joint labor in "Law and Economics." Research in management, political science, administrative science, sociology, and history should also stimulate the economic analysis of contracts by suggesting both propositions and hypotheses . . . or as a source of building blocks, empirical evidence, and issues to be addressed.

NOTE

Chapter 1 was originally published as "Economie des contrats et renouvellements de l'analyse économique," in *Revue d'Economie Industrielle* (92, 2000).

Appendix: canonical models of theories of contract

M'hand Fares

1 Incentives theory

The objective of incentives theory (IT) is to analyze situations in which a contract is contemplated under conditions of asymmetric information, that is, where one party (the agent) knows certain relevant information of which the other party (the principal) is ignorant. Usually two kind of situations are considered. In a *moral-hazard* situation, the principal cannot observe the agent's actions or decisions. The solution is then to define adequate contract terms in order to internalize incentives. In an *adverse-selection* situation, before signing the contract, the agent is aware of private information on his characteristics (his type). The solution is to let the agent choose between several alternative contracts in order to reveal his private information.

1.1 Moral hazard

Let e represent the effort of the agent (he) and $y = \theta e + \epsilon$ the production result observed by the principal (she), with θ a parameter of agent productivity and $\epsilon \rightsquigarrow N(0, \sigma^2)$. Following Holmström and Milgrom (1987), we assume that the principal offers a linear incentive scheme, $t(y) = B + \delta y$, to a risk adverse agent. The agent's risk aversion is captured by a CARA (Constant Absolute Risk Averse) utility function, $u(w) = -e^{-rw}$, where r represents absolute risk aversion and w wealth, with $w = B + \delta y$. As $y \rightsquigarrow N(0, \sigma^2)$, then $w \rightsquigarrow N(\overline{w}, \sigma_w^2)$. So, it is possible to evaluate the distribution of wealth using the function[1]

$$u(\overline{w}, \sigma_w^2) = \frac{\overline{w} - r^2 \sigma_w^2}{2}$$

The agent utility will be given by $B + \delta\theta e - \frac{r}{2}(\delta\sigma)^2 - g(e)$, where $g(e)$ represents the cost of effort. The agent program is then

$$\max_e B + \delta\theta e - \frac{r}{2}(\delta\sigma)^2 - g(e)$$

The first-order condition is

$$\delta\theta = \frac{\partial g(e)}{\partial e} \qquad (1)$$

The principal is supposed to be risk neutral. Her expected profit is given by $E_\epsilon[y - t(y)] = E_\epsilon[\theta e + \epsilon - B - \delta\theta e - \delta\epsilon] = (1 - \delta)\theta e - B$. She determines the optimal parameters δ and B that maximize her expected profit.

Under symmetric information, the principal observes the agent's effort. The linear incentive that maximizes her profit is the sure contract $B > 0$ and $\delta = 0$, such that $B = g(e)$.

Under asymmetric information, the principal cannot observe the agent's effort. Her program is then to maximize her expected profit subject to the incentive constraint (IC, given by (1)) and to the participation constraint (IR) so that the agent receives a non-negative utility

$$\max_{[\delta, B, e]} (1 - \delta)\theta e - B$$

$$\begin{cases} B + \delta\theta e - \dfrac{r}{2}(\delta\sigma)^2 - g(e) \geq 0 & (IR) \\[2mm] \delta\theta = \dfrac{\partial g(e)}{\partial e} & (IC) \end{cases}$$

Substituted into the objective function, this gives

$$\max_e \theta e - \left(\frac{1}{\theta}\frac{\partial g(e)}{\partial e}\right)^2 \frac{r}{2}\sigma^2 - g(e)$$

The first-order condition with respect to effort is

$$\theta^2 - \left[r\sigma^2\frac{\partial g(e)}{\partial e}\frac{\partial^2 g(e)}{\partial e^2}\right] - \frac{\partial g(e)}{\partial e} = 0$$

Using (1), we find the following optimal share

$$\delta = \frac{\theta}{1 + r\sigma^2\left(\dfrac{\partial^2 g(e)}{\partial e^2}\right)}$$

This result sheds some light on the trade-off between the incentives and insurance dilemma in a moral-hazard situation. If $\sigma^2 = 0$, there is no insurance. The optimal incentive scheme ($w = B + \theta y$) depends only on θ: the more productive the agent (increasing θ), the greater the payment. If $\sigma^2 > 0$, $\delta < \theta$ so that there is a risk sharing. And the greater the risk (increasing σ^2), the more the agent risk shares, the smaller δ.

1.2   *Adverse selection*

Now, we will consider two agents of different types, which differ only with respect to the disutility of effort function, which is

$$g_1 = \frac{\theta_1}{2} e_1^2$$

for type 1, and

$$g_2 = \frac{\theta_2}{2} e_2^2$$

with $\theta_2 > \theta_1$. Hence the disutility of any particular effort is greater for an agent of type 2. We shall refer to the first as a "good" type and the second as a "bad" type, since for the same effort, the principal will have to pay more to the second type than to the first. The principal will propose to the agents a compensation $w_i = w_i(e_i)$, $i = 1, 2$, relative to the effort level observed e_i in order to maximize her profit $\Pi = e_1 + e_2 - (w_1 + w_2)$. The choice of optimal contract (w_1, w_2) by the principal depends on the information that she holds on types before the contract design.

If there is no adverse selection problem, the principal can perfectly discriminate between the two types. The program is then to maximize her profit subject to the participation constraint (IR_i) that each agent receives a non-negative utility

$$\max_{[w_1, w_2, e_1, e_2]} \Pi = e_1 + e_2 - (w_1 + w_2)$$

$$\begin{cases} w_1 - \dfrac{\theta_1}{2} e_1^2 = 0 & (IR_1) \\[2mm] w_2 - \dfrac{\theta_2}{2} e_2^2 = 0 & (IR_2) \end{cases}$$

Substituting into the objective function and differentiating, we obtain

$$e_1^* = \frac{1}{\theta_1}, e_2^* = \frac{1}{\theta_2}$$

The optimum contract is then $\left(w_1^* = \frac{1}{2\theta_1}, w_2^* = \frac{1}{2\theta_2}\right)$. Because $\theta_1 < \theta_2$, $w_1^* > w_2^*$ and $e_1^* > e_2^*$. Agent 1 with the lower disutility of effort ("good" agent) is offered the higher payment and invests more effort than agent 2 ("bad" agent).

In the case of the adverse selection problem, the principal does not know which agent belongs to which type. As a result, if the principal offers the two contracts $\{(e_1^*, w_1^*), (e_2^*, w_2^*)\}$ to any agent allowing him to freely select the contract that he most likes, agent 2 will choose the contract that is designed for him, but agent 1 prefers (e_2^*, w_2^*) to (e_1^*, w_1^*) in order to receive a surplus $\delta = w_2^* - g_1(e_2^*) = \frac{1}{\theta^2}\left(1 - \frac{\theta_1}{\theta_2}\right)(>0)$. This result can be avoided if the principal restructures her payment so that the agent's i utility from choosing (e_i^*, w_i^*) is higher than his utility from choosing (e_{-i}^*, w_{-i}^*). These are self-selection constraints or incentive compatibility conditions (IC_i)

$$w_1 - \frac{\theta_1}{2}e_1^2 \geq w_2 - \frac{\theta_1}{2}e_2^2 \qquad (IC_1)$$

$$w_2 - \frac{\theta_2}{2}e_2^2 \geq w_1 - \frac{\theta_2}{2}e_1^2 \qquad (IC_2)$$

In order to calculate the best contracts that the principal can offer in this situation, let us assume that the principal considers the probability of an agent being type i is q_i. The principal's program is then

$$\max_{[w_1,w_2,e_1,e_2]} \Pi = q_1(e_1 - w_1) + q_2(e_2 - w_2)$$

$$\begin{cases} w_1 \geq \frac{\theta_1}{2}e_1^2 & (IR_1) \\[2mm] w_1 \geq \frac{\theta_1}{2}e_1^2 + \left(w_2 - \frac{\theta_1}{2}e_2^2\right) & (IC_1) \\[2mm] w_2 \geq \frac{\theta_2}{2}e_2^2 & (IR_2) \\[2mm] w_2 \geq \frac{\theta_2}{2}e_2^2 + \left(w_1 - \frac{\theta_2}{2}e_1^2\right) & (IC_2) \end{cases}$$

Only one equation from of each pair has to be used in the optimization procedure. The other inequality is automatically fulfilled.[2] The optimization problem of the principal becomes

$$\max_{[w_1,w_2,e_1,e_2]} \Pi = q_1(e_1 - w_1) + q_2(e_2 - w_2)$$

$$\begin{cases} w_1 - \frac{\theta_1}{2}e_1^2 = w_2 - \frac{\theta_1}{2}e_2^2 & (IC_1') \\[2mm] w_2 - \frac{\theta_2}{2}e_2^2 = 0 & (IR_2') \\[2mm] e_1^2 > e_2^2 \end{cases}$$

The first-order conditions give

$$\hat{e}_1 = \frac{1}{\theta_1} = e_1^*$$

$$\hat{e}_2 = \frac{1}{\theta_2 + \frac{q_1}{q_2}(\theta_2 - \theta_1)} < \frac{1}{\theta_2}(= e_2^*)$$

We verify easily that $\hat{e}_1^2 > \hat{e}_2^2$. The optimal wage offers are

$$\widehat{w}_1 = \frac{1}{2\theta_1} + \Delta$$

$$\widehat{w}_2 = \frac{\theta_2}{2} \left(\frac{1}{\left[\theta_2 + \frac{q_1}{q_2}(\theta_2 - \theta_1)\right]^2} \right)$$

with $\Delta = \left(\frac{\theta_2 - \theta_1}{2[\theta_2 - \frac{q_1}{q_2}(\theta_2 - \theta_1)]^2} \right)$. We can point out that if the "bad" type (agent 2) receives a smaller wage than under symmetric information $\left(\widehat{w}_2 < w^* = \frac{1}{2\theta_2} \right)$, the good type (agent 1) receives a higher wage $\left(\widehat{w}_2 > w^* = \frac{1}{2\theta_1} \right)$. The surplus (Δ) that he obtains is just big enough to make it of no interest to him to pretend to be the bad agent (agent 2).

2 Incomplete contract theory

Let us assume a vertical relationship between a buyer (B) and a seller (S) that runs over two periods of time. During the first period (*ex ante* period), the parties are supposed to be able to sign only an incomplete contract at date 0. At date 1, they invest in specific assets, respectively β and σ. These levels of investment are non-contractible because these are unverifiable by a court. During the second period (*ex post* period), the two parties set up the efficient quantity of exchange (q) (date 3) after the realization of a state of nature, which was unknown when they signed the initial contract (date 2). We denote $v(\beta, q, \epsilon)$ as the buyer valuation and $c(\sigma, q, \epsilon)$ as the seller cost of production. v is supposed to be increasing and concave in (β, q) and c decreasing in σ and convex in (σ, q). We distinguish two kinds of situation according to the degree of incompleteness of the initial contract: the *null contract* (sub-section 2.1) and the *simple contract* (sub-section 2.2).

2.1 Null contract *and property-rights allocation*

A *null contract* is a contract that does not specify a quantity provision (q). This can be explained by a difficulty describing the quantity variable and/or difficulty making this variable verifiable by a court (Grossman and Hart 1986, Hart and Moore 1990, Hart 1995). This has two implications. First, the only way to complete the incomplete contract is to define a property-rights allocation on a set of assets $K = \{k_1, k_2\}$, because ownership gives formal control over the asset for uses that have not been pre-assigned. It defines "residual rights of control" that give bargaining power during the renegotiation. Second, because there is a *null contract ex ante*, the parties have to negotiate about the possibility of trade taking place at date 3. There are two possible outcomes at this date: either the parties agree to trade or they go their own ways:

- If they agree to trade, a bilateral negotiation under perfect information defines an efficient quantity $q^*(\beta, \sigma, \epsilon)$, after β, σ, and ϵ have been observed. Then a total surplus $S(\beta, \sigma, q^*(\cdot), \epsilon) = [v(\beta, q^*(\cdot), \epsilon) - c(\sigma, q^*(\cdot), \epsilon)]$ emerges. If the parties can commit themselves *ex ante* to agreeing to trade *ex post*, the maximum social surplus at date 1 from choosing efficient levels of investment is then given by

$$\max_{[\beta, \sigma]} E_\epsilon S(\beta, \sigma, q^*(\cdot), \epsilon) - \beta - \sigma$$

We denote by β^* and σ^* the efficient levels of investment solution of the first-order conditions

$$\frac{\partial E_\epsilon S(\beta, \sigma, q^*(\cdot), \epsilon)}{\partial \beta} - 1 = 0 \tag{2}$$

$$\frac{\partial E_\epsilon S(\beta, \sigma, q^*(\cdot), \epsilon)}{\partial \sigma} - 1 = 0 \tag{3}$$

- If the parties fails to agree, the buyer receives her outside option $w_B(\beta \mid K_B)$ and the seller his outside option $w_S(\sigma \mid K_S)$, where $K_B(K_S)$ is the set of assets that the buyer (seller) has control over at date 3.

Assume that $S \geq w_B + w_S$. Then it is optimal to agree to trade and divide the total surplus such that the buyer obtains at least $w_B(\beta \mid K_B)$ and the seller at least $w_S(\sigma \mid K_S)$. If the surplus $S - w_B - w_S$ is split following Nash's solution (50 : 50), utilities are

$$u_B = w_B(\beta \mid K_B) + \frac{1}{2}\{S(\beta, \sigma, q^*(\cdot), \epsilon) - w_B(\beta \mid K_B) - w_S(\beta \mid K_S)\}$$

$$u_S = w_S(\sigma \mid K_S) + \frac{1}{2}\{S(\beta, \sigma, q^*(\cdot), \epsilon) - w_B(\beta \mid K_B) - w_S(\beta \mid K_S)\}$$

Foreseeing these date 3 payoffs, the buyer and the seller take their investment decisions at date 1. Let us assume that these decisions are made non-cooperatively and that a Nash equilibrium results. Let β^0 and σ^0 be the solutions to the following first-order conditions

$$\frac{\partial U_B}{\partial \beta} = \frac{1}{2}\frac{\partial w_B(\beta \mid K_B)}{\partial \beta} + \frac{1}{2}\frac{\partial E_\epsilon S(\beta, \sigma, q^*(\cdot), \epsilon)}{\partial \beta} - 1 = 0 \tag{4}$$

$$\frac{\partial U_S}{\partial \sigma} = \frac{1}{2}\frac{\partial w_S(\sigma \mid K_S)}{\partial \sigma} + \frac{1}{2}\frac{\partial E_\epsilon S(\beta, \sigma, q^*(\cdot), \epsilon)}{\partial \sigma} - 1 = 0 \tag{5}$$

The only endogenous variable influencing the parties' choice of investment is the allocation of assets K_B and K_S (through outside options). In order to analyze how assets allocation affects investment decisions, it is necessary to introduce further assumptions:

$$\frac{\partial ES}{\partial \beta}\left(\frac{\partial ES}{\partial \sigma}\right)$$

is increasing as the buyer (the seller) controls more assets; the cross-partial is positive

$$\frac{\partial^2 ES}{\partial \beta \partial \sigma} > 0$$

and the marginal returns of investment are supposed to be higher when the parties cooperate

$$\frac{\partial ES}{\partial \beta} \geq \frac{\partial w_B}{\partial \beta} \quad \text{and} \quad \frac{\partial ES}{\partial \sigma} \geq \frac{\partial w_S}{\partial \sigma}$$

The first implication is that the equilibrium level of investment is at or below the efficient level ($\beta^0 \leq \beta^*$ and $\sigma^0 \leq \sigma^*$).[3] Therefore, no property-rights allocation can replicate the first-best level of investment. The second implication is the definition of a *trade-off principle*: when B controls more assets (integration by the buyer), her outside option w_B increases which raises her incentives to invest (from (3)). But at the same time, S controls fewer assets which reduces his incentives to invest (from (4)). Analyzing symmetrically the situation where S controls more assets (integration by the seller) gives us the following comparison of efficiency under different property-rights allocations (Table 1A.1).

But who must integrate? Grossman and Hart (1986) define the following criterion: the property-right allocation which minimizes incentives distortions is the one which gives all the rights (integration) to the party whose investment has the prominent effect on social surplus.

Table 1A.1. *Efficiency under different property-rights allocations*

Property-rights allocation	Investment level
no integration ($K_B = \{k_1\}$; $K_S = \{k_2\}$)	$\beta^0 \leq \beta^*$ $\sigma^0 < \sigma^*$
Buyer integration ($K_B = K$; $K_S = \emptyset$)	$\beta^0 \leq \beta^B \leq \beta^*$ $\sigma^B < \sigma^0 < \sigma^*$
Seller integration ($K_B = \emptyset$; $K_S = K$)	$\beta^S \leq \beta^0 \leq \beta^*$ $\sigma^0 < \sigma^S < \sigma^*$

2.2   Simple contract *and first-best solution*

A *simple contract* is a contract which specifies a quantity provision in the contract. When the court can verify only that trade has occurred ($q = 1$) or not ($q = 0$), Hart and Moore (1988) show that a contract (*at will*), stipulating a trading price (p_1) and a penalty (p_0) when there is non-exchange, leads to surplus-sharing which depends on the state of nature (ϵ), whereby incentives to invest are not higher than under a null contract completed by a property right allocation. Nöldeke and Schmidt (1995) show, however, that if the parties can define a price contingent for the delivery of the good (*option contract*), a first-best solution can be obtained. But this *option contract* solution to the hold-up problem requires a higher degree of verifiability: a court is supposed to observe the party which is at fault in the exchange. Chung (1991) and Aghion, Dewatripont and Rey (1994) show that this additional verifiability assumption is not necessary if an initial contract (*specific performance contract*) can design a renegotiation framework that avoids this hold-up problem. This simple contract is such that :

- It allocates all the bargaining power to the buyer, such that she has the right to make a take-or-leave-it offer $(\overline{q}, \overline{p})$ in the renegotiation sub-game
- it defines a default option (q_0, p_0) that generates a status quo outcome to the seller in case of renegotiation failing (*specific performance*).

Given this framework, at the sub-game perfect equilibrium the buyer will always offer to the seller to deliver the efficient quantity $q^*(\beta, \sigma, \epsilon)$ at a price p which makes the seller indifferent between accepting and rejecting the offer

$$p - c(\sigma, q^*(\cdot), \epsilon) = p_0 - c(\sigma, q_0, \epsilon)$$

the seller's expected utility is then

$$U_S = p_0 - E_\epsilon c(\sigma, q_0, \epsilon) - \sigma \tag{6}$$

Let the initial quantity q_0 given by

$$E_\epsilon \frac{\partial c(\sigma^*, q_0)}{\partial \sigma} - 1 = 0 \tag{7}$$

By maximizing his expected utility (6), the seller chooses a level of investment σ investment such that (7) is verified. The assumptions on the function cost ensure that $\sigma = \sigma^*$.

The buyer's expected utility is

$$U_B = E_\epsilon\{[v(\beta, q_0, \epsilon) - c(\sigma, q_0, \epsilon)] + \varsigma\} - U_S - \beta \tag{8}$$

where ς is the net surplus from renegotiation that she captures

$$\varsigma = [v(\beta, q^*(\cdot), \epsilon) - c(\sigma, q^*(\cdot), \epsilon)] - [v(\beta, q_0, \epsilon) - c(\sigma, q_0, \epsilon)]$$

After simplification, her expected utility can be written

$$U_B = E_\epsilon S(\beta, \sigma, q^*(\cdot), \epsilon) - U_S - \beta \tag{9}$$

As the buyer captures the social surplus minus a constant U_S, she has the appropriate incentives to invest at the first best level ($\beta = \beta^*$). So the investment game equilibrium is such that the first-best level (β^*, σ^*) is achieved.

Now let us show that the extreme bargaining power allocation to the buyer can be sustained by a financial hostage provision. Let us assume that the seller rejects any offer $(\overline{q}, \overline{p})$ made by the buyer in the sub-game and makes a counter-offer $(\widetilde{q}, \widetilde{p})$ such that $U_S(\sigma, \widetilde{q}, \widetilde{p}, \epsilon) \geq U_S(\sigma, \overline{q}, \overline{p}, \epsilon)$. Then it is possible to design in the initial contract a hostage $t^* \in \mathfrak{R}$ such that $U_B(\beta, 0, t^*, \epsilon) \geq \max U_B(\beta, \widetilde{q}, \widetilde{p}, \epsilon)$. That is to say, the buyer prefers to capture the hostage and makes the offer $q = 0$ rather than accepting $(\widetilde{q}, \widetilde{p})$, which does not maximize her utility. At the sub-game equilibrium the seller never rejects the buyer's "take-it-or-leave-it" offer $(\overline{q}, \overline{p})$, and the buyer effectively obtains all the bargaining power. Then a simple contract (q_0, p_0, t^*) enables the parties to renegotiate the default quantities according to a bargaining rule that cannot be modified during this process. This ensures the credibility of the initial commitments and, therefore, the optimal levels of specific investment by each party.

But the Aghion, Dewatripont and Rey solution requires quite a strong constraint of verifiability (and actually a much stronger verifiability constraint than in the Hart and Moore model) because the judge needs to know the delivery and the payment date in order to be sure that he would be able to impose the performance of the contract.

3   Transaction-cost theory

The transaction-cost approach holds that the institutions of capitalism are to be understood in transaction-cost economizing terms. Such economies are realized in a discriminating way by aligning governance structures (market, hybrid forms, and firm) with the attributes of transaction, of which the condition of asset specificity is the most important (Williamson 1985, 1991). Unlike Incentives Theory, transaction-cost theory (TCT) analyzes only discrete choices because it assumes that economic agents choose between alternative governance structures and not a continuum of contracts. Moreover, as compared to ICT, incompleteness in the transaction cost approach is not due to verifiability problems but to the limited rationality of economic agents (contracting parties and courts) and the uncertainty of the environment.

We will extend the Riordan and Williamson (1985) model in order to formalize the trade-off between governance structures. Let $r(q)$ be the revenue from producing a quantity q, with $\frac{\partial r(q)}{\partial q} > 0$, $\frac{\partial^2 r(q)}{\partial q^2} > 0$, and $c(q, A)$ the production costs of governance structures procurement, with $\frac{\partial c}{\partial q} > 0$, $\frac{\partial c}{\partial A} > 0$ and $\frac{\partial c}{\partial q \partial A} < 0$. Asset specificity A is available at the constant per unit cost of γ. The profit is given by

$$\pi^*(q, A) = r(q) - c(q, A) - \gamma A$$

In a world without transaction costs, a first-best level of quantity (q^*) and asset specificity (A^*), solutions of the first-order conditions

$$\frac{\partial \pi^*(q, A)}{\partial q} = 0 \quad \text{and} \quad \frac{\partial \pi^*(q, A)}{\partial A} = 0$$

is achievable.

In world with transaction costs, the transaction costs of governance structure choice are defined by the function $TC = \beta + z(A)$, where β is the fixed cost of the chosen governance structure, and $z(A)$ an increasing function of asset specificity. $z(A)$ takes the form $v(A)$ when the governance structure is the market, $w(A)$ when it is an hybrid form, and $x(A)$ when it is a firm. Let the subscripts M denote market, Hy hybrid forms and F the firm. The transaction costs of these governance structures are given by

$$TC_M = v(A)$$
$$TC_{Hy} = \beta_0 + w(A)$$
$$TC_F = \beta_1 + x(A)$$

where $\beta_1 > \beta_0 > 0$ and $0 < \frac{\partial x(A)}{\partial A} < \frac{\partial w(A)}{\partial A} < \frac{\partial v(A)}{\partial A}$.

The corresponding profit functions for governance structures in a world with transaction costs are

$$\pi_M = r(q) - c(q, A) - \gamma A - v(A)$$
$$\pi_{Hy} = r(q) - c(q, A) - \gamma A - (\beta_0 + w(A))$$
$$\pi_F = r(q) - c(q, A) - \gamma A - (\beta_1 + x(A))$$

First-order conditions are

$$\frac{\partial \pi_i}{\partial q} = \frac{\partial r(q)}{\partial q} - \frac{\partial c(q, A)}{\partial q} = 0 \quad i = M, Hy, F$$
$$\frac{\partial \pi_M}{\partial A} = -\frac{\partial c(q, A)}{\partial A} - \gamma - \frac{\partial v(A)}{\partial A} = 0$$

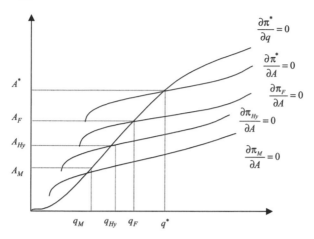

Figure 1A.1 Comparative efficiency of the three governance structures

$$\frac{\partial \pi_{Hy}}{\partial A} = -\frac{\partial c(q, A)}{\partial A} - \gamma - \frac{\partial w(A)}{\partial A} = 0$$

$$\frac{\partial \pi_F}{\partial A} = -\frac{\partial c(q, A)}{\partial A} - \gamma - \frac{\partial x(A)}{\partial A} = 0$$

In each case, optimal output is defined in order to minimize production costs $\left(\frac{\partial \pi_i}{\partial q} = 0\right)$. Optimal asset specificity is however chosen in order to minimize the sum of production costs *and* transaction costs $\left(\frac{\partial \pi_i}{\partial q} = 0 \text{ and } \frac{\partial \pi_M}{\partial A} = \frac{\partial \pi_H}{\partial A} = \frac{\partial \pi_F}{\partial A} = 0\right)$. As the first-order condition for the output is identical for the three governance structures, then $\frac{\partial \pi_i}{\partial q} = \frac{\partial \pi^*}{\partial q} = 0$. But the first-order condition for asset specificity is different. Indeed, as $\frac{\partial v}{\partial A} > \frac{\partial w}{\partial A} > \frac{\partial x(A)}{\partial A} > 0$, $\frac{\partial \pi_M}{\partial A} = 0$ is everywhere below $\frac{\partial \pi_{Hy}}{\partial A} = 0$, which is everywhere below $\frac{\partial \pi_F}{\partial A} = 0$. Then, the A solutions of the optimization problem are such that $A^* > A_F > A_{Hy} > A_M$ (see figure 1A.1). As $\frac{\partial c}{\partial A \partial q} < 0$, then the q solutions are such that $q^* > q_F > q_{Hy} > q_M$.

So, the optimal choice of governance structure depends only on asset specificity: market procurement supports transactions with slight asset specificity, whereas the hybrid form is more efficient as the condition of asset specificity deepens and internal procurement (firm) as asset specificity is high.

NOTES

1. If $w \rightsquigarrow N(\overline{w}, \sigma_w^2)$, the expected utility of the agent is

$$Eu(w) = -\int e^{-rw} f(w)dw = -e^{-r\left(\frac{\overline{w}+r^2\sigma_w^2}{2}\right)}$$

Because expected utility is increasing in

$$\frac{\overline{w} + r^2\sigma_w^2}{2}$$

we can take a monotonic transformation. Then we obtain the utility function given, which is equivalent to using the mean–variance criterion for choice under uncertainty rather than the expected utility criterion.

2. From (IR_2) and $\theta_1 < \theta_2$, we obtain

$$w_2 - \frac{\theta_1}{2}e_2^2 \geq w_2 - \frac{\theta_2}{2}e_2^2 \geq 0$$

we conclude that when (IC_1) holds, (IR_1) is also verified. Moreover (IC_1) is a binding constraint because the principal tries to keep his offer w_i as small as possible. Then substituting (IC_1) in (IC_2) we get $\frac{\theta_2}{2}(e_1^2 - e_2^2) \geq \frac{\theta_1}{2}(e_1^2 - e_2^2)$. As $\theta_1 < \theta_2$, this inequality is always strict when $e_1^2 > e_2^2$.

3. The seller's investment incentives, determined by (5) are such that

$$\frac{1}{2}\frac{\partial ES}{\partial\sigma} + \frac{1}{2}\frac{\partial ws}{\partial\sigma} \leq \frac{\partial ES}{\partial\sigma}$$

then they will push him to under-invest. The buyer's return of investment will be then lowered owing to the complementarity of the investments. So she will reduce her investment, which lowers the seller's incentives to invest, and so on . . . until a (sub-optimal) Nash equilibrium is achieved.

Part II

Contracts, organizations, and institutions

2   The New Institutional Economics

Ronald Coase

It is commonly said, and it may be true, that the New Institutional Economics started with my article, "The Nature of the Firm" (1937) with its explicit introduction of transaction costs into economic analysis. But it needs to be remembered that the source of a mighty river is a puny little stream and that it derives its strength from the tributaries that contribute to its bulk. So it is in this case. I am not thinking only of the contributions of other economists such as Oliver Williamson, Harold Demsetz, and Steven Cheung, important though they have been, but also of the work of our colleagues in law, anthropology, sociology, political science, sociobiology, and other disciplines.

The phrase, "the New Institutional Economics," was coined by Oliver Williamson. It was intended to differentiate the subject from the "old institutional economics." John R. Commons, Wesley Mitchell, and those associated with them were men of great intellectual stature, but they were anti-theoretical, and without a theory to bind together their collection of facts, they had very little that they were able to pass on. Certain it is that mainstream economics proceeded on its way without any significant change. And it continues to do so. I should explain that, when I speak of "mainstream economics," I am referring to microeconomics. Whether my strictures apply also to macroeconomics I leave to others.

Mainstream economics, as one sees it in the journals and the textbooks and in the courses taught in economics departments has become more and more abstract over time, and although it purports otherwise, it is in fact little concerned with what happens in the real world. Demsetz has given an explanation of why this has happened: economists since Adam Smith have devoted themselves to formalizing his doctrine of the invisible hand, the coordination of the economic system by the pricing system. It has been an impressive achievement. But, as Demsetz has explained it is the analysis of a system of extreme decentralization. However, it has other flaws. Adam Smith also pointed out that we should be concerned with the flow of real goods and services over time – and with what determines their variety and magnitude. As it is, economists study how supply and demand determine prices but not with the factors that determine what goods and services are traded on markets and therefore are priced. It is a view disdainful of what happens in the real world, but it is one to which economists have become accustomed, and they live in their world without discomfort. The success of mainstream economics in spite of its defects is a tribute to the staying power of a theoretical underpinning, since mainstream economics is certainly strong on theory if weak on facts. Thus, for example, in the *Handbook of Industrial Organization,* Bengt Holmström and Jean Tirole (1989, p. 126), writing on "The Theory of the Firm," remark that "the evidence/theory ratio . . . is currently very low in this field."

This disregard for what happens concretely in the real world is strengthened by the way economists think of their subject. In my youth, a very popular definition of economics was that provided by Lionel Robbins (1935, p. 15) in his book *An Essay on the Nature and Significance of Economic Science*: "Economics is the science which studies human behavior as a relationship between ends and scarce means that have alternative uses." It is the study of human behavior as a relationship. These days economists are more likely to refer to their subject as "the science of human choice" or they talk about "an economic approach." This is not a recent development. John Maynard Keynes said that the "Theory of Economics . . . is a method rather than a doctrine, an apparatus of the mind, a technique of thinking, which helps the possessor to draw correct conclusions" (introduction in H. D. Henderson 1922, p. v). Joan Robinson (1933, p. 1) says in the introduction to her book *The Economics of Imperfect Competition* that it "is presented to the analytical economist as a box of tools." What this comes down to is that economists think of themselves as having a box of tools but no subject matter. It reminds me of two lines from a modern poet (I forget the poem and the poet but the lines are indeed memorable):

> I see the bridle and the bit all right
> But where's the bloody horse?

I have expressed the same thought by saying that we study the circulation of the blood without a body.

In saying this I should not be thought to imply that these analytical tools are not extremely valuable. I am delighted when our colleagues in law use them to study the working of the legal system or when those in political science use them to study the working of the political system. My point is different. I think we should use these analytical tools to study the economic system. I think economists do have a subject matter: the study of the working of the economic system, a system in which we earn and spend our incomes. The welfare of a human society depends on the flow of goods and services, and this in turn depends on the productivity of the economic system. Adam Smith explained that the productivity of the economic system depends on specialization (he says the division of labor), but specialization is possible only if there is exchange – and the lower the costs of exchange (transaction costs if you will), the more specialization there will be and the greater the productivity of the system. But the costs of exchange depend on the institutions of a country: its legal system, its political system, its social system, its educational system, its culture, and so on. In effect it is the institutions that govern the performance of an economy, and it is this that gives the "New Institutional Economics" its importance for economists.

That such work is needed is made clear by another feature of economics. Apart from the formalization of the theory, the way we look at the working of the economic system has been extraordinarily static over the years. Economists often take pride in the fact that Charles Darwin came to his theory of evolution as a result of reading Thomas Malthus and Adam Smith. But contrast the developments in biology since Darwin with what has happened in economics since Adam Smith. Biology has been transformed. Biologists now have a detailed understanding of the complicated structures that govern the functioning of living organisms. I believe that one day we will have similar triumphs in economics. But it will not be easy. Even if we start with the relatively simple analysis of "The Nature of the Firm," discovering the factors that determine the relative costs of coordination by management within the firm or by transactions on the market is no simple task. However, this is not by any means the whole story. We cannot confine our analysis to what happens within a single firm. This is what I said in a lecture published in *Lives of the Laureates* (Coase 1995, p. 245): "The costs of coordination within a firm and the level of transaction costs that it faces are affected by its ability to purchase inputs from other firms, and their ability to supply these inputs depends in part on their costs of coordination and the level of transaction costs that they face which are similarly affected by what these are in still other firms. What we are dealing with is a complex interrelated structure." Add to this the influence of the laws, of the social system, and of the culture, as well as the effects of technological changes such as the digital revolution with its dramatic fall in information costs (a major component of transaction costs), and you have a complicated set of interrelationships the nature of which will take much dedicated work over a long period to discover. But when this is done, all of economics will have become what we now call "the New Institutional Economics."

This change will not come about, in my view, as a result of a frontal assault on mainstream economics. It will come as a result of economists in branches or sub-sections of economics adopting a different approach, as indeed is already happening. When the majority of economists have changed, mainstream economists will acknowledge the importance of examining the economic system in this way and will claim that they knew it all along.

NOTE

Chapter 2 was originally published in *American Economic Review*, 88(2), May 1998. It is reprinted with the permission of Ronald Coase and The American Economic Association.

3   Contract and economic organization

Oliver E. Williamson

1   Introduction

As discussed elsewhere, the New Institutional Economics works predominantly at two levels: the institutional environment, which includes both the formal (laws, polity, judiciary) and informal (customs, mores, norms) rules of the game, and the institutions of governance (markets, firms, bureaus) or play of the game (Williamson 1998). The transaction-cost economics approach to economic organization is concerned principally with the latter, with special emphasis on the governance of contractual relations. As it turns out, this approach to economic organization has wide application, generates a large number of refutable implications to which the data are broadly corroborative, and has many public policy ramifications – especially to anti-trust and regulation but to include labor, corporate governance, corporate finance, privatization, and the list goes on.

That the study of governance has such broad application is because any issue that arises as or can be reformulated *as a contracting problem* can be examined to advantage in transaction-cost economizing terms. Many issues present themselves naturally in this form – the mundane make-or-buy decision being an example. The comparative contractual choice to be made here is whether a firm should contract out for the provision of a good or service or take the transaction out of the market and manage it internally. The contractual nature of other transactions is more subtle – as with the corporate finance decision, where the choice needs to be made between debt and equity. Ordinarily debt and equity are treated as strictly financial instruments, but they are also usefully viewed as alternative modes of governance – where debt is the more market-like mode of contracting for project finance and equity is the more administrative form and is akin to hierarchy. Still other transactions need to be reformulated to bring out their contractual nature, the oligopoly problem being an example. The contractual issues surface here not when the problem is posed in Cournot or structure–conduct–performance (SCP) terms but as a cartel problem. When does the unenforceable and often illegal "contract" among members of a cartel work well or poorly, and why?

But there is a puzzle. If the comparative contractual approach to economic organization has wide application and generates new and testable propositions, why did it take so long to take hold? Also, where does it go from here?

2   Obstacles

Major obstacles to the comparative contractual approach to economic organization were that (1) orthodoxy was uncritical in its treatment of the firm in technological terms, partly because it was committed to full formalization, (2) contract had come to be viewed as unproblematic because of the presumed efficacy of contract law and its enforcement, and (3) organization was ignored, dismissed, or suppressed. Consider each in turn.

The theory of the firm-as-production function (or as production possibility set) was both a major conceptual achievement and a great analytical convenience for the progressive mathematization of economics in the immediate post-war era. To be sure, other social scientists were unpersuaded by some of the more arid abstractions of economics. The Graduate School of Industrial Administration at Carnegie Tech aside, however, the business schools lacked the academic credentials to dispute economic orthodoxy (Gordon and Howell 1959). And the gulf between economics and sociology was vast (witness the quip by James Duesenberry that "economics is all about how people make choices; sociology is all about how they don't have any choices to make," 1960, p. 233).

The ideas that contracts were complete and that the laws on contract (regarding offer and acceptance, breach, etc.) were well conceived and were enforced by well-informed courts in a legalistic way effectively removed contract from the research agenda. Upon treating contracts as unproblematic and fully within the purview of the law, the self-contained nature of the economics enterprise was reinforced.

The propensity of economists to delimit microeconomics to price and output served further to limit the scope. As Harold Demsetz put it, "It is a mistake to confuse the firm of economic theory with its real-world namesake. The chief mission of neoclassical economics is to understand how the price system coordinates the use of resources, not to understand the inner workings of real firms" (1983, p. 377). The contributions of organization theory to the study of economic organization and contract could thus also be set aside.

3 Growing discontent

In addition to the price and output purposes described by Demsetz, economists were also expected to advise on public policy. This very same theory of the firm was also used by Industrial Organization specialists to inform anti-trust and regulation. That was an embarrassment, in that the interpretation of non-standard and unfamiliar contracting and organizational practices in strictly technological terms invited convoluted and even preposterous public policy – although that was not evident until someone observed that the emperor was scantily dressed (Coase 1972). Concurrently, the legal centralism approach to contract law and its enforcement was also coming under criticism from lawyers, whence the readiness of economists to be dismissive of contract was being questioned. The growing importance of the modern corporation was also bringing issues of organization and governance more forcefully to the fore. The upshot is the economic, legal, and organizational foundations for the orthodox theory of the firm were all under assault. Consider each in turn.

So long as the firm was viewed in strictly technological terms, students of public policy were prone to condemn structures and practices that did not have obvious technological origins or serve technological purposes. For example, vertical integration that lacks a "physical or technical aspect," such as integrating the production of assorted components or forward integration into distribution, was believed to be lacking in economizing purpose and effect and, therefore, to be deeply problematic – whereupon excesses of vertical integration and firm size were projected (Bain 1968, p. 381). More generally, non-standard and unfamiliar contracting and organizational practices were believed to have anti-competitive purpose and effect, there being no legitimate economizing purpose that could accrue thereto. The then head of the Antitrust Division of the US Department of Justice thus treated "customer and territorial restrictions not hospitably in the common law tradition, but inhospitably in the tradition of antitrust."[1]

Reversing such a policy was not easy. It takes a theory to beat a theory (Kuhn 1970), and a rival theory needed to be fashioned. Ongoing developments in law and organization contributed to this purpose.

The legalistic approach to contract law had come under criticism from Karl Llewellyn in 1931, but that took time to register. Llewellyn's early distinction between the prevailing contract as legal rules approach and his proposed contract as framework approach is basic. The contract as framework approach recognizes that all complex contracts are unavoidably incomplete and holds that a contract between two parties "almost never accurately indicates real working relations, but ... affords a rough indication around which such relations vary, an occasional guide in cases of doubt, and a norm of ultimate appeal when the relations cease in fact to work" (Llewellyn 1931, p. 737). The main contractual action thus takes place between the parties in the context of private ordering, to which court ordering appears late for purposes of ultimate appeal, if at all.[2]

That reverses the "legal centralism" tradition, which holds that "disputes require 'access' to a forum external to the original social setting of the dispute [and that] remedies will be provided as prescribed in some body of authoritative learning and dispensed by experts who operate under the auspices of the state" (Galanter 1981, p. 1). The facts, however, reveal otherwise. Most disputes, including many that under current rules could be brought to a court, are resolved by avoidance, self-help, and the like (Galanter 1981, p. 2). That is because in "many instances the participants can devise more satisfactory solutions to their disputes than can professionals constrained to apply general rules on the basis of limited knowledge of the dispute" (Galanter 1981, p. 4). Private ordering through *ex post* governance is therefore where the main action resides.

A growing appreciation for the importance of organization and, more generally, of governance was also taking shape. Alfred Chandler's study of the modern corporation in the first half of the twentieth century revealed that significant organization form changes had taken place with the result that the managerial discretion problem with which Adolf Berle and Gardiner Means (1932) were concerned was being brought under more effective control (Chandler 1962). In that event, the firm was more than a production function. The structure of the corporation, especially as between centralized (U-form) and divisionalized (M-form), had governance/economizing consequences as well.

4   Fashioning a response

The comparative contractual approach to economic organization is responsive to all three of these critiques. Rather than hold law, economics, and organization apart, a combined law, economics, and organizations approach began to take shape. The firm is described as a governance structure in which (1) economizing transcends technology to include contract and organization, (2) comparison with alternative modes of managing contracts is featured, and (3) organization form matters.

Describing the human actors whose behavior we are studying turns out to be important to this project. So does naming the unit of analysis.

4.1   Human actors

According to Herbert Simon, "*Nothing* is more fundamental in setting our research agenda and informing our research methods than our view of the human beings whose behavior we are studying" (Simon 1985, p. 303, emphasis added). That challenges the propensity of economists to describe human actors in a fashion that served their analytical convenience – as illustrated by the triple of omniscience, omnipotence, and benevolence to which Avinash Dixit refers (1996, p. 6) in his description of old-style public policy analysis.

The transaction-cost treatment of human actors emphasizes three features: the cognitive ability of human actors, their self-interestedness, and their capacity for foresight. Describing human actors as boundedly rational – that is, intendedly rational, but only limitedly so (Simon 1961, p. xxiv) – undermines the idea of complete contracting. Instead, all complex contracts are unavoidably incomplete – hence contain errors, gaps, omissions, and the like. Such incompleteness is of special concern where human actors are given to opportunism, hence will not reliably self-enforce all promises. Instead, they will sometimes behave strategically – by sending false or misleading signals, by interpreting the data to their advantage, by costly repositioning, and by otherwise withholding best efforts to realize mutual gains. Mere promise, unsupported by credible commitments, is not self-enforcing by reason of opportunism.

A redeeming feature, however, is that human actors possess the capacity for conscious foresight. As Richard Dawkins puts it, the "capacity to simulate the future in imagination . . . [saves] us from the worst consequences of the blind replicators" (1976, p. 20). Parties to a complex contract who look ahead, recognize potential hazards, work out the contractual ramifications, and fold these into the *ex ante* contractual agreement obviously enjoy advantages over those who are myopic or take their chances and knock on wood. Human actors with conscious foresight will take steps to mitigate contractual hazards by crafting responsive governance structures.

4.2   Unit of analysis

But wherein do the potential hazards reside? What does working out the contractual ramifications entail? How does the *ex ante* contractual agreement get reshaped? John R. Commons' prescient insights apply. It was his position that "the ultimate unit of activity . . . must contain in itself the three principles of conflict, mutuality, and order. This unit is a transaction" (Commons 1932, p. 4).[3]

Taking the transaction to be the basic unit of analysis has turned out to be an instructive way of uncovering contractual hazards. If some transactions pose few hazards and others pose many, then presumably there are systematic differences between them. Identifying the key attributes of transactions that give rise to differential hazards has been instructive both for the theory of contract and economic organization and for empirical investigations that appertain thereto (which sometimes take the form of focused case studies, as with John Stuckey's study of vertical integration and joint ventures in the aluminum industry, 1983, but more often involve cross-section studies that employ conventional econometric techniques, as with Paul Joskow's study of coal contracting for electric power generation, 1987).[4]

4.3   Operationalization

The idea that the transaction is the basic unit of analysis needs to be harnessed to an economic purpose. The Commons' triple invites the concept of governance – where governance is the means by which *order* is accomplished in a relation in which potential *conflict* threatens to upset or undo opportunities to realize *mutual* gains. Economizing purposes that transcend technology are thereby realized.

Combining the idea that economizing is the main purpose served by economic organization with the proposition that mitigating contractual hazards (in cost effective degree) is among the chief economizing purposes to be served leads to the following hypothesis: transactions, which differ in their attributes, are aligned with governance structures, which differ in their cost and competence, so as to effect an economizing result. Transaction-cost economics realizes much of its predictive content from this discriminating alignment hypothesis.

Implementation of this hypothesis requires that alternative modes of governance be identified and their defining attributes described. There being no single, all-purpose superior form of organization, all evidently have strengths and weaknesses. That is because each generic mode of organization is defined by an internally consistent syndrome of attributes to which differential performance competencies accrue. As discussed elsewhere (Williamson 1991, 1999), key attributes of governance include (1) incentive intensity, (2) administrative controls, and (3) the applicable law of contract. Both different types of markets (spot markets and various forms of long-term contracting) and different types of hierarchies (firms, regulation, public bureaus) are distinguished. In general, incentive intensity decreases and administrative controls build up in moving

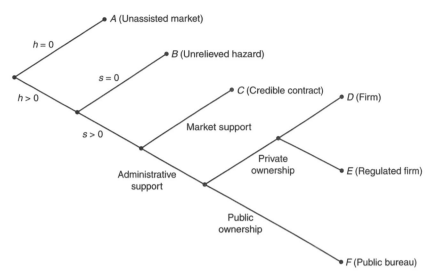

Figure 3.1   Incentive intensity and administrative controls

across the succession shown in figure 3.1 (where h denotes hazards and s denotes safeguards).

What is furthermore noteworthy is that each generic mode of governance is supported by a distinctive form of contract law. The contract law of spot markets is that of legal rules, which is the ideal transaction in both law and economics: "sharp in by clear agreement; sharp out by clear performance" (Macneil 1974, p. 738). This legal rules approach gives way to Llewellyn's concept of contract-as-framework as the importance of continuity builds up and incomplete long-term contracting is adopted. That in turn undergoes change when transactions are taken out of the market and organized internally. The implicit law of contract now becomes that of forbearance. Thus whereas courts routinely grant standing to firms engaged in inter-firm contracting should there be disputes over prices, the damages to be ascribed to delays, failures of quality, and the like, courts will refuse to hear disputes between one internal division and another over identical technical issues. Access to the courts being denied, the parties must resolve their differences internally. Accordingly, hierarchy is its own court of ultimate appeal. That firms and markets differ in their access to fiat is partly explained by these contract law differences.

The concept of contract thus has a pervasive influence on the study of economic organization. Consider the following five features: (1) the transaction (trade, exchange, contract) is the basic unit of analysis; (2) all complex contracts are incomplete (by reason of bounded rationality); (3) many contracts pose hazards (because mere promise, unsupported by credible commitments, is not self-enforcing – by reason of opportunism); (4) governance structures, which are the institutional frameworks within which the integrity of contract is decided, are hazard mitigating responses; and (5) each generic mode of governance is supported by a distinctive form of contract law.

4.4   Additional features

Omitted from the discussion but important to an understanding of contract and organization are (1) the institutional environment – constitution, laws, polity, judiciary – which define the rules of the game, (2) the central importance of adaptation, of both autonomous (Hayek 1945) and cooperative (Barnard 1938) kinds, to economic performance, and (3) the distinctive process attributes of organization, in auditing, accounting, informal organization, bureaucratization, and politicking, to include the ramifications of each on comparative economic organization. Suffice it to observe here that the study of contract and economic organization is an ambitious interdisciplinary undertaking. (For a discussion, see Williamson 1991.)

5   Looking ahead

The transaction-cost approach to economic organization has progressed through a series of stages. Beginning with informal (Coase 1937) and preformal (Williamson 1975; Klein, Crawford and Alchian 1978) stages, transaction-cost economics has moved into semi-formal (Klein and Leffler 1981; Williamson 1983, 1991; Riordan and Williamson 1985), and fully formal (Grossman and Hart 1986; Hart 1995) work.

Although full formalization is vital to a progressive research agenda, it can also be problematic. Here, as elsewhere, there are trade-offs. Thus although Simon once argued that "mathematical translation is itself a substantive contribution to theory . . . because it permits clear and rigorous reasoning about phenomena too complex to be handled in words" (1957, p. 89) and subsequently asserted that the "poverty of mathematics is an honest poverty that does not parade imaginary riches before the world" (1957, p. 90), provision also needs to be made for the possibility that core features of the theory are left out or obscured by the translation. There is, after all, such a thing as prematurely formal theory. David Kreps speaks to the issues as follows (1999, p. 122):

If *Markets and Hierarchies* has been translated into game theory using notions of information economics, it is a very poor translation . . . In particular, mathematics-based theory still lacks the language needed to capture essential ideas of bounded rationality, which are central to . . . transaction costs and contractual form. Anyone who relies on the translations alone misses large and valuable chunks of the original.

Kreps has reference especially to the "property rights theory of the firm," which is the fully formal theory to which I refer above. My reservations about this theory have been discussed elsewhere (Williamson 2000) and will not be repeated here. More to the point is that a series of promising full formalization efforts are taking shape "even as I write." These include the unpublished paper by Oliver Hart and John Moore (1999b), the unpublished paper by Patrick Bajari and Steven Tadelis (1999), and the unpublished paper by Gene Grossman and Elhanan Helpman (1999). I am confident that these are harbingers of more to come.

Such theoretical developments in combination with the vast and growing empirical literature in transaction-cost economics[5] lead me to project that the comparative contractual approach to the study of economic organization will remain an active area for research well into the new millennium. Public policy has been and will continue to be a beneficiary.

6 Concluding remarks

Whereas once the subject of contract was relegated to an obscure closet in the house of economics, that has changed as greater appreciation for more veridical attributes (as against analytically convenient attributes) of human actors has set in, the limits of legal centralism have been conceded, and the apparatus for doing comparative contractual analysis has been progressively built up. One of the most important developments with respect to this last has been to go beyond the "black box" theory of the firm (according to which the firm is a production function) to view the firm in comparative contractual terms – as a governance structure.[6] As Kreps observes (1990, p. 96):

The [neoclassical] firm is like individual agents in textbook economics . . . Agents have utility functions, firms have a profit motive; agents have consumption sets, firms have production possibility sets. But in transaction-cost economics, firms are more like markets – both are arenas within which the individual can transact.

This reconceptualization of firms and markets as alternative modes of governance with discrete structural differences has had ramifications for anti-trust and regulation and has promise for helping to reshape public policy analysis more generally. Avinash Dixit's monograph on *The Making of Economic Policy* has precisely that ambition (1996, p. 9):

Economists studying business and industrial organization have long recognized the inadequacy of the neoclassical view of the firm and have developed richer paradigms and models based on various kinds of transactions costs. Policy analysis also stands to benefit from such an approach, opening the black box and examining the actual workings of the mechanism inside. This is the starting point, and a recurrent theme, of this monograph.

I conclude that the examination of alternative modes of organization through the lens of contract and transaction cost economizing has been and will continue to be a productive research enterprise.

NOTES

Chapter 3 was originally published as "Contract and Economic Organization," in *Revue d'Economie Industrielle* (92, 2000).
1. The quotation is attributed to Donald Turner by Stanley Robinson, New York State Bar Association, Antitrust Symposium, 1968, p. 29.
2. Recourse to the literal language of the contract and access to the courts for purposes of ultimate appeal are important so as to delimit threat positions.
3. Such profound insights failed to impress critics of older-style institutional economics, who held that "Without a theory [American institutionalists] had nothing to pass on except a mass of descriptive material waiting for a theory, or a fire" (Coase 1984, p. 230).
4. Surveys of empirical transaction cost economics are reported in Howard Shelanski and Peter Klein (1995), Keith Crocker and Scott Masten (1996), Bruce Lyons (1996), and Aric Rindfleisch and Jan Heide (1997).
5. See n. 3.
6. This is responsive to Kenneth Arrow's advisory that "Any standard economic theory, not just neoclassical, starts from the existence of firms. Usually, the firm is a point or at any rate a black box . . . But firms are palpably not points. They have internal structure. This internal structure must arise for a reason" (1999, p. vii).

4   The role of incomplete contracts in self-enforcing relationships

Benjamin Klein

1   Introduction

A major advance in economics involves the recognition that contracts adopted by transactors are incomplete. This fundamental insight has produced two main strands of economic research. One strand of research emphasizes the importance of self-enforcement in assuring contractual performance. Building upon Stuart Macaulay's pioneering study[1] documenting that performance is secured in most business relationships not by the threat of court enforcement but by the threat of termination of the relationship, this work develops models of self-enforcement where a termination sanction is sufficient to assure transactor performance.[2]

The other, more extensive, unrelated strand of economic research flowing from incomplete contracts is the principal–agent contract design literature. This work examines the role of contract terms in minimizing transactor malincentives given that performance can only imperfectly be contracted on. The major point of this chapter is that the incomplete contract terms actually used by transactors in the marketplace can be understood only by combining these two strands of research. What follows is a summary of my research on contracts from this perspective of integrating our research on incomplete contracts.

One way to integrate the two lines of research on incomplete contracts is to add *self-enforcement* considerations to the principal–agent model.[3] The alternative way I have attempted this integration is by extending the simple model of self-enforcement to take account of the role of contract terms in facilitating self-enforcement. Contract terms are used as an aid to self-enforcement because the transactors' reputational capital through which the self-enforcement mechanism operates is limited (in the sense that transactors can credibly promise to pay only a finite maximum future amount to their transacting partners in return for current performance). Therefore, although Macaulay and others are correct in noting that many business relationships are self-enforced, transactors are not indifferent regarding the contract terms they choose to govern their self-enforcing relationships.

Rather than explaining the incomplete contract terms chosen by transactors in terms of the minimization of direct transactor malincentives, contract terms are considered here as devices that economize on transactors' limited reputational capital to facilitate self-enforcement. Transactors use contract terms to get close to desired performance without creating too much rigidity and to shift future rents between transacting parties so as to coincide more closely with each transactor's potential non-performance gain. In these ways contract terms assure that the transactors' business relationship remains self-enforcing over the broadest range of likely future market conditions. Within this framework where contract terms are used to efficiently define the self-enforcing range of the transactors' contractual relationship, self-enforcement and court-enforcement are not alternative enforcement mechanisms, but are complementary instruments used by transactors in combination to guarantee transactor performance.

2   Incomplete contracts

Contracts are incomplete because there are significant information and measurement costs surrounding most business transactions. When a large number of possible contingencies exist regarding future events, the use of the fully contingent complete contract of economic theory is too costly. Transactors use incomplete contracts in these circumstances not only to avoid the significant "ink costs" of writing fully contingent contracts, but, more importantly, because incomplete contracts avoid the wasteful search and negotiation costs that otherwise would be borne by transactors. The attempt to specify desired performance completely for a very large number of unlikely possibilities primarily involves the costly search by transactors for an informational and negotiating advantage over their transacting partner. Contractual specification of performance for such extremely low-probability contingencies creates potential wealth distribution effects, where one transactor will receive a transfer in the event some unlikely contingency occurs, with little or no allocative benefits in terms of creating proper *ex ante* incentives. Therefore, while these real resource costs associated with complete contractual negotiation will lead individual profit maximizing transactors to stop short of complete contract specification, transactors may jointly decide to reduce the wasteful rent dissipating activity of increased contractual specification even further. Transactors enter relationships knowing they have left some unlikely contingencies unspecified, recognizing that if such a contingency develops, it will have to be handled after the fact.

In addition to avoiding the rent dissipating search and negotiation costs involved in complete contractual specification, contracts are incomplete because of measurement costs. Some aspects of performance, such as the taste of a hamburger or the energy an employee devotes to a task, may be prohibitively costly to contractually specify in a way that breach can be demonstrated to a third-party enforcer. Therefore, performance along these not easily measured dimensions will not be fully specified in the contract.

Because the contract terms used by transactors are necessarily incomplete, transactors are cautious regarding what they write in their contracts. Incomplete contract terms may create opportunities for transactors to engage in a hold-up by using the court to enforce the literal imperfect contract term in a manner that is contrary to the intent of the contractual understanding.[4] This is one of the primary economic lessons of the General Motors–Fisher Body case. In that case Fisher took advantage of the long-term, cost-plus exclusive dealing contract designed by the parties to encourage Fisher to make GM-specific investments to hold up General Motors. The long-term contract used to protect Fisher's GM-specific investments which locked Fisher into GM-created contractual specificity that locked General Motors into Fisher. Fisher then took advantage of this long-term GM contractual commitment by refusing to locate an important body plant next to the GM assembly plant. As a consequence, Fisher produced very costly (but highly profitable) automobile bodies that General Motors was compelled to buy.[5]

The General Motors–Fisher example illustrates that, contrary to most models, increased contractual specification can make things worse.[6] Increased contractual specification not only produces benefits, but also creates costs. In particular, rigidity is created when an agreement is formalized in a long-term explicit contract. Only by declaring bankruptcy could General Motors have unilaterally opted out of not performing to the literal imperfect terms of the long-term Fisher Body contract. Unless a side payment was made to Fisher Body (and vertical integration was the form in which such a side payment was ultimately made), General Motors was forced to continue buying bodies at cost-plus from improperly located plants until the contract expired. If, on the other hand, the Fisher–GM understanding had not been formalized in a long-term written contract, the parties would have been able to flexibly alter their supply arrangements without being forced by the court to adhere to the conditions of the imperfect written agreement.

The extent of contractual specification chosen by transactors involves trading-off the obvious benefit of being able to use the court to enforce elements of performance with these less obvious costs of contractual specification. Increased contractual specification involves rent dissipating search and negotiation costs that results in an imperfect, rigid agreement which can then be used by transactors to hold up one another. The existence of these costs, not the narrow transaction costs associated with contractual specification, is why transactors often decide to intentionally leave some elements of performance unspecified.

3   Self-enforcing arrangements

Transactors can freely avoid the costs associated with complete contractual specification because they have available a self-enforcement mechanism to assure performance. Rather than court enforcement of written contract terms, a self-enforcement mechanism operates by threatening termination of the business relationship for non-performance of the unwritten contractual understanding. Transactors compare the short-term gains they can achieve by not performing consistent with the contractual understanding, W_1, with the discounted expected future profit stream they will lose if the relationship is terminated for such non-performance, W_2. Performance is assured when

$$W_1 < W_2 \tag{1}$$

W_2, the capital cost of the lost expected future profit stream that is imposed upon a non-performing transactor when the relationship is terminated,

$$W_2 = \Pi_0^* + \frac{\Pi_1^*}{1+r} + \frac{\Pi_2^*}{(1+r)^2} + \cdots \tag{2}$$

is called the *transactor's reputational capital*. The magnitude of each transactor's reputational capital determines, according to (1), the efficacy of the self-enforcement mechanism.

When sufficient reputational capital exists, transactors will rely on self-enforcement rather than court-enforcement. Self-enforcement avoids the costs associated with contractual specification described above and reduces the time lag and noise involved in court detection and sanction of non-performance. Court-enforcement entails an imperfect time-intensive process of contract interpretation to determine whether a contractual understanding has been violated or not, followed by a further period to determine an appropriate penalty. Rather than relying on necessarily imperfect contract terms to communicate the elements of agreed-upon performance to the court, such third-party contract interpretation and enforcement problems are avoided entirely with a self-enforcing mechanism. With self-enforcement, once transactors learn that their transacting partner has not performed, a termination sanction is imposed. Therefore, if sufficient reputational capital exists, transactors always will prefer to handle contract performance with self-enforcement.

If General Motors had possessed sufficient reputational capital, an explicit long-term contract would not have been used to induce Fisher Body to make its GM-specific investments and the subsequent costs associated with the contract would have been avoided. A long-term Fisher–GM contract would not have been necessary because General Motors would have had more to lose in the long run than it could gain in the short run from holding up Fisher Body for its GM-specific investments. Therefore, Fisher would have been assured that General Motors would not engage in a hold-up and would not have required the long-term exclusive dealing contract that later led to the Fisher hold-up of General Motors. It has been extensively documented that Japanese automobile manufacturers avoid these costs of court-enforcement in their dealings with parts suppliers in exactly this way.[7] By relying primarily on the threat of non-renewal of the relationship Japanese manufacturers induce their suppliers to make the required specific investments and to charge reasonable prices that are adjusted downward at regular intervals as sales increase and supplier costs fall.[8]

However, although self-enforcement is preferable to court-enforcement, transactors cannot always rely entirely on a self-enforcement mechanism because the magnitude of the private sanction that can be imposed for non-performance, W_2, is limited. Presumably, this is the reason why General Motors could not use a Japanese-type supply arrangement in its dealings with Fisher Body. General Motors' lack of sufficient reputational capital (W_2) compared to its hold-up potential given the magnitude of Fisher's required specific investments (W_1) made it impossible for Fisher and General Motors to use the superior, largely self-enforcing alternative. Instead, they were forced to rely to a large extent on court-enforcement.

4   Contract terms complement self-enforcement

In this framework the fundamental economic motivation for the use of court-enforceable contract terms is to supplement self-enforcement. Court-enforced explicit contract terms are a necessary evil that are used by transactors solely because the transactors possess limited reputational capital. This has broad implications for the economic analysis of contracts. Looking at contract terms in this way, it makes no sense to analyze the malincentive effects of contract terms in isolation from self-enforcement. It suggests that incomplete contract terms are likely to be used by transactors only to get close to desired performance, with transactors using a self-enforcement mechanism to move behavior the remainder of the way towards the desired level. As a consequence, the standard principal–agent view of incomplete contracts, where contract terms are considered solely as devices that create optimal incentives on imperfect court-enforceable proxies for performance, provides a biased view of contractual arrangements. Without considering self-enforcement, the malincentives that remain in most actual contractual arrangements are likely to be enormous. Incomplete contract terms cannot be understood without recognizing that their role often is to control W_1 so that it remains below W_2.

Recognition of the role of contract terms in facilitating self-enforcement explains, for example, why Fisher and General Motors used such seemingly inappropriate cost-plus/exclusive dealing contract terms. These contract terms may appear to have created an incentive for Fisher to increase the costs of auto bodies to the contractually "locked-in" General Motors. But the terms can be understood only within the context of self-enforcement, where contract terms, although imperfect, are designed to create conditions where each transactor has more to lose from termination of the relationship than it has to gain from not performing. Within this self-enforcement framework, the Fisher–GM contract terms were efficient when the parties entered into their contractual arrangement in 1919. In fact, although Fisher always had the ability to exploit the imperfect Fisher–GM body supply contract, the contract functioned extremely well for more than five years. Presumably, Fisher had more to lose from GM's non-renewal of the agreement than it had to gain. It was only in 1925, when GM's demand for Fisher bodies increased dramatically (along with new large required Fisher-specific investments) that Fisher began to take advantage of the contract. The next section discusses what occurred in the Fisher–GM relationship to make it no longer self-enforcing. But the role of incomplete contract terms in facilitating self-enforcement is first discussed in some more detail.

Equation (1) suggests that transactors can use incomplete contract terms to facilitate self-enforcement in two fundamental ways, by either reducing W_1 or increasing W_2. Reducing W_1 is the common motivation for contractual specification in the economic literature. By defining a particular element of performance, the ability not to perform along this dimension is directly controlled with court-enforcement. But, contrary to standard economic literature, the goal of such contractual specification is to make the residual W_1 (that is too costly to reduce further because of the contract specification costs discussed above) less than W_2.

In addition to contract terms operating on the left-hand side of (1) to reduce the expected gains from non-performance and hence the amount of reputational capital necessary to make the arrangement self-enforcing, contract terms also can operate on the right-hand side of (1). In particular, by shifting expected future rents and, therefore, reputational capital between transactors, contract terms can make each transactor's reputational capital coincide more closely with the transactors' potential expected gain from non-performance. This effect provides an economic rationale for many of the contract terms used in distribution arrangements, such as resale price maintenance (RPM) or exclusive territories.[9] By limiting the extent of intra-firm competition faced by a manufacturer's dealers, these contract terms create future rents that dealers operating under such contractual arrangements can expect to earn. Hence, these contract terms facilitate self-enforcement of dealer performance by, in effect, shifting some of the manufacturer's reputational capital to its dealers. The contract thereby increases the limited amount of dealer reputational capital relative to the dealers' non-performance potential, creating a situation where dealers have more to lose if they do not perform as desired.

Such a shift in rents can occur only if the manufacturer can credibly make such a commitment, that is, only if the manufacturer has more to lose if it reneges on the commitment than if it pays the dealer the promised future rents. This will depend on the cost to the manufacturer of organizing distribution in some less efficient alternative way. For example, in franchising arrangements franchisors can credibly commit to pay franchisees a future premium stream at most equal to the present discounted value of the cost savings of handling distribution with a franchising system than with the next most efficient non-franchising system, such as operating its outlets with employees. Any promised future franchisee premium stream greater than this will lead the franchisor not to pay the premium and, instead, bear such higher distribution costs. This implies the paradoxical result that a credible commitment is less likely to be made by a franchisor or manufacturer as the cost of the next most efficient alternative distribution arrangement decreases. Franchisees or dealers will believe they will receive the future profit premium promised by the franchisor or manufacturer only if paying it is cheaper for them than not paying it.[10]

Of course, both effects of contract terms in facilitating self-enforcement may operate at the same time. For example, consider exclusive territory arrangements, where a manufacturer designates a dealer as the exclusive supplier of the manufacturer's goods or services within a particular area. Such an arrangement increases the dealer's probability of repeat sales, internalizing dealer actions and thereby decreasing the dealer's short-run gain from non-performance, W_1. But granting a dealer an exclusive territory also may increase the dealer's future continuing profit stream, thereby creating a valuable dealer asset that can be lost by termination for non-performance, W_2.

This analysis illustrates a fundamental complementarity between court-enforcement and self-enforcement. The two enforcement mechanisms are substitutes in demand, in the sense of a positive cross-elasticity of demand, so that an increase in the price of one mechanism leads to an increased use of the other mechanism. (For example, an increase in the cost of using the court, such as in Russia, will lead to the increased use of self-enforcement by transactors.) But the two enforcement mechanisms are complements in supply, in the sense of a positive cross-elasticity of supply, so that an increase, for example, in the quantity of reputational capital leads to an increase in the marginal productivity of court-enforcement. That is, the two mechanisms work better together than either of them do separately.

5   The self-enforcing range of contractual relationships

Transactors will design their contractual arrangements, i.e., combine court-enforced written contract terms with self-enforced unwritten terms so as to optimally define the self-enforcing range of their relationship. In particular, as the Fisher Body–GM case illustrates, contract terms facilitate self-enforcement at the point of contracting but more generally how the contract terms minimize expected costs of hold-up possibilities over time. That is, since the future market conditions and hence the future gains from non-performance are uncertain at the time individuals enter into their contractual agreements, W_1 and W_2 should be thought of probabilistically.

The amount of each transactor's reputational capital, therefore, should be thought of as defining the self-enforcing range of the contractual relationship, or the extent to which market conditions can change (thereby altering the value of sunk specific investments and the gains to one or the other party from non-performance) without precipitating non-performance. Within the self-enforcing range, in spite of the change in market conditions, each transactor's gain from non-performance remains less than the self-enforcing sanction that can be imposed. Whether the contract terms chosen by transactors facilitate self-enforcement in either

of the two general ways outlined above, namely by controlling the expected gains from non-performance or by shifting reputational capital
between the parties, the intended result is to widen the extent to which
ex post market conditions may change unanticipatedly yet performance
remains assured.

This probabilistic self-enforcing framework explains why hold-ups
sometimes occur.[11] In the Fisher–GM case it does not make sense to
assume that Fisher Body took advantage of General Motors because
General Motors was naïve or because Fisher Body was able to deceive
General Motors into entering an imperfect long-term, exclusive dealing,
cost-plus contract.[12] Relying on the ability of transactors to deceive
their transacting partners is a highly unsatisfactory, usually untestable,
way to explain why hold-ups occur. General Motors and Fisher Body
were two large, sophisticated business firms that likely were fully cog-
nizant of the malincentive problems inherent in the imperfect contract
they entered into. General Motors and Fisher adopted the contract in
spite of these problems because they expected it to function satisfactorily
in combination with a self-enforcement mechanism. That is, Fisher and
General Motors expected their contractual relationship to remain within
the self-enforcing range defined by each transactor's reputational capital.
As noted above, the contract, in fact, worked well for more than five years
and, under normal circumstances, would have remained self-enforcing.

The Fisher–GM case vividly illustrates that the use of imperfect contract terms solves non-performance problems in some states of the world
but creates non-performance problems in other states of the world. If
General Motors' demand for Fisher's auto bodies had not grown so
dramatically after 1925 increasing Fisher's short-run gains from non-
performance, the contract Fisher and General Motors had adopted,
although imperfect, would have remained self-enforcing. The gains to
Fisher from taking advantage of the contract would have remained less
than Fisher's reputational capital and, therefore, the hold-up potential
associated with the cost-plus contract terms would not have mattered. It
was only after General Motors' demand for Fisher's bodies and Fisher's
required specific investments increased late in the contract term that the
contract's "inefficiencies" were acted upon by Fisher. It was only then that
Fisher found itself outside the self-enforcing range, where Fisher's reputational capital, or the private sanction that could be imposed on Fisher
by General Motors, became less than Fisher's short-term gain from not
performing. Fisher then found it profitable to violate the intent of the contractual understanding by taking advantage of the imperfect terms of the
agreement, refusing to make the necessary capital investments required
to produce bodies efficiently for General Motors.[13]

Fisher and General Motors presumably recognized when they entered their contractual relationship and made their specific investments that their reputational capital was limited, that the written contract terms they had chosen were imperfect and incomplete and, therefore, that there was some probability the contract would fail and a hold-up would occur if changes in market conditions moved either of them outside the "self-enforcing range," as occurred during 1925 when General Motors' demand for the bodies supplied by Fisher greatly increased. At that point the pressure placed on the imperfect contractual agreement used to facilitate self-enforcement became greater than the contract could withstand and the Fisher Body–GM relationship moved outside the self-enforcing range.

6   Vertical integration

The Fisher Body–GM analysis explains why transactors, when choosing the imperfect contract terms that govern their self-enforcing relationships, are more likely to use a vertical integration type of contractual arrangement when they expect future market conditions to be highly variable. When the uncertainty of future market conditions increases, the value of the hold-up potential present in every imperfect contract also increases. Parties entering contractual relationships can be thought of as buying and selling what amounts to options related to the probability of a hold-up occurring. As in standard options pricing theory, the values of these options increase as the value of the ratio of the underlying asset price increases relative to the exercise price (in our case, as the value of the hold-up potential increases relative to the transactor's reputational capital), and as the variance per period of the asset price multiplied by the number of periods increases (in our case, as the variance of underlying market conditions multiplied by the length of the contract increases).[14] Since transactors wish to avoid the costs associated with hold-ups even if they are not risk averse, this makes vertical integration, with its increased ability to make flexible post-contract adjustments, more likely.[15]

The alternative to vertical integration (in cases where the parties have made specific investments and W_1 is greater than W_2, i.e. where the relationship cannot solely be self-enforced) is an explicit long-term contract. The greater the uncertainty of future market conditions, the more likely it is that the arrangement defined by this imperfect long-term contract and the transactors' reputational capital will move outside the "self-enforcing range." In these circumstances the increased flexibility and control transactors gain from not using a rigid long-term contract to supplement their insufficient reputational capital is a primary economic advantage of vertical integration.[16] Transactors using vertical integration avoid the rigidity costs of long-term explicit contracts illustrated by the Fisher–GM case, at the cost of increased incentive inefficiencies associated with vertical integration (that presumably cannot be self-enforced because of the difficulty of detection). That is, vertical integration increases W_1, but makes the relationship more flexible and, therefore, self-enforcing (or decreases W_1 relative to W_2) in a wider set of *ex post* circumstances.

This analysis highlights the shortcomings in the pioneering Grossman and Hart model of integration.[17] While this model has the advantage of taking the incompleteness of contracts seriously, it does not consider the key aspect of the contractual arrangement we identify with the firm, namely that it involves less explicit contractual specification and more flexibility. Moreover, even within the context of this model, the primary conclusion that unspecified residual rights (what Grossman and Hart identify with the firm form of contract) should be allocated to the transactor that will misuse the rights the least makes sense only if we ignore self-enforcement. Because contract terms are not designed solely to minimize inefficiencies, how asset ownership is allocated is not determined independent of the reputational capital of the parties. Transactors must also take account of the reputational capital of the parties, in addition to their incentives to take advantage of residual rights not to perform, to determine who will be the owner of a particular asset. For example, even if ownership by one transactor causes increased gains from non-performance, this does not imply that the transactor is not the correct owner of the asset if its reputational capital is higher.[18]

7   Conclusion

To increase our economic understanding of contracts, it is necessary to get one's hands dirty and discover how particular contracts actually work in practice. However, to make progress in this empirical analysis one must have an appropriate organizing framework. In particular, one must recognize that the goal of contractual specification often is not to create optimal incentives on some imperfect court-enforceable proxy for performance. Rather than focusing solely on these direct incentive effects of contract terms now emphasized in the incomplete contracting literature, economic analysis of contract terms must also consider how contract terms may be used to facilitate self-enforcement. Contractual arrangements can be fully understood only by recognizing that transactors use court-enforced imperfect contract terms, including vertical integration, as a complement to their limited reputational capital in order to make a particular relationship self-enforcing over the broadest range of likely post-contract market conditions.

NOTES

Chapter 4 was originally published as "The Role of Incomplete Contracts in Self-Enforcing Relationships," in *Revue d'Economie Industrielle* (92, 2000).

1. Macaulay (1963).
2. See Klein and Leffler (1981) for an early example of such a model.
3. An important paper by George Baker, Robert Gibbons and Kevin Murphy (1999) does this by adding a self-enforcement mechanism to the standard Grossman and Hart (1986) principal–agent model of the firm. Although Baker, Gibbons and Murphy provide a number of valuable insights regarding the operation of the self-enforcement mechanism in this context, they do not identify what I consider to be the key advantage of vertical integration that facilitates self-enforcement discussed below, post-contract flexibility.
4. I am assuming for analytical and expositional simplicity that the court enforces written terms and does not enforce unwritten, understood terms. While courts in practice interpret both written and unwritten terms when enforcing contractual agreements, under English common law the amount of discretion exercised by courts with regard to unambiguous written terms is generally limited. In any event, as transactors cover additional contingencies with explicit imperfect contract terms, it is reasonable to assume that after some point there is an increased likelihood the court will effectuate a hold-up by enforcing the contract in a manner that is contrary to the parties' contractual understanding.
5. Klein, Crawford and Alchian (1978) and Klein (2000). These transitional hold-up costs conflict with the costless *ex post* renegotiation assumption generally made in the incomplete contracting/property-rights literature that has developed from the pioneering work of Grossman and Hart (n. 3). These models assume, contrary to what occurred in the Fisher–GM case, that in cases where a potential hold-up exists, *ex post* renegotiation of the contract instantaneously and costlessly takes place, so that, after a lump sum is paid to the transactor that can engage in the hold-up, price and cost quickly move to the efficient level. Therefore, instead of designing contractual arrangements to minimize the *ex ante* expected hold-up potential and, hence, the real resource costs incurred during the hold-up process (as the transactor engaging in a hold-up attempts to convince its transacting partner of the extent and magnitude of the hold-up), these models focus on *ex ante* investment inefficiencies as the economic motivation for contractual organization. Although the reduced willingness to make specific investments (as well as the wasteful expenditure of resources during the initial contracting process to protect against future hold-ups) are costs of potential hold-ups in this framework, the costless renegotiation formulation of the problem makes it difficult to justify the post-contract flexibility advantages of vertical integration discussed below.

6. Bernheim and Whinston (1998) present a model where increased contractual specification may make things worse by creating asymmetric non-
performance gains for one party.
7. See Asanuma (1989). Similar descriptions of Japanese auto parts supply
contracts are provided in Cusumano and Takeishi (1991) and Sako and
Helper (1998).
8. A self-enforcement mechanism may work well for Japanese automobile producers because of (until recently) the high level of expected future demand
growth and because of the increased social cohesiveness and likely communication of non-performance to other participants in the economy who may
also impose a sanction by refusing to deal with the non-performing transactor. Both of these factors imply a high level of the parties' reputational
capital.
9. See Klein and Murphy (1988) and Klein (1999).
10. See Klein (1995), pp. 22–3. In Kenney and Klein (1983), the ability of
DeBeers to commit to promise to pay siteholders a future profit premium
stream in return for not rejecting diamonds that have been only grossly
sorted analogously depends upon the cost savings of the DeBeers marketing
arrangement.
11. Klein (1996).
12. This is the basis of Oliver Williamson's definition of opportunism. He states
that "[b]y opportunism I mean self-interest seeking with guile. This includes
but is scarcely limited to more blatant forms, such as lying, stealing and
cheating. Opportunism more often involves subtle forms of deceit . . . More
generally, opportunism refers to the incomplete or distorted disclosure of
information, especially to calculated efforts to mislead, distort, obfuscate, or
otherwise confuse" (Williamson 1985, p. 47).
13. In particular, Fisher refused to build an important body plant close to a GM
production facility in Flint, Michigan. Fisher would not be expected to make
the new, large specific investments required by General Motors without a
renegotiation (e.g. extension) of the contractual arrangement. But as part
of this renegotiation Fisher took advantage of its existing GM contract to
engage in a hold-up. See Klein (2000).
14. See Klein (1996).
15. This effect of increased uncertainty on vertical integration when transactors are not risk averse is distinct from the effect increased uncertainty may
have on increased contractual incompleteness. If the parties are risk neutral, increased incompleteness, in itself, has no effect on vertical integration
in the standard property-rights (Grossman and Hart-type) approach to the
theory of the firm. If the parties are risk neutral, increased uncertainty and
increased contractual incompleteness does not affect organizational form (or
which party owns which assets) in these models because the models ignore
self-enforcement.
16. Klein (1988, 2000).
17. A summary of the continuing literature in the Grossman and Hart tradition
can be found in Hart (1995).
18. Klein and Murphy (1997).

5   Entrepreneurship, transaction-cost economics, and the design of contracts

Eirik G. Furubotn

1   Introduction

As a result of Williamson's pioneering work in relating the theoretical concept of transaction costs to real-world organizational and contractual activities, the field of transaction-cost economics (TCE) emerged and became the central force driving the development of the New Institutional Economics (NIE). Certainly, there can be no doubt about the importance of TCE in influencing neoinstitutional thought.[1] TCE took the analysis of the capitalist firm well beyond the abstractions of neoclassical theory and focused attention on actual institutional arrangements. In particular, it became possible to throw light on how variations in certain characteristics of transactions can operate to bring about differences in the specific contractual designs and organizational structures adopted by business units. Moreover, since transaction-cost analysis is deliberately oriented toward observable relationships, various hypotheses concerning such subjects as the internal organization of firms, the properties of contractual agreements, the role of vertical integration, etc. have become amenable to empirical testing. Thus, today, there exists a large and growing body of factual studies that provides greater understanding of many previously neglected aspects of enterprise behavior.

Despite the valuable insights that TCE has made possible, questions can be raised about the adequacy of the approach as a means for addressing the full range of issues that have relevance for contracting and the theory of the firm. In the standard presentation, TCE offers a somewhat specialized view of the capitalist firm's motivations and adaptive behavior. As Masten has put it: "The central tenet of transaction-cost economics is that the efficiency of alternative organizational arrangements turns on a comparison of the costs of transacting under each" (Masten 1996, 4). It is arguable, though, that more attention should be paid to what would seem to be the firm's fundamental objective – the need to maintain viability by earning an acceptable level of profit. We know, of course, that profit is always in the background of TCE analysis because it is impossible to say whether a particular action (and contractual arrangement) undertaken by the firm is desirable or not purely on the basis of the cost of transacting. The TCE approach recognizes that production costs as well as transaction costs play a role in determining appropriate enterprise behavior. Nevertheless, it is the alignment of governance structures with transactions that is stressed and, because of this, the impression can be conveyed that adequate profits will appear if only the firm is able to keep transaction costs down in reaching and enforcing agreements. There is reason, then, to give greater consideration to the question of how profits are generated. Quite simply, once attention is shifted in this direction, the way is open to examine various factors other than transaction costs that affect profits and hence the firm's organization and survival capability.

The total organizational structure of a firm has many dimensions and is based on decisions made about a variety of particular issues. Transaction-cost economizing can certainly be important, but the firm's complete organizational configuration and economic behavior depend as well on policies adopted with respect to such matters as the procedures the firm employs to reach decisions, the allocation of property rights within the firm, the way in which economic efficiency is perceived and sought within a "neoinstitutional" environment, etc. Relative to the last point, it should be emphasized that the economic environment in which decisions are made has a significant effect on the way the firm is able to perform. The so-called "neoinstitutional environment" is distinctive because it is one in which individuals operate subject to bounded rationality and face significant transaction costs in undertaking transactions. Research in the NIE has demonstrated that such "frictions," and the uncertainties to which they lead, exist in all real-world systems, and place severe restrictions on the ability of decision-makers to reach "idealized" solutions. Consequently, in practice, we must expect to encounter not only incomplete contracts but diverse and imperfect organizational arrangements.

When the firm's problem is viewed in the manner just suggested, there is reason to move beyond the usual strict interpretation of TCE and consider how the idea of transaction-cost economizing fits into a broader framework of analysis. Thus, the general objective of the chapter is to examine the forces that influence the firm's decision-making and contracting activities when its operations are conducted in a pure neoinstitutional environment and its goal is to achieve at least a minimally acceptable level of profit.

In developing the argument that contract theory should place greater emphasis on the way in which contractual arrangements affect enterprise profit, it will be useful to begin with a discussion of how the firm conducts itself when its operations are undertaken in a neoinstitutional environment. Thus, section 2 considers an economic system whose characteristics are different from those assumed in the neoclassical model and closer to real-world conditions. Specifically, individuals seeking profits are taken to be constrained by limited cognitive capacity and to face unavoidable deliberation and transaction costs in obtaining information about the economy, and in deciding on the policies to follow. Since decision-makers functioning in this milieu must contend with substantial uncertainty, they act as entrepreneurs rather than as mere managers who routinely implement clear-cut marginal rules. Against this background, section 3 indicates that optimization is a costly economic process in itself and that efforts have to be made to economize on the outlays made in this connection. The situation is such that firms are free to choose among different kinds of decision rules or procedures for optimization. And, in general, firms can be expected to differ in the rules they adopt and in the economic success they achieve. Under these circumstances, it appears that a firm's contractual activities are influenced by important factors in addition to those stressed by TCE. Section 4 pursues this theme further by explaining how the property-rights structure chosen by the firm affects both its decision-making processes and its ability to compete effectively in the drive for profits. In addition, the section indicates how ambiguities can arise in the interpretation of transaction-cost economization. Next, in section 5, the objective is to show that when the assumptions of neoclassical theory are abandoned, it is no longer possible to speak of economic efficiency in precise terms. Insofar as positive transaction costs and bounded rationality condition behavior, complex choice problems cannot be solved to determine "ideal" solutions. Rather, the firm can be understood to conduct a more or less continuing search for contractual and other arrangements that promise adequate profits and survival. Finally, section 6 offers some general observations concerning the manner in which the theory of the firm can be addressed by the new institutional economics.

2   Profit-seeking in a neoinstitutional environment

To understand economic behavior as it occurs in real-life economic systems, it is essential to come to terms with the fact that individuals have limited ability to acquire and process information, and recognize that, in practice, a large proportion of an economy's resources has to be devoted to the continuing task of facilitating exchange. Of course, the introduction of new assumptions concerning positive transaction costs and bounded rationality has far-reaching consequences. Indeed, all of the elements traditionally accepted as data in the neoclassical model undergo a change of status simultaneously. That is, given the constraints affecting the availability of information and human cognitive capacity, each decision-maker has only *partial* understanding of the options extant in society, and it is no longer possible to assume that each person knows everything about current technological alternatives, the nature and availability of all productive resources, the existence and true properties of every commodity in the system, etc. What takes place, in short, is a fundamental shift to a distinctive new economic environment – the "neoinstitutional" environment. And, as TCE has also noted, this new, more restrictive environment is a quite special one characterized by widespread uncertainty, asymmetrical information, opportunistic behavior, and many other "frictional" features not found in the orthodox neoclassical system.

It follows that insofar as a firm functions in the changed conditions of a neoinstitutional environment, it faces significant difficulties in determining a suitable operating configuration. The behavior of such a "neoinstitutional" firm, which must contend with this environment, differs from that of a standard neoclassical firm in respect to both the nature of the solution it reaches at any time and the process by which it achieves a solution (Furubotn 2001). Since the firm's decision-maker can be aware of only some of the myriad technological/organizational options extant and has modest powers of assessment and prediction, neoclassical-type "ideal" arrangements are beyond discovery and are not to be expected. Moreover, adjustments are not easily accomplished. Information is costly to obtain and, therefore, only limited additional knowledge of the system can be acquired and evaluated at any period. The result is that the individual guiding the neoinstitutional firm's policies has to make hard decisions and act as an *entrepreneur* rather than as a fully informed manager routinely implementing clear-cut marginal rules. In principle, the entrepreneur of a neoinstitutional firm would like its operations to yield very large profits, but she also appreciates that the realities of the firm's situation are such that straightforward profit maximization in the neoclassical sense is not possible – or necessary. More concretely, she understands that in an economy in which all firms proceed subject to highly incomplete information and uncertainty, the pertinent requirement is *positive profits* attained through relative efficiency (Alchian 1950, p. 20). What is critical is the position of the entrepreneur's firm relative to its actual competitors.

Granting the importance of relative efficiency, the entrepreneur must be concerned with controlling costs, including the costs incurred in reaching decisions (Göttinger 1982, pp. 223–4). This means, *inter alia*, that she must shape a production plan with the aid of decision rules designed to *economize* on search and deliberation costs. For example, rules of thumb, or some comparable devices, may be employed even though they do not lead the firm to a classic "optimal" equilibrium position. Such an outcome (which may depart greatly from a hypothetical ideal solution) presents no problem, however. This is so because, in the uncertain world in which she operates, the entrepreneur is content to achieve an "acceptable" solution (i.e. one that promises some positive level of profit). Subsequently, she may resume activity and search for a relatively superior technological/organizational configuration using trial and error methods. Nevertheless, under the circumstances of the neoinstitutional environment, no entrepreneur can have knowledge of all of the existing production options, or of what the theoretical "ideal" is[2] and, thus, there is never a possibility of comparing the "actual" with the "ideal" in order to range in on a hypothetical optimizing position. Moreover, there can be no assurance that trial and error processes in the system as a whole will force all firms to become elements of an ideal order (De Vany 1996). In general, firms in any given industry can be expected to show differences in organization and the profits they achieve.

Understandably, the special characteristics of the neoinstitutional firm have a direct bearing on the contractual process. Behavior is changed sharply from the neoclassical pattern. The decision procedures used in acquiring inputs are different, and even the types and quantities of inputs selected tend to be different. This development, however, is not given much attention by TCE which does not discuss how the firm's *overall* technological problem is solved. Rather, TCE focuses on governance, and argues that transactions, which differ in their attributes, should be aligned with appropriate governance structures. The latter, of course, differ in their cost and effectiveness so that the goal is to ensure that the value of hazard reduction to the firm is consistent with the cost of the safeguarding procedures. It is true, that, *ceteris paribus*, the firm has an interest in economizing on transaction costs. But, as noted earlier, this approach, placing emphasis mainly on the cost of transacting, can lead to some confusion, and it would seem that a better plan would be to consider how any given contract affects *firm profitability*.

Each input employed by a firm is associated with at least two economically significant effects. That is: (1) the act of contracting for and managing an input over time involves transaction costs, and (2) each input makes some contribution to the productivity of the firm. It is understood, of course, that TCE analysis must account for both the transaction-cost effect and the productivity effect. Obviously, a profit-seeking firm will not select an input, say K_1, *solely* because it promises lower transaction costs than another input K_2. The respective productivity effects of K_1 and K_2 must figure in the assessment of which option is preferable. For example, if K_1 and K_2 happen to have the same acquisition prices and productivity effects but are linked to different governance structures, the standard transaction-cost logic would prevail. The option having the lower costs of transacting would be chosen. When the firm's situation is viewed from this perspective, though, the TCE model seems to lose its distinctiveness. It really appears to be indicating that, ultimately, *profit-seeking behavior* rather than transaction-cost economizing is central to the firm's decision-making actions. But, if this is so, a question arises as to why a special (TCE) theory is needed. Indeed, if the firm's very survival depends on its ability to earn a positive economic profit, why should contracting activity not be associated directly with its consequences for enterprise profitability?

The issue concerning the firm's objective is especially important because, in a neoinstitutional environment, factors other than transaction-costs alone affect profit – and, hence, transaction-cost minimization does not imply (constrained) profit maximization. It is arguable that a more general theory of the contractual process should be formulated. In particular, it appears that closer study ought to be undertaken of: (1) the constraints imposed on enterprise behavior by the unique conditions of the neoinstitutional environment, and (2) the relationships that exist between contract design and the firm's ongoing search for profits.

Since the literature reveals that the analysis of contracts tends to be conducted with the aid of several different types of models, table 5.1 may be of some use in clarifying the arguments of the present study.

Table 5.1 gives a general indication of the differences that exist among the various models by showing the key assumptions underlying each. For example, in the first cell pictured in the upper left-hand side, it is apparent, from the headings at the top of the table, that the neoclassical case presupposes costless transactions. At the same time, it is also clear, from the second line of headings, that the neoclassical decision-maker possesses complete information on all options extant. Other cells are interpreted in similar fashion. Since the TCE model has not been formalized, it is somewhat harder to clarify with precision. Nevertheless, we understood from the literature that the model is a hybrid construct, drawing on elements of both neoclassical and neoinstitutional theory.

3   The process of decision-making

Neoclassical theory views economic choice as a straightforward and costless activity. Thus, it is asserted that the firm, although subject to certain constraints, is always able to select the best alternative from among the feasible options in a vast set of technological/organizational arrangements.[3] Detailed knowledge of technical processes and prices is

Table 5.1. *A comparison of models*

Model	Transaction cost	Deliberation cost	Total cost of optimization	Solution
	Information available	Cognitive capability	Economization procedure	Timing
Neoclassical	Zero Complete information on all options known to society	Zero Unlimited calculating capability	Zero No action needed	Ideal position reached Instantaneous
TCE	Positive Information on all feasible options	Some, but not all, costs are considered Substantial power to assess alternatives	Total cost of optimization is under-estimated Seek to minimize costs of transactions	Efficient sorting of transaction arrangements Variable
Neoinstitutional	Positive Budget allocation limits the collection of information	Positive Significant limitations on the ability to solve problems	Positive Seek low-cost methods (subjective decision)	Accept any solution that yields returns above minimum profit constraint Optimization process on-going in order to sustain or improve profit position

available in the system because transaction costs are zero and individuals are taken to be "completely rational." Supposedly, a decision-maker compares each option in the choice set with every other, in an exhaustive fashion, so that the true optimum can be found. This procedure suggests that optimization is automatic and errorless, and that a stable equilibrium end state is reached instantly. By contrast, the TCE model is aware of the various frictions present in a real-world environment, and recognizes the difficulties these forces represent for contracting and optimization. But, despite this recognition, TCE still shares some ideas in common with neoclassicism. In particular, TCE assumes that "efficient sorting" between transactions and governance structures will take place, and that something close to transaction-cost minimization will be achieved – in the long run if not immediately (Klein 1999, pp. 470–1).

The assumption made with respect to "efficient sorting" has importance because it points up certain deficiencies in the TCE approach. That is, TCE appears to give too little attention to the specific manner in which decision-making is actually conducted within a firm when information is costly and decision-makers are boundedly rational, and to suggest that the process a firm employs to discover usable organizational arrangements leads inexorably to *ideal, or near-ideal*, results.[4] What can be argued in opposition, however, is that: (1) different decision procedures will tend to be adopted by different firms to economize on search and deliberation costs, and (2) decision-making is always a costly and uncertain undertaking that does not promise optimal results. Moreover, since the firm's total technological/organizational structure has many dimensions and emerges as a consequence of decisions taken about various specific issues,[5] it is essential to distinguish among the numbers of separate policies the firm pursues as it seeks to achieve overall profitability. Judgments on many of these diverse policy matters need not involve narrow transaction-cost considerations, and it can be expected that decisions on some of the issues will be more costly to reach than decisions on others.

When a firm is about to enter an industry, an individual investor or group of investors must decide on how the "design" of the firm is to be established. In the classic case, a single owner-manager will take on the task of "designing" the production unit, but, in general, hired agents, responsible to the equity holders, will be used. Although all of the people involved are characterized by limited cognitive capabilities, critical decisions have to be made concerning such basics as the structure of authority in the firm, the specific choice methods to be employed, as well as the extent and allocation of resources earmarked for the acquisition and assessment of information on relevant economic matters. At this initial planning stage, the decisions arrived at have not been implemented.

These are entrepreneurial projections and are *independent* of actual transactions and contracting. Of course, the decision-making process is ongoing, not a once-and-for-all exercise. As experience is gained, as data is updated, and as conditions change, the original policies of the firm will tend to be modified. It is true, nevertheless, that entrepreneurial decisions, both at the outset and subsequently, play a key role in determining the institutional and technical arrangements of the neoinstitutional firm, and will decide the firm's success. Contrary to TCE, the overall organization and performance of the firm is not dictated exclusively by the properties of transactions.[6]

In order to put the decision-makers' plans into actual operation, contracts normally have to be negotiated with other individuals or organizations. While certain decisions made by the firm's authorities require no further action (as, for example, a decision by the firm's owners not to partition their property rights in the organization), most entrepreneurial decisions have to be embodied in contracts involving outside people and institutions, and lead to transactions of one sort or another. As TCE suggests, these transactions often require further decisions to be reached by the firm's authorities (using the firm's established decision procedures), and demand a greater or lesser expenditure of scarce resources. Even when a firm reaches the transacting stage, however, its *unique* decision-making characteristics must condition the contracting process and the particular types of contracts concluded. Understandably, in a neoinstitutional environment, choice among alternatives always constitutes a form of economic activity in its own right. Decision-making, as such, requires time and other resources. In effect, a "technology of choice-making" is involved, and constraints exist in the shape of the scarce inputs that have been allocated to the general task of choice making (Nelson and Winter 1982). Depending on the (subjective) judgment of the firm's entrepreneur, the total resources devoted to decisions and contracting, and the allocation of these total resources among different policy lines, will show one pattern or another. Yet, whatever the magnitudes of deliberation and optimization outlays in any given case, it is clear that the outlays, together with the decision rules adopted, will shape the characteristics of the firm.[7]

The amount and quality of the information possessed by a firm will influence its success. But the question of precisely how much information to acquire about alternatives, and how much effort to put into the evaluation of the alternatives, is not easily answered. This is so because there is a trade-off between the value of a more extensive and exacting optimization process, on the one hand, and the cost of such a process, on the other. Any decision made will be subjective and imperfect. This must be the case because of uncertainty, and because any attempt to discover a rule to aid the determination of "optimal optimization" will require its own rule (i.e. the rule to choose the rule). But, logically, still higher-order rules will then be needed to guide choice and, hence, the problem of infinite regress cannot be avoided. Ultimately, the rules structure chosen is decided in arbitrary fashion.

A firm's survival in a capitalistic economy depends critically on its ability to realize *at least some profits*. The firm, however, does not have to achieve ideal efficiency or maximize profits in the sense presumed by orthodox price theory. It follows, *inter alia*, that contracts need not be ideally formulated, and, in general, will not be. How intensively (and expensively) the optimization process will be carried out depends on a variety of factors – including the firm's existing profit situation, the severity of competition in the industry, the boldness and ambition of the decision-maker, etc. It is true, however, that, given the complexity of the firm's choice problem (and the difficulty of deciding on the total array of the contractual options from which a choice is to be made), an over-riding condition constraining behavior is the need to rely on some form of *cost-saving decision procedure* such as rules of thumb, imitation, random choice, convention, obeying an authority, etc. (Leibenstein 1985, pp. 5–8); Pingle 1992, p. 8). Thus, as Nelson and Winter have noted: "the decision rules employed by a firm ought to be regarded as an important part of its overall capabilities, in the same sense as the production activities in its production set" (1982, p. 68).

When attention is centered on the modern corporation, there can be considerable difficulty in trying to understand the various conditions that shape its actual decision-making procedure (Miller 1992). A corporation, however, can be recognized as having certain capabilities that are *firm-specific*. Thus, some writers argue that it is not contracts but the firm's "core competence" that is crucial: "firms exist because they are superior institutional arrangements for accumulating specialized productive knowledge, quite independently of considerations of opportunism, incentive alignment and the like" (Foss 1996 as quoted by Klein 1999, p. 469). However this may be, there can be little doubt that special problems are faced in the case of the corporation. Since a corporation is composed of many semi-autonomous parts, and since decision-makers exist at various levels, the decision process is not likely to be straightforward. Moreover, there may well be a different decision procedure for each kind of policy question that the corporation must address when solving its total organizational problem. At best, then, corporate decision-making faces a series of complicating factors: information is dispersed throughout the organization, different goals and points of view have to be reconciled, committees do not reach decisions in the same way as individuals, prevailing corporate culture tends to constrain behavior, group utility functions cannot be employed convincingly, etc. Under these conditions, different firms in the same industry can be expected to reach different solutions, and it seems too facile to say that the essential structure of the firm and its behavior is determined by the relative costs of organizing transactions under alternative governance arrangements.

A more fundamental objection to TCE has been raised by Hellwig, who finds difficulty with the very concept of transaction costs. He argues that insofar as the concept often refers as much to a *social* as to a technical phenomenon, its usefulness is compromised. Specifically:

> when there is incomplete information, Coasian transaction costs depend on the precise nature of the strategic interactions and cannot be assessed prior to a full analysis of the system. After such an analysis, when one understands the system anyway, it is not clear what additional purpose the concept can serve. (Hellwig 1988: 200)

In other words, if transaction costs represent simply the *technically given* costs of negotiating and transacting that must be incurred to establish a contract, they are said to be meaningful. In general, though, given uncertainty, and assuming that strategic behavior comes into play, the actual course of contractual negotiations cannot be predetermined or predicted accurately. Against this pessimistic view, of course, one might suggest that the parties seeking a contract are frequently willing to moderate strategic contentiousness because they are anxious to reach accommodation for long-term association and mutual gain.

While TCE may not be able to provide a truly comprehensive explanation of the firm's contractual activities and overall organization, this does not mean that the existing empirical studies on TCE topics are necessarily misleading. Rather, they shed light on how decision-makers can proceed when one particular dimension of the firm's operations is being considered and the associated choice problem is not too complex. Relative to this situation, it seems plausible to say that the extent to which scarce resources are used by decision-makers to find desirable arrangements is likely to be determined by perceived costs and benefits. Thus, a decision procedure similar to the orthodox neoclassical approach can be adopted to deal with certain policy problems that arise within the general framework of the firm. When the extent of the information that must be collected and assessed for a project is modest, the costs of optimization for this organizational feature will be acceptable. Then, the problem in question can be dealt with via exhaustive search and careful assessment. This understanding helps to explain why certain cases involving relationship-specific investments tend to justify the TCE logic. For example, Joskow's (1985) investigation of the duration of contracts between coal mines and electrical generating companies shows that a relatively small number of key factors (such as regional differences in the characteristics of coal, transportation distances, alternative markets, etc.) affect the length of coal contracts by firms located in different sections of the United States. Transaction-cost economizing in this limited sense can certainly be illuminating. Nevertheless, it remains true that the *complete* organizational structure (and success) of a firm is affected by other elements than those emphasized by TCE.

4   The firm's property-rights structure

The TCE literature asserts that property-rights analysis is misleading because it assumes that court ordering of contracts is costless and efficacious and that, in consequence, the full contracting process is given inadequate consideration. More concretely, it is argued that property-rights analysis, by placing virtually all emphasis on *ex ante* incentive alignment, suggests that bargaining action occurs only in the *initial* contracting stage. Supposedly, what is lacking is the anticipation of potential future conflicts, and, given this condition, it is said that the approach fails to provide for private ordering which may be able to establish adaptive mechanisms designed to settle disputes that occur over time (Williamson 1985, pp. 28–9). When this interpretation is made, and it is assumed that the main contractual action takes place in the context of *private ordering*, the essential problem of organization becomes one of "getting the governance structure right." A key proposition here is that, in developed market economies, where property rights are reasonably well defined and secure against expropriation by the state, the system moves from ($L2$) or first-order economizing ("get the institutional environment right") to second-order economizing ($L3$) – i.e. to the alignment of transactions with governance structures in an effort to enhance economic performance (Williamson 2000, p. 597).

It is true that firms cannot rely exclusively on court ordering to settle all disputes. Moreover, the fact that contracting becomes more important in developed economies is not in dispute (Scott 1996). Nevertheless, it is not clear that most of the *analytical action* moves from property to contract as development progresses. The significance of property rights for economic behavior does not end once a society has achieved an institutional environment in which basic rights are well defined and secure. The property rights held by the various participants in an enterprise influence incentives and hence behavior and enterprise productivity. If, as we assume, the firm's ultimate objective must be profitability, *incentive effects* can be more powerful in shaping the firm's organization and boundaries than transaction costs. TCE argues that the efficiency of alternative organizational arrangements (say, G_1 and G_2) turns on a comparison of the costs of transacting under each arrangement. But the firm, in comparing two possible situations based on different property-rights assignments to input owners, will not necessarily contract for the arrangement with the lower transaction costs. The reason is that the arrangement (or governance structure) G_2, although requiring higher negotiation and safeguarding costs than G_1, may also offer high-powered incentives to certain inputs, and thus promises the firm productivity results that offset, or more than offset, the higher transaction costs that will be incurred. A simple example suggesting the forces at work here is found in the case in which land, collectively owned by a group of cattle raisers, is subsequently distributed among individuals as private property. Under the new arrangement, transaction costs will normally be higher since each owner must now take action to enforce his property rights, but the more efficient incentive scheme that obtains with private ownership can bring about productivity (and profit) gains that will justify the choice of the governance structure having higher transaction costs.

What makes property-rights analysis significant for organizational questions is the possibility of devising different ways to *partition* the basic property rights associated with the classical capitalist firm (Alchian and Demsetz 1972). In the classical case, the owner has: full *control rights* (i.e. final authority over all of the policies pursued by the firm), full *income rights* (i.e. the unattenuated right to the firm's residual), and full *transfer rights* (i.e. complete freedom to assign his rights, in whole or in part, to others). Thus, for example, if the equity holders of a firm assign some of their rights to hired workers, a change in worker incentives and behavior can be anticipated. Depending on what specific rights assignments are made, and how the cost-benefit evaluations are established, the partitioning process may, or may not, promise advantage for the firm's profit position. If partitioning is agreed upon by the firm's owners, contracts have to be negotiated, and these contracts will imply, *inter alia*, certain transaction costs (for the initial period and into the future). But the crucial element driving analysis in this area is the *property-rights structure* being enforced (and the productivity results the structure implies), not simply the costs linked to the writing and monitoring of contracts and to the efforts required to treat contractual hazards. Indeed, as noted above, the incentive effects resulting from property-rights allocations may dominate transaction-cost considerations.

It is no exaggeration to say that the property-rights allocations within a firm affect its internal organization, the boundary between the firm and markets, and the specifics of the contractual arrangements formed between the buyers and sellers of commodities and services. As an example of how property-rights-induced changes can reconfigure enterprise behavior, consider a case in which the firm's original equity holders give up their exclusive right to the residual by offering hired labor certain stock options. Transaction costs arising in the labor market may be relatively *high* for the firm because it must search more intensively for capable workers who are willing to take a *lower than normal money wage* in early periods in the hope of securing large capital gains when they exercise their stock options in the future. Of course, for their part, the firm's original equity holders expect to gain the advantage of lower monitoring costs and higher productivity because they anticipate that workers will have a strong incentive to work hard and effectively to make the enterprise profitable. The firm may also expect to benefit from the fact that the lower wage bill for employees has the effect of increasing its apparent profit level in the near term and, thus, of making it somewhat easier to raise capital funds for expansion. Obviously, risk is involved for both the firm and the workers but firms in high-tech industries that seem to have opportunities for securing expanding markets and high future profits have used the device in practice.

Note, however, that with respect to the firm of our example, it is not necessarily clear whether it has violated the logic of TCE or not. Presumably, if most firms in the industry believe that the high transaction costs incurred in the search for special workers (relative to the transaction costs associated with the recruitment of workers who receive the standard higher wage and no stock options) *are not justified*, a problem exists. That is, the option-offering firm is making a mistake and is *not economizing* on transaction costs because the general view is that the potential gains in worker effort (and more easily available finance) are not large enough to outweigh the high transaction costs of searching through the labor market for the option-interested workers, plus any losses occasioned by the dilution of the stock held by the firm's original owners. On the other hand, if it is generally agreed by firms that the likely gains are greater than the higher transaction costs, TCE might say that the requirement of transaction-cost economizing is being met. The trouble with this approach, of course, is that the estimate of whether transaction costs are too high or acceptable rests on anticipations and subjective calculations. Different decision-makers operating in a neoinstitutional environment inevitably face difficulties because they have cognitive limitations and must work with imperfect information. Thus, they will often reach different conclusions about what is, and what is not, transaction-cost economizing. The situation here is very much like the well-known problem faced when individuals decide whether certain policies of the firm lead to the maximization of the present value of the stream of profits anticipated over time. Virtually any choice can be rationalized as being consistent with the assumed objective. Moreover, the issue is *untestable ex ante*.

Although the TCE literature suggests that property-rights analysis is concerned with incentive alignment and contract adjustment only at the outset of the firms' operations, this judgment is not correct. One way in which specific property-rights arrangements can be used in an attempt to forestall conflict and maintain worker–management cooperation over time is well illustrated in the case of *codetermination* – a policy of great importance in Europe. Equity holders may give up some of their *control rights* in the firm to labor either voluntarily or, in other cases, through legal requirement. Then, direct worker participation in the firm's decision-making process (via representation on the firm's Management Board) is supposed to moderate labor alienation, improve communication within the firm, reduce absenteeism and labor turnover, anticipate potential areas of conflict so that solutions can be worked out in advance, etc. In principle, by sharing policy-making power with the firm's stock holders, labor representatives on the Board are in a position to aid in the design of new modes of cooperation as they become necessary because of the changing circumstances of the firm. Whether significant efficiency advantages inhere in mandatory codetermination is a disputed question (Furubotn 1985, 1989). One difficulty, however, would seem to arise as a result of the "horizon effect" (Furubotn 1976). Insofar as a significant portion of the firm's work force looks toward a particular future date, say t^*, for retirement or exit from the firm, an incentive problem must exist. That is, workers may opt for policies that yield short-term, or medium-term, benefits to t^*, and oppose other policies (however desirable they may be for promoting enterprise wealth) that yield major rewards in periods after t^*. In brief, if workers have relatively short planning horizons, decisions may be taken with respect to investments, the work environment, job rights, etc. that do not contribute to the efficiency of the firm. It is also true that in the case of the legally mandated codetermined firm (in which workers have certain control rights but no claim on the firm's residual), the interests of the firm's capital owners and workers diverge substantially. By granting workers major control rights without regard to their actual investment position in the firm, state programs violate an important rule for ensuring rational allocation. Specifically, what the scheme fails to obey is the rule that those making decisions should bear the full consequences of the decisions they make. It follows, then, that codetermination can affect the terms of contracts, and possibly over-ride transaction-cost considerations.

The voluntary form of the codetermined firm (Furubotn 1988) has interest because it reveals another reason why minimization of transaction costs need not take place. Under voluntary codetermination, the firm's equity holders assign both control rights and income rights to workers in proportion to their investment in firm-specific human capital. The rationale for this action is that when workers finance their firm-specific investments, they supply one part of the total capital stock required by the firm for production. Thus, it is arguable that worker–investors should be regarded as equity holders like any others, and be granted control and income rights in the enterprise accordingly. From a motivational standpoint, there is good reason for the firm's participants to believe that this type of property-rights arrangement has the effect of enhancing enterprise productivity, and that it leads to *lower transaction costs* and a more rational allocation of risk. Despite these presumed advantages, though, experience has shown that this form of business organization has not been widely adopted in practice (Furubotn and Richter 1997, pp. 399–404). The preferred organizational scheme seems to be the traditional one which views labor inputs merely as hired workers who should have no direct control or income rights in the firm. Reward is then determined by union–management negotiations. But when workers secure all of their pecuniary reward and job rights through a multiperiod employment agreement, there are, inevitably, recurrent costs attached to renewing, adjusting, monitoring, and enforcing the agreement (plus third-party costs when strikes occur). While these costs of contracting are almost certain to be higher than the transaction costs under *voluntary* codetermination, the latter approach is resisted. Workers appear to believe that their best chance for gain lies more with reliance on strong labor unions and political influence (or with mandatory codetermination) than with worker–investor status. In other words, the (formal) institutional environment (Williamson's *L2*) together with informal institutions and social attitudes (Williamson's *L1*) can act to guide the choice of contractual design and, in some cases, may prevent the economization of transaction costs. Path dependence is, therefore, a force to be considered (Williamson 2000, pp. 596–9).

Given the different ways in which property-rights structures can affect the behavior of the firm and shape contractual arrangements, it does not seem appropriate that TCE should take Level Two institutions (*L2*) as no more than *given constraints* and assert that the study of economic organization involves, almost exclusively, Level Three (*L3*) operations (Williamson, 2000, pp. 597–9). We are told that, in the TCE interpretation, organization is determined largely by the process of aligning governance structures with the attributes of transactions and ensuring that transaction costs are as low as possible. But, as indicated above, property-rights arrangements are not confined solely to the formal legal rules extant, and the adjustment of contracts can be aided significantly by certain types of informally attained property-rights structures. Thus, these arrangements need not depend critically on court ordering. *Ceteris paribus*, it is important to keep down the costs of reaching and enforcing agreements so that the potential gains from trade can be realized. It is also important, however, to provide efficient *incentives* for the various members of the firm by establishing desirable property-rights allocations. In general, it would seem that *all* of the firm's organizational features that affect profits should be considered as factors that influence contracting.

5   The concept of efficiency

The literature has long recognized that a firm contemplating entry into an industry is free to choose its production arrangements from among a multitude of different input combinations and technical processes. Indeed, when multiperiod operation is considered, and it is understood that the firm can adopt different forms of internal organization, use inputs of varying quality, follow any of diverse types of corporate culture, etc., the existing "state of the arts" implies the presence of a vast number of feasible production alternatives. The fact that enormous technological/organizational complexity characterizes real-world conditions is something that has to be faced by an adequate theory of the firm. At the same time, however, if it is accepted that the firm's operations are to be conducted in a *neoinstitutional* environment in which transactions are costly and decision-makers are boundedly rational, the orthodox idea that the firm can move confidently and swiftly to an optimal configuration has to be abandoned. What seems evident is this basic truth: when a transition is made from the frictionless neoclassical world to the neoinstitutional, the process by which decisions are reached on the firm's organization must change profoundly. It also follows that ideas about the meaning of economic efficiency have to be reconsidered (Furubotn 1999).

Given positive transaction costs and bounded rationality, each firm in the system discovers that the general process of learning about technological opportunities and prices, and of choosing a favorable operating position, becomes a *costly* activity (Conlisk 1996). Inevitably, significant expenditures of time, human effort, and material resources become necessary even to achieve knowledge of only a small sub-set of the options that are, in theory, available in the society as a whole. Cost-saving choice methods are essential to enterprise survival. Yet, whether a firm is commencing production *de novo*, or is adjusting its structure to meet competition or improve its performance, all that an entrepreneur can do is undertake a limited trial and error procedure (for reviewing alternatives) with the object of bringing about an *acceptable* level of profit. How far any decision-maker should go in expending resources on search and evaluation activities, and what particular choice methods she should employ, are open questions. Presumably, though, different entrepreneurs will tend to solve this key allocation problem differently, and will reach *different results*.

It can also be noted that since Knightian uncertainty prevails, the firm is not in a position to adjust its structure optimally for operation over time. In particular, decision-makers cannot rely on probabilistic calculations. It is not possible to say that: if S denotes the possible set of states of the system, one of these states will emerge as the true state. When the future is unknowable, the problem is not simply that we do not know which state of the set S will be the actual future. What we do not know is the *content* of S. Hence, it is not feasible to establish credible probability values in the manner suggested by much of the current literature (Wiseman 1991, pp. 151–2).

From what has been said, then, it can be argued that the New Institutional Economics requires analysis to be very clear in explaining how the boundedly rational entrepreneur makes decisions and acquires information, and in indicating how much information he can reasonably be expected to acquire in any situation. Relative to this standard, Williamson's "remediableness criterion" for efficiency is open to criticism (Williamson 1996, p. 7). The Williamson concept holds that "an extant mode of organization for which no superior *feasible* alternative can be described and *implemented* with expected net gains is *presumed* to be efficient" (2000, p. 601, emphasis in the original). It is certainly useful for Williamson to emphasize that various obstacles exist in practice that can prevent the selection and implementation of organizational options that may appear, at first view, to be highly attractive. By distinguishing between the total set of alternatives and the economically feasible set, the number of possible organizational configurations open to use is reduced, but the number of possibilities remaining must still be very large. Williamson's definition, however, presupposes that it is practicable to discover the "best" feasible alternative from among extant or *newly proposed* options, and thus a question exists concerning how "best" is to be interpreted. Is the efficient alternative superior to others in the sense that it is the most rewarding (feasible) mode of organization to be found in the system as a whole? If this is the case, the implication is that each of the many feasible options known to society can be considered by a decision-maker and compared with all other feasible options in order to determine the optimal or efficient choice. Such an approach, involving very extensive information about the firm's alternatives, and exhaustive search among them, is clearly beyond the capacity of the boundedly rational decision-maker constrained by a limited budget. It is possible to point to at least five reasons why this kind of careful choice behavior cannot take place in a neoinstitutional environment, and why the "best" option is not discoverable:

(1) The number of different technological/organizational configurations that may conceivably be implemented by a firm anticipating long-run profitability is large even if options based on current innovation are ruled out.

(2) A clearly defined set of feasible technological/organizational blue-prints is not available for examination by interested parties – if for no other reason than that such knowledge is widely decentralized and in the possession of many different individuals (Nelson and Winter 1982).

(3) The cost of exhaustive search is prohibitively high because a firm pos-sessed of limited resources (including cognitive capacity) cannot allo-cate very large amounts of valuable factors to such a search program.

(4) Each firm currently in profitable operation has reason to keep the details of its technology and internal organization confidential.

(5) Each firm has its own characteristic decision procedures and will tend to establish a search budget that is different from that of other firms. Thus, each unit can be expected to employ (greater or lesser) resources differently and secure information on different sub-sets of the possibilities in the hypothetical grand set of feasible options. The overall result must be that each firm will reach a *different conclusion* concerning the nature of the "efficient" option (Hayek 1945).

To limit search outlays, and reduce uncertainty, a firm entering a com-petitive industry may seek to *imitate* existing production units that appear to be profitable. That is, the intention may be to adopt what is viewed as a "best-current-practice" arrangement that seems to be generating ade-quate profits. But even when imitation is the objective, precise duplication of a currently profitable enterprise is not so easily accomplished. The ex-istence of "noise" means that mistakes can easily be made. Uncertainty exists about the structural details and actual profit positions of the firms being copied, and there can be no assurance that any firm chosen for imitation is the best possible model since the search for an appropriate model by an entering firm will not be exhaustive. Entering firms, there-fore, will show deviations from the patterns chosen for duplication. The general result will be a scattering of solutions within a certain neighbor-hood representing technological/organizational options that have proved *relatively* successful, but neither these firms nor those that have searched more widely on a trial and error basis can be expected to discover the hypothetical optimum. An emergent order that is consistent with the neoclassical optimum is not an outcome that is assured even in theory (De Vany 1996, pp. 433–4). As a practical matter, of course, the situation is still less encouraging. Since the "ideal" solution cannot be known by any human agent in a neoinstitutional system, a decision-maker will never be aware that she has achieved it even if, by chance, she has done so.

Depending on the degree of success realized by entrepreneurs in designing basic enterprise structure, and in their search and contracting activities, the firms they lead will secure greater or lesser profits. The least well-adapted organizations may be forced to leave the industry as superior units cause price to fall. But, as indicated earlier, survival does not require a firm to attain some theoretically "ideal" configuration, or a configuration that is close to the "ideal." Positive profits and *relative efficiency* suffice for viability. How effective a firm must be in its production routines always depends on what other firms in the industry have achieved. This state of affairs, however, means that the concept of efficiency cannot be defined with great precision when a neoinstitutional system is being considered.[8] For example, efficiency defined as *constrained maximization* (De Alessi 1983, p. 69) suggests that every equilibrium reached is "efficient," but this approach denies the essential meaning of the term "optimization" (Leibenstein 1985, p. 11). It seems necessary, therefore, to move to some other (independent) standard for assessing outcomes in a neoinstitutional economy.

One possible solution is to interpret the efficiency criterion as a crude device that can be used simply to separate relatively more socially desirable activities from less desirable ones. Thus, in the case of complex (multidimensional) problems such as that of determining an appropriate technological/organizational configuration for the firm,[9] it is plausible to argue that efficient arrangements can be differentiated from inefficient arrangements on the basis of whether a firm is earning an economic profit or not. The core idea here is that, given transaction costs and bounded rationality, the system can do no better than to ensure that resources flow to those firms that are able to produce outputs that sell for prices that cover (or exceed) production and other legitimate costs, and to deny resources to firms that register losses. Unfortunately, however, this "positive profit" criterion is not very helpful. It reveals nothing about dynamic efficiency; and, indeed, even the fact that a firm makes large profits in one period does not imply that the firm in question is well organized to secure a succession of profits in future periods.[10] In the end, then, it seems that the notion of economic efficiency does not fit readily into the analysis of enterprise behavior in a neoinstitutional environment. What must be sought are not the marginal conditions for a stable equilibrium end state, but some understanding of how the firm conducts a more or less continuing search for arrangements that promise adequate profits and survival.

6   Concluding thoughts

The neoinstitutional firm, unlike the frictionless neoclassical firm, is assumed to consider a range of different activities (and costs) associated with the general process of optimization. Broadly speaking, the optimization costs that arise can be understood as the costs of planning and implementing a design for the firm, plus the monitoring and other supervisory costs of running the structure that has been created. The various uncertainties that characterize the neoinstitutional environment make it essential that the individual guiding the policies of the firm act as an entrepreneur and render judgments about how to employ the organization's limited resources for *decision-making* as well as for active use in production, marketing, finance, etc. In other words, in a neoinstitutional context, decision-making, as such, becomes an element of cost, and such cost must be accounted for in the overall profit-seeking program.[11] Some fraction of the firm's resources has to be allocated to secure and process information about economic alternatives but, as discussed earlier, how large the allocation should be is not easily decided. More investment in information and deliberation may lead to improved planning, more beneficial contracts, and superior institutional arrangements. Nevertheless, beyond some level, the accumulation of more information and the expenditure of more time on deliberation can involve costs that offset advantages, and so diminish profit. Given the complexity of the firm's multidimensional organizational problem, it seems clear that different entrepreneurs will reach different decisions concerning how to proceed with this aspect of profit-seeking behavior. Each entrepreneur will have to decide, *inter alia*, whether to allocate greater or lesser resources to information gathering and deliberation. Whatever the allocation made, however, each entrepreneur will, presumably, exert some effort to use the resources effectively. In this limited sense, then, it can be said that "economization" takes place.

The particular approach taken by a firm toward investment in the acquisition and assessment of information will be influenced by the personal characteristics of the decision-maker (including his willingness to accept risk), and by such factors as the level of competition in the industry, the ability of the firm to raise capital for its operations, and the apparent opportunities for technological change in production methods. Decision-making is subjective and since entrepreneurs will tend to hold different views of future economic developments, the possibility must exist that even firms in the same general circumstances will reach quite diverse solutions with respect to firm design. All firms, however, will not necessarily prosper or, indeed, survive. The critical condition for any firm is how well the design chosen for it at a particular point in time conforms to the requirements of the market, and how successfully the design is made operational through efficient contracting.

Once the firm's overall design has been established consistently with the entrepreneur's vision, contracts have to be negotiated with certain individuals and organizations so that the desired plan can be implemented. Contractual activity is obviously important, but it represents only one part of the firm's total optimization process. In other words, it is apparent that while effective contracting can contribute to the profitability of the firm, it does not guarantee that a survival profit will be achieved.[12] When viewed from this standpoint, it is also clear that TCE does not explain the total organizational structure of a firm, and economization on transaction costs, to the extent it occurs, is best understood as a procedure designed to realize a *sub-goal* of the firm. In short, it can be argued that TCE, by focusing largely on transaction characteristics and governance, neglects consideration of certain types of optimization costs, and fails to call sufficient attention to the role that entrepreneurial decision-making has on enterprise organization and the general direction that contracting takes.

In estimating the degree to which transaction costs can be reduced by careful selection of governance structures, a key factor influencing the outcome is the *complexity* of the choice problem. What must be emphasized is that, given a neoinstitutional environment, it is not appropriate to assume, implicitly or explicitly, that the decision-maker is free to devote unlimited time and resources to the task of finding an ideal solution. When the situation is such that numerous possible options exist, discovery of the ideal alignment of a transaction with a governance structure (via efficient sorting) may not be feasible even in the long run. An imperfect result can be expected because when the choice set is very large, exhaustive search is prohibitively costly. Thus, the entrepreneur's judgment concerning the amount and direction of expenditures on search is important, and there is an incentive to make whatever resources are allocated go as far as possible by using simplified decision procedures for both finding and administering contracts.

A further complication in establishing efficient contracts arises from the fact that the collection of information about alternatives and the assessment of the economic data collected has the character of an investment – with outlays and benefits spread out over a succession of time periods. Then, since accurate knowledge of future economic developments is crucial to the making of a sound investment, an entrepreneur in a neoinstitutional system faces difficulties. His information about the future is always imperfect and, thus, if he happens to make the wrong predictions, the solution he reaches will be much less than ideal. In other words, arriving at an "ideal" contract oriented toward circumstances that will never arise represents a policy error. And even if modification of the ill-designed contractual and organizational arrangements can take place over time, losses will be incurred. In the end, what seems to be true, given the preceding arguments, is that TCE comes into its own and has straightforward interpretation under certain special conditions. That is, when the choice set faced by the decision-maker is relatively small and the economic circumstances of prime importance to the firm's situation are relatively stable and predictable, the TCE paradigm yields valuable insights.[13] Such a result represents no small accomplishment, however, since many real-world cases in which TCE analysis has been applied seem to conform closely to the required conditions.

At any time when contracts are established and in play, the firm's optimization plan is proceeding in its operational phase. Inputs are secured and the production and sale of the firm's output takes place consistently with the various decisions that have been made. Attention now centers on whether profits are large enough to meet or exceed the minimum requirement for survival. In simplest terms, the firm's residual at any period can be defined as the total revenue from sales minus: (a) the planned outlays on factors of production, (b) the total transaction costs incurred in implementing contracts (including monitoring and transactions' safeguarding costs), and (c) the effective costs that are attributable to the investments in information search and deliberation. Profitability is important but neoinstitutional firms may display a wide variety of behaviors because relatively inefficient and marginally profitable firms can remain as active members of an industry. All firms, however, do face the need to preserve their viability by undertaking periodic adjustments to sustain or improve their competitive positions. In other words, a firm can be expected to alter at least some features of its organizational structure with considerable frequency since economic conditions are constantly being changed by industry members searching for improved institutional and contractual arrangements. Stable long-run equilibrium cannot be regarded as the characteristic outcome in a neoinstitutional world.

NOTES

1. It was, after all, Williamson who coined the term "New Institutional Economics" (1975, p. 1).
2. Only the "observing economist" of theoretical treatises is fully informed and capable of determining a Pareto-efficient solution.

3. Even with a simplified model of technology, it is easy to show that the number of alternative production arrangements capable of generating a given commodity can run in the millions. (See Furubotn 2001.)

4. See section 6 for a discussion of Williamson's remediableness criterion for efficiency.

5. Examples of some of these policies include: the flexibility built into the firm's technical facilities that enable it to adapt readily to different types of raw materials or to new lines of production, the tautness of managerial control over workers maintained to ensure high productivity, the measures taken to promote the safety of the firm's production workers, etc.

6. In the usual interpretation, TCE asserts that organizational form is a function of such variables as asset specificity, uncertainty, complexity, and frequency.

7. Since each firm tends to have its own decision-making procedure and to possess different stocks of information, it is reasonable to assume that firms will show quite different organizational configurations, have different boundaries between themselves and markets, and negotiate different kinds of contractual arrangements.

8. From a formal standpoint, a firm can be said to achieve a constrained optimal solution if it is assumed to move to the most advantageous position permitted by the particular set of constraints it faces.

9. While the firm's overall structural and organizational problem cannot be solved with the aid of orthodox technical methods, it is possible that the neoclassical approach can be employed to solve lower-level or sub-problems that appear within the firm.

10. The fact that profits can arise from monopoly or imperfect competition complicates the attempt to use the existence of profits as an indicator of efficiency.

11. As Conlisk has pointed out: "deliberation about an economic decision is a costly activity, and good economics requires that we entertain all costs" (Conlisk 1996, p. 669). (See also Conlisk 1988.)

12. Insofar as complexity and cost make it impossible to secure anything more than imperfect solutions for the firm's technological/organizational problem, it is not necessarily useful to find "ideal" answers to lower-level problems (See Ricketts 1994, pp. 346–8.)

13. It can be noted, however, that the criticism made by Hellwig (1988, p. 200) can hold even in this case. (See section 4.)

Part III

Law and economics

6   The contract as economic trade

Jacques Ghestin

1   Introduction

1.1   A contract as a legal concept

There is no such thing as "contractual pith and substance" (Truchet 1987) or "contract by nature" (Sinkondo 1993). Therefore, we must abandon any attempt to construe the contract in terms of a generalized abstraction, and accept rather that we must reduce it to a more modest, but precise, notion, that of a *legal concept*, whose only purpose is functional (Sacco 1999).[1] Moreover, this notion pertains only to a legal category, necessarily incomplete as an intellectual construct because of its diversity and inconsistency (Rouhette 1965), but nonetheless identifiable and distinguishable from other categories. This requires, however, that all contracts share at least one characteristic separating them from any other legal category and allowing them to be identified with certainty.

Sacco (1999) distinguishes between two different ways of defining a contract. The first consists of naming one essential element shared by all contracts and *necessary for their existence*. This aspect may not suffice to guarantee their recognition as contracts by substantive law, however. Additional features may be required to make contracts legally binding. The second way of defining a contract lists all the elements required for it to be *recognized as such under substantive law* – which may, in fact, be differentiated from the conditions under which it is enforceable. This route generates multiple solutions as to the domain of the contract. Under *common law* bequests are not contracts, nor is bailment, nor actions that transfer property or create securities, except in the case of the sale of movable property. In German law, the key element is the legal transaction, *Rechtgeschäft*, since the contract, *Vertrag*, is defined in the *Bürgerliches Gesetzbuch* (BGB) as a bilateral legal transaction. The contract transfers properties or creates securities only over the delivery of movables or the creation of a notarized deed in the case of immovables. In French law bequests are contracts, but they must assume certain forms to be recognized under substantive law. Conversely, the transfer of property is realized by simple mutual consent.

1.2   The contract domain

In our endeavors to fix a meaning for the word "contract" we thus find it necessary to retain the first method, even though this forces us to forgo the hope of assigning a specific meaning to the term. The question arises as to whether this method is not incompatible with a unique definition of the contract.

Sacco seems inclined to opt for this inconsistency, as he presents four possible definitions applicable to this domain. In the first instance he observes that the expressed meeting of minds seems characteristic of contracts, but also that the notion of free and sovereign wills underlying that definition may be qualified as metaphysical and unrealistic. He adds that *common law*, in emphasizing the *consideration*, treats the contract, and the trade it governs, as identical. English and North American laws distinguish between the *contract* and the *bargain*, i.e. the exchange of benefits or obligations. Moreover, the *consideration*, which may be largely symbolic, does not capture the essence of the exchange. The reference to economic analysis of the contract, also in Sacco, seems more significant (Poughon 1985). He again emphasizes the doctrine of the legal transaction, particularly developed in Germany, which creates a tight linkage between the transaction and autonomy and views the contract as an autonomous act. Finally, he retains a fourth definition, which he deems the most relevant to law and jurisprudence: the promise having given rise to an expectancy, a reliance, the need for two different wills, or of the meeting of an offer and an acceptance, disappears.

1.3   Unique concept of contract

The difficulty of establishing a unique concept of the contract is thus clear. It is nonetheless reasonable to hope that the various elements identified by Sacco, rather than being incompatible, may be combined and reconciled to create a synthetic definition of the contract. To simplify, we shall limit our discussion to the exchange of onerous goods and services for the moment. Indeed, according to von Mehren (1982), the classical contract model essentially corresponds to the *exchange of goods and services*, for which the contract is the preferred instrument. Michel Villey observes that, historically, the contract grew out of procedurally simple operations in which a good was transferred from one estate to another, with no requirement for consensus (Despotopoulos 1968; Gomaa 1968; Villey 1969).

This important function of the contract, the *transfer of value*, was emphasized by the celebrated thesis by Poughon "*L'Histoire Doctrinale de l'Echange et du Contrat*" (the doctrinal history of trade and the contact) (Poughon 1985), which transcends a simple historical analysis of a minor form of contract, barter. Indeed, for a long time trade was not viewed as a contract, but rather as a broader concept including all bilateral operations. This conception was abandoned by the authors of the *Code Civil*, but has been rehabilitated by economists.

1.4   Trade

Ever since Roman Law the act of trading has been conceived in two different ways. If trade, in the narrow sense of the word (*permutatio*), is in some sense a contract, it can also be said that *all contracts are trade in a broad sense*.

In legal tradition predating the civil code, the sixteenth-century doctrine assimilated the concepts of *permutatio* and *do ut des*. As to the economic aspect of trade, it was retained with the substitution of the concepts of nominate and innominate contracts by those of onerous and gratuitous contracts. Trade, which is nothing other than the *sunallagma* found in Aristotle, provides the model for the former, and bequests that for the latter. Trade, or the onerous contract, is typified by the *exchange of valuables*. This is the justification and the *cause*[2] of the contract, which appears more as an exchange of benefits than as an exchange of consents: trading the unnecessary for the necessary.

The school of natural law oscillates between the two conceptions of the contract. The same can be said of the seventeenth-century's *Domat*, which nonetheless represents a consensual view of the contract as an exchange of consents. This view was adopted by the architects of the *Code Civil*, who retained the notion of the onerous contract, however. As to trade in the narrow sense, in the *Code Civil* it loses all significance, remaining only as a shadow of the sale.

1.5   Reciprocated transfer

It was economists who, in the eighteenth century, rehabilitated the concept of trade. Their starting point was precisely that which legal scholars had neglected, the real and broad aspect of trade, from which they set out to reconstitute the law. For them, the trader is less a creature expressing a will than a person characterized by desires and needs. All trade is voluntary, of course, but it primarily serves to satisfy desires. Economists thus uncovered the idea, noticed and then abandoned by legal scholars, that trade is the pursuit of necessities. They completed this idea with the concept of value, concluding that *all trade is the reciprocated transfer, not of objects, but of values*; the object becomes irrelevant except as a repository of value. Each individual acquires or relinquishes a value, either of usage or trade. This broad definition of trade allows economists to reconstruct contract law. Distinctions between various private rights – sale, leasing, and lending – disappear and merge into a single definition of the exchange of values. Similarly for public rights, the government produces services and utilities and trades them for taxes paid by citizens (Poughon 1985, nos. 178 and following).

This *economic analysis* of the contract has attracted the attention of some legal scholars, who have drawn certain elements from it to justify a return to a more realistic conception of the law in general, and of the contract in particular. The contract is defined as "an economic operation founded on the objective or subjective equilibrium of the exchanged values" (Poughon 1985, no. 238). "All contracts can be reduced to an exchange of values. A sale, in particular, is only a trade" (Poughon 1985, no. 239).

1.6   *The meeting of minds*

While bearing in mind the importance of economic trade in the general theory of the contract, we must not neglect the particular form it assumes: the meeting of minds. Indeed, we must synthesize the strictly legal conception, which makes *the meeting of minds the essential subjective aspect of the contract*, and the notion, both ethical and economic, originating in our Greco-Latin and Judeo-Christian tradition, making *the useful and the just the objective end of the contract*.

2   The meeting of minds, an essential subjective aspect of the contract

Bearing in mind that the contract is a meeting of minds designed to carry legal weight, it must be specified that *its binding force depends upon its compliance with objective law* (Ghestin and Goubeaux 1994).[3]

2.1   *The contract is a meeting of minds designed to carry legal weight*

The creation of *legally binding rules by a meeting of minds* appears to be the shared feature of all contracts, thus constituting their specific character. When such an agreement does not underlie the legal situation under consideration, it cannot be considered a contract. Thus, a single-proprietor business cannot be construed as a contract of association, lacking a meeting of the minds, but rather as an institution whose purpose is to enable a single businessman to dedicate a certain amount of money to a specific economic activity (Champaud 1962; Chandler 1962).

The contract must be designed to have legal effect as a necessary condition for it to give full weight to the expressed wills (Viandier 1980). Its purpose, on the level at which it operates, is to create *legal rules* (Ghestin 1993; Ancel[4] 1999), and it requires that the signatories participate in their formulation. In this respect it is important not to confuse the ability to dictate rules with the ability to participate, through negotiation and dialogue, in their elaboration (Cadiet 1987). It is not negotiation that makes the contract, but rather the creation of the rules by a meeting of minds. Adhesion contracts remain contracts and negotiated regulations remain rules imposed on the signatories.

Contracts result from the meeting of minds and not from a unilateral dictate. Thus, it is essential that two wills, both free, join together to create a contract, which subsequently exists independent of the individuals' wills. The contract, *a voluntary act and free exercise, is at the same time a voluntary alienation of freedom* (Frison-Roche 1995). As Macneil (1980) observes, consent expresses a freedom to choose that disappears the moment it is exercised and that surrenders to the other party the right to restrict future incompatible choices. A freely given word cannot be freely withdrawn. The binding force of the contract is thus one of its essential elements; deriving from its definition as a procedure that creates legal effects.

Macneil (1980, pp. 4–5), however, contests the necessity of enforcing the binding character of contracts by *substantive law*. He deems the central issue, not the legal sanctioning of the parties' commitments, but rather the contract's ability to determine the terms of their future exchanges. Experience reveals, as I have personally witnessed in business as well as family matters, that there are cases of non-performance involving voluntary agreements that never make it to court or even arbitration. Nevertheless, the parties consider them binding – but are we still dealing with contracts?

However, this meeting of the minds should not be considered simply a necessary condition for qualification as a contract. It is rather its essential *subjective element*, necessary for its existence and underlying its fundamental role in social relationships. The will is the "motor," the dynamic subjective element that gives birth to the contract. It is over these wills that agreement between two people's self-interest can be achieved.[5] It is, indeed, *the interest, the distinctive utility,* that the contract holds for each party that motivates them to sign on. This is the "why," the *reason* for adhesion.

The will, transformed by the pursuit of this specific utility, is the preferred instrument of individual liberty and responsibility, and is its required complement. *Respect for the given word* is a moral precept that, in principle at least, appears to be universally accepted, though not necessarily always respected. This appears as a natural extension to the freedom to commit oneself. When a commitment is entered into freely, the obligation to follow through is perceived by the promissor as a moral duty, which justifies the legally binding force of the contract and governmental enforcement. Freedom of consent is thus an essential element of its effective performance. These various considerations leave room for each individual's freedom as well as for the responsibility that is its necessary complement.[6]

Wills must be free! However, this freedom needs to be subjected to some constraints; no one would argue that the law can sanction any and all meetings of minds. The definition of the contract must thus be completed by adding that *its binding force depends upon its compliance with objective law.*

2.2   *The binding force of the contract depends upon its compliance with objective law*

As a source of rules and regulations, the contract is binding. Normally drawn up by ordinary citizens, whence does it draw its binding force? The theory of the free will cannot answer this question.

Positivist analysis has the merit of effectively raising questions about the dogma of free will, demonstrating that it is *positive law* that confers the binding force to the contract, while the meeting of minds simply plays a role as a *specific procedure for the creation of effective rights*. The will, or agreement, expressed in contracts is no longer perceived anywhere as the true foundation of its binding force. Several authors have even explicitly ruled out the dogma of free will in favor of an external norm. Starck and Laurent and Boyer assert, rather radically, that "the free will is an outdated myth" (Starck, Roland and Boyer 1998). Terré, Simler and Lequette describe a remarkable evolution (Weill and Terré 1980; Terré, 1968) of the doctrine (Terré, Simler and Lequette 1999). To them, "The binding force does not originate with the promise, but rather with the value that the law imputes to the promise... The *Code Civil* does not escape from this rule. To contract is not only to express a will, but it is also to employ a *tool forged by law*" (emphasis in the original).[7]

The evolution of contractual relations and of substantive law has also prompted some authors to conclude that *free will cannot be absolute*. They recognize that the legislator and the judge must be able to ensure that the contract conforms to the public interest, public order, and the public weal (especially, Mazeaud 1998, no. 127; Flour and Aubert 1998, 128, p. 77).[8] Some persist, however, in maintaining that this autonomy is the underlying principle that must continue to inspire ordinary rules of contract law.[9] Solutions that are incompatible with this principle are presented as exceptions, qualifications, or limitations. We may wonder, however, whether this negative view of public order and, more generally, of the objective elements of the contract, with which the "voluntarist" interpretation of the nineteenth and first three-quarters of the twentieth century made us so familiar, is still reasonable (Hauser 1971).

The theory of free will survives to this day only because of its ambiguities. As the exercise of a sovereign authority parallel to, and in competition with, the law, it is now dismissed by most authors.[10] Nonetheless, there is no reason to deny a certain *delegated competence*,[11] granted to individual wills, to allow them to determine, or at least choose, the rules that will govern their specific relations for a given legal operation. It thus remains possible to speak of a certain freedom of the will, inseparable from a certain contractual freedom.[12]

Positivist analysis has also facilitated the evolution of legal civil-contract doctrine from the dogma of free will toward a debate on the *principles of freedom and contractual security*.

Whether or not they maintain freedom of the will as a fundamental principle, it is in fact the essential usefulness of this dogma that some authors defend, contending that the principle of contractual freedom, as a universal and timeless notion, is inherent in the concept of a contract, and that any limitation to this freedom must necessarily be exceptional. These same authors contend that the binding force of the contract, that is the privity of contract, must under these same conditions be immune from derogation to avoid interfering with the security of contractual relations. The true debate is thus engaged on the basis of liberty and security as fundamental, even exclusive, principles, which must underlie the contract regime.

Positivist analysis has demonstrated that the issue of contractual freedom is fundamentally metaphysical or political in the broadest sense, and is *not contingent on the nature of specific contractual relations*. No one contests that the contract has binding force only if it is not detrimental to the public order, which aims to ensure its compatibility with the public interest – break the basis, the end, and the check on the power of authorities charged with ensuring its performance, if necessary using coercion. Thus, it is reasonable that the public interest should underlie criteria for rules limiting contractual freedom. This is not a universal or timeless principle, being necessarily subordinate to ideological shifts that affect the relationship between public and private interests.

Unlike free will, contractual freedom is thus not fundamental to the notion of the contract, at least not as a principle that can be over-ridden only exceptionally. Public order is not outside the normal contract regime. It is rather a constituent aspect thereof, as it specifies the conditions under which the law recognizes its binding force.

From Kelsen's observations one can conclude that the contract derives its binding force from the *legislator's willingness to sanction it*.

Acceptance of this proposition is tantamount to recognizing that only positive law, i.e. law explicitly enacted by the individual or collective will of the legislator, is truly law. This is further equivalent to giving the legislator discretionary powers pertaining to contracts, such as the right to decide that they may be executed in bad faith.

Now, this type of power cannot be ceded to the legislator. Objective law (Ghestin and Goubeaux 1994) the concrete search for just solutions, supersedes positive law, which must strive to express the former as perfectly as possible. It is not the law established by the legislator that gives binding force to contracts. Courts did not await the arrival of article 1134 of the *Code Civil* to begin sanctioning them. The contract has binding force because *objective law confers it legal effect*, which it can do only because the public interest, some would say the common weal, requires it: first, the social usefulness of the contract and second, contractual justice, an element of social cohesiveness (Ghestin 1981, 1982).

That is why we have been advocating retention of utility and justice as guiding principles for the rules of law governing contracts since 1981. The meeting of minds is the essential subjective element of the contract, but it integrates into the latter's social utility as an instrument of trade that must occur according to justice.

Utility and justice are thus the ultimate aims of the contract.

3   Utility and justice are the ultimate aims of the contract

The contract cannot be studied independent of the issue of its social utility and justice. These two concepts are closely linked since both advance the public good, that is to say social harmony, and the institutional organization of contractual exchange is one of their principal instruments.

This analysis is buttressed by the position occupied by these two values in the various conceptions of the public interest originating in our European heritage of Greco-Latin and Judeo-Christian thought. This is particularly true of inter-individual relations and relations between individual and public interests, for which contracts are the preferred instrument.[13]

We may also note that today some authors define contractual freedom and the binding force of the contract from the perspective of social utility and justice.[14] Thus, Flour and Aubert, while retaining free will as a "principle" and a "rule," also see social utility and justice as vindicating limitations imposed on contractual freedom and on the binding force of the contract (Flour and Aubert 1998, 28, p. 32). For their part, Terré, Simler and Lequette retain the will as the motor, but subordinate the contract regime to justice and social utility (Terré, Simler and Lequette 1999). In Belgium, building on our work, Coipel (1999, 37: 28) has explicitly maintained that "utility and justice are the foundations for the binding force of the contract."

The contract is binding only because it is useful and if it is just.

3.1 The contract is binding only because it is useful

It has been demonstrated, notably by Friedrich Hayek (1976), that the contract is an essential element of a liberal social order. This utility translates into subordinate principles of *legal security* and *cooperation*.

3.1.1 The subordinate principle of legal security

The contract is an indispensable tool of individual foresight. Its binding force is necessary for the *promissee's confidence*.

It is primarily in its principal function of trade by the creation of obligations that the utility of the contract becomes manifest. "No seller would willingly surrender his good, no lender his money, no landlord would allow the use of his property and no individual would perform any service if the judicial principle of obligation did not guarantee them a return of the expected and promised equivalent value"(Gounot 1912, p. 355).

We here connect the notions of the *promissee's legitimate confidence*, as in Gorla, in Italy, and Atiyah, in Great Britain, with that of detrimental reliance, and more recently with legitimate expectancy, as in Dean Xavier Dieux[15] (Coipel 1999, 36: 27) in Belgium, into a foundation for the binding force of the contract (also Chirez 1977). While this confidence remains only one element of the contract's utility, it carries particular weight. Any reduction of the binding force of the contract diminishes the promissee's confidence and undermines the credit necessary for many operations of an incontestable social utility (von Mehren 1982, no. 25). For the utilitarian, "any action able to influence mutual confidence that human beings have to their words" (John Stuart Mill 1961) is an evil in itself.

The promissor's confidence is also, on a moral level, a *positive aspect of respect for the given word*. This moral rule may thus be justified, not only in reference to contractual justice, but also for its social utility.

The subordinate principle of security must, however, be balanced with that of cooperation.

3.1.2   The subordinate principle of cooperation

Economic analysis of the contract allows us to elaborate this cooperation. "Cooperation means preferring a collective outcome to individual gain" (Brousseau 1996, p. 23 citing Ménard 1995). This cooperation is the hallmark of the contract. It comes into play in varying degrees, depending on the type of contract. From the fraternity that animates gratuitous contracts to the shared liability typified by corporations, we see the need for basic coordination.

According to some economists, "The fundamental contractual mechanisms are responses to the great categories of known coordination problems: agents' limited rationality, opportunism, and risk" (Brousseau 1993, p. 74).

In the first instance, contracts limit the consequences of the *limited rationality* of economic agents by implementing "procedures and rules of conduct that free them from the need to calculate or imagine what they need to do at each point in time." However, transactions costs involved in writing and executing complete contracts covering all foreseeable contingencies may prove insurmountable. Furthermore, in situations of far-reaching uncertainty, when it is no longer possible to even imagine all possible states of the world, "completeness becomes impossible." Then it becomes necessary to resort to *authority*, that is to contractually entrench a right, normally residual, of one of the parties to "decide on the effective usage of the factors contributed by each" (Brousseau 1993, p. 75).

To discourage *opportunism* when the future is foreseeable, the signatories will attempt to deter it with specific incentives, such as the chosen modes of remuneration, so that each party will have an interest in honoring his word. This is the spirit in which economic theories of incentives and agency were developed. When uncertainty is far-reaching, it becomes necessary to resort to two types of measures to complete these incentive structures and render them useful under all assumptions. First, surveillance and appropriate penalties are applied to discourage manifestations of opportunism. Second, efficient procedures for negotiation and mediation, even arbitrage, are implemented to settle disputes relative to the allocation of the organization's quasi-rent (Brousseau 1993, p. 75).

In concrete terms, corporate schedules of conditions illustrate these types of antagonistic cooperation quite well. In matters of deadlines and costs, premiums are paid to, and penalties imposed on, the business person. Additionally, a principal contractor, an expert chosen by the principal but exercising a certain independence, will oversee the execution of the contract and censure any failure to comply, whereby recourse to an ad hoc joint committee or to an independent arbitrator remains possible.

Finally, a contractually defined procedure allows for constant adjustment of the contract to changing conditions, especially the addition of supplementary tasks and the consequential revision of deadlines and prices.

Finally, as to *risk*, many contracts, especially those governing labor relations, are characterized by a division of losses and gains that account for the relative level of risk aversion of one of the parties: for example, the employee *vis-à-vis* the employer.

These various mechanisms are both supplementary, as in the case of incentives and insurance, and complementary, as with routines and authority "The complexity of contracts springs from the formulation of these various types of solutions to coordination problems" (Brousseau 1993, p. 75). It thus becomes necessary to distinguish between types of contractual relations.

First, *memoranda of association or operation* of what Hauriou once called institutions, and what economists still call "institutions" (Williamson 1985) or "organizations" (Ménard 1995), such as firms, are treated separately. As demonstrated by the theory of transaction costs – founded by Coase (1960) and developed into an entire school of economic thought, notably represented by Williamson (1985) – while trade takes place in markets, institutions strive to shield their internal dealings from market forces (Coase 1937, 1988; Ménard 1995). Nonetheless, the birth and even the operation of these institutions is based on the meeting of wills: contracts of partnership, shareholder agreements, even labor contracts. The forms assumed by cooperation and opportunism differ here from those of their counterparts in contracts subject to the market, and also from those between shareholders or between employers and employees. The system of law for organization-contracts is necessarily affected (Didier 1999).[16]

Second, and even for contracts set in the market, it has become conventional, following Ian Macneil,[17] to distinguish between transactional contracts and relational contracts. The latter assume a contractual relationship of a fixed duration, and may consist of a single long-term contract or a cooperation based on repeated contracts (Brownsword 1996, p. 14). The phenomenon is all the more important because many transactional-type contracts, such as sales contracts, acquire a relational dimension by their integration into blanket contracts.

According to the economist Eric Brousseau, relational contracts require that future economic uncertainty be accounted for, leading to an incompleteness in their content that facilitates dynamic adjustment later. This incompleteness tends to reflect, on one hand, the objective commonality of interests that are at least partly and durably shared and, on the other hand, the distinctive confidence linked to habituation and the participants' knowledge of each other (Brousseau 1996). The sociologist Siegwart Lindenberg (1988) has demonstrated that solidarity resulting from the permanence and the strength of the bonds between the parties tends to curtail the pursuit of maximum benefits, creating a distinction between contractual relationships according to the degree of solidarity.

Finally, the concept of *antagonistic cooperation*, and the view that the contract is a means of organizing it, contrasts with the idyllic conception of a conflict-free world, in which no party is able to impose on the other choices that are counter to its interests and in which all trade necessarily benefits everyone. It also differs from the view of the contract as a means of hostile domination and exploitation of one party by the other (Brousseau 1996, p. 340).

With regard to the law, we see that the modern idea of cooperation within the contract lies somewhere between the classical model of entirely self-interested utility maximization and pure altruism. Cooperation is not limited to honoring one's own part of the bargain, or enabling the other party to do likewise (or obtaining the benefits of the contract), nor does it imply accommodating every demand made by the other party. Cooperation falls between the unconstrained pursuit of self-interest and the unqualified subordination of said interest.

It is the essence of cooperation to give rise to a *community of interests* between the parties. As already observed by Durkheim (1933), trade cannot be reduced to that brief moment in time during which an object changes hands, it creates important relationships between the parties within which their solidarity must not be disrupted. This community of interest does not eliminate each individual's self-interest, but rather restricts its, normally dominant, scope. In concrete terms, cooperation means that each party's selfish behavior must be compatible with the interests of the contracting community. This requirement, while congruent with a purely utilitarian view of the contract – at least for contractual relations characterized by long duration and having a personal-relationship aspect – also appears to have a certain inextricable moral side (Brownsword 1996, p. 18), as the *interests of others are taken into consideration* (Mazeaud 1999). It is also morality that makes contractual justice the other final aim of the contract.

3.2   *The contract is binding only if it is just*

Alongside social-utility considerations, the requirement for justice and reliability (Trigeaud 1983) gives rise to a moral and legal obligation to honor the given word. Similarly, considerations of justice and solidarity provide underpinnings for the need to cooperate, which can also be linked to the contract's social utility.

We are speaking of contractual justice in a very specific sense, that of *commutative justice* – borrowed from the classical distinction made by Aristotle and Saint Thomas Aquinas between distributive and commutative justice. Application of commutative justice leads to the *pursuit of equality of benefits*. Need we also seek *equality of the parties* (Thibierge-Gelfucci, 1997)?

3.2.1   The pursuit of equality of benefits

From a moral perspective, each party to trade must *receive the equivalent of what she surrenders*. This is the essence of how contractual justice is understood today. Considered in light of its principal function as an instrument for exchanging goods and services, the contract, like liabilities in general, is subject to the principle of *commutative justice*. It must not undermine the pre-existing equilibrium of endowments, implying that each party must receive the objective equivalent of what he has ceded (Gounot 1912; Gomaa 1968).

Georges Rouhette has further observed that, from a *sociological perspective*, the contract is deemed a commutative act, "normally establishing reciprocal obligations" that "must be equal for both sides" (Rouhette 1965, §85: 331 and the authors cited there).

Historically, James Gordley (1991, 1995) has shown how the moral philosophy of Aristotle and Saint Thomas Aquinas, being founded on the principle of commutative justice, was transmitted by the teachings of the late scholastics, especially Molina (1614), Soto (1553), and Lessius (1608), who elaborated a doctrinal construction of the contract. Despite a decline in the seventeenth and eighteenth centuries, these teachings inspired the work of Grotius, Pufendorf (Laurent), Barbeyrac, and then it influenced the authors of the *Code Civil* through Domat and Pothier.

On the moral, and especially the legal, level, commutative justice is reducible to the *relative equivalence of the benefits exchanged*.

Regarding commutative justice, writers as early as Saint Thomas Aquinas[18] emphasize the subjective nature of the value of trade and the difficulty of assigning an objective value to each benefit. We also find there the idea that, to establish strictly legal rules governing contracts, the importance of the security of the contract agreement must be unassailable on the basis of commutative justice, unless an imbalance is deemed to surpass a certain threshold or there is fraud.

The difficulty associated with establishing a just price leads to acceptance of a certain objective equivalence of benefits. The natural operation of the market does not allow a "just" price for fungible goods to be spontaneously determined, as even Friedrich Hayek (1976), a guru of liberalism, has recognized. Given the impossibility of objectively determining a just price, only when a marked injustice is clearly proven will it be directly addressed in order to reestablish the contractual balance.

What we must generally strive for is that each party find an interest in contracting. As we have seen, this interest, this *specific utility*, is the very motor of the will. *A priori*, it is necessary and sufficient that each party rationally believe that he is receiving more, or at least something of greater value to him, than that which he is surrendering. Thus the contract allows everyone to obtain more value, enriching everyone in the community. It remains true, however, that the subjective appreciation of the values must not be distorted. Therefore, emphasis must be placed on the *role of the contractual procedure*.

John Rawls has demonstrated that an *equitable procedure* transmits this quality to its result, but only on condition of being rigorously implemented (Rawls 1999). He vociferously argues the need for an *effectively* fair and equitable procedure (Audard 1988). To the extent that it is possible and necessary, commutative justice will be upheld by ensuring the *effective rectitude of the contractual procedure*. This rectitude can be realized only with true consent, the protection of which is thus the cornerstone of procedural justice.

The rectitude of the contractual procedure thus assumes the absence of coerced consent, but also extends to *controlling behavior.*

In France (Lyon-Caen 1946; Desgorces 1992; Tallon 1994; Le Tourneau 1995) as in most countries (Deschenaux 1969; Loussouarn 1992; Romain 1998), the essential instrument of control in positive law is *good faith*, in the sense of *Treu und Glauben* – deriving from our Roman-Christian heritage (Ranieri 1998; Gauthier 1999) – and, to a lesser extent, its converse, the *abuse of right* (Josserand 1939; Stijns 1990; Stoffel-Munck 1999). Good faith is required first and foremost during the elaboration of the contract (Jourdain 1992; Philippe 1992; Sacco 1992; Van Ommeslaghe 1992), to impose fairness in the negotiation, before and after the tender is issued, for confidentiality, for the obligation to neither deceive the other party nor take advantage of his relative weakness, and, most of all, for honest disclosure. It is also required by article 1134, paragraph 2, of the *Code Civil*, at the stage of performance of the contract (Bénabent 1992). This ensures that in its interpretation the spirit has precedence over the letter. It completes the contractual obligations by referring to the legitimate expectations of the signatories, revises these obligations even when the contract makes no such allowance, and assumes the good faith of both the promissor and the promissee when circumscribing its reach. Good faith is thus instrumental to the economic utility of the contract (Jamet-le Gac, 1998).

Finally, when the conditions under which a contract are concluded suggest a failure of the contractual procedure, especially in the case of adhesion contracts, the law will intervene directly to eliminate clauses that were *abusively imposed by one party on the other*.

Acceptance of an adhesion contract usually confirms the adherent's subordinate position. Must we look past the equivalence of benefits to the *equality of the parties*?

3.2.2   The pursuit of equality of the parties

Inequality between the parties may result from a given signatory's consent being compromised owing to error or fear, even to inexact or insufficient information. It may also be ascertained by taking into consideration the inherent inequality of entire groups of contracting parties, usually at a relative disadvantage because of constraints or ignorance. These groups may include consumers or employees, for example. In this situation it is legitimate to ensure special protection of the consent of these groups. Here inequality of the parties is not distinct from *inequality of the benefits*, of which it is the source.

In matters of distributive justice the issue is quite different. It consists of giving each their due, in accordance with nature as some would have it, in accordance with sociological or economic imperatives or the will of the government, others maintain. The goal here is no longer to ensure a fair and equitable contractual procedure, but rather a result deemed objectively just.

The evaluations required for distributive justice fall to *positive law*, in concrete terms to authorities competent to judge these matters. The danger is that these authorities will distort the natural unfolding of the contractual procedure in order to advance interests they deem, more or less arbitrarily, more worthy of protection. This statist form of distributive justice has been severely criticized, notably by Friedrich Hayek. In France, the *statut du fermage*[19] or, more recently, acts governing excessive indebtedness, provide good examples.

At this point in our reflection we may consider that, in our current system of private right, the contract governing the trade of onerous goods or services can be characterized as a category in law, as a meeting of minds (which constitutes its essential subjective aspect), and from the perspective of utility and justice (its objective goals). It thus remains a meeting of minds destined to produce effects in law, the binding force of which depend upon it conforming to objective law. On these grounds it must remain true to its objective goal: utility and justice. The goal of social utility gives rise to the subordinate principles of *legal security* and *cooperation*. The goal of contractual justice gives rise to the search for *equality of benefits* by the respect of a contractual procedure that is effectively fair and equitable.

NOTES

Chapter 6 was originally published as "*Le contrat* en tant qu'échange économique," in *Revue d'Economie Industrielle* (92, 2000).

1. It is also possible to contrast, on one hand, the *genotype*, a historical construct based on the idea of free will that is rooted in the general theory of the contract and of jurisprudence and, on the other hand, the *phenotype*, a concrete actualization of contracts, i.e. the various categories of actions recognized as contracts by substantive law, arising from legal practice. For more on the application of these terms to contracts, see Sacco (1999).
2. The word "cause" here is taken directly from the French, where it carries the meaning of a necessary condition for a contract to be valid. It pertains to the "why" of the obligation, i.e. in trade it accounts for the agreed consideration, the existence and lawfulness of which must be verified (trans.).
3. The heritage of statist positivism officially affirms the principle of obedience to rules, especially to the law. It is also acknowledged, however, that legal scholars, and particularly judges passing verdicts, must concretely search for solutions that are just. Reconciling these two principles is the goal of an intellectual process characteristic of judicial thinking. Objective law is the upshot of that concrete quest for a solution consonant with justice and social utility. (Cf. Ghestin 2002.)
4. Ancel objects to the traditional representation of contracts that emphasize the binding force and the creation of obligations. To him, beyond the creation of obligations, the contract has an essentially normative effect.
5. Cf. Demogue (1934), according to whom agreement "between people with conflicting interests is always of great significance." We prefer the term "self-interest", since the interests are not necessarily opposed and, as we shall see, a certain level of cooperation is always necessary.
6. Cf. Portalis (1844). Also, with respect to consumers, cf. Cornu (1973).
7. Cf. Ghestin (1982, pp. 4–5) for developments along the following lines, "The contract is only an *instrument* sanctioned by the law because it provides for socially useful operations"; "The contract is foremost an indispensable *instrument* for individual projections"; and "The contract is also the preferred *instrument* of individual freedom and responsibility."
8. Cf., especially, Mazeaud (1998); Flour and Aubert (1998).
9. For works previous to 1965, see Rouhette (1965, pp. 1–66). Cf. Coipel (1999), who observes that, "while avoiding the excesses of the theory of free will, traditional civil law doctrine continues to consider that the meeting of minds is the reason why objective law recognizes the binding force of the contract."
10. Even those who continue to see free will as the "principle," or the "rule," admit that "the will does not, as maintained by tenants of the pure theory of

free will, create rights that are simultaneously autonomous and prior," but that it "is only a delegated, and as such, regulated, authority," and that "the law defines, in light of the social interest (which surely includes the useful and the just) the extent and the specifics of the authority it cedes to individuals." This is combined with the uncontested observation that "the will remains an authority proper to each individual subject to the law, and which he may use autonomously within in the framework laid out by the law" (Flour and Aubert 1998, 128, p. 77).

11. We first presented this analysis in two articles on "*la notion de contrat*," in *Revue Droits* (1990, p. 7) and *D 1990, Chroniques* p. 147. Cf. a related concept presented later in Terré, Simler and Lequette (1993, 1999), in these terms: "The contract derives its binding force, not from itself, but from an external norm. The authority imputed to individual wills is not inherent, but *derived*" (emphasis in the original).

12. Cf., for another illustration from the area of moral law, the necessary distinction between freedom of the will or of reason and absolute sovereignty, John Paul II (1993).

13. Cf., for a rational conception of the relationship between utility and justice, Perelmann (1968). On utility and justice for social cohesion, see Baranès and Frison-Roche, (1994).

14. Cf., for Japanese law, Jun Sunaga (1985), which presents the importance to Japanese law of both the general theory of the contract and of nullities.

15. *Le respect dû aux anticipations légitimes d'autrui*, Pans, Bruylant and *LGDJ*, (1995).

16. Cf. Didier (1999), who defines the organization-contract as "a contract that, explicitly or implicitly, defines a task, divides it into constituent parts and allocates them in one way or another to the signatories."

17. Macneil (1974).

18. Aquinus, *Somme théologique*, qu. 77, art. 1, sol.

19. The *statut du fermage* is a law governing the relationship between farmers or sharecroppers and landowners (trans.).

7 Contract theory and theories of contract regulation

Alan Schwartz

1   Introduction

Discussions of regulation commonly focus on regulating particular industries, such as the airline industry, or regulating types of firms, such as natural monopolies. These discussions often concern the substance of the transactions that regulated firms make. Few regulatory discussions focus on regulating contracts as such. As an example of the distinction just drawn, a regulation discussion may ask what terms a regulated firm can include in its contracts with customers; a discussion of contract regulation may ask what terms the state should supply to firms to use in transactions with each other. In recent years, law and economics scholars have begun to add to the question which contract rule would be appropriate in particular cases the more abstract question regarding how the state should regulate contracts between business firms as a general matter. Contract regulation as a distinct area for scholarly inquiry is in its infancy, however.[1] This chapter's goal is to introduce the subject and to indicate its importance in the hope that more detailed treatments will follow.[2]

An economic theory of contract regulation will have a substantive and an institutional aspect.[3] The substantive aspect asks what the state should do. The institutional aspect asks which legal institutions should perform the needed regulatory tasks. Given the complexity of the subject and the necessary brevity of this chapter, any conclusions respecting these aspects must be tentatively held. With this disclaimer and beginning with substance, the state appears to do four things well: enforce contracts; police the contracting process for fraud and duress; supply parties with common vocabularies to use when writing contracts; and supply parties with governance modes for the conduct of transactions or the resolution of disputes. It should do only these things, and not the additional things that it sometimes attempts. An example of such an additional thing is the attempt to implement an *ex post* fair solution in a particular case when both contract and renegotiation have failed. Regarding the institutional aspect of the theory, only courts can perform the first two tasks just listed; only legislatures can do the last; and the third task commonly is and should be shared between the legislative and adjudicatory institutions.[4]

2　The substantive function

Law and economics scholars have proposed five regulatory functions for inter-firm contracts:

(1) *Enforcing a contract's verifiable terms*: Enforcement is specific when the state orders a party to perform the task or to make the transfer that the contract directs. Enforcement also can be by a damage sanction, as when the breaching party is required to pay to its contract partner the profit that the partner would have earned had the contract been performed.

(2) *Supplying contracting vocabularies*: The state cannot enforce a contract unless it knows what the contract says. A way to know this is to supply parties with a stock of common meanings, and this is done in three ways. First, the state can restrict parties to the dictionary meanings of the words they use, unless a contract at issue explicitly defines a commonly used word in an idiosyncratic manner. Second, a court when deciding cases or a statute can define commonly used words or phrases in the customary way. For example, the phrase "FOB Seller's place of business" has long meant that the buyer is to bear the expense and risk of transporting the goods once the seller delivers them to the carrier. Commercial statutes now define the FOB phrase in this way. As a consequence, if a contract uses the FOB phrase and the goods are damaged or destroyed while in transit, the seller is entitled to the price and the buyer bears the loss. Third, the state can adopt for purposes of adjudication the meanings that private trade associations have developed.[5]

(3) *Interpreting agreements*: The adjudicator asks what the parties to the contract before it meant by the words they used. It is the particular meaning that controls. If particular parties meant by the phrase "FOB Seller's place of business" that the buyer was to bear the expense of shipping the goods, but *not* the risk of their damage in transit, then on this interpretative theory if the goods were damaged, the seller could not recover the price unless it shipped new goods.

(4) *Supplying default rules*: The three principal types of default rules are[6]:

　A　*"Problem solving" default rules*: The state supplies parties with rules that maximize expected surplus. Awarding a party the gain it would have made under the contract had the other party performed is efficient with respect to the decision whether to breach the contract or to perform it. Hence, a legal rule that awards the gain if the contract is silent maximizes expected surplus, at least with respect to the breach decision.

B *Information forcing default rules*: The state supplies rules that seldom would be optimal for the party with private information. The effort of this party to contract out, it is hoped, will reveal information that is needed for efficient trade or investment. For example, suppose that one party can increase the probability of a successful performance by increasing the amount of effort it commits. This party could not choose the optimal effort level if it is uninformed as to the value that a successful performance would have. In this circumstance, a legal rule that would award the passive but informed party no remedy if performance turned out to be unsuccessful may induce this party to disclose its valuation, thereby facilitating the taking of efficient precautions by the uninformed performing party. (See Bebchuk and Shavell 1991, 1999.)

C *Fair default rules*: The state supplies parties with rules that are fair according to some normative conception. To illustrate, courts and commentators often think that it is fair for the seller to supply conforming goods when the buyer has paid a non-trivial price. The law generally implies a warranty – the seller must compensate the buyer if the goods are defective – and this is sometimes said to follow from the law's commitment to fairness.

(5) *Regulating the contracting process*: This function has several aspects:

A Not enforcing contracts that were procured by fraud, such as misrepresenting the quality of a performance that is to be rendered.

B Not enforcing modifications to contracts that were procured by exploiting sunk cost investment.

C Implementing the *ex post* efficient solution. As an example, when circumstances have materially changed between the time the contract was made and is to be performed, such that enforcement would benefit one of the parties but make society worse off on net, commentators urge courts not to enforce, and some courts heed this advice.

D Implementing the *ex post* fair solution. Continuing with the example, if performance would give one party a windfall gain, commentators urge courts to reduce the gain to a fair level, and courts occasionally attempt to do this.

3 The institutional aspect of contract regulation

3.1 What is possible?

In common law countries, courts today perform all five regulatory functions. The contract parts of Civil Law Codes tend to be written on a fairly high level of abstraction because the Codes regulate many different transaction types. This confers considerable discretion on courts, and it would be interesting to test the hypothesis that courts in Civil Law countries also perform these five functions. In any event, legislatures cannot perform functions (1) enforcement, (3) interpreting agreements, and much of (5) regulating the contracting process – because these are adjudicatory functions. To enforce a contract (function (1)) or to find what particular parties meant by the words they used (function (3)) requires case-by-case inquiries. Legislatures supply rules. Function (2), the supplying of contracting vocabularies, is shared between courts and legislatures. A statute cannot define every word or phrase that parties into the indefinite future may use in the contracts they will write. Courts, on the other hand, must give legal effect to the words in a contract; and the definitions they develop in the course of doing this often are held to specify the legally operative meanings when the same words appear in later contracts. Hence, courts necessarily play a residual role in supplying contracting vocabularies, even when the legislature has enacted a vocabulary itself.[7] The policing function (function (5)) also can be shared. For example, the legislature can direct courts to ignore windfalls when deciding cases or it can create standards by which courts must assess whether fraud has been committed. Legislatures seldom seem to perform these tasks, so the policing function (5) is today performed exclusively by courts.

This is not to say that courts can perform every aspect of this function well. Thus, a court seldom would have the information to implement the *ex post* efficient solution (function (5C)). This is because courts receive information only from the parties. If parties are symmetrically informed *ex post*, however, they will bargain to the efficient solution, so that courts will not see the case. If courts see only cases in which information is asymmetric, then they will lack the information to implement the efficient solution. As an illustration, let it be efficient to breach a particular contract because the seller's cost to perform would exceed the buyer's valuation, but suppose that the seller's cost is neither observable nor verifiable. The parties, suppose, cannot agree on a price for breach, the seller refuses to perform and the buyer sues. The court cannot know whether breach would be efficient or not; and since the seller's refusal to perform is itself verifiable, the court can only enforce the contract.[8]

A court also could not perform function (5D), implementing the *ex post* fair solution, because courts act subject to the institutional constraint that they decide according to either pre-existing legal or moral principles. Any division of *ex post* gains between two business firms would be arbitrary; that is, there is no legal or distributional principle that would permit a court to decide whether it is fair to give the plaintiff or the defendant particular shares. Since legislatures cannot perform functions (5C) and (5D) – implementing *ex post* efficient or fair solutions – these functions should not be performed for institutional reasons; that is, the limited competencies of legal institutions imply that the state should not alter the performances that contracts require to achieve either *ex post* efficiency or *ex post* fairness.

Before asking which of the remaining regulatory functions should be performed and by whom, it is worth noting that the two interpretative functions sometimes will be inconsistent. Parties will be less inclined to use judicially or statutorily defined phrases if courts will permit a party who turns out to suffer from a rigid application of a definition to introduce evidence that in pre-contract conversations the parties indicated that a rigid application was not their intention. Rather, parties will more frequently themselves define the words they use in the contracts they write, an effort that is more costly but more predictable than relying on pre-existing but malleable definitions. On the other hand, a rigid application of pre-existing definitions may impose obligations that some parties did not intend to assume. Thus, there is a tension between the "vocabulary-supplying" (2) and the "meaning-finding" (3) contract interpretation functions. (See Scott 2000.)

3.2   What is desirable?

The virtues of contract enforcement need not be stressed but there is a point to be made about enforcement modes. A contract can be "enforced" by awarding damages to the injured party or by specifically enforcing the actions that the contract requires. Solutions to the problem of inducing efficient relation-specific investment commonly involve the use of contracts that condition on verifiable sub-sets of information, and that require specific enforcement of the transfers that the contracts direct.[9] A practical objection to these solutions is that contract enforcement takes time, but subject to this difficulty European laws that make specific performance relatively easy to get are preferable to common law rules that make it difficult. Also, the desirability of preventing fraud and exploitation (functions (5A) and (5B)) is obvious.

Turning to functions (2) and (3), the vocabulary supplying function is non-controversial when it is stated in isolation, but becomes controversial when the tension between it and the interpreting agreements function of (3) is made explicit. This is because the two functions partly derive from distinct normative goals. The vocabulary-supplying function is efficient. Providing a contractual vocabulary is a public good. When parties have a common vocabulary, they can know what they are agreeing to and what will be enforced. The costs of supplying standardized contract terms will often exceed the gains for particular contracting parties. Also, a party who would be disappointed in the deal if it were enforced has an incentive to cheat *ex post*, by claiming that the parties made a different deal – that they intended the words they used to have a meaning particular to them. In sum, private parties will create sub-optimal sets of vocabularies, and a common contractual vocabulary could not survive unless it was made mandatory by judicial enforcement of the statutory or case-created meanings.

The meaning-finding function of interpretation follows from autonomy norms. Under these norms, a person cannot be made to take, or to be prevented from taking, lawful actions without his informed, voluntary consent. Hence, when a contract is sought to be enforced against a person, that person must be permitted to offer evidence as to the actual meaning that the parties intended the contract's words to have. Evidence relevant to this question can be found in what was said and done before the contract was made, from the customs of the industry or trade in which the parties exist, and from any conduct *ex post* that can shed light on what the written words meant to the people who actually used them. When a court permits such evidence to be introduced, it is said to engage in *contextual interpretation*, and when a court refuses to consider such evidence in favor of applying standard meanings in standard ways, it is said to engage in *acontextual interpretation*. Courts in the United States vacillate between these two modes of interpretation, but it is difficult to discern a principle underlying the decisions.[10]

Resolving the conflict between the vocabulary-supplying function (2) and the interpreting-agreements function (3) is beyond the scope of a short chapter such as this, but a remark is in order. Autonomy norms are strongest when a contract is sought to be enforced against an individual, and lose force as the defendants become companies. Hence, a normative theory of contract regulation whose subject is transactions among firms should prefer courts to abandon function (3) in favor of function (2). A less definitive solution is to let adjudicatory methods be default rules, so that courts which are using acontextual interpretation would switch to a more literal enforcement mode when the parties' contract so requested.[11] It is unclear how this suggestion would work in practice.

Function (3C) – supplying fair default rules – arguably should not be performed by any state institution. This is because the set of surplus maximizing rules and the set of fair rules, by any normative criterion, likely are disjoint. Business parties will contract out of "fair but inefficient" default rules. As a consequence, while a decision-maker may want to resolve choices among legal rules by fairness norms when all of the feasible rules are on the Pareto frontier, the supplying of fair default rules independently of their efficiency can be wasted effort for the rule creators and will impose unnecessary contracting costs on parties.

The remaining functions to consider are (5B) and (5C), supplying parties with problem-solving and information-forcing default rules. The problem-solving task can be divided into two sub-functions: (a) Providing modes of governance, such as a corporate form or a bankruptcy scheme; (b) Solving particular problems, such as the scope of the seller's obligation to supply product quality. The rationale for providing both functions is the same: supplying a governance mode or a solution to a complex but commonly recurring problem will often cost particular parties more than the gains that the mode or form could yield to them. A court could not supply a governance mode because courts exist to decide disputes, not create business-regulating codes. In addition, parties to a litigation will supply courts with information that may help to win a case, but will not supply information necessary to create an entire governance mode. Courts sometimes can supply rules to solve more particular problems. Thus, courts never but legislatures can and sometimes do supply parties with default governance modes, and both institutions sometimes attempt to solve particular problems.

The public goods aspect of supplying solutions to problems implies that problem-solving default rules should be created, but there is a distinction between supplying governance modes or dispute resolution schemes and the solving of particular problems. The former sets of solutions can be highly general, and applicable to a wide range of commercial behaviors. Thus, many different types of business activity can be conducted in the corporate form. In contrast, attempting to solve particular problems will often founder on the heterogeneity of large, modern economies. The state creates rules either through adjudication, which is expensive and time consuming, or by legislation, which also is costly and takes time. Consequently, state solutions to problems will not be cost justified unless the problems can be approached in a general way. Though commercial problems often are general – how to induce efficient sunk cost investment, for example – the solutions to these problems usually are specific. Contracts that may induce efficient investment thus condition on verifiable sets of information related to the costs and valuations of the parties to these contracts, and require transfers that are efficacious only in connection with these particular costs and valuations. (See, e.g., Hermalin and Katz 1993; Edlin and Reichelstein 1996; Maskin and Tirole 1999.) Hence, a set of state supplied default rules that attempted to induce efficient investment likely would approach in size the set of private contracts. This would not reduce social costs.

The disjunction between the need for state-supplied default rules to be general in form and the need for particularist solutions to commercial problems has led to dramatic legislative failures. As an example, the Uniform Commercial Code provides that, when the contract is silent, sellers assume all risks associated with product quality, as a consequence of which the sellers must pay compensation for any loss a buyer suffers from a non-compliant product. Sellers of products that may cause substantial losses, especially when the products are complex, *always* contract out of this default rule. The sellers then specify the precise quality obligation and damage risk they are willing to assume, and these specifications differ across products. Thus, the Code warranty sections impose contracting costs that are large in the aggregate but create no offsetting benefits. This story can be retold for other rules, and its lesson is that there are few commercial problems whose solutions are sufficiently general to justify the supply of problem-solving default rules by the state.

To the difficulty of heterogeneity must be added the related difficulty of asymmetric information. Parties will contract out of default rules that condition on unverifiable information because such rules would produce moral hazard. The pervasiveness of the verifiability problem thus seriously constrains the regulatory function of supplying default rules to commercial parties. And in sum, the related difficulties of heterogeneity and asymmetric information suggest that legislatures seldom should attempt to create contract law rules that have the purpose of maximizing surplus for parties who accept those rules.[12] These two difficulties do not plague to the same degree the function of creating default modes of economic organization, such as the standard partnership or business corporation.

The function of supplying information-forcing default rules (4C) also suffers from the difficulties of heterogeneity and asymmetric information. The goal here is to supply rules that will induce separating equilibria, but it will be difficult for courts or legislatures to obtain the knowledge needed for inducing separation when the economic actors function in highly heterogenous economies, and there is considerable private information. (See Adler 1999.) Analyses of third-degree price discrimination also suggest that separating agents is a context-specific task. While the issue is still under debate, one conclusion is clear: writing useful problem-solving or information-forcing default rules is a harder task than was originally thought.

4   Conclusion

Jean Tirole has written: "The challenge for the economist is to develop a theory of the optimal judiciary scope of intervention (the class of problems over which the courts have discretion) and instruments (the menu of choices they face)." The need actually is broader than this – to develop a theory of what the state in general should do regarding contracts and then to specify which legal institutions should perform which substantively desirable functions. This chapter has sketched the possible functions the state can perform and made a few preliminary remarks about which of these functions are possible and desirable to perform. Courts can and should enforce the verifiable terms of contracts, police the contracting process to deter fraud and duress, and help to supply firms with a common vocabulary to use when making contracts. Legislatures should also supply vocabularies and create default modes of economic organization. At this early stage in our understanding of these issues, these are the most defensible tasks and institutional roles that it is possible to do and to play.

Many additional topics remain to be explored. These include whether parties should be permitted to choose the interpretative practices that courts will apply to their agreements; whether courts should emulate the contracting practices of private associations; whether contextual interpretation helps parties to solve their own problems or hinders parties; and the appropriate level of generality that legal default rules should take. Contract theory regulation thus has an interesting research program.

NOTES

Chapter 7 was originally published as "Contract Theory and Theories of Contract Regulation," in *Revue d'Economie Industrielle* (92, 2000).
1. Early treatments of the topic are in Schwartz (1992a) and Tirole (1992). Citations to more recent work will appear below.
2. Courts will not enforce contracts that create externalities, such as agreements to fix prices. There also is considerable regulation of contracts between firms and consumers, commonly rested on the ground of an imbalance in sophistication and resources between these parties. Contracts that create externalities and consumer contracts are beyond the scope of this chapter.
3. A competing theory of contract regulation that is pursued largely by legal scholars holds that the state should enact contract rules that are fair and that promote community among contracting parties. An extensive treatment of this theory is in Collins (1999). Implementing a fairness theory is difficult when parties have the freedom to alter fair legal rules that do not maximize their expected gains. This point is developed in a little more depth on p. 120 below.
4. Private associations often create rules to regulate transactions among the members and between members and outside parties. These rules have the legal status of contracts made among an association's membership. The question

whether courts should treat these contracts as they do ordinary market contracts is unsettled in the law and among commentators, but there is a tendency for courts to enforce the contracts as written when the rules are clear. An interesting study of the contrast between the adjudicatory practices of courts and the adjudicatory practices of the institutions that private associations create is Bernstein (1996).

5. There are fewer such generally accepted, privately created meanings than had been supposed. See Bernstein (1999).

6. A complete taxonomy of default rule types is found in Schwartz (1994).

7. As an illustration, the American Uniform Commercial Code creates a set of default rules to regulate sales transactions. These rules use terms that are derived from commercial practice, but the Code defines them explicitly. Hence, parties who today use a statutorily defined term are held to intend the statutory meaning. The original Code's list of terms is not exhaustive, however, so courts are continually defining new terms, some of which have been incorporated into Code revisions. This process continues.

8. In addition to this theoretical difficulty, parties seldom would want a court to implement an *ex post* efficient solution in the rare cases when it could because commercial agents need prompt answers. Litigations take a long time, so that any otherwise efficient solution usually would be outmoded before it could be devised. Perhaps for the reasons given in the text and in this note, courts seldom attempt to implement *ex post* efficient outcomes. There are examples of these attempts in connection with long-term contracts.

9. For a review, see Schwartz (1998).

10. For a discussion, see Posner (1998).

11. This is suggested in Bernstein (1996).

12. Courts recognize these difficulties implicitly, and tend in asymmetric information environments to enforce only those terms that condition on verifiable information; they do not try to create new rules. (See Schwartz 1992b.)

8 Economic reasoning and the framing of contract law: sale of an asset of uncertain value

Victor P. Goldberg

1 Introduction

I have been teaching the basic Contract Law course for a few years now, and have been struck by the courts' frequent indifference to economic context. It is not so much a matter of the court arriving at the wrong answer as it is the court's asking the wrong questions. In too many instances the court frames the problem in a way which obscures the essential features of the transaction. A little – very little – sensitivity to some elementary economic concepts can go a long way toward illuminating a number of problem areas.

In this chapter, I want to illustrate this proposition by engaging in a close analysis of two American court decisions often featured in contracts casebooks: *Mattei* v. *Hopper*[1] and *Bloor* v. *Falstaff Brewing Corp.*[2] This is a piece of a larger project (Goldberg 2002). The other chapters in Part III have emphasized the manner in which contracting parties allocate to one party the discretion to respond to changed circumstances, but constrain that flexibility by conveying the counterparty's reliance interest. These decisions raise a different problem: production and transfer of information regarding the sale of an asset of uncertain value. Had the courts chosen to frame the problems this way, disposition of both cases would have been straightforward. The court's decision in the former case remains unaffected, but the implications for similar cases would be quite different. The decision in the latter case is simply wrong.

There are a large number of institutional responses to the information problem. I will focus on two which explain nicely the structure of the contracts in controversy. If, for example, the buyer is the most efficient provider of certain pre-sale information, then the parties might agree to give the buyer the option to buy while it collects further information. Such a lock-up provision was at the core of *Mattei* v. *Hopper*. Or, if the buyer fears that it is buying a "lemon," the seller could alleviate that fear by making some of the compensation contingent upon the future performance of the asset. Such was the case in *Bloor* v. *Falstaff*, although neither the court nor the litigators figured it out.

2   *Mattei* v. *Hopper*

Peter Mattei, a real-estate developer, entered into an agreement with Amelia Hopper to purchase a tract of land so that he might construct a shopping center on a tract adjacent to her land.[3] The purchase price was $57,500 and Mattei was given 120 days to "examine the title and consummate the purchase." He gave a $1,000 deposit to the real-estate agent. The agreement was evidenced on a form supplied by the real-estate agent, commonly known as a deposit receipt. The concluding paragraph of the deposit receipt provided: "Subject to Coldwell Banker & Company obtaining leases satisfactory to the purchaser." Before the 120-day period had run, Ms Hopper notified him that she would not sell her land under the agreed-upon terms. He then informed her that satisfactory leases had been obtained and tendered the balance of the purchase price. She refused; he sued.

Her defense was that the satisfaction clause rendered the promise illusory. He had promised to purchase only if he were satisfied, which, she argued, committed him to nothing at all. There was no consideration and, therefore, no contract. The trial court agreed. On appeal, the California Supreme Court reversed. If there were no limits on Mattei's right to claim dissatisfaction, then there would be no contract. However, the court held, Mattei was not so free. His invocation of the clause was subject to a good-faith limitation.[4] By binding himself to go forward unless he could in good faith claim dissatisfaction with the leases, Mattei provided the requisite consideration.

Real-estate transactions routinely make the transaction contingent upon information that would be developed after the contract has been entered into. For example, in *Omni Group, Inc.* v. *Seattle-First National Bank*,[5] another casebook favorite, the purchaser's obligation depended on its satisfaction with an engineer's and architect's feasibility report.[6] In a number of disputes, the seller has argued that the conditions rendered the promise illusory. And, as in *Mattei*, the courts have often rescued the deal by reading a good-faith requirement into the promisor's satisfaction condition. Indeed, in some instances they have done so in the face of contract language making the satisfaction a matter of the buyer's "sole judgment and discretion."[7]

Had the deal been structured a bit differently, there would have been no question of consideration or good faith. The transaction could have been conditional on the satisfaction of some independent third party, perhaps a lender or appraiser.[8] Mattei could have taken an option on Hopper's land, for, say $1,000. The $1,000 would provide consideration, hence there would be a contract, and Mattei could choose not to exercise the option for any reason at all.[9] Or Mattei could have made the $1,000 deposit non-refundable. If that were an exclusive remedy, then the situation would be identical to the option. There are two differences between the actual transaction and the $1,000 option. One is the language describing the conditions that would influence Mattei's decision to exercise the option. The other is the price. Hopper granted Mattei a four-month option with an exercise price of $57,500 and a price of $0. Is this by itself sufficient to find consideration, without resort to an implied duty to exercise his discretion in good faith?

The answer should be "Yes". Properly understood, the buyer's promise is valuable to the seller, even if the buyer reserved the right not to go through with the deal if he so chose. The agreement facilitates the production of information which can result in an enhanced price for the seller's asset (Goldberg 1997). The apparent paradox of the sale of a valuable option at a price of zero disappears upon recognition that the agreement is in reality two intertwined transactions. In the first, the buyer purchases an option: he pays a positive price to induce the seller to take the property off the market for a period of time. In the second, the seller pays the buyer to develop some information about the commercial prospects of the property. The seller believes that if the buyer had better information, the sales price would be higher and that the buyer is the most cost effective producer of that information. The netting of these two transactions could easily result in the buyer paying nothing. Indeed, we need not stop at nothing. The seller could agree to a negative price – the seller could pay the potential buyer up front or could agree to pay if the deal falls through, either because it or the buyer decided not to consummate the transaction.

The first half of the transaction – the option – is straightforward. The second – the lock-up – is less so. The seller faces two information problems. First, there is a possible information asymmetry with potential buyers fearing that the seller might take advantage of the information she developed while the property was in her possession. Potential buyers might discount their bid because of their fear that they might be buying a lemon (Akerlof 1970). The seller has a number of devices, none of them free, for providing quality assurance to purchasers. She might collect and publish information; she might provide specific representations and warranties; she might make some of the sale price contingent on the future earnings from the property (Gilson 1984). Or she might choose to subsidize the production of information by one (or possibly more) potential buyer(s).

Straight cash payments would not be the best way of accomplishing this, but let us put that aside for the moment. The simple point is that if the new information sufficiently enhanced the seller's credibility, the seller could receive more from the enhanced sale price of the land than it would lose from the payment to the prospective buyer. That is, the exercise price of the option is higher because the buyer and seller both know that if the property turns out to be less desirable, the buyer can walk away.

Second, given that the value of the land is uncertain and information about the value is costly to produce, the owner might not be in the best position to develop the information. The information might be on general matters of interest to most potential buyers, for example, soil conditions, traffic patterns, or the availability of potential anchor tenants. Or the information might be more specific to particular potential purchasers, for example, financing conditions or the availability of particular anchor tenants closely linked with a specific potential purchaser. If the buyer is the most efficient producer of this information, then, again, the seller might be willing to pay some of the buyer's expenses if doing so would increase the sale price by enough.

Why might sellers choose to make the payment indirectly, linking it to the option to buy, rather than simply paying cash? If the buyer's information costs are high, then the buyer must consider the real possibility that the expenditures would be for nought if the seller subsequently refused to sell. Even if the information were valuable only to the first buyer (say, the architectural plans and economic feasibility study for a unique structure), the buyer might be reluctant to incur the costs if the seller could sell to someone else or could take advantage of the buyer's sunk cost when negotiating the sale price. Potential buyers will balance the expected costs of additional information production against the expected benefits. If the seller can subsidize information production by certain buyers or otherwise increase the likelihood that the buyer would reap the rewards of its investment, it can influence the quantity and quality of the information produced. In particular, the seller must decide whether it prefers a large number of potential buyers each spending a small amount on information or a small number (perhaps one) studying the asset more intensively.

The seller might be able to use some of the information developed by the prospective buyer to its advantage in dealing with subsequent potential purchasers – in effect free-riding on the first prospective buyer's efforts. If, for example, Mattei had identified some retailers with a strong interest in being anchor tenants, Ms Hopper or a third party could approach those retailers directly. Later buyers could either use the information or draw some inferences about the content of the information from the first party's behavior. The potential purchaser must fear that others would free ride upon the information it produced, and without assurances or subsidies would likely produce too little information. Again, by providing those assurances or subsidies, the seller can influence the buyer's production of information.

Direct cash payments to the buyer would, in general, not work. Such payments would create two obvious moral-hazard problems. If the seller pays for information while buyers determine how much to produce, the buyers will not bear the financial responsibility for their investment decisions; they will have an incentive to over-spend. Moreover, the buyers would be reluctant to share the information with others; they would also be more inclined to tilt their information production toward information that would be of more value to them than to other possible buyers. A seller might be able to police this behavior by monitoring or by separating the production of information from the use of it (perhaps by insisting upon fire walls or by hiring information specialists who cannot benefit directly from the information generated). But if the potential buyers are indeed the best producers of information, the separation of ownership from use can be costly.

The lock-up provides an opportunity for a buyer to develop the information secure in the knowledge that if the information is positive, he will be able to reap the rewards. Mattei is free to explore the matter for 120 days and, if satisfied, he can buy Hopper's property for $57,500. The option means that if the value exceeds the strike price, all the benefits go to the buyer. If the information is negative, the buyer can refuse to exercise the option. It will, however, be out of pocket the information costs. Thus, the first moral-hazard problem is resolved. The seller bears some of the information cost in the negotiated exercise price, but the buyer bears all the direct costs of information production and, therefore, has the incentive to economize.[10] The cost of the option to the buyer is its expected expenditure on information. True, he does not promise to spend a dime on information production or to act upon any information produced. The seller's reward comes not from the buyer's explicit promise to produce information, but from the reward structure established by the bargain. This moral-hazard problem explains why the net price of the two transactions often ends up being zero. Sellers do not want to over-pay for the information. In effect, the net price of zero sets a limit on the amount of effort the buyer should put into the search.

The satisfaction clause suggests an all-or-nothing outcome. Either the buyer is satisfied and the option exercised, or he is not and the option expires. Good faith is obviously irrelevant in the former case; what about the latter? If we unpack that, it becomes clear that good faith adds almost nothing. Suppose that in the 120-day period after Mattei's deposit, the real estate market crashed and Mattei then chose not to exercise his option. One could argue that the non-exercise of the option because of adverse market conditions was bad faith, but that is a flimsy argument. After all, if the value of the property falls, the quality of the leases (that is, their economic value) falls too. Unless we insist that the contract meant that Mattei must be satisfied with the leases with rents determined on the date he and Hopper entered into their agreement, Mattei should be able to take into account changed market conditions when deciding whether or not to go forward with the sale.

If the information were only moderately disappointing, the buyer could make an alternative offer (perhaps waiting for the official expiration of the option). Nothing in the nature of the option precludes a subsequent sale to Mattei (or another buyer) at a new price below the exercise price. Of course, if Mattei's research gives him an informational advantage, he could exploit this advantage by acting strategically. Suppose that he finds the property worth a bit more than the exercise price. He could feign disappointment, telling Hopper that he cannot exercise his option, but that he would be willing to purchase the property at a new, lower price. Such strategic behavior might be less than admirable, but it is hard to imagine that it could trigger good-faith concerns. The questionable behavior occurs only in the renegotiation of the contract and the seller is hardly without recourse. If the seller were suspicious, after all, she maintains the right to refuse to sell to this buyer at any price below the initial contract price; she could shop the second offer to other potential buyers who might be able to draw some inferences from the original buyer's behavior.

In both cases, Mattei's decision not to go forward with the purchase would be the result of his having already performed his part of the agreement; that is, he would have acquired information on the value of the leases and acted upon the information by choosing not to exercise his option. What if Mattei had produced no information at all? If a better offer came along, the fact that Mattei had not yet spent anything searching for information about the parcel should not destroy Mattei's option. Surely, the buyer had bought the option to act on good news and the external offer is simply a manifestation of that good news. The only concern would be that Mattei for some reason wanted the property off the market and had no intention to either acquire information or consummate the deal. Perhaps Mattei entered into similar agreements on a number of parcels but intended to purchase only one. Even then, there was some likelihood that he would choose this particular parcel, so it would be unreasonable to characterize this as merely an attempt to put a parcel off the market for a period of time. It is difficult to imagine a plausible scenario in which a buyer would simply tie up a property with no intention of moving forward.[11] Yet that class of cases is the only one in which even a plausible case can be made for holding that the buyer's discretion undercut consideration. And then the legal response should not be "no contract"; rather, if anything, there should be a claim by the seller for fraud.

The foregoing is a somewhat convoluted path to a simple point. The seller and buyer both benefitted from the agreement, regardless of whether the buyer's discretion was limited by good faith. It was limited by a more significant, practical constraint, self-interest. The lock-up benefitted Hopper by increasing both the probability that the land would be sold by a certain date and the expected price of the asset. It benefitted Mattei by giving him a pure option and by giving him assurance that if he chose to expend resources on evaluating the property (as he most likely would, else why bother?), then he could purchase the land at the pre-set price if the information turned out positive. There is a bargain; both sides benefit and the seller suffers a detriment (her property is temporarily tied up). The buyer does not directly suffer a detriment, since he has the discretion to do nothing, even though exercising that discretion would almost certainly not be in the buyer's interest.

The contract could have left Mattei's decision, to his sole discretion, thereby making it a pure option. What purpose could be served by adding the satisfactory-lease clause (or satisfaction with engineering studies, approval of sub-division maps, etc.)? Such clauses can be viewed as a device for conveying information to the seller about the buyer's intentions. If the seller knows that the buyer's intended use is a shopping center, that information will affect the strike price of the option. The clause's effect is similar to a buyer's representation. Suppose, however, that Mattei had no intention of building a shopping center and that his real intent was to drill for oil (and that the land was much more valuable in that use). It could be argued that this deception should be actionable, perhaps as fraud, misrepresentation, or a breach of the implied covenant of good faith. But that is a far cry from concluding that there was no contract.

The option terminology suggests that the discretion be unbounded, but that need not be the case. The parties can, if they so choose, limit that discretion in various dimensions. They could even contract into a good-faith standard, however nebulous that might be. Indeed, the default rule could be that the discretion is constrained by good faith so that the parties would have to contract around it. My concern is twofold: (a) by making the buyer's good faith a necessary element of the contract (else no consideration), the doctrine needlessly raises good faith from a default rule to a mandatory rule, waivable only by concocting an alternative basis for enforceability (cash consideration or, that great wild card, reliance);

and (b) absent an understanding of the context, good faith does not provide a coherent constraint on the buyer's discretion.

3 *Bloor* v. *Falstaff* [12]

The owners of Ballantine beer (IFC) sold Ballantine's brand name and distribution network (but not the brewery) to Falstaff, another brewer, for $4 million plus a 50 ¢ per barrel royalty for beer sold with the Ballantine brand name for a six-year period. Had Falstaff maintained Ballantine's sales volume the royalty payment would have been over $1,000,000 per year. Falstaff agreed to use "best efforts" to promote and maintain a high volume of sales and further agreed to pay liquidated damages in the event of a substantial discontinuance of distribution under the Ballantine brand name. The seller subsequently went bankrupt and the bankruptcy trustee sued Falstaff under the contract claiming that Falstaff had not used "best efforts" in promoting Ballantine and that it had substantially discontinued production, thereby triggering the liquidated damages clause. The court found for the plaintiff on the first point, but not the second. The opinion has been well received, with commentators generally agreeing that Falstaff's breach was so egregious as to not provide much of a test of the boundaries of "best efforts." Farnsworth, for example, says: "Unfortunately, its decision did relatively little to add precision to the meaning of 'best efforts,' since Kalmanovitz [of Falstaff] fell so far short of the mark" (Farnsworth 1984).

Judge Friendly held that the "best efforts" clause required Falstaff to generate sales of Ballantine beer even if that came at the expense of Falstaff's profits:

While [the best efforts] clause clearly required Falstaff to treat the Ballantine brands as well as its own, it does not follow that it required no more. With respect to its own brands, management was entirely free to exercise its business judgment as to how to maximize profit even if this meant serious loss in volume. Because of the obligation it had assumed under the sales contract, its situation with respect to the Ballantine brands was quite different . . . Clause 8 imposed an added obligation to use "best efforts to promote and maintain a high volume of sales . . ." Although we agree that even this did not require Falstaff to spend itself into bankruptcy to promote the sales of Ballantine products, it did prevent the application to them of Kalmanovitz' philosophy of emphasizing profit *über alles* without fair consideration of the effect on Ballantine volume. Plaintiff was not obliged to show just what steps Falstaff could reasonably have taken to maintain a high volume for Ballantine products. It was sufficient to show that Falstaff simply didn't care about Ballantine's volume and was content to allow this to plummet so long as that course was best for Falstaff's overall profit picture, an inference which the judge permissibly drew. The burden then shifted to Falstaff to prove there was nothing significant it could have done to promote Ballantine sales that would not have been financially disastrous.[13]

The evidence was sufficient to convince the court that Falstaff had not tried hard enough to generate sales of Ballantine beer.

Judge Friendly takes it as axiomatic that the contract required Falstaff to trade off its profits for Ballantine's sales. Conspicuous by its absence in the decision is any analysis of why the contract included the royalty arrangement and the best efforts covenant. That is not entirely his fault, as the record was completely silent on this point. So, we are left with the somewhat peculiar spectacle of a court giving meaning to a context-sensitive phrase with no guidance as to the context. Had the court recognized that the royalty was, in effect, an "earnout," ancillary to the one-shot sale of some of Ballantine's assets to Falstaff, the outcome would have (or, at least, should have) been different.

An earnout makes part of the payment for an asset contingent upon some measure of future performance. Often it is a function of profits; here it is a function of sales. Most corporate acquisitions do not involve earnouts. In 1998, of the over 9,000 acquisitions only 153 included an earnout.[14] Earnouts rarely show up in appellate litigation – a LEXIS search found only 42 cases.[15] That might not adequately indicate the frequency with which they generate disputes. I suspect, based in part on my consulting experience, that the disputes are far more common, but that they arise in arbitrations, not litigation.[16]

IFC was, essentially, selling two assets – Ballantine's brand name and its distribution network. Its purpose was simple. It wanted to sell at the highest price. Other things equal, the fewer post-sale restrictions on Falstaff's exploitation of the assets, the more Falstaff would be willing to pay. That should be obvious, but the court's failure to recognize this basic point is the core of the problem. Falstaff's pursuit of "profit *über alles*," *ex post*, redounds to IFC's benefit, *ex ante*. So, any restriction, like the best efforts clause, immediately raises a red flag: how might the particular restriction raise the value of the Ballantine assets, *ex ante*?

The earnout was a response to the problem of asymmetric information. In some earnouts, the managers of the seller are expected to provide services to the buyer – the earnout serves a role similar to a covenant not to compete. That was not the case here, as the IFC managers were real-estate people with no useful knowledge about the beer industry and no intent to stay in the business. IFC was certifying the quality of the Ballantine assets. In sales of complex assets the seller typically has more information than the prospective buyer. If buyers cannot distinguish good assets from bad, then they are likely to be suspicious of any particular asset and to reduce their offer price accordingly. Sellers can get a better price if they can convince buyers of the quality of the asset. There are myriad ways of providing assurance.[17] The seller can provide extensive representations and warranties; the buyer can engage in extensive due diligence investigation. The parties have an incentive to economize on the joint production of information. By accepting some of its compensation in a contingent form, the seller provides some assurance to the buyer of the quality of the asset.

The parties want an arrangement which maximizes the value to the buyer *ex-ante*. But producing information and assurance is not costless. The process of maximizing the value of the asset can reduce the size of the joint pie. That would obviously be true if the parties had spent months negotiating elaborate representations and warranties and/or engaging in a due diligence investigation. In this instance the parties avoided all these costs using the royalty payment instead. It, too, is not costless. Earnouts in general have a number of value-reducing features. They do not track value perfectly; they can distort incentives; and they are not strategy-proof – that is, the buyer can operate the business in a way which exploits the mechanism. For example, if an earnout based on profits in the first three years, the buyer can make investment decisions which shift profits from the third to the fourth year. Anticipation of these costs will influence the final price of the asset.

The Ballantine royalty had the potential to alter Falstaff's incentives in two ways. First, the royalty acts as a tax (roughly 2 percent)[18] on sales which could induce Falstaff to market a somewhat smaller amount of Ballantine product than it would have, but for the royalty. So "best efforts" might possibly mean that Falstaff should push its sales effort a bit beyond the point that would otherwise be optimal, *ex post*. The distortion of incentives (which in this instance is quite minor) is a common problem in contingent compensation arrangements (franchise fees, percentage leases, oil and gas royalties, and so forth) and "best efforts" is just one of the devices for dealing with the problem.

The relatively low "tax" suggests that this was not the concern of the parties. The more likely concern was diversion: there were two assets being sold and the earnout tracked only one of them. If Falstaff could use the distribution network to sell Falstaff rather than Ballantine, the royalty would not track the value of the asset. The "best efforts" requirement could be viewed as one contractual device for protecting against this sort of diversion. But the context suggests how the clause should be read. "Best efforts" in this context means that Falstaff agreed that in its pursuit of "profit *über alles*" it would not opportunistically divert sales from Ballantine (the sales of which were to track asset quality) to Falstaff.

And that poses the central question: did Falstaff use the network to divert more sales than the parties should reasonably have expected? That might be a difficult question to answer for some fact patterns, but for the facts of this case the answer is easy and negative. When Kalmanovitz took charge he dismantled the distribution system. Falstaff did not divert resources to the more profitable brand, it simply terminated (or at least drastically pared) a project that did not work.

So, we are left with two plausible meanings of "best efforts" in the context of this transaction. First, it could be aimed at correcting Falstaff's incentives which were a bit distorted by the royalty "tax." Second, and more plausible, it could have been an attempt to limit diversion of revenue away from the device chosen to provide assurance of that value. Neither of these provides a basis for concluding that Falstaff's pursuit of profit *über alles* by revising its Ballantine marketing strategy and dismantling much of the Ballantine distribution network violated its obligation to Ballantine.

How to explain the liquidated damages of $1.1 million per year in the event of Falstaff's substantial discontinuance of Ballantine? If this proviso was included as part of the quality assurance mechanism, as I first thought, it makes no sense. In effect, it says: if the assets are really terrible so that they are unusable, then Falstaff pays Ballantine $1.1 million per year for the duration; if on the other hand, they are only pretty bad, Falstaff pays less. That is a perverse result, which I thought, could be explained only by poor drafting.

However, the clause makes more sense if it is viewed as being independent of the quality of the brand name and instead concerns diversion of revenues from the exploitation of Ballantine's distribution network. With this reading Falstaff says, in effect: we agree that we will not cheat you by diverting receipts from the metering device (Ballantine sales) and profiting by the use of the other valuable asset we have purchased, your distribution network; if we have done too much diversion, we agree to pay a penalty (although the law does not permit us to call it that). The trigger for the penalty would not be the *quantity* of Ballantine sold nationally, which is what the court focused on in ruling that there has not been a substantial discontinuance. Rather, it would be the *percentage* of Ballantine being sold through the old Ballantine network.

But this mechanism had one big hole. What if the network itself turned out to be of little or no value, as was in fact the case? Falstaff essentially abandoned the network, but continued to exploit the brand name as best it could. If the proviso's purpose was to thwart massive diversion of revenues, there was no diversion. Falstaff bore the direct risk of the distribution network being a lemon; it seems unlikely that *ex ante* the parties would have wanted Falstaff to post an additional bond against that prospect. But, and this must be emphasized, it is most likely that neither party expected the distribution network to be worth so little, and the contract reflected their failure to anticipate this possibility.

4   Concluding remarks

Two anecdotes do not a theory make. The analysis of these cases is meant only to illustrate the value of adopting a more transactionally sensitive perspective in contract litigation. I am not advocating that we try to ascertain the parties' true intent, a process Judge Easterbrook once characterized as inviting "a tour through Walters' cranium with Walters as the guide."[19] Certainly, in *Mattei* the parties were using forms and were largely unaware of the implications. And the lawyers drafting the Ballantine contract no doubt gave little attention to the possible meaning of "best efforts," a phrase they threw around liberally, using it six other times in the agreement.[20] The point is that the context of the transactions should constrain the court in interpreting what reasonable parties could (and should) have meant. An interpretation of a contract which begins with the presumption that the seller intended to restrict the buyer's subsequent use of the asset is bound to fail unless there is an understanding of the possible gains from tying the buyer's hands. Had Judge Friendly understood that – and I must emphasize that the litigators gave him no help whatsoever – then Falstaff would have been an easy case, but for the other side.

The case law is American, but the problem is universal. And the solutions – the option/lock-up and the earnout/royalty – are sufficiently obvious that I would be most surprised if they were not in common use outside the United States. I would speculate that the fit between what the parties do and the legal system's accommodation of their needs would be no better in the non-American legal systems; Falstaff would probably have fared no better elsewhere. I hope that this brief chapter will encourage a comparative analysis confirming my expectations on both fronts, and that such research might help nudge the doctrine in the proper direction.

NOTES

Chapter 8 was originally published as "Economic Reasoning and the Framing of Contract Law: Sale of an Asset of Uncertain Value," in *Revue d'Economie Industrielle* (92, 2000).

1. 51 Cal. 2d 119; 330 P.2d 625; 1958 Cal. LEXIS 213.
2. 601 F.2d 609 (2d Cir. 1979).
3. *Mattei* v. *Hopper*, 51 Cal. 2d 119; 330 P.2d 625; 1958 Cal. LEXIS 213.
4. Mattei could have been held to an objective (reasonable person) standard or a subjective (good faith) standard; the court chose the latter because of the difficulties in determining objectively the qualities of a satisfactory lease.
5. 32 Wash. App. 22; 645 P.2d 727; 1982 Wash. App. LEXIS 2819.
6. "This transaction is subject to purchaser receiving an engineer's and architect's feasibility report prepared by an engineer and architect of the purchaser's choice. Purchaser agrees to pay all costs of said report. If said report is satisfactory to purchaser, purchaser shall so notify seller in writing within fifteen (15) days of seller's acceptance of this offer. If no such notice is sent to seller, this transaction shall be considered null and void" at 3–4. See also *Horizon Corporation* v. *Westcor, Inc.*, 142 Ariz. 129; 688 P.2d 1021; 1984 Ariz. App. LEXIS 461 (approval of zoning, leases of major retail tenants, and financing); *Rodriguez* v. *Barnett*, 52 Cal. 2d 154, 338 P.2d 907 (1959) (satisfaction with and approval of a subdivision map); *Larwin-Southern Cal, Inc.* v. *J.G.B. Investment Company, Inc., et al.*, 101 Cal. App.3d 626, 162 Cal. Rptr. 52 (1979) (buyer's approval of a preliminary title report, its approval of its engineering report as to soil conditions, dirt balance, drainage, utility requirements and its economic feasibility study, and the approval of a tentative map).
7. *Horizon Corporation* v. *Westcor, Inc.*, at 134. See also *Resource Management Company* v. *Weston Ranch and Livestock Company Inc.*, 706 P.2d 1028. 1034; 1985 Utah LEXIS 884; 86 Oil & Gas Rep. 631.
8. The only good-faith issue would be whether the third party's independence had been compromised by a side deal with the buyer.
9. If the contract gives a false recital of the payment of nominal consideration ("in consideration of buyer's payment of $20,..."), the majority position in the United States is that there is no contract. See *Lewis* v. *Fletcher*, 101 Idaho 530 for majority position and *Smith* v. *Wheeler*, 210 S.E.2d 702 for the minority position.
10. One line of argument, developed in French and McCormick (1984), suggests that sellers invariably bear all the costs of pre-sale information production. As I show elsewhere (Goldberg 1997, pp. 475–81), they over-state the case. Nonetheless, it is correct to say that sellers will often find it in their interest to help potential buyers economize on their pre-sale information expenditures.
11. For a case in which the plaintiff alleged that the defendant entered into an option-like agreement with no intention of going forward, see *Locke* v. *Warner Bros.*, 57 Cal. App. 4th 354, 66 Cal. Rptr. 2d 921 (1997).
12. This discussion summarizes (and simplifies) a more complete analysis of the case presented in Goldberg (2000).
13. At 614–15.
14. For the number of deals, see "1998 M&A Profile," 33 *Mergers & Acquisitions* (March–April 1999, p. 42). For the number including earnouts, see "Deal Structuring: Earn-Outs Get Into More Deals," 33 *Mergers & Acquisitions* (March–April 1999, p. 35).

15. LEXIS search, 10 January 2000.
16. In 1999 I was involved, briefly, as a potential expert witness in two arbitrations concerning the interpretation of an earnout clause.
17. See Gilson (1984), note, pp. 262–4.
18. Ballantine's 1970 price was $26.60 per barrel (PX 9 at 1618) and the royalty rate was 50 ¢ per barrel.
19. *Skycom Corp.* v. *Telstar Corp.*, 813 F.2d 810, 814 (7th Cir. 1987).
20. See Goldberg (2000) p. 1471.

9   A transactions-costs approach to the analysis of property rights

Gary D. Libecap

1   Introduction

Property rights have been receiving considerable press from both policy-makers and academic scholars. As well they should. They are among the most critical social institutions, providing the basis for resource-use decisions and for the assignment of wealth and political power. As such, the property regime profoundly influences both economic performance and income distribution in all economies. Property rights define the accepted array of resource uses, determine who has decision-making authority, and describe who will receive the associated rewards and costs of those decisions. Accordingly, the prevailing system of property rights establishes incentives and time horizons for investment in physical and human capital, production, and exchange. Cross-country differences in property rights result in important differences in economic development and growth (Barro 1997; De Soto 2000).[1]

The property-rights structure also is critical for the environment and natural resource use. Complete and well-defined individual or group property rights internalize externalities and, thereby, guide decision-makers to consider the social consequences of their actions. In this manner, property rights minimize the losses associated with the tragedy of the commons or open-access resources (Hardin 1968; Johnson and Libecap 1982; Ostrom 1990; Deacon 1999; Brown 2000; Rose 2000). Finally, Pipes (1999) argues that private property rights are essential, not only for economic performance, but also for establishing and protecting individual social and political rights within a society.

Despite all of these advantages, property rights are controversial; often are very incomplete; and vary widely across societies in structure and scope. Recent experiences in transitional economies shows that property-rights regimes for valuable assets such as farm land and industrial enterprises cannot be transferred readily from one society to another, regardless of the anticipated benefits of doing so. The change in property rights redistributes wealth and political power and shifts the nature of production, which is often the motivating factor. But there is uncertainty as to the outcome; there are measurement problems; and there are winners and losers from property-rights changes.[2] Uncertainty and measurement issues make it difficult to determine what the gains from a new rights arrangement might be. Further, since property rights involve exclusion, some parties will be denied access to resources or revenues under the new system. Those that anticipate being harmed by the institutional adjustment mobilize to resist or modify the process. Those that expect to benefit are proponents, but under these circumstances, institutional change requires complex negotiation and compromise.

Even in more localized natural resource settings, it can be difficult to define a property-rights solution to mitigate the losses of competitive common-pool extraction. Except in cases where there are relatively small numbers of homogeneous parties using a resource in a limited area, agreements to control access and use typically occur late, after the costs of an inappropriate rights arrangement have been borne (Brown 2000).

Unfortunately, neoclassical theory offers little guidance as to why property institutions that otherwise would seem to improve economic welfare and performance are not quickly adopted or are openly resisted. The New Institutional Economics (NIE) with its emphasis on transactions costs (Williamson 1979; Eggertsson 1990; Furubotn and Richter 1997), however, offers important insights. A transactions-costs approach illuminates why the development of well-defined property rights in response to changing economic conditions will be more difficult than much of the traditional, neoclassical literature suggested (Demsetz 1967). Indeed, without consideration of transactions costs, it is hard to explain North's (1990) observation that property-rights institutions that promote efficient resource use are the exception rather than the norm.

In this chapter, I briefly outline the role property rights play in economic decision-making and resource use. I then focus on transactions costs by emphasizing distributional concerns and measurement problems that can prolong negotiations over property rights and raise enforcement costs. To illustrate these conceptual issues, I focus on efforts to assign property rights through unitization of oil and natural gas reservoirs in North American to mitigate common-pool losses. Unitization contracts both designate a single firm to exploit a hydrocarbon deposit and thereby eliminate the losses of competitive extraction and define property rights to oil-field rents. Yet, as outlined below these contracts typically are very difficult to write and often are incomplete. These results are surprising given the large potential gains from early agreement. Transactions costs associated with equity and measurement disputes delay and shape the nature of the agreements that can ultimately be reached.[3] Examination of the oil and gas case demonstrates the complexities involved in property-rights formation and modification.

2   Property rights: general concepts

Property rights are socially sanctioned uses of valuable assets by economic agents. They range from defining the access, use, and transfer of physical property, such as land, to the ownership of more intangible property, such as stocks and bonds. More broadly, they define the positions and responsibilities of parties in market exchange and within firms. In markets, property rights define sellers and buyers, the goods exchanged, the nature of payments, timing of transactions, enforcement, and dispute resolution. In firms, property rights define specialization of production, delivery, management, marketing, and the distribution of costs and returns among owners and employees (Demsetz 1995).

Property rights can assign ownership to private individuals, groups, or to the state, and each arrangement has different transactions costs for decision-making and resource use. How property rights are structured has important efficiency attributes because if complete, they can directly align individual decisions with relevant social marginal benefits and costs, eliminating externalities. Regardless of the nature of the allocation, property rights must be clearly specified, enforced, and exclusive to be effective, and the degree of specificity depends upon the value of the asset covered (Demsetz 1967; Libecap 1978).

For relatively low-valued assets and/or in cases where the number of parties is small and where there is a history of interaction, informal norms and local customs generally are sufficient for defining and enforcing property rights (Ostrom 1990). For higher-valued assets where the number of competitors is large and where new entry is common and profitable (so that the parties are heterogeneous and have little or no previous relationships), more formal governance structures, such as legally defined private property rights, become necessary. In this latter case, the power of the state is required to supplement informal constraints on access and use. State intervention involves politics and broadens the number and heterogeneity of constituencies that must be considered in negotiations for property-rights assignment and enforcement. Political competition among constituent groups may delay or limit the property rights that can be assigned. In the best case, formal documentation of ownership via title facilitates trade and investment. Trade is promoted through a broadening of the market beyond only those who recognize informal, local ownership arrangements (Alston, Libecap and Mueller 1999a). Investment is encouraged because title allows for property to serve as collateral for accessing capital markets (Feder and Onchan 1987; De Soto 2000). In the worst case, state intervention may not recognize informal property allocations and may not define property rights quickly or effectively. These problems have been evident on the Amazon frontier of Brazil where settlers have been slow to receive title from land agencies owing to bureaucratic and political factors (Alston, Libecap and Schneider 1996). Alternatively, the state may force a property-rights arrangement that harms some parties without compensation, potentially reducing aggregate welfare. Libecap and Smith (2001) argue that compulsory unitization regulation may have this effect by imposing unit agreements in oil and natural gas fields that had been resisted by some parties for legitimate measurement reasons.

Furubotn and Richter (1997) outlined the basic elements of property rights. They include: (a) the right to use the asset (*usus*), (b) the right to appropriate the returns from the asset (*usus fructus*), and (c) the right to change its form, substance, and location (*abusus*), including the right of transfer to others through market trades or to heirs through inheritance. This latter characteristic expands time horizons in resource use decisions because it forces owners to consider the impact of current uses on the longer-term value of the asset.

When property rights are not well defined or when they are restricted by a group or the state, there are implications for economic behavior and performance. The attenuation of property rights in an asset affects the owner's expectations about its use, timing, value, and, consequently, the terms of trade. Whatever specific form it takes, attenuation of property rights implies shrinkage of economic options for asset owners, and a corresponding reduction of the asset's value. Time horizons and incentives for investment and trade can be reduced. Lower-valued uses may be substituted for higher-valued uses, if the latter have become less attractive owing to weaker property rights. If widespread in a society, attenuation of property rights can result in lower economic performance, diminished wealth, and fewer economic opportunities for its members.[4]

Assessment of the impact of property-rights institutions on economic performance, however, is complicated because causality also runs in the opposite direction. That is, while more secure property rights can raise asset values, more valuable assets require more precisely defined property rights to avoid the rent dissipation associated with increased competition for control (Alston, Libecap and Schneider 1996). Technological change, population expansion, new sources of supply, and other changing market conditions exert pressure for adjustment of the existing rights structure to make it commensurate with higher asset values and to facilitate responses to new economic opportunities (Davis and North 1971; Libecap 1978).

Both historical and contemporary experiences, however, reveal that the process of institutional change is neither smooth nor complete. Indeed, most institutional change is incremental with the existing rights structure having a durable and in some cases, negative effect on long-term production and distribution (path dependence). In general, there can be no assurance that institutional change (property rights) will always be structured so as to bring about rational resource use and rapid economic growth (Libecap 1989b).

The process of institutional change is complex, and can become derailed by high transactions costs. The bargaining underlying the creation or modification of institutions involves debate over the aggregate benefits of the new arrangement and the distribution of those benefits among the various interested parties. Negotiations can break down if there are serious disagreements about either the net benefits of institutional change or their allocation. Conflicts, blocking cooperative solutions, can arise from, among other things, serious information asymmetries among the parties regarding anticipated benefits and costs, measurement problems, and an inability to devise side payments to compensate those who believe they will be harmed by institutional change. These problems increase with the size and heterogeneity of the bargaining group (Libecap 1989a). As a result, institutional changes that would be anticipated in a transaction-cost-free environment may not take place or emerge only in abbreviated form.

3   Transaction-costs issues in the assignment and modification of property-rights adjustment: equity issues

Any important redefinition of ownership of valuable assets brings about shifts in the distribution of wealth and political power within a group, or if broad, within a society. The response to proposed institutional changes depends upon how the various parties perceive their position under the new property arrangement relative to the status quo. In the unusual case that all parties can be made better off and these effects are broadly anticipated, then institutional change can be rapid. As described below, this situation is illustrated by the rapid unitization of oil reservoirs where deposits are relatively uniform and where the parties are homogeneous.

In the more usual case, the anticipated results will not be that obvious and some parties will not benefit without some form of compensation or modification in the proposed arrangement. Side payments will be demanded to entice support for institutional change, and disagreements over the size of such payments, their form, who will receive them, and who will pay for them will dominate most political negotiations over property-rights changes.[5] The slow and halting path of oil-field unitization where deposits are not distributed uniformly and where they include both oil and gas demonstrates this situation.

In negotiations, demands for compensation or other changes in proposed property rights can reflect legitimate concerns about the distributional and production effects of a new property-rights regime that may arise from incomplete information. Compensation demands also can be part of rent-seeking efforts as parties engage in extortion, holding up agreement unless they are offered more. The resulting political compromises may lead to the establishment of a rights structure that diverges sharply from what had been originally proposed and from what otherwise would have been viewed as optimal.

Accordingly, agreement on a new rights structure will be affected by the distribution of wealth that it authorizes. All things equal, very skewed rights arrangements lead to pressure for redistribution through further negotiations, a lack of enforcement of existing ownership, theft, and other forms of violence (Alston, Libecap and Mueller 1999b, 2000). If the wealth allocation under the existing property-rights regime is so highly concentrated that few have a stake in it, then it will lack legitimacy (viewed as "unfair") and likely be unstable. Enforcement costs will be high, and those costs will drain wealth and resources from productive endeavors. Further, if the property system is perceived to be closed; that is, if non-owners have few practical means of becoming owners (either through legal restrictions or through the size of the capital accumulation necessary to acquire assets), then owners and non-owners will have different incentives to maintain the property system. Some parties may prefer an incomplete specification of property rights because such an arrangement allows for greater redistribution. The tension that can exist between the wealth creation brought about by secure property rights and redistribution pressures to redress a skewed distribution of wealth presents problems for economic development.

By contrast, if entry is relatively open, that is, if there are recognized opportunities for social and economic mobility, pressures for redistribution may be mitigated. With economic mobility, the wealth assignment over time will be seen as more flexible so that more parties can anticipate improvements in well being. If that is not the case, however, and the proposed system of property rights is seen as having very narrow beneficiaries, then a broad group consensus for property rights change may not occur.

4   Transaction-costs issues in the assignment and modification of property-rights: measurement issues

The transactions costs of property-rights definition and change include the costs of negotiating the assignment and transfer of rights, which are affected by equity disputes, the measurement of asset value and individual allotments, monitoring compliance, and the enforcement of the rights arrangement. These costs determine how property institutions respond to changing economic conditions. In general, agreement on a new property structure depends upon a number of factors. These include (1) the size of the aggregate gains to be shared, (2) the number and heterogeneity of the bargaining parties involved, (3) extent of limited and asymmetric information, (4) the physical nature of the resource, including spatial constraints, and (5) the distributional issues discussed above (Libecap 1989a, 1989b).

The larger the expected aggregate gains, the more likely some agreement will take place. The total benefits of a new or modified property-rights regime often will not be controversial. The wealth losses associated with common-pool competition will be apparent to all. If the alternative of no agreement is so clear and dismal, then negotiations can proceed quickly. This notion is illustrated empirically by the desire among oil producing firms to unitize oil fields early to avoid the potentially large losses of common-pool extraction.

In some cases, however, the gains from agreement are not so obvious and developing a consensus for institutional change is difficult. The nature of the common-pool problem may not be clear or the relative advantages of the proposed property-rights or regulatory structure. For example, in many fisheries, incumbent fishers dispute the data presented by fishery biologists regarding depletion of the stock. They resist the imposition of regulatory controls. Only when the fishery is so depleted that there is little alternative will a new rights arrangement be accepted. This condition explains why institutional change frequently occurs late in the history of the exploitation of a resource after common-pool losses have become so large that distributional concerns are relatively unimportant (Wiggins and Libecap 1985). Unfortunately, by that time, much wealth has been lost.

The number and heterogeneity of the bargaining parties makes initial agreement and subsequent adherence to it more difficult. This is a standard outcome in cartels and other collective action settings (Schmalensee 1987). The greater the number of competing interests with a stake in the new definition of property rights, the more claims that must be addressed in negotiations to build a consensus on institutional change. But the problem is compounded if the parties are also quite different in their expectations, costs, wealth, size, or other important attributes. Under these conditions, it will be much more difficult to reach agreement on a definition and distribution of property rights that satisfies all parties.

For example in the unitization case described below, some firms with certain kinds of leases may decide they are better off under the status quo (competitive extraction) than under a new definition of property rights (unitization). They may chose not to join the unit, even though there is consensus that the group as a whole would be better off under unitization. Side payments are a way of compensating those who resist changes in property rights, but deciding the amount to be paid, the nature and timing of the payment, and the identities of the parties to fund and to receive the transfer can be contentious for a number of reasons.

Measurement problems complicate an accord on any side payments that are under consideration to draw in recalcitrant parties. Transfer payments require agreement on the amount to be paid, which in turn depends on agreement on the value of current holdings and of any losses that some parties expect as a result of the new definition of property rights. Asset valuation under the current and proposed property-rights structure can be a serious problem owing to uncertainty regarding income or cost projections or the physical characteristics of the resource. The physical nature of the resource can make it difficult to calculate share values for negotiations. It may make the costs of marking and enforcing property rights more difficult. Relatively non-observable, migrating resources are particularly difficult in the assignment of property rights, as experiences with fish, water (especially aquifers) and oil demonstrate. Stationary, observable resources with a history of stable prices are much more readily defined, valued, and traded in property-rights negotiations.

Disagreements over measurement will be compounded if there are information asymmetries among the parties regarding the value of individual holdings. These disputes will occur quite aside from any strategic bargaining efforts if private estimates of the value of current property rights and of potential losses from the new system cannot be conveyed easily or credibly to the other bargaining parties.

In addition to honest disagreements over the values of individual claims, the information problems encountered in devising side payments will be intensified if the parties engage in deception or opportunistic behavior. Deception can be used to increase the compensation given as part of an agreement on a new property-rights arrangement. It occurs through willful distortion of the information released by various interests to inflate the value of current property rights and the losses institutional change might impose. Widespread deception by competing parties can make agreements more difficult by reducing any trust that might otherwise promote the more rapid consideration of individual claims in side payment negotiations.

5   Equity and measurement issues in property-rights definition and change: oil-field unitization

5.1   The benefits of unit agreement: the incentive to assign property rights

Negotiation over the property rights implicit in oil-field unitization illustrates many of the equity and measurement problems discussed in the previous sections. Oil-field unitization involves the more precise assignment of property rights within oil and natural gas reservoirs. It is especially important in the United States where the production of crude oil and natural gas potentially involves serious common-pool losses (Libecap 1998a, 1998b; Libecap and Smith 1999). In the United States sub-surface mineral rights are granted to surface landowners, and land ownership is fragmented. For stationary resources, such as hard rock minerals, there is no serious common-pool problem. Owners can mark their claims and produce from their deposits with little incentive to compete with their neighbors. This is not the case with migratory hydrocarbons. Under the common law rule of capture, private property rights to oil and gas are assigned only upon extraction. Oil and gas can be attracted from one part of the reservoir to another through production, which lowers sub-surface pressures in that part of the formation, encouraging migration. Landowners grant production leases to producing firms, and these firms compete for the migrating oil and gas. At least initially, the more they produce, the more they can drain their neighbors' leases. Firms competitively produce to increase their private returns, even though these actions reduce the aggregate value of the reservoir.

Oil reservoir value or rents are dissipated as capital costs are driven up with excessive investment in wells, pipelines, surface storage, and other equipment. Rents also are dissipated as production costs rise with too-rapid extraction. Rapid production of oil results in the early venting of natural gas and/or water, which otherwise help drive the oil to the surface. As natural gas and water are voided from the reservoir, costly pressure maintenance or secondary recovery actions must be implemented. These actions involve the use of additional pumps and injection wells. Total oil recovery falls as pressures decline because oil becomes trapped in surrounding formations, retrievable only at very high extraction costs. Finally, rents are dissipated as production patterns diverge from those that would maximize the economic value of the reservoir over time.

Unitization grants more definite property rights to oil-field rents by assigning ownership shares to each of the leaseholders. It involves an institutional change from competitive extraction to coordinated production. Instead of multiple firms competing in production, a single unit operator is selected to develop the field with costs and revenues apportioned among the other parties according to a pre-defined allocation formula. The resulting individual shares are private property rights. Firm owners become shareholders in the ownership of the complete reservoir, rather than owners of individual production leases. Indeed, the production lease loses its significance. Under unitization, all leaseholders effectively are residual profit claimants, with joint incentives to develop the reservoir in a manner that maximizes its economic value over time. Wells and other equipment can be placed to maximize recovery and to minimize costs, and output can be controlled to maintain sub-surface pressures and to increase overall recovery. With unitized development and operation of reservoirs, no difference exists between the amount of oil and gas privately supplied and the socially optimal amount. When producers expect unitization to occur, exploration is encouraged because greater recovery rates and reduced costs are anticipated. Bonuses and royalties to landowners are higher because the present value of the oil and gas resource is greater with unitization.

Unitization can occur through private negotiation or through government-imposed units (compulsory unitization). The gains from unit agreement have been understood for a very long time, and they can be huge, both from savings in capital costs and from increases in overall production that can be from two to five times unregulated output.[6] With so much at stake and so many gains from agreement, owners of oil firms are motivated to form complete units early before the losses of the common pool are incurred.

5.2   *Equity and measurement problems in unitization negotiations*

Despite its advantages, complete unitization is much more limited than one would expect and negotiations often are contentious, taking a long time to conclude.[7] Even when unitization agreements are reached, many are not complete, leaving the potential for various forms of competition among owners that dissipate rents.[8] In an examination of seven units in Texas, Wiggins and Libecap (1985) and Libecap (1989b) showed that negotiations took from four to nine years before agreements could be reached. Moreover, in five of the seven cases, the area in the final unit did not cover the complete reservoir, allowing common-pool problems to persist as parties outside the unit competed for oil and gas lodged below unit members. As some firms became frustrated with negotiations, they dropped out to form sub-units. But sub-units led to a partitioning of the reservoir, the drilling of additional wells, and generally, did not minimize common-pool losses.[9]

Other costs of not completely unitizing are shown on Prudhoe Bay, North America's largest oil and gas field, first unitized in 1977. Two unit operators, separate net revenue-sharing formulas for oil and gas, and associated competition among the oil and gas owners resulted in protracted and costly conflicts among the parties on the field. This arrangement did not effectively address the common-pool problem. In 1996, concerns about wasteful production practices led the Alaska Oil and Gas Conservation Commission to initiate hearings on a mandatory restructuring of the Prudhoe Bay Unit. The April 2000 purchase of ARCO by British Petroleum and the subsequent reallocation of Prudhoe Bay holdings among Exxon, Phillips, and British Petroleum reduced the losses involved. But this event occurred after over twenty years of production.

These empirical examples reveal that although unitization increases the aggregate returns to be divided among the firms on a reservoir, those gains alone are not enough to bring about rapid agreement on unitization plans. There are a variety of equity and measurement issues to be settled in negotiations. The parties must negotiate a sharing rule that allocates the costs and revenues from production. The resulting property rights must be durable and responsive to considerable uncertainty over future market and geological conditions because field production often lasts twenty years or more. To protect exclusivity, entry or exit of parties from the unit must follow specified parameters if property rights are to be stable.

Further, property rights to the unit must take a particular form. To align all of the interests in maximizing the economic value of the reservoir, development, capital, and operating cost shares must be equal to revenue shares. In that case, each party will be a residual claimant to the profits from effective operation of the entire unit. Under these circumstances, the parties would not want to hold up needed investment or delay new production practices (such as drilling injection wells) in order to opportunistically force a re-negotiation of the contract. Such actions would not only reduce unit profits, but would invite similar strategic behavior by other parties, eroding the basis for any long-term cooperation to maximize the value of the unit. As such, the property-rights arrangement provides for self-enforcing, cooperative behavior among the firms.[10] Accordingly, although reaching agreement on the sharing formula can involve long and costly negotiations, if the property rights take this form they will reduce *ex post* enforcement costs.

If, however, the property-rights formula does not allocate costs and production shares in the same manner, then conflicts will emerge. The parties will have differential incentives for development depending on the nature of their individual benefits and costs, since they no longer are allocated in the same way. Certain lease owners will advocate actions that would skew development in the direction of those expenditures (such as injection wells) in which they would bear lower costs, but higher returns, even if that is inconsistent with maximizing the overall value of the unit. With costs and revenues portioned differently, every production and investment decision will involve individual calculations among the lease owners as to how the proposed activity would affect them. Dissension, delays, and even violation of the unit agreement, all with corresponding rent dissipation, are likely. Hence the need to distribute benefits and costs among the parties according to the same formula.

Because property rights within unit agreements must take this specific form in order to be effective, negotiations become even more difficult. They can be plagued by hold-outs seeking to gain larger revenue shares or by honest disagreements over measurement or equity. The latter occurs owing to disputes over the value of individual leases, which is the basis for assigning shares. To resolve such disputes, some parties (typically those with the largest leases and the most to lose) may devise side payments that restore consensus among the parties and allow the unit to proceed. For example, some parties may be granted a larger revenue share than their cost share. But as we have argued, this arrangement will not align incentives over the long term. New disputes and conflicts will emerge with the need for additional side payments, but these will only further distort the property-rights structure. The efficiency losses inflicted on the unit from disagreement and non-optimal production practices may be irreversible owing to resulting changes in reservoir dynamics. Accordingly, *ex post* efforts to align interests via side payments are not apt to be as effective as the *ex ante* proportionate assignment of costs and production shares to each party through the property-rights rule. This example illustrates how demanding the initial allocation of property rights can be and why it might take so long to reach agreement.

If the leases are homogeneous, then equity and measurement disputes during share negotiations are unlikely to be serious obstacles. Libecap and Smith's (1999) empirical investigation of sixty units in the United States and Canada reveals those with relatively simple and homogeneous geologic structures (no clustering of oil and gas in separate parts of the reservoir) and only one production phase (no secondary recovery) have no history of conflict.[11] These units have sharing or property rules that assign costs and revenues in an equal manner to each party and hence, align incentives for optimal unit-wide production. These conditions describe 78 percent (forty-seven of sixty) of the units, underscoring the importance all parties place on reaching effective agreement to maximize the value of the reservoir over the life of the contract; 22 percent of the units, however, do not have the requisite property-rights arrangement. These are more complex units with multiple production phases and/or separate concentrations of oil and gas, and the leases are much more heterogeneous. Because of complicated geological conditions and associated uncertainty over lease values, negotiating conditions are more complicated for these units, and such conditions affect the ability of the parties to reach agreement on an incentive-compatible property-sharing formula. Especially in formations where oil and gas are in separate pockets (gas caps), incomplete agreements exist, and conflicts and rent dissipation follow, as illustrated by the case of the Prudhoe Bay Unit.

In these cases, negotiating over unit shares amounts fundamentally to the trading of disparate assets among the parties. Because the reservoir has distinct physical properties that are not uniformly distributed, some leases have large amounts of gas and little oil, while others have more oil and less gas. Converting both into common values is necessary to determine lease values and unit shares. But measurement of the relative amounts of oil and gas and their value conversion from gas to oil are sources of dispute. Similarly, certain parties may hold leases that provide natural sites for production wells (for example, high on the formation) during primary production, while others may hold leases that are better candidates for water or gas injection (for example, low on the formation) during secondary production. Again, it will be necessary for the parties to adopt terms of trade based on the lease locations and the potential for enhanced recovery efforts to supplement the natural reservoir drive.

Through repeated negotiations, the parties typically are capable of translating differences in quantity of resources into ownership shares in the unit. However, differences in kind are more problematic. The basis for placing relative values on the oil and gas assets often is not obvious to the bargaining parties. Gas ownership presents a particular problem. The valuation of gas in the reservoir depends on whether it is assumed to be marketed, as opposed to being re-injected in support of enhanced oil recovery efforts. Gas values are more volatile than are those for oil and they do not always track one another, making valuation and exchange of gas and oil properties difficult. Further, owing to limited transportability in some cases, the existence of any external market for the gas may be doubtful, especially in remote locations. To the extent that the imputed value of gas is speculative, the parties find it difficult to adopt any conversion factor for gas to oil, and hence will be unable to agree on any particular distribution of equity in the unit as a whole.

In response to these conditions, the firms may elect to partition the unit in a way that isolates differences among tracts and permits them to be negotiated separately. When the reservoir is partitioned along any dimension, however, a boundary is created that may incite competition for resources and for value. The existence of such partitions may render the unit incomplete and hence, create conflicts of interest that dissipate reservoir rents.

Other complexities that lead to measurement and sharing disputes, raising the transactions costs of negotiation, include differences among the leases in terms of their structural advantage on the formation. Owners of leases that have a natural structural advantage will want to retain the value of this advantage in the unitization formula. Such individuals are unlikely to agree to a unitization contract that does not give them at least as much oil or gas, as they would have received by not unitizing. Even if the increase in ultimate recovery from unitization is so great that these parties will receive more from unit operations than from individual development, they have a much stronger bargaining position in negotiations than less-favored tract owners. They can hold out for the most favorable property-rights allocation, secure in the knowledge that the regional migration of oil will continue toward their tracts during any delay in negotiations. Indeed, holding out may increase the value of a structurally advantageous location. If the other firms form a sub-unit without the participation of the owners of better-located tracts, the pressure maintenance operations of the unit may increase the amount of oil migration toward the unsigned parties. The hold-outs then benefit from the unit without incurring any costs of the pressure maintenance activity.

These equity disputes require measurement of individual claims. Valuation is hindered by incomplete and/or asymmetric information about current lease values and the effects of unit-wide production, such as secondary and enhanced recovery, which are risky technologically and economically. Such actions change the time pattern of oil and gas production, perhaps lowering short-term payments to firms, while increasing payments over the long term. Production patterns, however, are estimated only imperfectly so that there may be disagreement as to the present value of individual leases and proposed unit shares. Some parties may refuse to join the unit because they have different information and assess the risks and rewards differently than do the proponents of the unit.

In negotiations, the level of information available to the contracting parties for determining lease values depends upon the stage of production in which contracting occurs. In exploration, little is known regarding the location of hydrocarbons and commercial extraction possibilities. At that time, all properties are relatively homogeneous, and unitization agreements can be comparatively easy to reach with low transactions costs, using simple allocation formulas to assign property rights, often based on surface acreage. Since no party knows whether the formula is to its particular advantage or disadvantage, negotiators can focus on the aggregate gains from unitization.

Information problems and distributional concerns, however, arise with development, as oil and gas reserves are proved and expanded. With the initial discovery well and the drilling of subsequent wells, lease heterogeneities emerge. Because reservoirs are not uniform, the information released from a well is descriptive of only the immediate vicinity. Hence, through drilling on their individual leases, firms gain knowledge of their portion of the reservoir. The full extent of the deposit and the productive potential of other areas of the reservoir will be revealed only through the drilling activities of other firms. Other parties will not hold this asymmetric information so that verifying claims based on it will be difficult.

Some of information is public, objectively measured, and non-controversial, such as the number of wells on the lease, its surface acreage, and the record of current and past production. Other data are more private, more difficult to measure, more subjective, and hence, more likely to be disputed, such as the amount of oil below lease lines, remaining reserves, net oil migration, and bottom hole pressure. As a result of disagreements over the measurement and interpretation of sub-surface parameters, unit negotiations often must focus on a small set of objectively measurable variables, such as cumulative output or wells per acre. These objective measures, however, may be poor indicators of lease value.

Conflicts over lease values and unit shares will continue until late in the life of a reservoir. With the accumulation of information released through development and production, public and private lease value estimates converge as primary production (production based on natural sub-surface pressure) approaches zero. At that point, a consensus on shares and the formation of the unit is possible. This suggests that unit agreements are more likely to be reached late in the life of the reservoir. Unfortunately, by that time most of the open-access losses have been inflicted.

6   Concluding remarks

Property rights are basic social institutions that determine incentives for production, investment, and trade. Neoclassical theory has long argued that a secure property-rights structure is necessary for encouraging production and exchange that maximizes wealth and minimizes rent dissipation. A growing body of empirical evidence supports this claim. Even so, property rights vary dramatically (historically and contemporarily), often straying from what would be considered optimal. Transactions costs associated with equity and measurement disputes can delay or block the development of effective property-rights arrangements. The example of oil and gas unitization negotiations illustrates the kinds of problems that can be encountered and shows why observed property rights often do not follow a theoretical ideal. Compromises and side payments in negotiations can modify the proposed property-rights arrangement with important efficiency implications.

It is useful to view property rights as contractual outcomes negotiated by parties informally in small groups or more formally in larger political settings, subject to transactions costs. By analyzing the details of property-rights negotiations, including the positions taken by the various parties, their characteristics, and the information available, one can determine why property rights emerge in the manner that they do. The larger the total benefits of devising new or modifying old property rights, the more probable is agreement. Further, the more homogeneous are the parties, the more likely that they will be able to construct and agree upon an assignment of property rights. Where the parties differ in important dimensions, such as production cost or access to information about the value of the asset, then agreement on property-sharing rules is going to be more difficult. And if the numbers are large, the transactions costs of reaching agreement will be increased. These points help explain the persistence of seemingly ineffective property rights arrangements across societies and across time.

NOTES

1. The material here draws on my chapter in Anderson and McChesney (2001).
2. Yoram Barzel (1989) emphasizes transactions costs and measurement problems in implementing property rights regimes.
3. The problem of the common pool was outlined early by Gordon (1954) and the notion of rent dissipation clearly described by Cheung (1970).
4. Of course, if the rights structure already is incomplete, such that there are divergences between the net private and social returns of resource use (externalities), then regulations on resource use can be socially beneficial.
5. These problems may be less critical in small-group settings where there is a history of interaction, relative homogeneity of the bargainers, and strong social norms (Rose 2000).
6. Libecap and Wiggins (1984) cite industry trade journals for predictions that unitization would raise oil recovery by 130 million barrels on the Fairway field in Texas.
7. Joe Bain (1947, p. 29) commented on the problem of fragmented lease holdings in the United States for unitization. He stated: "It is difficult to understand why in the United States, even admitting all obstacles of law and tradition,

not more than a dozen pools are 100 percent unitized (out of some 3,000) and only 185 have even partial unitization." Similarly, Libecap and Wiggins (1985) reported that as late as 1975, only 38 percent of Oklahoma production and 20 percent of Texas production came from reservoir-wide units.

8. Wiggins and Libecap (1985) and Smith (1987) examine some of the bargaining issues faced by unit negotiators. See discussion in Libecap (2001).

9. For example, after unsuccessful efforts to completely unitize the 71,000 acre Slaughter field in West Texas, ultimately 28 sub-units were established, ranging from 80 to 4,918 acres. To prevent migration of oil across sub-unit boundaries, some 427 offsetting water injection wells were sunk along each sub-unit boundary, adding capital costs of $156 million (Libecap 1989a, p. 106).

10. As described by Klein and Murphy (1997, p. 417), "the self-enforcing range measures the extent to which market conditions can change, thereby altering the gains to one or the other party from nonperformance, without precipitating nonperformance." (See Libecap and Smith 1999.)

11. The empirical investigation uses sixty unit-operating agreements from oil and gas reservoirs in Alaska, Alberta, Illinois, Louisiana, Oklahoma, New Mexico, Texas, and Wyoming.

Part IV

Theoretical developments: where do we stand?

10   Transaction costs and incentive theory

Eric Malin and David Martimort

1   Introduction

Over the last twenty-five years, incentive theory has been used as a powerful tool to describe how resources can be allocated in a world of decentralized information. The key achievement of incentive theory is that it provides a full characterization of the set of implementable allocations when resources within an organization must be allocated under informational constraints. The basic tool to obtain such a characterization is the Revelation Principle which has been demonstrated independently by several authors.[1]

The Revelation Principle stipulates that any contractual outcome achieved by an organization where information is decentralized among its members can equivalently be implemented with a simple direct mechanism where privately informed agents send messages on their own piece of information to a mediator who, in turn, recommends plans of actions to those agents. Moreover, the agents' messages are truthful in equilibrium, i.e. the mechanism must satisfy a number of *incentive compatibility constraints*. If the mechanism must be voluntarily accepted by the agents, some *participation constraints* must also be satisfied. These two sets of constraints completely characterize the set of *feasible allocations under asymmetric information*.

Once this first step of the analysis is completed, one can stipulate an objective function for the organization and proceed to further optimization. This optimization leads to an interesting trade-off between the achievement of allocative efficiency as Coasian bargaining would permit under complete information and the cost of insuring incentive compatibility. Under asymmetric information, conceding informational rents to privately informed agents must be done at the minimal cost and this has allocative consequences. The distribution of payoffs in the organization and the overall size of the cake to be shared among its members are determined simultaneously.

This two-step procedure has led to an enormous amount of work which is very much normative by nature and which, over the last twenty-five years, has changed our view of economics. Progress owing to incentive theory has spanned as many different fields as labor economics, the theory of the firm,[2] regulation and procurement,[3] public good provision,[4] optimal taxation,[5] and, more recently international trade.[6] Roughly and to simplify, any field in economics benefitted from being reconsidered through the lens of the rent–efficiency trade-off.

Interestingly, the optimal direct mechanism which is found following this two-step procedure may be implemented in many different ways by real-world institutions, i.e. by some sort of indirect mechanism. For instance, in the procurement context we analyze below, the optimal output produced by a privately informed seller (the agent) for an uninformed buyer (the principal) can equivalently be implemented by letting the agent report his information to the principal and having the latter choose the particular output target and compensation or by letting the principal offer a non-linear price and letting the agent choose within this menu his most preferred choice. In the first case, the agent has no freedom of actions except on his report to the principal who exerts formal and real authority. In the second case, the agent exerts some form of real authority within the constrained set of decisions proposed by the principal. As a consequence, the optimal scheme cannot explain the allocation of authority within the firm. Moreover, whether the agent works in the buyer's firm or owns his own productive unit has no consequence for the overall allocation of resources. Firms' boundaries are irrelevant in this context.

This indetermination in the implementation procedure has fascinating consequences since it amounts basically to an *Irrelevance Theorem*. One of the most striking applications of this Irrelevance Theorem is that ownership may have no impact on the optimal allocation of resources in the economy. For instance, Sappington and Stiglitz (1987) have shown that a publicly owned firm and a regulated privately owned one can both be induced to produce the same socially optimal output at the same incentive cost by a clever design of the procedure for auctioning the right to produce to the private sector. In this case, privatization has no impact on how resources are allocated between the public and the private sectors of the economy.

At first glance, this Irrelevance Theorem bears a strong resemblance to the traditional Coase Theorem which states that decentralized bargaining is enough to achieve allocative efficiency and that this outcome is independent of the allocation of property rights. First, note that this latter theorem presupposes that there is no asymmetric information and no transaction costs of any sort. For a given form of decentralized bargaining, asymmetric information introduces allocative inefficiency.[7] However, these inefficiencies depend on the allocation of property rights through the role that those rights play in determining the status quo payoffs of agents in the bargaining.[8] The Irrelevance Theorem differs from the Coase Theorem along several lines. First, it assumes a world of asymmetric information. Second, for a given set of property rights, it assumes that decentralized bargaining is replaced by a centralized design of the procedure for allocating resources in the organization. This is the implementation of this centralized design which is somewhat indetermined, since it can be realized in many different ways which have different observational consequences in terms of the distribution of authority in the organization (see our procurement example above). Third, if the procedure for allocating resources also includes the possibility of allocating ownership through *ex ante* auctioning, clever design makes the allocation of ownership irrelevant.

As a consequence, this Irrelevance Theorem has often been interpreted as implying that incentive theory has nothing to say about such things as the distribution of authority within an organization, the limits of the firm, the separation between the public and the private spheres of the economy, and, more generally, nothing to say about organizational forms and designs.

In our view, this criticism is clearly valid. However, we think that scholars who advocate this "criticism approach" fail also to give enough justice to what incentive theory is really. Those opponents of incentive theory have been too eager "to throw away the baby with the bath water." Indeed, the commonly held view of incentive theory provides us *only* with an ideal benchmark: it describes a world which is *frictionless*, a world in which *transaction costs* are absent or at least negligible. In other words, the Revelation Principle is a natural extension of the Arrow–Debreu world to asymmetric information settings. As it is almost nonsensical to explain market conduct and firm's performance within an Arrow–Debreu world, it becomes almost useless to discuss organizational forms with the Revelation Principle as the only tool at hand.

This chapter argues that simple and tractable extensions of standard incentive theory can nevertheless take into account various forms of transaction costs and that those forms of transaction costs lead to various contract incompletenesses which can be easily described. Indeed, those forms of incompletenesses are shown to preserve the great advantage of incentive theory, i.e. its ability to describe feasible allocations. To do this the standard Revelation Principle must be conveniently amended by introducing some *transactional constraints* which altogether with incentive and participation constraints again completely describe feasible allocations. This characterization, in turn, leads to interesting third-best optimizations which describe a world in which the Irrelevance Theorem does not any longer hold. Within this third-best approach, various organizational forms can thus be compared and, we believe, interestingly distinguished.

Section 2 presents the standard rent–efficiency trade-off to which we will refer throughout the chapter. It also solves for the second-best optimal contract in a transaction cost-free world. Section 3 discusses the assumptions underlying the applicability of the Revelation Principle and shows how various transaction costs correspond to relaxation of some of these assumptions and that the corresponding grand contract becomes then somewhat incomplete. Section 4 shows that those incompletenesses are in fact associated with contractual externalities which affect the third-best outcome. We show also that there exist quite general reduced-form formula describing the impact of these transactional constraints.

2   The rent–efficiency trade-off: a procurement example

As an example of the two-step procedure underlying the use of the Revelation Principle, let us consider the following procurement setting. A principal, the buyer, delegates production of an output to an agent, the seller. The principal gets a benefit $S(q)$ (with $S' > 0$, $S'' < 0$) from consuming q units of the procured good. The agent incurs a cost θq from producing q units. The marginal cost θ is privately known by the agent. It is drawn in a common knowledge distribution having for support $\{\underline{\theta}, \overline{\theta}\}$ (we denote $\Delta\theta = \overline{\theta} - \underline{\theta}$ the spread of the uncertainty) with respective probabilities ν and $1 - \nu$.

Of course, first-best efficiency obtained under complete information requires that production $q^{FB}(\theta)$ is set such that marginal cost equals marginal benefit, i.e.:

$$S'(q^{FB}(\theta)) = \theta \tag{1}$$

for both values of θ.

This contractual outcome can be easily implemented by allowing the principal to make a take-it-or-leave-it offer to the agent. For a given output target recommended to the agent, the principal compensates the latter with a lump-sum transfer so that the agent is just indifferent between producing or not for the principal.

This first-best solution can no longer be implemented under asymmetric information. Indeed, as can be easily shown, the efficient agent would like to claim that he is inefficient to produce the smaller output $q^{FB}(\bar{\theta})$ recommended by the principal to the inefficient agent. By doing so, he can save on the production cost an amount $\Delta\theta q^{FB}(\bar{\theta}) > 0$.

In what follows, we denote by $GC = \{(\underline{q}, \underline{U}); (\bar{q}, \bar{U})\}$ the grand contract offered by the principal to the agent. From the Revelation Principle, this is a direct mechanism which induces production and allocates informational rents $(\underline{q}, \underline{U})$ when the firm claims to be efficient and $(\bar{q}, \bar{U})$ when, on the contrary, it claims to be inefficient.

To induce information revelation from the efficient agent, the principal has to leave an informational rent $\underline{U}$ to the efficient agent which satisfies the following incentive compatibility constraint:

$$\underline{U} \geq \Delta\theta\bar{q} + \bar{U} \tag{2}$$

Similarly, the principal has to induce participation from the least efficient agent. The following participation constraint has thus to be satisfied:

$$\bar{U} \geq 0 \tag{3}$$

It is standard to show that the optimal contract solves the following reduced-form problem[9]:

$$\max_{\{(\underline{q},\underline{U});(\bar{q},\bar{U})\}} v(S(\underline{q}) - \underline{\theta}\underline{q}) + (1-v)(S(\bar{q}) - \bar{\theta}\bar{q}) - v\underline{U} - (1-v)\bar{U}$$

$$\text{subject to } (2)\text{--}(3) \tag{4}$$

In the last maximand, one can recognize on left the expected efficiency which would be maximized under complete information and on the right the expected cost of the informational rent which is now incurred by the principal under asymmetric information. Optimization leads to the following second-best outputs:

$$S'(q^{SB}(\underline{\theta})) = \underline{\theta} \tag{5}$$

and

$$S'(q^{SB}(\bar{\theta})) = \bar{\theta} + \frac{v}{1-v}\Delta\theta \tag{6}$$

Comparing second-best and first-best outputs,

$$q^{SB}(\underline{\theta}) = q^{FB}(\underline{\theta})$$

i.e. there is no allocative distortion for the most efficient agent; and

$$q^{SB}(\bar{\theta}) < q^{FB}(\bar{\theta})$$

i.e. there is a downward distortion of the output requested from the least efficient seller.

Therefore, (6) clearly highlights the rent–efficiency trade-off discussed earlier. By reducing output requested from an inefficient agent, the principal reduces the costly informational rent of an efficient one. The distribution of informational rents within the organization and the allocative efficiency cannot be disentangled under asymmetric information.

3   The ideal world of the Revelation Principle

That the Revelation Principle describes an ideal world can be easily understood by coming back to the assumptions underlying its applicability. Doing this is important first to understand the real domain of applicability of this Principle and second to define explicitly what should be a good definition of transaction costs from the point of view of incentive theory:

- **Definition of transaction costs for incentive theory:**   In our view, transaction costs should be understood as *all sorts of impediments* to the applicability of the Revelation Principle.

  Our definition is more precise than that given by Coase (1937) and Williamson (1985, 1996) who argue that transaction costs are all sort of costs incurred both the *ex ante* (negotiation or writing costs) and *ex post* (renegotiation, arbitration costs). Concerning *ex ante* transaction costs, this definition is somewhat imprecise since it puts under the same hat costs of different nature: costs owing to asymmetric information (negotiation) and costs owing to some limited ability to foresee contingencies or to think about their consequences. Concerning *ex post* transaction costs, again the definition is unclear. Indeed, renegotiation costs are the consequences of some form of limited commitment which can be explained only by introducing loopholes of the judiciary system, and thus other transaction costs ... Arbitration points instead to enforcement problems which are again linked to limits of the judiciary system in case of unforeseen contingencies. In other words, the actual definition of transaction costs *à la* Coase–Williamson is somewhat self-referencing.

  Our definition being stated, we can discuss all the different assumptions underlying the Revelation Principle and trace out the corresponding transaction costs which limit its applicability.

- **Assumption 1: full rationality and complexity** This is a rather simple observation to make but it deserves to be made. Implicitly, behind the Revelation Principle is the assumption that the mediator (or principal) is able to perfectly reconstruct the strategies of privately informed agents and to include their plans of actions into his recommendations about how the direct mechanism he proposes should be played.

As recognized by Williamson (1975), bounded rationality is one of the possible transaction costs which impedes contractual efficiency. This point is well taken, but neoclassical economics is still having difficulties dealing with this problem and the honest course is to recognize that transaction-cost economics (TCE) has not provided us with a powerful analytical treatment of this issue as well. As such, this obviously does not point to a weakness of incentive theory and we will have almost nothing to say on this issue in this chapter.[10]

- **Assumption 2: perfect communication** Once communication channels between the mediator and his agents have been opened, information flows up and recommendations flow down costlessly within the organization. This is of course an extreme assumption but little is known on contracting under *communication constraints*.[11] The methodological problem here is extremely close to that faced when one wants to deal with bounded rationality. It is quite easy to describe what happens with perfect communication (as with perfect rationality), it is much less easy to introduce convincing restrictions on communication (like convincing restrictions on the ability of agents to perform correct computations). The modeler here necessarily falls in the realm of adhocity.

  Clearly, incentive theory has not yet offered a satisfactory treatment of imperfect rationality and imperfect communication. But again, incentive theory is waiting for more fundamental developments of theory which would help the modeler to cope efficiently with those issues and which would benefit other fields of economic theory as well.

- **Assumption 3: full control of communication channels between agents** The mediator used in the Revelation Principle has full control of the communication channels he opens with the privately informed agents. This means that he can prevent at no cost bilateral communication among agents of the organization.

- **Assumption 4: full control of communication channels between agents and other mediators** The mediator used in the Revelation Principle can also prevent at no cost the communication of any of these agents with outsiders or external mediators who do not further communicate with the initial mediator and do not share his objectives.

  To understand the consequences of relaxing assumptions 3 and 4, assume now that there exist some unmodeled transaction costs which make the mediator unable to control all possible communications that an agent of his organization can open.

  The first limit on the ability of the principal to control communication channels among agents raises the issue of collusion and clique formation among workers or between agents and their supervisors. These collusions have been shown to impact quite significantly on the efficiency of an organization, as we have learned from industrial sociologists in the field of the theory of the firm[12] and from political scientists in the field of organization of government.[13]

The second limit on the ability of the principal to control communication channels between agents and outside mediators points to the fact that there is nothing like a single principal ruling all the activities of the economy. The norm instead is that agents report to several principals who may have conflicting interests. This is clearly the case of the management of the firm who is involved in several bilateral contracts with customers, shareholders, creditors, regulators, and so on . . . [14] But multiprincipal structures also abound within governments.[15]

Both contractual limits above can be dealt within an incentive theory framework. In both cases, the Revelation Principle must nevertheless be amended. When collusion among agents matters, the set of implementable allocations is conveniently described by appending to the initial individual incentive and participation constraints that must be satisfied by a direct mechanism, the *coalition incentive compatibility constraints* which guarantee that the possible coalitions which can form do not gain from collectively manipulating informational reports to the principal. This last step of the analysis was first performed in the early 1970s[16] but it received its most convincing treatment only with Tirole (1986, 1992) for collusion under symmetric information and Laffont and Martimort (1997, 2000) for collusion under asymmetric information. In that latter case, bilateral collusion is itself impeded by asymmetric information among colluding agents. Still, the set of implementable allocations can be easily described and the optimization within this set leads generally to a constrained optimum when collusion is a binding concern of the organization.

When communication with other principals matters, the set of equilibrium allocations of the game among non-cooperating multiprincipals is hard to describe by simple direct mechanisms.[17] However, as was initially suggested in Martimort (1992) and formally proved independently in Martimort and Stole (1999a, 1999b) and Peters (1999), the set of equilibria can be described with *a Taxation Principle*. This Taxation Principle stipulates that any equilibrium outcome of a game with competing mediators can be replicated when mediators offer non-cooperatively indirect mechanisms which leave to the common agents the choices of actions within those initially suggested by these mediators. In other words, when one moves from the one-principal setting to a multiprincipal setting, direct mechanisms becomes useless to describe equilibrium allocations. Instead, agents must now keep most decision-making and their information to themselves instead of sending it to their competing principals who would otherwise enter into infinite gaming to induce report manipulations into the mechanisms offered by their respective rivals.

Note that in both cases above, the existence of transaction costs which make a principal unable to control all communication channels within his organization does not make impossible a clear characterization of the set of implementable allocations. Incentive theory can still describe how transaction costs which make the control of all communication difficult or impossible for the principal to affect the set of feasible allocations.

- **Assumption 5: full commitment** An important assumption behind the use of the Revelation Principle is the fact that the mediator can commit to the mechanism he proposes to the agents. Commitment is the right benchmark for complete contracts. If parties to the contract find it beneficial to commit *ex ante*, they should be able to do so just by committing to pay large penalties in case of renegotiation. However, commitment is hard to justify if it is not sequentially optimal. Indeed, in the course of actions, information which would make beneficial a Pareto-improving recontracting may become available.[18] This issue naturally arises in the case of long-term contracting where the agent's choice of action in the first period reveals information to the principal before the second-period contract is implemented.[19] Also, it arises even within a single period of contracting when the principal uses a direct mechanism and learns the agent's report on his type before sending him a recommendation[20] or when the principal contracts *ex ante* with the agent (i.e. before the latter learns his information) and the agent's action is chosen after his own learning of the information. In the first case, the mechanism may be subject to *ex post renegotiation* taking place before the second-period contract is executed. In the second case, the mechanism may be threatened by *interim renegotiation* taking place just before its execution itself.

However, in both cases, the principal can perfectly anticipate the issue of the renegotiation and include this issue into his initial offer. By doing so, the principal ensures that the initial renegotiation-proof contract he offers will come unchanged as an equilibrium outcome of the game of initial contractual offer cum renegotiation. The *Renegotiation-Proofness Principle* is a natural extension of the Revelation Principle to this limited commitment environment. Incentive theory can again describe all equilibrium allocations by adding to standard incentive and participation constraints a set of *renegotiation-proofness constraints*.

Here, the impossibility of intertemporal commitments finds itself its origins in various loopholes of the judiciary system, if one is interested in private contracting, or of the Constitution if one is instead interested in public contracting. Transaction costs make those commitments difficult or impossible. Nevertheless, incentive theory can still describe the set of feasible allocations and can still allow us to optimize within this set.

- **Assumption 6: mediator's benevolence**   The mediator of the Revelation Principle is assumed to be a benevolent agent taking the objectives of the organization as his own. In reality, there is a substantial amount of delegation to those mediators. These may be political decision-makers to whom power has been given in elections or these may be CEOs to whom shareholders have delegated the control of the firm. Those principals have both private information on how the organization should be run and also private agendas that they may pursue.[21]

The delegation of decision-making to those non-benevolent mediators is thus itself plagued with transaction costs. Again, incentive theory can perfectly describe the contractual imperfections associated with these transaction costs by simply adding the necessary *incentive constraints* characterizing the behavior of these biased mediators.

- **Assumption 7: costless enforcement**   Within the realm of the Revelation Principle, the contract between the mediator and the agents is supposed to be perfectly enforceable. Contract enforcement is not an issue. In other words, the judiciary system is perfect and uncorruptible. Several problems arise when the judge enters into the picture. First, the set of verifiable variables which can be part of a contract is somewhat endogenous. It depends on the limited amount of attention and time that the judge is ready to spend on the particular contractual issue which is at stake. This is a moral-hazard problem. Second, the contract may specify outcomes for some contingencies which have to be clearly assessed by the judge. This raises the issue of collusion between the judge and one of the contracting parties.

The judiciary system is thus very much the source of various contractual inefficiencies which can be modeled only by making the judge be an actual player of the game with his own incentives and rewards. In a sense, the costly enforcement framework which is called for at this point is badly defined since introducing the judge as an actual player would call for another layer of enforcement device. One can think of reputations and more general repeated relationships as the potential glue to provide the right incentives to the judiciary system. However, if one believes in this last argument, costly enforcement of an imperfect judiciary system can only be a theoretical issue in the short run and this does not seem to be the case.

In this chapter, we will have little to say on this enforcement issue since little or, more precisely, nothing, is so far known about the role the judge in the design of incentive schemes.

4 Contractual externalities and transaction costs

To summarize section 3, the Revelation Principle presupposes a set of assumptions which describes an ideal world which is free of any transaction cost. Relaxing these assumptions amounts to introducing various transaction costs which impede the achievement of the second-best rent–efficiency trade-off obtained in the frictionless world. However, except for the case of bounded rationality and perfect communication, incentive theory still provides a useful description of the constrained feasible set. Once this first step of the analysis is completed it becomes easy to find the *constrained optimal* contract subject to incentive, participation, and some newly defined transaction-costs constraints.

Importantly, relaxing any of assumptions 3–6 amounts to introducing the possibility that the initial *grand contract* offered by the mediator to his agents is perturbed by further contractings. This may be collusive side contracting between agents of the organization (assumption 3), this may be external contracting with other mediators (assumption 4) or, finally, this may be explicit or implicit recontracting with the principal himself (assumptions 5 and 6). These further contractings introduce various *contractual externalities* which affect grand contracting.

Transaction costs thus imply some form of *incomplete grand contracting* and some kinds of contractual externalities associated with that incompleteness.

It is useful to classify contractual externalities with respect to their respective impact on the rent–efficiency trade-off discussed in section 3.

We will say that an externality is *negative* (resp. *positive*) if the rent–efficiency trade-off is tilted towards excessive rent extraction (resp. excessive efficiency). In this case, there is too much (resp. not enough) rent extraction in the organization with respect to the case without further contracting.

Coming back to our procurement example, it is easy to write *a priori* an ad hoc formula describing the optimal output choice of the organization when the optimal second-best trade-off between rent extraction and efficiency is achieved.

Since only the inefficient seller's output is affected by contracting under asymmetric information, let us write the third-best output of this agent when both incentive and transactional constraints are taken into account as:

$$S'(q^{TB}(\overline{\theta})) = \overline{\theta} + \frac{v}{1-v}(1-\lambda)\Delta\theta \tag{7}$$

λ is a parameter which is *positive* (resp. *negative*) in the case of a positive (resp. negative) externality.

Still in our procurement example, we now discuss how the various transaction costs previously discussed affect the value of λ.

4.1   *Vertical collusion*

Let us now assume that the buyer vertically integrates the production stage. To further control the production process, the owner–buyer sets up a monitoring system: a supervisor is used to report any informative signal that he may have learned on the seller's cost parameter.[22]

Let us further assume that these signals are hard information.[23] With conditional probability ϵ the supervisor learns that the seller is efficient. Otherwise, she learns nothing.

The fact that both the supervisor and the seller know some piece of information unknown to the principal leaves them the possibility of reaching a collusive side deal to manipulate this information and to share the gain of this manipulation.

In this case, the general expression for λ is the following:

$$\lambda = \epsilon(1 - k) > 0 \tag{8}$$

where $k \in [0, 1]$ is a parameter representing the efficiency of side contracting. k decreases when the collusive side contract suffers from greater transaction costs.

Here, the overall contractual externality is positive. Setting up a monitoring system improves incentives within the integrated firm and this definitively tilts the rent–efficiency trade-off towards efficiency. However and this last point illustrates Williamson's view of the large integrated firm as a bureaucratic structure,[24] that setting up a monitoring system also creates the scope for collusion between the supervisor and the seller unit. This last force is in fact a positive contractual externality. With respect to the case of no-collusion ($k = 0$), output should be reduced more as collusion becomes more efficient (k increases). Since the collusive stake is proportional to output, the cost of the binding collusion-proofness constraint necessary to induce information revelation from the supervisor is reduced with these downward distortions of output. The optimal contract moves towards a more bureaucratic rule leaving little discretion to the privately informed supervisor.

Several theories are now available to describe the behavior of these vertical collusions, i.e. to give foundations to the parameter k:

- **Exogenous k: hidden transfers**   Tirole (1992b) argues that, side transfers being implicit, enforced by a word of honor or by cultural norms within the organization, members of a collusive deal must incur some transaction costs of side contracting so that necessarily $k < 1$.

Laffont and Martimort (1999) show that the design of the monitoring structures and in particular the division of tasks[25] between supervisors helps to reduce the overall cost of implementing a collusion-proof allocation. Laffont and Meleu (1997) argue informally that the reciprocity of favors in an organization reduces these transaction costs of side contracting.

- **Endogenous k: repeated collusive relationships** Martimort (1999a) endogenizes this parameter by explicitly modeling the repeated relationship between a principal, his supervisor and his agent. Side contracts are now enforced as self-enforcing collusive equilibria of a repeated game.[26] More precisely, one has:

$$k = \frac{\nu\epsilon}{\nu\epsilon + r - 1} \tag{9}$$

where $r > 1$ is greater if collusive agents have a shorter life in the organization. More informative signals for the supervisor and greater future prospects of a continuing collusive relationship increases the efficiency of side contracting and tilts the optimal grand contract towards more rent extraction.

- **Endogenous k: delegated monitoring** Faure-Grimaud, Laffont and Martimort (1999a, 1999b) analyze hierarchical supervisory structures as nexi of bilateral vertical contracts between first, a principal and an informed supervisor, and, second, an informed supervisor and an even more informed agent. The design of the delegated contract can be viewed as the choice of a moral-hazard variable from the point of view of the top principal. With risk aversion at the supervisory level, there is an interesting trade-off between providing incentives to this supervisor to choose the right contract with the agent from the point of view of the overall organization and providing him insurance against shocks in the agent's cost parameter.

In those nested information structures, formula (8) is still valid provided that:

$$k = k(\epsilon, \rho, \Delta\theta\overline{q}) \tag{10}$$

Now the efficiency of side contracting is greater when the supervisor has more informative signals on the agent (ϵ greater), when he is harder to control (greater degree of risk aversion ρ) and when collusive stakes are greater ($\Delta\theta\overline{q}$ greater).

Note that with endogenous k, λ becomes now a function of various organizational parameters: information structures, preferences of the agents, technology, and bargaining power of the supervisor at the side contracting stage. In this third-best world, the exact design of the organization is no more neutral with respect to the rent–efficiency trade-off. The Irrelevance Theorem no longer holds in this context and there is scope for such things as authority structures, limits of the firm, ownership, and limits between the public and the private spheres[27] since these are all parameters which influence significantly the transaction costs of side contracting.

4.2   Delegation

Suppose that the buyer cannot procure the good directly but must rely on an intermediary to do the job. This intermediary acts thus as a principal for the seller, he may have a productive task himself or not. The impossibility of a direct contract between the final buyer and the seller creates a setting of sequential contractings between different layers of the hierarchy. Here, the exact timing of contracts signing and the information structure at the time of this signing is quite important to evaluate the true loss (if any) of delegated contracting.

Baron and Besanko (1992), Mookherjee and Reichelstein (1995), and Laffont and Martimort (1998) isolate conditions under which delegation *per se* does not affect the rent–efficiency trade-off, i.e. $\lambda = 0$. In those settings characterized by risk-neutrality of the intermediary and *ex ante* contracting, some form of the Irrelevance Theorem still applies even if the intermediate principal may be privately informed. The exact design of the organization does not really matter.

This is no longer true when there is some communication constraint and (or) some form of interim contracting[28] as in Laffont and Martimort (1998) and McAfee and McMillan (1995) or some form of moral-hazard constraint (veto constraint) on the intermediate principal as in Faure-Grimaud and Martimort (1999).[29]

In this case, summarizing various results in the literature, we have:

$$\lambda = -1 - \frac{v}{1-v}(1 - \phi(v, \rho, \Delta\theta\overline{q})) < 0 \tag{11}$$

where $\phi(v, \rho, \Delta\theta\overline{q}) \in [0, 1]$ and is equal to 0 in the case of a risk neutral intermediate and 1 in the case of an infinitely risk averse one. Moreover, as shown in Faure-Grimaud and Martimort (1999), $\phi(v, \rho, \Delta\theta\overline{q})$ is increasing in the stake $\Delta\theta\overline{q}$, capturing the fact that delegation becomes more costly as the intermediate principal has more stake to control.

The contractual externality here is negative. Indeed, the contractual chain of contracts induces distortions extremely close to the "*double marginalization effect*" of the industrial organization literature.[30] The top principal does not internalize the fact that the intermediate principal has already reached a balance between efficiency and rent extraction at the time of contracting with the latter.

4.3   Multiprincipals

A multiprincipal setting is extremely close to a model of delegation. The main difference is that there is no principal on top of the organization, i.e. sequential contracting has to be replaced by simultaneous bilateral contractings between the common agents and their non-cooperative principals.

Let us come back to our procurement example and assume that instead of one buying unit, there are two buyers each with a surplus $S_i(q_i)$ from consuming q_i units of the procured good.[31] Each of these buyers contracts independently with the common seller. Two cases must be distinguished.

4.3.1   The case of complements

Suppose that the seller is a Research and Development (R & D) venture which provides to both upstream firms an indivisible innovation. This innovation is in fact a public good from the point of view of both principals. In this case, we have[32]:

$$\lambda = -1 \tag{12}$$

Since neither of the principals takes into account the fact that the other principal is also paying the cost of information revelation, there is now excessive rent extraction and the contractual externality is negative. Achieving the right trade-off between efficiency and rent extraction becomes a public good and principals free ride in providing enough incentives to their common agent.

4.3.2   The case of substitutes

Suppose now that the seller provides to both parents q_i units from an essential input. More generally, the production cost of the common agent can now be written as $\theta C(q_1 + q_2)$ where q_1 and q_2 are perfect substitutes from the point of view of the agent's utility function (with $C'' < 0$).[33] Then, we have:

$$\lambda = 1 \tag{13}$$

With perfect substitutes, the setting is very close to an auction between the principals. The two competing principals are now bidding for the common agent's services. They do this by conceding a large amount of rent to the agent. Since informational rent is increasing with output, efficiency rises until the first-best output is achieved.

In both cases, substitutes and complements, allocative distortions depend on the set of outputs which are under the control of both principals. This third-best world leads again to failures of the Irrelevance Theorem. For instance, if ownership of an asset is associated with the auditing rights on the streams of profit generated by this asset, different ownership structures of a common venture yield different Nash equilibria between the upstream firms of this common subsidiary and different trade-offs between allocative efficiency and rent extraction. An optimal ownership structure should thus minimize the cost incurred by the organization because of these contractual externalities.

4.4   Renegotiation

Renegotiation of a contract can by the agent be accepted only if he gets more informational rent than without any limit on commitment, i.e., more rent than in the optimal contract without renegotiation described in (6). Since informational rent is increasing in output, allocative distortions implemented in a renegotiation-proof contract must induce more production than the second-best outcome.

Indeed, again summarizing results in the literature, a whole range of values of λ correspond to renegotiation-proof allocations and they can be written as:

$$\lambda = 1 - \mu > 0 \tag{14}$$

where $\mu \in [0, 1]$.

The tension between reducing the informational rent for incentive reasons and increasing the informational rent to make the allocation renegotiation-proof tilts the rent–efficiency trade-off towards efficiency. The possibility of further recontracting between the principal and the agent creates a positive externality on the initial grand contract.

Interestingly, this tension is the same whether one is interested in interim or in *ex post* renegotiations and renegotiation-proof final allocations (i.e. allocations taking place just after the renegotiation stage) can be expressed in the same way.

A priori, from the point of view of the execution of the last stage of contracting, there is always some cost of committing to a renegotiation-proof allocation which is not the second-best conditionally optimal outcome.[34] However, these commitments may have also some benefit in more complex environments.

First, such commitments make credible actions of the agent which may affect the behavior of some third party who interacts with the principal, as has been shown by Dewatripont (1988). For instance, by committing to excess efficiency with his seller, the buyer commits also to put lots of output on the final product market and this may help him to get a Stackelberg position on this market.[35]

Second, in long-term relationships, such commitment also makes information revelation easier in the first period. Since the efficient seller has a credible promise on the amount of informational rent he will receive in the future, he does not fear to reveal (at least partially) his type in the first periods of the relationship. It is this trade-off between first-period and second-period incentives which has been studied by Dewatripont (1988), Hart and Tirole (1988), and Laffont and Tirole (1993).

There have been very few works dealing with the organizational consequences of renegotiation. However, one can still prove here also that the Irrelevance Theorem fails. For instance, Poitevin (1995) argues that the distribution of information matters at the renegotiation stage and that an organization should be chosen to minimize the burden of renegotiation. Martimort (1999b) shows that combining renegotiation and multiprincipal considerations provides a theory of optimal renegotiation design among competing principals. The basic idea is that the positive externality of recontracting can be mitigated by introducing the negative externality of common agency. In the firm's context, various creditors should be given contracting rights on the firm's profit to harden renegotiation and improve the firm's overall ability to commit. In the context of the organization of the government, the separation of powers helps intertemporal commitment, as has been very often argued by political scientists.[36]

4.5   Biased principals

Let us now consider public procurement and let us assume that delegation of public decision-making is imperfect in the sense that social welfare is not maximized by elected biased political principals. Let us take the following example. With probability $1/2$, a rightist government gets elected and takes a pro-industry stance, putting a weight $\alpha \in]0, 1[$ on the seller's informational rent into his objective function. Here the motivation is that rightist parties are financed by the defense industry and their policy choice reflects somewhat the pressure of this industry. With probability $1/2$, a leftist government gets elected and, still because of reelection concerns, takes a stance against the industry putting now a weight $-\alpha$ on the seller's informational rent into his objective function. Hence, the political bias of the principal, i.e. his degree of non-benevolence, can be viewed as a random variable $\tilde{\alpha}$.

Third-best output can still be described with (7) provided that λ satisfies:

$$\lambda = \tilde{\alpha} \tag{15}$$

Contractual externalities are now positive (resp. negative) with a rightist (resp. leftist) party.

As shown in Laffont (1995), there are excessive fluctuations of the optimal policies around the socially optimal outcome. In this framework also the Irrelevance Theorem fails, organizational forms may still be designed to reduce those fluctuations and bring the outcome closer, at least in expectations, to the second-best outcome.

For instance, Laffont (1995) shows that simple policy instruments may be preferred to optimal contracts to reduce those fluctuations. Faure-Grimaud and Martimort (2000a, 2000b) and Gabillon and Martimort (1999) show, respectively, that independence of a regulatory agency and of a central bank from the political sphere improves expected social welfare and can be used strategically by the incumbent principal.

5   Conclusion

This chapter has given a definition of transaction costs which proves to be operational to adapt standard incentive theory and make it a better tool to describe real-world institutions and organizations. These transaction costs should be taken as primitives of the model. These transaction costs create contractual incompletenesses and not the reverse as often appears in the transaction-cost economic literature. These incompletenesses of the grand contract leaves scope for further contractings and as a result various contractual externalities emerge. These externalities, in turn, perturb the rent–efficiency trade-off of the standard incentive literature. Reduced-form formulae to analyze these perturbations were given. These forms should be viewed as guidelines for the modeler facing more complex and probably intractable settings than those described in this chapter. In those settings possibly multiple contractual incompletenesses may interact and a reasonable starting point of the economic analysis should be to see how the various contractual externalities add up and how far away the resulting organization is from the optimal rent–efficiency trade-off.

The approach followed in this chapter acknowledges some limitations: we did not talk about the hold-up problem, specific investments, and more generally the derived property-rights literature *à la* Grossman and Hart (1986). In our view, the profession as a whole has somewhat over-emphasized this hold-up problem in the definition of contractual incompleteness it has tried to come up with over the last fifteen years. Basically, it has become quite natural in the folklore of the profession to think of this type of incompleteness as the only possible explanation of organizational forms and authority structures. This approach may have been relatively successful in explaining firm boundaries, but we feel less convinced by its insights when it comes to understanding the internal structure of the firm itself or the design of political constitutions where, clearly, other contractual incompletenesses which have nothing to do with the hold-up problem are at work.

The point of this chapter is that some other types of contractual incompletenesses can still be analyzed with *almost standard tools* and this kind of analysis is clearly worth being made in a first step. In a second step, more ambitious work should be devoted to explaining and endogenizing what we have taken as the primitives of our approach: the various transaction costs which are the impediments to the use of the Revelation Principle. This seems an exciting challenge for further research.

NOTES

Chapter 10 was originally published as "Transaction Costs in Incentive Theory," in *Revue d'Economie Industrielle* (92, 2000). We thank the editor Eric Brousseau for the opportunity he gave us to participate to this issue. We also thank two referees for their remarks.
1. See Green and Laffont (1977); Dasgupta, Hammond and Maskin (1979); Harris and Raviv (1979); and Myerson (1979).
2. See Hart and Holmström (1987b) for survey of these two fields.
3. See Laffont and Tirole (1993).
4. See Laffont and Maskin (1982).
5. See Mirrlees (1971) for his seminal and pathbreaking paper.
6. See Brainard and Martimort (1997), for instance.
7. See Fudenberg and Tirole(1991, chapter 7). Moreover, Myerson and Satterthwaite (1983) have shown that the Pareto-efficient bargaining procedures under informational constraints require some allocative inefficiency.
8. See Cramton, Gibbons and Klemperer (1987), on this point.
9. Here, we have omitted the incentive compatibility constraint of the inefficient firm and the participation constraint of the inefficient one which both turn out to be strictly satisfied at the optimum.
10. In the property-rights literature, the debate between Maskin and Tirole (1999b) and Tirole (1999) and Grossman and Hart (1986) and Hart and Moore (1999a) also shows that the perfect ability to describe contingencies and the corresponding payoffs and to perform backward induction, in other words, unlimited rationality, is enough to recover efficiency even when no *ex ante* contract can be written as long as renegotiation of the revelation games used to implement this outcome is not an issue.
11. See nevertheless Green and Laffont (1986).

12. See Dalton (1959), Gouldner (1961), and Crozier (1963), among others.

13. See Moe (1984), for instance.

14. See Williamson (1985, chapter 11) for a clear overview of these bilateral deals and the corresponding contractual externalities.

15. See Wilson (1989), Martimort (1996b), and Dixit (1996), who all argue or formalize that the difference between public and private bureaucracies comes from the fact that bureaucrats are controlled by multiple principals in the former case.

16. See Green and Laffont (1977), and various contributions therein.

17. See Epstein and Peters (1996) for a definition of the set of relevant types to which the Revelation Principle should apply. This set includes both physical types and market-like information (the contracts of other principals).

18. Moreover, the French *Code des Contrats*, for instance, allows contractual partners to write a new contract if they wish so.

19. See Dewatripont (1988, 1989), Hart and Tirole (1988), and Laffont and Tirole (1993, chapter 9).

20. See Beaudry and Poitevin (1993).

21. In both examples above, the loss of control is particularly acute since there is a multiplicity of "principals of the principal" (voters and shareholders) who may fail to coordinate in exerting perfect control of the latter.

22. Note that the assumption of integration is important here, indeed under non-integration the buyer may not have such a monitoring technology at his disposal (see Williamson 1985, chapter 4) or even if he has this monitoring technology, he may not have the auditing rights to use it.

23. See Tirole (1986) for a discussion of this kind of informative signals which can be concealed but not manipulated by the supervisor.

24. See Williamson (1985, chapter 6).

25. These authors interpret this division of tasks as a *separation of powers* in their application of this idea to a regulatory framework.

26. Martimort (1997) applies the same idea and techniques to an instance of horizontal collusion between workers. This model also endogenizes the observation made in Laffont and Meleu (1997) that reciprocal deals are easier to enforce.

27. On this last issue, see Martimort and Rochet (1999).

28. I.e. contracting with the intermediate principal once he has learned some information on the seller.

29. These latter two authors explicitly model the possibility that the top principal and the intermediate one may have conflicting preferences on the sub-set of agents who must definitively produce. This adds a *"no-shut-down"* constraint which creates new agency costs.

30. See Spengler (1950).

31. The case of Type 1 externality (see Laffont and Martimort 1997 for a typology of these externalities in a common agency framework) where $S_i(q_1, q_2)$ depends on both outputs is fully analyzed by Martimort and Stole (1999b).

32. Martimort (1998) shows that there exist multiple equilibria in a two-type model with perfect complementarity as above. We select thereafter the Pareto-dominant one. In the case where θ is a continuous variable, Martimort (1992,

1996a) and Stole (1990) show also that there exist multiple ranked symmetric equilibria for imperfect complementarity.

33. In the case of imperfect substitutes, there exists no pure strategy equilibrium in the two-type model as shown in Martimort and Stole (1999b). Martimort (1992, 1996a) and Stole (1990) show also that there exists a unique symmetric equilibrium in the case of substitutes (perfect and imperfect) with θ being distributed continuously over an interval. In the case of a continuous variable, we have $\lambda(\theta) \in [0, 1]$ with $\lambda(\underline{\theta}) = 0$ and λ defined over the whole interval $[\underline{\theta}, \bar{\theta}]$ and where $\frac{v}{1-v}$ is replaced by the hazard rate $\frac{F(\theta)}{f(\theta)}$ of the distribution with $F(\theta)$ the cumulative distribution of θ and $F' = f$.

34. This is the expression coined by Laffont and Tirole (1993, chapter 10).

35. Of course, in such a setting, the objective function of the buyer can be written as $S(q, q_e)$ where q_e is the output put on the final market by his competitor.

36. See Moe (1984), among many others.

11   Norms and the theory of the firm

Oliver Hart

1   Introduction

Most standard models of incentives and/or organizations assume that economic agents are self-interested and must rely on formal contracts enforced by the courts to uphold their relationships. In reality, of course, many economic transactions are sustained by self-enforcing ("implicit") contracts, or norms of behavior, such as honesty or trust. An interesting question to ask is: does ignoring norms/self-enforcing contracts lead to misleading conclusions? That is, would a theory of incentives or organizations that incorporated norms look very different from the standard theory?

In this chapter, I will consider this question, focusing particularly on some of the attempts economists have made in the last ten years or so to integrate norms into the theory of the firm. I will argue that (a) although norms are undoubtedly very important both inside and between firms, incorporating them into the theory has been very difficult and is likely to continue to be so in the near future; (b) so far norms have not added a great deal to our understanding of such issues as the determinants of firm boundaries (the "make-or-buy" decision) – that is, at this point a norm-free theory of the firm and a norm-rich theory of the firm don't seem to have very different predictions.

2   Background

To begin with, it is worth mapping out some of the territory. I will follow Richard Posner in defining a norm as "a rule that is neither promulgated by an official source, such as a court or a legislature, nor enforced by the threat of legal sanctions, yet is regularly complied with" (see Posner 1997). I will focus on norms in and between organizations as opposed to societal norms, even though there is obviously an important connection between the two. For example, a society in which honesty is not taken very seriously is also one in which firms will have a lot of difficulty sustaining

180

trust. However, norms at the societal level are pretty slow to change, and, for many purposes, they can be taken as exogenous. In contrast, norms in and between organizations are capable of being designed.

A useful starting point is the idea that organizational norms matter when parties cannot write good contracts; more precisely, when transaction costs make contracts incomplete.[1] That is, in a world where parties can costlessly think and negotiate about the future, and judges are perfect, norms would not matter because parties' relationships could be governed by perfectly enforceable contracts. A leading source of contractual incompleteness stems from the fact that some economically significant variables are observable to the parties, but not to outsiders, such as a judge. (In the parlance of economics, these variables are "observable, but not verifiable.") For example, an ideal contract between an employer and an employee might specify that the employee would be given a bonus for good performance since this may encourage the employee to work hard. Both the employer and the employee may know after the fact whether the employee performed well or not, and therefore whether the bonus has been earned, but a judge may not have this information. As a result, the contract stating that the employer will pay the employee a bonus if the latter performs well is not legally enforceable. Here a norm of honesty would be very helpful. If the employer can be trusted to keep her word, the agreement that the employee will receive a bonus if he performs well can be sustained by informal means rather than by formal ones.

As another example, consider a company's promise to workers that it will not lay any of them off unless "things are really bad." Such a promise might serve an important role in providing risk averse workers with partial insurance about the future. However, enforcing such a promise in the courts is likely to be fraught with difficulty because of disagreement about the meaning of the phrase "things are really bad." (Without too much of a stretch of reality, it might be said that the event is observable but not verifiable.) Again, norms of honesty and decency can help here. If the firm can be trusted not to be opportunistic, then a flexible outcome can be achieved through an informal agreement: the company will reserve its right to shed workers if a disaster occurs, but will not abuse this right by laying off workers in events that are merely bad.

Given the link between norms and judicial imperfection, it is not surprising that much of the economic literature on norms in organizations goes under the heading of "self-enforcing contracts." However, it is important to realize that norms also matter when contracts are incomplete for other reasons, e.g. because the parties (themselves) are boundedly rational. For example, if the parties cannot think or negotiate ahead very well, then events will arise that their contract does not cover. A norm of fairness can help to fill in the contractual gap in an appropriate manner. For reasons of tractability, most of the economic literature rules out bounded rationality among the contracting parties themselves, and so the role of fairness-type norms has not been much explored in an organizational context.[2] In my discussion, I will follow the literature in this regard; it should be emphasized, however, that a consequence of this is that much of interest may be left out.

3   Modeling difficulties

As I have already noted, theoretical progress on analyzing norms and organizations has been slow. The main reason is that economists do not have a very good way to formalize trust. Three main approaches have been tried, and each has significant drawbacks. In this section I will briefly describe them.

The most commonly used approach is based on the framework of infinitely repeated games. Although this will be familiar to many, it is probably worth illustrating since I will use it later on. Suppose that a buyer B and a seller S want to trade a widget each period. S can deliver a high-quality widget or a low-quality widget; the former has value that exceeds its cost, while the latter has zero cost and zero value. The quality of the widget is observable (to B and S), but not verifiable (in a court of law). In a one-shot version of this game, trade will not occur if the parties are purely self-interested (and hence are not trustworthy). The reason is that if B promises to pay S as long as S supplies a high-quality widget, then it is always in B's interest to claim that the widget's quality was low, whether or not this is true, and, anticipating this, S has no incentive to supply high quality. (This example is isomorphic to the employer–employee example mentioned earlier.)

If this game is repeated infinitely often, however, trade at the high-quality level can be sustained. The way this works is (roughly) as follows. B promises to pay S a price P per period, where P lies between B's value and S's cost, as long as the widget quality is high in that period (recall that B observes widget quality). In return, S promises to supply a high-quality widget each period unless in some previous period B has broken her promise to pay, in which case S supplies low quality forever more.

It is easy to see that these promises are mutually self-enforcing, as long as the parties do not discount the future too much. The reason is that, while B can gain something each period by pretending that S's quality is low and withholding payment, this short-term gain is dwarfed by B's loss from never receiving a high-quality widget again.

Unfortunately, as is well known, this approach to explaining cooper-ation or trust runs into several difficulties.[3] First, it relies crucially on the assumption that there is no upper bound to the number of times the game is played. Suppose in contrast that it is known that the game will not be played more than τ times. Then, however large τ is, the parties will realize that in the last period B will break her promise to pay S (as in the one-shot game, there is no future to discourage her); anticipating this, S will supply a low-quality widget in the last period; hence B will have no incentive to pay in the previous period (she recognizes that this will have no effect on what happens in the last period), etc. In other words, the self-enforcing contract unravels. The conclusion is that, as in the one-period model, no trade will take place in any period, however big τ is.

Unfortunately, the assumption that there is no upper bound to the number of times the game will be played is hard to square with the fact that people have finite lives.

A second problem with the infinitely repeated game approach concerns the issue of renegotiation. Suppose B breaks her promise in some period. According to the equilibrium, S is meant to "punish" B by supplying a low-quality widget forever more (in effect, no trade occurs). However, by punishing B, S is also punishing himself since he won't get any payment. The question then is, why don't the parties let bygones be bygones and reinstate the cooperative outcome? After all, it is not as if S has learned anything adverse about B. B's characteristics are known, and the fact that B has broken her promise today tells S nothing about whether she will do so again.

The trouble is that, if B anticipates that cooperation will be restored after she breaks her promise, then this increases B's incentive to break her promise, and cooperation may not be sustainable. In other words, if the parties are rational enough to realize that they will renegotiate after a breach, then this may prevent cooperation occurring in the first place, i.e. the outcome may be as in the one-shot game.[4]

Partly because of these difficulties with the infinitely repeated game approach, another strand of the literature has instead supposed that the game is played finitely many times – t, say – but that the parties are not perfectly informed about each other: there is asymmetric information.[5] Suppose, for example, that there is a small probability that B is someone who always keeps her promises no matter what. (She is "irrational.") B knows whether she is the rational type or the irrational type, but S does not. Then in the early stages of the game, B has an incentive to pretend to be the irrational type even if she isn't, in order to encourage S to trade with her. In fact, it can be shown that, if t is large enough, then in every equilibrium of the t-period game, cooperation will be sustained almost all of the time.

The asymmetric information approach has the advantage over the infinitely repeated game approach in that it does not require an infinite horizon and can deal with the problem of renegotiation. However, it faces another difficulty. It turns out that the approach is very sensitive to the precise characteristics of the irrational type, about which we as modelers know very little. One way to see this is the following. Suppose that in addition to the irrational honest type there is another "irrational type," who is totally dishonest but, with some probability, has an irresistible urge to propose an agreement to trade in any period. Then there is an equilibrium of the following form. The parties do not trade in any period. The irrational buyer who has an irresistible urge proposes to S that they should trade: S turns her down because he rationally sees that this type of buyer will never pay him. The other buyer types propose nothing because there is no point: they would be confused with the irresistible urge type and thought to be dishonest and not worth trading with. This way the no-trade equilibrium is sustained however large t is.

The conclusion is that the asymmetric information approach does not provide a very solid foundation for the idea that cooperation will necessarily occur when play is repeated many times.

A third approach is to move away from thinking about the trustworthy type as a fringe, irrational agent and instead to recognize that all agents are trustworthy to some extent. One way to do this is to suppose that each agent incurs a psychic cost $\$C$ if she breaks a promise, where C is distributed in the population according to a known probability distribution and a person's C, although known to her, may or may not be known to others. This approach, like the asymmetric information approach, can explain cooperation in a finite horizon model.[6] However, not surprisingly, as with the asymmetric information approach, its conclusions are very sensitive to assumptions made about the distribution of C in the population and also about the nature of C – matters that again the modeler knows little about. For example, suppose B pays S slightly less than what she promised. Does she incur the whole psychic cost C or just part of it? Or suppose B promises n different sellers that she will pay them if they perform well (they are workers, say) and then simultaneously breaks her promise to them all. Does B incur a total psychic cost of $\$C$ or $\$nC$? The nature of the optimal self-enforcing contract is likely to be very dependent on these features of the model.

Not only are the asymmetric information and psychic cost approaches quite sensitive to the precise modeling assumptions made, but also it turns out that these approaches are not that easy to work with in a contractual or organizational setting. For these reasons, most researchers have used the infinitely repeated game approach, in spite of its shortcomings. In what follows, I will do the same. In the next section, I use the approach to illustrate the effects of self-enforcing contracts on the determinants of firm boundaries.

4   Norms and firm boundaries

A good application of norms in the organizational context is to the issue of the determinants of firm boundaries (the "make-or-buy" decision). Trust helps to sustain agreements both inside the firm and between firms. An interesting question to ask is: does trust favor one type of transaction relative to the other?

In the last fifteen years or so a formal literature – the property-rights approach – has developed that tries to explain firm boundaries in terms of the optimal allocation of asset ownership (see Grossman and Hart 1986 and Hart and Moore 1990).[7] This literature shares with the earlier transaction cost literature of Williamson (1975, 1985) and Klein, Crawford and Alchian (1978) the view that firms are important when contracts are incomplete. It departs from the transaction-cost literature in being more explicit about the role of decision rights and the link between decision rights and asset ownership. According to the property-rights view, the owner of a non-human asset has residual rights of control over the asset, i.e. the right to make all decisions concerning that asset that have not been specified in a contract or that are not inconsistent with some law. (When there are multiple owners of an asset or firm, they will typically delegate some of the residual control rights to a board of directors.) Residual control or decision rights are like any other good: there will be an optimal allocation of them. For example, suppose that individuals 1 and 2 are involved in an economic relationship. If it is important to encourage 1 to make an asset- or relationship-specific investment, it may be efficient to allocate ownership of some key non-human assets to 1. This way individual 1 is protected to some extent against "hold-up" by 2 since, if the economic relationship with 2 doesn't work out, 1 always has the option to take her assets away and trade with someone else. However, while allocating assets to 1 protects 1 from hold-up by 2, it has the opposite effect on 2: since 2 has fewer assets to take elsewhere, 2 is now more vulnerable to hold-up and so will be less willing to make an asset- or relationship-specific investment himself. Typically it will be optimal to divide the assets between the parties so that each party has some. If we view each set of assets with a common owner as a firm, this yields a theory of firm boundaries.

The property-rights theory has in the main been applied to static or one-shot situations where parties are self-interested and not trustworthy. However, it is natural to ask how the optimal allocation of assets or firm boundaries changes when norms and trust operate. Some papers that study this issue include Baker, Gibbons and Murphy (2002) and Halonen (2000). In what follows I will discuss some of the ideas behind these papers, using as a vehicle the paper on trucking by Baker and Hubbard (2000) (the Baker–Hubbard paper is not itself about norms or trust).

Consider a shipper S who at date 0 wants goods shipped from A to B. The shipper hires a trucker T to do this. The trucker may come with his own truck, in which case he is an independent contractor, or the shipper may provide the truck, in which case the trucker is an employee. We will assume that the shipper and trucker can contract on the shipment from A to B (known as the front-haul), but that they cannot contract on several other things. First, the shipper may sometimes want the trucker to engage in a back-haul, i.e. transport a second shipment of goods from B to another destination C. However, whether there will be a back-haul and its nature – how valuable the second shipment is, whether it is easy to transport, and the identity of the destination C – are variables that are hard to forecast and become known only when the trucker arrives at B, at date 1, say. So contracting about the back-haul must wait until then.[8] Second, the parties cannot contract on maintenance: how well the trucker drives the truck. The trucker may have an incentive to drive fast, take time off to visit a friend, and then speed again to reach B; this may be pleasant for the driver, but is bad for the truck. To make things simple, we will assume – at some cost of realism – that maintenance is observable to the trucker and shipper but is not verifiable.

Third, the trucker can spend time searching for alternative customers as he drives from A to B. (He has a mobile phone/access to the internet, etc.) For those searches to pay off the trucker must be able to drive the truck away at date 1. Some such searches are productive – they pay off in the absence of a profitable back-haul from B to C – but others are carried out to improve the bargaining power of the trucker when he negotiates over the terms of the back-haul at date 1. To simplify we will follow Baker–Hubbard in assuming that all search activities are on average *unproductive*, i.e. their return is less than their (effort) cost.

Finally, we will assume that the owner of the truck bears all the increases or decreases in the value of the truck; he is the residual income claimant. This may seem like a rather traditional view of ownership, and it is extreme (it rules out value-sharing agreements between the shipper and the trucker), but it is consistent with the residual control rights approach in the following sense: the owner has the (residual) right to decide to whom to sell the truck, when, and at what price. To the extent that the owner can always sell the truck for 1¢ (the verifiable price) and at the same time agree to supply another service to the buyer for an exorbitant price, he can ensure that he never has to share the sales revenue with anyone else.

The key question is: who should own the truck? In the static or one-shot version of the model, the trade-off is the following. If the trucker owns the truck he will maintain it (he bears the value consequences), but he will engage in search or rent-seeking activities (as owner of the truck, he can exploit these activities since he has the right to drive away the truck at date 1). On the other hand, if the shipper owns the truck, the trucker will not maintain it at all (he does not bear the value consequences), but neither will he engage in rent-seeking activities (these do not pay off given that the trucker does not have the right to drive the truck away).

To simplify matters, I will assume that in the one-shot model encouraging maintenance is more important than discouraging rent-seeking and so it is best for T to own the truck, i.e. T should be an independent contractor rather than an employee. To the extent that S owns other assets than the truck and T doesn't, I will refer to this arrangement as "non-integration," and to the arrangement where S owns the truck (and therefore has all the assets) as "integration."

So far we have analyzed asset ownership or firm boundaries in a trust-less environment. I now want to ask the following question: how does trust affect the boundaries of the firm? To the extent that there is a con-ventional wisdom on this matter, I suspect that it is that an increase in trust will make it more likely that the parties will "use the market," i.e., choose to be independent (non-integration) – and to be linked by a re-lational contract – rather than to become one firm (integration). This conventional wisdom can probably be traced to the fact that transaction-cost economics (TCE) tends to see the market as the first choice if it is feasible, and in a high-trust environment it is likely to be feasible.

To analyze this choice more formally, let us proceed as in section 3 and suppose that the relationship between S and T is repeated infinitely often and that both parties discount the future at the common discount factor Δ, where $0 < \Delta < 1$. We are led to consider the following self-enforcing contract: T promises to maintain the truck well and to engage in minimal rent-seeking activity (search). In return, S promises a fixed payment P per period. The self-enforcing contract is sustained as follows: if either party breaches, we revert to the equilibrium of the one-shot game described above forever more. (In contrast to section 3, this equilibrium involves some trade rather than no trade.) We will also suppose (following Baker, Gibbons and Murphy 2002, but in contrast to Halonen 2000) that ownership of the truck can be transferred at this point, i.e. if S owns the truck T will buy it. (Recall that, given our assumptions, it is efficient for T to own the truck in the one-shot game.)

Note that $\Delta = 0$ corresponds to the one-shot game, since, if the future does not matter at all, no cooperation can be sustained. At the other extreme $\Delta = 1$ corresponds to the case where trust can easily be sustained since the future overwhelms the present in importance. Thus an increase in Δ can be interpreted as a move to a higher-trust environment.

Thus the question: how does trust affect asset ownership or firm boundaries? can be rephrased as: how does an increase in Δ affect asset ownership or firm boundaries?

The answer is that it all depends: an increase in Δ does not have a clear-cut effect on the choice between integration and non-integration (see Baker, Gibbons and Murphy 2002). To see why, note that an increase in Δ improves all organizational forms. If Δ is close to 1, the first-best – where T maintains the truck well and does not engage in rent-seeking – can be sustained under a self-enforcing contract whether S owns the truck or T does. The reason is that no one wants to breach a self-enforcing contract since the future gains from cooperation are so large relative to the short-run gain from breaching. On the other hand, if Δ is close to zero, then non-integration is best (given our assumptions). This suggests that there is no simple monotonic relation between optimal organizational form and the discount factor Δ.

Specifically, it is easy to construct cases where integration is superior to non-integration when Δ is fairly close to 1, even though non-integration is superior to integration when Δ is close to zero. (Such cases turn the conventional wisdom on its head – a higher-trust environment favors large firms.) To see why, suppose that the cost of maintenance is very low but the value is very high. In the static model (one-shot game), there will be no maintenance under integration, which is highly inefficient. But in the dynamic model it is easy to get maintenance by offering T a small bonus if he looks after the truck. Since the bonus covers his (small) cost, T will maintain the truck as long as he expects to receive the bonus; and S will pay the bonus since, given that it is small, there is little gain from not doing so. Finally, there is no incentive for T to engage in rent-seeking under integration since he can't drive away with the truck. So in this case the first-best can be achieved under integration in the repeated game even for moderate discount factors Δ.

In contrast, under non-integration, while T will maintain the truck (as in the static model), he may need quite a large bonus from S to be deterred from engaging in rent-seeking behavior; but the promise of a large bonus gives S a strong incentive to breach. Hence it may be impossible to sustain the first-best under a self-enforcing contract for moderate levels of Δ when T owns the truck.

Note that, in spite of what I earlier called the conventional wisdom, there is some evidence that trust does indeed favor large firms rather than small ones; on this, see La Porta *et al.* (1997) and Kumar, Rajan and Zingales (1999).

It should be emphasized that, while in this example non-integration is optimal when Δ is small and integration is optimal when Δ is large, it is easy to construct another example based on the same model that yields the opposite conclusion.

I think that the correct conclusion to draw from this discussion is the following. The boundaries of the firm will be drawn to elicit appropriate actions from the parties – in this case, truck maintenance and (absence of) rent-seeking. In broad terms the choice between the two organizational forms will depend on the importance of these goals and the ease with which they can be achieved. It is easier to encourage maintenance if T owns the truck and to discourage rent-seeking if S does. This is true both in the static model and the repeated game. Thus in qualitative terms trust does not change things that much.[9]

5   The role of formal contracts

So far I have discussed the role of norms in situations where the opportunities for writing formal contracts have been quite limited. In section 3 formal contracts were impossible and in section 4 the only formal contracts concerned the allocation of asset ownership and spot (one-period) deals between S and T.

In this section I will make some brief remarks about the general impact of formal contracts on the sustainability of self-enforcing contracts, and mention one implication for judicial attitudes toward firms. Formal contracts have at least two effects on self-enforcing contracts. First, the better formal contracts are, the smaller is the surplus remaining for the parties to try to exploit via a self-enforcing contract. This reduces the incentive of parties to breach a self-enforcing contract, since, given that there is less at stake, the gains from opportunistic behavior are lower. Second, however, if a self-enforcing contract is breached, the penalty is also lower since the parties can always rely on formal contracts in the post-breach, no-trust environment; as a result, as argued by Baker, Gibbons and Murphy (1994), the incentive to breach may *rise*.

Because these two effects are opposing, it is hard to draw clear-cut conclusions about whether formal contracts will make it easier to sustain self-enforcing contracts (i.e. formal and informal contracts are complements), or more difficult (i.e. formal and informal contracts are substitutes). Which way it goes would seem to depend on the circumstances.

In their interesting recent paper, Rock and Wachter (2001) take the position that one would expect to see few formal contracts inside the firm given the concentration of residual control rights in the hands of one party (the board of directors): rather the firm is a place where informal agreements will flourish.[10] My interpretation of (one part of) their argument is that it is hard to imagine two divisions of a firm being bound by a formal contract. The reason is that either party can be prevented from fulfilling the contract by the board of directors, who can always *ex post* deny the members of the divisions (including the division heads) access to key non-human assets or key decision-making authority. Division members are unlikely to be prepared to enter into formal agreements which require them to pay damages in the event of breach, given that they have so little power to ensure that these agreements are implemented.

Not only do Rock and Wachter provide a persuasive argument as to why formal contracts may be difficult to sustain inside the firm, but also the discussion of this section suggests a reason why formal contracts may be undesirable even if they *are* feasible: they may in some cases make it harder to sustain self-enforcing contracts (the case of substitutes described above). This may provide some justification for the view that the courts should be hesitant to intervene in the firm's informal business; that is, they should take a hands-off attitude even in cases where they have the ability or expertise to intervene.

6   Summary and open questions

In this chapter, I have argued that it has been difficult to incorporate norms into the theory of organizations; and also that, although there has been some interesting recent work on this topic, this work has not to date greatly changed our views about the determinants of organizational form.

I want to conclude by making a further qualification about the material discussed above. The infinitely repeated game models of sections 3 and 4 are really models of individual reputation or trustworthiness. That is, while it is tempting to think of the buyer and the seller in section 3, and the shipper in section 4, as representing firms, an extra step is really required for the argument to work. This step involves explaining why a particular set of norms or reputation is associated with a firm or organization rather than with an individual or set of individuals who work there.

To put it in stark terms: what ensures that, when the CEO of a company that is known for high trust leaves, the high-trust reputation doesn't go with her? Somehow there has to be some stickiness in the firm or system, so that a firm's reputation can be separated from that of key personnel. To put it another way, a firm's reputation has to have some of the characteristics of a non-human asset. However, exactly how this comes about is far from obvious.

One attempt to explain how a reputation can be embodied in a firm rather than a set of individuals is contained in a paper by Tadelis (1999).[11] Tadelis considers the relationship between a firm and its consumers. Think of the way a firm treats its customers, e.g. the way it services its product, as a norm. Tadelis assumes that every consumer observes this norm, i.e. they know how past customers have been treated, but that consumers do not know who owns (or manages) the firm. If ownership changes, customers do not see this and so assume that the firm will continue to treat its customers in the same way. As a result a firm that has treated its customers well in the past will have a valuable reputation: moreover, outside buyers may be prepared to pay a lot for this reputation since at least in the short run – until and unless they show that they cannot maintain the reputation – they can charge more for their product than if they started from scratch (without a reputation).

The Tadelis model provides a useful starting point in helping to understand why a firm's intangible assets can be valuable. However, the idea that a firm's reputation matters only when (a significant fraction of) consumers cannot observe a change in ownership is not that plausible. It is to be hoped that in the future it will be possible to relax the informational assumptions of the model. For the moment the creation of a theory of norms attached to a firm or organization seems an even more challenging goal than the development of such a theory for the case of an individual.

NOTES

I would like to thank Antoine Faure-Grimaud, Bengt Holmström, Matthew Rabin, and Andrei Shleifer for helpful discussions and the National Science Foundation for financial support.
1. For a discussion of the implications of transaction costs for contractual relationships, see, for example, Williamson (1975).
2. But see Fehr and Gächter (2000) for a discussion.
3. For a discussion, see Fudenberg and Tirole (1991, chapter 5).
4. To be a bit more precise, suppose that the gains from renegotiation are split in a fixed (exogenous) way. Then if B gets most of the gains she has a large incentive not to pay S in any period; while if S gets most of the gains he has an incentive to renounce the self-enforcing agreement at the beginning of a period (i.e. refuse to supply) and negotiate a better deal.
5. See Kreps et al. (1982).
6. See, e.g., Hart and Holmström (1987).
7. For a summary of this literature, see Hart (1995).

8. For a formal justification of the idea that, when the future is uncertain, many aspects of a contract will be negotiated *ex post* rather than *ex ante*, see Hart and Moore (1999a).

9. A possible qualification should be noted. In the static models of Grossman and Hart (1986) and Hart and Moore (1990), joint ownership of an asset is never optimal. In contrast, the repeated game model described in this section can explain joint ownership of an asset if it is supposed that ownership of the asset cannot be transferred after the breach of a self-enforcing contract (see Halonen 2000). The reason is that, since joint ownership is sub-optimal in the static model, the threat of it can support cooperative behavior in the dynamic model. Note, however, that joint ownership can be optimal in more complicated versions of the static model, where it is important to discourage rent-seeking behavior of *both* parties (see, e.g., Rajan and Zingales 1998). (If neither party can walk away with the asset, then each party's incentive to search for alternative trading partners is reduced.) Thus in fact joint ownership (or joint ventures) can be explained both in the static (no-trust) model and in the dynamic (trust) model.

10. A related, but distinct, idea is that firms will arise in situations where it is important to suppress individual incentives and foster cooperative behavior. (See Holmström 1999.)

11. For earlier work, see Kreps (1990) and Tirole (1996).

12 Allocating decision rights under liquidity constraints

Philippe Aghion and Patrick Rey

1 Introduction

The debate on the foundations of incomplete contracts had focused essentially on the Grossman–Hart (1986) framework, in which actions (in that case, trade versus no-trade) are assumed to be *ex ante* non-describable but *ex post* verifiable. This class of incomplete contracts models focuses on how ownership allocation affects *ex ante* investments through its impact on the *ex post* bargaining between the contracting parties; since actions are verifiable, this bargaining is always *ex post* efficient so that the main source of inefficiency lies in the non-verifiability of *ex ante* investments. In this framework, Maskin and Tirole (1999a) shows that message games played *ex post* can often be used to circumvent the *ex ante* non-contractibility and even the non-describability of actions and states. A main response to this criticism (see Segal 1999, Hart and Moore 1999a, Maskin and Tirole 1999b) has been to add renegotiation and complexity considerations, in order to generate optimal mechanisms that can be easily interpreted as ownership and control allocations.

Another set of incomplete contracting models, starting with Aghion and Bolton (1992), focuses instead on *ex post* inefficiencies resulting from the non-contractibility of actions, combined with additional limitations on the ability to induce *ex post* efficient action choice through adequate transfers to the controlling party. In Aghion and Bolton (1992) (hereafter, AB), what limits the scope for *ex post* efficiency is the wealth constraint faced by the entrepreneur whenever the outside investor is in control (which prevents the entrepreneur from inducing the first-best action choice from the investor), together with *ex ante* participation constraints which can make it non-feasible to allocate full control to the entrepreneur (and then let the unconstrained investor make the *ex post* monetary transfers to induce efficient action choice). In Aghion and Tirole (1997) and the subsequent literature on authority, what prevents achieving *ex post* efficiency is the non-responsiveness of the agent to monetary incentives.[1] Now, as Maskin and Tirole did for the Grossman–Hart paradigm, one can also question the robustness of the control allocations in AB or Aghion and Tirole (1997) to introducing message games and optimal implementation mechanisms.

The main point of this chapter is to argue that there is no need to introduce complexity considerations in order to provide suitable foundations to this second class of incomplete contract models: that actions are *ex post non-verifiable* is sufficient. This non-verifiability assumption, together with the restrictions already introduced on the set of *ex post* feasible transfers, will often suffice to guarantee the optimality of control allocation contracts even when revelation mechanisms are allowed. This issue had already been discussed in the appendix to AB, but there the actions were implicitly assumed to be *ex post* verifiable and only Nash-implementation was being considered. Here, we analyze the extent to which *ex post* non-verifiability, combined with wealth constraints, limit the power of message games.

We consider a contracting problem between two parties who must decide about a future course of action which is *ex post* non-verifiable and generates non-verifiable payoffs to both parties. After the initial contract has been signed, the two parties negotiate *ex post* over the ultimate choice of action in a Nash-bargaining game in which one party can use monetary transfers in order to influence the ultimate action taken by the controlling party. While AB restricts attention to the case where only one party is liquidity constrained and where that same party has all the bargaining power *ex post*, the present chapter considers more general configurations of wealth and bargaining power distributions.

More specifically, we show that when actions are non-verifiable, the optimal contract consists essentially of a control allocation, together with an initial monetary transfer from one party to the other; in particular, revelation mechanisms have no bite, as there is nothing to reveal *before* the negotiation stage, and once *ex post* bargaining has fixed the choice of action, nothing "real" can be offered to reward information (monetary transfers do not suffice to reward information in an incentive-compatible way). Our framework thus provides simple foundations to control allocation contracts in a framework *à la* AB.

As in AB, the optimal allocation of control is indeterminate when agents are risk neutral and have deep pockets, but it matters when at least one party faces wealth constraints; who should get control ultimately depends upon how wealth constraints and relative bargaining powers affect both *ex ante* participation and *ex post* efficiency in the choice of action. We argue that *ex post* efficiency is easier to achieve when control is allocated to the poorer party, whereas *ex ante* participation may require giving control to the wealthier party. In addition, our discussion suggests that both *ex post* efficiency and *ex ante* participation considerations dictate that control would be optimally allocated to the party with the lower bargaining power.

The chapter is organized as follows. Section 2 outlines a simple contracting model with *ex post* non-verifiable actions, and establishes that the optimal contract boils down to a simple control allocation together with an initial monetary transfer from one party to the other. Section 3 explores how wealth constraints and relative bargaining powers affect the optimal allocation of control, emphasizing the interplay between *ex post* efficiency and *ex ante* participation considerations. Finally, section 4 concludes by suggesting avenues for future research.

2 The basic framework

2.1 Preferences and actions

Two parties, 1 and 2, can together run a project which requires the choice of an action, a, among a possible set of feasible actions $A = [a^1, a^2] \subset \mathfrak{R}$. Each party i has an initial wealth w_i, a reservation level of utility B_i, and derives a private benefit $b_i(a)$ from the chosen action. Party i has utility:

$$u_i = b_i + m_i$$

where m_i denotes the net wealth of i. The potential conflict of interest between the two parties is simply captured by the assumption:

*A*1: b_1 and b_2 are respectively decreasing and increasing in a.

That is, party i's preferred action is a^i. In addition, we suppose that b_1 and b_2 are both concave in a and that the Pareto-efficient action (assuming that transfers are feasible), denoted by a^* and defined by:

$$a^* \equiv \arg\max_a \{b_1(a) + b_2(a)\}$$

lies strictly between a^1 and a^2. We also assume that the project is *ex ante* viable:

*A*2: $b_1(a^*) + b_2(a^*) > B_1 + B_2$.

The following notation will be useful:
- for $i, j = 1, 2, b_j^i \equiv b_j(a^i)$ and $b^i \equiv b_1^i + b_2^i$
- for $j = 1, 2, b_j^* \equiv b_j(a^*)$ and $b^* \equiv b_1^* + b_2^*$

Assumption A1 then implies that:

$$b_1^1 > b_1^2 \quad \text{and} \quad b_2^2 > b_2^1$$

2.2   Contracting

If the action could be contracted upon and transfers were not limited by wealth constraints, the two parties could run the project and contract on $a = a^*$, together with an initial transfer that would guarantee that both parties' participation constraints are satisfied. In the remaining part of the chapter, we shall concentrate on the case where:

> $A3$: The action and private benefits are *ex post* non-verifiable by any third party.

We shall however assume that the parties can contract on who will choose the action,[2] as well as on monetary transfers.

Since a party's preferred action is inefficient, the parties have an incentive to renegotiate and exploit the potential for residual Pareto-improvements. As the ultimate choice of action is not verifiable by assumption $A3$, the extent to which the parties might be able to reach a more efficient agreement will depend upon the economic environment (frequency of interactions, reputation and credibility, information, lags between action choices and payments, etc.). As in AB, we shall assume that, *ex post*, the two parties can credibly trade a change in the action plan against a monetary transfer. We do not wish to argue here that this assumption is always relevant but rather, explore its implications for the design of the original contract. Aghion, Dewatripont and Rey (2000) analyzes situations where instead the two parties cannot credibly alter the choice of action through non-contractible bilateral negotiations.

Finally, we shall be interested in simple contracts that stipulate a transfer t_0 between the two parties, together with an allocation of decision rights on the choice of action; the next sub-section establishes sufficient conditions under which such contracts are weakly optimal. There are two possible allocations of control rights: to party 1 ("$\delta = 1$") or to party 2 ("$\delta = 2$"). In particular, contracts cannot affect the bargaining powers in the renegotiation game, but only the starting point of the renegotiation: this status quo is of the form $(a, t = t_0)$, where a is the preferred action of the party who has the decision right; thus, $a = a^i$ if $\delta = i$. In addition to setting the starting point of the negotiation, the initial contract can also stipulate a mechanism (e.g. a revelation game) to be implemented once the negotiation has taken place.

2.3   Renegotiation game

We assume that the outcome of the negotiation is given by the generalized Nash-bargaining solution, with bargaining powers α_1 and $\alpha_2 (\alpha_i \geq 0,$

$\alpha_1 + \alpha_2 = 1$) for the two parties; that is, starting from a status quo $(\hat{a}, \hat{t})$, and assuming that the set of transfers is restricted to $T \subset \mathfrak{R}$, the outcome of the negotiation is given by[3]:

$$\max_{a \in A, t \in T} [b_1(a) - t - (b_1(\hat{a}) - \hat{t})]^{\alpha_1} [b_2(a) + t - (b_2(\hat{a}) + \hat{t})]^{\alpha_2}$$

2.4   Timing

The timing of events can be summarized as follows:
- First, the two parties sign an initial "contract," which can specify (a lottery over) control rights[4] and initial transfers, and decide whether or not to run the project; if they have agreed to run the project, then
- Second, they "negotiate" the eventual choice of action, together with additional transfers;
- Lastly, they implement any additional mechanism stipulated in the initial contract.

3   The optimality of "decision-rights" contracts

3.1   Benchmark case: no wealth constraint

In the absence of wealth constraints (when both w_1 and w_2 are large), *ex post* negotiation leads to the efficient action choice a^* no matter what the initial allocation of decision rights: if the initial contract (δ, t_0) is signed in the first stage, the outcome of renegotiation is given by the solution to

$$\max_{a \in A, t} \left[b_1(a) - t - \left(b_1^\delta - t_0 \right) \right]^{\alpha_1} \left[b_2(a) + t - \left(b_2^\delta - t_0 \right) \right]^{\alpha_2}$$

and is thus characterized by $a = a^*$ and by a net transfer $t^*(\delta, t_0)$ such that:

$$\alpha_2 \left[b_1^* - t - \left(b_1^\delta - t_0 \right) \right] = \alpha_1 \left[b_2^* + t - \left(b_2^\delta - t_0 \right) \right] \tag{1}$$

The final levels of utility $u_1(\delta, t_0)$ and $u_2(\delta, t_0)$ are thus respectively equal to:

$$u_1(\delta, t_0) = b_1^\delta + \alpha_1(b^* - b^\delta) - t_0$$
$$u_2(\delta, t_0) = b_2^\delta + \alpha_2(b^* - b^\delta) - t_0 \tag{2}$$

Ex ante participation by party i then requires:

$$u_i \geq B_i, i = 1, 2 \tag{3}$$

Since the project is viable by assumption $A2$, for any $\delta \in \{1, 2\}$ there exists an initial transfer $t_0(\delta)$ such that the two individual rationality constraints are simultaneously satisfied. The allocation of decision rights thus does not play any prominent role in the absence of wealth constraints.

3.2   Simple contracts under wealth constraints

We now reintroduce wealth constraints (w_i small for at least one party i) and establish the optimality of control allocation contracts. Since contracts cannot affect the "rules" of the bargaining but only its starting point, there is little room for contracts more sophisticated than a simple "decision-right" contract of the form (δ, t_0), that simply allocates the right to choose the action and stipulates a monetary transfer. In particular, there is nothing to "reveal" before *ex post* bargaining takes place; and once *ex post* bargaining has fixed the choice of action, any subsequent revelation game would be a constant-sum game and therefore could not implement anything but a mere transfer, independent of the action chosen.[5] The parties might however wish to alter the outcome of the renegotiation game, and can do so by restricting the set of admissible transfers (beyond the restrictions already implied by wealth constraints). However, this is not the case when for example they wish (and are able to) reach *ex post* efficiency:

Proposition 1   *(a) There is no loss of generality in restricting attention to lotteries over contracts (δ, t_0, T) that simply: (i) allocate the control right to one party $(\delta = 1 \text{ or } 2)$; (ii) stipulate an initial transfer t_0; and (iii) restrict the set of final transfers to $T (\ni t_0)$.*

(b) Moreover, there is no loss of generality in restricting attention to lotteries over "simple contracts" (δ, t_0) that only allocate the control right to one party $(\delta = 1 \text{ or } 2)$ and stipulate an initial transfer t_0, when either of the following conditions holds:

(i) benefits are twice continuously differentiable and the parties focus on ex post *efficiency,*

(ii) limiting the set of transfers at the ex post *negotiation stage can only hurt both parties.*

Proof: (a) The optimal contract generates (possibly randomly) a starting point $(\delta, \underline{t})$ for the negotiation stage and a "game" to be played after the negotiation stage to determine the final transfer. The rules of this game can depend explicitly upon the transfer negotiated by the parties but not upon the negotiated action since it is non-verifiable[6] (the strategies may however depend both on the action and the transfer); we denote this game by $G(t)$. Since no information arrives before the negotiation stage, there is clearly no loss of generality in directly setting $(\delta, \underline{t})$ as the starting point of the negotiation and making the parties play $G(t)$ after the negotiation stage. We shall denote by $(\hat{\sigma}_1(a, t), \hat{\sigma}_2(a, t))$ the equilibrium strategies of this game and by $\hat{t}(a, t) \equiv \bar{t}(t, \hat{\sigma}_1(a, t), \hat{\sigma}_2(a, t))$ the transfer that is finally implemented when the outcome of the negotiation stage is (a, t).

The equilibrium transfer $\hat{t}(a, t)$ clearly cannot depend on a. To see this, first note that, necessarily, for any a and a':

$$\hat{t}(a, t) = \bar{t}(t, \hat{\sigma}_1(a, t), \hat{\sigma}_2(a, t)) \geq \bar{t}(t, \hat{\sigma}_1(a, t), \hat{\sigma}_2(a', t))$$
$$\geq \hat{t}(a', t) = \bar{t}(t, \hat{\sigma}_1(a', t), \hat{\sigma}_2(a', t))$$

The first inequality stems from the fact that by definition party 2 prefers playing $\hat{\sigma}_2(a', t)$ rather than $\hat{\sigma}_2(a', t)$ in the equilibrium that follows the negotiation outcome (a, t), whereas the second equality stems from the fact that party 1 prefers $\hat{\sigma}_1(a', t)$ to $\hat{\sigma}_1(a, t)$ in the equilibrium that follows the negotiation outcome (a', t). Similarly,

$$\hat{t}(a', t) \geq \bar{t}(t, \hat{\sigma}_1(a', t), \hat{\sigma}_2(a, t)) \geq \hat{t}(a, t)$$

where the first inequality stems now from the fact that party 2 prefers $\hat{\sigma}_2(a', t)$ to $\hat{\sigma}_2(a, t)$ in the equilibrium that follows (a', t), whereas the second equality stems from the fact that party 1 prefers $\hat{\sigma}_1(a, t)$ to $\hat{\sigma}_1(a', t)$ in the equilibrium that follows (a, t). Combining the two sets of conditions yields $\hat{t}(a', t) = \hat{t}(a, t)$.

It follows that the equilibrium transfer $\hat{t}$ depends only upon the negotiated transfer. Denoting by $\hat{t}(t)$ this function, the negotiated outcome (a, t) is then determined as the solution to the program[7]:

$$\max_{a \in A, t \in T} \left[b_1(a) - \hat{t}(t) - \left(b_1^\delta - \hat{t}(\underline{t}) \right) \right]^{\alpha_1} \left[b_2(a) + \hat{t}(t) - \left(b_2^\delta + \hat{t}(t) \right) \right]^{\alpha_2}$$

which is equivalent to

$$\max_{a \in A, u \in T'} \left[b_1(a) - u - \left(b_1^\delta - t_0 \right) \right]^{\alpha_1} \left[b_2(a) + u - \left(b_2^\delta + t_0 \right) \right]^{\alpha_2}$$

with $t_0 = \hat{t}(\underline{t})$ and $T' = \{u \mid \exists t \in T \text{ such that } u = \hat{t}(t)\}$. Therefore, the same equilibrium outcome could be achieved with the simple contract (δ, t_0, T').

(b) Part i. Let $(\tilde{a}(\delta, t_0, T), \tilde{t}(\delta, t_0, T))$ denote the outcome of the renegotiation when it starts from a status quo $(a = a^1 \text{ or } a^2, t_0)$ and transfers are restricted to $t \in T$, and $T_w \equiv [-w_2, w_1]$ denote the unrestricted set of transfers (apart from the wealth constraints). It suffices to show that for any (δ, t_0, T) such that $\tilde{a}(\delta, t_0, T) = a^*$, then $(\tilde{a}(\delta, t_0, T_w), \tilde{t}(\delta, t_0, T_w)) = (\tilde{a}(\delta, t_0, T), \tilde{t}(\delta, t_0, T))$.

Consider therefore a contract (δ, t_0, T) leading to $\tilde{a}(\delta, t_0, T) = a^*$. Note first that $\tilde{a}(\delta, t_0, T)$ is a solution to the first-order condition[8]:

$$\alpha_1 \left[b_2(a) + t - \left(b_2^\delta + t_0 \right) \right] b_1'(a) + \alpha_2 \left[b_1(a) - t - \left(b_1^\delta - t_0 \right) \right] b_2'(a) = 0$$

Differentiating this condition with respect to a and t yields:

$$[b_1'(a)\, b_2'(a) + \alpha_1[b_2(a) + t - (b_2^\delta + t_0)]b_1''(a) + \alpha_2$$
$$\times[b_1(a) - t - (b_1^\delta - t_0)]b_2''(a)]da + [\alpha_1 b_1'(a) - \alpha_2 b_2'(a)]dt = 0$$

where both the coefficients of dt and da are strictly negative. Hence, an agreement will be reached on a^* only if the negotiated transfer is $t = \tilde{t}(\delta, t_0, T)$. Now, consider the outcome of the negotiation without any restriction on the set of possible transfers (that is, $T' = \Re$); since in this case negotiation induces an efficient choice of action ($a = a^*$), it must therefore induce a negotiated transfer, $t^* = \tilde{t}(\delta, t_0, \Re)$ equal to $t = \tilde{t}(\delta, t_0, T)$. That is, $(\tilde{a}(\delta, t_0, T), \tilde{t}(\delta, t_0, T))$ solves:

$$\max_{a \in A, u \in \Re'} \left[b_1(a) - u - (b_1^\delta - t_0)\right]^{\alpha_1}\left[b_2(a) + u - (b_2^\delta + t_0)\right]^{\alpha_2}$$

But then, since: $T \subset T_w \subset \Re$, we necessarily have: $\tilde{t}(\delta, t_0, Tw) = t^*$.

Part ii. It suffices to note that, for a given starting point (δ, t_0), restricting the set of transfers T can lead only to a Pareto-inferior outcome. More precisely, denoting by $(\hat{a}, \hat{t})$ the solution to the program:

$$\max_{a, t \in T} \left[b_1(a) - t - (b_1^\delta - t_0)\right]^{\alpha_1}\left[b_2(a) + t - (b_2^\delta + t_0)\right]^{\alpha_2}$$

and by $(\bar{a}, \bar{t})$ the solution to the program:

$$\max_{a, w_1 \geq t \geq -w_2} \left[b_1(a) - t - (b_1^\delta - t_0)\right]^{\alpha_1}\left[b_2(a) + t - (b_2^\delta + t_0)\right]^{\alpha_2}$$

it is necessarily the case that $(\bar{a}, \bar{t})$ Pareto-dominates $(\hat{a}, \hat{t})$ if $T \subset [-w_2, w_1]$ since the function that is maximized is increasing in both parties' payoffs, $b_1(a) - t$ and $b_2(a) + t$. Therefore, without loss of generality we can restrict attention to lotteries over simple options of the form (δ, t_0). ∎

Proposition 1 asserts that there is no loss of generality restricting attention to simple contracts when the parties focus on *ex post* efficiency (and private benefits are smooth), or when restricting transfers hurts both parties. When private benefits are "smooth" (i.e. twice continuously differentiable), starting from an initial contract (δ, t_0) the outcome of the *ex post* negotiation is efficient ($a = a^*$) if and only if $t^*(\delta, t_0)$, defined by (1), is feasible. Any binding restriction thus involves a loss of efficiency. However, restricting transfers may still enhance one party's bargaining strength; that is, the outcome of the restricted negotiation is always less efficient but can be more favorable to one of the two parties. In that case, restricting transfers sacrifices *ex post* efficiency but may help meeting one party's participation constraint, as shown in the following example.[9]

Example 1: The two parties are respectively a wealthy buyer ($w_B > 0$) and a poor seller ($w_S = 0$) who must agree on a level of trade $a \in [0, 1]$. The buyer's valuation is $v(a) = a - a^2/2$, while the seller's cost is $c(a) = a^2/2$. Their utilities are thus respectively equal to: $B = v - t$ and $S = t - c$; the two parties have equal bargaining weights ($\alpha_1 = \alpha_2 = 1/2$) and reservation levels $B > 0$ and $S = 0$. First-best efficiency is achieved for $a^* = 1/2$, while wealth constraints imply $t \geq 0$.

To fix ideas, suppose that the status quo is $\delta = S$ (and thus $a = 0$) and $t_0 = 0$; then the outcome of the negotiation without transfer restriction, is:

$$a = a^*, v^* = 3/8, c^* = 1/8, t^S = 1/4, B^S = 1/8, S^S = 1/8.$$

Any larger transfer $t_0 > 0$ to the seller can only lead to a lower equilibrium utility for the buyer. If instead the transfers are restricted to $t \leq 7/54$, the outcome is $\hat{a} = 1/3, \hat{t} = 7/54, \hat{B} = 4/27 > B^*, \hat{S} = 2/27$. That is, restricting the transfers from the buyer to the seller reduces trade efficiency but *increases* the utility that the buyer gets out of the negotiation. Thus, the parties may find it mutually profitable *ex ante* to restrict the set of feasible transfers if for example the buyer's reservation utility B lies between B^* and $\hat{B}$.

An alternative would be to allocate control to the buyer ($\delta = B$); together with an initial transfer t_0, it will lead to efficiency only if the outcome is the same as with no restriction on transfers: $a = a^*$ and a net transfer t given by (1), that is here: $t = t_0 - 1/4$. Therefore, in order to reach efficiency, the initial transfer t_0 must be sufficiently large, namely such that $t = t_0 - 1/4 \geq 0$, or $t_0 \geq 1/4$. To be acceptable to the seller, the initial transfer t_0 must be even larger and satisfy $t - c^* = t_0 - 3/8 \geq 0$, or $t_0 \geq 3/8$. Conversely, in the absence of contractual restrictions on transfers, any initial transfer $t_0 < 1/4$ leads the seller to "buy-back" as much reduction in a as possible (i.e. the net transfer is $t = 0$) and thus gives the seller a negative utility ($-c(a) < -c^* < 0$).

Therefore, if (i) the buyer's reservation B utility lies between B^* and $\hat{B}$ and (ii) the buyer's wealth is too small ($w_R < 3/8$), then there is no contract without restrictions on transfers that is acceptable by both parties, whereas there exist contracts that further restrict transfers (e.g. $\delta = S$, together with restrictions $t \leq 7/54$ that are acceptable by both parties, even though they do not yield *ex post* efficiency.[10]

In what follows, we shall mostly focus on situations where either utilities are smooth and the parties want to reach efficiency ($a = a^*$) or relaxing constraints on transfers at the *ex post* negotiation stage benefits both parties. In both cases, without loss of generality we can restrict attention to simple contracts of the form (δ, t_0).

4   The determinants of control allocation

As pointed out in AB, wealth constraints raise two types of issues: they limit the efficiency of the *ex post* negotiation game and make it harder to meet one party's participation constraint *ex ante*. We consider these two problems in turn.

4.1   *Limited wealth and* ex post *negotiation*

In this sub-section we focus on the choice of action that results from *ex post* Nash Bargaining and abstract from *ex ante* participation considerations (assume, for example, that $B_1 > b_1^2$ and $B_2 > b_1^2$). We first stress that when parties differ in their initial wealth, giving control to the poorer party enhances the efficiency of the negotiation stage.

To see this, suppose first that one party, say party 2, has very little wealth ($w_2 \approx 0$), whereas the other party is unconstrained (w_1 large). Then, allocating control to the poor party (party 2) leads to the first-best action a^*, since it is always in the interest of the rich to compensate the poor for moving from a^2 to a^*. That is:

$$a^* = \arg \max_{a \in A, t \geq 0} \left[b_1(a) - t - b_1^2 \right]^{\alpha_1} \left[b_2(a) + t - b_2^2 \right]^{\alpha_2}$$

On the other hand, if control rights are allocated to the rich party (party 1), then the ultimate choice of action will be a_1 since party 2 lacks the resources needed to convince party 1 to move away from her most preferred action. More generally, achieving efficiency requires giving control to the poorer party whenever the initial wealth distribution is sufficiently uneven. This, of course, has also some implications with respect to the distribution of the gains from the partnership.

The following example helps illustrate this point and also allows us to briefly discuss the role of the two parties' bargaining powers.

Example 2:   Let $A = [0, 1]$, and suppose that the private benefit functions b_1 and b_2 are symmetric and piecewise linear, defined by:

$$b_2(a) = \overline{K}a \quad \text{for} \quad 0 \leq a \leq {}^1/_2$$

$$= \frac{\overline{K} - \underline{K}}{2} + \underline{K}a \quad \text{for} \quad a \geq {}^1/_2$$

where $\overline{K} > \underline{K} > 0$

and:

$$b_1(a) = b_2(1 - a)$$

The *ex post* efficient action is $a^* = {}^1/_2$ and yields a total utility level:

$$b_1^* = b_2^* = \frac{\overline{K}}{2}, b^* = \overline{K}$$

while the parties' preferred actions $(a^1 = 0, a^2 = 1)$ yield, for $i = j = 1, 2$:

$$b_j^i = 0, b_i^i = b^i = \frac{\overline{K} + \underline{K}}{2}$$

We first assume equal bargaining powers: $\alpha_1 = \alpha_2 = {}^1/_2$. If control is granted to party 1, in the absence of any initial transfer t_0, the outcome of the negotiation is determined as follows:

- if $w_2 < \underline{w} \equiv \dfrac{\overline{K}\underline{K}}{\overline{K} + \underline{K}}$, party 2 is too poor to induce party 1 to take the efficient action; the outcome of the negotiation in that case is defined by $\hat{t} = w_2$, and

$$\hat{a} = \arg\max_{a \in A} \left\{ \left(b_1(a) + w_2 - b_1^1 \right) \left(b_2(a) - w_2 - b_1^2 \right) \right\}$$

Using the fact that $a < {}^1/_2$, and thus $b_1(a) = \dfrac{\overline{K} - \underline{K}}{2} + \underline{K}(1 - a)$ and $b_2(a) = \overline{K}a$, the first-order condition with respect to a yields

$$\hat{a} = \frac{\overline{K} + \underline{K}}{2\overline{K}\underline{K}} w_2 < a^*$$

The corresponding utilities for the two parties are, respectively,

$$\hat{u}_1 = b_1(\hat{a}) + w_2 = \frac{\overline{K} + \underline{K}}{2} + \frac{\overline{K} - \underline{K}}{2\overline{K}} w_2$$

$$\hat{u}_2 = b_2(\hat{a}) - w_2 = \frac{\overline{K} - \underline{K}}{2\overline{K}} w_2$$

- if

$$\underline{w} \le w_2 < \overline{w} \equiv \frac{\overline{K} + \underline{K}}{4}$$

then party 2 can afford to bribe party into taking the efficient action but the negotiated transfer is still constrained by party 2's limited wealth; in that case

$$\hat{a} = a^* = \frac{1}{2} \quad \text{and} \quad \hat{t} = w_2$$

$$\hat{u}_1 = \frac{\overline{K}}{2} + w_2 \quad \text{and} \quad \hat{u}_2 = \frac{\overline{K}}{2} - w_2$$

- finally, if $w_2 \geq \overline{\omega}$, wealth constraints play no role; $\hat{a} = a^* = \frac{1}{2}$ and the net transfer $\hat{t}$ is simply determined by

$$\hat{t} = \arg\max_t \left\{ \left(b_1^*(a) + t - b_1^1 \right) \left(b_2^* - t - b_2^1 \right) \right\} = \frac{\overline{K} + \underline{K}}{4}$$

the utilities for the two parties are then:

$$\hat{u}_1 = \frac{3\overline{K} + \underline{K}}{4} \quad \text{and} \quad \hat{u}_2 = \frac{\overline{K} - \underline{K}}{4}$$

Both efficiency and the two parties' utilities increase with party 2's wealth w_2 as long as this party is severely constrained ($w_2 < \underline{w}$), whereas beyond this threshold increasing w_2 has no effect on efficiency but leads to a distribution of gains more favorable to party 1. Note, however, that $db_1/dw_2 \leq 1$, so that party 1 cannot gain from transferring wealth to party 2 through an initial transfer t_0.

The outcome of the negotiation when control is granted to party 2 can be derived by symmetry. Thus, *ex post* efficiency is achieved iff control is allocated to the poorer party (party 1, say), whenever

$$w_1 < \underline{w} \leq w_2$$

Furthermore, if

$$w_1 < w_2 < \underline{w}$$

so that efficiency cannot be achieved, the ex post *outcome is still closer to the first-best utility level b* when control is allocated to the **poorer** party, thereby letting the richer party make the* ex post *monetary transfers.* Note however that the richer party is better off being granted control.

We now consider the impact of the parties' relative bargaining power on the eventual choice of action.

The minimal wealth required from party 2 for achieving first-best efficiency when control is allocated to party 1 is determined by $a = a^*$ being a solution to:

$$\max_{a \in A} \left\{ \left(b_1(a) + w_2 - b_1^1 \right)^{\alpha_1} \left(b_2(a) - w_2 - b_2^1 \right)^{\alpha_2} \right\}$$

Taking the first-order condition with respect to a for $a = a^* = {}^1/_2$ yields:

$$\underline{w}_2(\delta = 1) \equiv \frac{1}{2} \frac{\overline{K}\underline{K}}{\alpha_2 \overline{K} + \alpha_1 \underline{K}}$$

This is strictly greater than the wealth required from party 1 for achieving first-best efficiency if control is allocated to party 2, namely:

$$\underline{w}_1(\delta = 2) \equiv \frac{1}{2} \frac{\overline{K}K}{\alpha_1 \overline{K} + \alpha_2 K}$$

This suggests that *it is easier to ensure* ex post *efficiency by allocating control to the party with the **lower** bargaining power.*

4.2   *Limited liability and participation constraints*

In contrast to *ex post* efficiency, participation constraints considerations call for allocating control to the richer party. To see why, consider first the following simple example:

Example 3:   Suppose:

$$w_1 = +\infty, w_2 = 0, B_1 = B_2 = 0, \alpha_1 = \alpha_2 = {}^1/_2$$
$$b_1^1 = b_2^2 = +100, b_2^1 = b_1^2 = -100, b_2^* = b_1^* = 50$$

Assume first that the initial contract allocates the decision right to party $2(\delta = 2)$. Then, since party 2 can offer no transfer to party 1, party 1 cannot hope to get more than

$$b_2^1 + \frac{b^* - b^2}{2} = 100 + 50 = -50$$

which is lower than his or her reservation level of utility. Hence no contract stipulating $\delta = 2$ would ever be accepted by party 1.

In contrast, allocating the decision right to party 1 can help meet this party's participation constraint. For example, together with an initial transfer of 100 from party 1 to party 2, it leads after *ex post* negotiation of the action choice to:

$$u_1(1, 100) = b_1^1 - 100 + \frac{b^* - b^1}{2} = 50$$
$$u_2(1, 100) = b_2^1 - 100 + \frac{b^* - b^1}{2} - 50$$

and thus satisfies both parties' participation constraints. This example thus suggests that, when at least one party faces wealth constraints, reaching efficient outcomes may require to allocate the decision right to the least wealth-constrained party.

We now further explore how the interplay between wealth and participation constraints governs the allocation of control in our more general setting. Assuming that the two parties' benefits are smooth, if control is allocated to party 1, say, together with an initial transfer t_0 to party 2, if *ex post* negotiation is efficient the final transfer t from party 1 to party 2 is equal to:

$$\alpha_2\left[(b_1^* - t) - (b_1^1 - t_0)\right] = \alpha_1\left[(b_2^* + t) - (b_2^1 + t_0)\right]$$

or equivalently:

$$t = t_0 + \alpha_2(b_1^* - b_1^1) - \alpha_1(b_2^* - b_2^1) \tag{4}$$

Since party 2 must compensate party 1 to convince that party to undertake the efficient action, this net transfer is lower than the initial transfer t_0.[11] And since the initial transfer must itself be feasible, the admissible range for the net transfer $\hat{t}$ is defined by[12]:

$$-w_2 \le t \le w_1 + \alpha_2(b_1^* - b_1^1) - \alpha_1(b_2^* - b_2^1)$$

To better focus on the role of participation constraints, assume that party 2 is sufficiently unconstrained (w_2 is sufficiently large) that *ex post* efficiency could always be achieved by granting control to party 1 (party 2 then bribes party 1 into choosing the efficient action). Yet, if party 1's wealth is too small, namely if:

$$w_1 < w_1^1 \equiv B_2 - \left[b_2^1 + \alpha_2(b^* - b^1)\right] \tag{5}$$

party 2 will never accept to sign a contract that allocates decision rights to party 1. To see this, note that if the contract ($\delta = 1, t_0$) is accepted and eventually leads to *ex post* efficiency ($a = a^*$), the final transfer, given by (4) gives party 2 a level of utility u_2 equal to:

$$u_2 = b_2^1 + t_0 + \alpha_2(b^* - b^1)$$

A contract granting control to party 1 can therefore be accepted by party 2 only if

$$\max_{t_0 \le w_1} u_2 = b_2^1 + w_1 + \alpha_2(b^* - b^1) \ge B_2$$

which in turn requires $w_1 \ge w_1^1$. In contrast, there exists a feasible transfer t_0 such that the contract ($\delta = 2, t_0$) is individually rational for both parties and efficient:

Proposition 2 *Suppose that: (i) one party, 2, say, is sufficiently unconstrained that it can always bribe the other party into choosing the efficient action ex post; and: (ii) efficient contracting would individually rational if the action choice were verifiable. Then, allocating control to party 1 may violate party 2's individual rationality constraint, whereas there always exists a feasible* *transfer t_0 such that the contract $(\delta = 2, t_0)$ is individually rational for both parties and efficient.*

Proof: If the contract $(\delta = 2, t_0)$ yields *ex post* efficiency, then the net transfer is given by

$$t = t_0 + \alpha_2(b_1^* - b_1^2) - \alpha_1(b_2^* - b_2^2)$$

and is larger than the initial transfer t_0. In addition, the two parties' equilibrium payoffs are respectively given by:

$$u_1 = b_1^2 - t_0 + \alpha_1(b^* - b^2)$$
$$u_2 = b_2^2 - t_0 + \alpha_2(b^* - b^2)$$

Such a contract will therefore be individually rational if and only if $u_i \geq B_i$. If party 2 is sufficiently unconstrained, the relevant constraints are thus the feasibility condition:

$$w_1 \geq t = t_0 + \alpha_2(b_1^* - b_1^2) - \alpha_1(b_2^* - b_2^2)$$

and party 2's participation condition:

$$B_2 \leq u_2 = b_2^2 + t_0 + \alpha_2(b^* - b^2)$$

These two conditions are compatible when:

$$B_2 - [b_2^2 + \alpha_2(b^* - b^2)] \leq w_1 - [\alpha_2(b_1^* - b_1^2) - \alpha_1(b_2^* - b_2^2)]$$

or:

$$w_1 \geq \hat{w}_1 = B_2 - [b_2^2 + \alpha_2(b^* - b^2)] + [\alpha_2(b_1^* - b_1^2) - \alpha_1(b_2^* - b_2^2)]$$
$$= B_2 - b_2^*$$

But this latter condition is trivially satisfied when efficient contracting is individually rational for party 2 if the action were verifiable. ∎

*Thus, allocating control to the **least wealth-constrained party**, together with an appropriate transfer towards the poorer party, makes the project acceptable by both parties and can eventually lead to the efficient action choice a^*. Giving instead control to the poorer party puts that party at an excessive advantage in the negotiation game, which in turn makes it difficult to meet the other party's participation constraint.*

Remark . In the more general case where both parties face (tight) credit-constraints, we saw on p. 204 that achieving *ex post* efficiency might require granting control to the poorer party. However, the above discussion suggests that doing so is more likely to violate individual rationality.

Whenever *ex post* efficiency and *ex ante* participation considerations conflict, in the sense that there does not exist an individually rational contract that leads to *ex post* efficient action choice after renegotiation, the participation constraints should dictate what the optimal control allocation will be, as suggested by the following example.

Example 2 (contd.):   Consider again our previous example with symmetric piecewise linear utility functions and, to fix ideas, symmetric bargaining power and reservation utilities:

$$B_1 = B_2 = B, \alpha_1 = \alpha_2 = \frac{1}{2}$$

In addition, suppose that:

$$0 \leq w_1 < w_2 < w_1 + w_2 < \underline{w}$$

so that achieving efficiency is impossible: no party can sufficiently "bribe" the other away from her preferred action, even if pooling both parties' wealth through initial transfers.

Maximal efficiency if achieved when the controlling party transfers all of her wealth to the other party. However, while both $(\delta = 1, t_0 = w_1)$ and $(\delta = 2, t_0 = -w_2)$ achieve this maximal efficiency, the latter yields more balanced utility levels:

$$u_1^1 \equiv u_1(\delta = 1, t_0 = w_1) = \frac{\overline{K} + \underline{K}}{2} + \frac{\overline{K} - \underline{K}}{2\overline{K}} w_2 - \frac{\overline{K} + \underline{K}}{2\underline{K}} w_1$$

$$u_2^1 \equiv u_2(\delta = 1, t_0 = w_1) = \frac{\overline{K} - \underline{K}}{2\underline{K}} w_1 + \frac{\overline{K} + \underline{K}}{2\overline{K}} w_2$$

while

$$u_1^2 \equiv u_1(\delta = 2, t_0 = -w_2) = \frac{\overline{K} - \underline{K}}{2\underline{K}} w_1 + \frac{\overline{K} + \underline{K}}{2\underline{K}} w_2$$

$$u_2^2 \equiv u_2(\delta = 2, t_0 = -w_2) = \frac{\overline{K} + \underline{K}}{2} + \frac{\overline{K} - \underline{K}}{2\overline{K}} w_1 - \frac{\overline{K} + \underline{K}}{2\overline{K}} w_2$$

so that[13]

$$u_1^1 > u_2^2 > u_1^2 > u_2^1$$

Therefore, whenever

$$u_1^2 > B > u_2^1$$

granting control to party 1 cannot be acceptable by party 2 (it cannot get more than u_2^1, even if party 1 gives away his wealth in exchange for getting control), whereas there exist contracts granting control to party 2 that are acceptable by both parties. In other words, ex ante *participation dictates that control be allocated to party 2 (the richer party), although this does not lead to ex post efficiency.*[14]

Remark 2: We saw on p. 205 that allocating control to the party with the lower bargaining power helps achieve *ex post* efficiency. The following example suggests that allocating control to the party with lower bargaining power can also help achieving *ex ante* participation.

Example 4: Let:

$$b_1^* = b_2^* = \beta; b_1^1 = b_2^2 = \Delta = -b_1^2 = -b_2^1; B_1 = B_2 = B; w_1 = w_2 = w$$

but with heterogeneous bargaining powers: $\alpha_2 >> \alpha_1$. When control is allocated to party 2 the participation constraints are:

$$w \geq B - \Delta - 2\alpha_2\beta$$
$$w \geq B + \Delta + 2\alpha_1\beta$$

When α_1 (resp. α_2) is sufficiently close to zero (resp. to 1), the latter constraint is harder to satisfy than the participation constraints when control is allocated to party 1, namely:

$$w \geq B - \Delta - 2\alpha_1\beta$$
$$w \geq B + \Delta - 2\alpha_2\beta$$

Remark 3: The above analysis can be easily extended in several interesting directions. Let us briefly mention two potential extensions:

- *Monetary benefits* When the project yields monetary benefits as well as private benefits, the additional wealth generated by the project can be used to soften the impact of limited wealth. In particular, the poorer party might give up his right to the monetary benefits instead of his right to control the action choice, as there is substitutability between revenue and control rights.
- *Moral hazard* If the party who "controls" the project is subject to moral hazard, this moral hazard is likely to be exacerbated by limited wealth problems (see, e.g., Sappington 1983 and Aghion and Bolton 1997). This, in turn, provides another reason for allocating the decision right to the wealthier party.

5   Conclusion

In this chapter we have investigated the issue of control allocation in a bilateral contracting framework with *ex post* unverifiable actions and limited wealth constraints. We have shown that the *ex post* non-verifiability of actions together with the limits that wealth constraints impose on transfers between the contracting parties, implies that the optimal contract boils down to an allocation of control rights to one party, together with an initial transfer from one party to the other, and possibly some contractual restrictions on the set of feasible transfers. We have turned our attention to the determinants of control allocation, which we have analyzed in the context of a few selected examples. These examples suggest, first that *ex post* efficiency is easier to achieve when control is allocated to the most wealth-constrained party, whereas *ex ante* participation constraints are most easily met when control is allocated to the least wealth-constrained party; second, that allocating control to the party with lower bargaining power at the renegotiation stage, helps both in achieving efficiency and meeting participation constraints.

Our analysis can be extended in several directions. One natural extension would be to open the "black box" of the bilateral trade between the party in control and the party making the monetary transfers. More specifically, we have assumed that, at this stage, the controlling party could credibly commit to changes in action choices in exchange for suitable monetary transfers; it would be interesting to explicitly analyze the credibility game between the two parties, for example using a dynamic model of reputation-building. Another extension would be to explore the interactions between contracting under *ex post* unverifiable actions and the strategic interactions between the contracting parties in a dynamic context, with a view to better understand the organization of firms. Two companion papers with Mathias Dewatripont (Aghion, Dewatripont and Rey 2000, 2001) provide preliminary attempts at exploring such a research agenda. The first paper shows how dividing formal control rights over a sequence of actions can enhance cooperation by creating "checks and balances"; the second paper shows how delegating real authority to a subordinate allows this subordinate to build a reputation regarding her willingness to cooperate in the future.

NOTES

1. Closely related to AB is the paper by Dewatripont and Tirole (1994), which includes an effort variable before the non-contractible action is chosen and investigates the ability of the action to provide effort incentives.

2. In Aghion, Dewatripont and Rey (2000), we refer to this type of actions as actions with contractable control, in contrast to non-verifiable actions over which the allocation of control is not-verifiable, although control may can be credibly transfered from one party to the other.

   As suggested by Bengt Holmström, one can interpret control allocation as giving the "key" to access a room, and where only those who enter the room can observe the action to be taken there. Control allocation (who gets the key) can then be verifiable, even though the choice of action is not.

3. Note that t refers to the overall *net* transfer, not to the additional transfer $t - t_0$ negotiated on top of the initial transfer t_0.

4. While allowing lotteries (e.g. random control allocations), we shall assume that the outcome of such lotteries is realized before the negotiation starts.

5. The situation would be different if for example subsequent actions had to be taken and the ultimate outcomes depended jointly upon all actions. Then, allocating future decision rights on the basis of reported actions might allow the parties to reveal their first choice of action – see Aghion, Dewatripont and Rey (2000).

6. Yet the two parties' strategies in this game may depend upon the negotiated action and also upon the negotiated transfer.

7. We assume that any restriction on transfers binds at every stage of the implementation of the contract. The reasoning still holds if the restriction only applies to the transfers that are finally agreed to.

8. Given the negotiated transfer $t = \widetilde{t}(\delta, t_0, T)$, reaching $\widetilde{a}(\delta, t_0, T) = a^* \in (a^1, a^2)$ requires an interior solution, which must therefore satisfy this first-order condition.

9. When private benefits are not continuously differentiable, restrictions on transfers may still be required to satisfy participation constraints without necessarily inducing a loss of efficiency (see example 2 below).

10. More precisely, *ex post* efficiency could be achieved (e.g. with $\delta = S, t_0 = 0$) if $1/4 \leq w_B < 1/2$, whereas no contract can induce efficiency if $w_B < 1/4$. In both cases, however, meeting both parties' participation constraints requires $\delta = S$, together with additional restrictions on transfers, of the form $T = [0, \overline{t}]$, with $\overline{t} \in [7/54, w_B)$.

11. This is easily checked in the above formula, since $b_1^* < b_1^1$ and $b_2^* > b_2^1$.

12. In particular, if

$$W \equiv w_1 + w_2 < \overline{W}_1 \equiv \alpha_1 \left(b_2^* - b_2^1 \right) - \alpha_2 \left(b_1^* - b_1^1 \right)$$

then it would not be possible to achieve *ex post* efficiency by allocating control to party 1, even with an initial transfer to party 2. Similarly, if

$$W < \overline{W}_2 \equiv \alpha_1 \left(b_2^* - b_2^2 \right) - \alpha_2 \left(b_1^* - b_1^* \right)$$

it would not be possible to achieve *ex post* efficiency by allocating control to party 2.

13. We have: $u_1^1 - u_2^2 = u_1^2 - u_2^1 = w_2 - w_1$ and

$$
\begin{aligned}
u_2^2 - u_1^2 &= \frac{\overline{K} + \underline{K}}{2} - \frac{(\overline{K} - \underline{K})^2 w_1 + (\overline{K} + \underline{K})^2 w_2}{2\overline{K}\underline{K}} \\
&\geq \frac{\overline{K} + \underline{K}}{2} - \frac{(\overline{K} + \underline{K})^2 (w_1 + w_2)}{2\overline{K}\underline{K}}
\end{aligned}
$$

and is thus positive since $w_1 + w_2 < \underline{w} = \overline{K}\underline{K}/(\overline{K} + \underline{K})$.

14. The most efficient acceptable contract is then $(\delta = 2, t_0 = -w_2)$; a smaller initial transfer (in absolute value, i.e. $t_0 > -w_2$) increases party 2's utility but reduces both party 1's utility and efficiency.

13   Complexity and contract

W. Bentley MacLeod

"The time is not here yet, but I hope it is coming when judges realize
that the people who draft . . . contracts cannot envisage all the things
that the future will bring."[1]

1   Introduction

Building upon the work of Simon (1957), Williamson (1975) observes
that a fundamental reason for transaction costs is the impossibility of
planning for all future contingencies in a relationship.[2] The purpose of
this chapter is to explore the conditions under which such complexity can
constrain the set of feasible contracts, and help us better understand the
contracts observed in practice. Specifically, a situation where agents are
asked to make decisions when unforeseen events occur, but cannot renegotiate the contract is one I call *ex post* hold-up. In these cases, complexity
can have an important impact upon the form of the optimal contract. The
chapter begins by comparing the structure of the *ex post* hold-up problem to other contracting problems in the literature and suggests that a
key ingredient in understanding the form of the optimal contract is the
timing of information and actions in a relationship. Secondly, a way to
measure contract complexity is suggested that has empirical implications.
Finally, the optimal governance of contracts facing *ex post* hold-up when
complexity is high depends upon the degree of correlation in subjective
beliefs between the contracting parties.

Beginning with Simon (1951), there is a large literature that takes
as given contract incompleteness due to transaction costs and then explores its implications for efficient governance. Simon argues that giving
one agent authority over another economizes on transaction costs by
allowing one to delay decision-making until after uncertainty has been
resolved. In a similar vein, the property-rights literature, beginning with
Grossman and Hart (1986), argues that problems of contract incompleteness are resolved by an appropriate reallocation of bargaining power in
a relationship through ownership rights. Agency theory, beginning with

Ross (1973), Mirrlees (1999), and Holmström (1979), focuses upon how asymmetric information can explain observed contracting arrangements. Holmström and Milgrom (1991) show that in a multitasking context when signals concerning one task are not available, then the optimal contract may ignore information regarding performance on other tasks.

While contract incompleteness and asymmetric information are central themes in this literature, the role of human cognition is not. One reason, as observed by Oliver Hart (1990), is that both agency theory and the property-rights literature assume that agents select their actions immediately after the contract is signed. The contract is designed to provide the appropriate incentives for performance at this stage, and hence if *ex post* unanticipated events occur these cannot affect actions that are sunk, and therefore cannot affect the structure of the optimal contract. Agents may anticipate events that cannot be described *ex ante*, but this is a different problem, and one which Maskin and Tirole (1999b) demonstrate that under the appropriate conditions does not affect the ability of individuals to optimally regulate their relationship, leading Tirole (1999) to conclude that there does not exist a satisfactory foundation for the theory of incomplete contracts (ICT).

How then do we reconcile these results in contract theory demonstrating the irrelevance of human cognition for contract formation with Williamson's (1985) view that bounded rationality is central to the theory of transaction costs?[3] My first point is that we can usefully categorize different contracting problems as a function of *when* information is revealed. In section 2 the sequence of moves for the agency model, the hold-up model, and Simon's authority model are reviewed. While these are important classes of problems that correspond to many interesting contracting situations, they are not exhaustive. In many principal–agent situations the agent is called upon to respond to unexpected events in a way that is personally costly, but for which there is not sufficient time to renegotiate the outstanding contract with the principal. I call this contracting hazard *ex post* hold-up, and show in section 3 that the nature of human cognition may play an important role in the optimal regulation of the relationship.

Many employment relationships have exactly this characteristic. For example, a fireman may have to respond quickly to events while a building is burning, and cannot renegotiate the contract with the city in mid-blaze. Emergency room doctors must deal with a variety of unexpected events, some of which are dangerous to the physician, especially when the patient has a communicable disease. In these situations hold-up can take one of two forms. First the agent after taking an action may not receive the compensation that he or she feels is appropriate. Secondly, the principal may worry that the agent may not have the correct incentives to take the appropriate action *ex post*.

Section 3 continues with a discussion of why contracting in these situations is difficult. If each event that an agent faces could be described beforehand, along with the appropriate response, then *ex post* hold-up would be solved with a complete state-contingent contract. However when the services to be provided entail multitasking with random benefits and costs, the number of contract contingencies grows exponentially with the number of tasks. This implies that even with a moderate number of tasks, complete state-contingent contracting is impossible. It is worth emphasizing that contract incompleteness in this case is *not* exclusively due to the bounded cognitive abilities of the contracting parties: when complexity grows exponentially with a variable of interest, the problem quickly becomes intractable for any finite computation device for even modest values of this variable.[4] This is an empirically useful result because it suggests that the number of tasks in a relationship is a measure of transaction costs that is independent of individual characteristics.

Anderlini and Felli (1994) take a complementary approach to contract incompleteness. They use the notion of a *computable* contract, namely any complete contract must have the property that it is possible to determine the terms and conditions using a finite number of computations. They give examples of contracts that are not computable, and hence are incomplete. Though this condition is *necessary*, it is not *sufficient* to ensure the existence of a complete contract. All the state-contingent contracts considered in this chapter satisfy Anderlini and Felli's necessary condition, however, like many problems in computer science, being solvable in finite time does not imply practical solution since the time needed to write a complete contract is an astronomically long period.[5] This approach is extended in Anderlini and Felli (1999) where they derive the optimal incomplete contract as a function of complexity costs.

In this chapter a somewhat different approach is explored. Even if contingent contracting is impossible, the contract may still provide a mechanism to determine what constitutes appropriate performance *ex post*, and ensure that the agent is rewarded for taking the appropriate action. This issue is addressed in section 4, where it is shown that the problem of performance evaluation is formally a problem in pattern recognition where the goal is to characterize event–action pairs into the sets acceptable or not acceptable. In cognitive science it is widely recognized that while humans are quite poor at thinking logically, they have very powerful pattern recognition abilities.[6] For example, the reason that humans are good at chess is not because of their ability to reason about the game, a skill for which computers are far more skilled, but rather their ability to recognize board patterns that represent strong positions.[7] This ability is so difficult to program that only recently have computers been consistently better than humans at chess, and only with programs that are highly specialized. This implies that human judgment of performance is in many situations superior to any mechanical measuring system, and hence optimal contracts should be designed to incorporate this ability.

Incentives can be provided in these cases by observing that both the principal and agent have subjective evaluations of an agent's performance. As long as these evaluations are sufficiently correlated, then it is possible to construct a mechanism that ensures efficient performance. The optimal contract in this case takes the form of a bonus payment by the principal to the agent when the principal has judged performance to be acceptable. Given that third parties, such as the courts, are at a disadvantage in determining if performance is acceptable, the optimal contract must depend upon the agent's self-assessment of performance. Should the principal not reward the agent when the agent believes he or she is deserving then the optimal contract requires the principal to pay a penalty to a third party. The difficulty with such payments is that they are subject to the hazard of renegotiation. In the event of a disagreement, the principal and agent have a strong incentive to renegotiate to avoid paying the third party. Two well-known solutions to this problem are discussed in section 5: enforcement with repeated interaction combined with the threat of termination and the use of rank-order tournaments. This is a useful exercise because it answers an open question in the legal theory of relational contract raised by Goetz and Scott (1981). They observe that the right to unilateral termination, while part of many bilateral relational contracts, is not a usual condition for collective agreements, and hence they question the efficacy of such termination rights. The results here show that unilateral termination clauses may be a necessary condition for efficiency when bargaining is restricted to two individuals, and can be modified only when there are three or more individuals in a relationship.

2   Contracting scenarios

Consider the following generic exchange problem between an agent (he) who produces a good or service for a principal (her) in exchange for compensation:

(1) The agent is expected to choose an action $\mathbf{y}$ from a set of possible actions $\mathbf{Y}$ (in general multidimensional) at a cost $C(\mathbf{y}, \beta)$, where β is a random parameter chosen by Nature.

(2) The benefit to the principal from this action is $qB(\mathbf{y}, \alpha)$, where α is random parameter chosen by Nature, and q is the quantity of trade, which is normalized to represent trade (1) or no-trade (0), or the probability of trade if $q \in (0, 1)$.

(3) The principal and agent write a binding contract at the beginning of the relationship conditional upon their expectations and information available. I assume that the principal has all the bargaining power at each stage.[8] The payoffs to the principal and agent are respectively given by:

$$U_P = qB(\mathbf{y}, \alpha) - W \qquad (1)$$
$$U_A = W - qC(\mathbf{y}, \beta) \qquad (2)$$

The principal is assumed to offer a contract that maximizes her payoff subject to the agent receiving his reserve payoff from the relationship. The term "contract" is used in the economist's sense rather than in the more restrictive legal sense. That is, the contract specifies a mechanism or game between the principal and agent, including expected actions and beliefs, even when these cannot be verified in court. In contrast the legal notion of contract refers to promises enforced by the threat of court-awarded damages in the case of default. In particular for the economist these damage awards are an explicit part of the agreement between the two parties, as are actions taken after events that only the contracting parties can observe. An important element of this broader notion of contract is the potential for one party (the principal) to reallocate bargaining power to the other party (the agent). This reallocation of bargaining power is central to the property-rights literature beginning with Grossman and Hart (1986). The purpose of this section is to illustrate how the form of the optimal contract and the nature of property rights are sensitive to the *timing* of information revelation. I briefly outline the three important classes of contracting problems that have been considered in the literature, agency theory and the hold-up problem of Williamson (1975) and Grossman and Hart (1986), and Simon's (1951) authority model, and discuss the relevance of theories of bounded rationality for each of these contracting problems. I then introduce the hazard of *ex post hold-up*, that is more appropriate for addressing the role of human cognition in contract formation.

2.1 Agency theory

Agency theory, beginning with Ross (1973) and Holmström (1979), is the starting point for the modern theory of contract. It is always possible to view the economic theory of contract as an application of agency

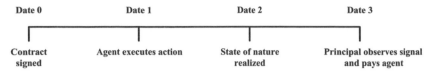

Figure 13.1   Time line for agency relationship

theory: namely observed contracts are the result of negotiations between a principal and an agent, who choose optimal contracts as a function of the available information. However, in this chapter I follow Hart and Holmström (1987), and adopt a narrower definition of agency theory corresponding to the class of models that focuses upon how to structure contracts as a function of mutually observed (and enforceable) signals of performance. In the context of our simple model let us fix β, and set $q = 1$. The timing of decisions are as illustrated in figure 13.1. At date 0 the contract is signed, then the agent chooses y, which is assumed to be a real number representing effort or some personally costly action: $\partial C / \partial y > 0$. The choice of effort affects the underlying distribution of α in such a way that more effort is beneficial to the principal: $\partial E(B(y, \alpha))/\partial y > 0$ for all α. The principal then pays the agent a wage that is a function of the observed benefit, or $W = f(B)$.

In agency theory it is typically assumed that the agent is risk averse, and hence he would prefer a wage W that is independent of the random shock α. In this case the agent has no incentive to work and would select y to minimize the personal cost of effort. A major insight of this literature, as discussed in Hart and Holmström (1987), is in order to avoid this moral-hazard problem the optimal contract should be a function of *any* signal that adds information regarding worker effort.

There is a great deal of evidence to suggest that the basic hypothesis of agency theory is correct, namely individuals do respond to incentives. Hence, if workers are paid a wage that is independent of income one expects to observe some shirking. Despite this fact, explicit pay-for-performance systems, while common, are far from being ubiquitous, leading many experts such as Gibbons (1997) and Prendergast (1999), to conclude that agency theory alone cannot explain all the variation observed in the data.

One solution, provided by Holmström and Milgrom (1991), begins with the observation that while effort is often multidimensional, performance measures may not be sufficiently rich to capture this variation. For example suppose that a home owner is contracting for the services of a contractor who must allocate effort between speedy completion of the project and quality, whose actions are represented by vector $y = \{y_s, y_q\}$, where y_s represents speed and y_q represents quality. In the absence of explicit contract terms, the cost-minimizing effort is strictly positive:

$$\{y_s^o, y_q^o\} = \arg\min_{y_s, y_q \geq 0} C(y_s, y_q) > 0$$

It is also reasonable to suppose that quality and speed are substitutes, and hence $C_{sq} > 0$.

In this simple example the benefit to the home owner is assumed to have no uncertainty and is given by $B(y)$. Given that the payoff represents the subjective preferences of the home owner, then one cannot write a contract conditional upon an explicit measure of B or for that matter quality y_q, also a subjective variable. Rather, the only contractible variable is y_s, speed. In this case, assuming that the problem is convex, it follows that under the optimal contract $\{y_s^*, y_q^*\}$ solves:

$$C_{y_q}(y_s^*, y_q^*) = 0 \tag{3}$$

$$B_{y_s}(y_s^*, y_q^*) = C_{y_s} + B_{y_q}(y_s^*, y_q^*)\left(\frac{C_{y_s y_q}}{C_{y_q y_q}}\right) \tag{4}$$

The first term is the consequence of the contractor minimizing costs in the quality dimension, while the second term is the first-order condition for speed. Since speed and quality are substitutes ($C_{sq} > 0$) then it follows that y_s^* is less than the first best.[9] Under Holmström and Milgrom's (1991) assumption, if the substitution effect is sufficiently strong, or C_{qq} sufficiently small, then $y_s^* < y_s^o$. In other words the optimal contract may entail providing either no incentive or negative incentive for speed.

Hence incomplete contracts in agency theory arise from a paucity of information regarding performance. Notice that the hypothesis of rational expectations is central to the theory. The principal structures the incentive contract as a function of her expectations regarding future performance by the agent. The introduction of bounded rationality regarding the formation of expectations would imply that we may sometimes observe incentive contracts with unintended consequences (a possibility that is often observed in practice, as the examples in Kerr's, 1975 seminal article demonstrate). However, aside from the potential for error, agency theory provides little guidance regarding the implications of bounded rationality for observed contract form.

Also, Holmström and Milgrom's (1991) explanation for the lack of high-power incentives for quality performance ignores the potential for incentives based upon non-contractible signals. In the case of the contractor, their model suggests that in a one-period relationship the contractor would simply choose his most preferred quality. Yet, disputes over quality are quite common during construction. In many cases contracts are structured so that in areas that the quality is lacking, the builder may ask the contractor to take corrective actions, even though some aspects of quality were not explicitly contracted upon *ex ante*. This type of *ex post* renegotiation over non-contractibles is central to the hold-up model considered next.

2.2   Hold-up

Suppose now that the contractor is building a custom-designed house. Given that time of completion is contractible, we focus only upon the provision of non-contractible quality. The main difference with respect to the agency model is the existence of a physical asset whose ownership rights can be transferred. Uncertainty plays a role in that *ex post*, it may be more efficient to allocate the good to another buyer in the market. Suppose that the value of the house to the principal and the market are, respectively, given by $B(y_q, \omega)$ and $B^o(y_q, \omega)$, where it is assumed that $B(y_q, \omega) - B^o(y_q, \omega) = k(\omega)$, and $k(\omega)$ is an uncertain amount of relationship-specific rent that depends upon the state of nature ω. When this is negative, it is efficient to breach the contract, while performance is efficient when $k(\omega) > 0$. Let the expected value of the relationship given that there is efficient breach, be positive and given by $\bar{k} = E(\max\{0, k(\omega)\}) > 0$. The time line for the contract is illustrated in figure 13.2.

The insight of the property-rights literature, beginning with Williamson (1975) and Grossman and Hart (1986), is that the *ex post* distribution of bargaining power is an important determinant of the efficiency of the relationship, and that this bargaining power can be reallocated via ownership rights. Consider first the case in which the principal owns the house. Given that the principal has all the *ex post* bargaining power we obtain exactly the same solution as in the agency model above: the contractor selects his preferred quality, y_q^o, and agrees to a fixed-price contract $p = C(y_q^o)$. In this case if *ex post* efficiency requires that the building be owned by another person, then the principal would simply sell the building to that person. Though this

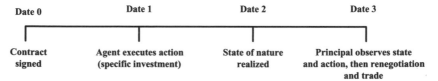

Date 0	Date 1	Date 2	Date 3
Contract signed	Agent executes action (specific investment)	State of nature realized	Principal observes state and action, then renegotiation and trade

Figure 13.2   Time line for hold-up problem

contract ensures *ex post* allocative efficiency, the lack of performance incentives implies that the contractor does not supply an efficient level of quality.

An alternative contract is for the principal to sell her right to the project to the contractor at price $p = \max_{y_q} E\{B^o(y_q, \omega)\} - C(y_q)$, with the provision that she must be given the chance to match any offer that the contractor might receive from the market. This is a contract that provides the principal with the *right of first refusal*, a contract that was common in Hollywood for some actors and producers.[10] Under this contract whenever $B^o(y_q, \omega) > B(y_q, \omega)$ the principal is unwilling to match the market price and the contractor receives $B^o(y_q, \omega)$. Whenever $B(y_q, \omega) > B^o(y_q, \omega)$, the principal simply matches the market offer, and again the contractor obtains $B^o(y_q, \omega)$. It is assumed that the marginal return from quality is the same in the market and for the principal, and hence this contract provides first-best incentives for quality, while ensuring efficient matching. More formally the payoff of the contractor is:

$$U_A(y_q) = E\{B^o(y_q, \omega)\} - C(y_q) - p$$
$$= E\{\max\{B^o(y_q, \omega), B(y_q, \omega)\}\} - \bar{k} - C(y_q) - p \quad (5)$$

This case is an example of general investment combined with turnover costs that are independent of investment. As in MacLeod and Malcomson (1993), it is also possible to obtain the first best in this case with appropriately chosen liquidation damages (proposition 5).

There is a literature that explores how the complexity of the *ex post* environment makes it impossible to write an efficient contract (Segal 1999, Hart and Moore 1999a). In these papers it is assumed that *ex post* there are a large number of potential goods that may be traded, but it is optimal to trade only one of these. When the nature of these goods cannot be specified *ex ante*, as the number of possible goods approaches infinity the optimal contract is a fixed price contract, which in turn implies that the level of investment in the relationship is inefficient. This result demonstrates how environmental complexity can cause individuals to optimally choose an incomplete contract, though this result is not an implication of bounded rationality and cognition *per se*. Both papers assume that contracting parties anticipate correctly the consequences of any mechanism they choose, hence do not explore the implications of unforeseen contingencies, and are rather concerned with "indescribable contingencies" (see Maskin and Tirole 1999b for a further discussion of these points).

Hart (1990) further argues that hold-up models provide an inadequate foundation for the study of the implications of human cognition for organization and contract design. For example, suppose there is an unforeseen event ω' for which it is efficient that the asset be sold to the market. *Ex post* renegotiation ensures that this indeed will be the outcome. However, given that specific investments have been sunk at the time individuals learn about ω', the occurrence of this event plays no role in setting *ex ante* incentives. Structuring relationships to efficiently deal with unforeseen contingencies is one of the motivations for Simon's (1951) original model of the employment relationship.

2.3   Authority

Simon's (1951) model of employment is concerned with the role played by authority. His idea is that in a complex world, rather than planning for all future events, one might gain by delaying decision-making until after an event occurs. The formal timing for his model is illustrated in figure 13.3. After the contract is signed the principal is able to observe the state of nature, denoted by $\omega = \{\alpha, \beta\} \in \Omega$, where Ω is the set of possible states, and can direct the agent to perform a task y as a function of this information (without loss of generality we set $q = 1$). In Simon's model giving the principal authority imposes costs on the agent *ex post* since he may be asked to carry out tasks with large private costs, $C(y, \beta)$. Simon supposes that the authority relationship is characterized by a wage, W, and a set of tasks $\mathbf{Y}^o \subset \mathbf{Y}$ from which the principal may choose. Giving the principal more authority corresponds to choosing a larger set of tasks, $\mathbf{Y}^o$, that the employee may be asked to carry out in exchange for a higher wage. Notice that since control is specified in terms of $\mathbf{Y}^o$, and not states, then the model incorporates a well-defined protocol to be followed when an unforeseen event occurs.

If this set is a single action, i.e. $\mathbf{Y}^o = \{y\}$, then Simon calls this a sales contract and the concept of authority has no relevance. Simon shows that the optimal contract gives the principal some authority over the agent when the benefits of flexibility outweigh the costs. Notice that the potential for renegotiation changes this result. Suppose that the agent accepts any sales contract $\{W^*, y^*\}$ satisfying $W^* - E\{C(y^*, \beta)\} = 0$, then it will follow that the expected utility of the agent is at least zero. After

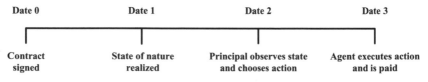

Date 0	Date 1	Date 2	Date 3
Contract signed	State of nature realized	Principal observes state and chooses action	Agent executes action and is paid

Figure 13.3   Time line for authority relationship

the event $\omega = \{\alpha, \beta\}$ occurs, under the sales contract the agent receives $U_A^*(\beta) = W^* - C(y^*, \beta)$ *ex post*. Suppose that the principal has all the bargaining power. In this case, she can offer a new *efficient* contract that would be accepted by the employee as long as the utility is at least $U_A^*(\beta)$. Hence we have the following result:

Proposition 1 *If renegotiation before the agent chooses his action is possible, then the sales contract results in the first best.*

For this contracting problem the allocation of bargaining power is not important, rather the key ingredient is the hypothesis that renegotiation can occur between the time the state is observed and the agent selects her action. In contrast to the hold-up problem, the addition of renegotiation in this case increases, rather than decreases, efficiency. However, there are a number of situations for which the hypothesis of renegotiation is not reasonable. For example firefighters must make second-by-second decisions on how to respond to a burning building, teachers need to be able to deal with new and unexpected questions and events in the class, surgeons must be able to deal with unexpected events during an operation. While not stated explicitly, it is likely that Simon had in mind situations such as these for which renegotiation to an efficient action in real time is not possible. Certainly, this is a case that is clearly not considered to be part of the standard hold-up model where renegotiation is assumed to be possible.

However, when renegotiation is not possible, the exercise of authority may also be imperfect. Alchian and Demsetz (1972) make this point when they argue that in employment relationships there is typically no real authority. The agent follows the principal's directives because he believes that he will be rewarded in the future. If the agent is dissatisfied then he is free to leave for another employment relationship. Alchian and Demsetz argue that the key point is the ability to *monitor* the agent's actions in order to be able to choose the appropriate level of compensation. Yet when performance is non-contractible, and the agent is unable to renegotiate her contract, she faces the prospect of taking a personally costly action, without any assurance that she will be rewarded because the principal can always claim that existing compensation is sufficient. This leads to a contracting hazard that I call *ex post hold-up*.

2.4   Ex post *hold-up*

In the contracting problems we have considered thus far, either the principal can observe the state of nature before the agent takes an action (authority) or the state of nature is revealed after the agent selects her

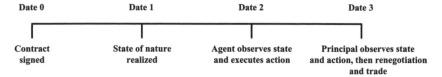

Figure 13.4   Time line for *ex post* hold-up

action (agency and hold-up). A case that has not been considered, but is ubiquitous in many employment relationships, is one where the agent is expected to respond to uncertainty before the principal has knowledge of the event or can guide the agent in selecting the appropriate action. I have already mentioned the case of fire fighters and surgeons, but this case also includes many employment situations where the employee is expected to internalize the objectives of the principal, and make decisions on the principal's behalf.

The hazard of *ex post hold-up* arises from the need to have an agent respond appropriately to events as they occur in the absence of an explicit and enforceable contract. The time line for this contracting problem is illustrated in figure 13.4. A defining feature of employment relations facing *ex post* hold-up is the need for the agent to allocate activity among a number of different tasks in response to the costs and benefits of the different tasks. More formally, suppose that the agent is facing a multitasking problem parameterized as follows:

(1) There are k tasks: $\mathbf{y} \in \mathbf{Y} = \{\{y^1, y^2, \ldots, y^k\} \mid y^1 + y^2 + \cdots + y^k \leq T\}$, where T is the agent's total time available to allocate between tasks.
(2) The cost function takes the form: $C(\mathbf{y}, \beta) = \sum_{i=1}^{k} c(y^i, \beta^i)$, where $c(y^i, \beta^i)$ is the cost of allocating effort to task i. If y^i is zero, then this cost is zero, otherwise it is $\beta^i y_i^2 + f$. The cost parameter β^i is a random variable that can take on one of m discrete values $\{d_1, \ldots, d_m\}$.
(3) The benefit function is assumed to take the form: $B(\mathbf{y}, \alpha) = \alpha^T \mathbf{y}$, where $\alpha^T \mathbf{y} = \alpha^1 y^1 + \alpha^2 y^2 + \cdots + \alpha^k y^k$ is the benefit to the firm from the agent's effort. The marginal benefit of task y^i is α^i, a random variable that can take at most n values: $\{a_1, \ldots, a_n\}$.

In this parameterization, the state space is given by the possible benefit and cost parameters: $\Omega = \{\{a_1, \ldots, a_n\} \times \{d_1, \ldots, d_m\}\}^k$. For each $\omega \in \Omega$, the optimal response is defined by:

$$\mathbf{y}^*(\omega) = \arg\max_{y \in \mathbf{Y}} B(\mathbf{y}, \alpha) - (\mathbf{y}, \beta) \tag{6}$$

An important assumption I make for the rest of the chapter is that both the benefit and cost measures are themselves non-contractible. In the case of the benefits, consider for example a secretary in a large firm. His or her keyboarding output is important to the firm, but there is no way to attach relative values to say keyboarding versus filing. Similarly, the dollar value of a research paper written by a professor, or an hour devoted to seeing students, is not known in practice. If the benefits were contractible, then the provision of an incentive contract would be straightforward. Similarly costs represent dis-utility to the agent, and hence are also difficult/impossible to verify accurately in practice.

2.5 State-contingent contracts and complexity

Though a single measure of performance may not be available, it may be reasonable to suppose that the principal can observe, or put into place a system that evaluates an agent's response to a specified state in a verifiable way. One way to avoid the potential for opportunistic behavior when an agent is simply told vaguely to do a good job is to outline explicitly what is expected for certain contingencies. For example, one may require a secretary to explicitly stop what he or she is doing if a client comes in and needs attention. Such an explicit condition may be necessary when an employee faces conflicting goals, for example if the secretary must decide between completing a keyboarding task immediately or addressing the needs of a client. For each possible state ω suppose there is an appropriate response, denoted $\mathbf{y}^*(\omega)$. Given that the agent is risk neutral, one may use a forcing contract that rewards the agent if and only if she achieves a satisfactory performance. This can be formally represented by the *judgment* function:

$$\mathcal{J} : \Omega \times \mathbf{Y} \to \{0, 1\} \tag{7}$$

where $\mathcal{J}(\omega, \mathbf{y})$ is 1 if the choice of $\mathbf{y}$ given ω is satisfactory, otherwise it is zero. In the case of an optimal complete contract, the principal defines the judgment function by $\mathcal{J}^*(\omega, \mathbf{y}) = 1$ if $\mathbf{y} \geq \mathbf{y}^*(\omega)$, and zero otherwise, and then offers a contract $\{w, b\mathcal{J}^*(\omega, \mathbf{y}^*(\omega))\}$, where w is a fixed payment and $b\mathcal{J}(\omega, \mathbf{y}^*(\omega))$ is the bonus payment. This forms an optimal contract if it satisfies the individual rationality constraints and the incentive compatibility constraints:

$$w + b - E\{C(\mathbf{y}^*(\omega), \beta)\} = 0 \tag{8}$$
$$w + b - C(\mathbf{y}^*(\omega), \beta) \geq w - \min_{\mathbf{y} \in \mathbf{Y}} C(\mathbf{y}, \beta) \tag{9}$$

With no restrictions on the sign of w, as long as costs are bounded then there always exists a contract satisfying these conditions.

Notice that in order to implement this contract one is required for every event ω to specify *ex ante* the expectations for the agent, and to reward the

Table 13.1. *Cost of a complete state-contingent contract*

Number of cost and performance levels	Number of tasks			
	2($)	5($)	10($)	15($)
2	0.16	10	10,000	10 million
3	0.81	600	35 million	2 trillion
4	2.56	10,000	11 billion	11,000 trillion
5	6.25	100,000	1,000 billion	10 million trillion
Cost of considering a contingency:	1¢			

agent if these expectations are met. However, when the number of tasks is moderately large this is simply impossible. In this model the number of tasks is k, and the number of productivity and cost levels are, respectively, m and n. The *complexity* of the contract is a measure of the costs of designing, writing and implementing the contract as a function of the data describing the relationship. Suppose that the cost of agreeing upon a contingency ω is γ, then since the number of possible events is $n^k m^k$, the cost of a complete contingent contract is $n^k m^k \gamma$. Since these costs are exponential in the number of tasks, they quickly rise to an astronomical level. For example, suppose that $\gamma = 1¢$, and that the number of cost and performance levels is the same ($n = m$), then table 13.1 presents the cost of a complete contract as a function of the number of tasks and effort levels.

As one can see from table 13.1, when there are several tasks, even with just two performance levels, the cost of even thinking about a complete state-contingent contract would be astronomical. Observe that it is the multitasking that increases the complexity costs, and not the number of cost and performance levels (the discreteness of the state space). In other words if the benefits and costs vary in a number of dimensions, then it is simply impossible to create a contingency plan for every possibility. This example illustrates the point made by Williamson (1975), and earlier still by Savage (1972), that in any realistic environment the number of possible contingencies is so large that complete state-contingent planning is impossible.[11] In particular, it is worth emphasizing that thinking in terms of human bounds on rationality is not helpful in these cases, rather one faces fundamental limits that make it impossible to construct complete contingent plans and contracts. To deal with this complexity, humans have developed algorithms and techniques for decision-making in complex environments that can be used for the design of more efficient contracts.[12]

3   The sales contract revisited: *ex ante* governance

Even though the contracting parties cannot consider every possibility, they can still write a complete contingent contract, of which Simon's (1951) sales contract is an extreme case. The sales contract is a form of *ex ante governance* requiring the agent to perform $\bar{y}$, *regardless* of the state of nature, and represents the polar opposite contract, in terms of complexity, to a complete state-contingent contract. Dye (1985) proposes that one endogenizes the complexity of the contract by specifying actions for a limited set of events. For example the event might be that there is a need to have a paper keyboarded, which is then associated with the action 'keyboard the paper today'. This event and response may not be efficient because demanding the paper be keyboarded immediately may lead to mistakes, or there may be more pressing tasks. The optimal contract trades off the quality of the contract against the cost of increased complexity. More formally, let $\Pi_N = \{E_1, E_2, \ldots, E_N\}$ be a partition of the state space Ω, and let $\mathbf{Y}_N = \{\mathbf{y}_1, \mathbf{y}_2, \ldots, \mathbf{y}_N\}$ be the associated actions. This defines a contract of complexity N, under which the agent in exchange for a wage W agrees to carry out the following actions:

$$c(\omega \mid \Pi_N, \mathbf{Y}_N) = \mathbf{y}_i, \quad \text{if and only if} \quad \omega \in E_i \tag{10}$$

Though this contract is complete in the sense that it defines an action for every state, it is not efficient. This is because all states in a single event E_i are associated with the same action, which many not necessarily be efficient.

For purposes of this example suppose that for each N the principal and agent agree upon a particular partition Π_N. Further suppose that if $N' > N$, then for every $E' \in \Pi_{N'}$, there is an $E \in \Pi_N$ such that $E' \subset E$. That is, if we agree upon a more complex contract, it refines the events of less complex contracts. Let $c_N^*(\omega)$ denote the optimal contract relative to Π_N defined by:

$$c_N^*(\omega) = \arg\max_{\mathbf{y} \in \mathbf{Y}} E\{B(\mathbf{y}, \alpha) - C(\mathbf{y}, \beta) \mid E_\omega\} \tag{11}$$

where $E_\omega \in \Pi_N$ is the unique event such that $\omega \in E_\omega$. Under these assumptions we have the following proposition, whose proof is straightforward.

Proposition 2   *The* ex ante *surplus generated by* $c_N^*(\omega)$,

$$S_N^* = E\{B(c_N^*(\omega), \alpha) - C(c_N^*(\omega), \beta)\} \tag{12}$$

is an increasing function of N.

Notice that this expression is strictly increasing when going from N to $N+1$ if and only if the additional partition causes the optimal action to change for some events. This reflects that well-known fact that information is valuable only when it causes a change in one's decision. For the multitasking problem of the previous section this is true for a generic choice of parameters α and β. The surplus *net* of transaction costs from the optimal contract of complexity N is $S_N^* - \gamma N$, where γ is the cost of adding a contract contingency. As illustrated in table 13.1, even if γ is very small, transaction costs for a complete state-contingent contract may be very large, and hence we are unlikely to observe such a contract. Suppose that the agents choose the complexity of the contract to solve

$$\max_{N \geq 1} S_N^* - \gamma N \tag{13}$$

then we have the following result:

Proposition 3 *Suppose that $\gamma \times \#\Omega > S^*$ where $\#\Omega$ is the number of states and S^* is the maximum surplus under a complete contingent contract then:*
1. *The optimal contract complexity is decreasing with contracting costs γ.*
2. *Keeping the transaction cost γ fixed, then a proportional increase in the value of trade: ζS_N, $\zeta > 1$, increases the optimal complexity of the contract.*

This result highlights the fact that increasing transaction costs lowers the complexity of a state-contingent contract. Secondly, as the value of trade rises, then so does the complexity of the contract, a result that is consistent with Macauley's (1963) observations regarding the commercial contracts. The benefit of *ex ante* governance is that the agent knows and understands exactly what is expected for every event E_i. However, it is precisely because of the fact that the contract is well defined and binding that the principal faces the hazard of opportunism. Consider the following example from the *Lincoln Electric* case in which the firm attempted to expand its system of piece rates to secretarial staff. Let ω denote the correspondence to be keyed in a particular day, and suppose that task i is the number of times that one strikes a particular letter. To improve productivity the company decided to reward individuals as a function of the number of keystrokes hit or $\sum y^i$. Clearly the intent is that the secretary keys a particular text at a higher speed, but what occurred is in one case a secretary repeatedly hit the same key during her lunch break to improve her earnings![13]

This is a rather stark example of Williamson's (1975) concept of opportunism. If the terms of employment simply specify the payment as a function of the number of keystrokes without mention of the quality of output, then even if the output is useless, the explicit terms call for payment to the secretary. The firm would argue (probably successfully) that the intent in this case is that the secretary produce useful documents, however the secretary could argue that this sophisticated firm had written an explicit contract and should be held responsible for its decisions. Unfortunately, organizations often make this kind of mistake, as highlighted in the famous article by Kerr (1975) who outlines several examples of workers responding to incentives in undesirable ways. As Kerr points out, many organizations are "rewarding A while hoping for B."

Yet, propositions 2 and 3 suggest that in principle a sufficiently contingent contract would be close to the first best, a view point that has led many economists to promote the increased use of pay for performance contracts (see for example Milkovich and Wigdor 1991). Moreover, as table 13.1 illustrates, the complexity of jobs involving multitasking is such that even very sophisticated firms may not be able to anticipate all the consequences of a contract. As Kerr observes, an explicit contract creates an incentive for the agent to discover ways to improve measured performance rather than a firm's performance, a behavior that is reinforced by the legal presumption that explicit contracts are legally binding. (This point is illustrated in the case of *Wakefield* v. *Telecom*[14].) In this case a salesperson, Wakefield, was employed on an explicitly at-will basis, but was also paid commissions for sales in his office. After several years of employment, he was dismissed just before he was to receive a commission payment from a significant sale. Northern Telecom did not pay this commission, arguing that the at-will nature of employment relieved it of this obligation. However, the court ruled that employment at will did not absolve the firm from its explicit obligation to pay a commission, and established the protection of explicit performance pay, highlighting the risk that a firm faces when using a poorly constructed contract.

In principle increasing the complexity of a contingent contract should enhance performance. However, not only does the complexity of the environment imply that a complete contract is impossible, it may also be the case that the contract provides incentive for an individual to discover *unanticipated* actions that are Pareto-inefficient but, under the terms of the explicit contract, are in the interests of the employee to implement. Section 4 discusses how subjective evaluations may be used to address this issue.

4   Judgment and subjective performance evaluation

An important insight of Simon's (1951) model is the idea that actions should be decided upon *after* the state of nature is revealed. Even when the determination of the appropriate action, given ω, is of low cost, the large number of potential states make such contingent planning impossible, a complexity that is dramatically reduced by delaying decision-making until after the state is revealed. The difficulty is that now we face the problem of the agent being held up. If he takes an appropriate, but costly, action how can he be sure that the principal will reward him appropriately?

Secondly, given that our maintained hypothesis is that there is no univariate measure of performance, in the absence of an *ex ante* agreement, how is the agent going to know what is appropriate performance, and how is the principal going to judge such performance? As Prendergast (1999) observes, in many cases both the principal and agent engage in subjective evaluations based upon *human* capabilities that cannot be replicated by any mechanical system. For example, the owner of a restaurant judges the performance of a chef by tasting the food. At the moment there is no known device that can automate such a process. When deciding upon whether to accept a paper for publication in a journal, once the referee has decided that the results are correct, the final decision turns upon the notoriously vague criteria of "importance" or "contribution to the literature."

In these examples, evaluation depends upon the *superior* performance of human versus mechanical evaluations of performance. From the cognitive science literature we know that humans have remarkable pattern recognition abilities that we are only just beginning to understand and model. The formal link of incentives to pattern recognition can be modeled with the introduction of a judgment function $\mathcal{J}(\omega, \mathbf{y})$. Formally this function is a *classifier* that divides the set $\Omega \times \mathbf{Y}$ into two sub-sets:

$$A = \{(\omega, \mathbf{y}) \in \Omega \times \mathbf{Y} \mid \mathcal{J}(\omega, \mathbf{y}) = 1\}, \quad \text{and} \tag{14}$$

$$U = \{(\omega, \mathbf{y}) \in \Omega \times \mathbf{Y} \mid \mathcal{J}(\omega, \mathbf{y}) = 0\}, \tag{15}$$

where A denotes "acceptable performance" and U denotes "unacceptable performance." When there is multitasking, then the state space Ω is very large, making a complete state-contingent contract impossible. Given that the classification problem simply involves dividing a space into two sets, then this seems an easier problem than writing a state-contingent contract. This is in fact not the case. Notice that any contract can be written as specifying whether or not performance has occurred in a state, and hence the complexity of a classifier is the same as the original contracting problem. Moreover, the seminal work of Minsky and Papert (1988) has proven that the identification of a classifier is a "hard" problem, a point that Anderlini and Felli (1994) have made explicitly in the context of contract formation.

While classification is a hard problem that challenges even the most sophisticated computing machines, research in cognitive science has found that the brain is specifically designed to be very good at pattern recognition (see for example Churchland and Sejnowski 1993). Though human classification is not perfect, it is the case that individuals can learn to be good at categorizing inputs. For the purposes of this chapter, the aspect of categorization I wish to emphasize is the ability to judge whether performance is acceptable or not (as opposed to providing a numerical measure of its quality). In the next sub-section it is shown that as long as the employer and employee have judgments that are correlated, then it is possible to construct contracts that are *not* explicitly state-contingent, yet nevertheless result in high performance.

4.1   Subjective contracting

Consider a situation for which a principal and an agent agree to a contract that requires the agent to formulate a response to a large number of events. When an event occurs, the agent is assumed to choose effort λ that determines the probability of good performance for that event. We do not explicitly model either the underlying state space, nor the set of possible actions. Rather, motivated by the previous discussion, it is assumed that both the principal and agent evaluate the response to the event, and decide whether or not performance is acceptable. Given that these evaluations are both non-contractible and that *ex post*, it is not possible to write a screening contract, this greatly constrains the set of possible performance contracts. In particular, it is shown that if judgment is not perfect, then the optimal contract necessarily entails the potential for conflict between the principal and agent.

More formally, suppose that the cost of effort $\lambda \in [0, 1]$ to the agent is $c(\lambda)$, where $c(0) = 0$ (cost of no effort is zero), $c', c'' > 0$ (more effort costs increase at an increasing rate) and $c'(\lambda) \to \infty$ as $\lambda \to 1$ (perfection is impossible). When success occurs, then a reward B^* is produced, otherwise there is no return. Hence the expected net surplus of the relationship for this reduced-form model is given by:

$$S(\lambda) = \lambda B^* - c(\lambda) \tag{16}$$

with the first-best level of effort, λ^{fb}, satisfying $B^* = c'(\lambda^{fb})$.

Let us assume that these parameters are commonly known, and that if success does not occur, then this is commonly known by both parties (this assumption can be relaxed at the cost of greatly complicating the analysis). Subjective evaluation is modeled by supposing that when success does occur, then the principal and agent may or may not agree upon this. In the event of objective success, let β_{ij}, i, $j \in \{A, U\}$, be the probability that the principal believes quality is i and the agent believes quality is j, where A and U denote "acceptable" and "unacceptable," respectively. Thus if the good outcome occurs, then β_{AA} is the probability that both principal and agent agree on this. It is assumed that the signals are positively correlated, that is $\beta_{AA}\beta_{UU} - \beta_{UA}\beta_{AU} > 0$. If the beliefs of the principal and the agent are perfectly correlated then $\beta_{AU} = \beta_{UA} = 0$.

Owing to the complexity of the relationship it is not possible to write a contract conditional upon the objective characteristics of output, nor can it be made binding upon the beliefs of the individuals. However the agents can agree to a contract that makes payments conditional upon messages sent by the principal and agent. Formally the contract between the principal and agent is given by:

$$c_{ij} = \{\pi_{ij}, w_{ij}\} \tag{17}$$

where π_{ij}, w_{ij} are the payments to the principal and agent under the contract as a function of the message i, $j \in \{A, U\}$, satisfying the constraint $\pi_{ij} + w_{ij} \leq 0$.[15] This constraint allows the total payments to be less than zero, a possibility that will prove to be crucial. The *ex post* hold-up problem has the following sequence of moves:

(1) The principal makes a take-it-or-leave-it contract offer to the agent, who accepts or rejects.
(2) An event $\omega \in \Omega$ occurs.
(3) The agent selects $\lambda \in [0, 1]$, which is his level of effort, in response to this event, to produce an observed response **y**.
(4) The principal and agent observe $\{\omega, \mathbf{y}\}$ and form subjective judgments regarding the success of the agent's action and simultaneously send messages from the set $\{A, U\}$ to the third party enforcing the contract.
(5) The payoffs are determined.

I assume that the principal is able to select the most efficient incentive-compatible contract. The payments under the contract to the principal and agent when they report k, but their true state is l are, respectively:

$$\pi(k \,|\, l) = (\pi_{kA}\beta_{lA} + \pi_{kU}\beta_{lU})/(\beta_{lA} + \beta_{lU}) \tag{18}$$

$$w(k \,|\, l) = (w_{Ak}\beta_{Al} + w_{Uk}\beta_{Ul})/(\beta_{Al} + \beta_{Ul}) \tag{19}$$

The principal's problem is to maximize expected payoff subject to the agent's individual rationality and incentive compatibility constraints:

$$\max_{\lambda, c} \lambda B^* + \lambda \pi(c) + (1 - \lambda)\pi_{UU} \tag{20}$$

subject to

$$\lambda w(c) + (1 - \lambda) w_{UU} - c(\lambda) = U^o \tag{21}$$

$$w(c) - w_{UU} = c'(\lambda) \tag{22}$$

$$\pi(l \mid l) \geq \pi(k \mid l), k, l \in \{A, U\} \tag{23}$$

$$w(l \mid l) \geq w(k|l), k, l \in \{A, U\} \tag{24}$$

$$\pi_{ij} + w_{ij} \leq 0, i, j \in \{A, U\} \tag{25}$$

where $\pi(c) = \sum_{i,j \in \{A,U\}} \pi_{ij} \beta_{ij}$ and $w(c) = \sum_{i,j \in \{A,U\}} w_{ij} \beta_{ij}$ are the expected transfers to the principal and agent, respectively, when the good outcome occurs. Constraint (21) requires the agent to earn at least his outside payoff, constraint (22) is the requirement that the agent select effort to maximize his payoff at stage 2. Constraints (23) and (24) are the stage 3 incentive compatibility constraints ensuring that the principal and agent truthfully report their subjective judgments to the third party enforcing the contract. The final constraint is the budget-balancing constraint for the contract.

Notice that if the contract is budget balancing, $\pi_{ij} + w_{ij} = 0$ for all $i, j \in \{A, U\}$, then the contract defines a constant-sum game at the message stage between the principal and agent. Such games have a unique value, and hence the payoff cannot depend upon subjective information. Thus in order that a subjective evaluation system induce positive effort on the part of the agent it is necessary that in some states there be a net loss to the relationship.[16] The next result provides a complete characterization of the optimal contract when we relax the budget breaking requirement.

Proposition 4 *Suppose that $\beta_{AA}\beta_{UU} - \beta_{AU}\beta_{UA} > 0$ then optimal contract with subjective performance evaluation has the form in table 13.2 where*
- *The optimal effort λ^* solves $c'(\lambda^*) = B^* - \frac{\beta_{UA}}{\beta_{AA}}(\lambda^* c''(\lambda^*) + c'(\lambda^*))$, where $\beta_{A*} = \beta_{AA} + \beta_{AU}$ is the probability that the principal believes performance is acceptable.*
- *The bonus satisfies: $b^* = c'(\lambda^*)/\beta_{A*}$.*

Table 13.2. *Contract payoffs*

		Agent's report A	U
Principal's report	A	$(-b - w, b + w)$	$(-b - w, b + w)$
	U	$(-P - w, w)$	$(-w, w)$

- *The fixed wage satisfies:* $w = U^o + c(\lambda^*) - \lambda^* c'(\lambda^*)$.
- *The penalty satisfies* $P = c'(\lambda^*)/\beta_A$.

The proof of this proposition is in MacLeod (2002). The optimal contract has the property that the agent's payment is independent of his report, and hence he has no incentive to misrepresent his self-evaluation. The principal provides the agent with effort incentives by paying him a bonus whenever she believes that he has provided acceptable performance. Given that we expect subjective evaluation to be used when explicit contracts are more expensive, then this implies that the incidence of bonus pay should be greater in jobs of greater complexity, an implication that has some empirical support, as shown by Brown (1990) and MacLeod and Parent (1999).

If the principal reports unacceptable performance when the agent reports acceptable, then she must pay a penalty P. It is the prospect of paying a penalty when the reports from the agent and principal differ that provides the appropriate incentives for truthful revelation by the principal. When correlation is imperfect and $\beta_{UA} > 0$, there is a positive probability that the principal will pay the penalty. Given that the size of the penalty depends upon the size of the bonus promised, the lack of correlation increases the marginal cost of providing incentives. This is reflected in the term

$$\frac{\beta_{UA}}{\beta_{AA}} (\lambda^* c''(\lambda^*) + c'(\lambda^*))$$

the amount by which the marginal benefit from effort is reduced in the optimal contract. Thus if the probability of the principal having an unacceptable evaluation while the agent has an acceptable self-evaluation is zero we obtain the first best. This result shows that the optimal contract is structured so that the principal's evaluation determines whether or not the agent receives a bonus, while the role of the agent's evaluation is to provide the necessary incentives for the principal to be truthful.

MacLeod (2002) extends this result to the case of risk averse agents and multiple signals of performance. In that case, the optimal contract with subjective evaluation entails a compression of the rewards to performance, relative to the optimal contract with objective measures of performance. The pooling is more extreme as the correlative between the principal's and agent's evaluations decreases. In the extreme case of no correlation in beliefs, Levin (1998) in the case of a risk neutral agent, and MacLeod (2002) in the case of risk aversion, have shown that the optimal contract pools all evaluations into two levels, acceptable or not.

4.2   *Relational contracts*

Goetz and Scott (1981) define a *relational contract* as one for which "parties are incapable of reducing important terms of the arrangement to well-defined obligations," a case that includes the problem of contracting with subjective evaluation studied here. They argue informally, as I do formally above, that such contracts arise when the number of contingencies is so large that it is not possible to write a complete contingent contract, creating problems for the interpretation and enforcement of contract terms and conditions.[17] This definition of a relational contract is not, however, universally accepted. The term originates with Macneil (1974), for whom the term refers to the complex set of behaviors and norms characteristic of individuals engaging in long term commercial transactions.

Following Axelrod (1981), the prisoner's dilemma problem is often viewed as capturing the essence of relational contracts. In this game two individuals simultaneously decide whether to cooperate or not each period. The model can capture the essence of the contracting with subjective evaluation when beliefs are perfectly correlated. In that case, the strategy cooperate can correspond to truthfully reporting one's evaluation. In these models it is typically assumed that budget balancing is imposed, and hence directly imposing a cost P is *not* possible. Since the principal has an incentive to report low performance if a bonus payment is required, then the only equilibrium in the one-shot game is to not pay the bonus, and hence the agent would choose low effort.

Equilibria with high levels of effort are constructed using a *self-enforcing contract*, modeled formally as a repeated game (see Bull 1987 and MacLeod and Malcomson 1989). The agent agrees to work hard, and in return the principal agrees to paying a bonus if the agent works hard. The relationship is terminated should either person renege. MacLeod and Malcomson (1989) provide necessary and sufficient conditions for the existence of a high-effort equilibrium in such a contract: it must be the case that the value of the relationship is strictly greater than the value of their next best alternatives by an amount exactly corresponding to the value of the penalty P derived above.

This result, in common with much of the literature on repeated games, takes the game form as given and then analyzes the set of possible equilibria.[18] These equilibria all share a common feature, namely in any given period there are a number of possible equilibria that can be played. Performance incentives are generated by a *norm of behavior* (equilibrium play) in which agents agree to move to an equilibrium specifying a lower payoff to any agent that cheats in the pervious period. The maximum punishment that can be inflicted upon an individual will therefore depend upon the structure of the constituent one-stage game. This approach creates a complex relationship between the structure of the game and the set of possible equilibria. (See in particular Kandori and Matsushima 1998 and Levin 1998.)

To better understand the role of cognition and contract incompleteness for the structure of the optimal contract, I have instead assumed that contracting parties have unlimited punishment ability. The result above illustrates a number of features of relational contracts that appear to be consistent with observed practice. The first is that the potential for conflict and disagreement that can generate a cost P, is a necessary ingredient of any productive relationship when subject evaluations are used and beliefs are not perfectly correlated. Given that organizational conflict is a ubiquitous phenomenon, this result is in some sense heartening because it implies that observed behavior is consistent with this theory! Moreover, as management consultants emphasize, such conflicts can be reduced when individuals have shared values, and there is general consensus that the system of evaluation is fair.[19]

Conflict is not the only mechanism that can generate such a cost. When disagreement results in the termination of a relationship, costs can also arise due to unemployment (Shapiro and Stiglitz 1984) or the loss of relationship-specific investments (Becker 1975 and Williamson, Wachter and Harris 1975). Other market mechanisms include reputation effects (Kreps *et al.* 1982 and Bull 1987), tournaments (Carmichael 1983 and Malcomson 1984), wages attached to jobs (MacLeod and Malcomson 1988), social networks (Kandori 1992 and Kranton 1996) and gifts (Carmichael and MacLeod 1997). In addition, the value of a relationship can be affected by the use of explicit pay for performance contracts, that can affect the set of self-enforcing agreements, as explored in Baker, Gibbons and Murphy (1994) and Pearce and Stacchetti (1998).

The common feature of these labor market institutions is that they can be seen as market responses to the problem of contract incompleteness arising from the use of subjective evaluation, which in turn is used to induce high performance in the case of *ex post* hold-up. This is a distinctively different problem from the standard hold-up model, whose implications for the theory of the firm have been explored in the work of Baker, Gibbons and Murphy (1997) and Bolton and Rajan (2000). One suspects that ultimately a complete theory of the firm will entail an integration of the problems of *ex ante* and *ex post* hold-up.

5 Discussion

Contract incompleteness is a ubiquitous phenomenon, yet the welfare theorems of economics require complete markets and contracts to ensure the existence of an efficient equilibrium.[20] Hence, a complete understanding of the efficiency of observed economic institutions depends upon understanding both why contracts are incomplete, and the extent to which such incompleteness generates inefficiencies. The traditional answer to this question follows from the research of Herbert Simon and Oliver Williamson, who argue that complexity and bounded rationality are the central ingredients of a complete theory. Yet, as Hart (1990) has argued, complexity considerations do not play an important role in the determination of the optimal contract for the hold-up model, a situation that corresponds to non-contractible investment decisions being made before resolution of uncertainty.

Moreover, there is a growing literature that demonstrates that in many situations contracting parties *choose* to write incomplete contracts. When there are costs for including contract terms, Shavell (1984) argues that in the case of low-probability events it is cheaper to let courts fill in the gaps. While Dye (1985) explicitly derives the optimal risk-sharing contact in this case, work that has been extended to dynamic contract formation by Battigalli and Maggi (2000). The example in section 3 illustrates that costly contingent contracting is a reasonable hypothesis when performance is multidimensional. In contrast, Ayres and Gertner (1989) and Bebchuk and Shavell (1991) show that the presence of asymmetric information may lead individuals to choose incomplete contracts, even when transaction costs for including additional terms are zero. Bernheim and Whinston (1998) demonstrate that strategic ambiguity can result in a similar effect.

In contrast, in the case of the hold-up model, renegotiation can introduce inefficiency, as emphasized by Hart and Moore (1999a). For example, Che and Hausch (1999) show that renegotiation in a hold-up model with cooperative investments may result in an optimal contract that is incomplete, but not first best. Segal (1999) shows that one obtains a similar result when the good being traded is complex in the sense that one cannot describe the good *ex ante*, while Schweizer (2000) derives necessary and sufficient conditions for efficient allocation to be implementable in a hold-up model with renegotiation. When renegotiation is not possible, Maskin and Tirole (1999a) have shown that one can achieve an efficient allocation even when the good is not describable *ex ante*.[21]

These conflicting results suggest not that incomplete contracts are unimportant, but that the term itself is possibly too encompassing of the different problems that arise from contract design. Rather, the main point of the chapter is to suggest that the extent to which complexity affects the form and efficiency of a contract is very sensitive to the timing of uncertainty and decision making in a relationship. The problem of *ex post* hold-up follows naturally from Simon's model of the employment relationship, and refers to situations for which it is not possible for an agent to renegotiate her contract between the time she learns the parameters of her decision problem and the time at which an action must be taken. The complexity of the environment makes a complete contingent contract impossible, and hence performance incentives depend upon *ex post* evaluation and reward by the principal.

My second point is that the focus upon *human* cognitive limitations is misplaced. In the case of *ex post* hold-up I have argued that the contracting problem is complex in an absolute sense. That is, complete contracts are physically infeasible, and thus not dependent upon constraints imposed by (very real) human cognitive limitations. In contrast, I suggest that the use of subjective evaluation is a way to harness the superior pattern recognition abilities that humans possess. The quality of the contract in this case is an increasing function of the correlation between evaluations of the principal and agent.

Finally, I have suggested that the hazard of *ex post* hold-up, or what the legal scholars refer to as the problem of relational contracting, can provide an economic explanation for a number of observed features of the employment relationship. These include the importance of corporate culture to ensure employees have a shared set of values,[22] the use of rank-order tournaments, bonus pay rather than explicit pay for performance, up-front gifts during recruiting in the form of dinners etc. Though in the end when appropriate incentives for employer performance do not exist, it may simply be optimal to lose one's temper when the boss gives you an unfair evaluation![23]

NOTES

Chapter 13 was originally published as "Complexity and Contract," in *Revue d'Economie Industrielle* (92, 2000).

I very much appreciate the comments of the referees, Tom Lyon, Eric Rasmusen, Sherwin Rosen, Eric Tally, and Oliver Williamson on this work, as well as seminar participants at the University of California Davis, Stockholm School of Economics, University of Oslo, University of Bergen, and the Yale Law School. I am also grateful to Mehdi Farsi for able research assistance. The financial support of National Science Foundation grant SBR-9709333 is gratefully acknowledged.

1. A. Denning, *The Discipline of Law* (1979, p. 56). As quoted in Farnsworth (1990, p. 543).
2. In particular the discussion in section 2.1 of Williamson (1975).
3. See chapter 1.
4. A point that is well appreciated in the computer science literature. See for example Garey and Johnson (1979). Williamson (1975, p. 23) makes a similar point in reference to the game of chess.
5. For example, decoding an encrypted message is a *computable* problem that it can be achieved in finite time. However, such messages are believed to be secure because the time required is sufficiently long as to be impracticable.
6. See Churchland and Sejnowski (1993) for an excellent introduction to these issues.
7. This was shown in a wonderful paper by Newell, Shaw and Simon (1963).
8. For simplicity, I follow Hart and Moore (1999a) and Maskin and Tirole (1999a) and assume that the principal has all the bargaining power in any *ex post* negotiation. This assumption can be dropped, but at the cost of unnecessarily complicating the argument.
9. A similar equation is derived by Baker (1992) who works out the optimal contract when the contractible variable is not perfectly aligned with benefits.
10. In personal correspondence relating his discussions with Ben Klein and Earl Thompson, Alchian (1998) observes that many Hollywood contracts for shows were exactly of this form. An actor or producer on a long-term contract could entertain outside offers. However, if the studio matched the offer, the individual had an obligation to stay with his or her studio. Alchian argues informally that the right of first refusal serves the purpose of providing incentives for efficient specific investment.
11. See Dekel, Lipman and Rustichini (2001) for an interesting axiomatic approach to modeling decision-making in complex environments.
12. See Churchland and Sejnowski (1993) for a good review of computational neuroscience exploring the algorithmic foundations of human decision-making.
13. See Irrgang (1972, p. 13).
14. *Wakefield* v. *Telecom*, 769 F. 2d 109 (20 Cir.), 1985.
15. From the Revelation Principle (e.g. Myerson 1979) we know that without loss of generality we can identify the message space with the information that is private to each individual.
16. This is a recurrent theme in the theory of incentives. See Green and Laffort (1979) for a discussion of the early Literature and Moore (1992) regarding the implications of implementation theory for contract formation.
17. See Schwartz (1992b) and Scott (2000) for discussions of relational contracts that argue against too much court intervention.
18. See Abreu's (1988) seminal contribution characterizing the set of equilibria in a repeated game, and the survey of cooperation and repeated game theory by Pearce (1992).
19. See Milkovich and Newman (1996, chapter 10).
20. See Magill and Quinzii (1996) for a comprehensive review of general equilibrium theory with incomplete markets.

21. Though Maskin and Tirole (1999a) also show that one can relax the renegotiation constraint with risk averse agents and the introduction of lotteries *ex post*.
22. See Hermalin (1999) for a review of this literature.
23. On the role of emotions and contracts see Hirshleifer (1987), Frank (1988), and Posner (1997).

14 Authority, as flexibility, is at the core of labor contracts

Olivier Favereau and Bernard Walliser

1 Introduction

From an external point of view, the treatment of labor contracts by modern microeconomic theory reveals an exceptional uneasiness. Either they are entirely unspecific, similar to sales contracts for a commodity (except that the commodity consists now of a service, rather than a good *stricto sensu*): this is the road followed by general equilibrium theory (see Debreu 1959, §2.4; for more subtle details, see Arrow and Hahn 1971, pp. 75–6); or they show some specific features, which makes them instances of more general types of contracts: insurance contracts (see Rosen 1985) or principal–agent relationships (see Salanié 1994). Indeed lawyers from any country in the industrial world (see Supiot 1994, part II) could only be surprised by the apparent reluctance of economic theory to deal straightforwardly with the essential property of labor contracts: the compliance of the salaried worker with his employer's authority (i.e. the acknowledged right of giving orders), in exchange for a predetermined wage, independent for the main part of the final proceeds.

Now the surprise is reinforced, not alleviated, by the fact that there is one – exactly one – such model of labor contract, in the economic literature: the one built by Simon (1951). Of course, some economists were aware that an authority relationship should lie at the heart of the contractual link between employer and employee (for an early mention, see Coase 1937). But it was not until 1951 that the first mathematical model of authority relationship was devised by Simon, drawing on the work of Barnard (1938), an expert in management and not an academic. What is even more surprising is that this pathbreaking paper had, to the best of our knowledge, no offspring at all: although quoted from time to time (Arrow 1974; Williamson 1975; Kreps 1990, 1996; Marsden 1999), it never gave rise to a new strand of literature, in spite of its appeal to realism. So there is a kind of a puzzle, also from an internal point of view: economic theory is most of the time silent about the defining feature of labor contracts and when at last a model appears to deal with that feature, it makes no use of it. It rather follows the opposite path, by stressing the autonomous behavior of the agent, with respect to the principal!

This chapter tries to offer a partial and tentative answer to the simple question: why is it so? Our thesis is that the true analytical structure of Simon's labor contract model has not yet been brought to light. We establish that, in order to prove the efficiency of employment contracts relative to sales contracts, Simon implicitly used the very framework Henry was going to use explicitly in 1974 (almost a quarter of a century later!) in order to measure the "option value," which ought to be integrated to the benefits of flexible decisions versus irreversible ones. Such an unexpected connection makes it clear, for the first time, that authority is at the heart of employment relationship because flexibility is at the heart of authority. We think this could give stronger foundations for a new way of devising models of labor contracts, more in touch with direct observations.

In section 2, we recall the results of decision theory in the context of irreversible actions and improving information, by means of a pedagogical model. In section 3, we show, through the same kind of model, that Simon's comparison between sales and employment contracts is simultaneously a prefiguration and an extension of these results; in the concluding section 4, we suggest some possible lines of research, beyond Simon's model.

2   Decision, irreversibility, and information

A two-period individual decision model combining considerations of flexibility of investment and acquisition of information was introduced by several authors (Arrow and Fisher 1974; Henry 1974) and later on nicely formalized (Jones and Ostroy 1984). In the first period, an available action is more or less flexible (or reversible) with regard to the actions it permits for the second period; more precisely, a given action is more flexible than another if the set of actions it allows for the future contains the set permitted by the other. Between the two periods, the uncertainty on the actions' results is reduced by additional information, either exogenous or conditioned by the first-period action; more precisely, a given message is more informative than another if the belief structure it induces on the states of nature is less dispersed. Since a flexible action is more able to take into account that information than an irreversible one, it can be shown that the former is preferable to some extent; a more informative message makes a more flexible action better under various sets of sufficient conditions.

For instance, a highway may be constructed in a reversible way (option a_1), i.e. first constructed with 2×2 lanes and further on widened

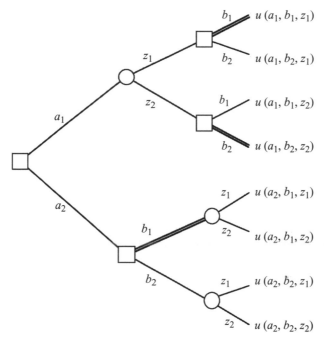

Figure 14.1   Highway construction

to 2×3 lanes (action b_1) or not (action b_2) according to the traffic observed, heavy (state z_1) or light (state z_2), after partial realization. It may also be constructed in an irreversible way (option a_2), i.e. immediately and definitely either with 2×3 lanes (action b_1) or with 2×2 lanes (action b_2), traffic being observed afterwards (states z_1 and z_2 of probabilities p_1 and p_2) (figure 14.1).

The utility of the decision-maker, aggregating the consumer surplus (related only to traffic) and the investment cost (related to option and action), obeys the following properties:

(1) Constructing 2×2 lanes always induces the same costs:

$$u(a_2, b_2, z_1) - u(a_1, b_2, z_1) = 0$$
$$u(a_2, b_2, z_2) - u(a_1, b_2, z_2) = 0$$

(2) Constructing 2×3 lanes immediately is less costly than widening from 2×2 lanes:

$$\mu = u(a_2, b_1, z_1) - u(a_1, b_1, z_1)$$
$$= u(a_2, b_1, z_2) - u(a_1, b_1, z_2) > 0$$

(3) For the reversible option, 2×3 lanes is better than 2×2 lanes with heavy traffic and reciprocally with light traffic:

$$\lambda_1 = u(a_1, b_1, z_1) - u(a_1, b_2, z_1) > 0$$
$$\lambda_2 = u(a_1, b_2, z_2) - u(a_1, b_1, z_2) > 0$$

(4) For the irreversible option, 2×3 lanes is better in expectation (only for convenience):

$$u(a_2, b_1) = p_1 u(a_2, b_1, z_1) + p_2 u(a_2, b_1, z_2)$$
$$u(a_2, b_2) = p_1 u(a_2, b_2, z_1) + p_2 u(a_2, b_2, z_2)$$
$$u(a_2, b_1) - u(a_2, b_2) = p_1(\lambda_1 + \mu) + p_2(-\lambda_2 + \mu)$$
$$= p_1 \lambda_1 - p_2 \lambda_2 + \mu > 0$$

By using "rightly" (to be explained below) the backward induction procedure (leading to the double-lined chosen actions on the tree in figure 14.1), the expected utility of each option can be computed:

$$u(a_1) = p_1 u(a_1, b_1, z_1) + p_2 u(a_1, b_2, z_2)$$
$$u(a_2) = p_1 u(a_2, b_1, z_1) + p_2 u(a_2, b_1, z_2)$$

The difference between both options can be written as:

$$\Delta = u(a_1) - u(a_2) = p_1(-\mu) + p_2(\lambda_2 - \mu)$$
$$= p_2 \lambda_2 - \mu$$

The rational decision-maker, maximizing his intertemporal utility, will choose the flexible (irreversible) option if Δ is positive (negative). Nevertheless, that is not the end of the story for the economist, even if it is for the (rational) *homo oeconomicus*. The recourse to backward induction has a deep analytical meaning, which was not correctly perceived before Henry as well as Arrow and Fisher (independently) in 1974 revisited the confusing notion of "option value" introduced ten years earlier by Weisbrod (see Favereau 1989). Backward induction allows to put to the fore a property of flexible decisions, hidden under a straightforward translation of expected utility criterion to intertemporal choices, as in the ususal definition of Net Present Value (see Hirshleifer 1970; Hey 1983; Kreps 1988; Dixit and Pindyck 1994). That property is the ability of flexible decisions to fully exploit forthcoming information: for instance, in the decision tree associated to our model (figure 14.1), the decision maker does not know today whether the traffic will be z_1 or z_2, but he knows today that he will know it tomorrow. So if he selects the flexible option today, he is sure to select the best action tomorrow: then backward induction enables him, at the last choice node, to compute the expected value of a "max," rather than the "max" of an expected value. That makes a difference, which Henry as well as Arrow and Fisher showed to be positive, under very general conditions, and which has an undisputable right to be called an "option value," since it is a supplementary benefit of flexibility.

Let us compute the "option value" in our model. Using the straightforward expected utility criterion is equivalent to reverse state ($\bigcirc$) and actions ($\square$) for the first option on the tree. The expected utilities of three plans of action have to be calculated, in order to choose between the two options:

$$u'(a_1, b_1) = p_1 u(a_1, b_1, z_1) + p_2 u(a_1, b_1, z_2)$$
$$u'(a_1, b_2) = p_1 u(a_1, b_2, z_1) + p_2 u(a_1, b_2, z_2)$$
$$u'(a_2) = p_1 u(a_2, b_1, z_1) + p_2 u(a_2, b_1, z_2)$$

The difference between both options (usually called "option price") according to the straightforward criterion of expected utility, can be written as:

$$\Delta' = u'(a_1) - u'(a_2) = \max_i u'(a_1, b_i) - u'(a_2)$$
$$= \max(-\mu, -\mu + p_2\lambda_2 - p_1\lambda_1)$$
$$= -\mu + \max(0, p_2\lambda_2 - p_1\lambda_1)$$

The "option value" v is then defined by the difference between the two preceding comparative results:

$$v = \Delta - \Delta' = u(a_1) - u'(a_1) = u(a_1) - \max_i u'(a_1, b_i)$$
$$= \min(p_1\lambda_1, p_2\lambda_2) > 0$$

The important (and highly intuitive) result is that v is always positive (but of course that is not true of either Δ or Δ' which may be positive or negative): keeping the opportunity of a flexible action is appreciated in the first period when further information is expected before the second; in fact, it could be shown that v corresponds to the "value of information" relative to the (certain) message received as a by-product of the implementation of the reversible action (Ponssard 1975; Freixas and Laffont 1984; Conrad, 1980). Last but not least, the reader should take notice of the formal (or paradoxical) nature of that concept of "option value" (see Favereau 1989): the decision-maker has not really to compute the option value; he is interested only in the difference Δ (which is the sum of the option price and the option value).

3   Contract, irreversibility, and information

We suggested, in the introduction to the chapter, that "a situation in which it may be advantageous to postpone a decision in order to gain from information obtained subsequently" was examined by Simon (1951) in a context of choice between two forms of contracts, relating a worker and a businessman. In an "employment contract," the worker gets a given wage from the employer, but accepts his authority to choose a task later on from a predetermined set, according to further information the boss will obtain exogenously about the uncertain result of the task. In a "sales contract," the worker's task is defined in advance and cannot be changed after it is accepted, but his wage depends on the specific task and is probably lower on average than before.

Simon's model is very similar to the general framework defined above (the first contract being reversible and the second irreversible), *except that the results of the decision-making process are evaluated by two players instead of one*. For instance, the employment contract (option a_1) and the sales contract (option a_2) may be compared for two tasks (actions b_1 and b_2) and two states of nature (states z_1 and z_2). The outcomes are evaluated by two utility functions, for the employer and worker, respectively, where each combines linearly the wage (depending on the contract and eventually the task) and the value attached to the realized task (depending on the task and the state, but not the contract) (figure 14.2).

Contrary to his later and definitive opposition to utility maximization, Simon concludes that the agents select the best actions by a (backward induction) maximizing procedure; in fact, he argued later (1978) that utility maximization is not necessary to support his conclusions, but less restrictive assumptions on agents' behavior are only suggested and not justified. More precisely, Simon states that in the second period of the employment contract, a task is chosen according to the employer's point of view while, in the first period, both types of contracts are compared from a collective point of view summarized by a collective utility function: $U = k_2 F_1(b, z) - k_1 F_2(b, z)$. It can be shown (more easily than he does) that all Pareto-outcomes may be generated with the task b maximizing the collective function. The wage w (assumed here not to depend on b) is variable (just constrained to give a positive utility to both players) and plays the role of a lateral transfer determining the distribution of individual utilities:

$$
\left|
\begin{aligned}
&\max_{b,w} u_1 = F_1(b, z) - k_1 w \\[4pt]
&u_2 = -F_2(b, z) + k_2 w \geq \underline{u_2} \\
&u_1 \geq 0, u_2 \geq 0
\end{aligned}
\right.
\quad \Leftrightarrow \quad
\left|
\begin{aligned}
&\max_{b} U = k_2 F_1(b, z) - k_1 F_2(b, z) \\[4pt]
&w \text{ s.t } u_1 \geq 0, u_2 \geq 0
\end{aligned}
\right.
$$

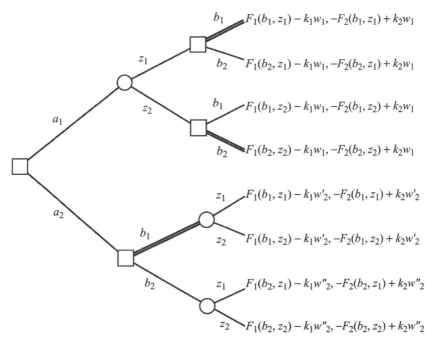

Figure 14.2 Simon's model

The further assumptions made by Simon on both utility functions are very similar to the assumptions made for the highway problem on the unique utility function:

(1) holds for each component F_1 and F_2, hence by combination for the collective function, but not for each individual one (if $w_2'' \neq w_1$)

(2) holds with $\mu = 0$ for each component F_1 and F_2, hence for the collective function, but not for each individual one (if $w_2' \neq w_1$)

(3) is stated only for component F_1, hence for the employer's utility function (since the wage is the same)

(4) is stated for the collective utility function U.

If the first- and second-period actions were both considered from the employer's point of view as far as utility is concerned, the employment contract would always be better. In that case, $\Delta = p_2\lambda_2$ is always positive because when z_1 happens, both options are equivalent and when z_2 happens, option a_1 is better than a_2. However, since Simon combines the employer's and the collective points of view, the sales contract may be collectively better if the worker has a strong enough preference for the first task. In that case, one computes:

$$\Delta = p_2[k_2(F_1(b_2, z_2) - F_1(b_1, z_2)) - k_1(F_2(b_2, z_2) - F_2(b_1, z_2))]$$
$$= p_1[k_2(F_1(b_2, z_1) - F_1(b_1, z_1)) - k_1(F_2(b_2, z_1) - F_2(b_1, z_1))] - v$$

In the first expression of Δ, the first difference is always positive and the second is of any sign. It expresses the fact that the employment and the sales contract lead to the action b_1 if z_1 happens, but to actions b_2 and b_1 respectively if z_2 happens, hence, a_1 is better than a_2 if for z_2, b_2 is collectively better than b_1. Moreover, if one puts $p_2 = 0$ in the first expression and $p_1 = 0$ in the second, the sales contract turns out to be better than the employment contract under certainty. Finally, the difference Δ (which is the only one calculated by Simon) is equal to the option value v since the option price is zero (according to assumption (ii) and (iv), $\Delta' = 0$). Hence, Simon implicitly used an option value, and moreover, in a non-formal way, since the option value had to be effectively computed in order to choose between the two contracts.

In that framework, Simon demonstrated two important theorems about the theory of contracts: a qualitative one and a quantitative one. First, should there be no uncertainty at all, the sales contract would always be optimal; in a world of certainty, there is no room left for a labor contract as an authority relationship. Second, considering a continuum of states of nature like Jones and Ostroy, the greater the degree of uncertainty (appropriately formalized through what is known as a mean-preserving spread; see Rothschild and Stiglitz 1970), the greater the advantage of the (reversible) employment contract over the (irreversible) sales contract.

The second result can be illustrated in our example, by considering in our model the following case for F_1 (F_2 being unchanged – and even a constant function for Simon):

$$F_1(b_1, z_1) = F_1(b_1, z_2) = \gamma$$
$$F_1(b_2, z_1) = (1 - \alpha)F_1(b_1, z_1) \qquad \alpha > 0$$
$$F_1(b_2, z_2) = (1 + \beta)F_1(b_1, z_2) \qquad \beta > 0$$

with $\alpha/\beta = p_1/p_2$

When γ is fixed (i.e. we arbitrarily choose the task b_1 as the benchmark) and α and β are increasing, we have a mean-preserving spread since the expected value of $F_1(b_2, .)$ is constant, and its variance growing, while $F_1(b_1, .)$ is unchanged. The first difference in the first expression of the option value can be directly computed (the second being unchanged): $\Delta_1 = p_2 k_2 \beta \gamma$. Hence, when β increases, the option value increases too, which enhances the possibility for Δ being positive, i.e. for the case where the employment contract becomes optimal. The reader will note the asymmetry in the increasing risk: the growth of β meaning a downward move in the expectation of the businessman (with respect to the consequences of an inappropriate selection of the task b_1, via a sales contract), our version of Simon's model replicates the "bad news principle" of Bernanke (1983; see also Dixit and Pindyck 1994, pp. 40–1).

4   Conclusion

When compared to the papers of Henry (1974), Arrow and Fisher (1974), and others, on irreversibility and uncertainty, which adopt the point of view of a single decision-maker and put irreversibility (and flexibility, as a consequence) as some material properties of an investment choice, Simon's contribution derives its originality from the deep collective meaning of his problem concerning the available actions as well as the pursued objectives. In the papers by Henry, Arrow and Fisher or later on Bernanke (1983), and Dixit and Pindyck (1994), the option value originates in technical/environmental features of a decision an individual has to take: for instance the adaptability of a piece of equipment (see Stigler 1939, for an early analysis of that kind of flexibility) or, more plainly, the opportunity of delaying the decision (as emphasized by the analysis of "real options": see Amran and Kulatilaka (1999)). Moreover, the option value is evaluated only by that single agent. In Simon's work, *it originates in a social construction shaped by two agents*, which enlarges the scope of individual sets of options (actually only the employer's set of options, but that could be easily generalized by taking into account the renewal of the employment contract), and is evaluated through a collective utility function.

Simon's contribution is also original by suggesting another argument in the long standing debate around the relative merits of markets and organizations, considered as combinations of different forms of contracts. Most current models relate the advantages of organizations to a few factors: negotiation and transaction costs, information costs and asymmetry of information, externalities and non-convexities, bounded rationality. Simon suggests a new argument by considering that organizations, in contexts of uncertainty, are a means for keeping a large set of possibilities open, and in that sense, appear as more flexible than the market!

More precisely, the employment contract, i.e. the admission into an internal labor market with its authority relationship and its binding rules, reveals much more flexibility than the so-called sales contract, with its typical "take-it-or-leave-it" structure. At first glance, it may seem surprising that Simon makes the institutional efficiency of organizations (rather than markets) rest on "flexibility", since markets are usually praised as a symbol of flexibility, in our deregulating times. There should be no surprise for an economist paying attention to micro-foundations: flexibility ought to be defined with respect to actions, not to prices. The ultimate strength of Simon's approach to coordination may be to give economic meaning to the classical distinction, in social philosophy, between "constitutive rules" which create new forms of behavior (e.g. the rules of chess) and "regulative rules" which regulate antecedently given forms of behavior (e.g. the Highway Code) (Rawls 1955; Searle, 1969, 1999); whereas the "regulative" approach to flexibility means simply alleviating constraints on existing opportunity sets, the "constitutive" approach – exemplified by Simon – means creating intertemporal devices for enlarging opportunity sets.

It was objected to Simon's work (Williamson 1975) that the terms of the truce were not fair, one kind of contract being flexible and the other quite rigid *ex definitione*. The objection is correct but it should be appropriately understood, when translated into a new program of research, beyond the great leap forward prompted by Simon as early as 1951. One obviously needs a truly dynamic framework, in which the two-period situation of his model would be repeated several times (on an undeterminate horizon) as well as a richer menu of contracts. But true dynamics should not be investigated where it could not be found. Without any doubt, it would be extremely fruitful to reconsider the growing stock of contract models with renegotiation, through the spectacles of "option values" (see Chaserant 2000, for a promising view of renegotiation along these lines). Nevertheless, the important point made by Simon would not be affected: flexibility of the employment contract does not come from any renegotiation of the contract, it comes from its very application.

Indeed the strongest piece of criticism of Simon's model has a paradoxical flavour: if it probably overstates rigidity of spot contracts, it also underscores flexibility of employment contracts. Real-world labor contracts are mostly incomplete, whereas contracts studied here rely on an exhaustive description of the tasks (for the worker) and the market risks (for the employer). If anything, the incompleteness of employment contracts will increase its potential for flexibility, by making it possible for both agents to develop individual and collective learning. So the main weakness of Simon's model of labor contract is the absence of learning and this is probably due to the absence of bounded rationality . . .

NOTE

Chapter 14 was originally published as "La subordination, en tant qu'elle est source de flexibilité, est l'essence du contrat de travail," in *Revue d'Economie Industrielle* (92, 2000).

We thank X. Freixas and C. Henry for their comments on a preliminary version of the chapter. We are also grateful for the critical remarks of three anonymous referees. Of course, we claim full responsibility for any remaining errors.

15   Positive agency theory: place and contributions

Gérard Charreaux

1   Introduction

One of the most-quoted articles of economic literature, by specialists in organizational economics or in management sciences – in particular, researchers in finance – is that of Jensen and Meckling (1976). This article provided the foundations of the positive agency theory (hereafter PAT), the influence of which extended considerably beyond finance. From the beginning, it was a part of an ambitious project (Jensen and Meckling 1998) initiated at the University of Rochester, at the beginning of the 1970s: to build a theory of organizational behavior based on the actors' rationality assumption, in particular of managers. This theory, originally founded on the property-rights theory and on the agency relationship concept borrowed from the principal–agent approach, is aimed towards a theory of coordination and control applied to organization management and centered on managers. It applies, in particular, to organizational architecture and corporate governance.

As Jensen and Meckling specified (1998, p. 8), their goal was to build a theory of organizations: "Our objective is to develop a theory of organizations that provides a clear understanding of how organizational rules of the game affect a manager's ability to resolve problems, increase productivity, and achieve his or her objective."

Since their first writings (in particular, Jensen and Meckling 1976; Jensen 1983), the founders of this theoretical current had clearly taken care to mark their difference in comparison to the principal agent theory, as much from the point of view of their objectives as of the methodological approach used. However, it appears that the specificity of PAT often remains ill-perceived. It is either regarded as a non-formalized alternative of the principal–agent theory, or it appears as a component of the contractual theories, which is less generally applied compared to that of the transaction-costs theory (hereafter TCT). These two interpretations are both, if not erroneous, at least simplifying; they are explained, in particular, by the methodological differences separating these various currents as well as by the fact that a major part of the work, based on PAT, was published in accounting and financial reviews, relatively marginal in the field of organizational economics, such as the *Journal of Financial Economics* or the *Journal of Accounting and Economics*. This origin, which was deeply marked by finance because of the relative isolation of the paradigms and disciplinary fields, led to the support of certain misunderstandings, even a certain ignorance of the central PAT characteristics or its many contributions, that are, however, important for organization and management sciences.

This chapter has three objectives. First of all, it points out the central components of PAT. Second, it aims at rectifying the reading of this theory, comparative to TCT,[1] proposed by Williamson (1988a). Third, it tries to show the variety of questions tackled by PAT in fields as diverse as finance, accounting, management control, human resources management, and corporate governance. The first concern of the founders of PAT was to offer an analysis framework to managers enabling them to understand the impact of organizational structure on performance and to guide their actions and decisions. The reading[2] thus suggested particularly attempts to show the continuity and the originality of the project of the Business School of the University of Rochester,[3] as much in its operational concerns, and its sources of inspiration, as in the methodology that it supports.

2   The principal components of PAT

To highlight the original place of PAT,[4] it is necessary to quickly reconsider its main ingredients and its principal theoretical message, in other words, the modeling of organizational architecture and the distribution of the economic activities that it proposes. Let us clarify that if PAT has evolved, its essential components are already present, to various degrees, in the seminal articles of Jensen and Meckling (1976), of Jensen (1983), and of Fama and Jensen (1983a, 1983b).

2.1   *The building blocks of the theory*

Jensen positions PAT as an "integrated" theory of organizations, directed at joining together two distinct research currents: the research into economic tradition centered on market operations, and those associated with the fields of psychology, sociology, organizational behavior, anthropology, and biology, directed at explaining human behavior, as much on the individual level as on the social one. Thus, Jensen's research group includes a personality like Argyris, well known for his work in organizational learning. PAT is thus conceived to be purposely integrative: it must allow for simultaneous embracing of organizational and market phenomena. In this sense, as well as in its multifield basis, it is close to the TCT, which moreover originally constituted one of its sources of inspiration.

PAT, according to the presentation made by Jensen (1998), includes four fundamental building blocks: a model of human behavior, the costs related to the transfer of knowledge, the agency costs, and the organizational rules of the game (figure 15.1).

Block 1: The model of human behavior

The article that Jensen and Meckling (1994) devoted to "the nature of man" includes an accurate presentation of the Resourceful, Evaluative, Maximizing Model (REMM).[5] This model falls under the paradigm of rational approaches of organizations. It is based on four assumptions:

- Individuals are concerned with all that is a source of *utility or disutility* and are "evaluators." They are in a position to trade off between the various sources of utility and their preferences are transitive.
- Individuals are *insatiable*.
- Individuals are *maximizers*. They maximize a utility function, the arguments of which are not exclusively financial, while under constraints. The constraints may be cognitive and the choices made take into account the acquisition costs of knowledge and information.
- Individuals are *creative and know how to adapt*; they are in a position to foresee the changes of their environment, evaluate the consequences, and respond by creating new opportunities that they are able to evaluate.

The design of rationality within PAT is close to that of Williamson, in other words, of bounded type, while remaining "calculative" under cognitive constraints. The rational expectations hypothesis used to build the model for optimal financial structure contained in Jensen and Meckling (1976), which implies a less bounded rationality, seems to have been adopted only by a concern for simplifying the analysis. It cannot be regarded as representative of REMM.

This rationality is socially "located." The social norms represent constraints and govern the actions; according to Jensen and Meckling (1994) "They serve as an external device that aids in the storage of knowledge about optimal behavior. In addition, they represent a major force for teaching, learning, disciplining, and rewarding members of a group, organization or society." They are supposed to evolve according to the changes in the environment and to those of knowledge, transforming individuals' theories, and influencing their actions by modifying all opportunities, costs, and gains associated with the actions. If the aspects related to social embedding are reflected in the individual's actions, they,

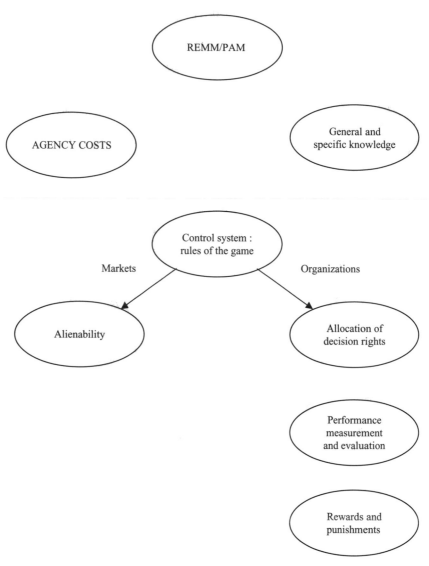

Figure 15.1   The building blocks of PAT
source: (Jensen, 1998, p. 3)

however do not dictate them. The status of the norms and institutions is
similar to that they hold in TCT: it is a matter of parameters. However,
like TCT, the theory does not allow an explanation (contrary to North's,
1990, institutional theory) of the institutional changes. The norms are
supposed to evolve when they impose costs that are too high in the new

environment, but the mechanism controlling their development process is not studied.

The possibility for the individual to be creative and to adapt gives the theory an implicitly dynamic character. The recognition of the adaptive character of behaviors allows us to take into account the active neutralizing behavior of certain mechanisms, central, for example, in the manager's entrenchment strategies, as well as, for that matter, the positive role that the latter may play in building all of the opportunities.

More recently, Jensen (1994) proposed an extension to REMM by adding the Pain Avoidance Model (PAM). Its goal is to explain, on the one hand, that in certain cases individuals acted, with defensive concern, in an irrational manner (from a consequentialist point of view) by making decisions that are apparently (for a neutral observer) contrary to their welfare and on the other hand, the limited character of the individual's learning capacity, in other words, of the adaptive behavior in view of the mistakes made. The individual would avoid changing their mental (or perceptual) model because of the resulting psychological costs ("the pain"). This dualistic model of human behavior would find its origin in the lessons from cognitive sciences and behavior. Let us specify that it may be possible, according to us, to avoid this problematic dualism from the methodological point of view. All that is necessary is the interpretation of the PAM model as an extension of the REMM model, (in a "calculative" sense), by invoking the high costs (in psychological terms) for individuals, related to the change of their perceptive models by learning.

Block 2: The costs of transferring knowledge between actors
Although Jensen uses the terms information and knowledge indifferently, knowledge is at the center of PAT that attributes it a determinant role in the constitution of the organizational performance. Efficiency basically depends on the capacity of the organization members to use the "relevant" knowledge, valuable in decision-making. The distinction, established by Hayek, between "general knowledge" and "specific knowledge," plays a central role. The solution to the organizational problem consists of finding the least expensive means to put the relevant knowledge at the disposal of the decision-makers. This availability, consisting of colocalizing decision rights and specific knowledge, can be achieved in two ways: (1) either, in a centralized manner, by transferring knowledge to those holding the decision rights; (2) or, in a decentralized manner, by transferring the decision rights to those having the knowledge. The choice depends on the respective costs of transferring knowledge and the decision rights. However, because of the importance of the non-transferable specific knowledge, the centralized solutions most often fail. The alignment of decision rights and

the localization of knowledge goes beyond the traditional centralization/ decentralization debate, insofar as specific knowledge is distributed on the whole hierarchy. The true question relates to the nature of decision rights to be centralized or decentralized.

Block 3: Agency costs

The decentralized allocation of decision rights creates agency relationships, sources of conflicts of interest, and of agency costs. The organizational must be conceived so as to reduce these costs creative of inefficiency, by implementing incentive and control systems intended to align the interests of the agents with those of the principal(s).

In PAT, the representation of the agency relationship – that would qualify more precisely as a "cooperation relationship" – evolves according to the analyzed problem. Beyond the traditional principal–agent asymmetrical relationship, for example between shareholders and managers, the relationship in certain models becomes bilateral or "dyadic" where the two parties can alternatively be regarded as principal or agent. Overall, the general formulation of the organizational problem in terms of efficiency and the representation of the organization as "a nexus of contracts," or rather a "contracting nexus," leads to the ability of going beyond these restrictive representations to locate the problem of the reduction of agency costs at the level of the simultaneous management of all the relationships between actors that can overlap and be interdependent. The same organizational mechanism, for example the board of directors, can be used to simultaneously manage conflicts of interests between shareholders and managers, but also between creditors and shareholders or between shareholders and employees.

Block 4: Alienability and the organizational rules of the game

The decision rights refer to the use of assets, of resources. They are, in fact, property rights, that Jensen and Meckling (1992) break up into two components: the actual decision right (the right to use the firm's assets) and that of alienating this decision right and appropriating the product of the transfer ("alienability" of the right).

Alienability is the basis for the existence of the market system, interpreted as a system of transferable rights. On a market, the colocalization of knowledge and decision is carried out by way of a transaction directed by prices, by the alienation of the decision right associated with a voluntary exchange. The decision rights are acquired by those who attribute the greatest value to them; they are agents who are in a position to use them for the best, because of the specific knowledge they hold. In the absence of externalities to the exchange, the colocalization by the market is efficient; it is not necessary to introduce a control mechanism. Only alienability solves the control problem by way of price, simultaneously representing a measurement of performance and an incentive system. On the other hand, the absence of alienability leads to the reappearance of the control problem.

For the intra-firm transactions, the transfer of decision rights does not accompany that of alienability. This leads to two consequences: (1) effective colocalization is no longer carried out in an automatic and decentralized manner; (2) an automatic system no longer exists for performance and incentive measurement, leading agents to use their decision rights in the interest of the organization. In this case, it is necessary to turn to a hierarchical authority to solve this problem as well as to various organizational mechanisms. Organization is explained only when the handicaps related to the absence of alienability are compensated by certain amount of advantages: for example, economies of scope and scale, reductions in transaction costs that cannot be obtained by independent agents, but also the "cognitive" argument put forth by Demsetz (1988): the firms allow us "to economize knowledge," in particular, because of the long-term character of the employment relationship.

2.2   *A theory of the organizational structure and distribution of the organizational forms*

The construction of PAT, based on optimal use of specific knowledge, results in the suggestion of two complementary application fields: (1) the internal field of organizational architecture and (2) the external field relating to the distribution of the organizational forms.

2.2.1   *Organizational architecture*
The argument presented results in the proposition of a theory of organizational architecture founded on the allocation of decision rights within the organizations. This allocation, which does not rest on the voluntary exchange of rights between actors, is carried out by way of an organizational policy. The rights are distributed by the managers and respect is assured by the incentive and control systems put in place taking into account the institutional environment. The distribution results from the arbitration between the costs related to the misuse of specific knowledge (insufficient decentralization of decisions) and those associated with the conflicts of interest (owing to decentralization). The distribution, incentive, and control systems constitute the "organizational rules of the game."

The theory of organizational structure is thus articulated around two dimensions constituting the base of the "taxonomy" central to PAT:

- *Allocation of decision rights within the organization*; this allocation may involve a distribution of decision rights between the decision management rights, which include the rights to initiate and implement the allocation of resources, and decision control rights that concern ratification and the monitoring of decisions.

This distribution of rights corresponds to the decision-making process in organizations as modeled by Fama and Jensen (1983b, p. 303), in four steps: initiative, ratification, implementation, monitoring (performance measurement of the agents, rewards, and punishments). The initiative and implementation functions, most often entrusted to the same category of agents, are regrouped to form the function of "decision management." Those of ratification and monitoring are associated in the definition of the "function of control" (decision control).

- *The design of the control systems*, while distinguishing:
  - the evaluation and performance measurement system
  - the incentive system, which allows us to specify the relationship between the performance measurement and its consequences in terms of rewards and punishments; it is the coherence and the complementarity between these two (or three) dimensions that is supposed to determine the level of organizational efficiency.

2.2.2   Distribution of organizational forms

PAT also allows us to understand the distribution of organizational forms. Fama and Jensen (1983a, 1983b) propose an explanation of the various organizational forms that relies on the central role of specific knowledge and the minimization of agency costs. Their argument comes from an analysis of the contracts considered as central in any organization, which are the contracts that specify, on the one hand, the nature of the "residual claims" and, on the other hand, the allocation of the steps of the decision-making process between agents. This results in establishing predictions for the distribution of the economic activity according to ownership structure, characterized by the distribution of residual claims that govern the bearing of risk.

By associating the concept of organizational complexity with that of dispersion of specific knowledge and by studying the efficiency of the various functional configurations (decision, control, and risk-bearing), Fama and Jensen (1983a, p. 304) construct two fundamental hypotheses:

- The separation of residual risk-bearing functions from decision management leads to decision systems characterized by a separation of the management and decision control functions
- The combination of the functions of management and decision control in the hands of a limited number of agents results in a concentration of residual claims with these same agents.

Fama and Jensen find a confirmation of their theory in the fact that almost all the organizations, characterized by a separation of the functions of decision management and risk-bearing, present the same structures of decision and control.

3   PAT compared with TCT: a second reading of Williamson (1988a)

While there is frequent opposition to contractual theories, of which the central argument is efficiency and the evolutionary theories in which cognitive aspects play an essential role, PAT, that bases efficiency on optimal use of knowledge, occupies in a certain way an intermediate position. This specificity of PAT implies, in particular, that it should not be confused with the TCT.

Many features attributed to PAT, as well as the distinctions contrasting it with the TCT, are often the outcome, because of Williamson's notoriety, of the comparison he carried out, in "Corporate Finance and Corporate Governance" (1988a). This comparison constitutes a useful starting point in understanding the origin of certain misunderstandings concerning PAT as well as its true nature. Even if PAT and TCT have evolved since then, the main foundations of the two theories had already been explicitly stated in 1988 – in particular, the role of specific knowledge and the presentation of the main arguments making PAT a theory of organizational architecture, and distribution of the organizational forms occupying a central place in the articles of Jensen (1983) and of Fama and Jensen (1983a, 1983b) quoted in the references of Williamson's article. The developments borrowed from subsequent articles on PAT only allow for reinforcement of the argument presented. The final objective of this second reading of Williamson's article, however, is not to make an exhaustive comparative assessment of the two theories, but to propose an analysis of PAT different from that of Williamson.

3.1   The common points: a critical discussion

Williamson identifies two principal common points: the *managerial discretion framework* and the *contractual efficiency*.

3.1.1   The first common point: the managerial discretion framework
The framework of managerial discretion regroups the conception of the nature of the firm and that of the man (bounded rationality, opportunism and risk neutrality).

Concerning the nature of the firm, in both theoretical bodies, according to Williamson, there is a rejection of the neoclassical conception of the firm as a function of production. In TCT, the firm appears as being of a particular governance structure, including a coordination directed by hierarchy as opposed to spontaneous coordination associated with the market. As for PAT, it would rest on the conception of a nexus of contracts that would also constitute an acceptable representation in the TCT.

These conclusions need to be moderated. There is not necessarily a contradiction between the representations of the firm as a nexus of contracts and as a function of production. Thus, Jensen and Meckling (1979) explicitly represent the firm as an enlarged function of production taking into account the organizational choices (the rules of the internal game) among the factors of production and conditioned by the institutional framework, when, simultaneously, they resort to the nexus of contracts metaphor. Should we see an inconsistency? The nexus of contracts concept means nothing other than that manager contracts in a centralized manner in the name of the firm with all the stakeholders, the partners who supply production factors or customers. Therefore, it is not contradictory to claim on the one hand, that the manager optimizes the production for others by taking into account the internal rules of the game as a production factor and in an institutional context and, on the other hand, that the nexus of contracts management is carried out so as to minimize agency costs by choosing an adapted organizational architecture. The first approach applies to "external" analyses directed towards the comparison of organizational forms, the second to "internal" analyses focused on organizational architecture.

The TCT approach, based on the firm as a mode of governance founded only on hierarchy, appears different from the representation that implies contract and production management within PAT. In the latter, the nexus of contracts does not necessarily imply an exclusive recourse to a mode of directed coordination. The only requirement is that the coordination be carried out so as to ensure the best use of the specific knowledge: therefore the firm can certainly use directed coordination, but it can also rely on spontaneous coordination (that does not compare to the simplistic outline of the price mechanism) or on concerted coordination. This plurality of coordination modes within the firm is, in particular, retained by Demsetz (1988, 1995), an author who greatly inspired Jensen and Meckling (1992). Moreover, it is useless to insist on the fact that the representation of the firm compared to the directed coordination is not easily compatible with the argument based on the optimal use of specific knowledge.

The conception of the nature of the firm seems rather different in the two theories. Reduced to the status of a particular mode of governance (directed coordination) in the TCT, the firm constitutes a complex system in PAT, the arrangement of which must allow for the best use of specific knowledge. The frequent references made to Demsetz may even lead to a conclusion that Jensen and Meckling (1992) would not reject the definition that he gives of the firms: "repositories of specialized knowledge and of the specialized inputs required to put this knowledge to work" (Demsetz 1988, p. 171).

Let us consider now the conception of the nature of the man retained in the two theories. The conception of rationality that the TCT implies is a "calculative" bounded rationality, allowing for a long-term view. It is of a consequentialist nature and not procedural. The presentation of the rationality models associated with PAT (a dualistic model: REMM and PAM) shows, at least for the REMM model, a very similar conception. The individuals evaluate, maximize (under cognitive and institutional constraints), are creative, and adapt; in particular they create new sets of opportunities to respond to environmental evolution. The insistence on the adaptive character, and more recently on the learning phenomena (by way of PAM, in particular), leads, however, to the conclusion that PAT will now retain a "broader" and more organic conception of rationality.

The opportunism hypothesis is often quoted as being central to the TCT. In fact, it does not imply that individuals are systematically opportunistic, but only that they may be. In PAT, opportunism does not have a particular role; its presence induces only an increase in agency costs. On the other hand, its absence does not induce the elimination of conflicts of interest. The fact that individuals have unequal access to information or have different cognitive models is enough to justify the existence of obstacles to cooperation and conflicts of interests.

Finally, according to Williamson, the risk neutrality hypothesis is not common to TCT and PAT, but to TCT and the principal–agent theory. In TCT, the justification of this hypothesis is of an instrumental nature; it allows us to focus the analysis on the most essential aspects of efficiency. PAT does not retain this hypothesis for it would lead to the inability to explain diversification behaviors. The risk aversion hypothesis, on the contrary, is retained; it allows for the explanation of the distribution of activities between the various organizational forms. In particular, it justifies the important role assigned to the risk-bearing function.

3.1.2   *The second common point: contractual efficiency*
Contractual efficiency ("efficient contracting") constitutes the second point common to PAT and TCT. The sources of efficiency would, according to Williamson, be within the capacity of organizational forms "to economize rationality" and to protect transactions against the risks from opportunism. He adds that PAT is concerned mainly about the

second aspect and pays almost exclusive attention to the contractual aspects *ex ante*. A reading, faithful to the spirit of PAT, focused on the central argument for the use of knowledge, leads to different conclusions. Concerning the sources of efficiency, the place attributed to the cognitive component in PAT leads, on the contrary, to the conclusion that both sources of efficiency are being considered. As for the exclusive attention paid to these aspects *ex ante*, it concerns only particular models, such as the financial structure model[6] proposed by Jensen and Meckling (1976), which rests on the rational expectations hypothesis and remains very close to the traditional models of the principal–agent theory. In the majority of PAT developments, this hypothesis is disappearing and the aspects *ex post* are being taken into account. Moreover, it is important to specify that in PAT, contrary to TCT, the conflict analysis is not carried out transaction by transaction, which is not very compatible with the representation of the firm in terms of a nexus of contracts. The management of conflicts is conceived globally, on the level of the considered organizational system, "the joint production team" (that is to say, all the cocontracting production factors), to employ the term used by Alchian and Demsetz (1972); it is this representation that constitutes the very foundation of PAT as a theory of organizational architecture.

3.2   The differences: a critical debate

If the common points identified by Williamson need to be moderated, his analysis of the differences also seems questionable. The main differences relate to the analysis unit, the distinction between agency and transaction costs, and the favored organizational dimension. To these three differences, he adds two others considered as secondary: the differences in *selection processes* and the *neutrality of the nexus of contracts*.

3.2.1   The main differences: the analysis unit, the nature of costs, and the central organizational dimension

Within TCT, the transaction is the basic unit of analysis. The study of organizational forms is done according to the transaction features. The explanation is based on the alignment of transactions/modes of governance in order to minimize transaction costs. The extent of the assets' specificity plays a central part. On the other hand, in PAT, according to Williamson, the central unit of analysis would be the individual, that would result in neglect of the transaction dimensions.

If the transaction is really the basic unit of TCT, the fact that it concentrates the attention should not mask the important role that actors preserve in this theory, based on methodological individualism. In fine, it is the actors who bear the costs and their analysis is done obviously from the point of view of the transaction participants. Let us recall furthermore that TCT gave rise to a certain number of criticisms, in particular, the imprecise character of the transaction concept and the central role attributed to the causal link between asset specificity and the choice of governance mode.

The status of PAT is rather similar to that of TCT. Although the theory also rests on methodological individualism, that does not imply that the individual is the basic unit of analysis. As in any modeling of organizational phenomena of this kind, the analysis on the individuals' level is of a relational nature and is located structurally within a system. Thus, in PAT, the basic unit is the agency relationship. If it sometimes takes the status of an asymmetrical relationship (shareholders with managers, for example), conversely in the most complex versions, the analysis relates to the whole of the nexus of contracts and organizational architecture. The representation of this agency relationship is contingent on the organizational phenomenon studied, which can be, according to the case, the board of directors, the total quality management (TQM)[7] or the financial structure (regarded as a particular organizational mechanism). For example, for the board of directors, the unit of analysis may be the agency relationship between shareholders and managers, but can be enlarged to become the nexus of relationships, shareholders/managers/employees/financial creditors/other stakeholders: the board of directors is therefore explained according to its capacity to minimize the agency costs on the whole nexus of relationships. In this approach, relationships between actors are overlapping; there is no single causality link, for example, between specificity and the mechanism of governance to be implemented. Thus, if the specificity of the manager's human capital implies that the board of directors may be interpreted as a mode of governance allowing for its preservation, PAT extends this kind of reasoning while claiming that the manager decides on his investment effort in specific human capital according to the nature of controls he submits to and, in particular, of his own capacity to control the board. The optimal solution, finally, depends in this context on the capacity to best use the manager's specific (present and future) knowledge.

The second difference referred to relates to the nature of costs: agency costs against transaction costs. Relying on the categories of agency costs (monitoring costs, bonding costs,[8] residual losses) identified by Jensen and Meckling (1976), Williamson concludes, regarding the only model of financial structure, that the agency costs are exclusively *ex ante*, and therefore restrictive. He then emphasizes that transaction costs also cover the costs *ex post* that, for him, play the most important role. This reading is also debatable because, as already mentioned, the hypothesis of rational expectation set out by Jensen and Meckling in their financial model has only one instrumental character specific to this model.

In addition, in the case of its restrictive character it takes the side of the concept of transaction cost rather than that of agency cost, because of the generality of the residual loss concept. From its very definition, the transaction cost is associated with a particular transaction (the basic unit). The same does not apply for the residual loss concept that constitutes the loss of value in regard to an ideal hypothetical situation associated with the absence of conflicts and an optimal use of specific knowledge. Thus, this concept is not dependent on one single transaction; it takes on significance only with regard to the organizational phenomenon, the subject of the research.

Finally, the third principal difference would relate to the favored organizational dimension. According to Williamson, because of the exclusive attention that PAT allegedly pays to the mechanisms *ex ante*, this theory would neglect the explanation of the organizational mechanisms as modes of conflict resolution *ex post*. Thus, PAT would not be concerned with internal organization, focusing only on the residual claims. Such a conclusion is wrong. On the one hand, agency costs *ex post* are not ignored by PAT and on the other hand, since its first developments, this theory was conceived to cover the internal organizational architecture and to simultaneously call on the external and internal governance mechanisms, relating to the market and organization.

3.2.2   *The secondary differences: the nature of the processes and the neutrality of the nexus of contracts*

According to Williamson, the modes of the natural selection process would differ between the two theoretical bodies. While the TCT, based on the remediability criterion, would be based on a "weak" form of the natural selection principle – only the more comparatively adapted, "the fitter," and not the most adapted (in the absolute sense of the fittest) would survive – it would be different in PAT. An attentive reading shows, however, that this difference seems to be illusory. Jensen and Meckling (1976, 1992), following the example of Williamson, are inspired by Coase and Demsetz. When Jensen (1983) evokes the concept of "the fittest," he does so in a context of constrained efficiency, in other words, relative to the existing organizational forms. He does not exclude the individual being creative, that more efficient organizational forms may appear.

As for the nature of the adjustment processes, even if the treatment offered by TCT may appear more thorough, one cannot conclude, as Williamson does, that the adjustments within PAT are all comparable to the market mechanism directed by prices. Since 1976, Jensen and Meckling invoked compensation, audit, and management control systems. More recently (Jensen and Meckling, 1992, p. 261), they wrote, in a very explicit manner, that the allocation and the implementation of decision rights in organizations depend on organizational policy, not on voluntary exchange[9] between actors. Within PAT, the adjustment mechanisms are based as much on hierarchy as on markets, or rather on the various forms of coordination (directed, concerted, spontaneous). Moreover, they must not be analyzed with regard to a single transaction, but relatively with the whole nexus of contracts, conceived as a complex equilibrium system.

The last difference would relate to the "neutrality" of the nexus of contracts, in the sense that all the contractual relationships are simultaneously determined, according to a complex balanced process. From Williamson's point of view, even if this hypothesis of neutrality is also shared by TCT, the structure of the latter would allow us, contrary to PAT, to take into account the strategic behaviors which can break up this neutrality, at least temporarily. For example, the manager, because of his central position, can broadcast information in a selective manner, profitable for him. Such a conclusion seems equally invalidated by the numerous developments of PAT, that explicitly takes into account the managers' entrenchment strategies to analyze the organizational mechanisms that adapt to assure a restoration of equilibrium.

3.3   A revised comparative assessment

The comparative assessment drawn up by Williamson thus seems to be a rectification. PAT is often presented in a restrictive manner, apparently because of a hasty comparison with certain models of the principal–agent theory or with the 1976 model of financial structure. In particular, the central role played by specific knowledge was not perceived by Williamson, the latter having placed, in his comparative table (1988, p. 575), a question mark in the heading "focal dimension" (translated as a fundamental variable of efficiency).

The revised comparative assessment may take the shape of table 15.1.

One may conclude from table 15.1 that PAT constitutes a more general and flexible analytical framework, in particular because of the following aspects:

- no central role is given to opportunism and asset specificity, which are only some dimensions among others in PAT
- adjustments are made at the level of the organizational system, the nexus of contracts, and not on the transaction level. PAT does not retain the

Table 15.1. *PAT versus TCT: a revised comparative assessment*

Common points	Dimensions	Differences	
		PAT	TCT
"Calculative" bounded rationality (more organic in PAT)	*Unit of analysis*	Agency relationship (with multiple representations)	Transaction
Principle of efficiency	*Focal dimension*	Specific knowledge	Asset specificity
Natural selection (remediability)	*Focal cost concern*	Residual loss (*ex ante* and *ex post* dimensions)	Maladaptation cost (more focused on *ex post*)
Organizational dimensions (internal and external)	*Contractual focus*	*Ex ante* and *ex post* governance using various mechanisms	Mainly *ex post* governance

direct causality link that is retained by TCT between the characteristics of the transaction and the mode of governance. Adjustments are made by displacement of the complex organizational equilibrium that aims for an assurance of optimal use of knowledge while minimizing agency costs.

4   Contributions and influence of positive agency theory

The central place that the manager occupies in PAT predestined this theory to play a determinant role in the development of management sciences. Reading the scientific journals, often considered as being among "the best" in their respective fields – for example, the *Journal of Financial Economics*, the *Journal of Accounting and Economics*, or the *Journal of Strategic Management* – allows us to grasp the extent of the influence of this theory on management sciences. If PAT initially appeared as a theory of finance, it quickly extended beyond the financial field to propose new analyses in accounting, management control, human resources management, manufacturing, or marketing management. Some works, for example, that of Watts and Zimmerman (1986) in accounting, revolutionized research in their field. In addition, PAT is at the origin of new theoretical fields such as "corporate governance." The corporate governance theory[10] permitted, in particular, a renewal or prolongation of the analyses regarding the comparison of the performance of economic systems (for example, the traditional debate opposing public to private companies) and the various organizational forms (companies, mutuals, cooperatives . . .).

Accompanied at times by TCT in which some features can be easily integrated, PAT became one of the main "grammars" used in management sciences. In particular, it allowed the establishment, if not restoring of, links between disciplinary fields, which had often evolved independently.

Rather than trying to do a survey of the multiple contributions of PAT to the various fields of management sciences, it seems preferable to examine the presentation made by Jensen and Meckling (1998, p. 17) of the four main axes constituting the PAT research program. This presentation will be complemented by that of another contribution of PAT, the enrichment of traditional methodologies through the use of clinical studies.

4.1   The four main axes of the PAT research program

- *The modeling of the nature of human behavior.* The objective is to build, in order to go beyond the existing models of REMM and PAM, a model of human behavior integrating the results of work from economists, psychologists, and neuroscience specialists in order to understand both rational (calculated) and non-rational behaviors. The goal is to undertake, on the level of the individual, the same effort as the one undertaken on the level of the organization, in other words, to burst the individual "black box" in order to better theorize human behavior.
- *The study of the promotion, compensation, and performance measurement systems.* In extension of the work of Baker, Jensen and Murphy (1988) and of Jensen and Murphy (1990), the goal of this axis is to provide a theory for the management of human resources that managers can rely on to design and implement systems allowing the best use of human resources within organizations, according to the argument that is implied by PAT, considered as a theory of organizational architecture. The theorization effort is also integrative, trying to take into account not only the teachings of labor economics and human resources management but also those of the human resources school in the field of behavioral sciences or the research in management control.
- *The study of the links between task structure, organizational boundaries, and nature of technology.* The goal is understanding how the overlapping systems, connecting organizations and markets, can allow us to benefit best from the opportunities offered by various technologies.[11] In other words, it is a matter of analyzing the relationships between the nature of technology and organizational architecture. This somewhat new axis

within the contractual perspective allows us to compensate for the gap frequently underlined in these theories, the neglect of manufacturing phenomena.

• *The study of the links between corporate governance systems, corporate finance, and organizational performance.* The objective of this is to understand how the relationships of the firm with its financial suppliers or, more generally, with all the stakeholders, influence the strategy, the processes of decision-making, and the creation and distribution of value.[12] This axis includes, in particular, work on corporate governance, focused on the organizational rules of the game, which constrain the top managers' decisions – for example, the board of directors. Work on corporate governance is in direct connection with corporate finance research, in particular that relating to financial and ownership structures.

Initially focused on an external vision of the organization, work of this last axis, in particular that realized in corporate finance, centered on valuation, tended to neglect internal aspects, but is nevertheless the most important to understand the creation of value. The current developments, by incorporating the lessons from research in organizational behavior, try to integrate the internal aspects of governance such as the formulation of strategy, the role of managers, or the distribution of decision rights within the hierarchy. These questions should permit an understanding as to how to make effective investment choices, a subject paradoxically neglected by financial research, as emphasized by Jensen (1993). Beyond investment decisions, the research topics also relate to restructurings or to the new forms of ownership structures, for example, leveraged buy-outs (LBOs) or employee stock ownership.

4.2   Methodological contribution of positive agency theory

Beyond the content of the research questions tackled, PAT built an original research methodology in the field of organizational economics, by developing the use of clinical studies as a legitimate research method. It is one of the aspects that separates PAT most significantly, on the one hand, from the principal–agent theory exclusively based on quantitative modeling and, on the other hand, from the traditional econometric approaches.

Jensen emphasized the limits of formal modeling approaches as much as econometric studies in order to understand organization behavior:

many important predictions of the research on positive organization theory and positive accounting theory will be characterizations of the contracting relations, and much of the best evidence on these propositions will be qualitative and institutional evidence ... By its nature, much of this institutional evidence cannot be summarized by measures using real numbers. (1983, p. 332)

Jensen also insisted on the nature of modeling in PAT (analytical but not mathematical) and on the central variables, very different from those of the principal–agent theory. Thus, the variables judged as important in the latter (preferences and information structures) are regarded as secondary in PAT, that favors the aspects relating to informational costs, institutional environment, or control systems.

This critical remark about the traditional tools of the competing theories resulted in the proposition, as an addition to the traditional approaches, of turning to clinical studies. As the editors of the *Journal of Financial Economics* (Jensen *et al.* 1989, p. 4) emphasized, clinical studies can direct the work of mathematical economists and econometricians towards more relevant theories by providing them with thorough analyses of the most important dimensions of real organizational phenomena. Many articles based on clinical studies were thus published in this journal. In July 1999, a conference was organized by Harvard Business School on the theme of the complementarity of the various methods of research in finance, insisting again on the contribution of clinical studies. This complementarity might, of course, be extended to other fields of management.

5   Conclusions

PAT occupies an original position, sometimes unrecognized, within organization theories; in particular, it should not be compared to the principal–agent theory or the TCT. If it remains positioned within the contractual paradigm, the central role that it attributes to specific knowledge, as well as the evolution of the rationality model on which it is based, tends to bring it closer, in particular in its most recent developments, to the evolutionary theory or strategic theories whose central focus is on resources or capabilities. It can thus, in some respects, be regarded as a first attempt at a compromise between the theories based on knowledge and those based on opportunism (Conner and Prahalad, 1996; Hodgson, 1998).

The current contributions are numerous and important. They strongly influenced the various fields of management sciences by renewing the analytical frameworks. The current developments of PAT lead, moreover, to a connection with the other traditional research paradigms in management, inspired in particular by the organizational learning, behaviorist, and managerial theories or certain streams of organizational sociology. Finally, the specific methodological orientations that it proposed, by recommending an important recourse to clinical studies, contributes to an emphasis of the influence on management sciences.

NOTES

Chapter 15 was originally published as "La théorie positive de l'agence: positionnement et apports," in *Revue d'Economie Industrielle* (92, 2000).
The author thanks the two referees for their comments and suggestions.

1. The differences between PAT and the principal–agent theory will not be specifically analyzed. These theories differ in particular in their underlying rationality models, in the basic variables of modeling, and in the methods used.
2. A more thorough analysis of PAT can be found in Charreaux (1999).
3. PAT was initially developed by Jensen and Meckling at the Business School of the University of Rochester where Meckling was the Dean. This theory could also in future be referred to as being of the Rochester–Harvard School, Jensen having left for Harvard University.
4. The texts which allow us to best account for the evolution and for the current state of PAT are, in addition to Jensen and Meckling (1998), Jensen (1998), and Brickley, Smith and Zimmerman (1997).
5. The first version of this article (Meckling 1976), written at the beginning of the 1970s, is contemporary with the 1976 article.
6. In fact, the majority of the interpretation errors seem attributable to an assimilation of TPA to this particular model that constitutes but one aspect of the 1976 article. This article furthermore contains more general developments of PAT which shows that this theory has a much more ambitious vocation.
7. For example, Wruck and Jensen (1994) developed a very innovative analysis of TQM.
8. Bonding costs are those associated with the mechanisms allowing the agent to reassure the principal on the credibility of his commitments, for example, the costs associated with a voluntary audit.
9. "The assignment and enforcement of decision rights in organizations are a matter of organizational policy and practice, not voluntary exchange among agents."
10. Detailed references, including the work realized in France, on the developments of PAT and, more particularly, on its applications to corporate governance, may be found in Charreaux (1997).
11. See, for example, Baldwin and Clark (1992).
12. See, for example, Jensen (1993) and Charreaux (1997).

Part V

Testing contract theories

16 Econometrics of contracts: an assessment of developments in the empirical literature on contracting

Scott E. Masten and Stéphane Saussier

1 Introduction

The growth in the analysis of inter-firm contractual relationships that has occurred in recent years is an indication of the importance economists associate with the issue of contracting and contract design. On the theoretical side, understanding how and why economic agents use contracts to coordinate their activities is crucial to understanding the organization and efficiency of economic exchange. For policy-makers, understanding the functions and implications of various contract terms is a prerequisite to distinguishing between efficient and anti-competitive practices and to developing appropriate policies with respect thereto.

Over time, two approaches have come to dominate the analysis of contracting: agency theory and transaction cost economics (TCE). Of the two, agency theory is widely regarded as having had the greater success developing formal models of contracting behavior.[1] But on the empirical side, the assessment is generally reversed. Compared to agency theory, TCE is seen as having been far more successful both at generating testable hypotheses and in explaining actual contracting practices.

In this chapter, we review the empirical research on contracting, with special emphasis on the relative contributions of agency and transaction-cost theories, first, in providing structural guidance to empirical researchers and, second, in identifying observable determinants of both the decision to contract and the design of contractual agreements. We begin in section 2 with a description of the underlying structure and specification of contracting and contract duration models, followed by assessments of, first, the contributions of agency and transaction-cost theories to the formulation of hypotheses about contracting decisions and, second, the evidence pertaining to those hypotheses. Section 3 extends the analysis from the decision *to contract* to the issue of contract design or, more precisely, to the relative success of agency theory and TCE in explaining the structure and content of contractual agreements. Section 4 comments briefly on the implications of empirical research on vertical integration for our understanding of contracting. Finally, in section 5, we provide an overall assessment of the literature's progress to date and discuss some remaining issues.

2 Why contract?

Agency and transaction-cost theories of contracting differ on the first and most basic question: why contract? Whereas the primary motives for contracting in the agency literature are risk transfer (insurance) and incentive alignment (see, generally, Hart and Holmström 1987), transaction-cost economists tend to view contracts more as devices for structuring *ex post* adjustments and for constraining wasteful (rent-dissipating) efforts to influence the distribution of gains from trade, including, especially, *ex post* bargaining and "hold-up" activities in transactions supported by relationship-specific investments (Williamson 1975, 1979; Klein, Crawford, and Alchian 1978) and *ex ante* sorting and search in contexts where additional information serves merely to redistribute rather than expand the available surplus (Barzel 1982; Kenney and Klein 1983; Goldberg 1985). Yet, despite these differences, the theories possess a common underlying structure. Before turning to the implications for empirical research of the differences in the theories, it will be useful to outline the basic decision structure that unites them.

2.1 Structure and estimation

2.1.1 The contracting decision
In its most general form, the decision to contract represents a standard discrete choice problem: Transactors will choose to contract if the expected gains (net of transaction costs) from doing so are greater than those of organizing the transaction in some other way, or formally,

$$G^* = G^C, \quad \text{if} \quad V^C > V^a, \quad \text{and}$$
$$= G^a, \quad \text{if} \quad V^C \leq V^a \tag{1}$$

where G^C represents contracting, G^a an alternative to contracting, V^C and V^a (the transactors' beliefs about) the corresponding values of the transaction under contracting and the alternative, and G^* represents the governance form actually chosen.

Because the returns transactors expect from governing their transactions in different ways are difficult, if not impossible, to observe, a testable theory of contracting requires that the theory relate the benefits and costs of alternative governance arrangements to observable features of the transaction.[2] To the previous arguments must thus be added relations of the form

$$V^C = V^C(X, e_c) \tag{2}$$

and

$$V^a = V^a(X, e_a) \tag{3}$$

where X represents a vector of observable attributes affecting the gains from trading under the relevant governance arrangements, and e_c and e_a are error terms that may reflect either variables omitted by the investigator or errors or misperceptions on the part of decision-makers about the true values of V^C and V^a.[3] If we assume, for practical reasons, that the preceding relations can be represented linearly as

$$V^C = \beta X + e_c \tag{2'}$$

and

$$V^a = \alpha X + e_a \tag{3'}$$

we can represent the probability that contracting will be chosen over the alternative governance form as $\Pr(G^* = G^C) = \Pr(V^C > V^a) = \Pr(e_a - e_c < (\beta - \alpha)X)$.[4] In words, an element of X whose effect on the expected gains from trade under contracting, β, is greater than its effect under the alternative arrangement, α, will increase the likelihood that contracting will be the observed form of governance. Theories of contracting inform the analysis by identifying which attributes empirical researchers should focus on and predicting the differential effects (i.e., $\beta - \alpha$) of those attributes on the value of transacting and, potentially, by providing guidance on the functional form of the $V(X, e)$s.

2.1.2 *Contract duration*

An alternative to the categorical formulation presented above is to treat the contracting decision as a question of contract duration: instead of choosing between contracting and not contracting, transactors could be viewed as choosing how many periods (if any) their contract should cover. The absence of a contract, under this formulation, would then correspond to the limiting case of contract duration equal to zero. Conversely, one could view the contract duration decision as a series of discrete choices, in which transactors decide, for each future period, whether or not to govern exchange by contract. Drawing on this correspondence, we could represent the continuous analog to the discrete choice decision represented by (1) as

$$\max_{\tau} V^C(\tau) + V^a(T - \tau),$$ (4)

where τ represents contract duration, T the potential (possibly infinite) duration of the relationship between the parties, $V^C(\tau)$ the cumulative value of contractual exchange over the τ periods covered by the contract, and $V^a(T - \tau)$ the value of trade in the periods following expiration of the contract. Optimal contract duration, τ^*, is the value of τ that satisfies the first-order condition

$$V_{\tau}^C(\tau^*) = V_{\tau}^a(\tau^*)$$ (5)

In words, the parties would continue to increase contract duration until the value of transacting under a contract for an additional period was just equal to the (forgone) value of transacting without a contract in that period.

As in the discrete choice case, our inability to observe the contracting parties' subjective expectations of V^C and V^a necessitates development of hypotheses that relate these values to observable attributes of transactions. Letting X and e again represent observable and unobservable factors, we can rewrite (5) as

$$V_{\tau}^C(\tau; X, e_c) = V_{\tau}^a(\tau; X, e_a)$$ (5')

Linearizing those functions as

$$V_{\tau}^C(\tau; X, e_c) = \beta_0 + \beta_1\tau + \beta_2 X + e_c$$ (6)

and

$$V_{\tau}^a(\tau; X, e_a) = \alpha_0 + \alpha_1\tau + \alpha_2 X + e_a$$ (7)

and substituting into (5') yields an expression for optimal contract duration, τ^*, of the form

$$\tau^* = \gamma_0 + \gamma_1 X + e$$ (8)

where

$$\gamma_0 = \frac{(\beta_0 - \alpha_0)}{\alpha_1 - \beta_1} \quad \text{and} \quad \gamma_1 = \frac{(\beta_2 - \alpha_2)}{\alpha_1 - \beta_1}$$

and $e = (e_c - e_a)/(\alpha_1 - \beta_1)$. For values of τ strictly between 0 and T, elements of X that increase the value of contracting for another period more than the forgone benefits of transacting without a contract in that period ($\beta_2 - \alpha_2 > 0$) will result in contracts of longer predicted duration. As in the discrete choice version of the model, the contribution of contract theories lies in identifying the attributes likely to affect the efficiency of contracting and its alternatives and in predicting the direction of their net effects.

Econometrically, (8) would seem to fit neatly the standard regression model. Two aspects of contract duration, however, necessitate departures from the standard model. One is duration's natural lower bound of zero, which affects how the distribution of the error term is parameterized. The second consideration is more peculiar to contracting. Because only contracts whose durations are at least as long as the difference between the sampling date and the contracting date "survive" long enough to appear in the sample – contracts written x years before the sampling date with durations greater than x years will appear in the sample but contracts with durations of less than x years will have expired and will not be represented – samples drawn from populations of contracts in existence at a point in time will tend to be over-represented by longer-term agreements. If the unobserved determinants of contract duration are correlated with the observed variables, ordinary least squares (OLS) estimates of the coefficients in (8) will be biased (see, e.g., Maddala 1983, pp. 166–7). Empirical research on contract duration has generally recognized this data censoring problem and has sought to account for the potential bias using maximum likelihood estimation techniques (see Crocker and Masten 1988 and Joskow 1987). A third issue, not addressed in the literature but relevant to studies of contract duration, is heteroskedasticity arising from the decreased precision with which contracting parties are likely to be able to assess the trade-offs from altering contract duration at more distant dates. In the data, this phenomenon is manifested in the tendency for contract duration to be more "finely tuned" for shorter-term agreements, which vary by intervals of days or months while the durations of longer-term contracts tend to cluster at discrete intervals of one, five, or ten years.

2.2 Predictions

2.2.1 Agency theory

Surprisingly, agency theory contains little explicit discussion either of the decision to contract or the choice of contract duration. Though seemingly a serious omission for a theory of contracting, the agency literature's inattention to those questions is consistent with the theory's inclusive use of the term *contract* to encompass any transaction (cf., for instance, Lyons 1996, p. 27). Under such a broad definition of contracting, it makes little sense to inquire whether contracting is desirable; the only question is what form the contract will take. Even where agency theorists nominally distinguish between explicit and implicit contracts, agency theory provides no reason for transactors *not* to make their agreements explicit: contracts deduced from agency axioms are complete, and therefore efficient, in the sense that (1) they specify each party's obligations for every possible contingency and (2) they yield the best possible outcome given the information available at the time the agreement is carried out and thus "never need to be revised or complemented" (see Holmström and Tirole, 1989, p. 68). Combined with the assumption that courts enforce verifiable provisions costlessly, issues of contracting and contract duration are effectively removed from consideration.

To generate testable implications for contracting or contract duration from agency theory, it is thus necessary to step outside the deductive agency framework by invoking contracting (transaction) costs (see Hart and Holmström 1987, pp. 131–3). Given some non-trivial impediment to contracting, we can extrapolate that factors that increase the benefits of contracting will increase the likelihood and duration of contractual agreements. Since in agency theory those benefits derive from the sharing of risk and alignment of incentives, the theory would predict contracting and contract duration to be positively related to the level of risk (or uncertainty) and to the importance of effort and information to payoffs.

2.2.2 Transaction-cost economics

In contrast with agency theory, the decision to contract and determinants of contract duration have been central concerns of the transaction-cost literature. First, transaction-cost economists, unlike agency theorists, tend to draw a clear distinction between contractual and non-contractual exchange, reserving the term *contract* for formal, legal commitments to which transactors give express approval and to which a particular body of law applies. By contracting, transactors expose themselves to potential third-party (judicial) sanctions for failing to honor their commitments and alter the procedures for resolving disputes and adapting to changing circumstances. In particular, whereas parties transacting without a contract are generally free to haggle, stall, or walk away as they please if dissatisfied with the terms of trade currently tendered, the law restricts the ability of contracting parties to extort concessions from their counterparts by unilaterally refusing to deal or threatening not to perform.

In terms of the models of section 2, the principal benefits of contracting, V^C, or, in the contract duration context, of contracting for an additional period, V_τ^C, in the transaction-cost framework are (1) the greater willingness of transactors to take actions whose value is conditional on the other party's performance, and (2) a reduction in the costs of (repeated) bargaining, while the costs of contracting (i.e. forgone benefits of not contracting), V^a, include (1) the costs of anticipating, devising optimal responses to, and specifying future contingencies (formation costs), and (2) the losses associated with efforts to enforce, evade, or force a renegotiation of the contract's terms and the "maladaptation" costs of failing to adjust to changing circumstances (execution costs). The benefits of contracting, according to the theory, increase with the value of relationship-specific investments, increasing the likelihood of contracting and the duration of contractual agreements. More complex or uncertain transactions, meanwhile, make performance specification and verification more difficult and increase the risk that the contract will impede desirable adjustments or induce costly evasion or renegotiation efforts, thereby discouraging transactors from entering formal, long-term agreements.

2.3   Evidence

2.3.1   Agency theory

We are unaware of any empirical studies of the decision to contract or of contract duration from an agency perspective. As we discuss below, however, where variables of interest in the theories overlap, evidence from transaction-cost studies offers little support for agency theory concerns.

2.3.2   Transaction-cost economics

At least two large-scale empirical studies of the choice between formal contracting and informal agreements using a transaction-cost perspective have been published. In the first, Allen and Lueck (1992b) examined the use of written versus oral leases for farmland. Farmers and landowners, they found, were more likely to adopt formal, written contracts for land requiring investment in and maintenance of irrigation systems (which are location-specific) while familial and other ongoing relations favored reliance on informal, oral agreements. In the second, a study of the contracting practices of UK engineering sub-contractors and their customers, Lyons (1994) found that the probability that firms adopted a formal contract was significantly higher the greater the share of the sub-contractor's output accounted for by the customer, the greater the percentage of that output specifically designed to that customer's requirements, and where production required significant investments in specific capital. The likelihood of a formal contract fell, on the other hand, where the subcontractor employed expensive, but flexible, equipment and where the firm produced an advanced technology product: the greater complexity and uncertainty likely to be associated with advanced technology products would tend to make contract specification and enforcement more difficult. The evidence is thus consistent with transaction-cost predictions regarding the benefits of contracting in the presence of relationship-specific investments and the liabilities of contracting in complex and uncertain environments.

The transaction-cost determinants of contract duration have also been the subject of several studies. An early and well-known example is Joskow's (1987) econometric analysis of the duration of approximately 300 contracts between coal mines and coal-fired electricity generators. Joskow's analysis exploited (1) regional differences in the characteristics of coal and transportation alternatives across the United States, (2) differences in the proximity of mines and power plants, and (3) variations in contract quantity to create proxies for the degrees of physical-asset specificity, site specificity, and dedicated assets. Joskow found the duration of coal contracts to be approximately eleven years greater in Western states, where coal is more heterogeneous, mines are larger, distances greater, and transportation alternatives fewer, than in the eastern United States, where coal tends to be more homogeneous, mines are smaller and more numerous, distances are shorter, and transportation alternatives abundant, with Midwestern coal contracts intermediate both in duration and characteristics. Longer still, by approximately twelve years, were contracts for coal supplied to power generators located at the mouth of a mine. Finally, contract duration increased by an additional thirteen years for each additional million tons of coal contracted for.

While Joskow's study provided evidence that contract duration varies with the benefits of contracting, Crocker and Masten's (1988) study of 245 natural gas contracts sought to assess variations in the costs as well as the benefits of contracting on the duration of contractual agreements. Like Joskow, Crocker and Masten found evidence of a positive relation between contract duration and appropriation hazards; contracts tended to be of shorter duration for wells in gas fields (1) served by larger numbers of producers and pipelines (reducing appropriation hazards) and (2) in which only a single producer operated, eliminating the risk of pipelines exploiting the common-pool drainage problem to extract price concessions. Crocker and Masten also found, however, (1) that natural gas contracts written during the period of greater uncertainty following the 1973 Arab oil embargo tended to be shorter (by an average of three years) than contracts written before the embargo, and (2) that misaligned incentive provisions (a byproduct of price regulation) reduced contract duration by an average of fourteen years. Finally, in addition to the study's substantive findings, Crocker and Masten developed a model of the contract duration decision that, though rudimentary, nevertheless yielded specific functional relationships for their estimations.

A pair of more recent studies by Saussier (1998, 1999) analyzing contracts for coal transportation in France also examined both the costs and benefits of contract duration.[5] Saussier found that the duration of these contracts was positively related to the value of investments in relationship-specific assets (as measured by the value of start-up investments and guaranteed contract quantities) and negatively related to the level of demand uncertainty over time. In addition, Saussier used two-stage least squares (2SLS) and a set of exogenous instruments to endogenize the level of specific investments, addressing a potential limitation of the earlier literature. He found his results to be largely robust to this refinement.

Finally, Bercovitz (1999) applied transaction-cost reasoning to analyze the duration of franchise contracts, an area of study otherwise dominated by agency-oriented research (see, generally, Lafontaine and Slade 2000). Consistent with the evidence from other contract duration studies, Bercovitz found that the duration of franchise agreements are significantly longer the larger franchisees' initial investments, which, she argues, are likely to be correlated with the franchisees' specific investment.[6] In addition, Bercovitz argues that the threat of non-renewal under shorter-term contracts allows franchisors greater ability to discipline opportunistic franchisees. Consistent with this, she found that franchise agreements tend to be of shorter duration in systems having the greatest potential for franchisee free-riding (as measured by the value of the system's brand name and the locational density of franchise outlets).

Although not specifically designed to test agency hypotheses, the results of several of these studies bear indirectly on the validity of predictions derived from agency concerns. Thus inasmuch as high-technology projects tend to be riskier than simpler procurements, Lyons' (1994) finding that engineering sub-contractors adopt formal contracts less frequently for projects characterized as high-tech conflicts with what would be expected if risk transfer was a primary motive for contracting. Crocker and Masten's (1988) and Saussier's (1998, 1999) findings that contracts tend to be of shorter duration in periods of higher uncertainty appear also to be inconsistent with the use of contracting as a mechanism to allocate risk.[7]

3   Contract design

3.1   Specification and estimation

The variety of possible contract designs is virtually unlimited: the structure of contractual agreements may vary with, among other things, the objectives of the contracting parties, underlying production relations, and the nature and size of informational and strategic impediments to contract formation and enforcement. As a consequence, theory provides no unifying structure for the specification and testing of contract design hypotheses.

At a practical level, contract provisions and their analysis, like the contracting decision itself, take both discrete and continuous forms. Contract terms such as price (Joskow 1988b); royalty rates and franchise fees (Lafontaine 1992; Bercovitz 1999); and take-or-pay provisions (Masten and Crocker 1985; Mulherin 1986) vary continuously, while other provisions such as price adjustment methods (Crocker and Masten 1991; Crocker and Reynolds 1993) and the assignment of authority or discretion often have a discrete, on-or-off character. In still other cases, researchers have chosen to treat contract terms as discrete choices empirically even though conceptually the "discrete" alternatives are actually the limit values of some continuous contract parameter. An example is the treatment of fixed and variable payment schedules as discrete alternatives (see Leffler and Rucker 1991, Allen and Lueck 1992a; and Masten and Snyder 1993) even though the "choices" represent corner solutions within a more general contract containing continuously varying fixed *and* variable components.[8]

The most common econometric issues to arise in the testing of contract design hypotheses consist of reasonably familiar simultaneity and endogeneity concerns and, for some continuously varying provisions, accommodations for limits on the range of the dependent variable. The only problem to arise so far that is even remotely peculiar to contracting concerns the systematic over-sampling of longer-term contracts discussed earlier, which could bias estimates of the coefficients in contract design regressions to the extent that the errors in contract duration and design equations are correlated. Empirical studies of contract terms that have recognized and made efforts to control for this potential bias include Joskow (1988b); Crocker and Masten (1991).

3.2   Predictions

3.2.1   Agency theory

Despite the profusion of agency theoretic models, neither complete nor incomplete contract theory (ICT) has produced much in the way of testable hypotheses. In the case of complete contract theory, the potential complexity of optimal incentive schemes and their "extreme sensitivity" to changes in information assumptions have prevented formulation of general hypotheses about contract form (Hart and Holmström 1987, pp. 80–1, 105). On the other hand, ICT, despite its name, is actually a theory of ownership rather than contracting that, by imposing severe restrictions on feasible contract forms, assumes in essence what a theory of contracting seeks to explain.[9]

Partly because of its relative tractability, the literature on linear sharing contracts has been more successful than complete and incomplete contract theories at generating predictions. The main prediction of that literature is that efficient sharing rules will balance incentives for one party against inefficient risk-bearing by that party or the incentives of trading partners; larger shares should tend to be assigned to the party with (1) lower aversion to risk and (2) higher marginal productivity of effort. More recently, the generalization of the linear agency model to multitask settings has augmented the list of agency predictions, most notably with the prediction that contracts should provide agents who perform multiple or multidimensional tasks, some aspects of which are difficult to measure, with low-powered incentives (Holmström and Milgrom 1991).

3.2.2 *Transaction-cost economics*

Transaction-cost economists acknowledge the role of contract terms in aligning marginal incentives but see an additional function of contract design in preventing wasteful efforts to redistribute existing surpluses. In contrast to moral hazard, which represents a deviation from joint surplus maximizing behavior within the terms of an extant contract, this second form of opportunism includes efforts to evade performance or to force a renegotiation of a contract's terms by imposing costs on one's trading partner. Because the incentive to engage in such efforts is likely to be related to the *ex post* distribution of contractual surpluses – parties greatly disadvantaged by the terms of a contract are more likely to want to evade or renegotiate a previous deal – contracting parties will seek to design contracts to divide *ex post* rents "equitably" (Masten 1988), keep the relationship within the agreement's "self-enforcing range" (Klein 1992), or, equivalently, achieve what Oliver Williamson has called "hazard equilibration" (1985, p. 34) (see, in addition, Goldberg 1985 and Goldberg and Erickson 1987). The more uncertain the environment and the harder it is to accommodate changing circumstances within the contract, the more likely it will be that parties will sacrifice the precision and ease of implementation of definite contract terms for more cumbersome but flexible "relational" contract terms that define performance obligations less precisely or establish procedures for negotiating adjustments in the terms of trade within the contract.

3.3   Evidence

3.3.1   Agency theory

In addition to its failure to generate testable hypotheses, complete contract theory has been criticized, by agency theorists themselves, for failing to account for even the most basic features of real-world contracts. Thus, whereas the theory predicts detailed and complex payment rules specifying each party's performance obligations for every possible contingency (in the case of discrete contingencies) and elaborate non-linear pricing rules (in the continuous case), actual contracts incorporate few if any explicit contingencies and generally use simple, typically linear, pricing schemes (Holmström and Hart 1987; Bhattacharyya and Lafontaine 1995).

Agency models that impose linearity at the outset thus start out with an obvious advantage in explaining observed contracts. Among the settings that have been analyzed in linear agency terms are franchising (Mathewson and Winter 1985; Lal 1990), agricultural share-cropping (Stiglitz 1974; Eswaran and Kotwal 1985), and product warranties (Priest 1981; Cooper and Ross 1985). Yet despite the variety of settings to which agency models potentially apply, empirical studies of the determinants of contract terms from an agency perspective have been limited (see Lafontaine and Slade 2000). One reason for this is the difficulty of finding workable proxies for contracting parties' relative risk aversion and the marginal contributions of their efforts to joint surplus. To the extent that these factors are difficult or impossible to measure, acceptance of the theory's predictions often turns on accepting non-falsifiable risk preference and marginal productivity assumptions (Stigler and Becker 1977; Allen and Lueck 1995).

Where risk arguments *have* been subjected to formal tests, they have not done well. For example, in franchising, where much of the recent empirical work has been directed, observed correlations between uncertainty and royalty rates are inconsistent with the standard assumption of franchisee risk aversion (Lafontaine 1992). Risk-sharing as a motive for contracting has fared poorly in other settings as well. Allen and Lueck (1992a, 1999), for instance, conclude that the incidence of crop-share versus fixed-rent contracts between farmer-tenants and land owners is inconsistent with the maintained assumption that farmers are more risk averse than land owners. Similarly, Leffler and Rucker (1991) reject risk-sharing as inconsistent with the incidence of lump-sum versus royalty payments in contracts between timber harvesters and land owners.

Predictions from agency models based on incentive (as opposed to risk) considerations have fared somewhat better in general. Lafontaine (1992), for example, found that royalty rates across franchises tend to vary with the relative importance of franchisor and franchisee effort. On the other hand, "franchise fees are in general not negatively correlated with royalty rates, despite the fact that the standard principal–agent model suggests that they should be" (Lafontaine and Slade 2000). Empirical research on agency contracting has also been criticized for focusing on such a highly limited range of contract terms (e.g. Bercovitz 1999).

3.3.2 Transaction-cost economics

Empirical transaction-cost research on contract design has looked primarily at three types of provisions: incentive provisions, pricing structures, and price adjustment methods. Like the agency literature, transaction-cost studies of incentive provisions have sought to determine whether contract terms align the interests of the contracting party and promote efficient adjustments to change. These studies have sought to explain more than just sharing rules, however. Studies by Masten and Crocker (1985) and Mulherin (1986), for instance, analyzed the incidence of take-or-pay provisions in natural gas contracts. Using data sets covering different periods in the history of gas contracting, the studies found that take-or-pay obligations varied with the alternative value of gas reserves, supporting an incentive interpretation over the alternative view that take-or-pay provisions served distributional or risk-sharing purposes (e.g. Hubbard and Weiner 1986).[10] Though these studies approached the issue of take-or-pay obligations from a transaction-cost perspective, their hypotheses and results are broadly consistent with an agency theoretic approach.[11]

The overlap between transaction-cost and agency theory predictions with respect to incentives can also be seen in two studies on the inclusion of "protective" provisions in franchise contracts. Although Bercovitz (1999) and Brickley (1999) analyze the use of various "non-price-related" restrictions on behavior in franchise agreements in similar terms and derive similar predictions, one describes her analysis as "building on the transaction cost framework" (Bercovitz 1999) while the other "uses agency theory to develop testable implications"(Brickley 1999).[12] The papers provide evidence that non-compete clauses (Bercovitz), passive ownership prohibitions, area development plans, and mandatory advertising requirements (Brickley) are positively related to proxies for the potential for franchisee free-riding and/or the size of initial investments.

Transaction-cost economists have taken a distinct approach to the analysis of pricing structures in contracts, however. Whereas agency theory analyzes pricing structures in moral-hazard and risk-sharing terms, transaction-cost economists have viewed the choice between fixed and variable payment terms as reflecting efforts to economize on transaction costs. An example is Leffler and Rucker's (1991) study of lump-sum versus per-unit pricing structures in timber harvesting contracts. In Leffler and Rucker's analysis, fixed-payment contracts give purchasers an incentive to engage in extensive pre-sale measurement of timber quality and quantity, whereas per-unit contracts discourage harvesters from harvesting timber efficiently and require greater post-agreement monitoring and enforcement efforts. Using a sample of 188 North Carolina timber contracts, Leffler and Rucker found the use of per-unit pricing to be more prevalent on relatively heterogeneous timber tracks for which pre-sale search costs were likely to be higher. Allen and Lueck's (1999) finding of a positive correlation between the variance in crop yields and the use of cash rent (fixed-price) contracts for farm land – the exact opposite of the prediction based on farmer risk aversion – is consistent with a hypothesis that farmers are better able to misreport crop yields as output variations owing to exogenous factors (weather, pest infestations) increase (see also Allen and Lueck 1998). Transaction-cost considerations also figure prominently in Masten and Snyder's (1993) analysis of pricing arrangements in equipment leases and in Bessy, Brousseau and Saussier's (2001) analysis of payment schemes in technology licensing agreements.

Empirical research also supports the role of "hazard equilibration" in contract design. Crocker and Masten (1991), for instance, conclude from their study of price adjustment in natural gas contracts that circumstances favoring the use of long-term, fixed-quantity agreements favor the adoption of relatively indefinite price adjustment provisions over formulaic adjustment mechanisms that, although less costly to implement, are more likely to induce efforts to evade performance obligations in extreme situations. As Goldberg and Erickson (1987) have noted, greater reliance on renegotiation provisions in fixed versus variable quantity contracts is difficult to reconcile with incentive alignment motives. Crocker and Reynolds' (1993) study of jet engine procurement contracts found that contracts tended to contain more flexible price adjustment mechanisms as performance horizons lengthened and technological uncertainty increased, while contractor litigiousness and the absence of alternative engine suppliers favored more definite price terms. More generally, Saussier (2000) provides evidence that the "completeness" of contracts, as measured by the number of dimensions of performance specified in the contract, varies with the attributes of the transaction: contracts for the transport of coal in France tend to contain more detail the greater the level of asset specificity but include fewer provisions as uncertainty increases. Thus, overall, the available evidence supports the notion that, in designing contracts, transactors are sensitive to the trade-off between the specification costs and rigidities associated with detailed performance obligations in uncertain or complex transactions, on the one hand, and the greater flexibility but higher expected cost of establishing terms of trade *ex post* with less definite "relational" contract provisions, on the other.

4   Contracting versus vertical integration

While our discussion of contracting in section 2 presumed that the alternative to contracting was a simple, arm's-length or "market" transaction, in practice the relevant alternative to contract is often vertical integration or "internal organization." For space reasons and because the empirical literature on vertical integration versus contracting has been discussed at length in several recent and extensive reviews (e.g. Shelanski and Klein 1995; Crocker and Masten 1996; Coeurderoy and Quélin 1997; and Lafontaine and Slade 1997, 2000), we confine ourselves here to a few observations.

4.1   Agency theory

Complete contract theory is unable to distinguish contracting from other institutional and organizational forms and thus unable to inform the choice between contracting and integration.[13] Incomplete contract theory, by contrast, was developed specifically to explain the existence of the firm and might therefore be expected to inform the contract versus vertical integration decision. Contracting and integration are not treated as alternatives in the incomplete contract framework, however. Rather, the theory asks only which of two (or more) parties to a contract should own a particular asset; the relationship between the parties themselves remains contractual regardless of who owns the asset.[14]

Given the limitations of complete and incomplete contract theories, linear contracting models have again, as in the case of contract design issues, been the primary source of predictions concerning the choice between contracting and integration within the broad agency framework. Or, to be more precise, models of the optimal linear share parameter have been used to extrapolate predictions about integration decisions: Assigning a large share of the residual to agents corresponds to the high-powered incentives associated with arm's-length contracts, while a low share generates the low-powered incentives conventionally attributed to integration (see Lafontaine and Slade 2000, pp. 5, 11). Agency theory thus predicts that integration is likely to dominate contracting where conditions favor allocating more of the risk to the principal, namely where the principal is the lower cost risk-bearer or the value of the principal's (non-contractible) effort is greater than that of the agent.[15] Although the evidence supports the predicted effect on relative effort contributions, the empirical literature "strongly rejects" the prediction that higher risk leads to more integration (Lafontaine and Slade 2000, p. 39). Finally, Holmström and Milgrom (1991) interpret Anderson and Schmittlein's (1984) and Anderson's (1985) findings that the importance of non-selling activities and difficulty measuring performance of sales agents leads to greater integration as support for the predictions of multitask agency theory; the inability to measure some of multiple dimensions of an agent's effort favors reliance on lower-powered incentives and the imposition of restrictions on agent behavior frequently associated with integration (Holmström and Milgrom 1994).[16]

4.2   Transaction-cost economics

The vertical integration, or make-or-buy, decision has been the most extensively studied question in the empirical transaction cost literature (for overviews, see Joskow 1988b; Shelanski and Klein 1995; Crocker and Masten 1996). For present purposes, two results are of particular note. First, the empirical literature reveals a consistent preference for integration over contracting as the specificity of investments increases. Thus, whereas asset specificity favors contracting when the alternative is simple exchange, contracting becomes *less* attractive as a way of protecting reliance or relationship-specific investments where the alternative to contracting is integrated ownership and production. Contracting thus appears to be only an imperfect response to the hazards posed by relationship-specific investments. Second, the evidence indicates that uncertainty and complexity also diminish the attractiveness of contracting relative to integration (e.g. Anderson and Schmittlein 1984; Masten 1984). Together with the evidence that uncertainty and complexity discourages contracting relative to simple exchange, these findings reinforce the conclusion that contracts are a costly and inflexible way to provide for future adaptations.

5   Some cautionary notes

The relative contributions of agency theory and TCE in explaining observed contracting practices derives in some degree to differences in methodology. Agency theorists, with their emphasis on axiomatic deduction, have been hesitant to incorporate into their models constraints, such as bounds on cognitive ability, that cannot be easily modeled (see, e.g., Hart 1990, 1995). Transaction-cost economists working in the tradition of Ronald Coase and Oliver Williamson, by contrast, have sought to develop and refine theory guided more by specific phenomena or puzzles than by the susceptibility of the theory to mathematical modeling. Although both have their place in the evolution of knowledge, it is not surprising in light of this difference that TCE – and, to a lesser extent, the more empirically oriented linear agency models – has turned out to have had more success empirically than the more mathematically elegant but ethereal complete and incomplete contract theories.

The term "success" can be applied only relatively, however; "tentative progress" would be a more apt description. Though not specific to empirical research on contracting, a variety of issues should temper our confidence in the findings to date. Probably chief among those is the quality of proxies used for the explanatory variables identified by the theory. Often, these proxies are crude and imprecise stand-ins for the variables of true interest or are endogenous themselves. Strictly speaking, the specificity of assets and the level of investment in those assets, which are treated as exogenous variables in much of the research, are themselves decision variables. The location of facilities, the adoption of specialized designs or equipment, and the scale of investments, all of which have been treated as exogenous in the literature, should, by rights, be treated as endogenous variables. Only a few studies have made tentative steps in that direction (see, e.g., Lyons 1995; Saussier 1999).

Another limitation of the existing research has been its tendency to analyze the individual provisions from complex contracts separately. Although focusing on individual contract terms has facilitated statistical analysis of the role of such terms, it has done so at the expense of ignoring potentially important interactions with and qualifications by other contract provisions that can radically alter or even negate their nominal meaning (see Masten 1998). Given that contract provisions will have been chosen simultaneously and are likely to interact with one another – often, as Goldberg and Erickson (1987) note, in subtle and unexpected ways – empirical contracting studies should, ideally, estimate the full set of contract provisions simultaneously. The econometric tools to handle such interactions and qualifications exist; Joskow (1987) and Crocker and Masten (1991), for example, have analyzed interactions among contract terms using standard simultaneous equation techniques.[17] The binding constraint is not technique but data availability. As the number of provisions analyzed increases, the number of explanatory variables and the size of the data set needed for statistical identification multiplies. Often, sufficient numbers of observations to analyze more than two or three provisions at a time will simply not exist. But even where the population is sufficiently large for statistical confidence, inadequacies in the scope and quality of the data that can be obtained on a large scale can temper conceptual confidence in statistical results.

For these reasons, case studies are an important, indeed necessary, complement to econometric analysis. Although case studies are often (justifiably) disparaged on the grounds that they lack generality and invite *ex post* rationalization, such concerns must be weighed against the aforementioned limitations of statistical analyses and the richer perspective that high-quality case studies can offer. What case studies lack in generality they often make up in depth. Data and measurement problems that would cripple econometric analyses often yield to intensive scrutiny of a single or small number of cases. And while a case study cannot disprove the general validity of a theory, a single, well-documented fact can refute the applicability of a theory to a particular case. Moreover, puzzles and anomalies encountered in case studies can and often have been the stimulus to refinements in the theory. Finally, some cases – the contracts between Microsoft and computer equipment manufacturers, for example – are important enough in their own right to warrant intensive analysis.

To compensate for lack of generality, a good case study will seek to account for a more complete range of details in addition to exploiting whatever variation exists over time and across transactions. The transaction-cost literature contains a number of excellent case studies that satisfy these but not the criteria for statistical confidence. Examples include Stuckey's (1983) analysis of organizational arrangements in the aluminum industry; Palay's (1984) work on rail-freight contracts; Gallick's (1984) analysis of the relations between tuna harvesters and processors; Joskow's (1985) preliminary exploration of vertical relations between coal mines and electric utilities; Goldberg and Erickson's (1987) study of petroleum coke contracts; Masten and Snyder's (1993) analysis of United Shoe Machinery Corp.'s lease terms; Pirrong's (1993) analysis of variations in ocean shipping contracts; Kaufman and Lafontaine's (1994) calculation of economic rents earned by McDonald's franchisees; and Ménard's (1996) investigation of organizational arrangements in the French poultry industry. What distinguishes these studies is their success in explaining the consistency among and variations in contractual details using a limited set of simple provisions. Such thoroughly researched and carefully argued case studies provide an important check that, in abstracting away from contract complexity to accommodate data limitations, econometric analyses do not misconstrue the purpose and function of particular terms.

Research on contracting has already begun to influence how courts think about contracting and resolve contract disputes (see, for instance, *PSI Energy* v. *Exxon Coal, USA*, 991 F.2d 1265 [1993]) and has normative implications for anti-trust policy and business decision-making as well. It is important, therefore, that positive theories of contracting behavior stand on as solid an empirical footing as possible. Although tensions are likely to persist between those who value axiomatic rigor and those willing to invoke empirical regularities to develop testable predictions, there are indications that agency theory and transaction-cost approaches to problems of contracting and organization are converging (cf. Tirole 1999). If that happens, the reality check provided by empirical research on contracting is likely to have played a significant role in that convergence.

NOTES

Chapter 16 was originally published as "Econometrics of Contracts: An Assessment of Developments in the Empirical Literature on Contracting," in *Revue d'Economie Industrielle* (92, 2000).
1. Reviews of the agency literature can be found in Hart and Holmström (1987) and Furubotn and Richter (1997), among other sources. For purposes of this chapter, we include under the heading "agency theory" complete contract theory (in the tradition of Myerson 1982), incomplete contract theory (such as Grossman and Hart 1986), and linear contract theory, the latter consisting of the set of models that restrict consideration to linear sharing rules (see, e.g., Allen and Lueck 1999 and Lafontaine and Slade 2000). See Masten 2000 for a discussion of the relation among these models.
2. For a more detailed discussion of the problems of identifying the efficiency of alternative governance arrangements, see Masten, Meehan, and Snyder (1991).
3. Potential differences in the set of attributes that affect efficiency under alternative governance arrangements are captured in the model by the possibility that the estimated marginal effects of particular attributes equal zero.
4. This correspondence between the discrete choice framework and transaction-cost hypotheses was first outlined in Masten (1982, 1984).
5. Saussier had access to the full population of the contracts written over the period covered by his study and therefore did not face the censoring problem present in Joskow's and Crocker and Masten's studies. Saussier's study, however, involved a smaller number of contracts (twenty-nine or seventy, depending on the specification).
6. Acknowledging that much of the equipment franchisees use is redeployable, Bercovitz includes only 10 percent of equipment expenditures in this figure.
7. Compare Goldberg and Erickson (1987, p. 398).
8. See Lafontaine and Slade (2000). Empirically, contracts often do contain only fixed *or* variable payments, not both, a fact that suggests discontinuities in how the terms operate.

9. While sympathizing with the view that individuals are not capable of dealing with unlimited complexity, purists complain that, in the absence of an accepted model of bounded rationality, restrictions on feasible contract forms are unavoidably arbitrary and ad hoc (e.g. Tirole 1994, pp. 15–17; Hart and Holmström 1987, pp. 133, 148).

10. Crocker and Masten's (1988) finding that distortions in the size of take-or-pay provisions significantly reduced the willingness of parties to engage in long-term contracting offered further support for the incentive interpretation of take-or-pay provisions. Case studies describing the use of minimum purchase requirements for coal (Carney 1978), petroleum coke (Goldberg and Erickson 1987), and bauxite (Stuckey 1983), among other products, also corroborate this finding (see Masten 1988, pp. 91–2, for a discussion).

11. Compare, for example, Shavell's (1984) theoretical development of efficient breach analysis with the characterization of the optimal take-or-pay provision in Masten and Crocker (1985).

12. In particular, Brickley (1999) interprets his results as being consistent with the multitask agency model of Holmström and Milgrom (1991, p. 747).

13. Models of vertical integration within the complete contract framework such as Crocker (1983) differentiate contracting from integration through the *deus ex machina* of eliminating information asymmetries upon integration.

14. On the potentially testable implications of incomplete contract theory with respect to ownership (as opposed to integration) and their relation to the empirical literature, see Whinston (2000).

15. The empirical literature on franchise contracting versus company ownership also generally shows that the larger the required initial investment of agents the more likely are outlets to be integrated. Depending on whether initial investment is regarded as a proxy for risk or for agent effort, this result may or may not be consistent with the predictions of agency theory (see Lafontaine and Slade 2000). To the extent that initial investment is correlated with the size of specific investments, the finding could also be interpreted as supporting transaction cost predictions (see Bercovitz 1999).

16. Lafontaine and Slade (2000) review these arguments and other evidence. Although Holmström and Milgrom (1991) frame the problem in agency terms, the effects of measurement costs on contracting and integration decisions has long been part of the transaction-cost literature (see, e.g., Barzel 1982). Several of the relevant empirical studies also describe the problem in transaction-cost terms.

17. Bercovitz (1999) and Brickley (1999) also analyze multiple provisions but do not systematically analyze possible interactions among them.

17 Experiments on moral hazard and incentives: reciprocity and surplus-sharing

Claudia Keser and Marc Willinger

1 Introduction

In the standard principal–agent model with moral hazard (Holmström 1979; Grossman and Hart 1987) the principal, who cannot observe the agent's effort, generally has an interest in proposing a contract with a variable remuneration that is a function of the realized profit. The model is based on the assumption of a stochastic relationship between the realized profit and the agent's effort; this relationship is common knowledge. As the agent's effort is unobservable to the principal, the contract has to provide an incentive for the agent to choose the effort level that is desired by the principal. In other words, the contract has to satisfy an *incentive constraint*. It also has to provide the agent with an expected utility that is as least as high as his utility without the contract. This is called the *participation constraint*. If the principal offered a contract with a fixed remuneration that is independent of the realized profit, the agent would provide the effort level that is least costly to him, which is in general the lowest possible effort. If the principal wants to induce a higher and more costly effort level by the agent, the contract has to be designed such that the agent maximizes his expected utility by choosing this effort level. Contract theory predicts that the principal keeps the entire expected surplus of the contract for himself and makes the agent just indifferent between rejecting and accepting the contract with the provision of the induced effort level.

This solution is based on the assumption that the stochastic relationship between the principal's profit and the agent's effort is common knowledge. Moreover, the principal has to know the agent's utility function in order to satisfy the incentive and participation constraints. Owing to the complexity of real phenomena and the presence of many sources of uncertainty the principal can, in reality, not base his contract policy on a given stochastic relationship between profit and effort. Often, the agent himself does not know this relationship, or, he has a different perception of it than the principal. Furthermore, in practice, the principal does not know the agent's utility function. Thus, real contracts are often incomplete and do not always satisfy incentive constraints. Given these difficulties, empirical verification of the accuracy of the theoretical predictions in a textbook principal–agent situation with moral hazard is problematic. Fehr, Gächter and Kirchsteiger (1997) argue that real contracts are often more equitable than in theory where the principal keeps the entire expected surplus of the contract for himself. Owing to a norm of reciprocity, the principal might be inclined to propose a positive share of surplus to the agent who, in return, will provide a higher effort than would be imposed by the incentive constraint (Akerlof 1982; Akerlof and Yellen 1990; Fehr, Kirchsteiger and Riedl 1993). A second verification problem, thus, results: if the real contracts are different from the predicted contracts by principal–agent theory, is this due to the incomplete information of the stochastic relationship or to a norm of reciprocity among the contracting parties?

Experimentation in a laboratory implies the creation of an environment that allows us to study the relationship between a principal and an agent in an artificial framework that largely satisfies the assumptions of the theoretical model. For example, the assumption that the stochastic relationship between the principal's profit and the agent's effort is known to both contracting parties can easily be implemented in such an experimental framework. Unfortunately, the non-observability of the participants' preferences remains a problem in experimental studies. In particular, it is difficult, if not impossible, to induce risk neutrality for those participants in an experiment who are assigned the role of principals and risk aversion for those who are assigned the role of agents. The efforts that Berg *et al.* (1992) and Epstein (1992) made in these directions lead to results that remain debatable. In spite of this difficulty, experimentation in the laboratory presents a great tool for testing the predictions of principal–agent theory.

Relatively few attempts have been made to date for testing principal–agent relationships with the help of experimental methods. The first principal–agent experiments that we are aware of are by Berg *et al.* (1992) and Epstein (1992). They produced results that were more or less compatible with the theoretical predictions. However, the principal was restricted in these experiments to the choice among an extremely limited set of predetermined contracts. The more recent experiments by Güth *et al.* (1998), Anderhub, Gächter and Königstein (1999), and Keser and Willinger (2000, 2001) allow for a much larger set of contracts. Their results generally contradict the predictions by contract theory.

The participants in an experiment are assigned the role of either a principal or an agent for the entire duration of the experiment. An experiment generally consists of several periods in order to allow the participants to become familiar with the strategic environment. We distinguish between two broad categories of experiments: those where the interaction between a principal and an agent is repeated in all periods by the same two participants and those where new pairs are (randomly) matched in each period. We denote the first category as experiments with *repeated interaction* and the second category as experiments with *one-shot interaction* between any two participants. Note that in one-shot experiments with random matching the probability of the same agent being matched with the same principal is negligibly small. We distinguish between repeated and one-shot experiments as they generally imply different theoretical predictions. When a contract is effectuated between a principal and an agent, each of the two participants realizes gains (or losses) that depend on the contract terms, the effort chosen by the agent and the result of a lottery. The gains are expressed in a fictive unit, the *experimental currency unit*. The gains are cumulated during the experiment and at the end of the experimental session converted into the monetary currency of the country to be paid to the participants.

The results of most of the experiments discussed in this chapter show that the participants' behavior is based on decision principles that are radically different from the principles on which the principal–agent theory is built. In one-shot interaction experiments (Keser and Willinger 2000) we observe that the principals propose contracts that are generally more favorable to the agents than predicted by contract theory and that often do not satisfy the incentive constraint. In particular, most of the contracts offer an assurance of no loss to the agent. The agents, generally, react in the predicted way to the incentives provided by the principal. Also in repeated interaction experiments (Güth *et al.* 1998; Anderhub, Gächter and Königstein 1999) we observe that the contracts offered by the principals rarely satisfy the incentive constraint. The participants' behavior seems to be guided by the principle of reciprocity: in general, participants in the role of agents provide higher and more costly efforts in response to more favorable contracts (see also Fehr, Gächter and Kirchsteiger 1997). These observations are in keeping with the concepts developed by Akerlof (1982) and Akerlof and Yellen (1990) with respect to equity considerations in employer–employee relationships.

In section 2 of this chapter we briefly survey the first principal–agent experiments that are characterized by the fact that their authors intended to induce specific preferences. We also discuss the methodological difficulties with these experiments. Section 3 presents the results of a series of experiments with one-shot interaction between a principal and an agent. Section 4 presents experiments where the same principal and the same agent interact repeatedly. Section 5 concludes.

2   Experiments with a mechanism to induce preferences

Experimental research on principal–agent relationship is relatively recent. The two experiments presented in this section (Berg *et al.* 1992; Epstein 1992) tried to control for the participants' risk attitude by using a mechanism of random remuneration.

2.1   Design and theoretical predictions

In the experiment by Berg *et al.* (1992) the principal may realize one of two profit levels, x_1 and x_2 (with $x_2 > x_1$), through the contractual relationship. The probabilities of these two profit levels depend on the agent's effort level, which can either be low, e_1, or high, e_2. The higher profit, x_2, is more likely with the high than with the low effort, i.e. $1 > p(x_2/e_2) > p(x_2/e_1) > 0$. The principal may propose a contract, defined as the pair (w_1, w_2) where w_i (with $i = 1, 2$) is the agent's remuneration that corresponds to a profit x_i of the principal. The principal has the choice among three contracts that exactly meet the agent's participation constraint: a contract with fixed remuneration that would be the optimal contract if the principal could enforce the high effort choice by the agent and two contracts with remunerations as a function of the realized profits. Both of the latter two contracts are designed to induce high effort, but one of them is more favorable (less costly) to the principal than the other. In the experiment, the effect of two treatment variables on the principals' contract choice and the agents' effort is tested. The two treatment variables are *observability* of the effort and the participants' *experience in the role of an agent*. In the treatments with effort observability the principal can enforce the choice of the high effort by imposing a high penalty if the agent defects from this effort. There is no moral-hazard problem in these treatments. In the treatments with acquisition of experience in the role of an agent previous to the actual play, all participants, whatever their role in the actual play will be, participate in a preliminary phase where they interact as agents with the experimenter. In this preliminary phase, each participant makes twelve effort choices, four for each of the three potential contracts. The idea is to test the sensitivity of behavior to the way in which common knowledge about the environment is conveyed to the participants in an experiment, an issue that had been raised by Binmore, Shaked and Sutton (1988) and Neelin, Sonnenschein and Spiegel (1988). Given a 2 × 2 treatment design, the experiment by Berg *et al.* (1992) consists of four treatments, resulting from a combination of the two observability conditions (with or without) and the two experience conditions (with or without). In all treatments each participant kept the same role until the end of the experiment (after the preliminary phase if there was one) and each participant knew that his interaction was always with the same other participant. The experiment consisted of either ten periods after the preliminary phase (with twelve effort choices in the interaction with the experimenter) or of twenty-two periods, of which only the final ten periods were analyzed, in the treatments without the preliminary phase.

Berg *et al.* (1992) aimed at inducing the participants' preferences by using a payment procedure in probability points, which had been introduced by Roth and Malouf (1979). This procedure is based on the conversion of the gain points accumulated over the experiment into the probability to win the high outcome in a binary lottery at the end of the experiment. The maximization of probability points is in this case the best strategy, independent of the attitude towards risk. By taking a transformation function from points into probabilities, which is linear for the principal and concave for the agent, it is claimed that one can induce preferences which satisfy the risk neutrality assumption for the principal and the risk aversion assumption for the agent.

In the situation without moral hazard (i.e. with effort observability), there exists a unique sub-game perfect equilibrium in which the principal proposes the risk-free contract with a fixed remuneration. The agent provides the high effort level in order to avoid the penalty. In the situation with moral hazard, the sub-game perfect equilibrium prescribes that the principal proposes the less costly of the two contracts where remuneration is a function of the realized profits. The agent should provide the high effort level.

2.2 Results and limitations

The observed contract and effort choices of fourteen, resp. sixteen, pairs of students participating in each of the four treatments are in keeping with the sub-game perfect equilibrium prediction both in the situation with and without moral hazard. The participants' experience in the role of an agent did not modify the behavior of the principals compared to the situation without previous experience.

These observations seem to support the major theoretical predictions of the principal–agent model with hidden action. However, this experiment suffers from three major weaknesses. The first weakness is that the principal's strategy space is limited to three options, which correspond to contracts for which the agent's participation constraint is binding in the case of the high effort. Among these three contract options are the optimal contract without moral hazard and the optimal contract with moral hazard. The difficulty with this particular set of contracts is that the principal is constrained to the appropriation of the entire surplus, which is part of the sub-game perfect equilibrium prediction. Thus, we are limited to the examination of risk-sharing between the principal and the agent, given that the agent is just at his participation constraint. A second problem results from the procedure to remunerate the participants in probability points. Selten, Sadrieh and Abbink (1999) show that this type of procedure, being far away from neutralizing the effects of risk aversion, can produce important biases in the participant's behavior. The third weakness is that the agents don't have the opportunity to refuse the proposed contract. This incurs problems for testing the predictions of contract theory relying on the assumption that the agent might reject a contract offer. Although all of the potential contracts satisfy the participation constraint, the agents who are forced to accept all contract offers do not have the opportunity for strategic rejection with the hope of obtaining a more favorable contract offer in the following period.

2.3   *Taking the agent's potential rejection into account*

With respect to the experiment by Berg *et al.* (1992), the major modification made by Epstein (1992) in his experiment is to introduce an explicit reservation utility by allowing the agent to refuse the contract. Epstein considers the situation with both moral hazard and experience in the role of an agent and compares his results to those of Berg *et al.* (1992). In his experiment, he uses an explicit reservation value of the agent in the case that he rejects the contract offer as a treatment variable: the agent's reservation value is either low and not binding or high and binding. The principal can, again, choose among three contracts, of which one corresponds to the unique sub-game perfect equilibrium of the ten-fold repetition of the game. Offered this contract, the agent should choose the high effort level. A second of the potential contracts consists of offering a fixed remuneration to the agent. In the treatment with a low explicit reservation utility, applying backward induction, the agent should never reject, whatever contract is offered to him. In other words, the explicit reservation utility is not binding. The third potential contract in this treatment is one that induces high effort but yields the principal a lower expected utility than the sub-game perfect equilibrium contract. In the treatment where the explicit reservation value is high, it is binding. The agent should reject the third contract if it is offered to him. Without the opportunity for the agent to reject, however, this contract would induce high effort and would maximize the principal's expected utility. Note that in both treatments the presence of the option to refuse the contract offer allows the agent to refuse an offer for strategic reasons with the expectation that the principal offers him a more favorable contract in the following period.

Six pairs of students participated in the treatment with a low reservation utility while eight pairs participated in the treatment with a high reservation utility. In the treatment with a low and non-binding reservation utility, the agents never refused the contracts offered to them. This result contradicts the hypothesis that the agents might use refusals in the early rounds for strategic reasons. The sub-game perfect equilibrium contract is chosen less often than in the experiment by Berg *et al.* (1992). Principals tend to offer the contract that is slightly Pareto-dominated by the equilibrium contract. This contract gives, compared to the equilibrium contract, a lower expected utility to the principal while giving the same expected utility to the agent. In the treatment with a high and binding reservation utility, the sub-game perfect equilibrium contract offer is less often observed than in the experiment by Berg *et al.* (1992). The principals tend to choose the equilibrium contract and the contract that is more favorable to them than the equilibrium contract but should be rejected by the agent equally often. This is not so surprising when we take the agents' choices into consideration. Even when offered the contract that should induce rejection, the agents choose the high effort in almost half of the cases.

Although the experiment by Epstein improved on the experimental design introduced by Berg *et al.* (1992) by introducing the agent's option to refuse the contract, it remains open to the two shortcomings mentioned above with respect to the experiment by Berg *et al.* (1992): the small number of predetermined contracts and the payment mode in probability points. Furthermore, Epstein provided only a vague explanation of the phenomena observed in his experiment, in particular that the sub-game perfect equilibrium contract was chosen less often than in the experiment by Berg *et al.* (1992), claiming that the adding of another dimension to the agent's action increased the participants' confusion.

3   The principal's behavior in one-shot interactions

In Keser and Willinger (2000, 2001) we present a series of experiments designed to test the static version of the standard principal–agent model. In these experiments the participants are assigned a role as either a principal or an agent for the entire experimental session. Each experimental session consists of one or two sequences of ten periods but in each period each of the participants is randomly re-matched with one of the participants in the other role. Thus, we consider the interaction of a principal and an agent in each period as a one-shot interaction; it is very unlikely for the same two participants to encounter each other again in the following periods. The parameters of the initial experiment (Keser and Willinger 2000) have been chosen such that the sub-game perfect equilibrium solution for a risk neutral principal and risk neutral agent is a unique contract under the restriction of integer numbers. Contract offers are, in contrast to the previously discussed experiments, limited only by lower and upper bounds on each of their components. All of the contract offers observed in the experiment are different from the sub-game perfect equilibrium prediction. The participants in the role of a principal offer contracts that do not tend to satisfy the incentive constraint and that are significantly more favorable to the agent than in equilibrium (i.e. the participation constraint is satisfied but not binding). We show that these results can be explained by behavioral principles of the principals, which are in contradiction with the behavior assumed in the principal–agent literature.

3.1   Design and theoretical predictions

In the experiment presented in Keser and Willinger (2000), the principal may offer one of a huge set of contracts. The model assumes two possible states of nature, which correspond to a profit of 50 (state 1) or of 100 (state 2) experimental currency units. The principal may propose a contract, defined as the pair (w_1, w_2) where w_i is the remuneration if state i is realized. The agent, if he accepts the contract, chooses one of two activities (effort levels): activity 1 induces a uniform probability over the two states of nature while activity 2 assigns a probability of 0.8 to state 2. Activity 2 incurs to the agent a higher cost than activity 1. The parameters of the model are summarized in table 17.1. If the agent rejects the principal's contract offer both players get zero payoff.

In the experiment the game was repeated in a first sequence of ten periods with random re-matching of each principal with an agent after each period. After a short break during which the participants could not communicate with each other, a second sequence of ten periods took place, again with random re-matching and each participant staying in the same role as either a principal or an agent. In the second sequence we consider the participants as experienced. Under the assumption of risk-neutrality of both the principal and the agent, we show that there exists a unique sub-game perfect equilibrium solution in integers in which the principal offers the contract (1,25) and the agent accepts and chooses activity 2. Note that this contract, to satisfy the incentive constraint, lets the agent suffer a net loss if state 1 occurs and a net gain if state 2 is realized.

Table 17.1. *Parameters of the experiment by Keser and Willinger (2000)*

	Probability that principal's profit is		
	50	100	Agent's activity cost
Activity 1	0.5	0.5	13
Activity 2	0.2	0.8	20

Under the alternative assumption of constant absolute risk aversion of the agent (i.e. $u(x) = -e^{-\gamma x}$, where $u(x)$ is the agent's utility function and x denotes his payoff) two types of equilibria are possible. The principal can induce activity 1 by proposing either (13,14) or (14,13). Note that for each of these contracts the agent has a utility which is superior to his reservation utility in one of the states of nature while (13,13) leaves the agent indifferent between accepting and refusing. The principal can also induce activity 2 by proposing a contract (w_1^*, w_2^*) such that $0 \leq w_1^* \leq 13$ and $w_2^* \geq 20$. The exact values of w_1^* and w_2^* depend on the value of the coefficient γ in the agent's utility function. The principal will choose to induce the activity which will maximize his expected payoff.

3.2   Results and interpretation

One hundred students of various disciplines at the University of Karlsruhe participated in the experiment. Note that, as the randomized pairing of principals and agents was effectuated within populations of five participants in the role of principals and five participants in the role of agents, we obtained ten independent observations. We do not observe any significant difference between inexperienced and experienced play. Among the total of 1,000 observed contracts, we never observed the sub-game perfect equilibrium solution under the assumption of risk neutrality of both the principal and the agent. The sub-game perfect equilibrium prediction with a risk averse agent was observed in only one of the contracts. The mean contract observed was (24,46) in the inexperienced play and (23,45) in the experienced play, and is, thus, in both cases and in both components far away from the predicted contract. About half of all contract offers satisfied the incentive constraint for activity 2; 95 percent of these contracts were accepted and 70 percent of those accepted led to the choice of activity 2 by the agent. Contract offers to which the agent's best reply would be the choice of activity 1, were accepted in 80 percent of the cases and then generally led to the choice of activity 1 by the agent.

To explain these results, in Keser and Willinger (2000) we identified three principles that seem to have guided the principals' decision-making: *appropriateness*, *loss avoidance*, and *sharing power*. Appropriateness implies that the principal offers a higher remuneration for a higher profit. Otherwise, the agent had no incentive to provide a high effort. The loss avoidance principle implies that the principal proposes only contracts such that, whatever the state of nature, the agent incurs no loss. This principle prescribes a lower bound to the remuneration in each state, which conflicts with the theoretical prediction that the agent's participation constraint should be binding. Many of the contracts that satisfy this principle also violate the incentive constraint. The sharing-power principle implies that the principal shares the surplus with the agent but in a way that it is not less favorable to himself than to the agent. This principle prescribes an upper bound to the remuneration in each state. It allows for many contracts where the participation constraint is satisfied but not binding. Thus, this principle conflicts with the theoretical prediction that the principal should keep the entire expected surplus for himself by just satisfying the agent's participation constraint. If we denote the agent's cost for activity i by c_i, the three principles can then be defined:

(1) Appropriateness: $w_1 \leq w_2$
(2) Loss avoidance: $w_1 \geq c_i$ and $w_2 \geq c_i$ $(i = 1, 2)$
(3) Sharing power: $w_1 \leq c_i + (50 - c_i)/2$ and
$$w_2 \leq c_i + (100 - c_i)/2 \quad (i = 1, 2)$$

Note that for the second and the third principles several variants are possible, depending on the costs (c_1 or c_2) to be considered. The same costs might be considered in the two different states of the world. Thus, for the second and third principle we have four possible variants each. The combination of the three principals (in whatever variant) describes a specific area of *fair offers* in the (w_1, w_2) contract space. Under the hypothesis that all of the contracts are equally likely to be proposed by a principal who chooses randomly within the strategy space, we may associate a probability to this fair offers area, called the *area rate*. The area rate is defined by the number of potential contracts in this area divided by the overall number of potential contracts in the contract space. We then define the hit rate of a combination of the three principals as the relative frequency with which the observed contracts fall into its predicted area. The difference between the hit rate and the area rate defines a measure of predictive success, S, for the considered combination of principles (see Selten 1991). The measure of predictive success, thus, considers the frequency of contracts satisfying a combination of principles, beyond the frequency that would be just due to chance. In the experiment, the combination of principle variants with the highest measure of predictive success corresponds to contracts

Table 17.2. *Activity costs in the experiments by Keser and Willinger (2001)*

Cost level for the agent	Activity 1	Activity 2
Low (Keser and Willinger 2000)	13	20
Medium	27	34
High	34	41
Very high	41	48

that are restricted by the following inequalities: $w_1 \leq w_2$, $13 \leq w_1 \leq 35$ and $13 \leq w_2 \leq 60$. This combination corresponds to costs of $c_1 = 13$ for the principle of loss avoidance in both states of nature (presenting lower boundaries of the area) and costs of $c_2 = 20$ for the principle of sharing power in both states of nature (presenting upper boundaries of the area).

These results show that whatever his profit level, the principal tends to offer to the agent a remuneration which is superior to the one predicted by the sub-game perfect equilibrium solution. Thus, the principal gives away part of the created surplus to the agent. Obviously, the principal avoids offering contracts where the agent might incur a loss. Thus, the agent does not have to bear the risk of a loss and receives a strictly positive share of the net surplus of the contract. The three principles, appropriateness, loss avoidance, and sharing power, which we have elaborated in an explorative way from the behavior of the participants in the experiment, are in conflict with the predictions of contract theory. Note that these experimental results do not necessarily imply that the principal wants to be equitable but rather tries to prevent rejection by the agent, which would eliminate an opportunity for the principal to make a certain gain. Thus, he offers a contract that yields a certain gain to the agent as well.

3.3 Validation of these principles

To test the robustness of the three principles of the principals' behavior, we ran an additional series of experiments (Keser and Willinger 2001). In these experiments we increase the agent's activity costs keeping everything else the same as in the previous study. We consider three different cost levels maintaining, however, the difference between the costs of the two activities constant at seven (see table 17.2). A total of 224 students (128 at the University of Strasbourg and 96 at the University of Karlsruhe) participated in these experiments; we obtained four independent observations for each cost situation in each of the two countries (additional to the ten independent observations in Germany for the lowest cost level).

By increasing the costs we reduce the principal's expected surplus from the contract in the sub-game perfect equilibrium solution. Furthermore, for these higher cost levels, there exist multiple equilibria (in integers) where both the agent and the principal are risk neutral. This renders the comparison of the results with the theoretical prediction less straightforward. The analysis of the average Euclidean distance of the observed contracts from the respective closest equilibrium contract shows that this distance becomes the smaller as activity costs increase. However, the contracts offered by the principals fail to satisfy the incentive constraint more frequently as activity costs increase.

As effort costs increase, the remunerations increase that the principal must offer to the agent in order to satisfy the loss avoidance principle and to make him accept the contract. The area that corresponds to the combination of the three principles, appropriateness, loss avoidance, and sharing power, that define the fair offers prediction, becomes smaller as costs increase. These experiments, thus, allow us to test the robustness of the fair offers predictions and the three principles on which it is based by having smaller and smaller areas described by the principles.

In the experiments with higher activity costs, the combination of the same variants of the three principles as in the previous experiment still yields the (second) highest measure of predictive success among all possible combinations. We observe a reduction in the measure of predictive success, though, when we increase the cost level. From the experiment with the lowest cost level to the experiment with the highest cost level the measure of predictive success of the fair offers prediction is reduced by 50 percent. This decrease reflects a reduction of the hit rate that is more important than the reduction of the area rate. Although the measure of predictive success remains at around 45 percent, we do observe many contract offers not satisfying the loss avoidance principle when the costs are very high. If we restrict, however, our analysis to those contracts that are accepted by the agents, the hit rate of the loss avoidance principle *per se* (such as the measure of predictive success of the fair offer prediction) is much higher than without this restriction.

In Keser and Willinger (2001) we determine the set of all possible subgame perfect equilibrium contracts under the assumption of a risk averse agent whose utility function belongs to the class of strictly increasing and concave functions. As neither the experimenter nor the participant in the role of the principal can know the agent's utility function, we predict that the solution should lie in a specific sub-set of the principal's strategy space. Comparing this equilibrium prediction under the assumption of a risk averse agent to the fair offers prediction, we observe that the latter yields significantly higher measures of predictive success as long as the effort cost is not very high. In other words, the fair offers prediction does better than the equilibrium prediction for a risk averse agent as long as the surplus of the contract to be allocated among the principal and the agent is not too small.

To summarize, the three principles remain a good predictor for the observed contracts as long as there is a more or less important surplus of the contract to be allocated between the principal and the agent. The loss avoidance principle appears to be the least robust one among the three decision principles when the surplus becomes unimportant. It appears that the principals want to keep the same share of the expected surplus, whatever the size of this surplus. Interestingly, principals in Germany offer more generous contracts to the agents than those in France.

4 Contract offers and effort in repeated interaction

The first experiments by Berg *et al.* (1992) and Epstein (1992) were based on repeated interaction between the same principal and the same agent. In this section we will report on two more recent experiments, which were designed to test the behavior of both the principal and the agent in repeated interactions. In these experiments the participants know that they will interact with the same other person during the entire experiment. The results of these experiments show the importance of reciprocity in the repeated interaction of a principal and an agent.

4.1 The experiment by Güth et al. (1998)

4.1.1 Design and theoretical predictions
Güth *et al.* (1998) study the behavior of a principal and an agent in a rather complex dynamic game context with both hidden action and hidden information. Their primary aim is not to test theoretical predictions as such but to provide empirical facts showing how incentives compete with trust and reciprocity. In the experimental game situation, the principal might be the owner of a firm whose management is conferred on an agent. The principal's interest is to accumulate capital to be liquidated at the end of the game. The agent plays a particular role in this game. On the one hand, as the manager of the capital he can let it grow by providing an effort. On the other hand, he has to decide in each period on how much of the profit he wants to distribute as a dividend. The distributed profit is allocated between the principal and the agent in a proportion that is specified in the contract.

In the beginning of the game the principal proposes at least one but not more than three contracts to the agent. A contract has two components (f_1, s_1) where f_1 (with $0 \leq f_1 \leq 4$) is a fixed salary and s_1 (with $s_1 \in \{0, 0.1, 0.2, 0.3, 0.4\}$) is the agent's share of the dividend. The principal's share of the dividend is $(1 - s_1)$. The agent has to accept one of the contracts. The interaction between the principal and the agent lasts between three and six periods in total. The principal may in each period, t (with $t > 1$), revise the accepted contract upward. Concretely, he may increase the fixed salary component and/or the agent's share of the dividend, such that $f_t \geq f_{t-1}$ and $s_t \geq s_{t-1}$.

At the beginning of the game neither the principal nor the agent knows the true value of the firm, W_1. They know that the firm can have one of two values, $W_1 \in \{3, 12\}$, where each value has a probability of one-half. After having chosen the contract in the first period, the true value of the firm is communicated to the agent. The agent then chooses an effort $e_t = \{0, 1, 2, 3\}$ the cost of which is given by $c(e_t) = e_t/2$. The agent's effort determines the random return of the firm $R_t = a_t \alpha_t$, where α_t is a random variable with a uniform distribution over $\{1, 2, 3\}$. Only the agent can observe the realization of the random variable, after the choice of his effort. The firm's profit in period t is defined by $\Pi_t = R_t - f_t$. Once the agent knows the firm's profit, he decides on the amount of the dividend D_t for the current period. The dividend must not exceed the sum of the firm's value (W_t) plus the profit of the current period. More concretely, $0 \leq D_t \leq W_t + \Pi_t$ if $W_t + \Pi_t > 0$, and $D_t = 0$ otherwise, with $W_t = W_{t-1} + \Pi_{t-1} - D_{t-1}$ for $t > 1$. Note that the principal is informed of the dividend (D_t) only, while the agent knows in each period also the firm's value (W_t) and the realized profit (Π_t). The payoffs of the agent (Π_t^A) and the principal (Π_t^P) in period t are defined, respectively, as $\Pi_t^A = f_t + s_t D_t - c(e_t)$ and $\Pi_t^P = (1 - s_t) D_t$.

From the second period on, the principal's decision is whether or not to increase the fixed pay and/or the agent's dividend share. In periods 4–5 he can end the game unilaterally. Otherwise the game ends after period 6. The agent's total payoff corresponds to the sum of his payoffs in each period, while the principal's payoff is determined by the sum of his dividend payoffs plus the residual value of the firm.

Under the assumption of risk neutrality of both the principal and the agent this game has multiple equilibria. However the authors propose a reference equilibrium to which they compare the experimental data. The reference equilibrium is a stationary one which is characterized by the fact that the dividend in each period is equal to the value of the firm plus the profit of the period $(D_t = W_t + \Pi_t)$, the principal never ends the game before the final period, and induces the maximum effort by offering a contract with a zero fixed salary component and a 30 percent share of the dividend for the agent ($f_t = 0$, $s_t = 0.3$). Note that the agent provides the maximum effort if $s_t \geq 0.3$ (incentive constraint); he provides the lowest effort if $s_t < 0.3$. Intermediate effort levels are never the agent's optimal choice.

Sixty-four participants (students of economics or business administration at the Humboldt University of Berlin) participated in this experiment. The multiperiod game was played twice in each session, with re-matching of pairs of a principal and an agent in the beginning of the second play. Each participant remained, however, in the same role as either a principal or an agent.

4.1.2 Results

The principal's behavior   The principals generally offer several contracts in the first period. More than 90 percent of the proposed contracts offer a positive fixed salary component, which is costly to the principal but should have no influence on the agent's effort choice. Almost all of the contracts offer positive dividend shares that are, however, not satisfying the incentive constraint in the first periods. Both the dividend shares and the fixed salary components increase over time. Note, however, that the increase of the two components is not so surprising since the rules of the game do not allow for a decrease. The average dividend share is around 30 percent toward the end of the game. Shares below and above the incentive-compatible share are observed. In about half of all cases the principals finish the game before period 6. The observed probability to finish the game early depends on the dividends paid: early termination is more likely after a zero dividend than after a positive one. These results hold for both inexperienced and experienced play.

The agent's behavior   The agents, when they have the choice among several contracts proposed by the principal in the first period, generally choose the one that offers the highest fixed salary. In only 19 percent of all cases did the agents choose the contract with the highest dividend share. The authors interpret this as self-selection by the agents. They observe that the agents who choose the contract with the highest dividend share tend to choose higher effort levels in the first period. About two-thirds of the efforts chosen over the two repetitions of the multiperiod game are different from the effort to be induced. We observe many intermediate effort levels (neither zero nor maximum effort) and also that the agents provide strictly positive efforts when their dividend share is below 30 percent. Furthermore, in each period the distributed dividends are inferior to the sum of the value of the firm plus the profit in that period.

However, the value of the firm decreases over time and becomes zero in many cases in the final period.

The authors show in a regression analysis that the effort level is positively correlated to the dividend share proposed in the contract and to the fixed salary component. In other words, agents respond to more favorable offers with higher effort levels. According to the authors' interpretation, the size of the fixed salary measures trust on the part of the principals and the positive correlation between the effort and the dividend share reveals reciprocal behavior on the part of the agents. Reciprocity becomes stronger in the course of an experimental game but is not carried over from one game (inexperienced game) to the next (experienced game, with a different partner). Fehr, Gächter and Kirchsterger (1997) show that reciprocity can be a powerful contract enforcement device.

If the objective is to test the predictions of principal–agency theory, this experiment implies several problems, in particular the one of the complexity of the game. The authors justify this choice by a concern for realism. They see the characteristics such as the repeated nature of the interaction, the downward rigidity of the remuneration, etc., as important elements of real contracts. Given its complexity, the experimental environment examined by Güth *et al.* leaves little chance for the theory to do well; in particular owing to the fact that the fixed salary component cannot be downward adjusted. Furthermore, the agent cannot influence the principal through strategic refusals. The conditions on which the theory is based are thus not met in this experiment. Some of these problems have been dealt with in the experiment by Anderhub, Gächter and Königstein (1999).

4.2   The experiment by Anderhub, Gächter and Königstein (1999)

4.2.1   Design and theoretical prediction

The experiment by Anderhub, Gächter and Königstein (1999) is based on the same type of contract as is the experiment by Güth *et al.* (1998). This means that the contracts are of type (f_t, s_t) where f_t is a fixed payment and s_t is a share of the profit realized by the principal. The principal can announce a desired effort level without the agent's obligation to satisfy it. The game is repeated over six periods by the same agents and then after a random re-matching repeated once again over six periods. Note several major differences with respect to the experiment by Güth *et al.*: the principal may propose a new contract in each period, the agent may refuse any contract, the agent's effort is *ex post* observable to the principal, and the relationship between profit and effort is not stochastic. Given the absence of risk the agent's behavior is not affected by his risk attitude. The fact that the effort will be observable to the principal *ex post* may affect the agent's behavior although the agent cannot be directly punished by the principal for deviation from the required contract. The agent might be afraid, however, of an unfavorable reaction of the principal in periods following little cooperative behavior by the agent. At the same time, the observation of reciprocity by the agent might be important for the building up of a cooperative relationship between the principal and the agent.

In period 1 the principal may offer a maximum of two contracts and only a single one in all subsequent periods. The agent has the possibility to accept or to refuse the contract(s) in each period t. In case of a rejection both players' payoffs are zero. If the agent accepts the contract he chooses an effort level e_t and then the principal is informed of his decision. The return of the effort is given by $R(e_t) = 35e_t$ and the effort costs are given by a piecewise linear function, $c(e_t)$, which is convex and increases with e_t. The payoffs to the agent and the principal in period t are $\Pi_t^A = f_t + s_t R_t - c(e_t)$ and $\Pi_t^P = (1 - s_t) R_t - f_t$, respectively.

The parameters of the experiment impose the following constraints on the decision variables: $f_t \in \{-700, -699, \ldots, +700\}, s_t \in \{0, 0.01, \ldots, 1\}, e_t \in \{0, 1, \ldots, 20\}$. The baseline game has multiple subgame perfect equilibria but a unique "trembling hand" perfect equilibrium (Selten 1975) in which the principal offers the contract $(-400, 100\%)$ to the agent who provides maximum effort. This solution prescribes that the principal sells the firm to the agent at a price corresponding to the revenue in case of maximal effort. Note that all sub-game perfect equilibria induce a relationship between f_t and s_t which is given by $f_t = 300 - 700s_t$ for all $s_t \geq 5/7$. Thus, $f_t \leq -200$.

4.2.2 Results

The principal's behavior In 70 percent of the 564 observed contracts (47 principals × 6 periods × 2 sessions, participants were students at the University of Zürich with various backgrounds other than economics) the principals have proposed negative fixed salaries. At the same time, about two-thirds of all contracts offered a profit share greater than 71 percent. In 82 percent of all cases the contracts aimed at inducing an efficient effort by the agent (suggested effort level). According to the authors these results show that the participants in the role of a principal have recognized the necessity to give an incentive to the agent for providing the desired effort level.

They observe a negligible number of contracts with purely a fixed salary component. Most of the contracts are of the mixed type ($s > 0, f \neq 0$). Contracts where both components are strictly positive are not incentive compatible. The "trembling hand" perfect equilibrium (selling of the firm to the agent) is observed in about 30 percent of all cases ($s = 1$, $f < 0$). The participation constraint is almost always satisfied (97 percent of all cases). However, we observe that the contracts offered imply a more equitable share of the surplus than predicted by the equilibrium solution according to which the principal keeps the entire surplus.

The agent's behavior   Although 97 percent of the contracts satisfy the agent's participation constraint, 112 of the 551 contracts that satisfy this constraint are rejected by the agents (about 20 percent). To examine the questions why agents rejected contracts, the authors pick up the hypothesis by Slonim and Roth (1998) for ultimatum bargaining games according to which the acceptance rate is positively correlated to the relative payment to the agent. The idea is presented in Anderhub, Gächter and Königstein (1999) by an equity assumption, according to which the acceptance probability for a contract is a function of the surplus share offered to the agent. The authors show the validity of this hypothesis in a logit regression that is run only for those contracts that satisfy the participation constraint and under the hypothesis that the agent chooses an effort level that maximizes his payoff. The results show that the surplus share significantly affects the acceptance probability. This implies that the acceptance depends not only on the absolute payment but also on the relative payment to the agent. In other words, equity considerations play a role in the decision-making.

The effort levels chosen by the agents, given an equitable contract, are the rational ones. More than 60 percent of all effort choices are rational. However, this also implies that a great number of the effort choices (almost 40 percent) are different from the rational choice. The authors argue that this may be explained by reciprocal fairness considerations. They observe that the deviations from the rational effort level (conditional on the contract offered) are positively correlated with the agent's surplus share. Contracts that are favorable for the agent trigger effort levels that are above the individually optimal effort level, and vice versa.

The major conclusion that the authors draw is that these results are not in contradiction to the maximization hypothesis but show the presence of other motivations such as equity and reciprocity that might influence the choices made by the principals and the agents.

5   Conclusion

In this chapter we have surveyed several contributions of the experimental literature to the understanding of the relationship between a principal and an agent. We distinguish between experiments that are based on repeated interactions and those that examine one-shot interactions.

In the experiments with one-shot interaction the contracts are almost always different from the predicted ones. Not even the repetition of the interaction with varying other participants brings a significant convergence to the predicted contracts. In the observed contract offers, the participation constraint is not binding and in about half of the cases, the incentive constraint is not satisfied. The principals are motivated by considerations other than those that correspond to the participation and incentive constraints when they design contracts. Most of the contracts avoid potential losses to the agent and imply a more equitable share of the surplus between the principal and the agent than the share predicted by principal–agent theory. The fair offer prediction proposed by Keser and Willinger (2000) is to a large extent robust to changes in the size of the surplus created through the contract.

The observed effort choices by the agents and their decisions whether or not to accept a contract tend to be compatible with the theoretical predictions. Note however, that the contract offers by the principal already reflect the principals' fear of rejection (loss avoidance principle) so that we cannot observe what the agents' reaction would have been to the theoretically predicted contract offers that are much more unfavorable to them.

When the interaction between the same principal and the same agent is repeated and the agent may choose among a set of effort levels larger than just a low and a high one, the agent's behavior also shows significant differences from the theoretical prediction. We observe here that the respect of the participation constraint in a proposed contract does not guarantee its acceptance by the agent but that the probability that the agent accepts a contract increases with its (absolute and relative) remuneration level. Also the agent's effort level is positively correlated with the remuneration level proposed by the principal. The agent's effort level is in many cases even higher than the effort level to be induced by the contract.

The question now presents itself as to whether the principal consciously proposes a contract that is favorable to the agent anticipating the reciprocity of the latter. This would suppose that the principal assumes that the agent is of a reciprocal type and that the agent would sanction an inequitable proposal by a rejection and recompense a favorable offer by a high effort level. An alternative explanation could be that the principal plays an incomplete information game where he does not know, for example the acceptance benchmark of the agent. Future experimental studies will likely consider the predictive power of these explanations in principal–agent situations. Note, however, that experimental results on other forms of repeated interactions (e.g. in ultimatum bargaining, investment games, voluntary contributions to a public good) also reveal the importance of reciprocity considerations on human behavior.

To conclude this chapter, recall that the principal aim of these experiments is not to understand the formation of real-life contracts but to test the predictions of the principal–agent model and the influence of considerations such as trust and reciprocity. We therefore need to construct frameworks that are appropriate to observe interactions such as they are described by the theory. The link between contract characteristics observed in the laboratory environment and in a real-life environment remains an open question. This question poses itself more generally with respect to the comparison of experimental results to observations in a real-life context.

NOTES

Chapter 17 was originally published as "La théorie des contrats daus une contexte expérimental: un survol des expériences sur les relations 'Principal–agent,'" *Revue d'Economie Industrielle* (92, 2000).

Part VI

Applied issues: contributions to industrial organization

18 Residual claims and self-enforcement as incentive mechanisms in franchise contracts: substitutes or complements?

Francine Lafontaine and Emmanuel Raynaud

1 Introduction

Franchising is a contractual relationship that has received a significant amount of attention in the empirical literature on contracting. In large part, this is because franchising is one of the few types of contractual relationships about which significant amounts of data are available from public sources. But franchising is also, as noted by Williamson (1991), a hybrid organizational form, which lies somewhere between complete vertical integration and spot markets. Thus insights gleaned from the study of franchise contracting have allowed researchers to develop a better understanding not only of this organizational form, but also of how firms organize their activities much more generally, both within and across firms.

Much of the literature on franchising has specifically been concerned with incentive issues and how these are managed in these contracts. This literature has identified two main categories of incentive mechanisms relevant to the franchise relationship: residual claims and self-enforcement. The former relates to the fact that franchisees get to keep their outlet's profits net of the fees they pay to their franchisors, giving them incentives to maximize those residual profits. The second relies on the presence of on-going rent at the outlet level, rent that the franchisee forgoes if his contract is terminated. Such rent is simply the difference between the (net present value of) returns that the franchisee earns as a result of being associated with the franchise network and the returns he could garner in his next best alternative. If the rent is positive, and franchisors can terminate franchisees, franchisees will have incentives to perform according to the standards set by the franchisor to reduce their chances of termination and protect their access to the rent.

In this chapter, we describe how these two types of incentive mechanisms work in theory and in practice in franchise contracting, and then explore the relationship *between* them. Our contention is that rather than being alternative approaches to aligning the incentives of contracting

315

parties, as suggested by much of the current literature, these approaches are in fact complementary. Specifically, we argue that residual claimancy rights motivate individual parties to a contract to invest greater effort as per standard agency arguments. At the same time, the existence of self-enforcement mechanisms prevents parties from engaging in individually profitable activities that can have a negative impact on the whole, or on other members of the franchise system. In fact, it is precisely the franchisee's status as a residual claimant that brings about the need to use a self-enforcement mechanism to curb his tendency to maximize his own profit at the expense of the brand or the rest of the chain. We argue that optimal contract design in this context must effectively balance the provision of high effort incentives for individuals with coordination incentives that preserve the value of group membership.

The chapter is organized as follows. To fix ideas, we begin in section 2 with a definition of franchising. In section 3, we describe the theory behind the two types of incentive mechanisms mentioned above. In section 4 we develop our main argument on the complementarity between residual claims and self-enforcement in these contracts. Section 5 describes more specifically how, in practice, various aspects of the franchise relationship or contract clauses support the two types of incentive mechanisms discussed herein. Finally, in section 6, we extend our analysis to non-franchised production and/or retail networks operating under common reputation concerns, such as, for example, production cooperatives in agro-food industries. Concluding remarks are found in section 7.

2   Defining franchising

From a legal standpoint, a contract is a franchise contract in the United States if three main conditions are met: (1) the franchisee operates under the franchisor's brand name and trademarks, (2) the franchisor provides on-going support and exerts, or can exert, significant control over the franchisee's operations, and (3) the franchisee is required, as a condition to obtain the franchise or to commence operation, to pay more than $500 to the franchisor before the end of the first six months in operation. The legal definition of a franchise in the European Union (EU) is similar except that it is more specific about the requirement that the franchisor transfer know-how to the franchisee.[1]

Within franchising, the US Department of Commerce further categorizes relationships either as "product and trade name," also called "traditional," franchises, and "business format" franchises. In a product and trade name franchise, the franchisor mostly sells a finished product to the franchisee who then resells it. Examples include dealer-owned gasoline stations and car dealerships. In such relationships, the franchisor's profits arise from the markups charged on products sold to the franchisee. In business format franchising, by contrast, the franchisor mostly sells the right to use her tradename and business methods to the franchisee. In this case, the franchisee is responsible for both the production and sale of the finished product, as in the fast-food or hotel industries. In exchange for the use of the trade name and business methods, the franchisee pays a combination of fees to the franchisor. These most often include a franchise fee, payable once, at the beginning of the period covered by the contract, as well as royalties and advertising fees which are usually defined as a percentage of the outlet's sales or revenues.[2] These fees are typically the same for all franchisees joining a chain at a point in time.[3]

As a result of the emphasis on franchisor know-how in the EU definition of a franchise, the EU version corresponds more closely to the US definition of a business format franchise. Within Europe, further slight differences in definition also arise across countries. Such definitional differences make it difficult or inappropriate to directly compare statistics on the extent of franchising across countries and jurisdictions. However, from an incentive perspective, franchisors involved in business format and/or traditional franchising face very similar sets of challenges. Consequently, the analyses below apply to both types of franchised relationships, except as specifically noted.

3 Residual claims and on-going rent as incentive mechanisms

Franchising fundamentally involves franchisors granting franchisees the right to operate under their trade marks and business processes. But as these intangible assets remain the property of the franchisor, the granting of these rights gives rise to incentive problems and agency costs. As noted above, two main types of incentive mechanisms have been identified in the literature on franchise contracting as ways to mitigate these problems: the granting of residual claimancy rights, as emphasized in the principal–agent literature (see, e.g., Rubin 1978; Mathewson and Winter 1985) and the reliance on self-enforcement, which involves the provision of a stream of on-going rent downstream that the franchisee forgoes in the event of contract termination (see in particular Klein and Leffler 1981; Klein 1995). In what follows, we discuss the theory behind the functioning of these two types of mechanisms in the context of franchising.

3.1   *Residual claims in franchising*

Franchisee-owned businesses are legally independent from the business of their franchisor. Franchisees can own one or several franchised outlets in a chain, and as owners, they have a claim on the profits generated by their outlet(s). Franchisees claim these profits net of the usual sales-based royalties and advertising fees they pay to their franchisors. As these payments normally represent 6–10 percent of revenues, franchisees obtain the bulk of every additional dollar of sales generated within their outlet(s). Also, since royalty and advertising fee payments are based on revenues and not profits, franchisees reap the full benefit from every additional dollar decrease in operating costs.[4]

When franchisee effort is not observable, and so cannot be contracted on directly, it is optimal for the franchisor to sell the outlet to the franchisee for a fixed price (assuming that the franchisee's effort is central to production). This outright sale makes the franchisee a full residual claimant, thereby giving him incentives to put forth the optimal level of effort (see, e.g., Rubin 1978; Mathewson and Winter, 1985). Specifically, assume that sales S depend on franchisee effort in the following way:

$$S = ae + \varepsilon$$

where e is franchisee effort and a measures the importance of the franchisee's effort in the sales generation process. ε is a random variable with mean 0 and variance σ^2 that prevents the franchisor from inferring e from observed S. If the cost of effort for the franchisee is $C(e) = e^2/2$ and F is the price at which the franchisor sells the outlet to the franchisee, the risk-neutral franchisee will want to maximize expected profits, namely

$$\pi = ae - e^2/2 - F.$$

The first-order condition for this maximization problem gives $e^{**} = a$, which corresponds to the first-best level of effort and, thus, to the level of effort that the franchisor would have chosen if she had control over it. In that sense, selling the outlet at a fixed price to the franchisee completely resolves franchisee incentive issues. The franchisor can extract all the profits from the outlet operations by appropriately setting the price, F, at $F = a^2/2$.[5]

In practice, franchisees usually do not acquire outlets at a fixed price. Instead, they pay a nominal fixed fee, plus a proportion of their revenues every period over the whole duration of the contract. The typical franchise contract thus involves sharing.[6] Yet, under our assumptions, sharing is counter-productive – it prevents the realization of the first-best outcome. In particular, the franchisee who must pay a portion α of his revenues to the franchisor (where $0 < \alpha < 1$ represents the sum of all revenue-based fees such as royalty rates and advertising fees), maximizes

$$\pi = (1 - \alpha)ae - e^2/2 - F$$

by setting effort $e^* = (1 - \alpha)a$. As this effort level is lower than the first-best level $(= a)$, which is readily achievable under a fixed-price sale contract, one would not expect sharing to occur in this setting.

The principal–agent literature provides two alternative amendments to the model above to account for the use, in practice, of sharing arrangements. The first amendment, which is the most traditional, involves introducing the assumption that the franchisee is risk averse rather than risk neutral (see for example Stiglitz 1974 for the first such model, applied to sharecropping). In this case, the franchisee no longer maximizes expected profits, but rather expected utility. Sharing in this model then becomes a means of shifting risk from risk averse agents (franchisees) to risk neutral principals (franchisors). The second amendment relies instead on the assumption that the principal (franchisor) provides some valuable input in the production process and that her behavior, like that of the agent (franchisee), is difficult to monitor. In this model, called a double-sided moral-hazard model, sharing arises from the need to provide incentives to the franchisor as well as the franchisee (see notably Rubin 1978; Eswaran and Kotwal 1985; Lal 1990; and Bhattacharyya and Lafontaine 1995).

Where the franchisee is risk averse rather than risk neutral, he maximizes his expected utility from outlet profits or his certainty-equivalent income. Assuming that ε is normally distributed, and that the franchisee has a constant absolute risk aversion parameter of ρ, his certainty-equivalent income is given by

$$R = E(y) - C(e) - (\rho/2) \, \text{var} \, (y)$$
$$= (1 - \alpha)ae - F - e^2/2 - (\rho/2)(1 - \alpha)^2 \cdot \sigma^2$$

where $E(y)$ are his expected revenues. The first-order condition for this maximization problem again yields $e^* = (1 - \alpha)a$. Once substituted back into the franchisor's maximization problem, who chooses α to maximize total surplus, we have

$$\max[(1 - \alpha)a^2 - (1 - \alpha)^2a^2/2 - (\rho/2)(1 - \alpha)^2\sigma^2]$$

The first-order condition for the franchisor's problem implies that $\alpha^* = [\rho\sigma^2/(a^2 + \rho\sigma^2)] > 0$. In words, the "best" contract from the franchisor's perspective now involves sharing. This sharing arises as a way to balance the need to motivate franchisee effort (which leads toward $\alpha = 0$) while providing insurance to now risk averse agents (which leads toward

$\alpha = 1$). Of course, while this solution is optimal from the franchisor's perspective, it does not give rise to the first-best level of effort and output as $e^* = (1 - \alpha)a < a = e^{**}$.

Assuming instead that the franchisor also provides some non-observable input that contributes to the franchised outlet production or sales process, then even under risk neutrality for both franchisor and franchisee the optimal contract will involve sharing.[7] The share parameter now trades off franchisor and franchisee incentives. To illustrate, assume that outlet sales are given by

$$S = ae + br + \varepsilon$$

where r is the franchisor's effort level. Assume further that the franchisor's cost of effort is given by $C(r) = r^2/2$. The franchisee maximizing his profits given α will again choose $e^* = (1 - \alpha)a$. The franchisor who gets a fraction α of outlet sales will set $r^* = \alpha b$. Substituting these two effort levels into the franchisor's maximization problem yields

$$\max[(1 - \alpha)a^2 + \alpha b^2 - (1 - \alpha)^2 a^2/2 - \alpha^2 b^2/2]$$

The first-order condition for this maximization problem gives $\alpha^* = b^2/(a^2 + b^2) > 0$, which once again implies sharing.

Three main testable implications arise from these principal–agent models. The share parameter α (here, the sum of royalties and sales-based advertising fees) will be higher:
(1) the lower the importance of franchisee effort, as captured by a above
(2) the higher the level of risk involved (σ^2) (assuming the franchisee is more risk averse than the franchisor)
(3) the more important franchisor effort is, as captured by b above (assuming this effort is non-observable).

The empirical literature on franchising has found support for (1) and (3), but not for (2).[8]

Our discussion thus far has focused on the incentives embedded in franchise contracts via residual claims. It is important to note, however, that employment contracts can also accord residual claimant status to employees. And an employee–manager whose compensation was directly tied to the profits of the outlet he manages would choose the same effort level as a franchisee as long as his contract entailed the same "level" of residual claims.[9] In practice, however, franchise contracts normally entail residual claimant status for franchisees whereas the compensation of managers of company units in franchised chains usually is not tied very closely to outlet profits (see Bradach 1997 for evidence.)

3.2 Self-enforcement

In this section, we turn our attention to the role of hostages (Williamson 1985), efficiency wages (Shapiro and Stiglitz 1984; Akerlof and Yellen 1986) and self-enforcement more generally (Klein 1980; Klein and Leffler 1981; Klein and Saft 1985) in franchise contracting. The common thread across all these analyses is the notion that parties to a contract can be given incentives to put forth effort by making sure that they derive a benefit from the relationship that is at risk if they do not behave as requested. The incentives embedded in a franchise contract in this context do not stem from residual claims, but rather from the combined effect of three elements: (1) an ongoing stream of rent that the franchisee earns within the relationship but forgoes if he "leaves" the franchised chain, (2) franchisee monitoring by the franchisor, and (3) franchisor ability to terminate the franchise contract. Since the ease or cost of termination is largely determined by the applicable legal system, the franchisor is left with the tasks of choosing the level of ongoing rent to be left with franchisees and selecting the frequency of monitoring so as to minimize the *ex post* cost of enforcing the desired level of effort.[10]

Specifically, let W_t^1 represent the (expected) gain that the franchisee can obtain when deviating from the franchisor's requested behavior, and W_t^2 be the present value of the ongoing rent that the franchisee can earn within the relationship. Then a franchise contract is self-enforcing iff $W_t^2 > W_t^1$ at every time t. In other words, for the contract to be continuously self-enforcing, the franchisee must have a minimum amount of rent to look forward to each period. W_t^2 must therefore include not only the rent expected over the remainder of the contract, which by definition decreases as the franchise gets closer to expiration, but also rent associated with future additional outlets and with the probability of contract renewal.[11]

In this framework, specific contract terms (described in more detail in section 4) play different roles (Klein 1995), influencing either W_t^1 or W_t^2.

(i) *Contract terms affecting* W_t^1: Some contract terms specify certain franchisee obligations, for example the mandatory level of input purchases from the franchisor, other procurement requirements, minimum local advertising expenditures, or staffing levels. These contract terms limit W^1 as they make it easier for the franchisor to detect non-conformance and quickly intervene to limit the associated benefit to the franchisee. They also make it less costly for the franchisor to rely on third-party or court enforcement as they provide more objective bases from which to establish non-conformance.

(ii) *Contract terms affecting* W^2: Other contract terms serve to ensure the existence of the stream of ongoing rent whose potential loss gives incentives to the franchisee. Although Klein (1980, 1995) does not specify exactly how the stream of rent is created, he suggests that clauses such as exclusive territories limit intra-brand competition and thus contribute to the franchisee's profitability.[12] As noted above, guarantees about future expansion opportunities and likelihood of contract renewal could further affect the level of expected rent positively.

Because of uncertainty, complexity and lack of perfect monitoring, all aspects of the behavior desired of franchisees cannot be specified by the franchisor in the contract *a priori*. Hence the franchisee always has some leeway, and W^1 is never zero. As a consequence, the contract must always give rise to positive rent W^2 if the incentive constraint above is to be continuously satisfied. At the same time, there exists a maximum amount of rent to which the franchisor can credibly commit. If the franchisor prefers franchising to company-managed stores, it is presumably because vertical integration (company management) is less profitable. This implies that $\Pi^F - \Pi^I > 0$, the difference in profit from operating a unit under franchising versus vertical integration, is positive. Then the franchisor's promise of rent to the franchisee is credible if the value of the rent is less than the discounted profit difference at every time t, namely

$$W_t^{\,2} < \sum_{t=1}^{\infty} \frac{(\Pi_t^F - \Pi_t^I)}{(1+r)^t}.$$

If this condition is met, then it is in the best interest of the franchisor to pay the rent. Otherwise, it is more economical for the franchisor to vertically integrate and appropriate the rent.[13]

Empirically, Kaufmann and Lafontaine (1994) have shown, through a detailed analysis of the economics of McDonald's restaurants in the United States, that there is indeed rent left downstream in that chain. Following a similar methodology, Michael and Moore (1995) confirmed the existence of rent in a number of other franchised chains. Moreover, Brickley, Dark and Weisbach (1991) have shown that the proportion of corporate units in franchised chains is higher in US states that restrict the termination of contracts compared to other states (see also Beales and Muris 1995). This result suggests that the cost of termination indeed affects franchisors' decisions to franchise or vertically integrate outlets, thereby lending support to the idea that franchisors rely on rent and termination in their dealings with their franchisees.

Finally, it is important to note that the use of rent and self-enforcement as an incentive mechanism is in no way limited to the franchise context. In fact, the huge literature on "efficiency wages" in labor economics shows that the provision of "rent" and its potential loss are used to motivate employees within firms just as they can be used to motivate franchisees. This suggests that a franchisor could well use efficiency wages to motivate her store managers and, in doing so, eliminate the need to give store managers residual claims or use franchisees.

4   Substitutes or complements?

In this section, we consider why both residual claims and self-enforcement coexist at McDonald's and in other franchise systems. This coexistence is puzzling given that the agency and the self-enforcement literature each suggests that its incentive mechanism is sufficient, in itself, to resolve incentive issues.

Specifically, the self-enforcement literature, and Klein in particular, never considers the use of residual claims as an incentive mechanism. In this literature, the combination of a stream of rent, periodic monitoring, and the termination option are sufficient to achieve the desired outcome. There is therefore no role for residual claims in the analysis.

Similarly, in the literature that emphasizes residual claims as a source of incentives, rent does not enter into play at all. If, *ex ante*, the franchisor has designed an optimal contract, i.e. a contract that satisfies the franchisee's incentive constraint as well as his participation constraint, the franchisee earns no rent. In some models franchisees do earn rent, but these arise from the need to use the right share parameter, α, while also satisfying some liquidity or selection constraint (see Mathewson and Winter 1985). The rent serves no direct incentive purpose in these models. Furthermore, as the contract is designed with the franchisee's optimal reaction in mind, the franchisee has no reason to deviate *ex post*, and the final outcome is exactly what the franchisor expects it to be.

Why, given this, do we see residual claims and self-enforcement being used together in franchise contracts? We believe that this coexistence arises because residual claims give franchisees the incentive to put forth effort and not shirk, while ongoing rent gives franchisees the incentive to maintain the value of the brand by acting in the chain's collective interests. In fact, we would argue that it is precisely franchisees' residual claimant status that reinforces the need to use a self-enforcement mechanism to curb the tendency of franchisees to maximize their own profit at the expense of the overall chain. In short, we contend that the two mechanisms work in tandem and complement one another rather than being alternatives for one another.

But what are those behaviors that franchisees might engage in to increase their profits at the expense of the chain? Franchisee free-riding on the value of the brand is one form of franchisee "misbehavior" that has been discussed frequently in the franchising literature. The issue, in essence, is one of externality: the franchisee bears the full cost of maintaining high quality in his outlet, but the benefit of his behavior accrues not only to him in the form of high outlet sales, but also to all others in the chain as well as to the franchisor as high quality in each outlet leads to higher sales overall in the chain. In that sense, the quality level that maximizes the franchisee's profits is always lower than that desired by the franchisor (see Brickley, Dark and Weisbach, 1991; Blair and Kaserman, 1994). Similarly, the prices that maximize a franchisee's profits are higher than those that maximize chain profits. This again stems from the fact that the franchisee does not appropriate the positive effect of his low prices on sales at other outlets in the chain (see, e.g., Barron and Umbeck 1984; Shepard 1993; Lafontaine 2001, for more on this). Finally, franchisees can refuse to implement new production processes or to sell new products that they don't expect will be profitable in their particular market even if they are expected to be worthwhile for the chain, or they may choose to modify processes or product offerings to better fit their particular market (see for instance Kaufmann 1987; Lewin-Solomon 1998).[14]

All of these franchisee profit maximization strategies correspond to "misbehaviors" from the chain's perspective. To understand why, one need merely reflect on the franchised chain's *"raison d'être"*: to offer consumers a predictable, homogeneous product across a large number of geographically dispersed establishments. In fact, homogeneity is the goal not only for product offerings, but also for building design, ambiance, service, and price as this is at the heart of sustaining the value of the franchised chain brand. If a particular franchisee offers lower service or less quality, consumers may well infer that overall chain quality is declining, and choose not to frequent any of the chain's establishments in the future. Similarly, a franchisee's effort to satisfy his local customers via special product offerings may affect the franchise chain negatively if consumers become confused about what to expect, or are disappointed when other outlets do not carry their favorite product. In short, franchisees' efforts towards individual profit maximization can adversely affect the franchisor and other franchisees by eroding the value of the brand on which all parties in the chain depend, and thus adversely impacting the value of group membership itself.

The need for homogeneity in franchised chains in fact gives rise to significant restrictions on franchisee behavior (see section 5 for more details). Such restrictions reduce the profit that the franchisee could derive from outlet ownership. The ongoing stream of rent earned by franchisees can be viewed as "compensation" for the profits they forgo owing to these restrictions. This compensation should then be such that the franchisee earns at least as much under the contract than by maximizing only his own profits. This will automatically be satisfied if the contract is self-enforcing since it implies that $W_t^2 > W_t^1$. Further, W_t^2 includes expected rent from the additional outlets that a franchisee might be given the right to operate in the future. As the cost of having their behavior constrained by the franchise system is likely to be larger for better, more highly motivated franchisees, it is important that their expected rent also be larger. This occurs automatically here since better franchisees are more likely to be given the opportunity to own several outlets.[15]

Our argument so far however raises an important issue: if the franchisee's residual claimant status leads him or her to behave in ways that are inconsistent with what is optimal for the chain, thereby requiring the use of supplemental incentive mechanisms, why don't franchisors simply use self-enforcement mechanisms without residual claims to motivate franchisees? After all, the self-enforcement literature suggests one can obtain the desired behavior simply with an appropriate combination of on-going rent, monitoring, and termination.

We would argue that the answer to this question lies in the different types of tasks required of franchisees. Specifically, some of the activities that franchisees engage in, such as all those related to day-to-day outlet operations, are very costly to monitor, especially for geographically dispersed outlets. Moreover, individual outlet sales and profits are fairly highly correlated to franchisee effort for these types of tasks. Residual claims are a particularly appropriate incentive tool in such contexts, i.e. when output measures (here sales and profits) are good proxies for effort and effort is difficult to monitor (see for example Lafontaine and Slade 1996 for more on this).[16] By contrast, a franchisee's decision to implement or not new production procedures or new product offerings, or to participate in various system-level activities, and more generally to comply with explicit contract clauses such as those that govern supplier choices and minimum advertising levels, are all fairly easy (low-cost) to monitor. Furthermore, as argued above, the correlation between outlet sales and compliance with all these policies need not be high at all. If sales and/or profits do not provide a good measure of such effort, residual claims will not provide the right incentives to implement these. Franchisors will therefore do better using a self-enforcement mechanism to get the franchisee to participate in these.

5   Specific contract terms and implementation

So far, we have focused our discussion on the role of residual claims and self-enforcement in aligning franchisee and franchisor incentives without providing much detail as to how these mechanisms are implemented or supported via specific contract terms. In this section, we briefly describe how specific franchise contract terms serve to implement these two mechanisms. We begin with residual claims.

5.1   *Franchise contract terms supporting franchisees' residual claimant status*

Contract terms defining the financial obligations of franchisees, along with contract terms that allow franchisors to ensure franchisee performance of these obligations, and finally franchisee prerogative to transfer ownership of a franchise all contribute to establish residual claimancy rights within franchise contracts. The financial terms define the apportionment of residual claims among parties to the franchise contract; the franchisor's access to specific type of information ensures that the defined apportionment of residual claims is correctly effected; and the franchisees' prerogative to transfer ownership of a franchise ensures that franchisees can appropriate the current and future profits due to their effort and investments.

As mentioned in section 3, residual claimancy incentives would be fully implemented if franchisees purchased their businesses for a fixed fee only. However, the optimal (second-best) linear contract involves sharing when the franchisee is risk averse or when there is a need to give incentives to the franchisor as well as the franchisee. In that context, the financial terms that implement residual claims in franchise contracts include not only the up-front franchise fee, but also most notably the royalty rate and advertising fee, both of which are normally defined as a proportion of revenues, and clauses specifying input purchase requirements when these inputs are sold at a markup.[17]

To the financial terms of the contract, one must add contract terms that allow the franchisor to obtain accurate accounting and sales information to calculate royalties and advertising fees. Specifically, one usually finds clauses defining precisely the store revenue that is subject to royalty payments and advertising fees. Other clauses indicate the method and frequency with which the relevant revenue data must be transmitted to the franchisor. Still other clauses stipulate the circumstances under which the franchisor will be able to conduct his own store audits and other forms of financial verification to ensure the validity of the information she receives.

Finally, contract terms that accord franchisees the right to transfer their franchise to someone else serve an important role in implementing residual claims as well as self-enforcement incentives. Franchisees usually own or finance much of the franchise's assets (which may, or may not include the actual building within which the franchise is housed), and are allowed to sell their franchise at any time (subject to approval of the buyer by the franchisor).[18] The ownership of the franchise, and its inherent transferability through sale, makes the franchisor's promise of future residual claims (and related future rent) credible (Lutz 1995). As such, they give franchisees' incentives to invest resources and effort in future as well as current revenues and returns.

5.2 *Franchise contract terms supporting the self-enforcement mechanism*

As explained earlier, self-enforcement incentives require that contracting parties always be better off by continuing to operate within the contract than by risking discontinuation. Contract terms can implement this condition by increasing the expected gains from continuation (W^2) and/or decreasing the expected gains from deviation (W^1). The former involves increasing expected ongoing rent through favorable financial terms as well as, potentially, entry restrictions, lengthy contract duration, a high likelihood of renewal, and a policy of allowing or fostering multi-unit ownership among franchisees. The latter involves restricting franchisee conduct through terms stipulating, for example, specific operating procedures, acceptable input sources, minimum advertising expenditure levels, or suggested pricing levels.

5.2.1 *Increasing expected rent (W_t^2)*

The financial terms of the contract described above determine the apportionment of revenues between franchisor and franchisee, and the amount of rent left downstream with the franchisee. In fact, as noted in section 3, once the optimal sharing parameter (sum of royalty rate and advertising fee) is determined, there is a maximum fixed fee that the franchisor can charge for the franchise. This maximum fixed fee is equal to the present value of the expected returns (*ex post* rent) of the franchise over the duration of the contract, given the chosen share parameter. If the franchisor sets the franchise fee at this level, there is no expected rent *ex ante* from owning the franchise. There is, however, *ex-post* rent downstream which may suffice to ensure franchisee performance. If the franchise fee is set at a lower level than this maximum, there is both *ex ante* and *ex post* rent left downstream in the franchised chain. The level of *ex ante* rent earned by the franchisee in fact is exactly equal to the difference between the present value of the stream of *ex post* rent expected over the duration of the contract and the initial fee. Thus holding the franchise fee fixed, factors that increase expected rent *ex post* also lead to higher expected *ex ante* rent.

Restricting new entry into the franchised chain ensures a degree of ongoing market power for individual franchisees. In concert with the allocation of exclusive territories,[19] such entry restrictions limit intra-brand competition and thus increase the amount of *ex post* rent for franchisees. After setting the financial terms of the contract, it is therefore through the number of franchises sold in each market that the franchisor most directly affects the level of revenues and rent for franchisees. Moreover, these decisions determine the density of outlets and thus the level of all forms of externality across outlets in the market.

By stringently qualifying prospective franchisees, the franchisor also helps ensure that chain homogeneity and quality, and thus franchisee rent, are maintained over the long run. The franchisor seeks motivated individuals with the demonstrated ability to manage the day-to-day operations of an outlet while respecting the franchise chain's restrictions and its rules. Furthermore, to acquire a particular franchise, a prospective franchisee must satisfy certain franchisor requirements, often including a minimum net worth and/or some level of prior business experience. During the training period the franchisor and the franchisee also each gain important information for assessing the fit between the two. The franchisor can assess the strengths and weaknesses of the potential franchisee while the franchisee can determine whether the business activity and franchisee role are right for that individual. The thorough selection process screens out prospective franchisees whose lack of motivation or ability could erode brand value, thereby providing current franchisees a measure of security against dissipation of their expected rent.

The length of the franchise contract also affects the amount of rent franchisees can expect to earn within the franchise relationship. The average length of franchise contracts in the United States is about fifteen years according to the US DOC, with most of them lasting from five to twenty-five years. The main advantage of longer-term contracts is that the franchisee can count on appropriating the returns to his long-term investments and is therefore more apt to make such investments. In addition, all else equal, long-term contracts directly imply higher levels of future rent (W^2), which in turn reduce free-riding problems. On the other hand, long-term contracts may increase the cost of self-enforcement by making it more difficult to "end" the relationship itself via non-renewal or termination. Courts may be more reluctant to endorse early termination of long-term contracts, or they may require that franchisors compensate franchisees more when they terminate a long-term contract. Moreover, a shorter-term contract makes it less costly for a franchisor to wait until contract expiration and simply refuse to renew. In this case, the use of short-term contracts would enable franchisors to avoid termination and its associated costs altogether.[20] In sum, decisions regarding contract duration must balance the need for franchisee investment and the costs of enforcement.

Finally, the probability of contract renewal and the availability of additional outlets within the chain play very similar roles as contract duration in the motivation of franchisees. Specifically, renewal implies that the franchisee can expect his stream of *ex post* rent to continue beyond contract expiration. The higher the probability of this event, the higher is the amount of rent associated with maintaining the relationship.[21] As for additional outlets, they can also serve to extend the period of expected rent *ex post* beyond the expiration of the first contract.[22] However, they can be even more valuable as an incentive mechanism if franchisees can expect to earn rent *ex ante* from these (i.e. if the franchise fee or purchase price for additional outlets is below the present value of expected returns from these generally, or for this particular franchisee because he already owns other units in the same market and will benefit from additional market power or efficiencies with the new unit).[23]

5.2.2   *Restricting the gains from deviation (W_t^1)*

Most franchise contracts include terms stipulating that the franchisee must operate his or her outlet according to the norms set by the franchisor in the operations manuals. In fact, these manuals and the detailed instructions they provide are often included in the contract by reference.[24] Moreover, the contract usually includes a clause indicating that the franchisor can modify these manuals as needed. The franchisor therefore can impose a large set of detailed rules on the franchisee's operations, and has the option of changing these rules in midstream. From an incentive perspective, these rules provide an evolving series of fairly objective criteria that can be used to justify and facilitate contract termination. They also limit the franchisee's opportunities to free ride and thus the profits he can obtain from free-riding generally.

Other specific contract clauses limit the franchisees' options and thus increase franchisor control. These include input purchase requirements or approved supplier clauses,[25] minimum advertising expense requirements, and suggested prices.[26] Non-compliance with such restrictions is easily verified by the court system. In that sense, their use reduces franchisees' opportunities to maximize their profits at the expense of the overall system.

Finally, if all these clauses and control mechanisms prove insufficient to induce the desired behavior from franchisees, or are simply too costly to implement, the franchisor can choose to vertically integrate any particular outlet. In that case, since managers are not typically paid based on profits or revenues (and do not have a stake in future profits or revenues either), the franchisor loses the incentive effects associated with residual claims. However, an efficiency wage can be put in place, and the store manager can be further motivated by the hope of promotion, in the form of a transfer to an outlet in a more desirable location, or to higher levels of the franchisor's corporate hierarchy. In fact, most franchisors own and operate a number of outlets in their system.[27] In that sense, the option of vertically integrating outlets is a very viable one.

In sum, franchisors use a number of contract clauses and incentive mechanisms that allow the franchise system to benefit from the effort and dedication of the individual franchisee/owner while limiting his or her ability to impose negative externalities on other franchisees or the franchised chain. Many of these clauses simultaneously support both types of incentive mechanisms used in franchise contracting. For example, financial contract terms simultaneously apportion residual claims and determine the amount of rent in the relationship. Similarly, sporadic audits are necessary to ensure that the revenues are declared and shared according to the terms of the contract, and termination, an essential component of the self-enforcement mechanism, is also the ultimate penalty imposed on a franchisee who does not fully disclose revenues. In fact, it should be clear from the discussion above that the terms of franchise contracts generally complement one another not only in their support of the two incentive mechanisms discussed here, but, fundamentally, in supporting the franchise system as a whole.

6   Non-franchised systems with common mark or reputation concerns

We have so far discussed how self-enforcement (and the many contract clauses that support it) work together with residual claims to give franchisees the right set of incentives. Fundamentally, we have argued that the franchised system relies on rent to prevent the profit maximizing franchisee from "hurting" the brand in his quest for higher profits. But the need to "protect the brand" or the system is not unique to franchising. In this section, we show through two examples how our analysis also applies to non-franchised systems with a common mark or common reputation concerns.

"Labels rouges" (literally red labels) are used in France to certify the high quality of various agricultural products. These "labels rouges" are government-endorsed marks that groups of producers can collectively create and work under. The creation of such a label requires that all producers in a vertical chain be involved, and that these producers collectively define a set of rules and specifications, codified in the "Cahier des Charges," under which they promise to operate (see Ménard, 1996; Westgren 1999, for a description of the organization of production under "labels rouges" in the poultry industry). Different groups of producers within the same agricultural sector can create different "labels rouges" with different rules and specifications. However, all of these must satisfy some minimum requirements to be approved as "labels rouges." From the consumer's perspective, the different "labels rouges" can be distinguished because they each have their own individual identity. For example, in the French poultry industry, there are now more than 80 different "labels rouges."[28]

When they create a "label rouge," producers must also organize and form a "Groupement qualité," which owns the collective mark and is responsible for the enforcement of the rules. This "Groupement qualité" is fundamentally an association of producers, and all producers must enter into a contract with this association before they can sell under this mark.

As each member of a "label rouge" is an independent and separate business, the producers are all full residual claimants. Consequently, they may free ride on the common mark or simply maximize their own profits without necessarily taking into account the effect of their behavior on others in the group. Thus the group must institute incentive and control mechanisms. And indeed, many of the clauses found in producer contracts with the "Groupement Qualité" are best understood as ways to make the contracts self-enforcing. In particular, the "Groupement Qualité" has the right to regularly inspect and monitor the behavior of individual producers, and the option to terminate the membership of any producer whose production does not satisfy the rules and specifications set forth in the "Cahier des Charges." Moreover, group members earn rent – they can sell their product at a premium because the label effectively differentiates it and identifies it as a high-quality product, and this price premium is protected by territorial exclusivity clauses (e.g. territorial exclusivity for slaughterhouses within a given label) (see Raynaud and Valceschini 1999 for details).

In sum, the contractual structure of a "label rouge," and in fact of production cooperatives more generally, tends to be very similar to that of a franchised system. Within these systems, individual producers are residual claimants as franchisees are. But the system also includes a central entity that contracts with all producers, as the franchisor does. This central entity also monitors individual producer behavior to make sure producers abide by the rules. Finally, like a franchisor, the central entity can exclude producers that do not abide by the rules and, as a result, cause them to lose access to a stream of rent.

In a similar vein, Arruñada (1996) shows the similarities between franchising and the way in which "Civil Law" notaries are organized as a profession in Spain. He notes that under Civil Law, notaries provide private contracting services for which their customers pay them directly. However, these notaries also provide a public good in that they keep records and perform research to ensure the validity of various contracts. The effort they put in these validation activities affects the quality of contracts in the economy, and thus entails significant externalities. The notary, as a residual claimant, would maximize his or her revenues by focusing effort on the production of the private good only. But without any validation activities, the whole civil notaries' system breaks down – the reputation of the whole system depends on each notary doing a thorough job of validating and record keeping. Arruñada (1996) argues that rent, owing to entry restrictions and price controls for notarized services, and the potential loss of this rent, complements the incentives associated with residual claimancy and ensures the provision of the public as well as the private goods.

7   Conclusion

The two types of incentive mechanisms found in franchise contracting are those related to the franchisee's status as a residual claimant, as captured in the principal–agent literature, and those related to self-enforcement. The latter focuses on giving franchisees something to lose if the relationship is ended, and combining that with some regular monitoring and termination rights so that the franchisee will indeed have to worry about this potential loss if he does not behave as requested. The literature has generally treated these mechanisms as separate and even substitute incentive mechanisms. Yet empirically they coexist. We have explained this coexistence based on the notion of complementarities. Specifically, we have argued that residual claims give strong incentives to maximize profits, sometimes at the expense of the brand and other group members. The combination of rent and termination rights in that context are tools that the franchisor can use to curb this profit maximization motive when it is harmful to the overall franchised system. Similarly, relying solely on rent and termination rights would leave the franchisor vulnerable to shirking by franchisees on the day-to-day operations as it would be very costly for the franchisor to do the type of monitoring necessary to prevent this type of misbehavior. Since outlet revenues provide a good measure of franchisee effort for these types of activities, residual claims are the more appropriate incentive tool.

Our argument that self-enforcement and residual claims go hand in hand in franchising and in other similar settings fits in particularly well with Holmström and Milgrom's (1994) work on the role of complementarities in the design and workings of incentive systems.[29] Though we have focused on a particular institutional setting, that of the franchise relationship, we have noted that the points raised here apply in many other settings where legally autonomous businesses share a common brand or reputation concern. Aside from production cooperatives, which we used as our main example, one can think for example of cartel enforcement and labor negotiations with common unions as other settings where the need to motivate individual members can conflict with the needs of the group and hence the value of group membership. Further work into the specifics of how these groups organize their joint activities would be most useful in clarifying further the role of complementarities in contracting and organization more generally.

NOTES

Chapter 18 was originally published as "Créance résiduelle et flux de rentes comme mécanismes incitatifs dans les contrats de franchise; compléments ou substituts?," in *Revue d'Economie Industrielle* (92, 2000).

We thank two referees and David Leibsohn for their comments, and our respective institutions for their support.

1. See FTC, "Disclosure Requirements and Prohibitions Concerning Franchising and Business Opportunity Ventures" (16 CFR § 436.1 *et seq.*), and EU rule 4087/88; 1988.
2. According to the US Department of Commerce (DOC) (1988), franchise contracts in the United States can last anywhere from five years to perpetuity, with an average of about fifteen years.
3. See Lafontaine (1992). Also, these fees are fairly stable over time. See Lafontaine and Shaw (1999) for empirical evidence on this.
4. In product and trade name franchising, franchisees do not pay these sales-based royalties. However, the markups charged by the franchisor on every unit of input can be equivalent to sales royalties under certain conditions. (See Lafontaine and Slade 2001 for more on this.)
5. To simplify the algebra, we ignore issues of contract duration and discounting. This in no way affects the generality of the result that a fixed price contract resolves all incentive issues when franchisees are risk neutral. Note that F could be set at any level not exceeding $a^2/2$. But any F below $a^2/2$ means that the franchisor does not make as much as he could, and the franchisee

does better than required by his participation constraint. We come back to this below.

6. Sharing occurs also, for example, in sharecropping, licensing, film distribution, and publishing contracts.

7. If the franchisee is risk averse while the franchisor is risk neutral, as in our previous setting, sharing will arise as an optimal response still. In this case, the share parameter will play the double role of providing incentives to the franchisor as well as insurance to the franchisee.

8. See Lafontaine and Slade (2001) for a review of the empirical literature on franchise contracting.

9. See Lutz (1995) for more on this.

10. For self-enforcement to work, the franchisor must be able to evaluate, *ex post*, whether or not the franchisee's performance is satisfactory even if the desired effort is too complex to specify in the contract.

11. Indeed, only high-performance franchisees can expect renewal and additional outlets within the same chain. These decisions therefore entail rent that gives further incentives to franchisees. See Kaufmann and Lafontaine (1994) for more on this.

12. This assumes that franchisees can earn profits in the long run, i.e. that they do not operate in a perfectly competitive or monopolistically competitive market. If profits were dissipated in the long run, there would be no rent in the long run, and thus no self-enforcement. In other words, Klein's analysis presumes that branding allows franchisees to differentiate their product enough that they earn positive profits in the long run (that the franchisor may or may not extract fully up-front – we come back to the issue of rent extraction below).

13. We assume that W_t^2 varies over time. See Williams (1996) and Brickley (2001) for an argument that as the market changes, the amount of rent may change in a way that makes integration the preferred option. The franchisor who then terminates or does not renew a franchise contract can be thought of as exercising the equivalent of a "call option."

14. Brickley and Dark (1987) also point out that franchisees tend to under-invest in their outlets as they must assume most of the investment risk. While this effect is due to risk aversion rather than the presence of an externality, it again implies that the franchisee will not act in the best interest of the chain as a whole.

15. Also, by granting franchisees several outlets that are close to one another, the franchisor may benefit even more as the franchisee then internalizes more of the horizontal effects of his behavior, and free-rides less. Consistent with this, Brickley (1999) finds that area development agreements – contracts through which franchisees are initially given the right to open several outlets – are significantly more likely to be used by franchisors involved in non-repeat customer industries, where free-riding is especially an issue.

16. Consistent with this, Kaufmann and Lafontaine (1994) present evidence that franchisors monitor the behavior of their store managers much more often than that of franchisees. Further, Bradach (1997) finds that the franchisors he studies use elaborate supervision and monitoring schemes for their store

managers, but that they shun the use of the same mechanisms for their franchisees.

17. In some business-format franchises, the royalty rate or advertising fee is replaced by an ongoing fixed payment. Abstracting from issues of termination or failure, these are equivalent to an up-front fixed fee from an incentive perspective.

18. Franchisors may also have a right of first refusal.

19. Various surveys indicate that in the United States, about two out of every three franchisors offer exclusive territories to their franchisees. Furthermore, "master franchise" agreements all involve some form of territory. Master franchise agreements take one of two main forms: area development agreements, where the selected franchisee normally develops and owns all the outlets on his territory, and sub-franchising agreements, where the "master franchisee" is expected to recruit and support (i.e. play the role of franchisor for) franchisees he establishes on his territory.

20. Legal rules against termination imposed in some US states apply also to non-renewals, but the latter remain easier and less costly to implement.

21. Often, franchisors request the payment of a new fixed fee upon renewal. This fixed fee should be deducted from expected *ex post* rent over the renewal period, and the result multiplied by the probability of renewal, to get an estimate of the *ex ante* expected amount of rent from renewal.

22. In fact, if the probability of renewal is very low, and the likelihood of additional outlets almost nil, the expected rent of the franchisee, and thus his incentives not to free ride or damage the brand, will diminish gradually over the duration of the contract.

23. See Kalnins and Lafontaine (2001) for further discussion of the potential benefits franchisees can derive from owning multiple units in a market.

24. Operations manuals are usually very detailed, to the point of including, for example, pictures of what plates should look like when served in a restaurant chain, including the position of each item on the plate.

25. *Siegel et al.* v. *Chicken Delight, Inc.*, 448 F. 2d43 (9th circuit, 1971) established that input purchase requirements were a form of tying for business format franchisors as long as the inputs were a separate product from the brand. As a result, business-format franchisors in the United States rely on approved suppliers rather than input purchase requirements to control input quality.

26. Resale price maintenance is *per se* illegal under US antitrust laws. However, a 1997 Supreme Court decision has made maximum resale prices for all intents and purposes legal. (See Blair and Lafontaine 1999 for more on this.)

27. On average, US franchisors operate about 20 percent of all their units, despite about 25 percent of franchisors operating none. Similarly, in France, about 78 percent of all franchised systems include both franchised and corporate units. See Lafontaine (1992) and Lafontaine and Shaw (2001) for US data, and Allam and Le Gall (1999) for French data. One finds a number of theories in the literature as to why franchisors might want to combine company-owned and franchised outlets within a given chain. It is beyond the scope of the present chapter to review this fairly extensive literature, but see Lafontaine and Slade (2001) for a review of the empirical literature on this topic.

28. For instance, "poulets de Loué" and "volailles de Challans" where Loué and Challans are different geographical regions.
29. See also Athey and Stern (1998) on this. Ichniowski, Shaw and Prennushi (1997) and Cockburn, Henderson and Stern (2000) provide evidence of complementarities in incentive mechanisms in steel production and the pharmaceutical laboratory context, respectively. Finally, Brickley (1999) considers complementarities between a few specific contract clauses in franchising.

19 The quasi-judicial role of large retailers: an efficiency hypothesis of their relation with suppliers

Benito Arruñada

1 Introduction

1.1 The problem

In recent years, public discussion concerning large retailers and their suppliers has been growing in intensity. It is often claimed that large retailers are endowed with overwhelming bargaining power and that they abuse this power in their relations with suppliers. New regulations have already been introduced and new regulatory initiatives are often proposed.[1] This work formulates and tests an alternative hypothesis, according to which large retailers efficiently perform a function similar to that of a court of first instance, that is, they act as second-party enforcers in their relationships with suppliers.

The empirical analysis is consistent with the argument that, in order to perform this function, large retailers exercise a set of implicit and explicit rights to "complete" or fill the gaps in the contract, to evaluate their own and the other party's performance and to impose due sanctions. Safeguards against opportunistic behavior in the performance of these quasi-judicial functions follow directly from the retailers' own interest in maintaining their reputation and the relationship with the suppliers, and in continuing to perform the double role of judge and interested party. It is rarely optimal, however, to eliminate opportunism completely. In retailing, failures in safeguards arise especially when the retailer's time horizon is unexpectedly shortened or his decentralized decisions are imperfectly controlled. Regarding these residual and potentially efficient distortions, it is claimed that regulation could hardly provide better incentives than market competition.

The chapter pays special attention to the most problematical aspects of the relationship between suppliers and retailers: the duration of the payment period, payment delays, and the revision of the clauses before the end of the contract term. Quantitative empirical evidence aiming to explain these phenomena in terms of efficiency is presented. On the one hand, payment periods vary according to an industry-wide pattern that is coherent with an incentive-based logic. On the other hand, statistical analysis of the average payment period and payment delay per country shows that administrative difficulties of the firms are the cause of both the longer payment period and the delay. This is coherent with the view of these two phenomena, payment period and payment delay, as being efficient contractual instruments. Finally, some empirical data concerning revisions before the end of the contract term are analyzed. It seems, first, that these revisions are related to phenomena that increase the total surplus of the relationship. Secondly, the possibility of suppliers being exploited is rejected on several grounds, such as the lack of specific investments because of the nature of the activity, the low concentration of the retail sector in Spain, the use of short-term contracts and, above all, the annual renovation of contracts.

The rest of the chapter has the following structure. The logic of the contracting process is examined in the second part of this introduction, where the theoretical background of the analysis is presented. Both the explicit (section 2) and the implicit (section 3) contracting between the two economic agents are studied, including the initial contracts, their revision, and the form and contents of the contracts. Special attention is paid to the payment period and payment conditions. The main sources of conflict are studied at length (section 4), and possible discipline mechanisms used by the retailer in his parajudicial role are analyzed (section 5). Finally, the safeguards assuring that these discipline mechanisms would not be abused are presented (section 6). The article ends with a summary of its basic conclusions.

1.2   *Asymmetric contracting*

Three main branches have been distinguished in the analysis of contracts (Masten 2000). First, in the economic theory of contracts, parties reach agreements on the content of the exchange and an external judge enforces these agreements perfectly. Secondly, law and economics comes closer to reality, by supposing that the judge also completes the contract, contributing to defining the terms of exchange. Different approaches within this perspective use more or less restrictive concepts. Sometimes the judge is believed to behave efficiently, trying to discover the hypothetical will of the parties. Alternatively, judges are assumed to take into account other considerations, such as equity, and sometimes their decisions are viewed as affected by the rent-seeking activities of the parties. Finally, the theories that consider contracts as relationships offer a more complex perspective, considering also the possibility that judicial intervention can be relatively inefficient. As a consequence, the main function of contracts is not to define the terms of exchange, but to frame the process by which these terms are decided (Macaulay 1963, 1985). Thus contracts define a variety of organs and decision rules, helping to create a framework, constitution, or governance structure for the corresponding economic relationship.

From this latter point of view, a basic option in contractual design consists of choosing whether to facilitate or to avoid the use of self-completion and self-enforcement mechanisms. "Self-completion" consists of the parties defining by themselves the conditions or contents of exchange, that is, the set of duties that the parties are obliged to perform for each other in any possible contingency. In general, these obligations can be specified through mechanisms that are internal or external to the parties. Internal solutions are implemented through organs and decision rules, but also through asymmetric authority, as in the case in hand. Alternatively, external institutional solutions may be used, consisting mainly of the law, for achieving *ex ante* completion, and of litigation and arbitration, for *ex post* completion. There is also a wide range of possibilities for enforcing the obligations resulting from the contractual relationship. They are also either internal to the parties, based on repetition and reputation, or external, using mainly the coercive power of the state.

Participants in economic transactions enjoy considerable information advantages with respect to third parties, including judges. For this reason, if one of the parties reaches a position of impartiality (either because of his reputation or because he contracts in a repetitive way), it is in the interest of all contracting parties to agree that this party possessing better information and incentives should be in charge of completing and enforcing the contract. This party thus performs tasks of a judicial nature. These include defining *ex post* any obligations that have not been agreed on *ex ante*, by adjusting the terms of trade to the latest changes and distributing unexpected gains or losses; evaluating whether each party has fulfilled its obligations or not; and imposing sanctions for poor performance.[2] In order to facilitate the exercise of these functions, it is necessary for the parties to choose contract solutions which strengthen the enforcing capacity of the internal judge (or which prevent opportunistic recourse to an external judge, as analyzed in Masten and Snyder 1993). The clearest of the examples studied in this chapter is the payment period between retailers and suppliers, which plays a much more important role than just exploiting comparative advantages of a strictly financial nature.

The resulting organizational structure therefore constitutes a hybrid between the two extremes that, following Williamson's typology (1975, 1985), represents the ideal types of market and hierarchy. Williamson views these hybrids as corresponding to neoclassical contract law subject to the "excuse doctrine," which is also an intermediate form between classical contract law and the principle of *forbearance* that governs the legal treatment of hierarchical relations (Williamson 1991, 1996, pp. 93–119).

The degree of judicial intervention places these intermediate solutions closer to one of the two extremes. In this case and with respect to the dimensions analyzed, we will see that the solution adopted in practice will be closer to the *forbearance* that is typical of the judicial treatment of hierarchical organization. This closeness, however, is not a consequence of active judicial abstention. In fact, judges are not given the opportunity of passing judgment on these matters because they are not litigated. Furthermore, if judges were given such an opportunity, precedents in other fields suggest that they would be likely to act in a way that would obstruct the performance of quasi-judicial functions by the retailer. This judicial inclination would motivate opportunistic litigation by suppliers. For this reason, this solution could work only when the relationship provides a large self-enforcement range or when this range can be enlarged by contractual means (Klein 1992, 1996; Masten and Snyder 1993; Klein and Murphy 1997).

These contractual mechanisms designed to avoid judicial intervention seem to be unnecessary between suppliers and retailers. Suppliers do not usually object to retailers' decisions, mostly because of the repetitive nature of the transactions. Interestingly, this happens even in cases of statutory rules which, because of their mandatory nature, can not be overruled contractually and which aim to establish a legal basis for litigation. An example of such a rule is the one giving creditors an irrevocable right to be paid interest and a penalty in the case of late payment by a retailer.

2   Explicit contracting

Typically, explicit contracting between suppliers and large retailers begins with the retailer making a thorough examination of the potential supplier. When the supplier passes the examination, a written contract is signed defining the terms of exchange, even if they remain open to systematic renegotiation and annual revisions.[3]

2.1   Contractual conditions

2.1.1   First negotiation
Large retailers usually examine their suppliers before signing the first contract to ensure that the quality of the product corresponds to the retailer's market position, thus effectively performing their quality assurance role.

They usually inspect the supplier's financial solvency, probably with the intention of estimating the potential duration of the relationship, and its incentives to maintain quality. Finally, they also evaluate the administrative organization of the supplier, as this is often a source of future conflicts.

Selling through a large retailer is valuable for small suppliers. If the retailer is an industry leader, suppliers even use this fact as a signaling device in their relations with other clients. The existence of an initial examination and this use of the condition of supplier as an informative signal indicates that large retailers effectively provide quality assurance services, which for many years has been one of their main objectives.[4]

2.1.2 Contract terms

At the beginning of every business year, the relations between suppliers and retailers are subject to exhaustive renegotiation. The process starts with the setting of objectives and follows with the signature of a new framework contract stipulating the price and other conditions. In the majority of relationships, a tariff and series of discounts related to specific variables (such as volume) are agreed. In this way, the retailer bears the risk of, for example, unexpectedly low sales which would prevent it from benefitting from any such discounts. In other contracts, these risks are borne by the supplier because annual "guaranteed prices" are agreed. In this second case if, at the end of the business year, after computing all the sales and promotions the resulting average price exceeds the guaranteed price, the supplier should pay the difference to the retailer. A small number of retailers try to go further, negotiating a "net price" plus a detailed schedule of all the promotions planned for the whole year. In this way, both parties have incentives to achieve common goals.

2.1.3 Payment period

Payment conditions such as the term and the instruments to be used are a central element of the contract. The established patterns show remarkable regularities, which can be seen most clearly in the duration of the payment periods. (a) Purchases of perishable goods are generally paid for within thirty and forty-five days, or on the spot. The only spot payments that are really immediate, however, are those for purchases of fresh fish, the rest having a payment period of about ten days. Payment periods are shorter for those products where a longer payment period would not facilitate supervision of the supplier by the retailer (short product life and no-return policy for perishables) or where such supervision would generate more trouble than good (fresh fish). The argument can be extended to other attributes of the transactions and products that influence the parties' capacity to observe any possible defect in product quantity or quality. In this case, the problem is solved by the intervention of a third party, usually an independent transport company, that gives information about the quantity of the merchandise delivered and the date of delivery. (b) Consumer products such as packaged food and drugstore items are paid for within a period of sixty–ninety days, while household goods are generally paid for in ninety days. (c) Textile products, which have the longest trade cycle and whose quality is thus known with the greatest delay, are paid for in 120–180 days. (d) Finally, any merchandise that is distributed with a right to return unsold items is paid for in periods longer than the return period, thus the payment period avoids possible opportunism associated with credit balances.[5]

There is also some variation among suppliers within the same industry that is sometimes explained by differences in the suppliers' bargaining power. However, it is not clear how the retailer benefits if he exploits his hypothetically greater bargaining power over a longer payment period rather than over the buying price. In fact, international data confirm the existence of a positive correlation between the price paid by purchasers and the payment period, both in general for all kinds of purchasers, and in particular for retailers (see table 19.1, in which the purchase price is proxied by the commercial margins, assuming that the selling price is unaffected). Explanation of the variety observed would therefore consider the payment period as an implicit modification of the product's price. The discount implied in a longer payment period is less evident both for the negotiator himself and for an employee who negotiates for his superiors. Differences among retailers with respect to their average payment period are also difficult to explain on the basis of bargaining power. They are neither related to the respective market share, nor do these shares reach a sufficiently high level, at least in Spain, in order to exert an influence. Given that there are also considerable variations in other dimensions of the retailers' strategies, such differences could be interpreted as an integral part of their strategic variety. In particular, retailers with longer average payment periods can be understood as developing comparative advantages in financial management.

In conclusion, the patterns in payment periods are coherent with the argument that the payment period serves not only to achieve comparative advantage of a financial nature, but also to lessen the intensity of conflict in contractual relationships. Bargaining power explanations are not satisfactory because they are unable to account for sectorial and product patterns. It is difficult to believe that bargaining power varies according to sectors and products, especially considering that sectorial and product patterns are not correlated with concentration of supply.

Table 19.1. *Average profit margin as a function of credit and payment periods in EU countries*

	Average net margin[a]		Average gross margin[b]
Constant	38.203	40.592	1.037
	(5.906***)[c]	(5.375***)	(15.199***)
Ln (Contractual credit period granted to clients)	−6.796 (−3.758***)	—	—
Ln (Actual average payment period)	—	−6.838 (−3.532***)	—
Ln (Actual average payment period)	—	—	−0.222 (−3.222**)
R^2_{adj}	0.467	0.433	0.652
F	14.123**	12.473**	10.379**
N	16	16	6

Notes and sources: [a]Regressions based on country averages for the net commercial margin, obtained through a survey of manufacturers (Intrum Justitia, 1997). This survey, carried out in 1996 by NOP Corporate for Intrum Justitia, covered 3,000 European companies and was part of a research into payment patterns supported by the European Commission. [b]Regression based on country averages for the gross margin of large retailers, given by Strambio, González and Contreras (1995, p. 53). [c]Two-tail *t*-statistics are in brackets, with *** = significant at the 99% confidence level; ** = significant at the 95% confidence level.

2.1.4 Legal formalization

The first agreement and successive annually revised ones are formalized in writing. Considering that litigation is very rare, these written contracts are mostly used to help the parties during the progress of their relationship. In this sense, the written form rationalizes the parties' behavior in at least three dimensions. First, it facilitates annual revision of the contract, which starts out on a sounder and less controversial basis, reducing the cost of bargaining. Secondly, it facilitates completion, as the danger of forgetting or distorting previous mutual agreements is avoided. Finally, it provides a precise reference when judging performance, whether this judgment is made by one of the parties or by a third independent one.

2.2 Annual revision of contracts

The relationship between the large retailers and their suppliers usually lasts for a long time, although its conditions are revised by writing new contracts annually. (This is separate from the revision of the contract before the end of the contract term, which will be analyzed in section 3.) This revision of the annual contract lasts from three to six months. The time and resources spent in these annual negotiations is understandable when considering that failure, which happens sporadically, would interrupt the relationship, causing substantial costs to both parties.

The duration of the negotiations is justified because it is necessary to know how the relationship functioned the previous year. In addition, retailers are overloaded with work at the end and the beginning of each year and therefore force the negotiations to start long after the beginning of the year during which the parties bargain. Furthermore, it is believed to be a disadvantage to be the first supplier to reach an agreement with a retailer, and this helps to delay the agreement further. However, signing a contract with a retailer should strengthen, rather than weaken, the bargaining position of a supplier in his negotiations with other retailers. Maybe transaction costs *within* both firms are also relevant, with both negotiating agents wanting to demonstrate to their superiors the effort they have made.

Apart from the direct costs, the long duration of the annual negotiations on revising the contracts is in itself a source of conflict and misunderstanding. During the months of negotiating, the conditions from the previous business year are still in force. However, once a new agreement is reached, the new terms are applied to all transactions during the year, including those already carried out before the agreement. Outside observers frequently misinterpret this retroactive effect of the annual price agreement, considering it as a forced discount over the previously agreed price.[6]

3   Implicit contracting: dynamic adjustment of the terms of exchange

In addition to the annual formal revision, the conditions established in the annual contracts are occasionally but systematically revised during the life of the contract. The most striking revision is what the industry jargon calls "wedding presents," alluding to the discounts which suppliers are asked for by retailers that have recently merged with or acquired other retailers.[7] Similar discounts are associated with promotion activities such as new center openings or anniversaries. There are two types of explanation for these revisions and discounts. One is based on the creation of efficiency incentives, and the other on the retailer's exploitation of his improved position.

3.1   *The efficiency argument*

The retailer's effort is important if the relationship with his suppliers is to result in the highest possible benefits for both parties. It is no longer true that the supplier provides all the product attributes and the retailer is a mere, passive distribution *channel*. An increasing number of attributes are now produced by retailers, not only the physical availability that is typical of passive distribution channels. Retailers are responsible for a growing part of the marketing effort and, in the case of products with insufficient reputation, for quality assurance, as was explained in section 2. For this reason, the incentives of retailers to exert effort and to invest are increasingly important. They also need to be precisely fine-tuned, which might require revision of the conditions during the course of the year.

The fact that revisions are related to investment and expenditure initiatives (openings, mergers, and promotion campaigns) which increase the total benefits of the relationship supports the above explanation. In addition, mergers create a situation in which suppliers' costs may be substantially reduced for a number of reasons: a bigger purchase volume generates bigger order and production batches; the acquiring retailer usually takes all the responsibility for logistics; the logistics of the supplier become simpler because deliveries are centralized; administrative work decreases because only one buyer is concerned; and financial risk decreases because it is usually the more financially sound retailers that acquire the weaker ones.

The efficiency hypothesis is also supported by other data. Generally, large retailers which are better placed to affect the sales volume of the product through effort and investment are more inclined to carry out the revisions. However, both parties share the consequences of some misfortunes, which indicates once again that the distribution of the gains from trade between the parties is continuous and dynamic.[8] The fact that suppliers often accept discounts without objection is also coherent with this explanation, except for the case when the retailer's bargaining power is substantially higher in the middle of the contract period. This possibility takes us directly to the second hypothesis.

3.2 The monopoly arguments

Certainly, these occasional revisions may be due to abuse by the retailer of its bargaining power, which may be caused by an existing advantage or may be a consequence of the contract itself.

There are several arguments against the *ex ante* monopoly hypothesis. Mainly, it is unclear why this method should be used, when it would be enough to fix lower prices. In addition, the degree of concentration of the retail sector is low, especially in comparison with the concentration of supply in most markets.[9] The argument is not supported, either, by the relative size of the firms in the two sectors. Furthermore, it has not been found that bigger suppliers reject the revisions to a greater extent than smaller ones. Neither do smaller retailers apply this practice less often, because the quasi-integration of small retailers through purchasing organizations permits them to renegotiate and reduce their buying prices.[10]

Despite *ex ante* competition, suppliers could find themselves obliged to accept these revisions *ex post* if some of their assets are "dedicated" to the retailer (Williamson, 1985, p. 96). In such cases, if the retailer were to threaten to cancel or delay orders, it would be difficult for the supplier, in the short term, to find an alternative use for the assets, even if they are not physically specific to the retailer, and it would have to accept the downward revision of prices. This possibility, however, is not convincing, for both theoretical and empirical reasons. From a theoretical point of view, given that these occasional revisions are applied to all suppliers, the power of a retailer to sanction recalcitrant suppliers by a cut in their orders finds a natural limit in the number of non-compliant suppliers. As the probability of rejection is greater in the case of opportunistic revisions, these will be less feasible as they carry with them the risk that the retailer would not be able to react when faced with rejection by several suppliers of the same product line. The empirical indications go in the same direction because suppliers do not break off their relations with their retailers in the short run. Furthermore, they do not seem to gradually adapt their clientele of retailers, selling more to those retailers which are known for not revising contractual conditions in the middle of the year. This behavior by suppliers is not coherent with the possibility that their bargaining power changes substantially after signing the contract with the retailer and designing their annual production plan. The fact that they do not take other precautions against the possibility of revisions is especially revealing when considering that it is common to negotiate additional safeguards (in most cases, a longer contractual period) when the contract involves investments which are dedicated to a specific retailer, as when producing goods with the retailer's own label.

4   Sources of conflict

Like all complex relationships, those established between suppliers and retailers suffer from substantial conflicts. Claims of faulty performance, either intentional or unintentional, are the main source. Other common discrepancies concern prices and deliveries. Discussion frequently arises about whether the invoiced prices are or are not in accordance with the previously agreed levels. There are also delivery delays that are punished by the retailer when they cause stockouts and losses of sales. Clarification of these arguments is difficult. Price schedules are intricate and it is hard to evaluate the cost caused by imperfect performance. Opportunism is possible on both sides. For instance, it is possible for a return of merchandise with the allegation of late delivery to be due to opportunistic behavior on the part of the retailer because sales did not go as well as planned when ordering the goods.

Errors in the administration circuits are also a main source of conflict. Examples of these are differences in the quantities and prices between the time of ordering and delivery of the merchandise, or accounting errors, where the quantity in the invoice and the delivered quantity do not correspond. Retailers claim that administrative problems are common because the administrative systems of small-size suppliers are under-developed. There are cases when the supplier issues the invoice and the delivery note at the same time so, if the delivery suffers from some defect, this is discovered only when the whole invoicing process has started. This makes fixing the problem cumbersome and slow. In other cases the transportation agent may fail to return the delivery notes to the supplier, causing administrative chaos. The importance of the supplier's administration is supported by the fact that some retailers refuse to work with suppliers that lack reliable administrative systems.

How important contractual and administrative factors are becomes clear when we observe the empirical relation that exists between the average duration of the payment periods in each country and the importance attributed to the different kinds of phenomena that cause payment delays. It has been observed that the average payment period is positively correlated with the importance of debtors' financial difficulties resulting in delays and *negatively* correlated with the importance of both disagreements between creditor and debtor and administrative errors. In other words, in countries with longer payment periods, debtor insolvency is more important while disagreements and administrative errors are less important, arguably because there is more time to solve both problems before the end of the contractual credit period (table 19.2). This can mean that a longer payment period worsens problems with a financial origin, while it lessens those related to contractual and administrative issues.

The macroeconomic data are also coherent with the argument that improved administration tends to reduce payment periods and payment delays. As shown in table 19.3, in the most developed countries in which companies are supposedly better organized, both average payment period and payment delay are lower. In fact, the administrative competence of the supplier is probably as important as that of the client. On the one hand, the best-organized suppliers are the ones that meet their obligations best.

Table 19.2. *Correlation coefficients between country averages of credit and payment periods and causes of late payment in domestic transactions*

	Contractual credit period (%)	Actual average payment period (%)	Days overdue (%)
Causes of late payment			
Debtor in financial difficulties	54.75**	58.72**	39.98
Disputes	−55.78**	−50.02**	−15.94
Administrative inefficiency	−52.00**	−64.31***	−59.56**

Note: ***,** = Correlation is statistically significant at a confidence level of 99 and 95 percent, respectively.
Source of data: Intrum Justitia (1997), see notes to table 19.1 for details.

Table 19.3. *Average payment periods, average delays, and economic development*

	Contractual payment period	Actual payment period	Delay
Constant	390.877	564.142	173.265
	(4.369)***	(6.186)***	(3.424)***
Ln (GDP per head)	−35.201	−51.065	−15.863
	(−3.936)***	(−5.602)***	(−3.136)***
R^2_{adj}	0.509	0.685	0.387
F	15.494***	31.385***	9.837***
N	15	15	15

Notes: Two-tail *t*-statistics are in brackets. *** = Significant at the 99% confidence level.
Source of data: Intrum Justitia (1997, p. 5) and national accounting data.

On the other hand, the best-organized clients are the ones that are most capable of verifying the supplier's performance in a short time.

5   Disciplinary mechanisms

In relationships between the large retailers and their suppliers, the parties themselves undertake the tasks of completing the contract and sanctioning the most usual non-fulfillments. Even when the default is claimable, the parties are unlikely to go to court, because repeated contracting provides them with a cheaper solution. The parties even find it efficient to divide the supervision and control rights – including the rights to complete the contract and to punish defaults – in an asymmetric form, assigning both rights to a greater extent to the retailer. In this quasi-judicial role, it is common for the retailer to evaluate the level of performance and to take disciplinary actions. Let us analyze now what these actions are and how they work.

5.1   Payment delay as safeguard and sanction

Payment postponement strengthens the retailer's position as a judge, enabling it to take precautionary and punitive measures for possible non-fulfillment on the part of the supplier. In this function, it can either delay the payment until the defects are rectified or discount compensation if the defects are not corrected. Obviously, on the negative side, the retailer can abuse this authority, using delay or other instruments in an opportunistic manner, extracting benefits from his suppliers. However, if this opportunistic behavior is controlled (there is more on this in section 6), this quasi-judicial role can be a helpful and efficient mechanism in the contracting process. This efficiency is based on the fact that both parties have an important information advantage in their role as judges, because they know the particularities of the trade and can observe the defaults and conflicts at a very low cost, as a by-product of being in the business and trading.[11]

This interpretation provides a simple explanation for a common practice found in many countries, where no supplier pretends to be paid interest in instances of payment delay.[12] It is thought that such interest is not requested because of the high litigation costs. This factor may be of importance in cases of insolvency, but not in the case of delay, especially in countries in which the party that is found guilty pays the other's party litigation expenses. The persistent remission of this interest can be better explained by the continuous nature of the relationship, which easily survives episodes of late payment. Furthermore, this continuity is coherent with the possibility that apparent late payments may not be real or may have efficient causes, stemming from previous defaults by the creditor or being related to the provision of financial slack to the debtor in times of hardship.

5.2   Explicit sanctions: discounts for inexact debits

It is also common for retailers to apply discounts for "inexact debits," usually on the basis of differences between the prices agreed and those invoiced.[13] The existence of administrative costs, allegedly burdensome for suppliers, helps to explain why it is the retailer that resolves this issue.

The retailer is the one who writes the framework contract which is equivalent in its consequences to a contract of adhesion, while most suppliers sign a different contract for each of their distributors.[14] This variety, compounded by decentralization, means that suppliers with standard organizational capabilities do not have complete and current knowledge of the terms under which they are trading.

5.3   *Quasi-judicial taxes*

Most disagreements between retailers and suppliers are discussed by suppliers and "settled" through negotiation. This fact hints that retailers exercise self-restraint and do not use their self-enforcement role opportunistically. Furthermore, a process is constituted which is very similar in its characteristics to court litigation: the unsatisfied supplier "appeals" before the decision-maker or frequently before a superior within the hierarchical structure of the retailer. This negotiation process is subject to problems similar to those affecting court litigation, including frivolous litigation. To avoid this phenomenon, some retailers have introduced a penalty payment for ungrounded claims. In a well-known case, suppliers of a chain of supermarkets who made ungrounded payment claims had to pay 3 percent of the sum claimed as well as a fixed fee for administrative expenses.[15] These payments raise a question similar to that of charging fees to the parties for court proceedings. Not imposing fees may motivate parties to present trivial or opportunistic claims, while imposing them may prevent parties from making justified claims. If, in our case, the retailer does not impose claim fees, treats everybody equally in its initial decisions and these decisions are subject to errors, the suppliers have an incentive to claim even in cases when it would be efficient not to claim, because of the small stakes involved or doubtful grounds. In such circumstances, a system of fees for ungrounded claims could probably help to prevent excessive claiming.

5.4   *Merchandise returns*

If we ignore the wholesale phase, the most simple trading cycle is the one starting with a retailer's purchase and ending, after a storage period, with a sale to a final consumer. However, in modern economies many sales are accompanied by an explicit or implicit right to return. This prolongs the cycle by one or two phases and makes it even more unstable, because the duration of these additional phases depends on the return period the supplier and the retailer may want to introduce in their relationship, which is generally shorter than the return period for the consumer. This extension of the trade cycle may induce a corresponding extension of the payment period in order to facilitate the enforcement of the right to return. If the consumer buys with a right to return, his return decisions function as a disciplinary mechanism which helps to assure product quality. It seems logical that the retailer and the supplier should share the cost of returns to the extent to which their decisions affect the quality in question. Likewise, it seems reasonable for the retailer to be assigned an explicit or implicit right to return. An arrangement that assigns to the retailer the right to return unsold merchandise intensifies the suppliers' incentives to produce relevant information and to adjust their product to the final demand, while at the same time it reduces the retailer's incentives in these connections. For this reason, such an arrangement is more likely when suppliers are in a better position to organize productive resources according to final demand, either in the information producing activity or in the coherent adaptation of product design and the corresponding change of the production system. This conjecture is coherent with the observation that the arrangement discussed is most commonly used with products for which sales vary seasonally, and for which retailers are in a relatively worse position to produce information about demand.[16]

5.5   *Breaking off and cooling of relations*

The long-term relationships of retailers with their suppliers may be interrupted in two ways. Final termination, which is relatively rare, is motivated by deficiency in product quality or in the services provided. A cooling-off of relations during short periods (a duration of several months, although there are cases of up to two years) may also take place as a consequence of irreconcilable disagreements over buying prices. This, however, is not common. Most retailers do not put a definite stop to their purchases, especially of branded products. Instead, they keep buying the product, although they sell it at a higher price, either because its buying price is higher or because the product in question is not included in the retailer's promotion activities, which results in a substantial decrease in the product sales.

6   Safeguards and regulation

It can be deduced from the above that the retailer is in a situation to behave opportunistically with his suppliers. Moreover, some observers interpret as opportunistic many of the practices that we have rationalized by efficiency arguments. To understand some of the conflicts subsisting in these relationships, it is useful to analyze how the safeguards against opportunistic behavior function and why they occasionally fail, giving rise to conflicts.

6.1   *The efficient safeguard is imperfect*

The basic safeguards are the repetitive character of the exchange and the contractual reputation of the retailer.[17] The reputation affects in particular the possibility of further contracting under the asymmetry conditions that have just been described. Reputation also inspires enough confidence to convince suppliers to invest in assets which are specific to the retailer. This is becoming increasingly important with the growth in sales of products under retailers' own labels.

Given that these safeguards are costly, it would not be optimal to have perfect safeguards, freeing the relationship of all opportunism. In particular, incentives to perform well lessen when the decision-makers' time horizon shortens. This is especially true for firms whose survival is in question. Some retailers that acquired other financially troubled retailers realized the importance of this issue, when observing that the acquired firm had followed dubious practices with their suppliers, usually in the form of late payments.

Similarly, on a more general level and irrespective of the type of firm, problems also appear with decentralized decision-making, because of misalignment between the optimal behavior of the decision-makers and the behavior that is optimal for the company as a whole. In large retailers this situation arises because of substantial delegation of decision-making to store and product-line managers at store level, whose time horizon is shorter than that of the company. When these division managers are subject to high-powered incentives and there are no mechanisms to control long-term effects, these managers are tempted to take decisions that boost their apparent performance at the cost of cheating the suppliers, no matter how much such cheating of suppliers damages the reputation of the retailer company.

When discussing the importance of these cases of opportunistic behavior, the long-term incentives of the parties and the inescapable nature of transaction costs have to be considered. First, given that the retailer suffers a net loss, he has an interest in resolving the conflict. Otherwise, he will be subject to worse contract conditions. Second, because of the existence of contractual costs in the relationship with the divisional managers and while decentralized decisions are needed, it is not optimal to avoid these agency costs completely. Today, even in the presence of strong differentiation among retailers, there is a powerful tendency towards centralization, which reduces the importance of these dysfunctional phenomena.

In some retailers, store managers no longer have the authority to influence the payment process. These retailers have centralized the decisions that affect the whole market, with respect not only to product range and prices, but also to the physical location of products on the shelves and, for the majority of products, the selling price and promotions. The task of store managers is therefore to implement these decisions at minimum cost, and the role of in-store product-line managers is limited to incorporating specific local information and controlling, confirming, or correcting the ordering decisions. Such decisions are automatically generated by the management information system (MIS), which controls the stock level and sales flows. Similar consequences result from the development of logistics platforms and centralized storehouses, which increase the distance, even physically, between suppliers and the points of sale, and also separate shop managers from the contracting process with suppliers. Obviously, the possibilities for centralization vary according to the type of product and it can be expected that decentralized decisions will be still needed for perishable products.

6.2   No clear scope for regulation

In view of all the possible failures in the system of private safeguards, a relevant question concerns the role of regulation. As is usual with regulatory matters, the answer depends on the assumptions. In this case, the important assumptions to consider are, on the one hand, the capacity of the private agents to anticipate (and also penalize through their pricing decisions) possible non-fulfillment and, on the other hand, the regulatory capacity to prevent them. As for insolvency and the deterioration of incentives that precede it, the predictive capacity of the parties is probably not very high. But regulation similar to bank regulation, like that discussed in Spain at the beginning of the 1990s, would not be effective either. Moreover, it would be costly. This is why, in the absence of systemic risk, which might justify such bank regulation, it would not be reasonable. As for payment delays, the repetitive character of the transactions inclines us to think that creditors, to a great extent, are able to anticipate delays and the problems arising from them. When delays occur, suppliers penalize the retailers that behave worst and, in consequence, the latter will strive to improve their internal control. Empirical evidence regarding the existence of these penalties is the differences in retailers' reputations concerning their internal organization capacity and their inclination to engage in this kind of conflict.

In view of the above, the analysis indicates that regulation in this field will most likely result in a reduction and distortion of competition, among both retailers and suppliers, rather than a balance of suppliers' bargaining powers with respect to retailers. To the extent that regulation in fact would oblige retailers to perform better, the ones that have been complying worst would be at a disadvantage, because they would have to include this additional cost of change in their policy, and this would lead to less decentralization and a tighter control of decentralized decisions. Obviously, these retailers would obtain a benefit because of lower prices in the agreements given the higher rate of compliance, but probably this benefit would not compensate for the cost in question, because if it had, they would have followed this policy before the change in regulation. Moreover, since regulation would oblige some retailers to adopt a policy that is not beneficial for them, it would indirectly benefit those for which the new policy was already beneficial. The same argument can be applied to the differences that exist among suppliers, either in their capacity to foresee insolvency or in their capacity to accumulate information on the rate of compliance of their clients. As a result, regulation would probably favor suppliers with a smaller capacity for prediction.

7   Summary

Contractual practices that are typical of the relationships between large retailers and their suppliers may respond to efficiency considerations. This efficiency explanation contradicts the hypothesis of systematic abuse on the part of retailers but does not imply perfect functioning of the safeguarding mechanisms. The recurrent nature of the relationships generates incentives for compliance and makes it possible for most conflicts to be solved through negotiation between the parties without third-party enforcement. The retailer is assigned and performs quasi-judicial tasks possibly because of its advantageous position regarding availability of information, which is needed to evaluate suppliers' performance. Thus, retailers act as courts of first instance, exercising a right that is implicitly assigned at the beginning of the relationship and with each annual renovation of the contract.

The main ways by which this quasi-judicial role is exercised is by delaying payments associated with defective purchases and invoices, as well as debiting discounts for inaccurate debits or incorrect invoices. Coherent with this analysis is the variability in standard payment periods across different groups of products. Payment periods vary systematically according to the types of product and the differences observed seem to correspond to the ultimate objective of reducing conflicts in the parties' financial and commercial relations rather than to their relative bargaining power. This conclusion is also supported by the fact that there are no relevant differences in payment periods, even in the special cases of exclusive suppliers and suppliers delivering products sold under the retailer's own labels.

This quasi-judicial role of retailers permits them not only to motivate suppliers' performance but also to adjust the distribution of the additional surplus produced by the efforts of each party which are too costly to contract explicitly *ex ante*. The mechanism used is that retailers request bonuses and discounts below the contracted buying price, these requests being made, and mostly accepted, throughout the life of the contract. The fact these requests are triggered by retailers' initiatives – retailer mergers, openings of new stores and logistics platforms, special promotions – that benefit their suppliers supports an interpretation of these contractual revisions as being efficient. According to this interpretation, the possibility of modifying the contracted conditions allows for modification of the distribution of any gains from trade resulting in both changes in the environment and efforts and investment by the parties.

The long-term behavior of suppliers also refutes the hypothesis that delays and the revision of contract conditions constitute an abuse on the part of retailers. In the short run, suppliers might accept these delays and contract modifications because they have no other option. However, in the long run, they keep contracting repeatedly with the same retailers, in spite of such practices. This persistence would not be reasonable if such delays and adjustments were expropriatory.

A final word of caution is in order, however. The qualitative and casuistic nature of much of the evidence in this study recommends a prudent conclusion. It is hoped, however, that the arguments in the chapter will hold relatively well if a similar level of circumspection is applied to alternative explanations.[18]

NOTES

Chapter 19 was originally published as "The Quasi-Judicial Role of Large Retailers: An Efficiency Hypothesis of their Relation with Suppliers," in *Revue d'Economie Industrielle* (92, 2000).

The author acknowledges the cooperation received from IDELCO and its personnel and the assistance of the managers and experts interviewed who provided most of the information on which this study is based. The author also expresses his thanks for the comments made by Luis Garicano, Fernando Gómez-Pomar, Manuel González, Luis Vázquez, Pedro Schwartz, Decio Zylbersztajn, numerous workshop participants, and two anonymous referees, and the help of Demián Castillo and Veneta Andonova as research assistants. Usual disclaimers apply.
1. See, for example, the French 1996 "Galland" Act (*Loi* 96–588), modifying the 1986 *Ordonnance* (86–1243) on freedom of pricing and competition, and the Spanish Retailing Act of 1996 (*Ley* 7/1996). More recent examples of

this regulatory trend are the proposal for the EU Directive on late payments (*OJEC*, December 3, 1998), even if the text finally adopted was less strict (Directive 2000/35/CE, *OJEC*, August, 8, 2000); the failed project for a Code of Good Commercial Practice prepared by the Spanish Ministry of Finance in 1998; the extension of the concept of unfair competition to include the exploitation of economic dependence, the termination of a commercial relationship without a six-month notice period and the attainment of discounts under threat of termination introduced in the Spanish Unfair Competition Act by *Ley* 52/1999; and the initiative taken by the French Government in January 2000 to modify the Galland Act (*Les Echos*, January 14–15, 2000; p. 24).

2. For an empirical test of this theory in the car distribution sector see Arruñada, Garicano and Vázquez (2001).

3. Unless stated otherwise (mainly with respect to the econometric tests in sections 2 and 4, which are run over aggregate European data), the evidence on the structure and functioning of contractual relations comes from case studies and interviews conducted with a sample of representatives from all the parties in the sector in Spain. This sample contained large and small, multinational and Spanish retailers and manufacturers. While special care was taken to cover a variety of operators, it was not possible to assess the statistical significance of the sample.

4. It should be expected that suppliers sell at a lower price and accept worse conditions from retailers that give them more additional services of this nature. For this reason, the comparisons of selling prices which are often employed in discussions on competitive conditions may lose much of their relevance, because it is possible to observe only the net price (the nominal price less the implicit discount that the supplier accepts in exchange for services that are not explicitly paid). This net price is no longer comparable across retailers of different reputation and size, because the value of the reputation services they provide to suppliers is not the same.

5. Payment periods have been discussed in more detail in Arruñada (1999a, 1999b).

6. For example, *Expansión* (June 1, 1998, p. 8).

7. See two examples in *Expansión* (February 3 and June 1, 1988).

8. This makes the relationship between suppliers and retailers closer to the type of relationships which can be observed more and more frequently in industries in which the intensification of competition induces the use of decreasing price clauses (see an example from the automobile sector in Aláez *et al.* 1997, p. 100, n. 14). These clauses do not prevent car manufacturers from asking for and occasionally receiving additional discounts from their component suppliers. Several varieties of asymmetric contracting have been studied in different industries and the conclusion is that this kind of contracting is typical for services provided under a franchising regime, both under a strict franchise arrangement (Rubin 1978) and under allied activities (for example, in Arruñada, Garicano and Vázquez 2001, we analyze its use in automobile distribution).

9. See Ormaza (1992); Schwartz (1999).

10. See, for example, Padilla (1996).

11. There is more on this in Arruñada (2001 and 2002, chapter 3, generally; see also 1999c, 2000, for an application to financial auditing).
12. For information about the situation in different European countries, see CCE (1997, p. 7).
13. In some cases the impact of these discounts is substantial. For example, in the relationship between one of the biggest retailers and one of the biggest consumer good suppliers, both multinational firms, these discounts were evaluated in 1998 at 1.67 percent of the turnover, according to the supplier. In the same year and with the same retailer the supplier recovered 13 percent of the total value of the discounts (0.2171 percent of his turnover with the retailer).
14. The fact that retailers have a greater capacity for control does not mean that they have either perfect or homogeneous control. This issue is highlighted by the policy of some retailers who contracted specialists to detect irregularities in the contracting and accounting of their purchases. Operations over the previous five years were investigated and the specialist received half of the amount recovered. The mere existence of this practice highlights the high degree of error that exists in the administrative processing of transactions.
15. *Expansión* (1 June, 1998, p. 8).
16. Obviously there are more factors that influence the efficiency of contracting with or without right of return. (See Kandel 1996.)
17. See Klein and Leffler (1981) and Shapiro (1983) for the basic formulation of the role of reputation in contracting.
18. In fact, the studies that currently guide European legislative proposals in this field do not seem more reliable. See, in particular, the study that provided the basis for the Directive on late payments (CCE 1997) and, for a criticism, Arruñada (1999b).

20 Interconnection agreements in telecommunications networks: from strategic behaviors to property rights

Godefroy Dang-Nguyen and Thierry Pénard

1 Introduction

Interconnection regulation is a major issue for the liberalization of energy and telecommunications networks. Certainly, it is a focal point for tensions and interest conflicts among operators. In France, for example, the Telecommunication Regulatory Authority (ART) has to settle disputes concerning interconnection. These conflicts, opposing most often the incumbent operator France Telecom to its new competitors, deal with the unbundling of the local loop or the termination charges of calls from fixed to mobile networks.

Generally, interconnection has a precise objective: the subscribers of the interconnected networks are given the opportunity to have access to more subscribers (telecommunications) or more suppliers (energy or water). Interconnection requires a technical harmonization, as well as a contractual, often bilateral, arrangement among network operators. More precisely, in an interconnection contract operators define the conditions of access to their networks and the corresponding usage rights. In this chapter we will consider mainly telecommunications networks (voice and data). But many economic issues raised are equally relevant, *mutatis mutandis*, for other interconnected networks.

In telephone networks, interconnection agreements have been strongly influenced by the institutional framework in which they have emerged. For a long time, the telephone services relied on the principle of "network integrity." This notion appeared in the United States at the beginning of the twentieth century, under the influence of T. Vail, the AT&T's CEO of that time, to justify the monopoly given to his private company. As long as only national monopolies provided voice services, interconnection was merely a problem of international, diplomatic bargaining. For data networks, the relationships concerning the right of usage have been strongly influenced by the academic origin of the Internet. Interconnection took the form of peering agreements, in which networks convened to exchange traffic without monetary compensation.

With the development of competition in the telephone services and the rise of a "business" Internet, one can expect a reassessment of the strategies and governance structures for interconnection. What is the most relevant framework to analyze this evolution?

Network economics is one of these frameworks. The first theoretical papers on network economics were stimulated by the AT&T breakup in 1984. In this literature, interconnection agreements are treated as strategies for compatibility (Economides 1996). Interconnection or compatibility choices depend on the initial structure of the market and on competition modalities. In the case of telecommunications networks, interconnection is obviously different in a market with a former monopoly incumbent (fixed telephone) and a market without an historical leader (mobile telephone). Briefly, two interconnection issues are possible. The first one deals with the access to an essential facility; there is an asymmetric relationship for vertical compatibility. Without interconnection, some operators cannot deliver their services to the final customer, and have to quit the market. In the second case, interconnection leads to horizontal compatibility among competing services. It is a symmetric relationship, since each operator has a direct access to its customers. Without interconnection the operators can provide services but do not fully exploit the network externalities. Papers dealing with those two issues stress the anti-competitive effects of interconnection agreements, when operators freely bargain. Some of those agreements may deter entry or favor a collusion on prices. A public intervention seems thus necessary to control the operators' behaviors and possibly to establish interconnection and usage rules, particularly in the asymmetric case.

If this first approach highlights the impact of interconnection strategies on the competition game, it says nothing on the institutional setting in which these agreements are convened. Interconnection is a meta game in which not only operators, but also their suppliers, their customers, and the public authorities (government, parliament, regulation agencies) intervene. The stake is about the definition of property rights and their assignment to the network operators. To study this issue, the neo-institutional theory is better suited. This approach enables us to better understand the links between technical and institutional changes in the networks. In particular, the possibility provided today by technical progress to split the networks very finely is accompanied by institutional innovations, with which the interconnection strategies of the operators have to cope.

In section 2, we analyze the interconnection agreements as a strategic dimension of the competition game, by using network economics. In section 3 we analyze interconnection agreements through the lens of neo-institutional theory.

2   Interconnection agreements as a strategic game

For an operator, its interconnection choices have an overwhelming influence on the diversity of its services, their quality, and their price. They also condition its profitability, hence its survival in the market. Moreover, although operators always have the possibility of revising or renegotiating their agreements, it seems that interconnection decisions are less flexible or are more complicated than tariff decisions. For all these reasons, interconnection strategies have to be analyzed in a sequential game in which the operators set their interconnection policy as the first step, then define their provision of service in a second step. This game theoretical framework enables us to deal with two issues: on the one hand the decision to interconnect or not with another operator, on the other hand the contractual conditions of this interconnection. Those questions are raised differently whether operators have an asymmetric relationship (sub-section 2.1) or a symmetric one (sub-section 2.2).

2.1   *Asymmetric interconnection and essential facilities*

An asymmetric interconnection agreement reflects a vertical relationship, whereby an operator needs the other for its own service provision. The latter, who owns a facility essential for the former, benefits from a strategic advantage which he can abuse. If he has the possibility of freely determining the access conditions to his network in conformity with his own interest only, he is in a situation of a regulator of the competition game. The establishment of a public regulation is deemed necessary to limit this power and to give the control of the competition game back to the public authorities.

2.1.1   *The access to an* essential facility
A carrier owns an *essential facility* if the others cannot duplicate such an infrastructure with reasonable costs. In telecommunications and energy networks, the access to subscribers is such a facility. In particular, the local loop in telecommunications and the distribution network for gas and electricity are bottlenecks through which competitors have to pass. The joint use of an infrastructure by competing operators thus raises the issue of access conditions. A limited access at high prices may curb the development of competition and new services.

However, the problem is different whether or not the owner of the essential facility provides himself competitive services. If he provides interconnection only, his objective will be to extract the profits of the operators using his network. Thus, he will set an access charge to his facility high enough to capture all their profits. Meanwhile it is in the owner's interest to provide end-user services himself (Economides and Woroch 1992). This vertical integration strategy may even be favorable for consumers, since the price of the end user service may decline. This result holds from the elimination of the double margin when the supply of the service is vertically integrated, a classical result shown by Cournot (Economides and Salop 1992; Economides 1999).

Vertical integration, however, reinforces the risk of monopolization. The integrated operator may well deny the access to his essential facility in order to obtain or maintain a monopoly on the final service. This strategy is called "foreclusion." In telecommunications for example, the operator that controls the local loop (the local network), can easily monopolize the market for long-distance calls.[1] For this, he can use either the access price or access quality to the local loop, in order to raise rivals' costs or to downgrade their quality of service (Economides 1998; Economides and Lehr 1995; Beard, Kaserman and Mayo 1996).

If competition is about strongly substitutable services, or if operators have no capacity constraints, it is clear that a *vertically integrated operator* has a strong incentive to exclude his competitors, to prevent them from stealing his business. Conversely, if operators have capacity constraints or if they provide differentiated services in quality or in variety, the incumbent can in principle gain by letting them enter: he can account for new revenues from the access to his essential facility, thereby balancing the profit losses on competitive services (Economides and Woroch 1992; Pénard 1999). But these results hold in a static framework. In the long run, operators can always overcome capacity or variety constraints and foreclusion seems the most robust strategy. Beyond the concern about anti-competitive behaviors, fairness issues are also raised: it seems questionable to leave to an operator who has, for historical reasons, inherited from an essential facility, the right to establish the rules of the competition, namely the right to decide who can use his infrastructure or not. Efficiency and equity arguments thus call for a regulation of access conditions to essential facilities.

2.1.2 Access regulation

The objective of regulation is to open the access to the essential facility and to promote competition on the complementary services. In such a perspective, the regulator must intervene on the rights and obligations of each operator. He can make interconnection compulsory or establish some modalities in the contractual agreements among the operators (point of access, tariffs...). However, the regulator must be conscious of the dilemma faced by the owner of the essential facility. When the latter invests in the capacity or quality of his facility, he can provide better services to the end-users, but his competitors that have access to his infrastructure can also improve their services. In other words, he partially benefits from his investments. This situation may lead the integrated operator to under-invest in his essential facility as shown by Amstrong, Cowan and Vickers (1994) in the case of the United Kingdom. This trend is even stronger if the incumbent expects an unfavorable evolution of the regulation (increase of the access points to his network or decrease of the access tariffs). Thus the regulator has to make sure that the former monopoly is paid enough for the use of his network and for his investment. Conversely, high access charges may lead the competitors to invest in inefficient bypass infrastructures (Curien, Jullien and Rey 1998). What should the appropriate tariff for the access to the essential facility be?

The regulation of access tariffs to an essential facility is complex, when one considers that most of the network costs are fixed and shared with other activities of the incumbent. Several rules of efficient regulation have been proposed, in order to recover the costs of usage of the facility. Baumol and Sidak (1994) recommend tariffing the access at its opportunity cost that corresponds to the marginal cost of giving access to the infrastructure, plus the loss of revenue for the owner, owing to the competition on the complementary services. This rule is called ECPR (Efficient Component Pricing Rule). Its advantage is to prevent the entry of less efficient operators than the incumbent. The efficiency of this rule has been theoretically put in doubt (Armstrong, Doyle and Vickers 1994; Economides and White 1995, 1998). Spulber and Sidak (1997) claim that the regulated access tariffs should comply with at least one condition of voluntary interconnection: that means that the interconnection must be profitable for the owner of the essential facility. Finally Laffont and Tirole (1994) suggest applying a Ramsey–Boiteux tariff for the access to a local facility. This rule recommends setting access charges inversely proportional to the price elasticity faced by each of the alternative operators. Interconnection charges paid by an operator will thus be lower whenever the price elasticity of his services is high. Laffont and Tirole generalize these results to the situation where the regulator knows imperfectly the costs and behavior of the incumbent. Therefore an efficient regulation consists in a menu of interconnection contracts proposed to the incumbent, to induce him to reveal his true cost and to provide enough productivity efforts. But these incentive schemes leave an informational rent to the incumbent.

The implementation of these efficient rules, although analytically convincing, is difficult to apply. Most regulatory agencies in telecommunications have chosen a method grounded first on accounting costs (or historical costs) and then, when their knowledge of the costs improves, on the long-run incremental costs, to which profit margins on invested capital are added. Only New Zealand has tried to apply the ECPR rule, but abandoned it after several litigations triggered by new operators (Blanchard 1995). In France, as in most European countries, the public authorities have heralded the principles of transparency, fairness, and efficiency in interconnection regulation. Moreover, they have forced the incumbent to answer positively to interconnection demands and to offer cost-oriented prices. The latter is also subject to accounting separation as a first step towards a better knowledge of the operator's cost, in conformity with the concern of the regulator to fix the interconnection prices as close as possible to the usage costs of essential facilities. Regulation thus reduces the contractual freedom of the incumbent, both for the choice of counterparts and the choice of tariffs. Recently, public authorities wished to go further in this way, by enforcing an interconnection obligation for the incumbent, as close as possible to the subscriber: this is the unbundling of the local loop.

Interconnection to essential facilities is not the only type of agreement examined in network economics. Agreement among symmetric networks are also subject to numerous although more recent papers.

2.2 Symmetric interconnection and compatibility

An interconnection is symmetric when two operators have a direct access to their customer on the one hand and are in competition on the other: for example, an agreement between a fixed and a mobile network operator, or an agreement between Internet Service Providers (ISPs). Symmetric interconnection raises the issue of both quality and prices of services that operators provide to each other.

2.2.1 Competition and compatibility

Symmetric interconnection is first an issue of compatibility. Operators have to know whether they allow their customers to access the networks and services of competing operators, while providing as a counterpart their own services to the latters' customers. This choice will depend on two opposite effects. On the one hand interconnection enables the customer to benefit from network externalities. Since the network size and the number of services increases, the customers' willingness to pay increases too. Operators can thus raise the price of their services without reducing customer utility. On the other hand, interconnection brings networks closer with regard to the quality of service. By reducing differentiation, it increases substitutability and price competition among operators.

The network effect supports interconnection while the substitution effect (or business-stealing effect) restrains it. The net effect will depend on several conditions concerning the size of externalities, the characteristics of demand and of operators (Encaoua, Michel and Moreaux 1992; Katz and Shapiro 1985). For example for Automatic Teller Machines (ATMs), the compatibility decision will depend, among other things, on the initial size of the networks and interbanking fees (Matutes and Padilla 1994).

This theoretical framework fits well with interconnection among Internet networks. Many ISPs refuse to be interconnected even if they could benefit from network externalities. Thus Baake and Wichmann (1999) show that a large ISP (with a large number of subscribers) may deny interconnection with a small ISP to keep a quality of service advantage. Dang-Nguyen and Pénard (1999) show also that ISPs have more incentives to interconnect if they have similar qualities. But compatibility in the case of the Internet is less a discrete (whether or not to interconnect) than a continuous (which interconnection quality to adopt) choice. Each operator chooses the quality of interconnection through the maximum and the guaranteed bandwidth of the connections set up with other operators.

Few theoretical works finally are devoted to interconnection choices among telephone networks. First, compatibility is compelling: in Europe as well as in the United States, any open voice network has to accept interconnection demands, in conformity with quality standards imposed by the regulator. Moreover network effects are considered so large that compatibility issues seem irrelevant.

2.2.2   Financial transfers and collusion

Whether voluntary or mandatory, interconnection requires an agreement between operators on tariffs and financial transfers. The financial counterpart to the service may be fixed or usage-sensitive charges. Moreover, they can be set either independently or cooperatively. In most cases the operator directly receives revenues from the subscribers and transfers part of them to operators terminating the service or the communication.

Compared to this principle, the Internet exhibits a specificity since most interconnection agreements, called *peering agreements*, contain no financial counterpart to traffic exchanges. Each operator keeps all revenues stemming from its network customers.

When operators agree to set positive access charges, they face the following dilemma: a high access charge augments the revenue on each incoming call, but limits their number. The net effect will depend on price elasticity of the interconnected users. Laffont, Rey and Tirole (1998a) show that when the operators choose interconnection tariffs non-cooperatively, the result is non-optimal, with too high tariffs, since operators do not internalize the adverse effects upon the utility and the demand of users. The authors then study the case of a collective determination of interconnection charges. The cooperative choice may reduce competition and increase the retail prices of calls, reflecting a possible collusion among operators. These effects are strengthened when the regulator imposes a non-discrimination principle between incoming and outgoing calls, as well as a reciprocity of access charge (the same charge for incoming calls of all networks).[2] If these regulatory constraints are upheld, a cooperative determination of access charges leads to less collusion (Laffont, Rey and Tirole 1997, 1998b).

One of the limits of these papers is to describe competition in a static framework. Only the impact of interconnection on current profits is considered, without taking its consequences on competition dynamics into account. In particular, the link between access charges and collusion is never analyzed in an intertemporal context. Without going into details, one can say that the transition from a static to a dynamic framework often reverses the results: this is the topsy-turvy principle underlined by Shapiro (1989). For example, if operators want to sustain a tacit collusion on prices, they can punish those who cheat or breach the agreement, by reverting to the competitive static equilibrium. As a cooperative determination of access charges increases static profits, it reduces the severity of punishments and makes collusion less likely. Then a practice that increases current profits may appear as collusive in a static framework, while being pro-competitive in a dynamic one. The results of the previous models, most of them static, should thus be accepted with caution to evaluate the efficiency of a regulation which is essentially dynamic.

To sum up, network economics has the virtue of exhibiting the strategic motivations of operators in interconnection agreements. This approach focuses on the way operators, but also regulators, interact in the competition game. However, it underestimates the coordination problems met by operators, in a context of strong uncertainty and imperfect information. Moreover, it considers the institutional framework as given, whereas it is well known that operators constantly try to influence the rules of the game and to modify the regulation. The competition game is thus embedded in an institutional game on which depends, in the end, the rules and rights for interconnection. In section 3 we will complete the strategic approach with an institutional one.

3   Contract theory and interconnection

Through an interconnection agreement each operator gets a usage right on a network capacity of another operator. This right is normally reciprocal, but each party is not in a symmetric position, as seen above. Contractual difficulties may result from asset specificity and opportunistic behaviors. The usage right defined in an interconnection agreement may conflict with the operator's property right upon its own network. Thus, the parties have to set up "governance structures" which reconcile the right of usage and the property right. But the choice of a governance structure is not independent of the institutional framework designed by public authorities. The latter can limit or transform any property right on the network. We show that this actually happened in telecommunications, thus illustrating a theoretical issue raised by Williamson (1993), in continuity from Commons (1934) and North (1990): how institutions affect governance structures.

3.1   *Network evolution, property rights, and rights of usage*

In a transport network, flows are commanded through an overlay network called a "command network." For example, in a railway network, the "command network" is the set of signaling and switching devices. Previously, the command network and the infrastructure network were combined into a *system*, intended to globally optimize the performance of the network. In that context, interconnection meant the interoperability of two systems, both for the command and the infrastructure networks. International agreements for telephone networks followed this principle.

In the 1980s, it became possible to split the command and the infrastructure networks. This unbundling was established in 1987 in the United States by the Open Network Infrastructure (ONA) doctrine of the Federal Communications Commission (FCC). It gave the new operators the opportunity to freely combine "modules" leased to incumbent operators. Telecommunications, as well as computer networks, were then functionally broken down. This led to redefining usage as well as property rights on each module. The question is thus raised of the efficiency and fairness of this redefinition: the analysis of interconnection agreements cannot neglect the breaking down of the networks into modules.

Hence transaction-cost theory (TCT) analyzes the possibility of separating or integrating several modules depending on their asset specificity. These modules can be either assembled or leased. But TCT says nothing on the initial definition of modules, on the assignment of property and usage rights, which seems to refer to an institutional power. Thus TCT assumes that modules exist before their possible integration and does not explain how they do emerge. One hypothesis is that the definition of these modules is an institutional issue, which evolves and has to be explained theoretically. Some examples show how this process occurs. The splitting of a system into modules is often *functional*, and may be linked to a *horizontal* (AT&T's geographical breakup in 1984) or *vertical* (the breakup of IBM's complementary activities, such as software and hardware in the 1960s) institutional separation. This splitting also occurred in electricity networks (Joskow 1996). However, modularity appears to be a major feature of information technology goods and services. The question is thus raised of the effectiveness of this institutional intervention.

3.2   Institutions, transaction costs, and assignment of property rights

Functional splitting can be explained by technical progress. Splitting should provide the firms with the possibility of creating more efficient modules, later recombined into more complex services or goods. Williamson (1993) claims that technology provides a *semi-weak* determination upon organizational choices, in as much as well-known technological options would limit the governance structures. Institutional intervention would thus ratify technological opportunities. Given the state of the art in technology, separable and well-identified modules could be individually appropriated and their ownership rights could be transacted. In the network industries, those modules could be interconnected through contractual arrangements, in order to provide a complete service to the customer.

But the module appropriation is not so clear. Technology provides practically no limit in the separability into modules: it is now technologically possible to split elementary particles or genetic codes. The technical frontier is thus beyond what society considers as a property right, economically or socially sustainable. An intuitive answer to this issue is that the principle of the first mover should apply. Those who elaborate or create the module should be the owners. But all that happened in information technologies (IT) suggests that a subsequent reconsideration of the initial assignment of property rights is always possible, precisely through a finer definition of modules. Then only *institutions* have the coercive right to assign and to question those rights. It is thus essential to know the motives and criteria of institutional actions.

Williamson does not explicitly treat this question. He is more interested in the evolution of "governance structures" than in the initial assignment or the subsequent institutional reallocation of property and usage rights (Williamson 1981). Nonetheless, he puts forward a principle of "remediableness" to guide institutional actions (Williamson 1996): one should implement only institutional reforms which, once achieved, would provide a "net gain." Similarly, Commons (1934) suggests that institutions comply with the principle of "artificial selection": public institutions choose to

favor institutional rules which favor more efficient but also "fairer" transactions (Ramstad 1994). Following the categories of Commons, the
"institutional environment" (institutions) should be conceived to facilitate better "institutional arrangements" (governance structures), in terms
of equity and efficiency.

Advocates of the property-rights school emphasize the role of property-
rights structures upon economic performance (De Alessi 1983). For
Demsetz (1998), non-institutional conditions, such as the initial endowment of factors or the evolution of exogenous parameters like transportation costs, are essential for the definition of the rules and may lead to the
revision of the ownership-rights structures. Technology and its evolution
could be interpreted as a form of non-institutional determination.

Very differently, evolutionary theorists suggest that institutional rules
rely on a principle of path dependency (Magnusson and Ottosson 1996).
Once established upon an institutional trajectory, public authorities could
not put them into question so easily.

This brief discussion of the motives for institutional intervention raises
the following question: Why do public authorities periodically decide to
modify the "institutional rules" that are applied on markets? Who initiates
these changes? We will try to answer these questions through the example
of the modularization process that has been occurring in telecommunications networks. However it is necessary to distinguish between voice
networks and data networks, where "modularization" has taken a different form.

3.3   Modularization and assignment of property rights in voice networks

The existence of "integrated systems" in telephony is historically explained by interconnection difficulties among early operators (Muller
1993). Indeed, networks were initially developed by local governments
because intercity networks were too expensive. Competition did exist in
the United States, but also in France, where state intervention is a tradition. But in the United States, the dominant network of the Bell System
denied interconnection to their competitors; their argument was that interconnection would undermine the competitive advantage and expropriate the shareholders of the Bell System. T. Vail, the CEO of Bell, pleaded
for the uniqueness of the telephone system with the motto: "one policy,
one system, UNIVERSAL SERVICE." Institutionally, this point of view
has become dominant and telecommunications developed through a
monopolistic organization, theoretically grounded on the "theory of
the natural monopoly" (Sharkey 1982): duplication of infrastructures
seemed costly and inefficient. Moreover, complementarity between the

local and the long-distance networks justified integration into one system, to economize transaction costs. In some countries (the United States, Canada, Finland, Denmark...) local and long-distance networks were run separately, but coordination structures did exist among the local and long-distance monopolies.

In the 1980s, a liberalization process took place which can be interpreted as the calling into question of monopolies' property rights on their networks. However, with the noticeable exception of the United States, there has been no vertical or horizontal separation of ownership, namely no breakup, but a *functional separation* which limited the property rights of the operators on their networks. The unbundling of the local loop is an example of this process. Modules are defined by regulation and incumbent operators continue to own the modules, but a usage right is recognized of the competitors to lease them. Now the new operators choose between "make" or "buy" (or, rather, "lease") not on the basis of "market" versus "integration," as in the TCT paradigm, but on "institutionally guaranteed lease" against "integration." The guarantee goes as far as to define prices, technical interfaces, availability conditions, etc. .... It thus remains to examine why previously an exclusive (and monopolistic) right of ownership was institutionally recognized for the monopolies up the 1980s, and why this exclusive right has been called into question since then.

Clearly, technology is part of the explanation, as suggested by Williamson and Demsetz: the decrease of transmission costs has enabled the duplication of long-distance capacities. Vertical separation between long-distance and local networks was a kind of "institutional remediableness" in accordance with this evolution. But interestingly, this separation occurred in one country only, the United States. In other countries, it was limited only to an accounting separation, without breakup.

On the other hand, unbundling was more the consequence of lobbying than the search for optimal governance structures. Indeed, the separation of the command and the infrastructure network, the definition of ONAs, was set up at the monopolistic operators' initiative. The latter were eager to buy equipment in separable modules, in order not to be locked-in by one equipment manufacturer. Later, when competition was institutionally admitted in telecommunications services, the competitors of the incumbent operators took advantage of the existence of these modules to get access, and lease only a sub-set of modules rather than entire systems with the help of regulatory agencies.

The method that regulatory authorities, such as FCC in the United States, Oftel in the United Kingdom, or ART in France, have used to modify the institutional rules on telecommunication markets is rather original. Instead of proceeding bluntly (breakup, obligation to sell and thus to abandon property rights on specific activities), they have adopted a more flexible and "fine-tuned" approach, based on property rights and usage rights. They have been searching for a fine balance between property and usage rights. To some extent, regulation has appeared as an *institutional innovation*, which has created the conditions of challenging the property rights of telecommunications operators for the sake of promoting competition. However, from a "governance structure" point of view, the new operators do not take a "make-or-buy" decision, but a "make-or-lobby" decision.

We can thus say that former monopolies initiated modularization to improve their governance structures with their equipment suppliers, but this subsequently led to an *institutional innovation*, which is the enforcement and regulation of leasing contracts among competitors and the former monopoly. This had the consequence of limiting the latter's property rights on its network, and promoting competition. This institutional innovation had several advantages. First, through the guarantee of interconnection, it reconciled the beneficial effects of competition and network externality: everybody could access anybody whoever his or her telephone supplier was. Second, as the former monopolists avoided breakup, they more easily accepted the transition to competition.

It is not clear, however, whether the governance structure emerging from this decision process is really optimal. In other words, do the regulatory agencies provide the right signals and incentives to both the incumbent and new entrants, to stimulate innovation, since the benefits of their ownership of some assets may be upheld and shared with their competitors? Also, lobbying is not an efficient business *per se*, and may lead to opportunistic behavior: it might be cheaper but socially more detrimental to obtain an extended usage right upon somebody else's asset, rather than negotiate directly for a lease contract, or establish one's own asset.

3.4   Ownership-rights assignment for data networks

In the data networks, a modularization process has also happened with the emergence of the Internet. The Transmission Control Protocol/Internet Protocol (TCP/IP) clearly defines a boundary between what is "below the IP layer," namely the infrastructure of data flows transport, and "above the IP layer," namely the command network and all Internet services and applications. Hence, an Internet service uses at least two components: a "transport module" and a "service module." The latter may itself be cut into smaller modules provided by different suppliers: access, browsers, applets, . . .

The infrastructure layer consists in thousands of heterogeneous interconnected networks. Most of the time, interconnection among ISPs is tacitly convened. ISPs often agree to cooperate on data flow transports without financial counterparts (*peering agreements*). For applications "above the IP layer," many innovations such as the Web and its tools (html, http), browsers, search engines, operating systems (Apache, Linux), and programming languages (Perl) have been the outcome of a collective development by the Internet community, and disseminated freely (Stallman 1999). The Internet has thus provided an original solution to the coordination issue: *users* themselves have set up the "governance structures," thereby reducing opportunism and transaction costs, that may come out of the sharing of tangible or intangible assets. In such conditions, the public institutions have not had to intervene, and modularization has been achieved on a strictly technical basis. The question of assignment of property rights has been avoided. It is clear that the specific origin (military and academic) of the Internet has been of paramount importance to explain such an evolution. There has been a "path-dependant" institutional evolution in the development of the Internet which explains why so many services are "free" and why it is so difficult to earn money on the Net. But the diffusion of the Internet in the market economy may lead to a profound evolution.

For example peering agreements are beginning to be replaced by formal interconnection contracts. At the applications layer, companies like Microsoft and to a lesser extent Sun, have attempted to individually appropriate the collective benefit of the Net. This shows that the public good nature of Internet may perhaps disappear in the future. Conflicts between the advocates of individual intellectual property rights and proponents of the collective appropriation (exemplified by the Free Software Foundation) are becoming more and more relevant. From a public policy point of view, it remains to be seen whether the denial to assign individual property rights on the modules is efficient and fair in the Commons' sense.

The collective organization of the Internet at the applications level may be justified by the following features: first, software is never finished and benefits from the subsequent improvement of users adapting it for their own needs. Second, by abandoning Intellectual Property Rights (IPR) the innovators may trigger a network effect more quickly (Katz and Shapiro 1986; Church and Gandal 1992). Innovators will benefit by increasing their reputation and by providing ancillary (and charged) services.

4   Conclusion

The analysis of interconnection contracts in network industries has underlined the strong interdependency between the competition and the institutional games, where the latter permits us to define the property rights, as well as the rules of the competition game. It establishes in particular the role and the scope of intervention for the regulatory authority. We have shown in this context that the regulator has to take into account the asymmetries among operators and the dynamics of competition.

In telecommunications networks (voice and data), modularity has been, without a doubt, not only a technological but also an institutional innovation, which has allowed the stimulation of competition. Its implementation has depended on the nature of the network: in voice transport, it has been accompanied by a partial expropriation of the former monopoly, a *sine qua non* condition of the effective functioning of competition. In the case of data networks, there has been rather, at least initially, a "collectivization" of some modules. These difference of institutional choices may be explained by a path dependency: because it was born in the academic community the Internet has favored and still favors communitarism. Because telephone operators initially held a monopoly upon a full-fledged network, institutions have redistributed some property rights.

Convergence between voice and data networks may lead to a partial elimination of these institutional differences. Indeed, some practices of data networks (peering, free software) do not rely on a stable institutional framework. This framework has to be designed and the property rights explicitly assigned. A convergence of the institutional frameworks is likely to occur for both the Internet and telephone networks.

NOTES

Chapter 20 was originally published as "Les accords d'interconnexion dans les réseaux de télécommunications: des comportements stratégiques aux droits de pvopriété," in *Revue d'Economie Industrielle* (92, 2000).

1. This was AT&T's attitude when MCI entered this market in 1963.
2. Economides, Lopomo and Worock (1996) show, however, that if a network dominates (with a strategic advantage), the reciprocity rule enables us to prevent this network monopolizing all the subscribers. But non-discrimination rules (access price equals internal price) and an unbundled supply of service are less efficient.

21   Licensing in the chemical industry

Ashish Arora and Andrea Fosfuri

1   Introduction

A firm wishing to protect its intellectual property from imitation has different options, notably patents, first-mover advantage, lead time, and secrecy. Although patents are often thought to be less effective at enabling the inventor to benefit from the innovation than other alternatives (Levin *et al.* 1987; Cohen *et al.* 2000), they have an important socially valuable feature that the alternatives lack. Specifically, patents can be used to sell technology, typically through licensing contracts.

This is our point of departure beyond the traditional approach to patents that has mainly focused on patents as means to exclude others. By reducing transaction costs, patents can play a key role in facilitating the purchase and sale of technology, or in other words, the development and functioning of a market for technology. A market for technology helps diffuse existing technology more efficiently; it also enables firms to specialize in the generation of new technology. In turn, such specialization is likely to hasten the pace of technological change itself. The reason for focusing on the development and functioning of a market for technology is that it greatly reduces the transaction costs involved in buying and selling technology, implying that innovators have the option of appropriating the rents from their innovation by means of simple contracts, instead of having to exploit the technology in-house.

However, the development of a market for technology is not an automatic outcome. It depends not only on the efficacy of technology licensing contracts (and on the strength of patents that underpin these contracts), but also on the industry structure itself. This is an important issue – whether firms contract for technology depends not only on the transaction costs, as commonly understood, but also on historical factors. Thus, in chemicals, the presence of specialized engineering firms that licensed technology, and in other cases provided complementary know-how for technologies developed by chemical firms, played a key role. The increasing competition has also fostered the willingness of even the largest chemical firms to license their technology, while globalization and entry since the Second World War has meant that there exists a substantial number of chemical producers that are potential buyers of technology.

The chemical industry provides a natural framework within which to explore these themes. It is a technology-based industry with a long history of patenting and licensing. Further, as we show, transactions in technology have become widespread, with substantial variations across products.

Section 2 reviews the contribution of the economic literature on licensing contract design, whereas section 3 underlines the role of patents in facilitating the diffusion of technology. In section 4 we show how, in the past, chemical firms have used patents as one of the ways of excluding competitors and creating monopolies. However, after the Second World War firms started to use licensing contracts (underpinned by patents) as means to profit from innovation, leading to the development of a market for chemical process technology. As section 5 argues, patents have also facilitated the entry of specialized engineering firms and a progressive division of labor. Furthermore, as discussed in section 6, this has profoundly influenced how even large chemical producers appropriate rents from their innovations. Section 7 discusses the specific features of the chemical industry that have favored the creation of a market for technology. Section 8 summarizes and concludes the chapter.

2   Review of the economic literature on licensing contract design

Most of the early works of the literature on licensing contract design (see Kamien 1992 for a survey) have analyzed the optimal licensing contract for a non-producer innovator in a framework with perfect information and homogeneous goods. The two main findings are that an auction is the mechanism that maximizes profit extraction from the licensees, and that licensing by means of a royalty is inferior to a fixed-fee payment both for the non-producer innovator and for consumers. However, Muto (1993) finds that a royalty might be superior to a fixed fee in a differentiated goods duopoly with Bertrand competition, and Rockett (1990) shows that output royalties can be optimal when the licensor and the licensee compete in the same product market.

Since Arrow (1962) it has been well known that licensing contracts are plagued with information problems which may result in imperfect appropriability. (See also Caves, Crookel and Killing 1983.) Indeed, in a framework with asymmetric information in which one party might not know the other party's type, a licensor endowed with a technology with a low commercial value can pretend to have a much more profitable technology. An uninformed licensee would be willing to pay no more than the expected value of the technology. As a result, higher-type licensors want to offer a contract which a lower type would never find in her best interest to offer. Gallini and Wright (1990) show that performance-based royalties may allow separation because higher-type contracts can base a large fraction of the total payments on output when it is commonly known that a higher-value innovation will result in greater output than a lower-value innovation. (See also Macho-Stadler and Perez-Castrillo 1991.) Beggs (1992) obtains a similar result in a model in which it is the licensor who lacks information about the "type" of the licensee.

The design of the licensing contract is further complicated by the tacit nature of the technology. Tacit technology is typically transferred as know-how, but contracts for know-how are marked by double-sided moral-hazard problems (Arrow 1962; Teece 1986). For instance, once the licensor has received the payments, she may not send her best engineers or managers over to the licensee to provide the technical service, or she may provide the licensee's engineers with only limited exposure to her own operations. Some important trade secrets may not be revealed to the licensee. Given this possibility of moral hazard on the part of the licensor, the licensee would like to make the bulk of the payments after being satisfied that the full technology, including the tacit part, has been transferred. However, once the licensee has learned the know-how, she cannot be forced to "unlearn" it. Hence, a licensee may refuse to pay the agreed-upon amount in full after the know-how is transferred.

There are ways through which the efficiency of contracts for know-how can be enhanced. These include reputation-building in the context of repeated contracting, and the use of output-based royalties. However, output-based royalties may not solve the moral-hazard problem. Indeed, the amount of output produced by the licensee is often private information and hard to assess by the licensor or a third party. In addition, output-based royalties can handicap a licensee in the product market, especially in oligopolistic markets (e.g. Katz and Shapiro 1985) and possibly for this reason, it has been shown that the use of output-based royalties to compensate the licensor for technical assistance is uncommon (Contractor 1981). Reputation-building through repeated contracts, while a potential solution, requires a greater degree of integration among the partners.

Arora (1995) shows that efficient contracts for the exchange of technology can be written by exploiting the complementarity between know-how and any other technology input, most notably patents, that the licensor can use as a "hostage." With complementarity, the use of the know-how, which cannot be taken back from the buyer once transferred, is more valuable when used in conjunction with the complementary patents. This allows the licensor to use her patents to protect herself against opportunistic behavior by the licensee. On the other hand, the licensee protects herself by postponing a part of the payment till the know-how has been transferred. If the licensee does not make the second payment, the licensor can withdraw from the contract and withdraw the patents. As long as the additional benefit of having the know-how and the complementary patents is greater than the second-period payment, the licensee will make the payment. As long as the second payment is greater than the cost to the licensor of supplying know-how, the licensor will honor the contract as well. Thus, the problem of opportunism can be mitigated through simple and self-enforcing contracts.

Empirical research has shown that the vast majority of licensing contracts involve performance-based royalties, often used in combination with fixed fees. For example, Macho-Stadler, Martinez-Giralt and Perez-Castrillo (1996) found royalty provisions in 72 percent of 241 Spanish technology transfer contracts while Bessy and Brousseau (1998) found such provisions in nearly 83 percent of French contracts. However, the available evidence seems to suggest that royalty rates tend to vary very little across licensing contracts for any given industry, and are typically established by "rule of thumb" (Contractor 1981). This suggests that factors other than royalties may be important in reducing transaction costs.

3   The role of patents as a transaction-cost reducing mechanism

Patents can play an important role in determining the efficiency of knowledge flows, which are critical to any knowledge-based division of labor. First, the direct costs of knowledge transfer are lowered when the knowledge is codified and organized in a systematic way. Since the innovator has always some discretion in how she codifies, stores, and organizes knowledge, strong patent protection provides incentives to codify new knowledge in ways that are meaningful and useful to others. This is particularly important when innovation systematically originates in firms that will not develop and utilize the knowledge themselves.

Second, patents might help to make licensing contracts more efficient by reducing the transaction costs of transferring know-how in licensing contracts. As noted earlier, patents can function well as a complementary input provided by the licensor. Thus, a prototypical case would be one in which the technology to be transferred is composed of both a patented (possibly codified) component and complementary know-how (e.g. experience with using the technology). Arora (1996) uses a sample of 144 technology licensing agreements signed by Indian firms to test the empirical relevance of patents. He uses the provision of three technical services – training, quality control, and help with setting up an R&D unit – as empirical proxies for the transfer of know-how. Arora (1996) finds that the probability of technical services being provided was higher when the contract also included a patent license or a turnkey construction contract. Interestingly enough, machines and equipment merely increased the probability of training being provided, whereas patents and turnkey contracts were more strongly associated with the provision of services relating to quality control and R&D.

In the technology licensing agreements discussed below, the vast majority are contracts that involve the transfer of know-how and unpatented technology. However, for the most part, these contracts are underpinned by patents. Industry executives we interviewed strongly believe that strong patent protection is vital for technology licensing and that absent such protection, firms would drastically reduce the extent of technology licensing.

Arora and Gambardella (1994) and Merges (1998) argue that patents are likely to have a greater value for small firms and independent technology suppliers as compared to large established corporations. Whereas the latter have several means to protect their innovations, including their manufacturing and commercialization assets, the former can appropriate the rents to their innovation by only leveraging the protection that patents provide. At the margin, an increase in the strength of patents and intellectual property rights increases the returns from investments in technology development more substantially for smaller technology specialists and start-ups than for the larger integrated companies.[1]

In a more recent paper Arora and Merges (2001) use the incomplete contracting approach (Grossman and Hart 1986; Hart and Moore 1990) incorporating not only opportunism but also information spillovers. Information spillovers arise owing to the supplier's effort to customize its generalized technology to the specific needs of the buyer. Arora and Merges (2001) argue that stronger intellectual property rights enhance the viability of specialized firms by reducing buyer opportunism. As the examples of technology-sharing agreements in the chemical industry, discussed below, show, patents play an important role in structuring complex contracts involving the exchange of technology between large firms.[2]

Arora and Merges (2001) provide several examples of the role that patents play in the specialty chemical industry, specifically from firms like Lonza or SepraChem specializing in the design and production of optically pure or "chiral" compounds used as inputs by the pharmaceutical industry.[3] These firms must typically expend considerable effort in developing new molecules (or processes for developing new molecules) for their customers, the large pharmaceutical firms. They hope to recoup this cost by supplying the molecules over a period of time. This up-front cost, analogous to the cost of transferring tacit knowledge, makes the firm vulnerable to hold-up by the customer. Ownership of patents covering the design of their input products provides these firms with some security if future trades with the customer firms do not come through, a possibility that the financial disclosure documents of chiral suppliers explicitly note. Indeed, a case study of the contractual relationship between Alkermes and Genentech in Arora and Merges (2001) shows how patents are used to structure technology licensing agreements. Alkermes has a proprietary, microencapsulation, drug delivery technology which routinely patents microencapsulated versions of highly successful drugs. This it does in close collaboration with the large drug firms that own the rights to the drugs: Alkermes has deals with Schering-Plough, Johnson and Johnson, and Genentech, among others. Drug firms enter into these deals to access Alkermes' proprietary delivery technology, which makes the drugs easier to take, and in some cases opens up new sub-markets not available using conventional delivery techniques.

The basic structure of the Genentech–Alkermes deal illustrates the role of patents in such transactions. There are two stages to the transaction: (1) Alkermes adapts its microencapsulation drug delivery technology to Genentech's successful therapeutic product, a genetically engineered form of the naturally occurring protein called Human Growth Hormone (HGH); and (2) Alkermes manufactures the product for Genentech and sells it at a pre-agreed price, with Genentech then marketing and distributing it. Note that Alkermes is required to make substantial investments in adapting its technology to Genentech's product and in creating the production process needed to manufacture it, and licensing this know-how to Genentech.

Arora and Merges (2001) argue that that Genentech is technically able to duplicate the production process if it wanted to. So what protection does Alkermes have? The major source of protection for Alkermes is its patents. Alkermes currently has 43 patents covering (1) its microencapsulation process; (2) novel polymers and preparations that make up the coatings; and (3) microencapsulated formulations of the drugs it delivers under its collaboration agreements. These patents provide a fallback in the event that Genentech does not continue with the agreement. They would prevent Genentech from using the Alkermes technology after the agreement is terminated.

4 The market for chemical process technology

The way in which patents have been used in the chemical industry has evolved over time. Patents played an important role in the development of organic dyestuffs, the first major product area of the modern organic chemical industry, in the 1850s and 1860s. Chemical technologies, strongly based in science, were easier to codify and patent compared to mechanical technologies. The properties of synthetic dyes were dependent heavily on the structure of the molecules. Thus, understanding the structure of the dyestuff molecules and how to produce them implied that the innovator could protect the innovation through patents. German companies skillfully combined secrecy and patents to exclude competitors, both at home and abroad (see Arora 1997 for a full discussion).

Domestic licensing was not common during this time because the dominant producers also controlled technology, not because of problems in technology licensing. Instead, the dominant producers in each market tended to form licensing and market-sharing agreements with each other to keep out entrants. Indeed, the pre-Second World War international chemical market has been characterized by many as a sort of a "gentlemen's club" (e.g. Spitz 1988; Smith 1992). These cartels used a number of instruments, including patent licensing agreements, to maintain market shares and deter entry.

Some cartels were organized around a common technology, and were often initiated by the patent holder. The patent would be licensed, often in return for an equity stake, with technology flow-back agreements. For instance, the Solvay process licensees were required to share all improvements with the Solvay company, and the latter would share it with other licensees. To the extent that there were benefits to all licensees from having the Solvay process become the standard process for the production of alkali, such technology-sharing cartels were mutually beneficial. In other cases, particularly during the 1920s and 1930s, there were some prominent technology- and market-sharing agreements, with the agreement between Standard and IG Farben that involved technology sharing in butyl rubber, TEL, and arc acetylene (from Standard), and Buna S (from IG Farben) being one of the best-known examples.

Though anti-competitive in intent, these arrangements did economize on scarce assets. For instance, although ICI obtained the basic patent on polyester, Du Pont had developed significant expertise in the production process based on its experience in nylon, and controlled the melt-spinning process that was crucial for successful commercialization. ICI and Du Pont had a long-standing agreement that involved technology licensing as well as the extensive sharing of information and know-how.

As a result, the two companies quickly settled on a suitable cross-licensing agreement.

However, it is only after the Second World War that firms start to use licensing as a means to profit from innovation and a market for chemical technology began to arise. Indeed, starting from the 1950s an increasing number of chemical processes became available for license. Landau (1966, p. 4) writing two decades after the end of the war, noted that "the partial breakdown of secrecy barriers in the chemical industry is increasing... the trend toward more licensing of processes." Importantly, these were not exclusive licenses. As Spitz (1988, p. 318) put it:

> some brand new technologies, developed by operating [chemical] companies, were made available for license to any and all comers. A good example is the Hercules-Distillers phenol/acetone process, which was commercialized in 1953 and forever changed the way that phenol would be produced.

Our data analysis confirms the presence of a well-established market for chemical technology during the 1980s.[4] Indeed, figure 21.1 shows that during the period under study only a fifth of the technology used in new chemical investments world-wide was developed in-house by the investors, while the rest was licensed in from unaffiliated sources. However, there are important differences across geographic areas, chemical sub-sectors, and investors' sizes and nationalities in the propensity of chemical producers to rely on the market for technology. Firms investing in North America (Canada and the United States) have the highest share of plants developed in-house (more than 40 percent), closely followed by firms investing in Western Europe. This share is the smallest for firms in Eastern Europe, Africa, the Middle East, and South America (less than 5 percent). Multinational firms tend to rely more on in-house technology

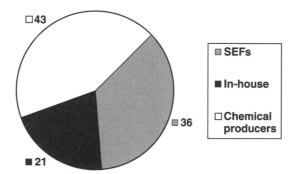

Figure 21.1   Who was licensing chemical technologies, 1980s (percent)

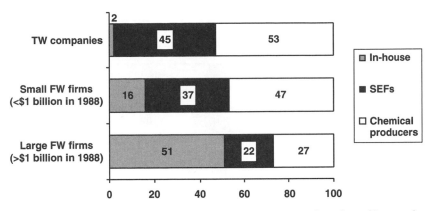

Figure 21.2   Market for chemical technology as a function of investor's type (percent)

although this share is still sensitive to the final location of the investment. Size and nationality of the investors, which might proxy for the degree of technological capability, seem to play an important role. Large chemical corporations from advanced countries acquire less than 50 percent of their technology from unaffiliated sources. By contrast, third-world firms rely almost completely on the market for technology (see figure 21.2).

Differences across chemical sub-sectors are remarkable as well. In the aggregate, technology licensing is most common in sectors with large-scale production facilities, with relatively homogeneous products, and with a large number of new plants. It is less common in sectors marked by product differentiation, custom tailoring of products for customers, and small scales of production. Indeed, in pulp and paper, gas handling, fertilizers, industrial gases, and organic refining more than 90 percent of the plants involve the sale of technology between firms that are not linked through ownership ties, whereas in pharmaceuticals, organic chemicals, and plastics the share is close to 50 percent.

Finally, the market for chemical technology is more prominent in large product markets. As shown in figure 21.3, the extent of the market for chemical technology moves from close to 90 percent in "large" product markets (those accounting for more than thirty plants world-wide during the period under study) to 50 percent in "niche" product markets (one–two plants).

Contracts typically involve a lump-sum payment that is paid in install-ments, starting when the contract is signed and ending when the plant is commissioned. In addition, there may be royalties on output for a spec-ified period of time (royalties are more or less set by industry norms,

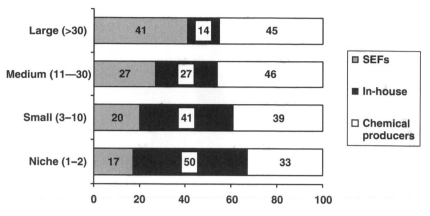

Figure 21.3   Share of SEFs licensing, by size of product markets (percent)

typically between 2 percent and 5 percent). These carry with them the right to audit, a right which is occasionally exercised. Specialized engineering firms tend to favor lump-sum payments, being unwilling or unable to track how the project does after commissioning.

5   Specialized engineering firms and division of labor

An important reason for the dramatic surge of licensing transactions after the Second World War has to do with the rise of specialized process design, engineering and construction firms (hereafter, SEFs). SEFs originated as an American phenomenon. From very early in the twentieth century, the oil firms used specialized sub-contractors in various capacities: to procure or manufacture equipment such as pumps and compressors, valves, and heat exchangers, and to provide specialized sub-systems such as piping and the electrical systems. As these specialized engineering–construction firms grew in their ability to handle more sophisticated tasks, process design became a part of their activities as well. By the 1960s, SEFs dominated the design and construction of new plants and were important sources of process innovation (Freeman 1968, p. 30). SEFs reaped the advantages of specialization. By working for many clients, they benefitted from learning by doing, and by repeatedly selling their expertise (through licenses or engineering services) they could spread the cost of accumulating that expertise over a larger output.

The importance of the SEFs lies not only in the fact that they were sources of innovations but also in how they appropriated the rents from innovation. Lacking the downstream assets required to commercialize their innovations themselves, SEFs used licensing as the principal way of profiting from their innovations. Freeman (1968) showed that for the period 1960–6, SEFs as a group accounted for about 30 percent of all licenses. During the 1980s the importance of SEFs as a source of technology has increased somewhat. Figure 21.1 shows that in the 1980s SEFs supplied the technology for more than one-third of plant investments in the world as a whole, which implies that about 45 percent of all technologies coming from unaffiliated sources were licensed by SEFs.[5]

With some prominent exceptions such as UOP and Halcon/Scientific Design, SEFs did not focus on breakthrough innovation. However, they did improve and modify processes developed by chemical firms and offer those for license. SEFs encouraged technology licensing in two other ways. First, as discussed below, they induced chemical firms to license their own technology. Second, they often acted as licensing agents for chemicals firms. Chemical producers often lack licensing experience and are unwilling to provide the various engineering and design services that licensees need in addition to the technology, and therefore use SEFs as licensing agents. A chemical firm will license its technology to an SEF. The latter offers a complete technology package, consisting of the core technology licensed from a chemical producer, along with know-how and installation and engineering services. This arrangement enables the licensor to benefit from the superior ability of SEFs to manage technology transfer. It also provides a buffer between the chemical firm and its licensees, limiting accidental leakage of information. From the point of view of the customer, dealing with a single source for technology, construction, and engineering reduces transaction costs. The SEF can also provide better operational guarantees than if the contract were a pure technology licensing contract. (See Grindley and Nickerson 1996 for further discussion of this topic.)

Interviews with industry executives have confirmed the important role of SEFs as integrators, bundling technology licensed from a technology supplier like UCC or BP with engineering and procurement services. It appears that whereas established firms in the United States or Europe are more likely to negotiate directly with the technology supplier, and then ask SEFs to bid for the engineering and construction contract, chemical firms in developing countries rely very heavily on SEFs. For them, SEFs act like one-stop shops, procuring technology and equipment, and providing engineering and construction services.

Our data confirm this. In the 1980s, SEFs were more important sources of technology for small chemical companies and third-world firms. For instance, large chemical companies from advanced countries (those with a turnover of more than $1 billion in 1988) purchased around a fifth of their technologies from SEFs. For smaller first-world companies (with less than $1 billion of turnover in 1988) this percentage was 37 percent, and close to 50 percent for third-world chemical firms. (See figure 21.2.)

Finally, figure 21.3 shows that SEFs accounted for a larger share of total licensing in larger product markets. Furthermore, although not evident from figure 21.3, larger markets also tend to have a larger fraction of the total investment from small firms and third-world companies.[6] In other words, the evidence is consistent with the notion that SEFs encourage investment, particularly by small firms and third-world companies.

6   Licensing by chemical firms

6.1   Empirical evidence

The licensing activities of the SEFs have had a major effect on the rent appropriation strategies of the other players in the market as well. In a marked departure from their pre-Second World War strategy of closely holding onto their technology, a number of chemical and oil companies began to use licensing as an important (although not the only) means of profiting from innovation. Licensing by chemical producers is now a significant share of all licensing in the industry. As figure 21.1 shows, although SEFs play a major role as licensors, at least half of the licenses sold to unaffiliated firms are by other chemical producers themselves.

Table 21.1 shows the licensing strategies by a number of selected chemical corporations from advanced countries, which were especially active as technology suppliers during the 1980s. In particular, columns (E)–(F) of the table report the share of licenses directed to the national market, to the rest of the first world and to the third world, respectively. All companies are more likely to use licensing in dealing with overseas investments, although some firms (e.g. Union Carbide, Monsanto, Exxon) also license in their home markets. On average, slightly more than one in ten licenses goes to the national market. To put this in perspective, the weight of the national market *vis-à-vis* the world market is also one-tenth, implying that the bias towards international licensing is moderate.

Not only do firms license extensively, many of them now explicitly consider licensing revenues as a part of the overall return from investing in technology. For instance, Union Carbide is reported to have earned $300 million from its polyolefin licensing in 1992 (Grindley and Nickerson 1996). Both Du Pont and Dow, two chemical firms with a long tradition of exploiting technology in-house, have indicated that they intend to license technology very actively. In 1994 Du Pont created a division with the specific task of overseeing all technology transfer activities. Reversing

Table 21.1. *Licensing strategies by some selected chemical producers*

Company name	Turnover (1988)	A	B	C	D	C/D	E	F	G
Air Liquide	FRA 3539	129	45	233	120	1.94	0.12	0.36	0.52
Monsanto	USA 7453	113	31	204	590	0.35	0.26	0.22	0.52
Union Carbide	USA 8324	106	37	192	59	3.25	0.22	0.42	0.36
Shell	UK 11848	101	71	183	773	0.24	0.02	0.43	0.55
ICI	UK 21125	93	55	168	1020	0.16	0.0	0.31	0.69
Air Products	USA 2237	59	29	107	72	1.48	0.19	0.24	0.57
Amoco	USA 4300	55	23	99.5	NA	NA	0.18	0.40	0.42
Phillips	USA 2500	55	22	99.5	NA	NA	0.16	0.40	0.44
Rhône-Poulenc	FRA 10802	44	28	79.6	632	0.13	0.0	0.23	0.77
Texaco	USA 1500	44	9	79.6	NA	NA	0.18	0.32	0.50
BASF	GER 21543	37	45	66.9	1,010	0.07	0.03	0.49	0.48
Exxon	USA 9892	35	49	63.3	551	0.11	0.23	0.37	0.40
Mitsui Toatsu	JAP 2991	35	15	63.3	NA	NA	0.09	0.11	0.80
Hoechst	GER 21948	34	44	61.5	1,363	0.05	0.03	0.3	0.94
Du Pont	USA 19608	33	66	59.7	1,319	0.05	0.03	0.12	0.85
Total		973	569	1,760	7,509	0.23	0.12	0.32	0.56

Note: A = Total number of licenses in 1980–90, B = Total number of self-licenses in 1980–90, C = Estimated annual average licensing revenues, D = R&D expenditures in 1988, E = Share of licenses at home, F = Share of licenses in the rest of the first world, G = Share of licenses in the third world.
All figures (except shares) in million US dollars.
NA = Not available.

its tradition of treating in-house technology as the jewel in the crown, Du Pont has started to exploit it through an aggressive outlicensing program. Starting in 1999, this was expected to be a $100 million per year business. On its own web page, Du Pont advertises the technologies available for licensing in several areas: fibers-related, composites, chemical science and catalysis, analytical, environmental, electronics, biological. The words of Jack Krol, Du Pont's president and CEO, at the 1997 Corporate Technology Transfer Meeting, emphasize this new trend:

For a long time, the belief about intellectual property at Du Pont was that patents were for defensive purposes only. Patents and related know-how should not be sold, and licensing was a drain on internal resources... Our businesses are gradually becoming more comfortable with the idea that all intellectual property... is licensable for the right price in the right situation.

Dow has also long had a reputation for "never licensing breakthrough technology, and there was an emotional bias against licensing"

(Ed Gambrell, Vice President, Dow). In 1995, it formed a licensing group with the purpose to "create more value" from its technology. Before the group was formed, Dow had licensing revenues of roughly $10–20 million per year. It expected to earn a $100 million/year business by 2000.

Finally, we have estimated the average annual licensing revenues (during the period 1980–90) for a sample of large chemical producers. These revenues amount to $26 million, or about 10 percent of the mean R&D expenditure in 1988 (for our sample). Some firms are performing well above this average. For instance, Union Carbide has licensing revenues as large as its total R&D expenditure. Other firms like Monsanto, Shell and ICI cover, respectively, about 35 percent, 24 percent, and 16 percent of their R&D expenditures through licensing revenues. In table 21.1 we report for a selected number of firms the annual average licensing revenues (column (C)) and their total R&D expenditures in 1988 (column (D)).

6.2   Why is there so much licensing by chemical producers?

This behavior of the chemical firms runs contrary to the orthodox management prescriptions (e.g. Teece 1988). Traditional wisdom holds that licensing is undesirable because the innovator has to share the rents with the licensee, and because licensing implies increased competition and rent dissipation.

There are two, related, reasons for the change in strategy: increased competition, and technology licensing by SEFs. The presence of competing technologies drastically changes the payoff to the strategy of trying to keep one's technology in-house. For instance, suppose there are two viable processes for the production of a particular product, each owned by a different firm. If one of the firms is going to license out (sell) its technology, the best response of the other innovator may well be to license out (sell) as well.

A search of the trade publications in 2000 turned up further evidence that shows that, at least in some markets, chemical and oil companies are aggressively competing to sell technology, often in collaboration with an SEF which undertakes the provision of the engineering and other know-how. Sometimes, competitors in the market for licenses are other chemical producers. In other cases, the major competition is provided by SEFs.

In Arora and Fosfuri (1999) we develop a model of oligopolistic competition with potentially more than one technology supplier. We consider the case where at least one of the competing innovations is patented by an SEF. Lacking production facilities, an SEF has little option but to license its technology to others.[7] Therefore, when one of the innovators is an

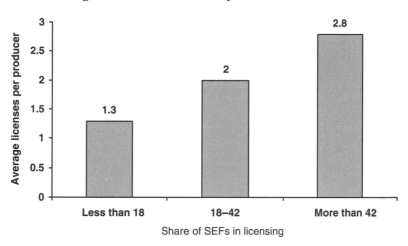

Figure 21.4   Market share of SEFs and licensing, by chemical producers (percent)

SEF, the other innovator's dominant strategy is to license its innovation
as well. Put differently, in product markets where SEFs are widespread,
chemical producers have no other strategic choice, but aggressively licensing themselves. Figure 21.4 shows that in all chemical sub-sectors in
which SEFs had more than 42 percent of market share during the 1980s,
the average number of licenses sold out by chemical producers was 2.8,
whereas in the sub-sectors in which SEFs had less than 18 percent of the
market, it was as little as 1.3.[8]

Even without SEFs, a technology holder may license if the net licensing
revenues are greater than the loss in profits owing to increased competition in the product market. However, whereas the licensing revenues
go only to the licensor, all incumbent producers potentially lose from
the increased competition. In other words, licensing imposes a negative
pecuniary externality upon other incumbents, which is not taken into
account by the licensor. As a result, licensing can be privately profitable
even if it reduces the joint profits of all incumbents.

This is exemplified by the different ways in which BP Chemicals has
approached acetic acid and polyethylene. In acetic acid, BP Chemicals
has strong proprietary technology, but it licenses very selectively, typically
licensing only to get access to markets it would otherwise be unable to
enter. By contrast, in polyethylene, BP has less than 2 percent of the
market share. Although it has good proprietary technology as well, there
are a dozen other sources of technology for making polyethylene. Thus,
BP has licensed its polyethylene technology very aggressively, competing

with Union Carbide which was the market leader in licensing polyethylene technology. Even here, BP initially tried not to license in Western Europe, where BP had a substantial share of polyethylene capacity. However, other licensors continued to supply technology to firms that wished to produce polyethylene in Western Europe, with the result that BP found that it was losing potential licensing revenue without any benefits in the form of restraining entry.

In Arora and Fosfuri (1999), we formally show that the more homogeneous the product, the greater the negative externality to other incumbents, and the greater the incentives to license. We find that technology licensing is most common in sectors with large-scale production facilities, with relatively homogeneous products, and with a large number of new plants. It is less common in sectors marked by product differentiation, custom tailoring of products for customers, and small scales of production. Figure 21.5 confirms this finding. It classifies all chemical sub-sectors reported in CAPF in three broad categories of product differentiation: homogeneous, intermediate and differentiated. Figure 21.5 shows that the average number of licenses per patent holder increases as the product market becomes more homogeneous.[9]

Finally, most of the licensing takes place for processes. New products are far less likely to be licensed, at least in the initial stage of their life cycles. In this case, the profit loss due to competition would be felt almost entirely by the licensor since by definition there would not be any other incumbent producers of the product. These incentives are reinforced by the unimportance of SEFs in product innovation.

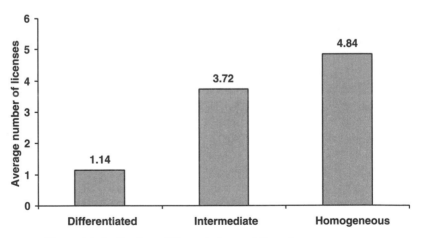

Figure 21.5   Product differentiation and licensing

7   Why in chemicals?

Licensing and the presence of a market for technology are not limited to the chemical industry. In Arora, Fosfuri and Gambardella (2001) we provide evidence of extensive licensing in sectors such as semiconductors, electronics, industrial machinery, equipment and business services, biotechnology, and several examples of licensing strategies by large established producers such as IBM, Texas Instruments, Boeing, Philips, Procter & Gamble, and General Electric. Nevertheless, it is true that the use of licensing as a strategy of rent appropriation is less developed outside of chemicals, particularly for processes (see also Anand and Khanna 2000).

As discussed earlier, technology licensing may be hindered either because licensing contracts are very inefficient or because it is not in the strategic interest of the technology holder to license the technology. Licensing contracts can be inefficient owing to the need to transfer know-how and owing to information asymmetries. Both are closely related to the strength of patent protection.

In the chemical industry, unlike most others, chemical processes can be effectively protected through patents. As a result, even the valuable unpatented know-how, needed to use the technology, can be licensed. Patents pertain to that part of the discovery that is codified. Therefore the effectiveness of patents depends on how cheaply and effectively new ideas and knowledge can be articulated in terms of universal categories. When innovations can not be described in terms of universal and general categories, sensible patent law can provide only narrow patent protection. During the 1860s, when synthetic dyestuffs first appeared, their structure was poorly understood, as were the reaction pathways and processes. Thus broad patents led to extensive litigation and retarded the development of technology. In France, an excessively broad patent on analine red was construed to include all processes for making the red aniline-based dye, even though it was quite clear that the structure of aniline dyes was as yet unknown. There were long and bitter disputes in England about the validity of the Medlock patent for *magenta* (another aniline dye) that turned on whether the appropriate definition of "dry" arsenic acid included the water of hydration (Travis 1993, pp. 104–37).

Arora and Gambardella (1994) point out that technological knowledge that is closely related to broad engineering principles and physical and chemical "laws" is more readily codifiable. Chemical engineering developed more general and abstract ways of conceptualizing chemical processes, initially in the form of unit operations, and later in terms of concepts such as mass and energy transfer. A number of different processes could be conceived of in terms of these more elementary units. A chemical engineer could therefore see common elements across a number of processes that might appear very different and diverse to a chemist from an earlier generation. Chemical engineering (and the concomitant developments in polymer science and surface chemistry) thus provided the language for describing more precisely the innovations to be protected.

In other words, patents work well in the chemical industry because the object of discovery can be described clearly in terms of formulae, reaction pathways, operating conditions, and the like (e.g. Levin *et al.*, 1987). But it is not merely that the object of discovery is more discrete in the sense of being a particular compound. Rather, it is the ability to relate the "essential" structure of the compound to its function. This allows a patent to include within its ambit inessential variations in structure, as in minor modifications in side chains of a pesticide.[10] In fact, chemical patents frequently use Markush structures to define the scope of the claim.[11] The use of Markush structures permits a succinct and compact description of the claims and allows the inventor to protect the invention for sets of related compounds without the expense (and tedium) of testing and listing the entire set. The ability to explicate the underlying scientific basis of the innovation allows the scope of the patent to be delimited more clearly. The obvious extensions can be foreseen more easily and described more compactly.

8   Conclusions

We have argued that there exists a functioning market in chemicals where process technologies are sold through arm's length license contracts. We have documented the substantial extent of technology licensing in the chemical industry, involving both specialized engineering firms and chemical producers themselves. The existence of this market for technology has contributed to a faster world-wide diffusion of the chemical technology and to making the chemical industry a truly global industry. This process has progressed to the point where licensing is an integral part of the technology strategies of even the largest chemical firms.

Such widespread licensing would be unlikely without a well-functioning patent system: transaction costs involved in contracting for technology would be larger and contracts for know-how less efficient. Although further research is needed, we believe that patents have worked well in the chemical industry because the underlying knowledge base – chemistry and chemical engineering – has been very successful in clarifying the relationship between structure and function. A chemical invention can be described clearly in terms of structure, reaction pathways, or operating conditions, with a reasonably clear sense of the limits of the invention.

While patents are necessary for a market for technology, they are by no means sufficient. Firms that specialize in the design, engineering, and construction of chemical plants emerged and some developed proprietary technologies that they offered for license, at a time when many firms, all over the world, were looking to acquire chemical technologies. SEFs induced chemical firms to license their technology as well. In addition, SEFs reduced transaction costs by acting as licensing agents for chemical firms and by bundling technology with complementary engineering, design, and construction capabilities valuable to potential buyers of technology. The presence of SEFs, induced entry by a number of firms, increasing the number of potential technology buyers. The net result was a "thicker" and a more efficient market for technology.

NOTES

Chapter 21 was originally published as "The Market for Technology in the Chemical Industry: Causes and Consequences," in *Revue d'Economie Industrielle* (92, 2000).

Financial support from the TSER project, "A Green Paper on the Chemical Industry: From Science to Product," is gratefully acknowledged. We are indebted to Alfonso Gambardella and Robert Merges for ongoing suggestions and discussions. We thank Eric Brousseau, Jean-Michel Glanchant, and participants in seminars at Stanford University, University of Stuttgart, Universitat Pompeu Fabra and University Carlos III (Madrid) for helpful comments on a previous draft. Ralph Landau and Martin Howard have shared their extensive knowledge of licensing practices in the chemical industry, for which we are very grateful. All errors, of course, remain our own.

1. In some cases, policies designed in the naïve hope of encouraging small inventors have encouraged the abuse of the patent system. In the United States, for instance, there have been well-known cases where patents filed in the 1950s were ultimately issued more than twenty years later. In the meantime, the patentee could legally amend the application so that it covered inventions made well after the filing date. Since patents in the United States are published only upon issue, such patents (sometimes referred to as "submarine" patents because they are not visible for long periods after they are filed) have surprised many established firms. The move towards patent harmonization, which will require publication of all patent applications after a certain period, will be helpful in this respect.

2. This is not specific to the chemical industry. Grindley and Teece (1997) report that, in cross-licensing agreements in electronics and semiconductors, the quality and the market coverage of the patent portfolios of each party is used in the calculation of balancing royalty payments. (See also Hall and Ham 1999.)

3. Briefly, many molecules can exist in two mirror-image forms; they are said to be "chiral." The majority of biomolecules occurring in the human body exist in only one of the two possible forms. Because the wrong chiral form can be ineffective or harmful (as in the case of the drug thalidomide), sophisticated catalysts are required to ensure that the manufacturing process for a pharmaceutical product yields only the desired form of the molecule. (See Ball 1994, pp. 77–8.)

4. All figures reported in this chapter refer to our calculations of the Chemical Age Project File (CAPF), a comprehensive data set on world-wide investments in chemical plants during the 1980s, compiled by Pergamon Press (London). The data set covers about 14,000 plants constructed or under construction during the period 1980–90. CAPF discloses the information about the licensor only in half of the plants. Most of the figures provided in this chapter are based on the assumption that the missing information about licensors is selected randomly.

5. The role of SEFs varies across different sub-sectors. For instance, in pharmaceuticals, plastics, and agricultural products, SEFs account for less than 10 percent of all technologies from unaffiliated firms, compared to 60 percent in sub-sectors like fertilizers, and textile and fibers.

6. The market share of big chemical companies (i.e. all firms with a turnover of more than $1 billion in 1988) is 28 percent in "large" product markets (more than thirty plants), whereas it is about 45 percent in "niche" product markets (one-two plants).

7. Our data confirm that the average number of licenses sold out by SEFs is larger than the average number of licenses sold out by producers in basically all chemical sub-sectors.

8. Figure 21.4 classifies all chemical sub-sectors (twenty-three) reported in CAPF in three broad categories characterized, respectively, by small, medium, and important presence of SEFs. It reports the average number of licenses per chemical producer.

9. Our measure of product differentiation was computed as follows. CAPF classifies the chemical plants within each sub-sector in more disaggregated process technology classes. We use the counts at this disaggregated level to compute an equidistribution index at the sub-sector level. Our index of product differentiation takes the value of 0 if the products are homogeneous and the value of 100 if they are totally differentiated. We have also tried alternative measures of product differentiation, such as the entropy index and the Herfindahl index, with substantially similar results.

10. In some instances, seemingly minor variations in side chains can have significant biological effects. Therefore, what is a "minor" variation is itself determined by the state of the current understanding of the relation between structure and function.

11. A Markush structure is best understood as a language for specifying chemical structures of compounds, which allows generic representation for an entire set of related compounds. See Maynard and Peters (1991, p. 71) for details.

Part VII

Policy issues: anti-trust and regulation
of public utilities

22 Inter-company agreements and EC competition law

Michel Glais

1 Introduction

In a free-market economy, suppliers are supposed to adopt their strategic decisions in a totally independent manner. In this respect both tacit and explicit agreements are forbidden by the texts governing competition within Europe, as in the United States. However, Community law has seen fit to include a proviso for possible dispensations from the rule concerning independence of behavior between competitors, when agreements between them enhance production, distribution, or the promotion of economic progress and so long as competition in the ongoing market be maintained to a sufficient degree. Many agreements may therefore be considered to be in accordance with this principle when the advantages they represent outweigh the accompanying competition restraints. Given the impossibility of making an individual examination of each agreement because of their number, the Brussels Commission is now authorized to decree "exemptions by category" for certain types of agreements. Candidates for a cooperation operation are presented with two procedures when they seek validation by community authorities of the operation in question. In accordance with the contractual clauses of their project within the legal framework laid down by the exemption, regulations also afford them, in principle, exemption from any prior notification. Otherwise, companies are required "to present the Commission with the supporting documents needed to establish justification of individual exemption and, where the Commission might raise objections, to propose alternative action."[1]

One of the greatest merits of Community authority intervention in the field of free-market functioning control is to have recognized very early that the promotion of technical progress could be ensured only if companies could be made largely exempt from the principle of independence (section 2). Conditional validation of certain distribution contracts duplicates this desire to see the promotion of economic efficiency when the positive results to be expected significantly outweigh the effects of restrictions (section 3).

2   A voluntarist concept of the promotion of technical progress

A more rapid diffusion of economic progress within the Community represents one of the priorities the Commission has assigned itself. License or patent agreements, formerly covered by various regulatory texts, have become since 1996[2] the object of a unified legal framework (sub-section 2.1). Cooperation projects established at the research-development stage also fall under a specific regulation. Established between competitors holding substantial market shares, they are nonetheless validated on the basis of individual rulings in which the Commission has shown real concern for the most recent developments of economic analysis (sub-section 2.2).

2.1   Block exemption to certain categories of technology transfer agreements

This concerns equally licenses for patents and know-how, and "mixed" licenses covering both types of transfer.

Principally established to validate transfer technology agreements between non-competing firms in the markets concerned, this regulation is nonetheless open, under certain conditions, to cooperation agreements between rivals.

Exempt by nature from the principle of independence, transfer agreements within this Community legal framework must leave sufficiently effective competition in the market concerned. This is why exemption from certain competition restriction provisions is granted only for a limited duration and applies only so long as the agreeing parties refrain from including certain clauses considered illicit *per se* (so-called *black clauses*).

2.1.1   Agreements covered by the new exemption: regulation 240/96

The standard contract to benefit from block exemption comprises three main characteristics. The agreement must be concluded between two companies only, neither of which are to be competitors or to have any contractual links. The agreement should contain only obligations relative to the Common Market territories. Any contract of this type which respects the provisions laid down by the regulation is, *a priori*, exempt from the provisions of article 81 §1 of the Community Agreement Law.

However, the Commission reserves the right to withdraw such exemption benefit when: "the effect of the agreement is to prevent the licensed products from being exposed to effective competition in the licensed territory from identical goods or services or from goods or services considered by users as interchangeable or substitutable in view of their characteristics, price and intended use"(article 7-1).

This may be the case when (1) the licensee holds a market share of more than 40 percent, (2) circulation of goods is illicitly hindered within the community space.

The very restrictive nature of the obligation preventing companies from being rivals on the same market is nonetheless lessened by the existence within the regulation of two significant adjustments:

(1) Exemption applies to licensing agreements concluded between competitors with participation in a joint venture (or between one of the two and the joint venture) when the licensed products and other goods and services of companies involved (considered as interchangeable or substitutable) represent only: (a) no more than 20 percent, in cases of a license limited to production, (b) no more than 10 percent, when extended to production and distribution of the whole range of interchangeable or substitutable products competing on the market in question (article 5 §2-1).

(2) This also applies to agreements concluded between competitors granting reciprocal technology transfer licenses when the parties are not bound by any territorial restriction within the common market concerning manufacture, use, and commercial application of the products concerned by the agreement or the use of technologies in common (article 5 §2-2).

2.1.2   *Contractual clauses concerned in this new regulation*

Three types of contractual clauses are evoked by the new block exemption regulation. *Clauses or restrictions declared exempt* are those considered to be favorable to the diffusion of technological progress, since by their nature they incite the holder of a patent or of a certain know-how to concede licenses to companies which, in turn, will readily agree to investments (and assume further expenses) necessary to the diffusion of these new products on their geographical markets. Thus, for limited periods of time, *non-active and passive competition clauses* are declared exempt.

The aim of the former (restriction of active competition) is to oblige the licensor not to exploit his license (in any way whatsoever) within the territory of the license holder nor to authorize other companies to do so, the licensee making a similar commitment to the licensor as well as to other licensees within the territories conceded to them. The aim of the latter is to forbid each partner to reply to unsolicited demands on the part of buyers situated outside the territory of the licensee concerned (territory of the licensor or other licensees). Investments set up by licensees often fall into the category of sunk costs expenses and as such the exemption of such clauses proves indispensable to the efficiency of a technical progress diffusion policy. Nevertheless, these provisions should not protect the parties in question beyond the period deemed reasonably necessary to cover the expenses incurred and the initial risk of putting the product or technology covered by the license onto a new geographical market.[3]

Clauses which do not prevent exemption first concern the obligations imposed on licensees to respect the quality level of the goods under license and to ensure the protection of the technology conceded (non-disclosure of the know-how communicated, interdiction to grant a sub-license, obligation to inform the licensor of misappropriation of the know-how or of infringement of the licensed patent, etc.). They also cover (1) provisions relative to access by the parties to improvements or to new applications which each of the parties could apply to the technology in question (for example, reciprocal obligations to grant licenses, exclusive or not, in these fields), (2) financial aspects of the agreement (calculation of fees, clause of "most favored nation", etc.), (3) conditions for anticipated termination of contract (for example, in the case of contesting of the secret or substantial nature of know-how or of the validity of the patent, of non-respect of active/passive competition restrictions, etc.), and (4) provisions relative to second-source agreements (in particular, concerning the limitation of production volume when the license was granted solely with the aim of supplying a number of customers with a second source of supplies within the conceded territory).

In accordance with well-established case law forbidding, *per se*, any prior consultation concerning prices and any other interference in strategic rulings falling under the rule of independent behavior, exemption is refused when the agreement comprises "*black clauses*" such as: (1) fixing, by the licensor, of prices imposed or of a discount system granted to the licensee's customers, (2) limiting of the quantities of products manufactured under license[4] beyond those necessary to manufacture on the part of the licensee for his own products, and (3) reciprocal interdiction to compete in fields such as research and development (R&D), manufacture, use, or distribution of competing products.

Equally important is the need to allow free play to "*parallel imports*" within the Common Market, and with this aim the Community authorities refuse to grant block exemption to agreements comprising restrictions without objectively justified reasons for the free circulation of products in question when companies fix different prices according to the geographical areas concerned.

Finally, the authorities also forbid the following clauses: (1) obliging the licensee to cede all or part of his rights to improvements he has made to the conceded technology without reciprocal agreement of this sort on the part of the licensor, and (2) having for object or effect to be exempt from the regulations limiting exclusive rights or export prohibition.

2.2   An analysis of requests for individual exemption in accordance with contemporary economic theory

Breaking with the very neoclassical methodology analysis of "traditional" agreements concerning prices or production levels, the Community authorities looked to a much more "Austrian" framework of analysis to establish an attractive jurisprudence in the field of validation of agreements non-eligible for block exemption regulations relating to transfers of technology or R&D agreements.[5] Analysis methods used for validation of cooperation operations make a distinction between agreements directly falling under the provisions of article 81 §1 of the EC Treaty (collusive agreements) and those covered by regulations relative to concentration operations (projects involving the creation of a *concentrate joint venture or a "full function" joint venture"*).

2.2.1   Conditions for individual exemption from the provisions of article 81 §1 of the treaty

As P. Laurent points out quite rightly (1993, p. 40): "Even when efficient, an agreement [between competitors] constitutes an anomaly the legitimization of which may only be accepted within the strict confines set forth by article 81 §3 [formerly 85 §3]". Only those competition restrictions indispensable to the efficiency of an agreement allowing the subsistence of sufficient competition may be eligible for exemption. Therefore it is only after a precise analysis of the net welfare effects of the project that a projected consensus agreement between competitors might be validated after an individual exemption ruling. The demonstration must first be made that the agreement envisaged will produce beneficial results inaccessible through simple competition and which will outweigh the disadvantages engendered by restriction of independence of the parties in coalition.

Objectively, the hoped-for advantages have to be sufficient to justify the agreement, without comprising restraints superfluous to the individual freedom of the agreement partners. Moreover, it is necessary that the

positive effects be shared equitably with end-users. Of necessarily limited duration, the agreements favorable to the promotion of economic
progress must not allow the companies involved to be able to eliminate
competition for a substantial part of the products concerned.

In order to remove the presumption of efficiency attributed to competition, partners to an agreement must therefore establish the fact that
their cooperation constitutes the only means to give increased efficiency.
Such proof implies two successive findings. First, it must be proved that
the constraints inherent to competition make it impossible for each individual partner to accede to a new market, or to create a new product,
given the significance of the investments involved and the risks run. Second, there must be clear demonstration of the fact that the projected
consensus agreement alone can achieve the efficiency objectives aimed at
by the agreement. The proof of the efficiency of an agreement therefore
supposes that a causal link be established between it and the advantages
invoked as well as the indispensable and unavoidable character of the
agreement.

It is encouraging that Commission jurisprudence sanctions several
advances in contemporary economic analysis which underline the importance of: (1) the temporal dimension of production, (2) sunk costs'
commitments stemming from theory of contestable markets, and (3) coordination needs of both complementary and competitive investments,
resulting from information failings and insufficient mobility of productive
resources. Thus, innovation as the creation of new resources constitutes
the typical example of qualitative changes causing firms to lose stability
(Amendola and Gaffard 1998), that is, towards a situation where they are
required to manage the progressive destruction of their former production capacities and the creation of new productive schemes. The difficulty
posed by such management comes from the fact that, during transition,
the costs for each period are disassociated from receipts for reasons of
intertemporal complementary natures and coordination failings. Only cooperation between complementary firms, though often in competition,
may make it possible to manage this transition phase efficiently (Glais
and Gaffard 1999).

In 80 percent of the main individual rulings made by the Commission
since 1990, the gestation periods for innovation and the risks run by
the companies concerned have been explicitly recognized as sufficient
to allow validation of organizational structures which nonetheless may
comprise significant accessory competition restrictions over time periods
lasting up to fifteen years (see Glais 1996).

Although a number of projects submitted for the appreciation of the
Community authorities link companies possessing specific resources of

different natures but strongly complementary, it is not unusual that at the same time partners to the agreement are currently in competition (or potentially competitive) on the markets concerned. So it is in perfect conformity with an economic analysis founded on production theory that the rulings applied took account of the fact that the innovations envisaged would have required *excessively long gestation periods and might not even have been implemented*. Moreover, the promotion of more incremental technical progress is recognized by the Commission when it implies, for the companies concerned, substantial irrecoverable investment costs. Specialization agreements are also validated when their positive effects are proved, particularly in the case of their *contribution to the reduction of transaction and distribution costs*. This is the case when agreements affect products subject to a vertically differentiated offer, liberating each partner from the worries of small-series production and are accompanied by a standardization and normalization program whose effects may, finally, prove favorable to the emergence of stronger competition. Therefore, the speedier diffusion of know-how resulting from these cooperation operations is now taken into account in individual exemption rulings made by the Commission. However, the benevolence with which cooperation projects targeting the promotion of efficiency are received does not prevent the Commission from carefully checking that the exemption period corresponds to the time limit necessary for the execution of the innovations envisaged.

Once the objectives fixed by its members have been reached, the coalition no longer has any reason to continue. It should be dissolved immediately to give way to fresh competition. However, whatever the quality of information available to the Commission, it remains difficult to define with precision the time limit needed for the agreement to produce its beneficial effects. This is why the provisions relative to the application of community competition law (regulation no. 17, article 8) specify that any individual exemption ruling for a determined period may be renewed, or modified, or even revoked, when an excessive time limit granted would unduly prolong a situation harmful to the Community economy. Too short a time limit would disproportionately weigh down administrative control by multiplying the numbers of exemption requests and weaken efficient supervision of competition within the Community. Initially not lasting more than five years, the exemption time limit has since 1990 been extended to ten years, sometimes even longer, depending on the *length of the gestation period for research innovation*. However, in such cases, the Commission generally accompanies its decisions *by precise charges allowing effective supervision of the evolution of the agreement* (regular activity reports, communication of quantities sold and fixed prices, modifications made to the agreement and, where applicable, any arbitration rulings made in cases of conflict between associates, etc.).

2.2.2   *A new analysis procedure of joint venture creation projects (new provisions of regulation no. 1310/97)*

It is rare that agreements limit cooperation to the initial stage of R&D. More often this is extended to production and commercialization of the products in question within the companies created for this reason. Until the adoption of the CE no. 4064/89 regulation (December 21, 1989) relative to control of concentration operations, this type of agreement could be only validated under the provisions of collusive agreement law. When the no. 4064/89 regulation appeared, Community authorities sought to operate a distinction between two types of joint ventures. A specific type of concentration may be constituted following this regulation: "The creation of a joint venture durably fulfilling all the functions of an autonomous economic entity without involving any coordination of competitive behavior between founder companies, either between themselves or the joint venture" (article 3 §2 of the regulation). Such a company, also called "full function," must be able to dispose of all necessary resources (financial, staff, tangible and intangible assets) in order to carry out durable activity. It should therefore be able to operate on a market, carrying out all the functions usually carried out by other companies present on this market. Thus, the following companies were excluded from the regulation on concentrations: (1) joint ventures applying only one of the functions specific to the activity of a company (joint ventures limited to the promotion of R&D or production when this merely represents a sales counter), (2) companies, while fully operational, may allow the coordination of competitive parent companies on the same market.[6] Initially the dissociation operated between a joint concentrative venture and a full function joint venture, but deemed cooperative, led to analysis methods which were very different in their effects on competition. The *compatibility of a concentrative project with the maintaining of sufficient competition* was (and still is) declared after a purely competitive analysis, the purpose of which is to check the absence of any risk of strengthening (or creating) a dominant position consecutive with the emergence of the new company. Conversely, a full function cooperative joint venture had to continue to be subjected to the *"economic analysis" stipulated by the application of article* 85 §3 (*now* 81 §3), its life expectancy being furthermore limited.

Aware of the difficulties inherent in the interpretation of these initial rulings and thus of the relatively tenuous nature of the distinction between the two types of joint venture evoked by the regulation on concentrations, the Community authorities amended their initial text in order to include, within regulation no. 4064/89 all full function joint ventures (regulation no. 1310/97 EC, consideration no. 5). Since 1998, the creation of a joint venture performing on a lasting basis all the functions of an autonomous economic entity therefore lies in the field of *concentration control*.

However, when its purpose or effect enables coordination of the competitive behavior of companies remaining independent, this coordination is assessed, within the framework of the procedure established by the concentration regulation, according to the criteria cited in article 81 §3 of the EC Treaty.[7]

Finally, during the creation of a joint venture, it is not unusual for the project submitted for assessment by the community authorities to be accompanied by "*ancillary restraints*" (non-competition clause, buying or delivery commitments, transfer of know-how, patent licenses, etc.). Such restrictions are validated only if they are linked to and necessary to the carrying out of the concentration project. Thus, they should not entail limits on freedom of behavior except between the parties, and in no case should they be detrimental to a third party. Second, they may not concern any object different in nature from that directly resulting from the operation concerned. Tangible proof must be given of their necessary character (cost savings, reduction of risk, or time periods pertaining to the application of the projected innovation obtained thanks to these restrictions).

The legal security obtained by the parties following a decision reached through the application of the regulation on concentrations, and the speed with which this decision is made, have no doubt been related to the increase in the number of concentrative joint venture projects witnessed since 1990. It would therefore be justified to ask whether some of these legal arrangements have not occasionally been adopted in order to avoid the regular controls operated by the Commission in the case of simple cooperation agreements (or of the creation of common cooperative channels). But the question may also be asked whether the proliferation of concentrative joint companies will not entail structural rigidities in market functioning. Even if a concentrative joint venture may have to disappear or see its shareholders change identity, the life expectancy of such an organizational structure is often lengthened beyond those generally imposed on simple cooperation agreements. Very often, agreements restricted as to time periods are quite as profitable regarding the promotion of technical progress but contribute more efficiently to the protection of more intensive competition.

3   Conditional freedom of vertical agreements:
         new category Regulation dated December 22, 1999

In the early 1980s the Community authorities engaged in deeper reflection concerning the effects of exclusive distribution contracts and
franchising agreements on the play of competition as well as on the promotion of economic efficiency.[8] Moreover, at that time, theoretical work
on these specific vertical relations were of only very moderate interest to
the community of economists. Abundant jurisprudence first allowed the
Commission to fine-tune the limits of its benevolence regarding this type
of contractual formulae. The new category Regulation no. 2790/1999
dated December 22, 1999, aimed at unifying their legal framework (apart
from the sector of automobile distribution), therefore represents the fruit
of this experience, backed up by certain works of economic theory carried
out since 1990.

Although the often beneficial character of these vertical contracts has
been reaffirmed from the viewpoint of the objective of promoting economic efficiency (section 3.1), the risks of excessive infringement of the
freedom of behavior of resellers as well as freedom of entry onto the
markets concerned has nonetheless been abundantly clearly described
in the very structuralist "guidelines" accompanying this new regulation
framework (section 3.2).

3.1   Vertical contracts and efficiency promotion

The creation of intangible assets potentially able to build consumer loy-
alty constitutes one of the fundamental reasons for the success of a company on a market, as well as its contribution to economic efficiency.
To invest in the promotion of recognized and appreciated brands is not
enough to ensure the promoter of durable commercial success in the absence of similar actions on the part of those whose aim is to ensure the
retail sale of the products concerned. The respective interests of both
parties do not always converge, so only sufficiently incentive contracts
prove able to avoid the adoption of discretionary behavior detrimental to
producers.

To ensure perfect conformity with the commercial strategies of suppliers and resellers does not, however, represent the sole objective of such
contracts. The temporal coordination of investments by each of the partners may also justify the introduction, in such agreements, of specific
clauses able to further limit their strategic latitude. The state of dependence in which certain signatory retailers to commercial agreements with
one supplier sometimes find themselves in fact may bear economic and

financial risks which can be reasonably covered only by specific measures of protection such as territorial exclusivity whose second advantage is also to stimulate inter-brand competition.

3.1.1 *Vertical restrictions and brand protection*
Breaking with traditional economic analysis which considers the cost of brand promotion as vector of reduction of competitive rivalry, the developments of contemporary microeconomic analysis have worked to rehabilitate informative content. The brand name, also underlined forcefully by management experts, must be analyzed as a kind of implicit contract which, in the long term, links a manufacturer to his customers. According to these analyses, it would be as if the latter agreed to grant the products offered by promoters of recognized brands increased confidence, based on the fact that these brands represent the symbol of a gradual accumulation of knowledge and the permanent search for excellence. Conversely, costly communication about mediocre-quality products would have little impact since the trick would soon be apparent during the learning stage undertaken by the end-users. A brand, even a well-known one, may nevertheless become an wasting asset when the efforts made by its owner are not sufficiently followed through with similar activity by the resellers.

Distributors are the drive belts between manufacturers and consumers, and as such may behave as loyal partners or not, according to how they define their role as service providers. The risk of seeing these partners behaving uncooperatively would entail the producers opting for an organizational plan based on total integration of the channel in question, unless the cost of such a strategy proved prohibitive. The logic of seeking optimal sharing out of resources has thus led manufacturers to opt in favor of contractual solutions consisting in giving distribution activity to specialists spread over the geographic market concerned. But can all candidates for the role of distributor be taken on without prior selection and restrictive contractual clauses?

Both business experience and contemporary economic analysis shows this to be out of the question as soon as one recognizes the possibility for distributors to behave in an opportunistic manner when carrying out contracts lacking in incentives. Permanent supervision of distribution activities would involve prohibitive costs, especially since the number of distribution agents is often high. Forcing resellers to invest in sunk costs assets and imposing contract clauses detailing the precise commitments to which they would be held makes it possible to avoid the danger of commercial parasitism (such as: the call price technique, pirating of selective networks, or insufficient supply of advice and services).

In the recent past and particularly during disputes raised by dissatisfied distributors,[9] the Community authorities had already engaged in recognizing the strong interest of protection strategies for the value of intangible assets created by manufacturers. The merit of the guidelines laid down by the Commission in support of its new category exemption regulation is to recognize explicitly that:

A vertical restriction may enable a manufacturer to increase his/her sales by imposing a certain uniformity and certain quality standards on distributors so as to acquire a good brand image and attract end-users. Selective distribution and franchising are examples of this. (*JOCE* C 270, September 24, 1999, p. 27)

However this does not imply that this type of commercial relations may be applied to the resale of any product. In compliance with the teachings of economic analysis considering that vertical restrictions are really justified only when there is insufficient information on the end users arising from sporadic purchases of the product in question, the guidelines expressly specify that to benefit from a favorable *a priori*, the restrictive contract should cover *a new or technically complex product* and have a *certain value*. (*JOCE* C 270, September 24, 1999, p. 26)

3.1.2   *Time coordination of suppliers' and distributors' investments*

Within the context of a more long-term development strategy of their activities, producers must be confident that their resellers are in a position to increase their production capacities at the same rhythm as theirs.

In compliance with certain developments in the theory of incomplete contracts, the introduction of appropriate contractual clauses can enable them first to limit the resellers' rights of control over variations in their volume of activity and to control *ex ante* the investment choices of the commercial partners. In some theoretical constructs like those proposed by Grossmann and Hart (1986), the fact that one of the parties can fail to persuade its partner to increase its activity in its favor when the latter has other openings at its disposal is particularly stressed. By acquiring the "residual" control rights (vertical integration) or by limiting their use (contractual formula) the coordination of complementary activities can be carried out in a more optimal manner. In this theoretical construct, the by-contractors' investment decisions are nevertheless made independently. It is however more efficient to draw up contracts allowing (as shown by Perry 1989) prior control over the commercial partner's investment choices. The risk of seeing the former choose levels of production capacity differing highly from those of their by-contractor appears frequently in the case of high indivisibility of the capital factor, all growth of capacity and supplementary expenditure on investment at sunk costs expenses being redeemable only over a relatively long period.

The right to' add contractual clauses allowing the management of this type of problem is also recognized today by the guidelines under clearly stated conditions :

They first specify that certain investments must be made, either by the supplier or by the purchaser, as in the case of special equipment or specific training...It is then possible that the by-contractor should not commit himself to carrying out the necessary investments before having reached an agreement with this partner as to certain arrangements in terms of supplies. (*JOCE* C 270, September 24, 1999, p. 27)

The legal validation of such commitments nonetheless implies that certain conditions be met. The assets concerned must first be undeniably characterized as sunk costs investments, redeemable only after a fairly long period; the projected investments must secondly be asymmetrical, one of the parties investing more than the other. Two specific situations are particularly taken into consideration within the guidelines. First, specific investments made on the premises of the other party may not have been completely recovered on expiry of the commercial cooperation contract. Their resale to the partner concerned generally proves to be the best solution in consideration of the high cost of their recovery by the investor. In this case the Commission considers that a vertical restriction of limited length can be justified when such a resale leads to high transaction costs. According to whether the investment has been made by the supplier or the distributor, restrictions may be applied in the form of non-competition or purchase quotas clauses (first hypothesis), or exclusive distribution or supply rights (second case).[10] Imposing an exclusivity clause on one's by-contractor constitutes, secondly, an obligation proportional to the degree of benefit conferred on a distributor in the case of granting of substantial know-how; such a clause constitutes in fact protection for the assignor[11] from the risk of very rapidly seeing his know-how benefit some of his competitors. Moreover, without such protection, it is only with the greatest reservation that its holder would accept to share the sum total of his knowledge in the domain of activity concerned.

3.1.3 *Territorial protection, promotion of inter-brand competition, and risk limitation of resellers*

To allow one's distributor the sales monopoly of a well-known brand over a particular geographical area appears on the first analysis to be hardly compatible with the free market ideal of neoclassical theory. The introduction of a territorial protection clause for each reseller seems nonetheless to benefit from the application of a favorable economic analysis when it appears to arise from a search for a balance in the contractual relationship between the parties involved and to reserve for the final users an equitable part of the resulting profit. It is moreover in the area of franchising that this type of contractual clause proves most justified.

The reasons adduced from several court decisions of individual exemption made by the European Commission prior to the adoption of its first ruling of category exemption are particularly pertinent.[12] The restriction of intra-brand rivalry to which territorial protection leads is often, in fact, more than compensated for by the growth of more active inter-brand competition, particularly when it is stimulated by producers who are efficient but new arrivals on the market and not having at their disposal enough of their own resources to allow them the rapid extension of their commercial circuits. It is, in fact, franchise applicants who make the necessary investments to establish new sales points. *Per contra*, the exclusive territorial rights the franchises are allowed can be considered indispensable:

No franchise applicant would realistically have been willing to make the investments necessary and to pay a not inconsiderable standard charge to integrate such a distribution system if he had not been sure of a certain territorial protection from the competition of other franchisees and from the franchiser himself. (*Y. Rocher et Pronuptia* verdict, *JOCE* L. 8 and L. 13 of January 10 and 15, 1987, no. 36)

As a factor of inter-brand competition, this type of contract undeniably contributes particularly to the improvement of consumer welfare. Gaining first from the advantages provided by a coherent distribution network offering products of uniform quality, the former also reap the benefits of the interest the franchisee, as an independent reseller and with a personal interest in the management of his business, finds in "looking after, helping and carefully following up his clientèle" (*Y. Rocher et Pronuptia*, *JOCE* L. 8 and L. 13 of January 10 and 15, 1987, no. 35).

3.2   *Validation conditions of vertical contracts*

Adhering faithfully to economic analysis methodology, the Community authorities have taken particular care to restate that these contracts should nevertheless not allow an unconsidered reduction of the action of intra-brand and inter-brand competition.

3.2.1   *Maintaining sufficient intra-brand competition*
Contingent on the restrictive contract complying with the efficiency criteria previously mentioned, it is still important to ascertain that the selection

means are not discriminatory (the case of selective distribution) and that the contractual clauses allow real competition between the selected distributors.

(1) The new legislation first considers that *selective distribution* founded on purely qualitative criteria[13] is not covered by article 81 §1[14] in so far as it imposes no direct limit on the number of re-sellers.

Furthermore, the selection criteria must be objective and non-discriminatory. The exclusion from a selective network of large-scale distribution companies would thus not be acceptable when they agree to respect the totality of the criteria defined by the manufacturer. In the two cases described previously (*Leclerc* v. *Commission*) the Court thus particularly stressed that a hypermarket may not be excluded from a selective network simply because other products are sold there. According to these two rulings, such a sale is not in itself harmful, for example, to the image of luxury products since the location or space allocated to the sale of similar products is so arranged as to present them in an attractive way. One can, however, have reservations about adopting the court's way of thinking. In fact there can be a real problem of image compatibility between suppliers of highly well-known brands and large-scale distribution resellers. It is not usually in the interests of a manufacturer having always chosen to position himself in the "up-market" segment to accept that part of his sales should be made by a distribution circuit having chosen to position itself on the sale of products which come from far more downmarket segments. The fact of accepting to respect the qualitative criteria imposed by a provider of superior quality products (or from the luxury market) on only this type of product is not sufficient for its less prestigious image to be modified. It is thus legitimate to wonder if commercialization by large-scale distribution (particularly food products) of products packaged with a well-known brand name might not lead to a certain trivializing and affect the value of the producers' intangible assets. Large-scale distribution being considered (and often rightly so) to privilege competition by price, it is not irrelevant to consider that in the eyes of competition authorities this form of rivalry should be encouraged and take over from any other forms of competition, and this, whatever the characteristics of the products concerned. So the break with the "neoclassical" competition model would be far from sufficient.

(2) Secondly, in spite of the reservations of economic analysis concerning an absolute prohibition of the strategy of fixed prices, the new legislation excludes from category exemption the agreements which intend,

directly or indirectly, to *restrict the buyer's capacity to freely determine his sales price*.[15] The effects on competition of a minimum price or a fixed price are twofold according to the guidelines: total elimination of intra-brand competition in terms of price and, secondly, the reinforcement of transparency favorable to the emergence of horizontal collusion between manufacturers and distributors in relatively concentrated markets.

While it cannot be denied that fixing imposed prices may constitute a factor favorable to the emergence of collusive agreements in oligopoly markets, such is not the primary objective of producers when they use this type of price scale. According to an exhaustive study of lawsuits filed in the United States between 1890 and 1983, against companies having had recourse to imposed prices practices, it is only in a third of cases that the former could possibly have served to support a horizontal agreement. In all the other cases, the adoption of imposed prices had been carried out by only one company (Ornstein 1985). Now, in such a case, this practice can simply serve to incite distributors to offer a better quality of service (see, for example, Posner 1976[16]; Tirole 1985[17]), or to stop some from succumbing to the temptation of using the technique of loss leader (Marvel and McCafferty 1984). In a more general manner (Rey and Tirole 1986), the choice of an optimal control policy over the distributors' action cannot take place without an in-depth analysis of the sources of uncertainty affecting the resellers' activity as well as the importance of the latter's aversion to risk-taking. The conclusions of the model designed by these authors illustrate that there is no objective reason to analyze vertical practices differently whether or not they focus on the variable of price.

If free circulation of products between participants in the same network constitutes a rule which tolerates no exceptions, the prohibition of delivery to distributors outside the network can not only be licit but is judged to be the most effective means of guaranteeing protection of the distribution circuit concerned (case of selective distribution). On the other hand, the restriction of passive or active sales to final users by the members of a selective distribution system operating as resellers on the market means loss of eligibility for category exemption for the contract. What is authorized, however, in an agreement such as a franchise or exclusive distribution is:

the restriction of active sales into the exclusive territory or to an exclusive customer group reserved to the supplier (or allocated by the supplier to another buyer) where such a restriction does not limit sales by the customers of the buyer. (article 4 of Regulation no. 2790/1999)

3.2.2   Maintaining efficient inter-brand competition

A distribution agreement can quite clearly obtain exemption from the terms of article 81 §1 only to the extent that this does not substantially contribute to a reduction of inter-brand competition for a given market. Rather than relying on expertise based, for example, on calculation of concentration indexes (such as, for example that of Herfindahl–Hirschman) the Commission has opted for the criteria of market share:

Over the market share threshold of 30 percent there can be no presumption that vertical agreement following within the scope of article 81 §1 will usually give rise to objective advantages of such a character and size to compensate for the disadvantage which they create for competition. (Subsection 9 of Regulation no. 2790/1999)

In such a case, the Commission services will be invited to carry out a virtual "check-up" of the market in question, based on the analysis of its structural characteristics, when they are called on to evaluate the probability of seeing the agreement in question produce anti-competitive effects.

Therefore, contracts which force a purchaser to procure goods or a given service from the same supplier (the case, for example, of mono-brands), as well as situations where a juxtaposition of restrictive contracts leads to added effects generating closure of markets with potential competition, are particularly relevant. At this level, the position adopted in the guidelines proves in conformity with jurisprudence established by the Court of Justice on the occasion of disputes in the area of the beer industry.[18]

However, in spite of an often mixed analysis of the effects on inter-brand competition of the most common types of restrictive contracts, the guidelines nonetheless have what could be qualified as surprising reservations about selective distribution contracts. These are often judged first to be of a nature to create strong barriers to entry insofar as they apply particularly to branded products: "It will often take a long time and considerable investments for foreclosed resellers to launch their own brand or indeed to obtain competitive supplies."

Such a statement clearly gives the impression that the combination "selective distribution" and "well-known brands" comes from the phenomenon of an artificial rise in competitors' (or of distributors') costs described by Krattenmaker and Salop (1986).

Contemporary economic theory refuses nonetheless to evoke the concept of barriers to entry (along with the attendant negative connotations) when the absence of a total porosity of the frontiers of a market is explained essentially by the fact that companies in place have succeeded (thanks to continuity and the seriousness of their business relations) in building up business goodwill, allowing them not to be afraid of losing their market position at any moment.

Numerous studies (see, for example, Von Weizsäcker 1981) have also concentrated on demonstrating that the "goodwill" possessed by a company does not fall into the category of inefficient barriers. Secondly, free entry into the market does not mean "easy entry." It is, in fact, in the nature of the competitive process to recognize as legitimate the fact that a new entrant should work (as the sellers in place did in their time) to find a durable position in the market.

The guidelines accompanying the new legislation tend therefore to confirm the somewhat unfortunate jurisprudence prohibiting the exclusivity clauses featuring in certain distribution contracts with the motive that, given the large market share of the company in question, it would prove difficult for other competitors to penetrate the market concerned. It is thus that Unilever was prohibited from continuing to include an exclusivity clause in their freezer supplies contracts on the Irish market for ice-cream for immediate consumption. The size of the Unilever market share, the quasi-impossibility for most distributors of using several freezers in their commercial spaces certainly made the entry of new competitors difficult. Nevertheless, in this instance the Commission made light of the degree of satisfaction displayed by the distributors in terms of their commercial relationships with their supplier and moreover did not pay enough attention to the existence of powerful potential competitors such as Nestlé or Mars. Within the framework of a more "Austrian" analysis of the competitive process it would not have been superfluous to recognize that, according to Kirzner's (1973) definition, the company in place would have been the first to discover a non-exploited opportunity on the market concerned, that the market position the former had achieved was economically legitimate, and finally that followers would logically have to assign large investments to compete with this position. The solution adopted by the Commission, prohibiting the leading operator from using a distribution strategy that his competitors, on the other hand, were allowed to use, largely amounts to penalizing the operator who showed signs of alertness (a particular state of vigilance) in the sense used in competitive process theory.

Secondly, should the doctrine of the cumulative effect of similar contracts be applied to purely selective contacts, as is suggested by the guidelines?

The real business world shows, quite on the contrary, that the existence of selective distribution networks constitute a highly favorable factor for the penetration of a market by new providers. The latter are not, in fact, constrained to invest heavily at the distribution stage to be able to offer their products to end-users. In fact there are already numerous specialized resellers, recognized as such, on the market, ready to receive new products in their sales spaces insofar as these products correspond to the criteria of quality and distinctiveness appropriate to the concept of selective distribution. It is indeed the distributors rather than the suppliers already in place who then judge the advisability of accepting new brands in their shelf-space. The error of analysis in the guidelines, in this particular case, is clearly through a hasty assimilation of the effects of selective distribution to those of exclusive distribution in terms of risks of market closure. The selective distributor retains real freedom in the choice of an assortment of brands that he intends to offer to the end-purchasers. If there was a time when, in certain contracts offered by suppliers, there were clauses said to be of "brand environments" likely to allow the birth of collusions within a group of suppliers, this risk has disappeared today following the prohibition of such procedures by manufacturers.

In other words, by allowing the emergence of distributor networks selected only on the basis of qualitative selection criteria whose objectivity and character in proportion to the demands which they are required to meet are verified by the competition authorities, the supplier "first entrants" on the markets concerned offer, to some extent, positive externalities to new entrants who are providers of products of a comparable quality. The ease with which the latter may have access to these networks allows them, moreover, to valorize their brands more rapidly and reduces their communication and promotion expenditure.

4   Conclusion

This brief analysis of the texts adopted by the Community authorities and the broad tendencies of jurisprudence relative to cooperation agreements leads to a slightly attenuated evaluation.

As far as contractual relations aiming for the promotion of technical progress are concerned, the Community authorities have shown real open-mindedness concerning the integration of certain currents of thought (in particular of "Austrian" essence) They have, thereby, published decisions endorsing the merits of an analysis based on the process character of competitive rivalry. On the other hand, in other areas of inter-firm cooperation they have shown a greater reluctance to integrate the developments of contemporary theory of company and market organization. A real wish for transparency in their methods of appreciation of the competitive effects of the agreements concerned should certainly be noted as a positive result of their action.

Nevertheless, as far as the area of distribution contracts is concerned, the guidelines which have been divulged prove to be relatively casuistic and particularly still over-influenced by the teachings of traditional theory. The role of non-price competition, while it is tentatively recognized, clearly does not carry as considerable a weight as that of price as the vector of promotion of economic efficiency. Secondly, the fear (permanent within the guidelines) of seeing the markets concerned with the extension of restrictive agreements polluted by the emergence of situations of collusion is witness of an extremely insecure belief in the fundamental robustness of competitive rivalry.

NOTES

Chapter 22 was originally published as "Les accords inter-entreprises et le droit communautaire de la concurrence," in *Revue d'Economie Industrielle* (92, 2000).

1. CJCE, 17/01/84, VBVB, no. 52; decision dated February 5, 1992, "Construction aux Pays Bas."
2. Regulation no. 240/96 dated January 31, 1996 (*JOCE* L. 31 dated February 9, 1996)
3. Active competition may be forbidden: (a) as long as the patent under license is protected by parallel patents granted in the territories of the licensees (case of pure patents license), (b) for up to ten years (pure know-how license), or according to the more advantageous of the two time limits just mentioned (mixed licenses). The validity of a non-passive competition clause is limited to five years from the date when the licensed product was first put on the market by one of the licensees within the Common Market.
4. Except in second-source contracts.
5. Regulation no. 4/8/85 dated December 19, 1984 (*JOCE* L. 53 dated February 22, 1985) modified by text 161/93 dated December 23, 1992 (*JOCE* L. dated January 29, 1993). This R&D regulation is presented in a form similar to that concerning technology transfers (same typology of contractual clauses, for example). Competing firms holding, at the time of the agreement, a market share of over 20 percent of the products concerned (or a substantial part of the latter) are unable to benefit from the categorical exemption.
6. The case of founding companies continuing to carry out significant activities on the same markets as those of the joint venture, on neighboring markets or on upstream or downstream markets, the joint venture being their main economic partner (supplier or customer).
7. It should be noted that a venture may not be defined as "joint venture" without supervision by at least two shareholders who are to reach understanding on all major decisions relative to the activity of the company under supervision. It is not a joint venture when one of the founders may alone supervise its own activity or when no minority shareholder holds a veto.
8. Reflection which was sanctioned by the adoption of categorial exemption regulations relative to: exclusive distribution contracts (no. 1983/83 dated June 22, 1983); distribution and after-sales service automobile agreements (no. 123/85 dated December 14, 1984, modified by regulation no. 1475/95 dated June 28, 1995); franchising contracts (no. 4087/88 dated November 11, 1988).

9. Thus in two notable judgments, the Communities' court of first instance implicitly validated the thesis supported by the manufacturers according to which "competition targeted on elements other than price has advantages, given the substantial investments required and the need to prevent 'parasite' resellers from living at the expense of those who accept the economic constraints of the manufacturer's economic policy" (Affaires "Groupement d'achat E. Lerclerc c./Commission," rulings dated December 12, 1996).

10. Such vertical restraint may also allow avoidance of the parasitism of this investment by the investor's competitors.

11. Furthermore, the competition authorities have responsibility for verifying the essential character. In compliance with the present, well-established jurisprudence, this know-how (as a whole or in the configuration or precise assembly of its components) may not be already known or easily assimilated. It must provide the reseller with significant information in the area of sales techniques or of supplementary services. Finally, it should reasonably allow the latter to improve his/her competitive position by aiding penetration of new markets and increased profits.

12. See for instance, the following rulings: *Y. Rocher et Pronuptia*: *JOCE* L. 8 and L. 13 of January 10 and 15, 1987; *Computerland*: *JOCE* L. 222 dated August 10, 1987; *Service Master*: *JOCE* L. 332 dated December 3, 1988; *Ch. Jourdan*: *JOCE* L. 35 dated February 7, 1987.

13. Such as the training of sales personnel, service provided by the supplier, the range of products sold, the quality of the outlet site, and its facilities.

14. Such would not necessarily be the case of quantitative selection criteria (limiting the number of resellers, fixing minimal or maximal sales levels . . .).

15. A maximal or suggested sales price is nevertheless authorized in so far as it is not equal to a fixed or minimal sales price after pressure applied by one of the parties or incentive measures taken by them.

16. An analysis of the reasons for the existence of imposed retail prices constitutes one of the tests suggested by Posner when it is a question of separating situations of tacit agreements from those arising from simple parallel behavior. In the eyes of this author, it is only when imposed prices are adopted by a group of companies belonging to the same market that this test can have any conclusive value.

17. According to Tirole (1985), this type of practice, by guaranteeing a sufficient profit margin for the reseller, can incite him/her to provide a better service. Otherwise, the advantages thus offered to consumers when they improve the manufacturer's reputation are not totally internalized by the reseller. Fixing a retail price confers on the reseller/purveyor of commercial information property rights pertaining to the information supplied to his/her supplier.

18. On several occasions, the Court has considered that a contract for the supply of beer was prohibited, in compliance with the agreement law when two cumulative conditions combine. First, on account of the economic and legal context, the national market should be difficult to access by competitors who could operate there (or who could expand their market share). Secondly, the litigious contract should contribute significantly to the blockage effect generated by the entirety of these contracts.

23   Incentive contracts in utility regulation

Matthew Bennett and Catherine Waddams Price

1   Introduction

Incentive contracts transformed the theory and practice of regulation in the last quarter of the twentieth century. Emphasis shifted from control and prescription to incentives and discretion, with significant implications both for outcome and for the distribution of benefits and risk. We trace the development of this change, illustrating it with the British experience of utility regulation where the shift from public ownership to explicitly regulated private companies has been particularly stark. This chapter provides a broad-brush analysis of recent issues and developments in this rapidly changing area of economics, rather than attempt to detail all the individual problems. Our main focus is on key issues such as welfare, efficiency, and the development of competition. This last category has drawn increasing attention from regulatory economists, as governments race to introduce competition in utilities and theory strives to keep pace with practice. Where issues are only briefly discussed, we suggest articles that cover specific topics in more detail, and in particular seek to update the arguments since 1995. In section 2, we first address the question of why regulation is needed, identify experience in the past, and examine regulation as a simple principal–agent model. In section 3 we trace the growth and development of incentive contracts such as the price cap. Section 4 suggests that introducing competition may not prove to be the regulatory panacea once envisaged, and identifies practical issues including distribution concerns, which have marred the original concept of incentive contracts in regulation, and assesses their prospects; section 5 concludes.

2   Public ownership, cost of service, and incentives in regulation

2.1   *Problems and solutions for natural monopolies*

Generally, the market failure which provides the case for regulation in utilities, derives from the problems created by natural monopolies and economies of scale in production. Other examples of market failure (for example, externalities) may also require government intervention, either through direct regulation or through taxation, and many of the utilities operate in markets which also exhibit such externalities; however, here we focus on their natural monopoly network characteristics. We include among utilities the traditional network industries of water, electricity, gas, and telecommunications (though some now dispute whether telecoms still exhibits these characteristics); transport is also sometimes included because of its fixed network. Competition in networks is generally both impractical and inefficient. Moreover a second market failure, asymmetry of information between firm and consumers, also affects some of the products; for example a customer cannot know that water is safe until after it has been drunk. But government intervention itself creates a new information asymmetry, between the firm and the regulator, which is crucial in devising regulatory mechanisms.

The very nature of the services supplied by the utility industries affects the design and execution of policies. Their products are essential to household life and participation in society, and are also crucial to businesses. Economic welfare has traditionally been divided into efficiency and equity concerns. The classic economists' argument is that equity is best addressed by instruments specifically devised for this purpose, such as income taxes and benefit transfers, and that efficiency should be separately analyzed. We follow this convention, but note that in the case of these particular industries the political reality may not enable such a separation to be maintained in practice. We return to this in our assessment in section 4.

Market failure within the utilities may be rectified through some form of government intervention, and it is useful to identify benchmark positions for reference. Marginal cost pricing maximizes efficiency under certain assumptions, but where average cost exceeds marginal cost (as is typical of natural monopolies) a government subsidy is required. Without such a transfer, marginal cost pricing results in unsustainable losses for the firm, which then closes down, resulting in lower overall welfare. If lump-sum subsidies are ruled out, a second-best tariff must be devised to cover the firm's costs. Ramsey–Boiteux pricing is a benchmark solution to the problem of welfare maximizing in such a multiproduct monopolist with uniform tariffs. The general method was first defined by Ramsey in 1927 and applied in the well-known regulation context by Boiteux in 1956. The regulator maximizes social welfare across a number of products subject to a firm's budget constraint. In the simple case where product demands are independent, the optimal departure from marginal cost pricing is inversely proportional to the price elasticities in each market. Where it is necessary to raise price above marginal cost, it is better to do so where consumers are least sensitive to increases in price. This minimizes demand distortion from the first-best levels for a given amount of additional revenue. Consumers with rigid demand contribute more to cover the fixed costs. Despite the attraction of Ramsey–Boiteux pricing for economists, there remain problems which prevent its regular implementation.

First, the optimal pricing rule requires enormous amounts of information on both costs and demand, and use of incorrect information may actually reduce social welfare; even when Boiteux directed Electricité de France a simpler doctrine of uniform increases above costs was adopted. Secondly, the optimal tariff is discriminatory in the sense that price depends on demand as well as cost characteristics, and consumers with lower elasticities pay a relatively higher price. This is a contentious policy to which we return in considering the regulators' concern for distribution and undue discrimination issues.

The focus on the relation between price and costs has led to the two traditional responses to market failure in utilities: public ownership (particularly in Europe) and cost of service regulation (typical of North America). Where the firm is owned by the state it can be directed to implement the government's chosen policies (including pricing); alternatively the government may direct a private firm to do the same, in particular dictating how prices should be related to costs. However in either case the government suffers from asymmetric information. It does not know enough about the market to define Ramsey–Boiteux pricing; and, as has become increasingly apparent, even if it can observe realized costs, it cannot identify *efficient* cost levels. This raises principal–agent issues which underlie much of regulation.

When the utilities were nationalized and owned by the government, contractual problems associated with a separation of ownership and control were internalized. However both the aims of the nationalized utilities (at least in the United Kingdom), and how far the managers' incentives were aligned with those of the government, were unclear (see Markou and Parmar 1999). The managers (agents) were likely maximizing the size of their operations or bureaucracy (Jackson 1982; Rees 1984) rather than meeting the government's (principal's) objectives. The latter were particularly difficult to identify because of typical political reluctance to identify objectives and trade-offs explicitly. The consequent management discretion and weak incentive structure led to a perception that the nationalized industries were generally inefficient. In the United Kingdom it was decided that the best way to rectify this problem (and coincidentally to balance a large budget deficit) was to privatize the industries and allow the shareholders to incentivize the firm, rather than create managerial incentives within a nationalized framework. This raised new problems of the different objectives pursued by government and shareholders, which are discussed below.

2.2   Cost of service regulation

First, however, we turn to cost of service regulation, an alternative to public ownership which had been widely practiced in the United States. The most common form of such regulation was to constrain the firm's rate of return on capital. This "rate of return" regulation allows the monopolist what is deemed a fair return on capital, to prevent it from abusing a monopoly position. The "fair" rate of return is generally above the market cost of capital to ensure the company continues production and may be supplemented by a requirement that investments are prudent (since the mechanism guarantees their profitability). Prices are generally set at average cost (including the cost of capital) and remain fixed until either the regulator, consumers, or the firm initiates a regulatory review. This can be thought of as direct regulation at a micro level.

Rate of return regulation has come under heavy criticism.[1] First, Averch and Johnson (hereafter, AJ) showed, in their influential 1962 paper, that the rate of return reward induces the firm to engage in inefficiencies. As the level of regulated return approaches the cost of capital, the optimal ratio of capital to labor, rises above the efficient level for that output. This may induce the firm to produce more output and charge a higher price in comparison to an unregulated firm, but not to expand output to the optimal level. Rate of return regulation does not induce wastage of capital (defined as capital investment with a negative net present value (NPV)), as the firm produces as large an output as possible for each capital–labor ratio. However the inefficiently high capital–labor ratio sometimes leads to an accusation that the scheme induces wastage.[2] One example of these perverse incentives is the reluctance of US companies to adopt off-peak pricing even though it would generally enhance economic welfare. Under rate of return regulation, the larger the peak demand, the larger the network and the capital base upon which profit can be earned (Sherman 1989).

A second criticism is that with price always at average cost, there are few incentives for cost minimization under the continuous time regulatory framework which AJ assume, since gains are immediately passed onto consumers through lower prices. Bawa and Sibley (1980) show that although a time lag between regulatory reviews does not get rid of the capital bias, as the rate of return tends towards the cost of capital, this bias is less serious than in the static case. The introduction of demand uncertainty may however increase the bias as firms raise capacity to meet the demand fluctuations (Crew and Kleindorfer 1979, pp. 140–3). Rate of return regulation is ambiguous in its effect on quality. There is an implicit incentive to excessive levels in the form of "gold-plating," as return is guaranteed on investment, but the firm has no *direct* interest in increasing quality. Over-capitalization is as likely to take the form of increased managerial expenses as of quality enhancement.

Finally, the practicalities and informational requirements for rate of return regulation make the regulatory burden very high. Apparent details, such as allocation of costs and the basis for depreciation, have a huge impact upon the level of permitted profits. These difficulties with cost of service regulation raised interest in alternatives, especially incentive-based contracts, in North America at much the same time as the UK government was privatizing its nationalized industries.

2.3   Introduction of incentive contracts

When the nationalized industries were privatized in the United Kingdom, ownership moved from government to private shareholders. This new structure of ownership changed objectives and contract relationships, raising a new set of principal–agent issues. The new owners (shareholders) are expected to maximize profit rather than welfare as the government might wish.[3] Consequently the principal (government) may need to appoint a supervisor (regulator) to oversee the whole process and ensure that the government's objectives are met. Managers are now answerable to the shareholders rather than government; their objectives may be aligned more closely with those of the new owners through share options, but a basic conflict between risk-sharing and the power of the incentive remains. The best attainable contract for the shareholders has more high-powered performance incentives the lower is the managers' risk aversion, the lower the marginal cost of effort, the higher the marginal benefit of effort, and the easier it is to measure performance (Besanko, Dranove and Shanley 2000).

In reality the regulator's and shareholders' problems are similar, since neither can observe the level of effort exerted by management, and direct effort-based reward is therefore impracticable. Left to their own devices, managers will exert less effort (and generate less overall utility) than that required to deliver both the social and the profit maximizing optimum. Just like the shareholders, the regulator needs to devise a regulatory framework that induces firms to achieve the optimal outcome given the market asymmetries. It is possible to view this as managers being answerable to two principals (shareholders and regulator). An alternative model is one of principal–supervisor–agent, allowing for the development of a separate set of objectives by the regulator. However to illustrate the issues of incentive regulation, and for reasons of space, we treat management and shareholders as a single agent, the firm/shareholders, with a single principal, the regulator.

We have noted the divergence between government and firm objectives which makes regulation necessary. The shareholder-owned firm maximizes profit by pricing above the social optimum, creating incentives for misrepresenting true costs, or demand, or both. This poses problems for regulation by detailed prescription, whatever the ownership of the industries, because of the regulator's inferior information.[4] However, in an ideal incentive regulation framework, a mechanism is created so that the firm chooses the socially desirable outcome without the need for detailed knowledge on the regulator's part. This may be facilitated (and the information asymmetry minimized) by the introduction of competition to any sections of the industry where it is appropriate, while regulating remaining elements of natural monopoly. This last outcome is possible only where the natural monopoly markets in the industry can be separated from those which are potentially competitive. The benefits of such separation depend on whether the transactions between different vertical levels of the industry are amenable to external explicit contracts rather than internal arrangements. Where quality, for example, is very complex and difficult to define it may be preferable to determine this within a vertically integrated company. This problem arose with railways where complex contracts and penalties between train operating companies, rolling stock companies and Railtrack had to be devised when British Rail was vertically separated. Difficulties in determining appropriate compensation to train operating companies for delays caused by an extensive emergency maintenance programme in 2000–1 indicated that many of these contractual relationships had not been resolved satisfactorily at privatization. Where new entry results in imperfect competition in a market with a monopolized input, continued regulation of the upstream industry is required to prevent double marginalization, and regulation of the new entrants may be needed if they possess significant market power. Such a partial regulatory/competitive state is currently that of the United Kingdom's network industries and this interaction of competition and regulation has attracted an increasing literature to which we return in section 4. Section 3 traces the development of incentive regulation.

3   Development of incentive contracts

3.1   Incentive contracts and introduction of price caps

Incentive regulation contracts were largely developed to meet the criticism of rate of return regulation described above. Because of information asymmetry the regulator needs to incentivize the firm to produce at or close to the Ramsey–Boiteux optimum without the necessity for the firm to reveal cost and demand information (which it may not even have known completely itself as a nationalized industry subject to different objectives and constraints). Where demand information is general knowledge but cost information is known only to the firm, Armstrong, Cowan and Vickers (1995) show that rebalancing prices away from a single uniform price will generally increase profits whilst avoiding a reduction in consumer surplus. This model is similar to Ramsey–Boiteux pricing with profit maximizing subject to a given level of consumer surplus instead of maximizing consumer surplus subject to a given level of profit.

Although this method reduces the need for cost information, it still requires the consumer surplus function and demands to be known within a static time framework. Where a dynamic framework is considered, we assume that the firm's last-period cost and output information can be learned at the start of the next period. Using this assumption, Vogelsang and Finsinger (1979) propose a regulatory regime which relaxes the requirement of current cost and demand information. However this is replaced by other strong assumptions such as a myopic firm which will not engage in strategic behavior to maximize future profits. The regulator constrains prices so that with period t prices, the firm generates no more revenue, with prices weighted by output in period $t - 1$, than that period's total observed costs. Thus with one product, the current price must be lower than the previous period's average cost. This produces a long-run stationary equilibrium with firms making zero profit and charging Ramsey–Boiteux prices, but makes the fundamental assumption that average costs are non-increasing over time; if this is not true the regime may produce negative profits. Most importantly, Sappington (1980) demonstrates that where the firm is not myopic it may indulge in wasteful expenditure in early periods to ensure higher profits in later periods, although Hagerman (1990) shows that with lump-sum transfers the wasteful expenditure can be reduced.

Price cap regulation, first introduced in 1982 for contraceptive sheaths (MMC 1992), is similar to the Vogelsang–Finsinger mechanism as both deal with constraining price over time. Price caps, like many innovations in regulation, were in place before full theoretical analysis, which often developed later and produced mixed verdicts. The Littlechild Report (1983) first proposed RPI-X, the British form of price cap regulation, for the utilities. Under this regime the firm is allowed to charge any price so long as the average price of the specified basket does not increase faster than RPI-X. RPI is the UK Retail Price Index and X is some number set initially by government, and subsequently by the regulator. At the end of the period, the level of X is reset until the next price review. Unlike the Vogelsang–Finsinger mechanism, information on past costs is not required within the price cap period, but is likely to influence the resetting of X. In the original scheme devised for British Telecommunications (BT) the firm had to choose current prices so that when weighted by the previous period's revenues, the total (hypothetical) charge was no higher than the previous period's revenue. Vogelsang (1989) assessed the price cap scheme based on a Laspeyres index but without the automatic tightening of the constraint (as under the Vogelsang–Finsinger mechanism). He showed that a non-myopic firm maximizing the discounted value of its profits subject to the tariff basket constraint will set prices that satisfy the Ramsey condition.

Since its conception there have been many comparisons between this incentive-based scheme and rate of return regulation, including Littlechild (1983), Vickers and Yarrow (1988), and Waterson (1992). Essentially there are three perceived advantages. First, RPI-X is less vulnerable to cost-plus inefficiency and over-capitalization, because the firm retains any cost efficiencies it undertakes at least until the next review of X; secondly, RPI-X allows the company greater flexibility to adjust the structure of prices within the chosen basket; and lastly RPI-X is simpler and cheaper for the regulator and the company to operate. However as incentive regulation developed, a number of issues arose. We discuss these in turn.

3.2   Practical questions in incentive regulation of monopolies

The first is a time consistency problem for the government in determining X. We discussed above the regulation of the firm in the principal–agent framework, and the question of who is the principal. Before privatization the firm is owned by the government, but at flotation, the government sells ownership of the firm to a diversity of shareholders. After privatization the government is no longer a principal with direct interest in the firm's financial performance and has more general interests for welfare, with implications for the level of X at privatization and at the first price review. The initial level of X was set not only to ensure consumer and producer welfare, but also to maximize the government's revenue when it sold the company. By increasing producer welfare through lowering X, the government could raise the striking price and its own revenue, but only before its shares are sold. So a time consistency problem exists between the optimal initial level of X when the government is the owner, and the best level of X at subsequent reviews.[5] Littlechild (1983) does not acknowledge this time inconsistency problem when he rates RPI-X as being both the best for "proceeds and prospects from privatisation" and for "consumers' welfare".

In practice, X must be repeatedly reset to ensure that prices do not deviate too far from costs, creating allocative inefficiencies and welfare loss. Vickers and Yarrow (1988, p. 97) argue that resetting X on the basis of a fair rate of return will in practice ensure that "RPI-X is simply another form of rate of return regulation". In his original proposals in 1983, Littlechild made clear his beliefs on the longevity of explicit regulation (1983, p. 1): "Competition is by far the most effective means of protection against monopoly. Vigilance against anti-competitive practices is also important. Profit regulation is merely a 'stop-gap' until sufficient competition develops." It is clear that he did not envisage that aspects of telecommunications would still be regulated seventeen years after privatization (constraints on retail prices were extended for a further year in 2001). Waterson (1992) makes the point that while RPI-X incentive regulation is not the zero-cost option it was once thought to be, the regulatory burden of all the regulators is still less than the smallest of monopoly welfare loss predictions. He estimated that the incentive regulation burden was less than one-half the regulatory burden of the US rate of return.

However in recent years the regulators' budgets have increased, largely because of the degree of accounting knowledge required to recalculate the price cap, while initial caps seem to have been snatched from thin air.[6] It is now common to see discussion moving away from the general form of incentive contract, and centering more on detailed arguments such as what types of accounting, productivity measure, and forecasting determines the initial prices.[7] The price reviews of water and electricity in the United Kingdom show that these financial forecasts are often the pivotal aspects in determining the level of price.

Sappington (1994) makes the point that much of the underlying regulatory contract literature assumes that the firm may be able to control the level and quality of output through effort; however, where there is no correlation between output and effort incentive regulation will be ineffectual. Where performance is stochastic in its outcome, incentivizing this structure is likely to create uncertainty for the firm. This lack of certainty increases the cost of capital and reduces the level of investment away from the efficient rate, which in the long run may lead to higher prices and welfare loss.

One suggested way of mitigating this is to link rewards and penalties to average performance across other firms within the industry. Where the firm performs below the target, but proportionately better than other firms within the same industry it may well be due to exogenous factors and hence would not attract a penalty. The creation of this penalty "dead zone" maintains the incentive to perform but reduces the uncertainty derived from the contract. However care must be taken that only risks beyond the control of the firms are linked in this way, as weakening a direct link between effort and outcome will result in dampening the incentive structure. Such links between the firm's performance contract and industry performance are an example of yardstick competition, which has been increasingly used in both the United Kingdom (especially for water, sewerage and electricity regulation) and the United States.[8]

One means to reduce uncertainty in variables beyond the firm's control is to allow some form of cost pass-through. In its most basic form this is reflected in the basic RPI-X formula for BT where inflationary costs may be passed on; other industries' regimes have adopted some form of explicit cost pass-through. Where complete pass-through is permitted (that is, the firm is regulated at price equals cost) the firm will make no profit and allocative efficiency is satisfied; this is essentially cost of service regulation, providing no incentive for cost reduction and resulting in cost of service regulation and production inefficiency. Armstrong, Cowan and Vickers (1994) show that the optimal level of pass-through depends upon the firm's level of risk aversion and the extent of uncertainty. If the firm is risk neutral or there is no uncertainty, a pure price cap is optimal, while the optimum degree of cost pass-through increases if the firm is risk averse or there is uncertainty in costs. The cost pass-through enables the firm to share risk with consumers, but provides incentives to substitute costs away from those which are fully within the cap to those which can be passed on. Examples are the initial (1986–91) cap for gas where gas purchase costs could be passed on, and upstream costs for electricity supply. More generally it is important to note than any cost pass-through element, particularly RPI or input costs, should be entirely exogenous to avoid any possibility of strategic behavior.

There are alternatives to incentive regulation which have been implemented in various degrees. Instead of encouraging competition *within* the market some form of competition *for* the market can be devised. In such a system firms bid for the right to supply (usually for a fixed period); the government aims to extract the expected rent from market power through the franchise fee. The United Kingdom has introduced a form of franchising through auctions in railways, a similar procedure to that in France for the allocation of rights to service water. The literature on auctions is extensive and is only briefly described here; a more thorough treatment of auctions in the framework of regulation can be found in Laffont and Tirole (1993). The idea of franchising is old, contemplated by Demsetz in 1968 and developed formally by Riordan and Sappington (1987). Most franchising models are subject to the criticisms made by Williamson (1976): difficulties in complete and simple specification, effective competition for first and subsequent auctions, and ensuring that where the old firm is displaced, it receives proper compensation for transferable investments it has made. In reality franchising often goes hand in hand with developing competition, although its success has arguably been limited.

In contestable markets, where there are low sunk costs and a lag between entry and price response, the monopoly is forced to price at the competitive level to prevent entry. If the monopoly increases price above this level, entry can occur with the entrant taking all the market share and making a profit. The criticisms of this theory are well known and there are many convincing arguments that such a market is seldom found in reality. However it does provide an interesting insight into the link between market structure and the level of entry. Where sunk costs are high, as in most utilities, competitive entry is neither possible nor desirable, but if it is possible to separate the natural monopoly from the operation of the utility then partial competition can be encouraged, as we have discussed above.

3.3   Strategic behavior by firm and regulator

As incentive regulation has developed in the United Kingdom, there has been a parallel debate in the United States on introducing an explicit institutionalized regulatory lag rather than maintaining the endogenously determined lag. In the United Kingdom the price cap review, while allowing the consumer to benefit from realigning prices to cost, provides scope for the firm to engage in strategic behavior much like Sappington's (1980) "ratchet effect" criticism of the Vogelsang–Finsinger mechanism. Immediately after the review the incentives for cost reduction are high. As the time before the next review shortens, the firm's investment and cost decisions will increasingly depend upon the benefit that manipulating the next price review entails. At some point before the review period, the immediate gain for the firm from reducing its costs is outweighed by the loss incurred through their effect in triggering lower prices after the next review. This results in incentives to reduce effort or increase costs.

Hence when looking at the profile of effort over time, it takes the same ratchet structure as Sappington showed with output under the Vogelsang–Finsinger mechanism. Armstrong, Rees and Vickers (1995) explore a simplified version of such a trade-off in which both regulator and firm have the same information. They confirm that the firm's effort to reduce costs decreases as the review approaches. Additionally, as demand elasticity falls and costs become more sensitive to the effort to reduce them, the regulator may improve welfare through increasing the time period between regulatory reviews. A valuable extension to this model would include asymmetry of information, inducing strategic behavior by the firm in an attempt to signal that it is a high-cost type.

Initial discussion of this type of behavior by Sappington (1994) shows that where firms differ in ability between high- and low-cost types in a one-period game, the firm should be allowed to choose between two contracts designed to reveal their ability type. When the game is extended to multiple periods the firm might choose the steeper reward schedule in the first period and then reduce expenditure (costs). In the second period it will choose the flatter reward schedule, undertaking excessive expenditure (costs) to make up for the lower effort in the first period. The strategic shifting of costs allows the firm to make a large profit in the first period and incur only a small penalty in the second period. This results in strategic cycling of effort/costs, potentially reflected in output quality, to manipulate the contract and raise profits. There is some evidence of such a cyclical pattern in investment expenditure which is delayed until immediately before the next review (for example in the UK water industry). BT provided evidence of similar behavior immediately prior to their first review. Having rebalanced prices in every year since privatization, they declined to do so in 1987, despite an opportunity to raise prices within the cap (Bradley and Price 1988b). One interpretation of their behavior is that such rebalancing gave the regulator "too much" information on potential profits, in this case through prices rather than costs. Although both price caps and rate of return regulation suffer from the possibility of manipulation, price caps may be a better means of regulation owing to the exogeneity of the regulatory lag (as opposed to endogenously determined reviews within the US system).

Firms may have incentives to manipulate prices across markets as well as over time. This poses the significant question as to whether welfare is actually enhanced under price cap regulation even in a static model. Bradley and Price (1988a) first address this question in their study of an average revenue regulated monopolist such as that applied to many of the UK industries. In this case the prices are weighted by current demand, rather than previous consumption or revenue levels, and the firm is induced to restrict supply to the higher-cost markets (through raising price) and expand supply in the lower-cost markets (through lowering price). This results in incentives to charge prices in some markets that may be higher than those charged by an unconstrained monopolist. (However analysis of the initial years of price caps applied to UK regulated industries showed that they were much more responsive to informal regulatory guidance than to the incentives contained within the formal price caps themselves, Giulietti and Waddams Price 2000.) Armstrong and Vickers (1991) compare the welfare results of allowing price discrimination with that of uniform pricing under an average revenue constraint. They find that the welfare result depends upon the tightness of the price constraint, with some degree of price discrimination being optimal as the constraint is relaxed.

Sappington and Sibley (1992) show that for an average revenue lagged tariff, the strategic incentive to manipulate prices through a non-linear tariff may result in loss of welfare even though a linear tariff may enhance welfare. Armstrong, Cowan and Vickers (1995) strengthen this result by showing that the optimal non-linear tariff is distorted and other types of regulatory constraint may be preferable to a tight average revenue constraint. Law (1995) returns to differing costs and shows that a tightening of a price cap can lower aggregate consumer surplus, confirming Bradley and Price's (1988a) result that tighter regulation induces the firm to reduce the number of high-cost consumers by raising the price in this market and lowering the price in the low-cost market. Cowan (1997a) confirms that total welfare may fall as a result of an average revenue cap that is "too tight".

Crew and Kleindorfer (1996) consider a total revenue constraint as applied to UK regional electricity companies. They show that the revenue cap has a much larger potential than an average revenue constraint to distort output incentives, producing prices above the monopoly level in some markets. Cowan (1997b) compares the dynamic case for three different types of regulatory constraints: average revenue, Laspeyres base-weighted tariff basket constraint, and the average revenue lagged regulation first studied by Sappington and Sibley (1992). He confirms that the average revenue lagged constraint and average revenue may not only be inefficient but is likely to reduce overall levels of welfare, while a Laspeyres index-based constraint can induce efficient prices even when the firm is not myopic.

This section has made it clear that there are substantial difficulties in attempting to design an optimal incentive contract for regulation while taking account of factors such as consistency, uncertainty, and welfare. More generally, where a principal seeks to create incentives for multiple tasks, there is a risk that the one may create adverse incentives for the other. In particular, multiple objectives need to be carefully balanced. Baron (1985) shows that if an economic and environmental regulator develop their constraints independently, the firm will produce a higher environmental standard, less output, charge higher prices, and make more profit that in the maximum efficiency case. This is exactly the conflict which arose in the UK water industry as new price levels were set from 2000. Baron shows that the optimum can be restored if the regulators can internalize the trade-off between their different objectives before setting the constraints, a result with wide-reaching implications for regulatory structure.

Uncertainty for the firm raises questions of regulatory commitment. If a firm has an investment choice that will result in a return only at some future date, lack of commitment by the regulator to enable recovery of the investment may result in the abandonment of a cost reducing investment. The regulator's time inconsistency problem arises from the initial desire for reduced costs, followed by the wish to minimize prices by not allowing the costs of the investment itself, once it has been undertaken. The optimal reward *ex ante* for the investment (to ensure it is undertaken), is no longer optimal *ex post*, tempting the regulator to change the rules and strand the invested assets. Where it is possible to write some form of binding contract upheld by both parties or some third party (such as the introduction of judicial reviews in the United Kingdom) the time inconsistency problem may be mitigated. One infamous example of stranded assets has arisen as a result of regulatory reform in the UK gas industry. The incumbent monopolist signed several take-or-pay contracts which committed it to paying for gas supplies even if they were not used. As competition was introduced the incumbent lost large portions of its market, especially for industrial consumers, and found itself committed to pay for gas which it could no longer sell. In the United States the Federal Communications Commission adjusted prices downwards for local telecom exchange carriers in 1995, arguing that productivity had been substantially higher than forecast. Such a manipulation of the contract could result in reduced incentives and increased uncertainty, especially where firms' previous investment decisions had been based upon the original productivity assumptions.

Clawing back profits *ex post*, whether explicitly or implicitly, has the result of dulling the firm's incentives, to the extent that the regulated firm may prefer an earnings-sharing plan within the regulatory contract. Such arrangements reduce incentives to lower costs and innovate because the regulated firm will receive only a proportion of its earnings. In the United States this has been recognized since 1993, when no incentive contracts have incorporated an explicit earnings-sharing portion. In general some level of flexibility in incentive regulation is optimal to allow exogenous shocks to be factored in and the reasonable recovery of stranded assets, but frequent changes in regulatory rules create uncertainty and a corresponding reduction in investment.[9]

One major difference between UK and US regulatory bodies is the degree of transparency in decision-making. The UK regulator has more discretion and less need to reveal the basis for decisions than its US counterpart. It is an interesting quirk of the UK regulatory system that because of the lack of transparency, the price review is often something of a bargaining process between the regulator and the firm. If agreement cannot be reached, the Competition Commission acts as arbiter, and typically supports the arguments of the regulator.

4   Incentive regulation and competition

The Conservative Government of the 1980s and 1990s believed that regulation should be only an interim stage in the drive towards competition. This desire was at first tempered only by the practicalities of ensuring that competition did not open up a host of other problems such as the wasteful duplication of sunk costs, and incorrect billing of consumers. Criticism of the government's treatment of BT and British Gas, which were privatized as vertically integrated monopolies, induced the government to separate transmission from generation, and introduce some horizontal separation of generation when electricity was privatized in 1990–1. The possibilities of competition in water were much more limited owing to the absence of a national network and geographical problems, and the companies were left as vertically integrated regional monopolies. Although competition has proved successful in many of the industries such as telecoms, gas, and electricity, there now exists a mix of old regulatory problems and new issues created through the introduction of competition.

4.1   Industry structure

Development of competition has raised new questions about the boundaries of regulation. Parts of the industries which are intrinsically naturally monopolistic will require some form of long-term control, while technological advances continually expand the areas where competition is viable. This raises questions about the optimal structure of the industry, the development of competition, and terms of access to natural monopolistic elements which are "essential facilities" for competition. There may be a danger that policy-makers lose sight of the final goal during the quest for competition, which is fundamentally a means to engender higher welfare. Especially in the rapidly changing telecoms market, the assumption that competition brings higher welfare is being questioned, and if competition should be allowed, how should it be structured? Gilbert and Riordan (1995) compare a vertically integrated monopolist producing the end-good with that of a vertically separated monopolist who is prevented from operating in the end-market, and fringe competition bidding in the form of an auction with the right to enter the end-market. An integrated monopolist avoids the cost information asymmetry that results in an effect analogous to double marginalization, but this benefit may or may not be greater than the benefit derived through the competitive auction to supply the downstream market; the balance depends on the degree of complementarity between the upstream and downstream products.

Industries which have remained vertically integrated (such as telecoms) have proved more difficult both to regulate and for the introduction of competition, than those where the natural monopoly element has been separated. However there may be a loss in economies of scope through separation, and an overall reduction in welfare. Further loss results from a potential problem of double marginalization, if both the upstream and the downstream firms are imperfectly competitive or inadequately regulated. In this case the regulator must ensure that the upstream firm (i.e. the natural monopoly that supplies an input for the downstream firms) prices at or close to marginal cost, raising practical problems of providing subsidy. This is equivalent to internalizing the transaction, resulting in greater final output and welfare for all. Vertical restraints such as franchise contracts or price ceilings by the monopoly may generate the same problems as vertical integration and are best controlled by an external regulator.[10]

Comparing models of integration and separation, Vickers (1995) looks at the trade-off between allowing a vertically integrated monopolist to operate downstream under Cournot competition with entrants, and forbidding the monopolist to enter the market downstream. He shows that because of the link between the number of firms downstream and the access price, it is optimal to have the access price higher than marginal costs to prevent duplication of fixed costs. The monopolist's incentive to raise rivals' costs may be outweighed by the advantage of producing at a lower average cost if fixed costs are not duplicated. However where there is no link between the number of firms and the access price (Bertrand competition), the access price should be set below marginal cost to compensate for the incentive to raise rivals' costs, and it is less likely that the monopolist should be allowed access. Thus the excess entry result common in many product differentiation models drives the incentive to integrate.

This basic framework has been extended by Lee and Hamilton (1999) by relaxing the assumption of identical constant marginal costs between the monopolist and downstream firms. However they still maintain the somewhat unrealistic assumption of the regulator knowing the costs of the downstream firms (owing to difficulty in assuming asymmetric information both upstream and downstream). The advantage in cost for the incumbent increases the likelihood that the integrated structure will be optimal. Iossa (1999) presents a similar model looking at asymmetrical information in demand rather than costs, finding that the optimal market structure depends upon the level of correlation between the upstream and downstream goods.

4.2   Access pricing, bypass, and cross-subsidies

Where the incumbent is vertically integrated and owns an essential facility, the access price itself becomes a crucial issue. In the United Kingdom, even as the telecoms industry becomes increasingly competitive, the access price is now controlled by a network price cap. With a vertically integrated upstream network and downstream consumer supplier, the incentive for the monopoly to favor its own business with lower access prices than the entrant's is strong. De Fraja and Waddams Price (1999) show that welfare can be higher when the incumbent's access price is not directly regulated but he is rewarded according to the level of entry downstream. Laffont and Tirole (1990) model a multiproduct monopolist where the regulator cannot observe effort.[11] The model illustrates a number of interesting points when considering the trade-off between consumer gain through allocative efficiency and possibly harmful distribution effects. Asymmetric cost information between the regulator and firm increases the likelihood of bypass, as the access cost is higher. The greater the asymmetry in costs the higher the access cost is likely to be and hence the more chance that an entrant will build its own network. If the competitors are unregulated and their profits take away incumbent profits used to subsidize social obligations, then competition may be undesirable.

Curien, Jullien and Rey (1998) use a model similar to Laffont and Tirole (1990) to show that bypass can increase welfare for all consumers connected to the network, while the incumbent's profits are reduced and the regulator's subsidies increase at the expense of the tax payer. They demonstrate that where subsidies to the incumbent are not allowed, it is the largest consumers that benefit from bypass, while small consumers who have been supported by the social obligations policy face falling welfare through exclusion. Such exclusion may be mitigated through the diversification of the incumbent into other markets in which it is free to adjust prices.

The most useful models look at the cross-subsidization problem and the incentive to increase access price trade-off as a whole rather than separately. Laffont and Tirole (1993) provide some insight into this problem where the regulator is able to control both the access price and the final product price of the monopolist. The optimal access price will exceed the marginal cost of access in proportion to elasticity (for Ramsey reasons). This access price will be greater when the regulator attaches higher value to the monopolist's profit than to that of the competitive fringe (perhaps for financing social obligations). To facilitate social obligations and bypass problems of asymmetric knowledge, one suggestion has been the use of "global" price caps on the entire incumbent's output. Laffont and Tirole (1996) argue that when access is simply added into a weighted basket of products, the incumbent is induced to choose the optimal Ramsey prices, subject to the consumer surplus weights in the basket. This regime allows the incumbent to change prices as long as the average value remains within the global price cap, but has been criticized as potentially leading back to subsidizing predation by the incumbent.[12]

4.3   Competition in telecoms networks

These issues have been reflected in practice through the gradual creation of new telecoms networks bypassing the existing incumbents, and creating problems as well as benefits. Laffont and Tirole (1998a, 1998b) model an unregulated telecoms industry characterized by several interconnected networks. Their findings cast doubt on the general conclusion that increased competition results in lower prices. Assuming that there is balance between outflows and inflows of calls, a non-price-discriminating firm that reduces the usage price increases the number of consumers joining the network, but does not increase profitability (owing to balancing). The greater number of consumers on the network increases the number of calls made, raising the number of off-network calls and triggering an access price deficit to the other network. Where price discrimination is allowed, firms are able to charge relatively high prices to calls off the network compared to on network calls, reducing the access deficit. Consequently high access prices may trigger intense competition for market share and consequently low "on-network" prices. Where firms are forced to adopt uniform prices, reducing final price results in a higher market share, but this increases the call volume, resulting in a higher access deficit and a loss in profitability. Hence they conclude that under uniform pricing there is little incentive to reduce prices and competition is weakened. This result is strengthened by disincentives for a new limited coverage entrant (under uniform prices) to undercut the full network incumbent, as it will again incur an access deficit. The entrant may prefer to under-invest in coverage (taking the role of "puppy dog") to transform the incumbent into a pacified "fat cat".

The introduction of non-linear price competition increases competition among the networks as the firms can reduce the fixed fee and build market share without incurring an access deficit (keeping usage price high). Laffont and Tirole find that price discrimination may increase competition but creates inefficiencies compared with uniform prices. For small-scale entry, an incumbent may use price discrimination to squeeze the small firm out by raising terminating access charges. The high access charge results in a large access deficit for the entrant and eventual eviction from the market. Unless entrants can quickly build a large network they are unlikely to remain in the market. This implies that in reality where price discrimination is practiced it may well be necessary to regulate access prices until the networks are of a similar size.

Whether the firm is vertically integrated or not, competition has usually been introduced in the presence of the former monopolist as incumbent. How, then, might a competitive fringe behave? Caillaud (1991) analyzes the optimal regulation of a dominant firm facing Bertrand competition from a fringe of competitive firms which are not regulated. He finds that the fringe will potentially produce more efficiently than the regulated firm, and its presence reduces the asymmetry in cost information when the fringe's costs are correlated with the incumbent.

Taylor and Weisman (1996) discuss an incentive contract proposed for regulating Canadian Radio-Television and Telecommunications. The contract is designed to avoid some of the problems of price cap regulation discussed in this chapter. They consider the introduction of a yardstick means of sharing productivity gains. Where the firm's productivity is higher than industry productivity, the firm is allowed to keep some specified proportion of this increase in the form of a proportionately higher revenue constraint. The new contract also incentivizes increasing the quality of service through comparison with the last period's quality, and through managing the weights may provide an effective disincentive to manipulate quality. Lastly they explicitly adjust for the loss of the incumbent's market share to entrants. Each service has a weight attached to it dependent upon the incumbent's market power; as market power decreases the weight of that service within the tariff basket falls, until eventually at some set level it is removed altogether.[13] The authors propose that the strategic manipulation of two-part tariffs along the line of Sappington and Sibley (1992) will be welfare enhancing as long as consumers may choose between the non-linear and original tariff. This type of incentive contract illustrates the development of practice through a detailed contract specifying as closely as possible the optimal price for the firm, while preserving the incentive structure for cost reductions and efficiency savings.

4.4   Competition and distributive concerns

The issue of access deficit charges for social obligations raises more general questions about the nature of these "utility" industries, which are likely to form part of a larger social distribution policy. The "Universal Service Obligation" (USO) policy found in many developed economies is based on the argument that each citizen has a right to clean water, electricity, and other basic utilities, regardless of income or location. Consequently many of the prices for goods in such monopoly industries do not fully reflect costs. One example of this is in the gas industry's charges. In the United Kingdom, British Gas traditionally charged the same amount for gas regardless of the level of costs their service entailed. Those consumers whose costs of service are low (i.e. customers that pay by direct debit) indirectly subsidized those with high costs of service (customers paying by coin meters). When competition in domestic gas was first introduced in 1996, the entrants logically targeted the most profitable direct debit market. This resulted in a reduction of the incumbent's profits that were further reduced by the regulator initially preventing British Gas from raising prices to customers not paying by direct debit.[14] Had this continued, over time British Gas Trading would no longer have been able to fulfill its social obligations to higher-cost consumers and still make a profit. To compensate for this, the regulator has allowed some rebalancing of prices between the high- and low-cost consumers, though it has limited the extent to which the incumbent is able to do this, ostensibly on grounds of discrimination. Direct regulation was removed from the retail gas market in April 2001, with the only remaining constraint (initially for one year) being an undertaking that the difference between charges to the less and more competitive markets should not increase.

Because of these social dimensions and the desire for universal service, there may be greater weight attached to profits made by the incumbent monopolist than by the entrants when social obligations and cross-subsidization are issues. All the privatized industries have inherited such cross-subsidies, hence the challenge is to incorporate such objectives within the incentive contract in the presence of competition.

The solution to the conundrum of promotion of competition and social obligations such as a USO may be finally solved only through the unravelling of cross-subsidized products, leaving price regulation only on services deemed essential. The problem however is how to treat this in the transitional period. Helm and Jenkinson (1997) propose four possible policy responses: allowing a long transition time; increasing prices to deal with costs; relying on social security policy; and relying on the efficiency gains to offset the cross-subsidies. Another approach is through a competitively neutral tax on the revenues of all providers. The provider of a universal service would then receive a lump-sum subsidy to compensate for the difference in price and cost of the service. The solution requires the controversial deregulation of many of the incumbents' markets once they are deemed competitive. The energy regulator appointed in 1999 has addressed this issue directly, recognizing the potential of these concerns to prevent or distort the development of competition (Ofgem 1999). The best solution is often to reinstate the efficiency/equity division and provide direct government support for vulnerable groups to replace the cross-subsidies. Unfortunately governments are not always amenable to such solution, despite their benefits. Particular problems may arise if there are simultaneous changes across several industries which adversely affect some vulnerable or politically sensitive group (Waddams Price and Hancock 1998).

A sign of the increasing importance that the government has placed upon the consumer welfare aspects of competition has been the passing of the Utilities Act 2000. This changed the primary task of the energy regulator to one of protecting consumers and introduced a new duty to take account of the interests of individuals with low income, providing an explicit (if unspecific) distributional remit. The Act also provided for the government to issue guidance on environmental or social concerns which the regulator must take into account, but need not act upon. As important as these remit change has been the new institutional framework which the Act introduced. The powers of the individual regulator have been transferred to an Authority, with a majority of non-executive directors, which "the regulator" now chairs. A new consumer body has been created with both a representative and an advocacy remit, although there remain questions about what differentiates this role from that of the Regulatory Authority with its own new consumer-oriented duties. Similar legislation was expected to be introduced for the water industry (except that the regulator will remain an individual) and the communications sector in 2002.

5   Conclusions

The very success of incentive regulation in generating cost reductions and profit increases led to political calls to reform the UK system, because of perceptions of excessive profits from lax regulation. The "windfall tax" introduced by the Labour government in 1997 runs contrary to the original spirit of incentive regulation. Because gains to consumers through the price cap are independent of the firm's earnings, announcement of high profits generates political pressure to claim that the price cap is flawed and consumers should gain a larger share of the realized gains. The clawback may take place explicitly (i.e. through a "windfall tax") or implicitly through higher demands for quality or increasing competition at an earlier date, but we have already seen that this weakens incentives.

This chapter shows that there is no simple answer to creating the optimal regulation regime. Over time regulatory contracts have become more incentive-based under the different types of price cap and tariff basket schemes. However there still remain many problems such as quality control, strategic manipulation, and cross-subsidization, among others. Consequently the design of an optimal incentive contract depends largely on the regulator's main goal.[15] The goal itself depends on the regulatory structure, and the institutional relationship between regulator and government. How much discretion should the regulator have in determining objectives and the means to achieve them? Who sets the goals, how well are they defined, and how closely do they reflect society's preferences? These are the very issues which prompted the second round of regulatory reform leading to the Utilities Act in the United Kingdom.

These reforms underline the trade-offs inherent in the regulation process itself. The literature demonstrates that identifying the correct level of incentive is like walking a tightrope: too much discretion to the firm may result in a reduction of total welfare; too little dulls the incentives for cost reduction. In designing an incentive contract it is almost impossible to shift all of the producers' gains into consumer gains without destroying the incentives which the original contract so carefully sought to create. At the same time the overall system needs to be politically acceptable in terms of the distributional consequences.

What is clear from application in the United Kingdom and United States is that regulatory contracts are no longer simply matters of price caps concentrating on a single performance measure. Incentive contracts must be designed to take account of several different dimensions, and have become increasingly complex. In the United Kingdom this has generally evolved behind closed doors at the discretion of the regulator, whilst the United States has adopted a more transparent methodology using their system of public hearings. A parallel may be drawn with Williamson's (1976) criticism of franchising in that for an efficient regime to exist, the contract must by specified in its entirety. Even where the aims are explicit, it is doubtful whether such a detailed contract is compatible with the original aim of light handed regulation.

The question is how regulation should proceed where such complete contracts are not feasible. Some regulators (notably in the United Kingdom) have moved to an informal contract framework in which the regulator has considerable unofficial influence over the actions of the monopolist. Several economists have argued that one of the main advantages of the UK system over the US is the United Kingdom's ability to use judgment in setting prices. A range of factors may be considered when setting price constraints which do not necessarily explicitly enter the contract. Littlechild (1983) saw the process of resetting X as a bargaining process between the regulator and firm taking account of a whole range of factors, rather than relying heavily on total factor productivity measurements, as had been common in the United States. However we return to the danger of weakening regulatory commitment where the ability of the regulator to manipulate the rules may result in stranded assets, uncertainty, a reduction below optimal investment levels, and higher costs.

In reality, all regulation constitutes a series of choices with various associated trade-offs. Incentive mechanisms within utilities are limited both by the nature of the industries and the need to achieve political consensus in the design and outcome of their regulation.

NOTES

The authors acknowledge funding from the ESRC under grants R00429834287 and R022250147, respectively, and are very grateful for many helpful comments from Morten Hviid, though he bears no responsibility for the outcome. The first version of this chapter was written when both authors were members of the Centre for Management under Regulation at the University of Warwick.
1. See Sherman (1989, chapter 8), for a detailed discussion of these criticisms.
2. For empirical evidence of the AJ model hypothesis, Courville (1974) finds that for all 110 rate of return regulated plants analyzed, the ratio of input prices exceeds the ratio of marginal products as the AJ model suggests. He finds that costs are up to 40 percent higher than the minimum efficient level, with the average being 11.6 percent higher. See also Petersen (1975) and Jones (1983) for other studies confirming the general bias result.
3. The possibility that the government's attitude to industry profits changes post-privatization is considered in section 3.
4. The problem of completely specifying a contract is discussed in more detail at the end of sub-section 3.2.
5. This issue is explored in Green and Waddams Price (1995).
6. The estimated budget for Oftel in 1999 was £12.6 million, which may still be thought of as a regulatory bargain when considered against the turnover of a UK telecommunications market estimated at £22 billion. Similarly Ofgas' budget of £12.9 million in 1998 may be compared to Centrica and Transco's combined revenue of £11 billion. What is less clear is the cost of the regulatory burden placed on the companies to meet the regulator's information demands, and in pursuing rent-seeking behavior.

7. See Tardiff and Taylor (1996) for a good summary of some of the detailed issues.
8. See Shleifer (1985) for the formal theory behind yardstick competition.
9. See Crew and Kleindorfer (1999) for a discussion of stranded assets and a means of allowing fair recovery.
10. A good introduction to the problem of vertical integration and restraints can be found in Waterson (1996).
11. See Baron and Myerson (1982) for an influential model of asymmetric information in which they assume that the firm's effort to reduce costs is exogenous and concentrate on the information asymmetry between the regulator and the firm.
12. See Armstrong, Doyle and Vickers (1996) for an analysis of this criticism.
13. Taylor and Weisman are clear that market share is not a sufficient indication of market power, as first it may not be a good measure of power in nationalized industries, and secondly it may be strategically manipulated by both the incumbent and the entrants.
14. See Waddams Price and Bennett (1991) for an account of domestic gas competition and the types of consumers who have switched their gas supplies from British Gas Trading to the new entrants.
15. See Sappington and Weisman (1996) for a description of the limits and myths of incentive regulation.

24 Contractual choice and performance: the case of water supply in France

Claude Ménard and Stéphane Saussier

1 Introduction

A great variety of contractual arrangements coexist today in the provision of public utilities such as water supply, urban transportation, and electricity. In the extensive set of modes of governance to which these arrangements correspond, the "purely" integrated form of a service provider owned and managed as a public "bureau" appears as a very specific case, and maybe one in extinction. The general reexamination of public provision for these services that developed in the 1980s raises the issue of the extension of government activities. This question by far exceeds the problem of privatization, with which it is too often identified. Beyond the transfer of property rights, important decisions must be made about the choice of the most satisfactory mode of governance for providing these services. Research by Hart, Shleifer and Vishny (1997) and Williamson (1999) looks for more rigorous analytical foundations to the resulting trade-off.

With regard to these issues, the case of water supply is a particularly rich domain. There is no doubt about the importance of guaranteeing safe and regular provision of water to the population. However, the choice of the most relevant mode of governance for doing so efficiently, i.e. at a low price and with high quality, remains an open question. Studies such as Ménard and Shirley (1999) show a significant dispersion of results for similar contracts, suggesting a major impact of institutional factors. Depending on the context, public providers sometime perform quite well while, symmetrically, private operators also fail. Other studies claim that disengagement of local authorities in favor of private sector participation systematically improves performance, at least under certain conditions (World Bank 1995; Gatty 1998). Last, empirical surveys show innumerable malfunctions, whatever the mode of governance is (Cour des Comptes 1997).

The French situation presents an exceptional terrain for studying these questions. Water supply has been under local responsibility for centuries, generating a wide variety of solutions. At the same time the rules of the game constraining choices (e.g. environmental laws) are the same for all, making the institutional environment continuous, stable, and homogeneous. Thus, it becomes feasible to compare alternative modes of governance that monitor similar activities. In this chapter, we take advantage of this situation to shed light on two questions. How much does the choice of a governance structure for providing public utilities depend on economic choices related to characteristics of the good to be distributed and the transactions that are involved in doing so? And do some modes outperform others systematically?

More precisely, this chapter presents results based on a detailed comparative analysis of performance for different contractual arrangements in the water sector. The study put aside factors that may depend on institutional elements (e.g. political influence) in order to focus on variables related to the governance *per se*. We used a database that provides information on all units supplying water (WSU) to towns of more than 5,000 inhabitants. This panel includes 2,109 WSU, for a period of three years (1993–5); it represents 73 percent of the French population.[1]

After a short overview of the organization of the water sector in France (section 2), we introduce our analytical framework, based on recent developments in transaction cost economics (section 3). The propositions derived from that framework are then tested on our data set, in order to shed light on the economic rationale behind the choice of a mode of governance (section 4) and on the links between the arrangements chosen and their performance (section 5). We show that these choices, although they are made in a sector that is particularly sensitive to political decisions, obey significant economic determinants. Neglecting the latter in making the choice of a contractual arrangement translates immediately into decrements in performance.

2   Contractual arrangements: characteristics of our sample

Before proceeding to the analysis itself, we need to briefly introduce some major characteristics of the organization of the water sector in France. Considering the goal of this chapter, we will not report strictly institutional characteristics (e.g. laws regulating the entire sector).

Water supply is different from other French network industries providing services to the public, such as mail, rail transportation, and electricity, in that it has traditionally been decentralized. The choice of the mode of governance and its monitoring depend primarily on local authorities. Successive laws have defined the general rules within which these choices operate. There are three main types of law that govern the sector: (1) Laws defining quality standards, because of the externalities on public health; (2) Laws compelling decision-makers to obey rules intended to make these choices transparent, in order to reduce risks of "capture" by operators and risks of corruption; (3) Laws oriented toward the protection of the environment and of a scarce resource.

Within these general rules, which allow flexibility unknown in most other public utilities in France, there is a wide variety of contractual arrangements and of their accompanying modes of governance. It is standard to differentiate three families of arrangements.

The first one is that of public bureaus ("Régies") involving direct ownership and control by local authorities. This mode is called "*gestion directe*" (direct management). Three sub-varieties can be identified. The "régie directe" is actually a public department through which local authorities directly manage the provision of water. The "régie autonome" characterizes a situation in which the agency providing water acquires financial autonomy but remains without legal independence: legally, it is not distinct from the local government. Last, the "régie personnalisée" identifies a public agency with financial autonomy and some autonomy in its corporate governance (with a Board of Administration, usually appointed by local authorities, and a director elected by the Board).

A second mode of governance is characterized by the involvement of an external partner, a private operator acting as a manager, while the water system remains publicly owned. This is called "*gestion intermédiaire*" (intermediary management), with an associated governance structure identified as "Régie assistée". In one sub-variety, the "régie intéressée," the operation and maintenance of the service are outsourced to a contractor, while local authorities remain responsible for investments and financial risks. The operator is involved in determining the price of the service and is paid a fixed amount for the service provided, usually complemented by revenue based on performance. The other sub-variety, the "gérance," differs essentially with regard to the incentive mechanism, since the operator is not involved in price-setting and receives a fixed amount for his services.

The third family covers different forms of "franchising" and is called "*gestion déléguée*" (delegated management). Typically, this is a contractual arrangement in which the franchiser, i.e. the local government, delegates to a franchisee, i.e. a private operator, the responsibility of providing water. In the case of "affermage," which corresponds to a lease, the franchiser delegates the operation and maintenance of the system as well as some investments to the franchisee, with the contract specifying goals and constraints (e.g. delays for connections), while the local government remains in charge of all major investments and bears financial risks. The franchisee assumes the risks related to the daily maintenance

Table 24.1. *Permanent average population, by type of arrangement*

Contractual arrangements	Observations	Average population	Std error	Min	Max
Direct management	534	18,704	41,745	528	606,147
Lease	1,416	16,619	32,709	200	586,501
Concession	102	58,112	116,550	3,065	698,127

Source: Direction Générale de la Santé.

and operation, and is paid by collecting bills from users according to rules (e.g. prices) negotiated in the contract. The other case is that of a "concession," in which local authorities delegate investments, maintenance, and daily operation (connecting, billing, collecting) to a private operator through a long-term contract. The operator bears the financial risks and gets its revenues by collecting bills from users, under constraints (e.g. prices) negotiated in the contract. At the end of the contract, all assets remain the property of local authorities.

One last arrangement to be mentioned, although it is extremely marginal in France, as in almost all countries,[2] is privatization, in which case a private operator fully owns and operates all assets related to the provision of water.

To summarize, there is a wide spectrum of arrangements, and all of them are present in France (see table 24.2). However, most of our study will focus on the three dominant forms, i.e. public bureaus, lease and concessions, notwithstanding the diversity introduced by the sub-varieties. Together, these three forms represent over 95 percent of the arrangements. The number of fully private operators in our sample is too small to be significant in our tests.[3] The distribution of contractual arrangements among the three forms is provided in table 24.1. We have indicated the size of populations concerned, since this variable is important in measuring the full significance of the distribution system adopted; moreover, this variable will play an important role in our analysis.

One last thing needs to be mentioned. All the operators, whatever their status, are coordinated and partially supervised by regional agencies ("Agences de l'Eau"). These agencies correspond to the main rivers defining the major basins that provide water.[4] These agencies are designed to coordinate the usage of a collective resource by the different users and to prevent and control pollution. Their main interest for our study is that they provide us with a geographical dimension, thus allowing a more precise distribution of contractual arrangements that includes

Table 24.2. *Distribution of contractual arrangements, by regional agencies*

Contractual arrangements		Regional agencies						
	Seine-Normandie	Loire-Bretagne	Rhône-Méditerranée	Adour-Garonne	Départements d'Outre-mer	Rhin-Meuse	Artois-Picardie	Total
Direct management	16.7	24.6	23.1	22.7	0	43.2	30.9	**23.8**
Assisted direct management	1.1	1.5	1.2	1.8	15.1	3.4	2.3	**1.5**
Lease	71	61.5	74.3	65.5	84.9	53.4	57.6	**67.1**
Concession	7.8	6.9	1.2	5.2	0	0	8.6	**4.8**
Privatization	2.5	0	0.2	0.3	0	0	0.6	**0.8**
Others	0.9	5.5	0	4.5	0	0	0	**2**
Observations	438	468	520	287	73	148	175	**2,109**

Source: Direction Générale de la Santé.

geological and climatic factors. These factors have an important impact on costs and on consumption. In 1995, for the WSU serving more than 5,000 inhabitants, table 24.2 shows the distribution of contractual arrangements.

These data demonstrate the interest of a study of the water sector for the economy of organizations and contracts. They show that, for the same sector, producing goods and services that are relatively homogeneous, using well-known technologies, and sharing characteristics with most network industries, we have a large variety of contractual arrangements. This raises questions that are at the core of our study: How do we explain such a diversity of arrangements for organizing similar transactions? Does this diversity translate in significant differences in performance? And is there a logical and coherent distribution of these performance differences (if they exist) among the modes of governance?

3   Our analytical framework

Three main approaches to the problem of the choice of contractual arrangements have been developed in recent economic literature.[5] A first approach put the emphasis on asymmetry of information between the government and the operator as the key factor in the provision of public utilities (Laffont and Tirole 1993). Choosing the best information revealing scheme *ex ante* is therefore at the core of the trade-off among alternative modes of governance. For example, if asymmetries are such that the franchiser (the government) can not obtain the relevant information, it may be better for him to provide the service directly, which is a form of integration. As a result, this type of analysis focuses essentially on the incentive mechanisms and neglects *ex post* adaptation that requires devices built into the mode of governance. A second approach emphasizes the allocation of residual property rights in the decision to outsource a service versus providing it "in-house" (Hart, Schleifer and Vishny 1997). There is a trade-off between quality and cost in providing a collective service with the assumption that there exists an adverse effect between quality and cost (i.e. it is not possible to increase quality and decrease cost at the same time). The choice of the mode of governance must be made according to the priority, with public bureaus emphasizing quality factors, since their lack of control over residual rights provides them little incentive to reduce costs, while private operators react the other way around. This analysis raises important issues, since the trade-off between quality and cost is so central in the provision of water; but it ignores the variety of potential contracts between the polar cases of private versus public operators. A third approach analyzes the choice of a mode of governance as the search for a form that proposes relevant incentives *ex ante* without neglecting the role of contractual hazards that will require adaptation *ex post*. The degree of adaptability required, and therefore the form of the contract, will depend on the characteristics of transactions at stake. Initially developed for explaining the trade-off between making or buying, and progressively extended to take into account intermediate modes of governance ("hybrid arrangements"), the framework of the economics of transaction has recently been applied to the decision that a government must make between providing a service itself, or outsourcing it through contractual arrangements (Williamson 1999).

In order to answer the questions raised at the end of section 2, we will use this last approach that has been so successful empirically.[6] The analytical framework, largely developed in Williamson (1985; see also 1996), is now well known. Let us assume that agents are looking for efficient modes of organization, i.e. arrangements that will minimize both their costs of production *and* their costs of transaction, under the constraint that represents the risk of opportunistic behavior of their partners. The theory then predicts that the trade-off among different possible arrangements and the adequacy of the resulting choice depend on the characteristics of the transaction that the mode of governance has to organize. Identifying these characteristics makes the central proposition testable: efficient modes of governance are those in correspondence with the degree of specificity of the assets required by the transaction and the degree of uncertainty surrounding this transaction. As a consequence, misalignment of an arrangement increases transaction costs, providing incentives to shift to another arrangement. A very large number of econometric tests confirms the robustness of this prediction, particularly for cases in which the trade-off for a firm is between buying on the market or making in-house.

More recent studies have extended the initial model, showing a wide array of arrangements between markets and integrated firms. Moreover, some of these studies have shown circumstances in which several substantially different arrangements coexist, without significant differences in performance (Ménard 1996). At first sight, the data above suggest that this is the case for water supply in France, since several modes of governance have persisted over time within the same institutional environment. A main goal of this chapter is to determine whether there is a relationship between modes of governance and performance. If performance were similar across very different arrangements operating on the same transactions within the same environment, then transaction-cost theory would be weakened. On the other hand, if performance differs, then the persistence of different forms would have to be explained by other factors, e.g. the political dimension involved in choosing the mode of governance for providing water, path dependency, and so forth.

In order to explore the determinants of the mode of governance and the resulting performance, we will define propositions based on the hard core of transaction cost economics, i.e. the hypothesis that a mode of governance performs much better if it fits the characteristics of the transaction it supports, namely, specificity of assets and uncertainty. Space constraints prevent us from looking at these determinants and their rationale,[7] we will restrict ourselves to applying the basic propositions to the case under review, in order to focus on our data and our test.

Proposition 1 *The more a geographic area requires specific investments to provide water, the lower is the probability of outsourcing these investments (i.e. delegating), everything else remaining constant.*

This proposition results directly from Williamson's hypothesis, one of the most often tested, according to which a higher degree of specificity in investments pushes towards more integration. In our version, this means that when highly specific investments are required, it is likely that integrated forms (i.e. "régies") will prevail over arrangements that are closer to market forms (e.g. concessions).

Proposition 2 *With specific investments required for distributing water in a certain area, the higher the uncertainty in that distribution, the lower the probability of outsourcing these investments (i.e. delegating), everything else remaining constant.*

Again, this proposition simply expresses Williamson's hypothesis that there is a close relationship between the degree of uncertainty surrounding a transaction and the degree of integration. Indeed, increasing uncertainty pushes us towards the adoption of a mode of governance that allows tight control, the polar case being full integration. In our typology of arrangements, direct management by a public bureau ("régie directe") is the extreme expression of such integration.

These two propositions, now quite standard in transaction-cost economics (TCE), do not shed light on the institutional dimension involved in the decision to choose a specific mode of governance. Indeed, the logic underlying these propositions focuses on economic determinants. So far, we have assumed that agents have a strong incentive to choose the most efficient mode of governance. This assumption is quite reasonable when we study actors operating in highly competitive markets. It can be seriously challenged, however, in an analysis of the decisions made by local authorities for utilities that are largely protected from competition. In these circumstances, it is likely that important factors other than economic efficiency, e.g. support of key political constituencies, will play an important role. For example, local authorities may choose a form that will allow them to influence local employment, a much easier task with a public bureau ("régie") than with a private operator whose autonomy of decision is protected by a long-term concession. Political orientation may also be a factor.[8] We plan to come back to these issues in another paper.

One last thing that we want to consider, because of its importance to local authorities, is the role of financial constraints. Specific investments are usually costly and can hardly (or not at all) be redeployed. Water is a sector with very important sunk costs, and these costs represent a very high proportion of total costs (up to 80 percent: Shirley and Ménard 2002). Many local governments will therefore be subject to financial constraints that do not allow them to chose the mode of governance they would otherwise prefer for that type of investment. This can actually be considered as another side of specific investments. We translate this into the following proposition:

Proposition 3 *Local authorities with limited budgets are more likely to choose to outsource than to provide the service themselves, when significant specific investments are involved, everything else remaining constant.*

4   The choice of the mode of governance: our variables

Our analysis is based on a sample of 2,109 Water Supply Units (WSU), serving all towns of over 5,000 inhabitants, for the period 1993–5. These units represent only 7.3 percent of the total units providing water to the French population, but they cover the needs of 72.6 percent of the total population. In order to test our propositions, we have identified for each unit, during the period under review, information relevant to the characteristics of transactions identified in our theoretical framework, namely: investments, uncertainty, and the financial constraint.

4.1   Investments

According to our proposition 1, geographical areas that require large investments to guarantee a reliable supply of water should push toward integration by local authorities, i.e. WSU should be under their direct control ("régie"). So far, we do not have coherent data on investments required for each WSU. However, we were able to identify proxies that are closely correlated with the level of investments.

4.1.1 Properties of raw water

One indicator of the volume of investments needed is the quality of raw water available and the related treatment it requires from the WSU. The worse the quality of raw water, the greater the investments required for its treatment. Quality of surface water is indicated by a standardized typology: A1 is for raw water that requires only simple mechanical filtering with light disinfection; at A2, raw water requires a combination of physical and chemical treatment, plus disinfection; for A3, raw water needs all of the previous treatments, plus a refining process; last, the level OS ("out of standard") designates quality that poses exceptional problems. To represent this quality factor, for which we have the relevant information, we use the variable $A3OS$ which takes value 1 if the WSU operates in departments (the French administrative unit) where there exist raw water of quality A3 or OS, 0 otherwise.

4.1.2 Origin of water

As for underground water, we do not have information on its initial quality before treatment. However, it is well known that underground water is of much better quality than surface water. Hence, units for purifying underground water are less complex and less expensive. On the other hand, underground water is more costly to exploit. Pumping requires investments significantly larger than does routing surface water into canalization. For similar quality, different sources of water therefore require significantly different amounts of investment. To capture this characteristic, we have isolated the WSU that operate in departments where all water comes from underground. This variable is labeled $WATUND$.

4.1.3 Population affected

Last, the size of the population for which a WSU provides water also plays an important role in the size of investments as well as in the dependency of local authorities on a potential private operator. First, the larger the size of a population, the more rapid amortization can be. This will reduce the incentive to have long-term contracts in which control is more diffuse, thus favoring the risk of opportunistic behavior by the operator. Second, the size of the population also influences the economic and technical capacities that local authorities can mobilize. Small towns have fewer internal resources either to produce water themselves or to monitor and control private operators, while using external expertise is costly, since private operators have little interest in managing smaller systems. This may explain the tendency of small towns to create pools, either to provide water directly through a joint bureau or to outsource. When the population is large, local authorities can much more easily hire technical expertise and, simultaneously, their market is more attractive to the private operators. With a large population, the choice of a contractual arrangement is much more open. We capture this effect with the variable *PERMPOP*.

To summarize, we have three proxies that can indicate the degree of specificity of investments required: *A3OS, WATUND*, and *PERMPOP*.

4.2   Uncertainty

Our proposition 2 suggests that areas in which transactions are plagued with a high level of uncertainty should be "integrated," i.e. water should be provided through direct management ("régie"). Sources of uncertainty may include climate (rainfall, drought) and other unknown factors that influence the volume of water to be distributed (economic development of the area, variation of future population) or its quality. The available data do not provide us with fully satisfying proxies for these factors. However, taking into account the basins through dummies allows us to approximate part of the problem, since they correspond to natural geographic area (climate) and to areas with specific urban and economic development.

4.3   Financial constraints

Last, our proposition 3 emphasizes that the size of investments also translates into financial constraints. In addition to the size of the population, which obviously affects the potential budget of local authorities (see our variable *PERMPOP*), another factor plays an important role: the gap between average and permanent population, a factor largely owing to seasonal variation. Indeed, such variations, when they are substantial (e.g. winter resorts, or the Riviera in the summer) require substantial investments to meet the seasonal demand, and these investments are often very significant relatively to the financial resources available to local authorities. We capture this with our variable *DELTAPOP*.

4.4   Performance

In our introduction, we stressed that one important goal of this chapter was to evaluate performance of each mode of governance. Indeed, a key point of our analysis is to identify whether or not we can observe significant differences according to the mode of governance chosen, and to determine if there is a mode better adapted to the characteristics of the distribution of water. As is well known, choosing the relevant variables for measuring performance is not trivial. Several dimensions can be taken into account, and several indicators can be chosen: financial, economic, or even physical. In this chapter, we adopt a simple criterion with a clear rationale for water service, the capacity of WSU to provide water that meets legal standards.[9]

In France, standards of quality are defined by a legal decree (no. 89.3, from January 3, 1989).[10] Their implementation and control are under the responsibility of powerful regional administrations ("Directions Departementales des Affaires Sanitaires et Sociales, DDASS). Any anomaly detected by controllers of the DDASS or of specialized organizations must be reported to DDASS. It is followed, according to the severity of the anomaly, by additional controls, by imposition of measures to correct the situation or, when threat to health is serious, by prohibition of the incriminated water for consumption.

Standards of quality changed significantly over the twentieth century, with increasingly tighter requirements. At the beginning of the century, drinkable water was defined through six chemical parameters and the identification of two microorganisms. Before the decree of 1989, twenty-one parameters were taken into consideration. Now there are sixty-two parameters used for determining quality of drinkable water. Obviously, these parameters cover a very diversified set of factors. Some serve essentially as indicators of the good condition of facilities (e.g. indicators of turbidity), so that they do not necessarily signal a risk for consumers. But most have a direct relation to health. Another important point to mention relates to the potentially large variation in the quality of water. The quality of raw water depends on where it is captured. It is subject to hazards related to natural conditions (hydrogeology, meteorology) as well as to temporary pollution. It also varies according to the type of treatment. Last, it changes in the distribution process, by getting mixed with other sources of water, by contact with materials used, and by exogenous sources of pollution. Since our goal here is to measure as directly as possible performance of contractual arrangements, we focus on the quality of water after treatment but before transportation and distribution to final consumers.[11] We use the variable *DETECT*, which takes value 1 for a WSU that has been identified as producing water not meeting the standards, zero otherwise.

4.5   Checklist of our variables

Table 24.3 summarizes all variables used in our econometric tests.

Table 24.3. *Variables and their meaning*

Variables	Definition
Dependent variables	
REGIE	Variable taking value 1 when the mode of organization is direct management
DELEG	Variable taking value 1 when the mode of organization is direct management; value 2 for leasing; value 3 for concession
DETECT	Variable taking value 1 for a WSU that has been identified distributing bad-quality water, at least once within a year, 0 otherwise
Investments	
DELTAPOP	Variable equals the gap between average and permanent population
PERMPOP	Variable equals the permanent population concerned by the WSU
A3OS	Variable taking value 1 when the WSU operates in a department where there exists raw water of bad quality (A3 or OS quality levels)
WATUND	Variable taking value 1 when the WSU operates in a department where all water comes from underground
Control variables	
SN	Variable taking value 1 when the WSU operates in an area supervised by the Seine-Normandie regional agency
LB	Variable taking value 1 when the WSU operates in an area supervised by the Loire-Bretagne regional agency
RMC	Variable taking value 1 when the WSU operates in an area supervised by the Rhône-Méditérannée-Corse regional agency
AG	Variable taking value 1 when the WSU operates in an area supervised by the Adour-Garonne regional agency
DOM	Variable taking value 1 when the WSU operates in an area supervised by the DOM regional agency
RM	Variable taking value 1 when the WSU operates in an area supervised by the Rhin-Meuse regional agency

5   Results

As already mentioned, our econometric regressions intended to clarify two main issues: what are the determinants of contractual choice? And what is the relationship between the arrangement chosen and its performance? Our results confirm the robustness of the predictions we made using transaction cost economics.

5.1   *Determinants of contractual choice*

In order to analyze the determinants of the choice of the arrangement which characterizes a WSU, we have defined a variable *DELEG*. This variable reflects the degree of delegation chosen by local authorities (see table 24.3). It takes value 1 when the mode of organization is direct management by local authorities ("régie"), i.e. there is no delegation to a private operator; value 2 for leasing, which corresponds to a partial delegation of authority to a private operator; and value 3 if the contract is a concession, which is the maximum involvement of a private operator short of full privatization.[12] The results of our tests are in table 24.4.

A preliminary comment is necessary with regard to column *DELEG* (1) in table 24.4, in which there are significant differences according to the basins. This was already noticeable in table 24.2. Local authorities in the Seine-Normandie basin delegate much more water provision than in other regions. Conversely, local authorities in Rhin-Meuse delegate much less. Other basins are in between.[13] A similar result has been observed previously on a much more limited sample of WSU (Derycke 1990).

Let us now introduce the variables that measure the key characteristics of transactions involved in the choice of the mode of governance. For all of them, results are significant (see column *DELEG* (2) in table 24.4). Indeed, these choices are unambiguously related to the explanatory variables that we have identified.

First, our results show a clear impact of *PERMPOP*. The larger the population concerned, the more we observe delegation by local authorities. This supports proposition 1: the larger the population, the smaller the investment *per capita*,[14] and the better the profitability for an operator. Indeed, anticipation of good profitability gives local authorities the choice between providing "in-house" or delegating to an operator; it also provides an incentive for operators to bid, since they can reasonably expect normal amortization of their investments within the limit of the duration of the contract.[15] In these circumstances, there is an incentive to delegate.

Second, for the WSU operating in areas in which water comes exclusively from underground, or in areas in which there exist surface water of bad quality, our test shows a clear predominance of direct management through public bureaus ("régies") and, to a lesser degree, of lease contracts. These modes allow local authorities to exert tighter control over the operator, public ("régie") or private (lease), than they could over a concession. This result substantiates proposition 2. Raw water of bad quality or of underground origin requires much larger investments; shaving costs or being vulnerable to opportunistic behavior by a private operator would have a negative effect on quality of water and on the health of the population, with political consequences as a direct effect.[16]

Third, our test shows that the more variable the population served by a WSU, the more likely it is that the arrangement adopted will be delegation to a private operator. Indeed, these modes relax the financial constraint for the local authorities. The result confirms proposition 3.

Table 24.4. Determinants of contractual choice

Independent variables	Ordered logit		Multinomial logit DELEG (3)[#]		Multinomial logit DELEG (4)[#]		Logit
	DELEG (1)	DELEG (2)	Régie	Concession	Régie	Concession	REGIE (5)
SN	0.67 (3.41)***	0.72 (3.47)***	−0.81 (−4.48)***	1.03 (3.034)***	−0.87 (−3.99)***	−0.07 (−0.19)	−0.84 (−3.94)***
LB	0.21 (1.09)	0.20 (1.04)	−0.20 (−1.24)	1.23 (3.63***)	−0.25 (−1.29)	0.05 (0.156)	−0.23 (−1.21)
RMC	0.15 (0.803)	−0.06 (−0.31)	−0.50 (−3.33)***	−1.44 (−2.90)***	−0.56 (−2.79)***	−2.65 (−5.09)***	−0.37 (−1.90)*
AG	0.23 (1.135)	0.13 (0.63)	−0.30 (−1.69)*	0.59 (1.53)	−0.36 (−1.67)*	−0.54 (−1.28)	−0.28 (−1.33)
DOM	0.50 (1.68)*	0.28 (0.90)	—	—	—	—	−1.03 (−2.79)***
RM	−0.75 (−3.30)***	−0.99 (−4.15)***	—	—	—	—	0.55 (2.34)***
PERMPOP	—	0.043 (3.70)***	0.018 (1.21)	0.077 (4.47)***	0.01 (0.26)	0.32 (4.83)***	−0.001 (−0.14)
PERMPOP^2/10^{12}	—	—	—	—	−0.042 (−0.13)	−0.97 (−2.83)***	—
PERMPOP^3/10^{18}	—	—	—	—	−0.068 (0.17)	0.85 (2.03)**	—

DELTAPOP	—	0.30	−0.63	−0.28	−0.65	−0.25	−0.61
		(1.87)*	(−2.37)**	(−0.63)	(−2.42)**	(−0.63)	(−2.31)***
WATUND	—	−0.55	−0.018	−2.96	−0.50	−3.20	0.13
		(−3.33)***	(−0.10)	(−4.04)***	(−0.29)	(−4.35)***	(0.75)
A3OS	—	−0.34	−0.19	−2.23	−0.21	−2.41	−0.042
		(−2.63)***	(−1.44)	(−5.43)***	(−1.52)	(−5.85)***	(−0.31)
Constant	0.85	1.02	−0.56	−2.72	−0.47	−1.94	−0.69
	(5.22)***	(5.68)***	(−4.91)***	(−9.88)***	(−2.50)***	(−5.63)***	(−3.94)***
Log likelihood	−1522	−1505	−1458		−1285		−1145
Observations	2052	2052	1831		1831		2052

Notes: For all our estimations, we took into account the possibility that *PERMPOP* would have non-linear effects on the decision to choose a mode of governance. There were no significant effects except in regression *DELEG* (4).

*** Significant at the 1 percent level; ** significant at the 5 percent level; * significant at the 10 percent level.

WSU operating in overseas territories (DOM) and in the basin monitored by the Rhin-Meuse agency have been removed from the regression, because in these two cases, there is no concession contract. Hence, the total number of observations is down to 1,831. Results are identical in the constraint model in which the variable *DELTAPOP* intervenes only in the decision whether or not to outsource water provision (i.e. it is not involved in the decision to choose the specific form of outsourcing, lease versus concession).

Considering the quality of the data available, we decided to go a step further and to check the robustness of our results. One possibility is to proceed to an estimation in assuming that the variable $DELEG$ is a qualitative variable, but not an ordered one.[17] The results, based on a regression in a multinomial model, confirm our propositions (see $DELEG$ (3) in table 24.4). They also provide more precision on the effect of each variable on the choice of arrangements open to local authorities. The most noticeable effect is that strong seasonal variation in the population ($DELTAPOP$) has a significant impact on the decision to not provide water through a public bureau ("régie"). The other variables do not play a determinant role in that choice with this model. This is confirmed by another estimation, in which the dependent variable is binary (see column $DELEG$ (5) in table 24.4). One interesting result is that larger populations ($PERMPOP$) increase significantly the probability that water will be provided through a concession contract rather than a lease, with the possibility of a non-linear effect (see column $DELEG$ (4) in table 24.4). On the other hand, bad water quality, or an underground source of water, increases the probability that distribution will be through a public bureau ("régie") or a lease, rather than through a concession that would escape the control of local authorities.

To summarize, our results seem robust. They also suggest that *the choice of a mode of governance proceeds in two steps*. The decision to outsource or not depends centrally on the financial constraint, particularly when investments are major ones. If the decision is to outsource, then the choice between a lease and a concession depends largely on the density of the population and the concomitant investments. This last point reinforces the idea that control over potential opportunistic behavior plays an important role in the decision process. Indeed, local authorities have much more control over the private operator under a lease than under a concession. In the former arrangement, investments that the operator will engage directly are almost always much less than in the latter, and major investments remain under the control of local authorities. Moreover, the duration of a lease being significantly shorter, control over the private operator and the capacity to put him under competitive pressure are easier.

Therefore, it seems that the choice of a mode of governance is not random, nor is it based purely on political determinants. There are factors involved that suggest economic rationale in these choices. This being said, we must also acknowledge that, with the data available for this chapter, a significant part of the variation in choices remains unexplained, which suggests that important explanatory factors have been neglected.

5.2 Mode of governance and performance

Another goal of our chapter is to test if there is a close relationship between contractual arrangements and performance. One puzzling aspect that confronts transaction-cost economics (TCE) is the coexistence in some sectors, for long periods of time, of different modes governing the same transactions (Ménard 1996). Again, our data set is particularly useful for examining aspects of this issue since, within the same rules of the game, we have an array of arrangements that have been operating for years, some for decades. If the theory is right, different modes of governance monitoring transactions with similar characteristics should have different performance. Indeed, local authorities having chosen the "wrong fit," i.e. a contractual arrangement that is not well aligned with the transactions having the characteristics that we have identified above, should be much more exposed to opportunistic behavior from the operator, e.g. under-investments, repeated renegotiations. These malfunctions should reflect in the quality of the product delivered, which is precisely what our data measure.

As mentioned very briefly in sub-section 4.4, in order to measure the impact of contractual choice on performance of our WSU, we selected a simple, observable, and unchallenged criterion when it comes to provision of water, i.e. quality (which involves safety in this sector). More precisely, we considered the probability for a WSU to be identified as failure to meet at least one parameter of quality as defined by the law, at least once a year, whatever this parameter is.[18] Hence, our variable *DETECT* takes value 1 for a WSU that has been identified as failing at least one quality parameter, at least once within a year, 0 otherwise.

Our sample covered three years. Data were available for 1,942 of the 2,109 WSU of our initial sample. Results of our econometric tests are summarized in table 24.5.

Results of our tests show that concession is the mode of governance that performs the best (see column *DETECT* (1) in table 24.5), even when the specific characteristics of the different basins are taken into account. In contrast, public bureaus ("régies") have the worst performance, in that their probability of distributing water that is below some legal standards is significantly higher.

More precisely, this is the result we obtain if we assume that the contractual arrangement is given, i.e. we consider the arrangement as exogenous. But one important contribution of TCE is to make the choice of the mode of governance endogenous: each mode has its advantages and its disadvantages, with the "right" choice depending on the characteristics of the

Table 24.5. *Modes of organization and performance*

Independent variables	Logit *DETECT* (1)	Logit *DETECT* (2)[#]	Logit *DETECT* (3)[@]
SN	−0.50 (−4.11)***	−	−0.94 (−3.70)***
LB	0.47 (4.22)***	0.45 (2.53)***	−0.86 (−2.44)***
RMC	0.69 (6.03)***	−3.80 (−5.19)***	0.41 (1.27)
AG	1.19 (9.79)***	1.01 (4.88)***	−
DOM	4.43 (6.09)***	−	−
RM	0.53 (3.73)***	−	0.32 (0.25)
PERMPOP	2.64 (2.99)***	6.65 (2.68)	3.41 (1.21)
DELTAPOP	2.90 (3.30)***	−	−
WATUND	0.78 (7.75)***	−	−
A3OS	0.68 (9.14)***	−	−
CONTROL NUMBERS	−0.10 (−2.95)***	−0.27 (−2.59)***	−0.14 (−1.19)
AFFERMAGE	0.55 (3.57)***	−	−0.27 (−0.82)
REGIE	0.89 (5.64)***	0.10 (0.70)	−0.12 (−0.33)
Constant	−1.76 (−10.16)***	−0.24 (−0.08)	0.42 (1.05)
Log likelihood	−3650	−673	−504
Observations	5826	1101	795

Notes: In all our estimations, variables $PERMPOP^2$ and $PERMPOP^3$ are not significant.
*** Significant at the 1 percent level; ** significant at the 5 percent level; * significant at the 10 percent level.
[#] This estimation concerns only small units (less than 50,000 inhabitants) in which there is no significant variation of population during the year ($DELTAPOP = 0$) and operating in areas with water surface of bad quality ($A3O3 = 1$).
[@] This estimation concerns only small units (less than 50,000 inhabitants) in which there is no significant variation of population during the year ($DELTAPOP = 0$) and operating in areas with underground raw water only ($WATUND = 1$).

transactions that the arrangement will have to organize. In that respect, the decision for a government to make "in-house", i.e. through its own "bureau," rather than outsourcing, should correspond to the same logic (Williamson 1999). If it is so, there should be situations in which the "integrated" form that is a public bureau ("régie") should perform at least as well as other forms. According to the theoretical explanation of integration (and a public bureau is a form of integration into the government), this should occur in areas that require heavy investments *per capita* to produce and distribute water that meets quality standards and in areas in which costly water treatment installations are required.

In order to test this proposition, we first focused on WSU serving less than 50,000 inhabitants and operating in areas with bad quality surface water (A3 and OS). WSU operating in areas in which raw water comes exclusively from underground sources (i.e. is of much better quality) are excluded. Thus, we are concentrating our analysis on areas in which important investments are required and in which quality is a real problem. Our sample then shrinks to 1,101 WSU, among which only nine operate under a concession; we eliminate these nine units in order to focus on the measure of the respective performance of public bureaus ("régies") and lease contracts. In the situation thus described, public bureaus perform at least as well as lease units (see column *DETECT* (2) in table 24.5); this is consistent with what the theory suggests.

In other terms, we need to reexamine our initial result that showed a comparative advantage of concessions over all other forms. More precisely, a more refined test shows that WSU under lease or concession perform better than public bureaus only when the latter do not correspond to what the theory suggests to be the most adapted form with regard to the characteristics of the transactions. But when these characteristics correspond to those for which one would expect integration according to predictions made by TCE, then the comparative advantage of lease and concessions disappears. In a second step, we extended our analysis to WSU operating in areas with raw water of underground origin and with populations of less than 50,000 inhabitants. The result is identical to the previous one (see *DETECT* (3) in table 24.5). Hence, the two approaches converge: when public bureaus ("régies") have been chosen in situations with characteristics that correspond to what TCE predicts, these integrated forms perform at least as well as lease or concession.

Therefore we obtain quite consistent results. First, the choice of the mode of governance seems to follow an implicit economic logic that conforms to what TCE predicts, notwithstanding the influence of other factors, e.g. politics. Moreover, this choice of a mode of governance does have a direct impact on the performance of the WSU, as measured by the criterion of quality relative to legal standards. There are significant differences in performance among WSU. But these differences do not express the absolute advantage of one mode of governance over the others. Rather, they follow logic predicted by TCE. Indeed, integrated arrangements ("régies") are used in situations in which problems of raw water quality are the most acute, and in which investments required are significantly greater. To put it the other way around, when the integrated form ("régies") is adopted in such circumstances, its performance is comparable to and sometimes better than the performance of private operators working in similar conditions.

6   Conclusion

Very few empirical studies have analyzed the trade-off among different contractual arrangements in provision of public utilities. There is a vast literature on the decision to integrate or not, including econometric tests, particularly in TCE. But, to our knowledge, there have been no previous econometric tests that used the same theoretical apparatus for understanding decisions made by governments either to provide a service directly ("in-house") or to outsource part of the service (lease) or all of it (concession or privatization) to a private operator.

Our chapter proposes a test of that type. Our study relies on a detailed set of data that have never been used for that purpose so far. We used these data to explore with the help of econometrics two questions that are central in industrial organization: What determines the choice of a specific mode of governance among a set of possible forms? How do alternative modes of governance perform with regard to the same type of transactions? The first question has generated many econometric studies in TCE but to our knowledge, none on the decision by a government to outsource or not. As for the second question, there is an extremely small set of empirical tests of this issue, since it is very unusual to have data on several alternative arrangements, operating on the same type of transactions, with no interference of changes in technology or the institutional environment. In the French water system, we found such a set of data, and have developed preliminary results on our two questions.

Although this is still an exploratory chapter, with more data to analyze in future studies, our initial results are very encouraging. In a sector in which most interpretations of the choice of the mode of governance have relied heavily on political factors, we have shown that there is room for an economic explanation. Characteristics of transactions at stake do impose at least part of their logic on the choice of decision-makers. Our results also strongly suggest that there is no absolute advantage for one specific mode of governance. We observe instead some comparative advantages that depend crucially on the characteristics of the transactions that modes of governance organize. In our sample, the integrated form with public ownership ("régies") often performs well, sometimes even better than privately operated utilities. But this occurs only when transactions have some specific characteristics that we have identified here. We are now developing our data set in order to include more direct measures of investments and costs. We are also collecting data on prices, and extending the period under review. More results can be expected.

NOTES

Chapter 24 was originally published as "Contractual Choice and Performance: The Case of Water Supply in France," in *Revue d'Economie Industrielle* (92, 2000).

1. A forthcoming study will complete these data by a set of contracts that covers all the main cities, with information about a wide variety of variables (such as size, demography, and geological factors).
2. The United Kingdom is the only significant exception so far, with the privatization of water in England and Wales in 1989. The sector remains highly regulated by OFWAT (the Office of Water Services).
3. In an on-going project we are planning case studies to examine their performance.
4. Corsica and Oversea Territories (DOM) are exceptions: they correspond to an area, not a basin.
5. What follows is a highly simplified summary of the different approaches. Space constraints notwithstanding, it is important to make explicit and in comparative terms some reasons for our choice of the approach developed in this chapter.
6. For surveys of this empirical literature, see Joskow (1988a); Klein and Shelanski (1995); Crocker and Masten (1996); Coeurderoy and Quelin (1997), and Masten and Saussier see chapter 16 in this volume, pp. 273–291.
7. The heuristic model is in Williamson (1985, chapter 4). More is developed in Williamson (1996) and, with more technical details, in Saussier (1997, 1999).
8. A previous study, based on a limited number of cities, concluded that the political orientation of local authorities did not play any significant role in the choice of the mode of governance (Derycke 1990). But political factors may still be involved that transcend delineation of political parties (e.g. influence, corruption).
9. France being a highly developed country, we assume that all population is connected. Rate of connection is a major issue in developing countries (see Shirley and Ménard 2002).
10. General quality standards are based on those established by the World Health Organization (WHO) in 1986. Sanitary standards for water for human consumption are defined more precisely in another decree (no. 98-3,

from January 3, 1989). Also relevant are the decrees adopted by the EU (no. 75-440, no. 79-869, and no. 80-778).

11. Indeed, in transportation and distribution, several factors can interfere to change the quality of water without the responsibility of the WSU being involved (e.g. negative effects of roadwork, or of pollution originating outside of the water system).

12. We have already mentioned that for towns of more than 5,000 inhabitants in France, which is the base of our data set, there are not enough cases of fully privatized modes of governance to be significant in our tests.

13. Overseas territories (DOM) are an exception, since they virtually all use lease arrangements. The only possible explanation we can see for that is political and/or administrative origin.

14. In our sample, size of population is strongly correlated with demographic density. Therefore, we infer that it is *per capita* investment, not the absolute value of investment, which explains the result.

15. It must be mentioned here that duration of contract is regulated. A law adopted in 1993 (Loi Barnier) stipulated that duration cannot exceed twenty years. Lease contracts usually have duration within the seven–twelve years' range. Concessions are almost all for more than fifteen years (and now less than twenty by the Loi Barnier).

16. Indeed, we do not suggest that local decision-makers are purely oriented towards maximizing the well being of the population; but they make their choice with awareness of the political consequences of responsibility for water of bad quality being delivered to their constituencies.

17. The error in applying an ordered model to a non-ordered variable is much higher than the converse (Maddala 1983).

18. Some of these parameters, e.g. turbidity, pose no risk to public health.

25 Institutional or structural: lessons from international electricity sector reforms

Guy L.F. Holburn and Pablo T. Spiller

1 Introduction

The widespread privatization of national electricity sectors across both the developing and developed world provides a broad base of experience to assess the relative performance of various countries in attracting private sector participation in the industry. Since 1980, when Chile commenced a radical restructuring, and later privatization program, over sixty countries have introduced reforms in the electricity sector. These reforms have been generally designed with the purpose of increasing the levels of private ownership and investment, thereby reducing the dominance of the state-owned vertically integrated enterprise, the traditional mode of organization. There is substantial variability in the nature of these reforms. Some countries have invited private investment in the generation sector only, financed by long-term supply contracts to state-owned utilities (e.g. China, India, Indonesia, Mexico); some have vertically separated the industry but privatized only part of the sector (e.g. Colombia, El Salvador, Kazakhstan, New Zealand); while others have privatized the entire industry and additionally created competitive generation markets (e.g. Argentina, Chile, United Kingdom).

The degree of private sector interest, however, has been markedly mixed across countries. There have been some notable successes in attracting significant levels of private investment in all sectors of the industry (e.g. Argentina, Australia, United Kingdom). On the other hand, private investors have shown little interest in purchasing state-owned enterprises or in financing *de novo* infrastructure assets in countries such as Mexico, Turkey, or the Ukraine, to name only a few. Indeed some countries, including Hungary and Venezuela, have had to postpone planned privatization programs owing to lack of investor interest. In these countries, despite substantial state encouragement, governments have been unable to reverse sustained periods of under-funding in state ownership with large inflows of private capital.

As a consequence of the mixed experiences, and of the variety of alternative approaches undertaken, a debate has emerged on the design of "optimal" restructuring policies. Much of this debate has focused on classic industrial organization issues, such as the optimal degree of vertical integration between transmission, distribution and generation functions (Newbery 1999), the extent of horizontal fragmentation, the design of competitive generation markets, the sequencing of reforms, and so on. In practice, however, there is no clear empirical correlation between the method of restructuring implemented and the ultimate success of the reforms, casting some doubt on the notion of an "optimal" structural approach. Rather, the main lesson that emerges from the accumulated reform experience since 1980 is different. Here we claim that the design of what Levy and Spiller (1994) call the sector's "regulatory governance" regime is more important for attracting long-term private investment than the specific choice of industrial structure. Levy and Spiller's (1994) approach to regulation is rooted in the transactions-cost framework. They see regulation as having the features of an implicit contract between the government and the company. Under this contract, one of the parties, the operator, undertakes heavy specific investments, while the other party, the government, has strong incentives to behave opportunistically. In such an environment, *governance*, and in this case, regulatory governance, becomes crucial in order to motivate the operator to invest and to restrain the opportunistic behavior of the government. Thus, regulatory governance frameworks that provide a credible commitment to safeguard the interests of potential investors and customers alike, particularly when economic shocks create political pressure to shift the balance of power among competing interest groups, are better suited to attracting the levels of long-term private capital necessary for securing an adequate and reliable supply of electricity. Weak regulatory governance institutions, however, offering few or no credible assurances against direct or indirect expropriation of private property, have difficulty in encouraging private investment. Indeed, the disappointing experiences with sectoral reforms observed in various countries are generally the result of design flaws at the level of the regulatory governance regime, and also of weaknesses in national political, legal, and administrative institutions, rather than the result of the chosen industry structure. For policy-makers, our analysis suggests that the key to successful reforms is first to establish a credible regulatory environment, and only then to ponder on refinements of the chosen organizational structure for the industry.

We illustrate the critical role of regulatory governance and institutional structure by considering how several countries have responded to a common problem that has afflicted many wholesale generation markets, namely the alleged presence and exercise of market power. While each of the countries we examine has recently experienced strong political forces for policy reform in the generation sector, the speed and nature of adjustments to regulatory policies varies dramatically among the countries. This "natural experiment" therefore allows us to analyze the extent to which different regulatory institutions protect investors' interests while simultaneously providing sufficient flexibility to adjust to the appearance of unexpected shocks, some of which may require some tinkering with the "rules of the wholesale market game."

We provide first a general discussion of the utilities' problem, and of the meaning of regulatory governance and regulatory incentives. Then, based on this framework, we discuss some common myths on structural reforms, showing how these common presumptions, normally found in international aid agency recommendations, are unsupported by the existing evidence, and how "having the institutions right" is more important than "having the structure right." Finally, we go into the detail of three specific countries' responses to the appearance of high wholesale electricity prices.

2 The utilities' problem: regulatory governance and regulatory incentives[1]

In order to understand the relationship between the design of regulatory institutions and performance in the utility industries, it is helpful first to appreciate the particular features of the utilities sector that distinguish it from other industries: first, their technologies are characterized by large specific, sunk investments;[2] second, their technologies also exhibit important economies of scale and scope; and third, their products are massively consumed. What separates the utilities sector from the rest of the economy is then the combination of three features: specific investments, economies of scale, and widespread domestic consumption. These features are at the core of the contractual problems that have traditionally raised the need for governmental regulation of utilities.[3] In turn, they make the pricing of utilities inherently political.

The reason for the politicization of infrastructure pricing is threefold. First, the fact that a large component of infrastructure investments is sunk implies that once an investment is undertaken the operator will be willing to continue operating as long as operating revenues exceed operating costs. Since operating costs do not include a return on sunk investments (but only on the alternative value of these assets), the operating company will be willing to operate even if prices are below total average costs.[4] Second, economies of scale imply that in most utility services there will be few suppliers in each locality. Thus, the whiff of monopoly will always surround utility operations. Finally, the fact that utility services tend to be massively consumed implies that politicians and interest groups will care about the level of utility pricing. Thus, massive consumption, economies of scale, and sunk investments provide governments (either national or local) with the incentive and opportunity to behave opportunistically *vis-à-vis* the investing company.[5] For example, after the investment is sunk, the government may try to restrict the operating company's pricing flexibility, it may require the company to undertake special investment, purchasing or employment patterns, or it may try to restrict the movement of capital. All these are attempts to expropriate the company's sunk costs by administrative measures. Thus, expropriation may be indirect and undertaken by subtle means.

Expropriation of the firm's sunk assets, however, does not mean that the government takes over the operation of the company, but rather that it sets operating conditions that just compensate for the firm's operating costs and the return on its non-specific assets. Such returns will provide sufficient *ex post* incentives for the firm to operate, but not to invest.[6] Indeed, the expropriation of sunk assets has been more prevalent in Latin America than direct utility takeovers or expropriation without compensation.[7] While the government may uphold and protect traditionally conceived property rights, it may still attempt to expropriate through regulatory procedures.

2.1   The political profitability of expropriation

Sunk assets' expropriation may be profitable for a government if the direct costs (reputation loss *vis-à-vis* other utilities, lack of future investments by utilities) are small compared to the (short-term) benefits of such action (achieving reelection by reducing utilities' prices, by challenging the monopoly, etc.), and if the indirect institutional costs (e.g. disregarding the judiciary, not following the proper, or traditional, administrative procedures, etc.) are not too large.

Thus, incentives for the expropriation of sunk assets should be expected to be largest in countries where indirect institutional costs are low (e.g. there are no formal or informal governmental procedures – checks and balances – required for regulatory decision-making; regulatory policy is centralized in the administration; the judiciary does not have a tradition of, or the power, to review administrative decisions, etc.), direct costs are also small (e.g. the utilities in general do not require massive investment programs, nor is technological change an important factor in the sector), and, perhaps, more importantly, the government's horizon is relatively short (i.e. highly contested elections, need to satisfy key constituencies, etc.). Forecasting such expropriation, private utilities will not undertake investments in the first place. Thus, government direct intervention may become the default mode of operation.

2.2   The implications of government opportunism

If, in the presence of such incentives a government wants to motivate private investment, then it will need to design institutional arrangements that will limit its own ability to behave opportunistically once the private utility has undertaken its investment program. Such institutional arrangements are the design of a regulatory framework, stipulating, *inter alia*, price-setting procedures, conflict resolution procedures (arbitration or judicial) between the parties, investment policies, and so on. In other words, regulation, if credible, solves a key contracting problem between the government and the utilities by restraining the government from opportunistically expropriating the utilities' sunk investments.[8] This, however, does not mean that the utility has to receive assurances of a rate of return nature, or that it has to receive exclusive licenses.[9] In some countries, however, such assurances may be the only way to limit the government's discretionary powers.[10]

Unless such a regulatory framework is credible, though, investments will not be undertaken or, if undertaken, will not be efficient. Investment inefficiencies may arise on several fronts.[11] A first-order effect is under-investment. Although the utility may invest, it will do so exclusively in areas where the market return is very high and where the payback period is relatively short.[12] Second, maintenance expenditures may be kept to the minimum, thus degrading quality. Third, investment may be undertaken with technologies that have a lower degree of specificity, even at the cost of, again, degrading quality.[13] Fourth, up-front rents may be achieved by very high prices which, although they may provide incentives for some investment, may be politically unsustainable.[14]

A non-credible regulatory framework then, by creating strong inefficiencies and poor performance, will eventually create the conditions for direct government take-over. Thus, government ownership may become the default mode of operation, reflecting the inability of the polity to develop regulatory institutions that limit the potential for opportunistic government behavior.

2.3   Sources of regulatory commitment

In Levy and Spiller (1994) it is argued that the credibility and effectiveness of a regulatory framework – and hence its ability to facilitate private investment – varies with a country's political and social institutions. Political and social institutions not only affect the ability to restrain administrative action, but also have an independent impact on the type of regulation that can be implemented, and hence on the appropriate balance between commitment and flexibility. For example, relatively efficient regulatory rules (e.g. price caps, incentive schemes, use of competition) usually require granting substantial discretion to the regulators. Thus, unless the country's institutions allow for the separation of arbitrariness from useful regulatory discretion, systems that grant too much administrative discretion may not generate the high levels of investment and welfare expected from private sector participation. Conversely, some countries might have regulatory regimes that drastically limit the scope of regulatory flexibility. Although such regulatory regimes may look inefficient, they may in fact fit the institutional endowments of the countries in question, and may provide substantial incentives for investment.

Levy and Spiller (1994) look at regulation as a "design" problem.[15] Regulatory design has two components: regulatory governance and regulatory incentives. The governance structure of a regulatory system comprises the mechanisms that societies use to constrain regulatory discretion, and to resolve conflicts that arise in relation to these constraints.[16] On the other hand, the regulatory incentive structure comprises the rules governing utility pricing, cross- or direct subsidies, entry, interconnection, etc. While regulatory incentives may affect performance, one of the main insights from Levy and Spiller (1994) is that the impact of regulatory incentives (whether positive or negative) comes to the forefront only if a regulatory governance framework has successfully been established.[17] Regulatory governance is a choice, although a constrained one, since the institutional endowment of the country limits the menu of regulatory governance mechanisms available. Thus, regulatory commitment has two sources: the institutional endowment and regulatory governance.

2.4   Institutional endowment[18]

Levy and Spiller (1994) define the institutional endowment of a nation as comprising five elements. First, a country's *legislative and executive institutions*. These are the formal mechanisms for appointing legislators and decision-makers, for making laws and regulations (apart from judicial decision-making); for implementing these laws; and for determining the relations between the legislature and the executive. Second, the country's *judicial institutions*. These comprise the formal mechanisms for appointing judges and for determining the internal structure of the judiciary, and for resolving disputes among private parties, or between private parties and the state. Third, custom and other informal but broadly accepted *norms* that are generally understood to constrain the action of individuals or institutions. Fourth, the character of the contending *social interests* within a society, and the balance between them, including the role of ideology. Finally, the *administrative capabilities* of the nation. Each of these elements has implications for regulatory commitment. We focus here on the first two.

The form of a country's legislative and executive institutions influences the nature of its regulatory problems. The crucial issue is to what extent the structure and organization of these institutions impose constraints upon governmental action. The range of formal institutional mechanisms for restraining governmental authority includes: the explicit separation of powers between legislative, executive, and judicial organs of government;[19] a written constitution limiting the legislative power of the executive, and that can be enforced by the courts; two legislative houses elected under different voting rules;[20] an electoral system calibrated to produce either a proliferation of minority parties or a set of parties whose ability to impose discipline on their legislators is weak;[21] and a federal structure of power, with strong decentralization even to the local level.[22] Utility regulation is likely to be far more credible – and the regulatory problem less severe – in countries with political systems that constrain executive discretion. Note, however, that credibility is often achieved at the expense of flexibility. The same mechanisms that make it difficult to impose arbitrary changes in the rules may also make it difficult to enact sensible rules in the first place, or to efficiently adapt the rules in the face of changing circumstances. Thus, in countries with these types of political institutions, the introduction of reforms may have to await the occurrence of a drastic shock to the political system.

Legislative and executive institutions may also limit a country's regulatory governance options. In some parliamentary systems, for example, the executive has substantial control over both the legislative agenda and legislative outcomes.[23] In such countries, if legislative and executive powers alternate between political parties with substantially different interests, specific legislation need not constitute a viable safeguard against administrative discretion, as changes in the law could follow directly from a change in government.[24] Similarly, if the executive has strong legislative powers, administrative procedures and administrative law by themselves will not be able to constrain the executive, who will tend to predominate over the judiciary in the interpretation of laws. In this case, administrative procedures require some base other than administrative law.

A strong and independent judiciary could serve as the basis for limiting administrative discretion in several ways. For example, the prior development of a body of administrative law opens the governance option of constraining discretion through administrative procedures.[25] Also, a tradition of efficiently upholding contracts and property rights creates the governance option of constraining discretion through the use of formal regulatory contracts (licenses). This option is particularly valuable for countries where the executive has a strong hold over the legislative process. Further, a tradition of judicial independence and efficiency opens the governance option of using administrative tribunals to resolve conflicts between the government and the utility within the contours of the existing regulatory system. Finally, it provides assurances against governmental deviation from specific legislative or constitutional commitments that underpin the regulatory system.

The regulatory challenge therefore lies not just in designing regulatory incentive structures that restrain utilities' monopoly behavioral tendencies but also in designing regulatory governance frameworks that constrain the political and administrative actors who have ultimate jurisdiction over the industry. Designing regulatory institutions that are *flexible* enough to make balanced policy decisions in response to unanticipated events but that are also *rigid* enough to insulate policy from political pressures is a difficult task, however. In the United States, the country with the longest history of private ownership in the utilities sector, the regulatory solution that emerged in the electricity industry during the early twentieth century was to move regulation one step up from local politics. Regulatory authority over electric distribution utilities was moved away from the highly politicized municipal environments towards state-wide independent administrative agencies (state Public Utility Commissions or PUCs) with statutory authority to monitor utility performance and to set final rates. Since PUCs normally operate in systems where legislative power is divided among the executive and two legislative chambers, they generally have substantial autonomy to determine regulatory policy without the threat of legislative over-ride or overwhelming political interference. While PUCs operate under vague statutory objectives ("reasonableness" is the typical criterion for rate structures) and have the power to disallow imprudent or anti-competitive managerial behavior, their decisions cannot be made in an arbitrary fashion. First, the evolution of constitutional interpretation implies that utilities are allowed to earn a fair return on their investments. Second, due process requirements enshrined in states' administrative procedure acts also ensure that PUC rulings must be based on the facts and evidence of the case (Vanden Bergh 1998). In the event of disputes, utilities are able to challenge the PUC on both statutory and constitutional grounds in state and federal courts which, given the nature of judicial appointments (and in the state courts, of the reelection

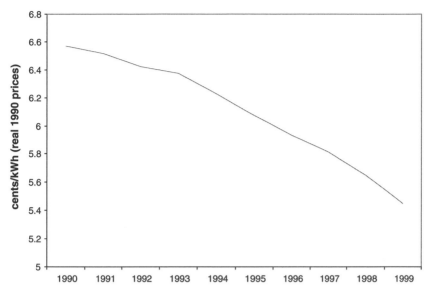

Figure 25.1   US retail electricity rates, 1990–1999
Note: Price is calculated as average revenue per kWh.
Source: US Energy Information Administration.

process), normally operate independently of the political establishment (Spiller and Vanden Bergh 1997). In the electricity sector, a second level of protection against local opportunistic behavior resides in the fact that wholesale electricity generation markets, given the interconnection across states of transmission grids, are regulated at the federal rather than at the state level.[26] Given their independence and nation-wide range of interests, federal agencies are less able to be manipulated by local or state officials. Private investors thus have some assurance that regulatory policy will be protected from immediate political pressures as well as from agency arbitrariness. Although hard to assess, it appears that this regulatory arrangement has balanced utility and political tensions reasonably well: electricity costs, for example, are low compared to most other countries (IEA 2000), and investment levels in generation, distribution, and transmission capacity have usually ensured reliable network operations. Furthermore, since the deregulation process started across the states, electricity costs and prices have been falling (see figure 25.1),[27] and investment levels in generation have been gathering speed (Rose 2000).

In contrast to the United States, the utilities sector in almost all other countries operated under state ownership for most of the second half of the twentieth century. This, however, did not exempt utilities from the risk of governmental opportunism.[28] As many of these countries have sought to partially or fully privatize their electricity sectors over the last two decades, they have needed to create regulatory institutions that simultaneously restrain private operators from exploiting their incumbency advantage and yet credibly commit to not expropriate their returns. Designing regulatory frameworks that satisfactorily achieve this balance is not a straightforward task, though. The ability to infuse credibility depends not only on the willingness of the current government, but also on the country's broader political, administrative, and judicial institutions. Regulatory institutions, then, must be tailored to the specific circumstances of the country at hand and may not be simply transplanted from other countries (Levy and Spiller 1994).

In sections 3 and 4 we illustrate the critical role that regulatory institutions play in the performance of privately-owned electricity sectors. In section 3, we examine some recent international aid agency proposals for electricity sector reforms that emphasize industry structural solutions over regulatory institutional reform. By introducing an institutional perspective, as described above, we suggest that structural reform by itself, without attention to the reform of regulatory institutions, will have only a minimal impact on industry performance. While we propose these arguments at a general level, we go on in section 4 to explore in detail the impact of regulatory institutions on industry outcomes in three countries, El Salvador, the United Kingdom and the United States (California), each of which differs in its regulatory incentive and governance frameworks.

3   "Optimal" restructuring myths in the electricity industry

The decision to privatize state-owned electricity assets naturally raises a series of questions about the optimal organizational approach to transferring assets to private owners. Should all asset types, whether generation plants, high-voltage and distribution networks, be privatized or should private ownership be limited to the sectors where competitive markets can be feasibly implemented? And, if markets are small, should competition be attempted? In the former case, what is the optimal degree of vertical integration between privately owned generation, transmission, and distribution activities, bearing in mind that investments or operational decisions in one sector can have important consequences for operational efficiency in other sectors? Similarly, given the need for investment and real-time operational coordination between, as well as within, geographic regions, what is the optimal level of horizontal fragmentation?

Although policy-makers and government advisors have paid considerable attention to these and other issues in the development of reform programs, there is little empirical evidence to suggest that one particular structural configuration of a fully or partially privatized electricity industry is more conducive for long-term private investment than another. In spite of the heated debate among advocates of particular reform policies, the experience of various countries suggests that no single organizational structure obviously trumps another.[29] To illustrate, we examine several of the common structural prescriptions for encouraging private investment in transmission, distribution, and generation assets.

3.1 Transmission investment

Myth 1 Large economies of coordination imply that vertical separation of transmission and generation or lack of a transmission monopoly will lead to inefficient investments

Transmission networks play a critical role in ensuring a low-cost and reliable supply of electricity. In the absence of transmission-capacity constraints, electricity generated in one region is able to flow to other regions where local generation supplies are either insufficient to meet demand, or else are relatively costly compared to out-of-area supplies. The construction of additional transmission infrastructure can therefore serve as a partial substitute for building extra generation capacity when demand and supply are uneven across regions. For this reason, vertical integration between transmission and generation functions is sometimes seen as an efficient organizational structure for a newly privatized industry, particularly when the size of the market is small. A vertically integrated owner faces incentives to invest in generation and/or transmission assets in a manner that minimizes combined generation and transmission costs, whereas under separate ownership contracting difficulties may prevent such an outcome, potentially leading to under-investment.

While efficiency rationales have led to proposals for vertically integrated, horizontally concentrated industry structures, concerns about the exercise of market power on the other hand have led to opposing recommendations. Difficulties in setting and regulating efficient transmission charges, so it is argued, enable vertically integrated suppliers to devise charging structures that favor their own generation plants over those of competitors in dispatch decisions (Newbery 1999). By separating the ownership of transmission and generation assets, the incentives for transmission owners to discriminate against particular generation companies are reduced, thereby encouraging efficient entry into the generation sector.[30]

Table 25.1. *Organizational and ownership structure of competitive wholesale electricity markets*

| Country | Ownership | | | Installed capacity (MW)[1] | Vertical integration allowed[2] | # Firms | |
	Generation	Distribution	Transmission			Transmission	Distribution
Argentina	Private	Private	Private	22,000	No	7	25+
Australia (Victoria)	Private	Private	Private	6,700	No	1	5
Chile	Private	Private	Private	8,000	Yes	4	20
UK	Private	Private	Private	70,000	No	1	12
Peru	Mostly private	Mostly public	Public	5,000	No	2	7
Bolivia	Mostly private	Mostly public	Private	950	No	1	24
Colombia	Mostly private	Mostly public	Public	15,000	Yes	1	25+
Spain	Mostly private	Mostly private	Mostly private	43,000	No	1	17
USA	Mostly private	Mostly private	Private	779,000	Yes	200+	3000+
Guatemala	Mostly public	Mostly private	Public	1,300	Yes	1	15
El Salvador	Mostly public	Mostly private	Public	850	Yes	1	5
Finland	Mostly public	Mostly public	Mostly private	16,000	No	2	130
New Zealand	Mostly public	Mostly public	Public	8,000	Yes	1	42
Norway	Mostly public	Mostly public	Mostly public	27,000	No	1	240
Portugal	Mostly public	Mostly public	Mostly public	9,000	Yes	1	4
Sweden	Mostly public	Mostly public	Mostly public	34,000	No	1	270
Ukraine	Public	Public	Public	55,000	No	1	27

Notes:
[1] *Source:* Energy Information Administration, US Department of Energy.
[2] Vertical integration between transmission and generation functions.

The presence of market power concerns thus suggests that the policy of vertically integrating transmission and generation ownership will not necessarily be the optimal restructuring approach, and that the decision will depend on a careful consideration of the pros and cons in each individual situation. Indeed, among countries adopting competitive wholesale markets, there is no uniform preference for vertical separation or integration; approximately 40 percent allow integration, 60 percent forbid it (see table 25.1), suggesting that a "one-size-fits-all" policy of integration is inappropriate.

For the same reasons motivating vertical integration proposals, it has been argued that since efficient investment in national transmission networks also requires coordination *among* operators in various regions, the optimal degree of horizontal fragmentation in transmission under private ownership should be low. Dynamic concerns again contradict efficiency-driven policy recommendations. Generation companies require access to transmission networks in order to compete effectively against rival generation companies. When transmission is organized as a monopoly franchise, implying that generation companies are not free to invest in their own transmission assets, transmission owners are in a position to "hold up" generators through a variety of means. Monopoly transmission owners have an incentive to extract rents from generation companies by manipulating access to the network; for example, by using uncontracted network upgrades or maintenance schedules as bargaining points. A natural solution to this problem is to remove ownership restrictions in the transmission sector to allow generation firms to invest in their own competing transmission assets, thereby creating an *a priori* argument for horizontal fragmentation.

Turning again to the evidence, we find no common consensus in the degree of transmission concentration or fragmentation, raising further doubts about the optimality of the former policy prescription. Out of the eight countries with predominantly privately-owned transmission networks, three have systems that are quite fragmented with four or more owners (see table 25.1).

Myth 2 Public ownership of transmission assets is required to facilitate coordination and efficient investment

Recognizing the plethora of conflicting tensions under private ownership, still others (in particular Labor Party-led European governments) have argued that the best policy is in fact to retain transmission networks under public ownership (Newbery 1999). An important assumption underpinning this proposal is that the government has less incentive to hold up private generators than a private owner of the transmission network.

As we discuss below, however, the highly politicized nature of electricity consumption in all countries makes the industry especially susceptible to government control, irrespective of the ownership structure. Under public transmission ownership, the government may actually find it easier to hold up private generation firms since it has direct control over day-to-day managerial decisions than in the private ownership case where the government may have to pressure a regulatory agency to implement its preferred policy. Thus, while public ownership may allay concerns over the exercise of private market power in transmission it also exposes generation firms to greater political hazards. Indeed, by transferring transmission assets to private owners and by establishing an independent regulatory agency – both actions that are politically difficult to reverse – the government can send a strong signal to the private sector that it will not readily meddle in operational affairs for political ends, thereby encouraging higher levels of private entry in all parts of the electricity sector. Eight out of seventeen countries implementing competitive wholesale markets during the 1990s have done so under private transmission ownership regimes (see table 25.1).[31]

3.2   Generation markets

Myth 3   Economies of scale in generation limit the potential for competition in relatively small markets

In addition to the organization of transmission, governments have several options for reform in the generation sector. Chief among these is the decision to create a competitive wholesale generation market where sellers bid against each other to supply electricity on a continuous basis, with prices determined by a market-making mechanism. Following the lead of Argentina in the 1980s, a number of jurisdictions have made competitive generation markets a central component of privatization and restructuring programs (e.g. Australia, California, Chile, Finland, Norway, Sweden, United Kingdom, Ukraine). Although the introduction of wholesale markets is generally perceived as being a desirable policy goal, questions have been raised about the feasibility of implementing similar reforms in smaller countries where, it is argued, only a small number of generation companies can be supported, leading to an oligopolistic situation. Competitive markets have been established, however, in several small countries where installed capacity is a small fraction of that in larger wholesale markets, such as Bolivia, El Salvador, and Guatemala.[32] Similarly, there have been disastrous results in some large countries; in Ukraine, for instance, repeated attempts by the government and international aid agencies to breathe life into the spot generation market have failed since 1996, and most generation trades are now arranged on an ad hoc bilateral basis among generators and distributors or final consumers.[33] Legal uncertainties about the status of contracts and private property in Ukraine, as well as strong concerns over bureaucratic corruption,[34] have undermined the incentives for entrants to invest in new, more efficient generation capacity, to write long-term contracts and to engage in the spot market. The experience of Ukraine suggests that, rather than geographic or population size, the main constraint on the operational feasibility of wholesale markets is the ability of new generation companies to enter the market, access transmission resources on a non-discriminatory basis, and enter into enforceable contracts with new or existing buyers.

3.3   Distribution investment

Myth 4   Large economies of scale in distribution imply that too much fragmentation of distribution facilities will lead to high distribution costs

Within the distribution sector, perceptions about the degree of scale economies have also led to prescriptions for the optimal level of geographic fragmentation for inducing private sector investment. A common concern is that while horizontal fragmentation of the distribution sector creates regulatory benefits – in that a larger number of companies facilitates "yardstick" regulation – it may also increase distribution costs and encourage inefficient investment decisions if economies of scale are ignored. For this reason, low levels of fragmentation are frequently prescribed in reform programs.

The hypothesized relationship between geographic fragmentation and distribution costs and investment is questionable, however, on several grounds. First, economies of scale in distribution are driven by the *density* of customers, implying that optimal geographic footprints can be very small, and that the degree of fragmentation can be quite large. Thus, in Norway, distribution activities are divided among more than 240 firms and in New Zealand among more than forty. Chile, which started its reforms with a dozen distribution companies, has doubled its number over the period. Secondly, the ability to induce efficient levels of distribution investment depends on private sector expectations about future regulated rates of return and the possibility that once assets have been put in place, attempts will be made by political actors to expropriate their rent streams.

3.4   Summary

Although it is hard to empirically identify the relative success of alternative structural reform policies in terms of encouraging new private investment, the absence of a clear pattern linking the structural nature of industry reforms to performance casts some doubt on the assertion that a single structural approach is uniformly optimal. We suggest that the lack of empirical consensus is not an accident but the indirect result of a commonly held implicit assumption in the debate on optimal restructuring policies, specifically that the supporting regulatory institutions have a neutral impact on the players' behavior. In practice, however, the design of the regulatory governance of the sector has a critical effect on investors' incentives to make long-term asset commitments. In section 4 we explore this proposition in some detail by focusing on the recent experiences of three countries, each of which differs substantially in its regulatory institutions but each of which came under significant political pressure during the period 2000–1 to reform its wholesale electricity market. As we shall argue, the nature of the regulatory institutions, by more or less insulating regulatory policy from political forces, played a critical role in determining the direction of regulatory reforms.

4   Regulatory responses to market power allegations in the generation sector

Market power allegations have emerged as an unanticipated major policy concern in many jurisdictions that have implemented competitive wholesale power markets over the last decade (Borenstein and Bushnell 2000; Joskow 2000). Unlike most other industries, power generation firms with small as well as large aggregate market shares are sometimes in a position to exploit local market power by raising prices above a competitive level. Given the physical characteristics of electricity network operations, including the need to maintain system reliability, the impossibility of storing electricity, and the existence of local transmission constraints, individual generation plants must occasionally be operated under certain demand and supply conditions to maintain the stability of the network. If generators anticipate that they will be called upon by the system operator to supply electricity to the network almost independently of the offered price, they can bid very high prices for their services in auction settings. Since the short-run price elasticity of demand is relatively low,[35] such prices can reach almost any level unless restrained by demand or capped by administrative rules. Thus, under specific supply and demand rules and scenarios, generators will enjoy substantial local market power. This market power may be limited, however, by contracts between the dispatch entity or final users and the generator, by transmission investments that relieve congestion, or by *de novo* entry.

In addition, the auction rules that govern wholesale generation markets in many jurisdictions are highly complex and susceptible to "gaming" by generators. In the United Kingdom, for example, generation firms were able to withhold capacity from the market in order to drive up the spot market prices for other generating plants, and also employed bidding strategies that achieved the same result but without withholding capacity (Wolfram 1999; Ofgem, 2000). Similar results obtained in California, particularly in the market for ancillary services, leading to significant increases in wholesale prices and in retail rates in some regions.[36] El Salvador also experienced a serious increase in wholesale prices during early 2000, leading to drastic retail price increases.

As a result of the increasing concern with generators gaming trading systems to their advantage,[37] political actors came under pressure during the late 1990s to "fix the system" and to reform regulatory policy through a variety of means. In spite of common political forces, however, regulatory policy responded in dramatically different fashion in the three countries whose recent experiences we examine in greater detail below. While the United Kingdom redesigned the rules governing the power market taking care as much as possible to follow established administrative rules, providing a level of protection for the generation companies, El Salvador responded by shifting *ex post* some of the costs of increased wholesale market prices onto the distribution companies, effectively expropriating some of their quasi-rents, and also by diminishing the role played by the wholesale market. California also reduced the role of the wholesale market though political attempts to move the accumulated costs of high wholesale prices onto the distribution companies, and also onto the generation companies, were limited by the prospect of independent judicial review.

We argue that differences in regulatory governance frameworks, in particular in the rules governing the relationships between regulatory agencies, the courts, and political institutions, played a central role in explaining why different countries adjusted their regulatory policies differently to an unexpected common shock.

4.1   *Market power and regulatory reform in the United Kingdom*

After the Conservative government privatized and restructured the UK electricity industry in 1990, concerns were voiced about the structure and operation of the generation sector, notably over the degree of competition in the newly created power pool. Critics argued that two characteristics of the generation market reforms enabled incumbent generators to exert a strong degree of market power. First, at the time of privatization the government essentially established a generation duopoly by dividing the state-owned Central Electricity Generating Board (CEGB) into two private companies, National Power and PowerGen, with a combined share of national capacity of more than 80 percent, and a third state-owned corporation, Nuclear Electric, holding the CEGB's nuclear assets. Studies have suggested that the presence of two dominant players in the electricity pool facilitated Cournot-style implicit collusion, raising prices, on average, 20–25 percent above marginal costs (Wolfram 1999).[38] The second source of market power lay in the design and governance arrangements of the power pool, the electronic quasi-marketplace that balanced demand and supply on a continuous basis and that generated a single spot price, the System Marginal Price (SMP), in the process. Unlike other competitive wholesale markets, such as in California, El Salvador, or Scandinavia, the UK power pool did not allow negotiated bilateral prices and trades among buyers and sellers, either within or outside the pool, and operated purely on a day-ahead basis.[39] It was compulsory for licensed generators to sell the vast majority of their output through the pool, and contracts were based on the SMP.[40]

The emphasis on the day-ahead price as the lone market clearing mechanism created strong incentives for the generation companies to develop trading strategies that manipulated the pool price through a variety of means. A chosen one was the withholding of capacity to drive up the capacity payments for electricity purchased from other plants in the company's portfolio.[41] The limited involvement from the demand side in the pool also reduced buyer pressure on prices, leading to higher prices overall and taller price spikes than otherwise.[42] Since the committee responsible for the operation of the pool was governed entirely by the industry,[43] administrative attempts by the Director General (DG) of Ofgem, the regulatory agency, to significantly reform the system – so as to reduce the inherent biases in favor of the generation firms – were not surprisingly stymied.[44]

As a consequence of these features, while fuel, operating, and capacity costs for generation fell by 50 percent in the decade after 1990, and in the face of substantial entry by combined cycle operators, wholesale prices for electricity remained largely unchanged,[45] lending considerable support to the claim that incumbent generators exploited a position of market power.

The United Kingdom's *de facto* single-chamber parliamentary system that unites legislative and executive functions might offer the government unbridled opportunities to implement regulatory reforms through legislative means or else by directly pressuring regulatory agencies. As a consequence, at the time of industry privatization, the government undertook a variety of institutional designs precisely to, on the one hand, provide the government with flexibility in the design of regulatory policies while at the same time safeguarding the rights of interested parties. This allowed the UK government to respond to the market power issue and to commence a broad consultative process of redesigning the generation sector.

At the administrative level, regulation is primarily implemented through the award of long-term licenses to generators that specify their rights and obligations, as well as those of the regulatory agency, Ofgem, which has broad oversight responsibility for the industry. Licenses include the procedures for firms to appeal Ofgem decisions, which in this case consists of a complex set of checks and balances involving appeals to the Competition Commission (the UK anti-trust agency, formerly known as the "Monopolies and Mergers Commission") and a potential veto by the Secretary of State.[46] Thus, the appeals process provides some protection to the firms by limiting the ability of the DG to unilaterally change regulatory policy. Within this framework, Ofgem retains considerable flexibility in the design of policy since few quantified objectives or constraints are written in statute. For example, Ofgem has considerable discretion over final rates, making periodic determinations about price cap levels, without requiring formal political approval.

The formal authority enjoyed by Ofgem to regulate the industry on an independent basis is reinforced by the existence among the highly expert civil service of a strong norm of administrative independence, making direct political interference in the design of regulatory policy, except in highly unusual circumstances, damaging to the government in terms of its public reputation and support within the administration. In addition, the judicial system has a strong tradition of probity in upholding contracts. Indeed, the courts have ruled against the government in the past, providing further reassurance for license holders against administrative expropriation (Baldwin and McCrudden 1987).[47]

The balance of flexibility (through administrative means) and protection of private-property rights (through the use of licenses, administrative constraints, and judicial norms) inherent in the UK regulatory governance framework is apparent in the way that the Labour government reformed the generation sector after coming to office in 1997. In the first instance, the government enacted reforms mostly through the existing "rules of the game" (i.e. administrative procedures specified in company licenses), and did not initially resort to legislation.[48] The DG sought to introduce a "market abuse" clause in the generation companies' licenses – allowing the DG to penalize anti-competitive behavior in the new wholesale market – using the amendment procedure specified in the licenses, rather than relying on the government to achieve a similar end with targeted legislation.[49] Indeed, two generation companies, after exercising their right to refer the matter for independent determination to the Competition Commission, succeeded in gaining a ruling from the Competition Commission that struck down the DG's proposal.[50] While the Secretary of State for Trade and Industry could have overridden the Competition Commission, using the powers provided by the Utilities Act 2000 to unilaterally modify existing licenses as part of the provisions for establishing NETA, it elected instead to defer to the agency's decision.

Reforming the workings of the wholesale market (i.e. the pool), on the other hand, required the government to resort to legislation since under the original system the DG had no administrative authority to initiate changes in the rules governing the pool. After it became clear that the generation plant divestments that occurred under the Conservative government during the mid-1990s had not effectively reduced the ability of incumbents to manipulate the pool price, the Labour government elected in mid-1997 quickly initiated a consultation exercise on reform options. Although the government announced its intention to legislate, it placed considerable emphasis on allowing Ofgem, and interested parties, through an extensive consultation process, to shape the design of the NETA. The DG published initial proposals for reform in July 1998.[51] These were accepted by the government in October 1998 in the form of a White Paper,[52] which commenced a lengthy public review exercise,[53] and which culminated with the issue by the DG and the Secretary of State for Trade and Industry of the NETA in October 1999.[54] Implementation of the NETA eventually occurred during mid-2001.[55] Affected parties, then, had substantial opportunity to organize, to lobby ministers and Ofgem, and in general to make their views known publicly and privately.[56] As a result of this process, although the NETA implied a drastic reform of the operation of the wholesale market,[57] it achieved a substantial level of consensus among industry players.

4.2   *Market power and regulatory reform in California*

While the new Labour government in the United Kingdom moved relatively quickly and in a considered manner to mitigate market power issues with a series of significant legislative and administrative reforms, regulatory reform in California proceeded at a slower and more ad hoc pace. This was not the result of a more smoothly operating generation market, however. The California Power Exchange (PX) and the Independent

System Operator (ISO)[58] differed from the original UK "Pool" in that buyers and sellers – excluding, however, most of the demand that arose from the main investor-owned utilities who had to buy all their requirements from the PX – were able to negotiate bilateral trades, which were then submitted for dispatch to the ISO. The presence of local transmission constraints meant that individual generation plants were sometimes able to charge prices well above long-run competitive levels, especially in the market for ancillary services. One study estimated that energy purchase costs in California averaged 16 percent above competitive levels during 1998 and 1999, with substantially greater multiples during periods of peak demand – including the summer of 2000 (Borenstein, Bushnell and Wolak 2000).[59] Such discrepancies over long-run marginal costs were also reinforced by a lengthy and cumbersome state-approval process for new generation projects. Out of 20,000MW of new capacity that reached the planning stages after deregulation (representing a 44 percent increase on the installed capacity base of 45,000MW), only a small fraction had come on-line by 2001 (Oren and Spiller 2000). Also, new entry by Energy Service Providers (ESPs) was impeded by the original restructuring legislation (Assembly Bill AB 1890) in 1996 that fixed retail rates at a 10 percent discount over June 10, 1996 levels, reducing the incentives for ESPs to market stable rate plans to consumers. Market structure and impediments to new entry thus both contributed to increased wholesale electricity prices.

Crisis level was initially reached during the summer of 2000 when the combination of high natural gas prices, warm weather, and extremely limited spare capacity reserves pushed spot energy prices to unprecedented levels (see figure 25.2). In the PX Day-Ahead market, for example, spot prices reached a peak of $470/MWh during May 2000, more than nine times the peak during the previous May.[60] For the investor-owned distribution utilities, who had been required to purchase all their supplies through the PX and were subject to retail rate caps, this meant a substantial postponement in the recovery of their uneconomic costs, as increased power purchase costs could not be passed through to consumers.[61] When retail caps were released for one utility in the southern parts of the state, as per the original legislative schedule, PX prices were passed straight through to consumers leading to final bill increases of two or three times in magnitude.[62] Naturally, these large and unexpected wealth transfers away from final consumers increased political pressure for regulatory reform.

By December 2000 the crisis had intensified rather than abated. Sustained high spot prices throughout the latter half of 2000 had substantially depleted utilities' cash reserves and generated accumulated operating

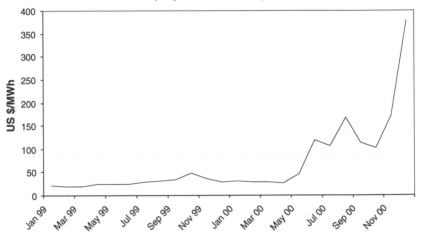

Figure 25.2   Unit spot price, California wholesale market, January 1999–November 2000

losses of $12 billion, leading to concerns about their ability to finance fuel supply and non-utility energy purchases. Independent power producers, who in early 2000 had been willing to sign long-term contracts with the utilities but were prohibited from doing so by the CPUC, were now unwilling to sell electricity on any credit terms, demanding immediate payment up-front.[63] When the utilities defaulted on nearly $1 billion in short-term debt in early February 2001, by which time credit agencies had already downgraded their bond ratings, fuel supplies were assured only by a FERC emergency ruling ordering natural gas suppliers to continue sales to the Californian utilities. The rapid deterioration in the utilities' financial position, as well as that of the ISO, eventually led to a precipitous fall in the stock prices of Pacific Gas and Electric (PG&E) and Southern California Edison, the two major Californian utilities, and PG&E's filing for bankruptcy in early 2001.

In addition to the financial stresses in the electricity sector, increasing strain was being placed on the physical infrastructure as available generation capacity, both within and outside the state, proved insufficient during peak demand periods. Although Stage 1 and Stage 2 network emergencies had occasionally been declared in previous months, January was the first time that Stage 3 emergencies were declared and, in addition, for successive days and weeks, with large sections of the customer base experiencing rolling blackouts.[64] Thus, for the first time, large numbers of voter–consumers were feeling the real and financial effects of what was commonly referred to as the "energy crisis,"[65] ultimately forcing the state governor, Gray Davis, to declare a state of emergency on January 17, 2001.

Compared to the United Kingdom, implementing regulatory reforms at legislative and administrative levels in California, and in the United States more generally, is frequently a more difficult and lengthy exercise, lending considerable weight to status quo policies. First, as a result of the nation's federal structure, as well as of its separation of political powers, legislative policy changes require the agreement of multiple institutions, all of which are subject to judicial review. Thus, in the presence of divergent interests it can be difficult to find mutually preferable new proposals that also survive judicial review.[66] Consequently, drastic changes in regulatory policy – those that entail a redistribution of wealth among competing interest groups – are difficult to implement as the losing coalition will lobby against adoption. Thus, when political interests are fragmented, dramatic legislative proposals tend to be watered down with compromises reflecting political rather than economic logic.

Second, while the US system of political checks and balances insulates interest groups against unfavorable *legislative* reforms, the logic of political delegation also ensures that regulatory agencies do not rapidly implement substantial policy changes against the wishes of their political principals through *administrative* means. A variety of governance mechanisms are used to safeguard against rapid administrative decision-making which may distort legislators' preferences. Legislators undertake committee hearings, appointments of officials are reviewed, and agencies are subject to administrative procedures and due process requirements that provide interest groups with a role in decision-making procedures. Thus, even if the threat of legislative over-ride is not credible, agency decisions cannot drift too far too fast from the status quo.[67]

The combination of multiple legislative veto points, administrative controls, and independent judicial review tends to insulate status quo public policies and the interests of stakeholder groups from dramatic reform. This is especially apparent in the political acrobatics undertaken by the Calfornia legislature and governor in their attempts to reform the wholesale market and at the same time to protect ratepayer interests.[68]

Owing to potentially adverse electoral consequences, the government, which consisted of the first Democrat legislative and executive coalition in several decades, was unwilling to make consumers directly feel the pressure of high wholesale prices. Although higher retail prices were needed both to promote conservation and to bring the utilities back to credit-worthiness, the legislature instead enacted a bill, AB 1X, that made the state the main intermediate energy purchaser, by-passing almost completely the wholesale PX market. In early February the state commenced negotiations for up to $10 billion in long-term supply contracts with generation companies within and outside California, which would then be sold on to the distribution utilities, eliminating the credit risk inherent in the poor financial situation of the utilities. This had two politically beneficial effects. First, by effectively disbanding the PX in favor of negotiated contracts, the governor claimed to have eliminated the exercise of market power by generation companies during times of peak demand, thereby substantially lowering average energy prices. The operating losses of the utilities would therefore be staunched and consumers would be protected against future additional rate increases. Secondly, by controlling the price at which the distribution utilities purchased their power, the government gained the option to not pass on the full costs of energy purchases to final consumers. Thus, although consumers would ultimately pay for this arrangement indirectly through higher state taxes and/or through partially increased rates, the impact would be less visible than in the case of full rate increases, and the government retained greater flexibility to spread the tax burden away from voter–consumers and over future tax-paying generations. This would limit the immediate political damage of the crisis but also postpone the resolution of the problem.

While ratepayers found a natural ally in the governing Democrat political coalition, institutional structures afforded a strong degree of protection for the generation companies and their shareholders, in this case from the intense adverse political pressure within California. The original governance arrangements of the California ISO, which was responsible for the operation of the transmission network, reflect the principle of incorporating multiple interest groups in administrative structures. The enabling statute specified that the governing board consist of representatives of "investor-owned utility transmission owners, publicly owned utility transmission owners, nonutility electricity sellers, public buyers and sellers, private buyers and sellers, industrial end-users, commercial end-users, residential end-users, agricultural end-users, public interest groups and nonmarket participant[s]."[69] Since ISO decisions required a majority vote, the diversity of interests represented on the board ensured that radical proposals would likely be vetoed.[70] The generation companies could thus organize against, and potentially veto, reforms proposed by competing stake holder groups that would threaten their interests, for example regarding price cap levels or sanctions for facility operation or maintenance transgressions.

Further protection for the generation companies stemmed from the fact that most major policy decisions concerning the operation of the power markets still required the agreement of FERC, which had jurisdiction over transmission pricing issues. Proposals for changes in ISO price cap levels, for example, had to acquire FERC approval before being implemented. Similarly, ISO decisions to impose sanctions on transmission facility owners for inadequate operation or maintenance practices were also subject to FERC approval. Although dramatic proposals for regulatory reform were unlikely to emanate from the ISO, FERC had the authority to implement changes at the ISO that reduced incumbent generation companies' market power. However, as a federal agency, FERC had little incentive to make changes that simply gained political capital within California. Although it could "punish" generation companies and appropriate past financial gains without demonstrating abuse of market power, as a federal agency the implications for investments throughout the nation would overcome any rush to expropriate rents within the California market.

In sum, the plurality of interests embedded within the administrative structure of the wholesale markets implied that agencies could not drastically swing regulatory policies to consumers' short-term advantage – tightening wholesale price caps or otherwise recouping windfall profits – in response to external political pressure. The generation companies and shareholders that profited from relatively high wholesale energy prices were therefore fairly secure from having their gains directly or indirectly expropriated.

While political and institutional factors insulated the interests of two major stake holder groups, ratepayers and generators, in the reform process, the experience of the distribution utilities was more mixed. The utilities' profits were highly exposed to wholesale price fluctuations since the 1996 restructuring legislation originally froze retail rates at a specified level until either the utilities' stranded generation costs had been recovered or until January 2002 at the latest. Without the fulfillment of either of these conditions, the utilities were unable to automatically pass on higher purchased energy costs to consumers in the form of higher rates, resulting in substantial accumulated financial losses by early 2001.

The utilities' financial distress need not have been the default outcome, however, since the CPUC had some discretion to revalue the utilities' generation assets during 2000 and hence to relax the fixed retail rate constraint. According to the original 1996 restructuring legislation, AB 1890, the CPUC was required to value the utilities' generation assets, in order to estimate their stranded assets, by the end of December 2001 at the latest.[71] Despite repeated requests by the utilities to revalue their assets during 2001, the CPUC refused to do so. Given the high wholesale energy prices at the time and thereafter, a revaluation would have resulted in a large downward revision of the magnitude of the utilities' stranded costs, thereby triggering the removal of the retail price caps. Exposing consumers to the full cost of wholesale energy purchases, however, could have created a political backlash similar to that which took place in San Diego. The Governor, and the CPUC, however, did not seem interested in releasing retail rates. Instead, the CPUC utilized its discretion to avoid having to evaluate PG&E's stranded assets, and, thus, force it to finance the rate freeze. This is the type of opportunistic behavior which by not following the intent of the 1996 legislation – to provide a fair valuation of the utilities' stranded assets – effectively expropriated much of the utilities' sunk investments.

Despite the apparent opportunism of the CPUC in this instance, the US regulatory governance system provides measures that can reverse such outcomes or else restrict their frequency of occurrence. Specifically, the courts provide an additional check in the determination of regulatory policy. Agency decisions are subject to judicial review and federal legal precedent stipulates that utilities are entitled to a fair rate of return on their investments.[72] Furthermore, agency decision-making procedures are governed by a well-developed body of administrative law, limiting their ability for making rulings, and agencies and legislatures cannot penalize utilities without first demonstrating managerial imprudence or malfeasance. The role of the courts in the broader public policy process was evident in California where the utilities turned to the state and federal courts in an attempt to shift regulatory policy in their favor. PG&E filed a case in the California Supreme Court concerning the losses it had sustained in the PX during 2000 and also a case in a federal court requesting an injunction against the CPUC to raise consumer bills by more than $3.4 billion.[73] Although PG&E ultimately filed for bankruptcy, its timing may be interpreted as a strategic move to seek judicial resolution in the absence of a political solution to its inability to pay creditors. Southern California Edison also adopted a judicial strategy, using a previously filed lawsuit against the CPUC to gain leverage in negotiating a settlement with the agency in October 2001.

Litigation thus provides utilities with an additional avenue to protect their interests, though the emphasis on due process in the judicial system guarantees that in complex cases with multiple intervenors, ultimate resolutions are reached only after a substantial time interval.

While market events in the Californian electricity industry eventually catalyzed political pressure for regulatory reform, the complex set of checks and balances characteristic of the US policy-making environment suggests that the market power issue would be unlikely to trigger policy changes that drastically disadvantaged the major interest groups involved.

Although one of the California utilities was driven towards bankruptcy, and another lost half of its market value, the political acrobatics undertaken by the governor and the legislature were intended to avoid both judicial review and a political backlash. Thus, the web of judicial protection and multiple layers of authority in a fragmented polity assure investors, to a large extent, that their quasi-rents will not be easily taken away by administrative fiat. Although the unexpected shock associated with the increase in wholesale market prices generated a serious financial crisis for the utilities and substantial political heat, the basic governance provides for multiple checks on arbitrary decision-making, such that a resolution of the crisis could be in sight without affecting the long-term investment incentives of the various players.[74]

4.3   Market power and regulatory reform in El Salvador

El Salvador started to consider the reform of its electricity market in 1991 when the government created the Executive Committee for the Energy Project as an inter-ministerial committee to participate in a World Bank funded project whose purpose was to promote competition in the sector. In 1995 a private generation company started operating a 127MW thermal plant in the form of a Build–Operate–Own (BOO) project with CEL, the public generation and transmission company.[75] In 1996 the Salvadorean Assembly passed the 1996 General Electricity Act. Among other things, the 1996 Act created a wholesale market with programmed dispatch based on bilateral or multilateral contracts coupled with a balancing market, eliminated franchise monopolies in the distribution and transmission sector, created an independent dispatch operator (composed, as the California ISO, of stake holders), instituted open access to transmission and distribution facilities, regulated charges for the use of both types of networks, and required the publicly owned generation and transmission company to create a separate transmission company.

The wholesale market started operating in January 1998 following the privatization of four distribution companies. The initial effect of the creation of the wholesale market was a slight drop in wholesale prices. While prior to the start of the wholesale market in 1998 prices to distributors were around 8¢ per kWh, from January 1998 onwards, prices tended to move in the 6–8¢ range (see figure 25.3). In August 1999, CEL sold its thermal park composed of three thermal plants to Duke Energy International. As figure 25.3 shows, prices started to increase shortly thereafter, reaching a peak of 17¢ per kWh in April 2000, and falling then to more normal levels in May 2000 following the signature of a long-term contract between CEL and Duke for approximately 50 percent of Duke's capacity.

US¢/kWh (May 2000 Prices)

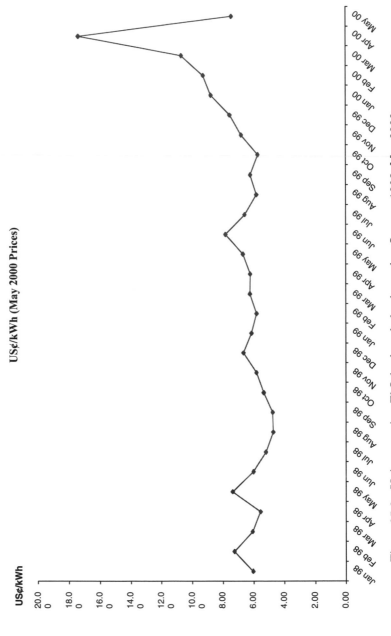

Figure 25.3   Unit spot price, El Salvador wholesale market, January 1998–May 2000

The drastic price increase in early 2000 generated substantial political problems. The 1996 Act required the indexation of the retail tariffs to the evolution of wholesale market prices. An Executive Decree interpreted the indexation to have two components: a quarterly indexation and an annual indexation. Once a year tariffs would be "reset" so that the average increase in the previous year would be translated into the new tariff structure. Within the year, tariffs were adjusted quarterly if the price increase during the quarter exceeded 10 percent. In July 2000 the quarterly indexation would have implied a substantial increase in prices, as wholesale prices in the first quarter of 2000 were more than 50 percent above prices in the prior quarter. This, on top of an important increase in the retail tariffs for the first quarter,[76] triggered substantial political concerns. Although a careful analysis of the situation shows that Duke and CEL were essentially keeping prices high during the last quarter of 1999 and the first quarter of 2000,[77] the government and the press placed the emphasis on imports from Guatemala and on the presumed high profits of the private distribution companies. Pressure grew to reverse the 1996 Electricity Act to regulate wholesale prices and to further regulate the profits of the distribution companies.

The government responded to the political pressure in three fundamental ways: first, it amended its interpretation of the 1996 Act, second it instituted direct subsidies to the residential users, and, third, CEL entered into a contract with Duke Energy for a substantial portion of Duke's capacity. The impact of these three acts was, first, to expropriate a substantial part of the distribution companies quasi-rents: the change in the Executive Decree interpreting the 1996 Act was undertaken in August 2000, just prior to when the third-quarter indexation was to take place. It essentially eliminated the adjustment that would have compensated the distribution companies for the losses they had incurred when the wholesale price was above the retail tariff. By modifying the interpretation of the law just prior to the introduction of the compensating adjustment, the intertemporal compensation was eliminated. The second effect was to expropriate a substantial portion of the public generation company's quasi-rents: during 1999 the subsidies that the government required CEL to provide to the distribution companies were approximately equal to all of its pre-tax operating profits.[78] Finally, via the contract with Duke, the government monopolized the operation of the wholesale market in the hands of CEL.[79]

Although these three actions had a direct impact on retail tariffs, thus alleviating an important short-term political problem, they may have a major impact on the viability of the competitive framework, creating a long-term problem for the country. On the one hand the contract with

Duke eliminated the incentive that Duke might have had to limit supply into the market.[80] Since the CEL/Duke contract price is based on Duke's operating costs, Duke will not benefit from limiting the availability of its remaining 15 percent of the generation capacity.[81] Thus, the fall that took place in prices in May 2000 can be directly related to the CEL/Duke contract. On the other hand, the subsidies granted by CEL[82] and the reform of the interpretation of the 1996 Act softened the impact of the price spike on consumers.[83] Indeed, following the reduction in the spot price, the government substantially reduced the subsidies.[84]

The speed with which the government, and government entities like CEL, moved, and the redistributive character of the reforms, raises substantial questions about the nature of the governance structure of the sector. Indeed, a close examination shows that the regulatory governance of the sector is very weak, raising questions about its ability to sustain private investment in the long run.

El Salvador is a Presidential republic with a single-chamber Legislative Assembly.[85] The Salvadorean Supreme Court justices do not have life tenure, and the legislature renews the justices' appointments. As a consequence, the judiciary is highly sensitive to political issues and is subject to substantial legislative control. The lack of judicial independence is particularly problematic given the ability of the president to interpret legislation via Executive Decrees.[86] Since attempts to overturn Executive Decrees that have support in the legislature are unlikely to be supported by the courts, it is not surprising that, differing from the distribution companies in California, the Salvadorean utilities have not filed suits against the government for a change in its interpretation of the 1996 Act which has cost them several million dollars.

The regulatory governance regime, then, provides for a high level of regulatory flexibility, and hence may generate credibility problems which, in the long run, will tend to discourage private investment. The 1996 Act, however, provides no further instruments to limit the government discretion. Although the Act could have been substantially more specific and, in particular, it could have not granted the government the ability to regulate retail prices, it did. Granting the government the ability to regulate final tariffs, the legislature opened a Pandora's box, where the executive, via decrees, can modify more or less at its pleasure the nature of such regulation. Had the 1996 Act not granted the government the right to set retail prices, the government could have still expropriated CEL's quasi-rents and entered into a contract with Duke,[87] but it would not have been able to affect the profitability of the distribution companies.

This case shows, then, that in institutional environments with few checks and balances, regulatory frameworks have to place particular emphasis on limiting the discretion of the government, rather than in granting flexibility. The 1996 Act failed to do so, and thus created a serious credibility crisis.

5   Final comments

Electricity reforms are being undertaken throughout the world. Much emphasis is being placed on industry-structure issues. This chapter emphasizes that although industrial structure is important – affecting market power and efficiency considerations – a more fundamental issue is the regulatory governance of the sector. By looking at how three countries reacted to alleged instances of exploitation of market power in wholesale energy markets, we show how governance structures determine the degree to which regulatory policies respond to partisan political pressures. The case of El Salvador illustrates how weak governance regimes, characterized here by a paucity of legislative checks and balances, a politicized judiciary, and considerable executive discretion, can lead to policy reforms in the presence of economic shocks that effectively expropriate certain interest groups. Here, the government insulated final consumers from the full impact of increased wholesale prices by implementing substantial subsidies. It did so at the expense of the private distribution companies by *ex post* manipulating the pricing mechanism such that the distribution companies could not fully adjust final rates to compensate for higher wholesale prices in the recent past, thereby expropriating some of their quasi-rents. The government also appropriated the profits of the state generating company to further subsidize final consumers.

On the other hand, countries such as the United Kingdom, with stronger regulatory governance structures can weather the political storms associated with spiking wholesale prices without engendering credibility crises in the industry. In the United States, the presence of multiple checks and balances, at legislative, administrative, and judicial levels, limits the scope for implementing policy changes that drastically redistribute rents between interest groups. The generation companies, being regulated primarily by *federal* agencies, were insulated from direct *state-level* political pressures to appropriate some of their financial gains previously earned in the power market. The distributors, however, were exposed to opportunistic behavior by the CPUC. However, the option of independent judicial review, including bankruptcy proceedings, provides an opportunity for the distribution companies to recoup some of their losses by challenging agency and legislature policy decisions. In the United Kingdom, strong norms of judicial and agency independence, and a complex system of administrative checks and balances, also provided reassurance for investors while simultaneously allowing the government to implement policy reforms.

In the United Kingdom and to some extent in California, strong regulatory governance structures protected regulatory policy, and investors' interests, from the immediate political pressures to implement industry reforms that would directly or indirectly expropriate their assets or revenue streams.

Finally, for policy-makers, our chapter argues that governments should emphasize the appropriate match of the sectoral regulatory governance framework to the nature of their political, judicial, and administrative institutions. In instances where institutions do not provide for a system of substantial checks and balances, the regulatory governance regime should be substantially rigid, so that unexpected shocks, which will always come, do not reverse the progress already undertaken in reform programs.

NOTES

We would like to thank Ioannis Kessides and David Newbery for their persistent questioning and Richard Green for helpful comments. All remaining errors are naturally our own.

1. This section draws heavily on Spiller (1996).
2. Specific or sunk investments are those, once undertaken, whose value in alternative uses is substantially below their investment cost.
3. See, among others; Goldberg (1976); Williamson (1988b); Barzel (1989); North (1990); Levy and Spiller (1993, 1994).
4. Observe that the source of financing does not change this computation. For example, if the company is completely leveraged, a price below average cost will bring the company to bankruptcy, eliminating the part of the debt associated with the sunk investments. Only the part of the debt that is associated with the value of the non-sunk investments would be able to be subsequently serviced.
5. Observe that this incentive exists both for public *and* private companies. (See Spiller and Savedoff 2000.)
6. The company will be willing to continue operating because its return from operating will exceed its return from shutting down and deploying its assets elsewhere. On the other hand, the firm will have very little incentive to invest new capital as it will not be able to obtain a return. While it is feasible to conceive loan financing for new investments, as non-repayment would bring the company to bankruptcy, that will not however be the case. Bankruptcy does not mean that the company shuts down. Since the assets are specific, bankruptcy implies a change of ownership from stock holders to creditors. Now creditors' incentives to operate will be the same as the firm, and they would be willing to operate even if quasi-rents are expropriated. Thus, loan financing will not be feasible either.
7. Consider, for example, the case of Montevideo's Gas Company (MGC). Throughout the 1950s and 1960s the MGC, owned and operated by a British company, was denied price increases. Eventually, during the rapid inflation of

the 1960s it went bankrupt and was taken over by the government. Compare this example to the expropriation by the Perón administration of ITT's majority holdings in the Unión Telefónica del Rio de la Plata (UTRP), (UTRP was the main provider of telephones in the Buenos Aires region). In 1946 the Argentinean government paid US$95 million for ITT's holdings, or US$623 million in 1992 prices. Given UTRP's 457,800 lines, it translates at US$1,360 per line in 1992 prices (deflator: capital equipment producer prices). Given that in today's prices, the marginal cost of a line in a large metropolitan city is approximately US$650, the price paid by the Perón administration does not seem unusually low. See Hill and Abdala (1996).

8. See, Goldberg (1976) for one of the first treatments of this problem. See also Williamson (1976).

9. Indeed, the Colombian regulation of value added networks specifically stipulates that the government cannot set their prices, nor that there are any exclusivity provisions. Thus, regulation here means total lack of governmental discretion.

10. On this, see more below.

11. Williamson's basic contracting schema applies here. See Williamson (1995).

12. An alternative way of reducing the specificity of the firm's investment is by customers undertaking the financing of the sunk assets.

13. In this sense it is not surprising that private telecommunications operators have rushed to develop cellular rather than fixed-link networks in Eastern European countries. While cellular has a higher long-run cost than fixed link, and on some quality dimensions is also an inferior product, the magnitude of investment in specific assets is much smaller than in fixed-link networks. Furthermore, a large portion of the specific investments in cellular telephony is undertaken by the customers themselves (who purchase the handsets).

14. The privatization of Argentina's telecommunications companies is particularly illuminating. Prior to the privatization, telephone prices were raised well beyond international levels. It is not surprising that, following the privatization, the government reneged on aspects of the license such as price indexation. The initial high prices, though, allowed the companies to remain profitable, even following the government's deviation from the license provisions. See Levy and Spiller (1993).

15. The concept of regulation as a design problem was first introduced in Levy and Spiller (1993). Here we use the terminology subsequently developed in Levy and Spiller (1994).

16. Williamson would call such constraints on regulatory decision making "contractual governance institutions." (See Williamson 1985, p. 35.)

17. Commenting on the interaction among technology (institutions), governance, and price (regulatory detail) Williamson (1985, p. 36) says, "[i]n as much as price and governance are linked, parties to a contract should not expect to have their cake (low price) and eat it too (no safeguard)." In other words, there is no "free institutional lunch."

18. This section draws heavily on Levy and Spiller (1994).

19. For analysis of the role of separation of powers in diminishing the discretion of the executive, see Gely and Spiller (1990) and McCubbins, Noll and Weingast (1987, 1989), and the references therein.

20. Non-simultaneous elections for the different branches of government tend to create natural political divisions and thus electoral checks and balances. (See Jacobson 1990.) For an in-depth analysis of the determinants of the relative powers of the executive, see Shugart and Carey (1992).

21. Electoral rules also have important effects on the effective number of parties that will tend to result from elections, and thus, the extent of governmental control over the legislative process. For example, it is widely perceived that proportional representation tends to generate a large number of parties, while first-past-the-post with relatively small district elections tends to create bipolar party configurations. This result has been coined *Duverger's Law* in political science. More generally, see Taagepera and Shugart (1993). For analyses of how the structure of political parties depends on the nature of electoral rules (with applications to the United Kingdom) see Cain, Ferejohn and Fiorina (1987) and Cox (1987).

22. On the role of federalism in reducing the potential for administrative discretion see Weingast (1995), and the references therein.

23. While parliamentary systems grant such powers in principle, whether they do so in practice depends upon the nature of electoral rules and the political party system. Parliamentary systems whose electoral rules bring about fragmented legislatures would not provide the executive – usually headed by a minority party with a coalition built on a very narrow set of specific common interests – with much scope for legislative initiative. By contrast, electoral rules that create strong two-party parliamentary systems – as well as some other kinds of non-parliamentary political institutions – would grant the executive large legislative powers. For an in-depth discussion of the difference between parliamentary and presidential systems, and the role of electoral rules in determining the relative power of the executive, see Shugart and Carey (1992).

24. In the United Kingdom, regulatory frameworks have traditionally evolved through a series of acts of Parliament. For example, major gas regulation legislation was passed in 1847, 1859, 1870, 1871, 1873, and 1875. Similarly, water regulation legislation was passed in 1847, 1863, 1870, 1873, 1875, and 1887. Systematic regulation of electricity companies started in 1882, only four years after the inauguration of the first public demonstration of lighting by a public authority. The 1882 Act was followed by major legislation in 1888, 1899, 1919, and 1922, and culminating with the Electricity (Supply) Act of 1926 creating the Central Electricity Board. See Spiller and Vogelsang (1993), for discussions of the evolution of utility regulation in the United Kingdom, and the references therein.

25. This has traditionally been the way administrative discretion is restrained in the United States, as regulatory statutes have tended to be quite vague. For an analysis of the choice of specificity of statutes, see Schwartz, Spiller and Urbiztondo (1994). Observe, however, that administrative law may not develop in a system where the executive has strong control over the legislative process.

26. They are under the supervision of the Federal Energy Regulatory Commission.

27. The US Energy Information Administration estimates that competitive pressures in the generation sector will reduce retail electricity prices from an average of 6.3¢/kWh in 1996 to 4.2¢/kWh by 2005 (J. Alan Beamon, "Competitive Electricity Pricing: An Update", 1998).
28. See Spiller and Savedoff (2000).
29. For example, private investment in transmission networks has been secured under a variety of ownership and structural arrangements. Substantial investment has occurred in Argentina (private, vertically separated, fragmented transmission) and in Chile (private, vertically integrated between generation and transmission, concentrated transmission). Low levels of transmission investment have occurred in the United Kingdom (private, vertical separation between generation and transmission, concentrated transmission), in California (private, vertical integration between distribution and transmission, and some generation), and in New Zealand (public, vertical separation, concentrated transmission). Similarly, among countries implementing competitive wholesale markets, there is no discernible pattern of vertical integration between transmission and generation functions or in the ownership of transmission assets and their relative performance (see table 25.1).

    Indeed, it could be argued that independently of market structure, as long as the regulatory governance of the sector is properly designed, the following six structural conditions are sufficient for generating incentives for private investment in liberalized electricity markets, and hence for developing a competitive generation market:
    (a) free entry into generation
    (b) some amount of direct access, including access to large users
    (c) fragmented demand (in most cases this implies a fragmented distribution sector)
    (d) dispatch operations run by an entity independent of the generation companies
    (e) open access to transmission and distribution grids
    (f) incentive regulation of transmission and distribution charges.
30. This, however, assumes that dispatch is run by the transmission company, which violates condition (d) in the list of sufficient conditions for a competitive environment in n. 29.
31. As we discuss below, the proposal by the California Governor in 2001 to take over the transmission system was designed not to alleviate investment or market power issues, but rather to effect a cash transfer ("bailout" according to critics) to the utilities that would otherwise have been politically infeasible.
32. For further analysis of this particular issue, see Spiller (1999).
33. *Power Economics*, September 30, 1998; *East European Energy Report*, October 25, 1996 and August 1, 1997; *Utility Week*, June 1, 1998; *International Private Power Quarterly*, Fourth Quarter 1998.
34. *The Electricity Daily*, May 10, 1999.
35. The demand elasticity is often made lower by not allowing the demand side to bid into the spot or balancing markets.
36. Similarly, in California, auction rules and particular regulations (particularly, the requirement that the large distribution companies trade exclusively in

the formal power exchange, and that wholesale market prices are capped), provided some distributors with the incentives to bring down their costs by under-scheduling demand in the day-ahead market. Under-scheduling demand generates prices in the day ahead market which are below the price cap. The remaining demand traded in the real-time market would be priced at the cap. Were the distribution company to schedule its whole demand on the day-ahead market, the day-ahead price would have hit the price cap limit, increasing the distribution company's overall energy payments.

37. It should be emphasized that so far there has not been a claim of the coordinated exercise of market power, an action that is illegal in both the United Kingdom and the United States but not in El Salvador, which has no antitrust legislation.

38. See also Green and Newbery (1992) and Newbery and Pollitt (1997) for theoretical and empirical analyses of the operations of the UK electricity pool.

39. Buyers and sellers are free, though, to enter into financial forward contracts known as "Contracts for Differences."

40. See Gilbert and Kahn (1996) for an extensive discussion of electricity regulation arrangements across fifteen countries including an insightful chapter by Newbery and Green (1996) on the UK electricity industry.

41. Capacity payments have been extensively criticized as an ineffective way of promoting capacity investment. For a critique, see Oren (2000).

42. Office of Gas and Electricity Markets, The New Electricity Trading Arrangements (NETA), July 1999, p. 3.

43. The Pool committee consists of generation and supply company representatives. In order to protect minority interests, such as small generators and suppliers, and potential entrants, changes in the operational rules of the pool may be implemented only upon a supermajority vote of the committee.

44. *Ibid.*, pp. 28–9.

45. *Ibid.*, p. 2.

46. See Spiller and Vogelsang (1997) for a discussion of how the UK system of administrative checks and balances provides a measure of credibility to the UK regulatory process not otherwise found in its polity.

47. See also Spiller and Vogelsang (1997).

48. Office of Gas and Electricity Markets, NETA, October 1999, p. 1.

49. Competition Commission, Statement by Callum McCarthy, Director General of Ofgem Addressing the Scope for, and Experience of, the Abuse of Market Power by the Generators Under the Wholesale Electricity Pool in England and Wales.

50. AES and British Energy challenged the DG's move at the Competition Commission. Similarly, in the mid-1990s the DG promoted plant divestitures from the main generators under the threat of a reference to the Monopolies and Mergers Commission (MMC) for a forced license modification (through the Electricity Act) or a structural remedy (through the Competition Act). The ability to make a reference to the MMC requesting a license modification forces the generators to consider to what extent the MMC will side with the DG.

51. Office of Electricity Regulation, Review of Electricity Trading Arrangements: Proposals, July 1998.
52. *White Paper on Energy Policy*, HMSO Cm 4071.
53. Office of Electricity Regulation, Review of Electricity Trading Arrangements: Framework Document, November 1998.
54. See, Ofgem/DTI, "The New Electricity Trading Arrangements: Ofgem/DTI Conclusions Document," October 1999, available from http://www.ofgem. gov.uk/elarch/anetadocs.htm.

    Using the power granted to the Secretary of State for Trade and Industry by the Utilities Act 2000, the Secretary designated new license conditions requiring the licensees to sign the required documents to implement the NETA. These documents include the Balancing and Settlement Code, licensing changes and the implementation schedule. See Ofgem Press Release August 14, 2000, PN 89.
55. See Ofgem Press Release October 27, 2000, PN 114.
56. See http://www.ofgem.gov.uk/elarch/05forums.htm for a list of industry forums undertaken by Ofgem.
57. The NETA will base dispatch on a system of bilateral and multilateral trading coupled with a balancing market in which the buyer is the dispatch operator who buys balancing services from both demand and supply utilizing – so as to discourage the use of the balancing market as a scheduling device – "pay as bid" rather than a single price to all participants. The bilateral trading and balancing mechanism will be accompanied by a series of forward markets to be developed by the industry.
58. These institutions were established in late 1996 by the state legislature as the two central institutions to develop and operate a competitive wholesale market.
59. See also Joskow (2000, pp. 79–107), and California ISO Market Surveillance Committee Report, October 1999, for discussions of the California electricity wholesale market.
60. At one point, ISO prices for replacement reserves reached just shy of $10,000 per MWh until the ISO requested Federal Energy Regulatory Commission (FERC) authority to cap prices at $250 per MWh.
61. Distributors subject to the price cap regulation started charging their customers *negative* Competition Transmission Charges (CTCs), which meant that the CTC became an instrument to subsidize customers, rather than for customers to pay for stranded assets, as originally intended. As a consequence, their recovery of the uneconomic generation costs – as defined in the Electricity Restructuring Act 1996 (AB 1890) – was postponed further into the future, which increased their risk of never recovering such amounts, driving them closer to bankruptcy.
62. The California Public Utilities Commission (CPUC) Decision of May 27, 1999 limited price increases for the summer of 1999, but completely liberated prices thereafter.

    San Diego Gas & Electric (SDG&E) ended its "transition period" during mid-1999 and hence was allowed to start passing through the energy costs to its – so far – captive customers. See CPUC Decision 99–05–051 of

May 27, 1999, which approved the end of the transition period, implying that SDG&E had recovered all its uneconomic generation costs subject to AB 1890 provisions. The decision can be found in http://www.cpuc.ca.gov/static/electric/electric_restructuring/decisions.htm.

63. *San Francisco Chronicle*, "PG&E Bargains with Wary Gas Suppliers," February 3, 2001.
64. A Stage 1 Emergency Notice is declared by the ISO any time it is clear that an Operating Reserve shortfall is unavoidable or, when in real-time operations, the Operating Reserve is forecast to be less than the minimum after utilizing available resources. A Stage 2 Emergency Notice occurs when the Operating Reserve is forecast to be less than 5 percent after dispatching all resources available. During 1999 there were four Stage 1 and one Stage 2 Emergency Notices. A Stage 3 Emergency Notice is declared when the Operating Reserve is forecast to be less than 1.5 percent after dispatching all resources available. No Stage 3 Emergencies occurred during 1998 or 1999 and only one occurred in 2000 (see ISO Event Log).
65. Although some have emphasized that the crisis of winter 2001 was more a liquidity than an energy crisis.
66. In the case at hand, judicial review of legislative acts would be based on their constitutionality, while judicial review of administrative acts would be based both on their legality (i.e. whether they follow the various statutes) and their constitutionality.
67. On the relationship between regulatory agencies and legislatures, and on the role of administrative procedures, see McCubbins and Schwartz (1984); McCubbins, Noll and Weingast (1987, 1989); Epstein and O'Halloran (1994, 1996); Tiller and Spiller (1996); Tiller (1998); Holburn and Vanden Bergh (2000).
68. The need for political compromise is also evident in the 1996 bill that restructured the Californian electricity industry, which was enacted by a Republican governor and Democrat-controlled legislature who held differing positions on a wide range of policy issues including electricity reform. While incumbent utilities were allowed to recover their stranded assets through a CTC levy on all bills, consumers were guaranteed retail rates fixed at 10 percent below their historic levels during a pre-specified transition period. This approach was politically expedient – it gave consumers a rapid benefit from restructuring – but a major consequence was the elimination of retail competition in the supply market. At the same time, it generated the presumption of price stability even in the presence of substantial wholesale energy cost changes, reducing large users' incentives to enter into demand-side management programs. Once the transition period in southern California finished in July 1999 and retail price caps were removed, retail customers were confronted with volatile prices but with no options to buy alternative rate plans offering price stability, triggering substantial calls for regulatory reform. As discussed above, the retail price cap also generated a negative CTC when wholesale prices skyrocketed, bringing the major utilities close to bankruptcy. To a large extent, therefore, the foundations of the Californian energy crisis were rooted in the political logic that shaped the initial restructuring legislation of 1996.
69. AB 1890, Section 337

70. FERC disbanded the existing ISO Board on December 15, 2000 and ordered its reconstitution with new members who were not stake holders or participants in ISO operations.
71. Article 367, AB 1890.
72. The *Hope Natural Gas* and *Bluefield* cases set the precedent of "just and reasonable" profits as the norm for regulated industries (see Bonbright 1961).
73. *San Francisco Chronicle*, November 9, 2000, "New Angle to PG&E Bid to Raise Rates: Utility Files Complaint in Federal Court."

   Although a federal court decision in early February 2001 cast some doubt on whether the utilities would be allowed to raise final rates in order to gain full compensation for their distribution business losses, the determination of this issue is made by a disinterested party (i.e. the courts) on the merits of the case (while the distribution operations of the utilities made large financial losses during 2000, their generation businesses naturally benefited from high PX prices, leading some to argue that full compensation is not required). The courts therefore provide an important check against the risk that the state government, seeking political favor with its constituents, may prevent the utilities from recovering their sunk costs (see *Southern California Edison* v. *Lynch* (California Public Utilities Commission), US District Court, Central District of California, Case no. 00-12056-RSWL (Mcx).
74. More than anything, the California example shows the political risk of placing all the weight in spot markets, and the need for promoting long-term contracts between load-serving companies and generators.
75. CEL, which stands for Comisión Ejecutiva Hidroeléctrica del Río Lema, was also the owner of various distribution companies.
76. See, "Cargo de Energía sube 52 percent", *El Diario de Hoy*, Thursday April 6, 2000, San Salvador, and "Energía: el alza no tocará los hogares", *El Diario de Hoy*, Tuesday April 4, 2000, San Salvador.
77. See Spiller (2000).
78. See Memoria de Labores, CEL (1999).
79. Prior to signing the contract with Duke, CEL had control over approximately 70 percent of the domestic generation, and Duke of the remaining 30 percent. Since the contract transfers to CEL control more than half of Duke's generation capacity, it essentially granted CEL control almost completely over the wholesale market.
80. Spiller (2000) claims that such restrictions were what triggered the increase in price during the fourth quarter of 1999 and the first quarter of 2000.
81. See "Costosa energía no generada," *El Diario de Hoy*, El Salvador, October 18, 2000.
82. See "La fuerza de la Generación," *Más!*, El Salvador, October 3, 2000.
83. See "Subsidio cuesta a CEL c1, 470 millones," *La Prensa Gráfica*, October 17, 2000.
84. See "CEL invierte más de mil millones en generación," *La Prensa Gráfica*, El Salvador, October 17, 2000.
85. The nature and timing of presidential and legislative elections imply that the President does not necessarily have a majority in the assembly.
86. Indeed, a simple reading of the original Executive Decree interpreting the 1996 Act would suggest that such an interpretation violates the Act. The Act

says in its article 79 that retail prices should be adjusted based on "the average price of the energy in the wholesale market in the respective node during the year prior to the filing of the tariffs." The Executive Decree introduced a 10 percent adjustment clause and a quarterly adjustment.

87. Since the contract with Duke is voluntary, it is reasonable to expect that Duke receives from CEL at least what it could obtain from the wholesale market.

26 Electricity sector restructuring and competition: a transactions-cost perspective

Paul L. Joskow

1 Introduction

One of the most important changes in industrial organization that has taken place around the world in the last fifteen years is the restructuring of industries which were historically considered to be natural monopolies and were subject to strict government price and entry regulation (and were often state-owned as well). These industries include telecommunications, electric power, natural gas transportation, and railroads. The primary goals of these restructuring initiatives have been to promote competition in those horizontal segments of these industries which are conducive to it, to shrink the scope of industry output organized as a regulated monopoly, and to introduce new regulatory mechanisms for residual regulated monopoly segments to provide better incentives for cost reduction and efficient pricing.[1]

In Joskow (1991) I argued that transaction-cost economics (TCE) provides an indispensable set of tools for understanding how the organizations subject to reform had emerged, how they are likely to respond as economic and regulatory conditions change, and how effective industry restructuring can be accomplished.[2] A major thrust of these restructuring initiatives has involved vertical separation of potentially competitive segments (e.g. electricity generation) from natural monopoly segments (e.g. electricity transmission).[3] It has been my view that there are very sound TCE reasons why these industries evolved with vertically integrated structures.[4] Other things equal, vertical integration conserves on a variety of transactions costs compared to an unintegrated governance structure. Accordingly, vertical restructuring to promote competition in certain horizontal segments must necessarily confront a trade-off between the potential benefits of market forces replacing inefficient regulated monopolies and the potential costs associated with various inefficiencies arising from vertical de-integration. The challenge for the development of new governance arrangements in these industries is to keep the costs of vertical separation low while obtaining the benefits of competition. These challenges are especially great when the performance of the competitive segments (e.g. electricity generation) depends critically on the details of relationships with segments which were previously under common ownership (vertical integration) and that continue to be regulated monopolies (e.g. electricity transmission) which buyers and sellers in the competitive segments depend upon to support competitive trading relationships:[5]

Major vertical restructuring of industries that involve significant non-redeployable sunk investments, the operation of complicated networks, and significant costs of system failure, necessarily raise precisely the kinds of organizational issues that transaction cost economics is supposed to be able to deal with well. However, while transaction cost economics has played a role in the debates about vertical restructuring in these industries, and the precise form that such restructuring would take, it is my sense that the direct role of transaction cost considerations in influencing the direction of public policy has, so far, been quite modest.[6]

We now have an additional decade of experience with industry restructuring in these industries since I made these observations in 1991. I focus here on the experience with electricity sector restructuring and competition programs. I first wrote about the challenges that must be confronted to create well-functioning competitive wholesale electricity markets, drawing heavily on the early TCE, literature almost twenty years ago.[7] I have continued to follow the evolution of electricity sector reforms and evaluate their results since then.[8] While the electricity sector reform programs in many countries have been successful in the sense that the benefits of the reforms exceed the costs of the reforms,[9] a number of common problems have emerged in many of them.[10] Moreover, in countries whose "traditional" electricity sectors performed reasonably well, recent experience has raised questions about whether in reality, rather than in theory, the benefits of these reforms necessarily exceed their costs.

There are two important elements of TCE thinking that I will focus on here. First, I want to emphasize the importance of adopting the conceptual framework of "comparative institution choice" to evaluate whether structural regulatory and competition reforms are desirable, and, if they are, what form the new governance arrangements should take.[11] Resource allocation to and within an industry can be organized in a variety of different ways. None of these alternative institutional or governance structures will yield "perfect" performance compared to some abstract "social planner's" ideal. Each set of alternative institutional arrangements will have some net costs compared to that abstract ideal. The task of policymakers is to choose among alternative institutional designs to find the one that minimizes the total costs of governing the transactions at issue, carefully accounting for direct production costs, transactions costs, including the costs of opportunistic behavior and costs incurred to mitigate it, and other market and institutional imperfections. That is, to choose the best governance structure from a set of *imperfect* governance structures. From this perspective, concluding that some industry structure and associated governance arrangements are "inefficient" compared to some abstract ideal is not enough to justify a proposed reform. The alternative market structure, governance, and institutional arrangements must be defined and their performance properties carefully evaluated. A movement to the alternative governance arrangements is justified when the new institutional framework is less costly than the incumbent framework – that is, the reform makes things better than the status quo. And ideally, the reforms will adopt the governance structure from the set of potential alternatives that maximize these gains.

The second important set of issues that I emphasize is associated with a variety of potential transactional problems that arise when a complex existing market structure and supporting institutions are fundamentally changed. I will focus here on transactional problems that arise because of the presence of long-lived capital investments that had been made in the past under then-prevailing institutional arrangements and are now not easily redeployable. The historical pattern of investments that created the existing configuration of generating, transmission, and distribution assets was well adapted – in a transactions-cost conservation sense – to the governance arrangements in which they were made – regulated vertically integrated monopolies. In particular, the asset configuration did not reflect efforts to economize on the transactions costs that could arise in an industry with a very different structure. These incumbent or "legacy" long-lived sunk investments create potential hold-up and coordination problems *ex ante* when the existing industry structure is de-integrated vertically and horizontally into independent firms pursuing their own self-interest. As I will discuss presently, these problems are revealed post-restructuring in the form of supplier market power problems, coordination difficulties between the generation, transmission, and distribution segments, sub-optimal investments in transmission capacity, and excessive consumer prices. Historical investments in metering and communications equipment which make it virtually impossible quickly to provide end-use consumers with good price signals reflecting supply and demand conditions in the wholesale market reduce the effective elasticity of demand and further enhance the ability of suppliers to engage in opportunistic behavior.

When industries are subject to mandatory restructuring and the imposition by governments of new sets of firm structures, market designs, and supporting institutional arrangements, long-lived sunk investments cannot be expected to adapt instantly to the new governance structure. If the new governance arrangements are not sensitive to the configuration of non-redeployable sunk investments inherited from the past, and take into account this configuration of sunk investments and the potential for opportunistic behavior and coordination problems in designing new market and regulatory institutions, then the new market organization is likely to run into costly opportunism problems, costly responses to them, and coordination and investment inefficiencies. Obviously, the key to avoiding these problems is for responsible policy-makers to take these problems into account in the design of new firm structures, market rules, contractual arrangements, and regulatory mechanisms.

2   Basic characteristics of electricity supply and demand

The supply of electricity is generally divided into three or four separate functions:

1. The generation (G) of electricity using falling water, internal combustion engines, steam turbines powered with steam produced with fossil fuels, nuclear fuel, and various renewable fuels, wind-driven turbines, and photovoltaic technologies. In most developed countries there are typically many generating plants in service dispersed over a large geographic area.
2. The distribution (D) of electricity to residences and businesses at relatively low voltages using wires and transformers along and under streets and other rights of way.
3. Related to distribution, a set of power procurement and retailing (R) functions. They include making arrangements for supplies of power from generators, metering, billing, and various demand management services. The dividing line between distribution and retailing is still murky and controversial.
4. The transmission (T) of electricity involving the "transportation" of electricity between generating sites and distribution centers, the interconnection and integration of dispersed generating facilities into a stable synchronized network, the scheduling and dispatching of generating facilities that are connected to the transmission network to balance demand and supply in real time, and the management of equipment failures, network constraints, and relationships with other interconnected networks. These latter functions may be aggregated into a set of System Operating (SO) responsibilities.

The attributes of electricity demand, electricity supply, and physical constraints associated with the operation of synchronized alternating current (AC) networks are highly relevant for understanding the organizational structure of the electric power sector that evolved over the twentieth century. These attributes are also highly relevant for designing transmission network and competitive wholesale power market institutions with good performance attributes.

Electricity usually cannot be stored or inventoried economically, and demand varies widely from hour to hour during an individual day and from day to day over the year. The aggregate short-run elasticity of demand is inherently very small and the effective short-run elasticity of demand reduced further by the absence of hourly metering, communications, and pricing arrangements. Moreover, there is generally no meaningful direct physical relationship between a specific generator and a specific customer and no economical way to curtail an individual customer's consumption when specific generators fail to perform.[12] Since consumers continue to draw power as long as the circuits are closed and they are connected to the network, the aggregate generation of electricity and the consumption of electricity must be balanced continuously for the entire network to meet certain physical constraints (frequency, voltage, stability) on network operations. That is, electricity consumed at a specific point in time must be manufactured in a generating plant virtually contemporaneously with its consumption; it is the ultimate in "just-in-time" manufacturing.

A modern AC transmission network makes it possible to utilize generating facilities dispersed over wide geographic areas efficiently in real time to meet continually changing demand levels through the substitution of increased production from low marginal cost facilities (say, in New Mexico) for production from high marginal cost facilities (say, in California). In principle, an efficiently operated network would constantly equate the marginal costs of supplying an additional kWh of energy at all generating nodes adjusted for marginal losses, thermal and operating constraints throughout the network. It would also economize on the reserve capacity required for any given level of reliability (responses to equipment outages and unanticipated swings in demand) by effectively aggregating loads and reserve generating capacity over a wide geographic area and by providing multiple linkages between loads and resources that can provide service continuity when transmission facilities fail. To accomplish these tasks, the network must be operated to maintain its frequency and voltage parameters within narrow bands and to respond to rapidly changing system conditions on the demand and supply sides, especially short-term demand swings and unplanned equipment outages. Generating facilities must be called upon almost continuously to provide a variety of network support or reserve services in addition to providing energy to run customer appliances and equipment. These "ancillary services" include spinning reserves, standby reserves, blackstart capability, frequency regulation (Automatic Generation Control), scheduling and dispatch control, and others.

Electric power networks are not switched networks like railroad or telephone networks where a supplier makes a physical delivery of a product at point A that is then physically transported to a specific customer at point B. A free-flowing AC network is an integrated physical machine that follows the laws of physics (Kirchoff's Laws), not the laws of financial contracting. Electricity produced by all generators goes into a common pool of electric energy and demand by consumers draws energy out of that common pool. The network operator must ensure that the pool stays filled to a constant level, balancing inflows and outflows. The electric energy produced by a particular generator cannot be physically associated with the electricity consumed by a particular consumer. When a generator turns on and off, it affect system conditions throughout the interconnected network. Large swings in demand at one node affect system conditions at other nodes. A failure of a major piece of equipment in one part of the network can disrupt the stability of the entire system if resources are not available to the network operator to respond quickly to these contingencies. Moreover, efficient and effective remedial responses to equipment failures can involve coordinated reactions of multiple generators located remotely from the site of the failure. These attributes create potential network externality and network "commons" problems. The physical attributes of AC networks also make is difficult to define a well-defined set of property rights. As a result, it is unlikely that market mechanisms can be relied on entirely to internalize network externality problems effectively.

Everywhere on earth electric power systems evolved with similar governance structures, which I have previously argued reflect these special attributes of electricity supply and demand.[13] Electricity suppliers typically had *de facto* exclusive rights to serve all consumers in a particular geographic area and an obligation to supply them with reliable supplies of electricity at "cost-based" regulated prices. Electric utilities typically met their supply obligations by vertically integrating into all four supply segments, owning generation, transmission and distribution facilities, operating them in an integrated fashion using internal operating protocols, and providing consumers in their franchise areas with a single bundled electricity supply product.[14] The physical and economic attributes of generation and transmission in particular led to vertical integration as an efficient governance arrangement.[15]

The economic rationale for vertical integration between G&T is that it internalizes the operating and investment interrelationships between generation and transmission inside public or private organizations where the potential public goods and externality problems that arise as a consequence of the physical attributes of electric power networks, as well as the challenge of coordinating operations in real time to adapt to changing demand and supply conditions, can be solved with internal operating hierarchies rather than markets. However, vertical integration between the network functions which have natural monopoly characteristics and the generation function effectively turns the supply of generating service into a monopoly as well even if there are numerous generating plants connected to the network and limited economies of scale associated with generation *per se* in isolation from the coordination functions performed by the network (Joskow and Schmalensee 1983). This in turn leads to the extension of public regulation of prices, costs, investment decisions, service quality, etc. and in most countries state ownership of the entire vertically integrated entity – both the potentially competitive segments and the "natural monopoly" segments.

In many countries, especially those with a government-owned electricity sector, regulation of prices, costs, investment decisions, etc. was the responsibility of a government ministry, with varying degrees of legislative oversight. The regulatory process in these countries was generally closed to public scrutiny, based on often opaque cost of service principles, and often became highly politicized. In some countries, these regulatory responsibilities were fully or partially decentralized to the state, provincial, or municipal level, with ministries or councils at these levels of government responsible for regulating the behavior of local monopoly electricity suppliers. Both the United States and Canada have a long tradition of relying on independent regulatory commissions which operate with clear regulatory responsibilities, well-established principles governing cost accounting and price setting, and very open administrative procedures in which various interest groups have opportunities to participate. The original rationale for independent commissions in the United States was to create expert regulatory bodies that followed well-defined public interest principles and which would be insulated from political pressures created by powerful interest groups. Complete insulation from political pressures is, of course, impossible when regulators are appointed by government officials, depend on government for the funds they need to perform their jobs effectively, and are ultimately subject to changes in the laws under which they operate. Nevertheless, the open independent commission system places significant constraints on special political deals and corruption because they are more difficult to hide.

3   Performance problems with regulated electricity monopolies

Successful reform requires understanding how resource allocation decision were made under the existing governance arrangements and the nature and magnitude of their performance problems. All resource allocation tasks that had to be accomplished under the old governance structure will still need to be accomplished under a reformed governance structure, but are likely to be performed differently – e.g. through transactions between firms subject to competition rather than within regulated monopoly firms. The combination of legal supply monopolies, "cost-plus" pricing rules and political pressures on price levels, price structures, and resource utilization decisions should be expected to lead to inefficiencies compared to the social planner's ideal allocation of resources. Electricity sector reforms are generally based on the proposition that these production and allocational inefficiencies can be reduced by narrowing the expanse of economic activity organized around legal monopolies and public regulation, turning as much of the resource allocation decisions as possible to competitive markets, while reforming residual regulatory tasks so that they induce more efficient sector performance.

The historical performance of the traditional electric power sectors around the world varies widely. The sectors in most *developed* countries have performed fairly well based on a variety of "macro" performance criteria. In particular, the systems provide electricity with high levels of reliability, investment in new capacity can generally be readily financed to keep up with (or often exceed) demand growth, system losses (both physical and those owing to theft of service) are low, electricity is available virtually universally, customers can get hooked up for service relatively quickly and cheaply, there is a long record of rapid productivity growth (at least until the early 1970s), the average price of electricity typically covers the total cost of supplying it, including a reasonable return on investment, and the real price of electricity fell almost continuously until the early 1970s and then again in the 1990s. Moreover, the rate of growth in the demand for electricity in most developed countries has slowed considerably since 1980 in response to slower overall economic growth, shifts in industry composition, rising real electricity prices (until the mid- to late 1980s) in many countries, and improvements in end-use energy efficiency. On average in the OECD countries, projected electricity demand growth over the decade to 2010 is about 2 percent per year.[16]

However, a closer examination of various performance indexes across developed countries and across electric companies in countries with multiple suppliers (especially the United States), reveals substantial performance variation within these general sector performance attributes. There was significant variation in the cost of building reasonably comparable generating facilities across countries and between suppliers within the same country. These variations have been revealed most starkly in the context of nuclear generating facilities, but are revealed as well for large fossil-generating plants (Joskow and Rose 1985). The operating performance (e.g. availability) of both fossil and nuclear units also varied widely even after controlling for age, size, and fuel attributes (Joskow and Schmalensee 1987). There were also wide variations in the labor intensity of power sectors. For example, the pre-reform sector in England and Wales had about twice as many workers per unit of output as did the US sector. Other costs were incurred as a result of the use of public and private utilities to pursue a variety of social goals via "taxation by regulation." Whether it was protecting the domestic coal industries in England and Wales, Germany, and Spain, or promoting domestic equipment manufacturing enterprises, as in France and other countries, or promoting costly renewable energy and energy conservation programs as in the United States, or extensive cross-subsidies among customer classes, the costs of these programs were hidden from the public in electricity prices and these prices were necessarily distorted from efficient least-cost based levels.

These inefficiencies are properly attributed to the combination of cost of service regulation, public ownership, and severe limitations on competition. Price regulation weakens incentives for cost minimization, public ownership often further exacerbates the problems by softening budget constraints and further weakening incentives, and the institution of regulated private or public monopolies is conducive to the politicization of input choices and cross-subsidization.

Whatever the performance problems of the traditional electricity sectors in developed countries, in the broader scheme of things they are small compared to the performance problems of the traditional sectors in many *developing* countries.[17] Under pre-reform institutional arrangements, the electric power sectors in many developing countries have been unable to mobilize the capital necessary to finance needed investments in generating, transmission, and distribution capacity at a time when these countries are at a phase in their development when the demand for electricity should increase rapidly. The performance of existing facilities is often poor by world standards, with high losses, poor distribution system reliability and power quality, high heat rates, and poor generator reliability. There are long queues for service hookups, and extraordinary levels of excess employment of workers in many electricity sectors in developing countries. The average price of electricity often does not recover costs on an historical accounting cost basis and is often far below the long-run incremental costs of expanding the system, making it difficult to finance new investments and to maintain capital facilities in good operating order, increasing the extent and social costs of supply shortages. The poor performance of the electricity sectors in many developing countries could have significant adverse consequences for economic development in these countries.

Accordingly, the performance targets that electricity sector reforms are aimed at are clear: more efficient operation of existing facilities; shedding of excess labor and other cost burdens in the fuel and equipment areas resulting from the sector's historical politicization; creating a contractual, regulatory, and industry structure framework that will attract investment to support new supply facilities required to meet electricity demand at least cost; improving system reliability; bringing electricity prices into balance with the costs of supplying it; and de-politicizing the sector. The best way to go about achieving them quickly will vary from country to country, and, most importantly, between developed and developing countries. Nevertheless, the basic restructuring and competition models being pursued in many countries are based on the electricity restructuring program introduced in England and Wales in 1990.[18]

4   The basic reform model[19]

In response to real or imagined performance problems with these traditional governance arrangements, many countries have or are in the process of implementing a new model for their electricity industries.[20] The new model has the following general features: generation would be fully separated from transmission and distribution; regulated distribution and transmission charges would be "unbundled" from generation and retail service charges; wholesale generation service prices would be deregulated; generators would compete *de novo* in regional markets both to supply distribution companies purchasing on behalf of their retail customers (full wholesale competition with exclusive retail supply) and to supply retail customers as well ("retail wheeling") either directly or through financial intermediaries (wholesale marketers and retail Energy Service Providers, or ESPs). This model of a restructured electric power sector that would reduce the expanse of regulated monopoly to transmission and distribution functions and rely on competition to supply generation and transmission services at wholesale and retail is depicted in figure 26.1.

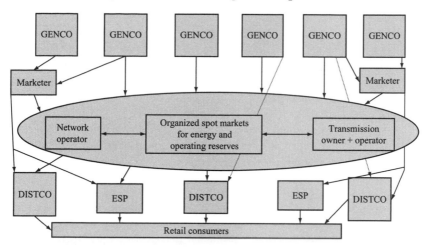

Figure 26.1   Competitive wholesale and retail markets

The core of most electricity sector reforms is the creation of reasonably competitive wholesale spot and forward (financial) markets for electric energy, capacity, and a variety of operating reserve services (also referred to as ancillary services).[21] In addition, free entry of new generating capacity to make sales in these unregulated power markets in response to economic opportunities is a critical component of these reforms. Competitive generation markets on electric power networks are most appropriately conceptualized as spatial markets with demand (or loads) and differentiated generators dispersed across the network's geographic expanse. These demand and supply locations are generally referred to as "nodes" on the network. Though the generation suppliers produce more or less the same product – electric energy (reserve services and differences in adjustment speeds complicate this) – they are differentiated from one another along three major dimensions: (a) marginal costs of production, (b) transportation costs owing to congestion and thermal losses, and (c) the speeds with which they can adjust their output from one supply level to another, including starting up from zero. The transportation costs in turn vary widely with system conditions – supply and demand – at all nodes on the network. In additional, generators can produce multiple services, consisting of both energy and various reserve services.

Accordingly, the basic framework for thinking about competition among generators should be based on a fairly complicated spatial competition model with competing multiproduct firms at different locations which are "separated" by congestion costs and thermal losses. The suppliers of generation service are asymmetric, the costs of transportation vary widely over time as congestion varies, and the elasticity of supply around the competitive equilibrium varies widely over time as demand that must be met by just-in-time (JIT) production fluctuates between very low and very high levels. Markets with these attributes are unlikely to be perfectly competitive and policies designed to facilitate competition and to constrain inefficient strategic behavior should be an important feature of the reform program.

As in other commodity markets, wholesale and retail electricity markets play the traditional role of balancing supply and demand and allocating supplies among competing generators in the short run and provide economic signals for entry of new suppliers in the long run. However, wholesale electricity market mechanisms also play another important role. They are relied upon to provide generation resources, and economic signals for using these resources efficiently, that the operator of an electric power transmission network must rely on for maintaining the reliability and power quality of the network (frequency, voltage, and stability) and to manage congestion and related network constraints at the same speed at which electricity supply and demand attributes change – which is very fast. These resource-allocation functions were traditionally performed within vertically integrated firms using internal scheduling, dispatch, and emergency response protocols that depended on a combination of computer optimization routines, marginal cost signals, and "band aids" applied by system operators to deal with unusual circumstances. The short-run operating functions and the associated physical attributes of electric power systems just listed are perhaps the primary factors that led to vertical integration between generation and transmission. They are also the most challenging resource-allocation activities to mediate through market mechanisms.

All of the credible models for creating new competitive electricity markets, recognize that there must be a single network operator responsible for controlling the physical operation of a control area, coordinating generator schedules, balancing loads and resources in real time, acquiring ancillary network support services required to maintain reliability, and coordinating with neighboring control areas – performing Systems Operations (SO) activities. In most countries, organized spot auction markets have also been created both to allow generators to trade energy with buyers and with each other and to allow the network operator to purchase options on capacity to allow it to manage network congestion and other reliability and physical constraints. The performance of these auction markets depends critically both on there being robust competition among generation suppliers and the implementation of a set of auction rules that are compatible with the physical operating constraints on the system and do not facilitate gaming and market power problems that may be exacerbated by these physical constraints.

5 Performance improvements resulting from recent electricity sector reforms

Regulated monopoly electricity supply sectors, especially those that were state-owned, tended to have more workers than was necessary to produce their services efficiently. From England and Wales to Chile and New Zealand, restructuring for competition has led to significant labor shedding.[22] However, because electricity is not a labor-intensive production activity, the overall effect on prices of improvements in labor productivity is relatively small. At the same time, the magnitude of the costs involved may make it possible to structure early retirement and other worker incentive programs to facilitate staff downsizing without causing major labor unrest.

The experience in England and Wales also indicates that significant cost savings can be achieved by moving away from procurement based on national politics toward procurement that reflects least-cost principles. In those countries with a "coal problem," electricity restructuring simply places more pressure on coal sector restructuring efforts that are already underway.

Another dimension of performance improvement is related to increases in generating unit availability, as well as savings in both physical and financial losses (theft of service) on the distribution system. These cost-saving opportunities are most significant in developing countries with objectively poor sector performance, but have also been observed in developed countries that have restructured. The increases in the availability and the operating cost savings in the nuclear sector in England and Wales since 1990, and the increases in availability of fossil and hydro facilities in Argentina since 1992, are especially impressive examples, as are the improvements in the performance of nuclear power plants in the United States.

Cost-based regulatory rules and political constraints have historically led electricity suppliers to continue to operate some generating facilities beyond the date they would be retired if they had to live on the revenues they could obtain in competitive markets. Many old inefficient generating plants have been retired in England and Wales since restructuring in 1990. The pressures of emerging competition have also led to the early retirement of nearly a dozen nuclear reactors in the United States in the early 1990s.

Many electricity sector restructuring programs have also been very successful in attracting investment in new generating plants and in controlling the construction and operating costs of these new facilities. Traditional electricity sectors in *developed* countries were generally reasonably successful in attracting investment capital to expand production and distribution capabilities. This is the case because the institution of regulated monopoly effectively shifted risks associated with construction cost over-runs (and under-runs), as well as market risks that change the economic value of generating facilities, to consumers. Regulated electricity firms were generally viewed as having relatively low financial risks for equity investors and high credit ratings for bond investors. Indeed, one of the standard criticisms of traditional regulated monopolies in the United States was that they built too much capacity and had poor incentives to control construction costs. In these countries, capital attraction has not been the problem. Rather, the problems have been associated with pervasive excess capacity and construction cost over-runs. The challenge for reform is to rely on markets to increase incentives to control construction and operating costs, and to reduce any tendencies for excess capacity, by shifting market and cost risks to investors from consumers, without creating markets that have so much market and residual regulatory risk that they veer to the other extreme, discouraging investment in adequate generating capacity to properly reflect consumer preferences for reliability. Replacing a system that is "too reliable" with one that has a significant number of blackouts owing to the failure to attract investment in new capacity at the right time and in the right places will not be viewed favorably by consumers.

The experience with investment in new generating plants in the restructured markets in England and Wales, Argentina, Australia, and the United States has generally been favorable.[23] There has been substantial entry and costs and market risks have been transferred to suppliers providing high-powered incentives to them to control costs. The experience with investment in new transmission capacity has been more mixed, with network investment problems emerging in a number of countries, including the United States.

On the other hand, electricity sectors in many *developing* countries had a great deal of trouble attracting adequate investment to expand networks to reach the entire population and to balance supply and demand efficiently. The cause of this problem typically was the inability of the regulated monopoly suppliers to charge prices high enough to cover their operating costs and to service their financial obligation and to finance new investment. Internal cash flows could not fund needed new investments, government subsidies or capital grants were generally limited by general fiscal constraints, and private capital markets would not provide investment capital to entities that were not credit-worthy. From this perspective, it is important to understand that no electricity supply framework will yield good performance if prices are constrained to levels that do not allow for cost recovery and if theft of service is widespread. Accordingly, any successful reform in developing countries typically requires price increases and a crackdown on thefts of service. Privatization and competition may be the excuse for implementing broader reforms on the price and theft of service fronts that are unlikely to be politically popular.

6   Problems encountered by reforms

A number of market performance problems have also arisen in several of these new electricity markets. These problems fall into several categories. First, there have been problems that appear to be a consequence of the legacy of long-lived sunk investments made in the context of a vertically integrated monopoly system. These long-lived sunk investments create potential hold-up problems when the system is broken up and decentralized. Investments in generation and transmission facilities in particular were made under the assumption that they would be under common ownership and operation. Opportunistic behavior that may arise when separate profit maximizing organizations own and operate these assets were not taken into account when the investments were made since they were under common ownership and integrated operating control. As I will discuss, the opportunism problems of particular concern include "local market power" problems caused by transmission network constraints, the management of network congestion, and generator market power problems that are exacerbated by the absence of metering and communications infrastructure which limits the ability of the system to give end-use consumers good short-run price signals and further reduces the effective short-run elasticity of demand.

One might view these problems as transition issues, though with long-lived investments the transition can take a long time. Ideally, the potential for opportunistic behavior associated with the existing stock of non-redeployable assets configured to match traditional governance arrangements should be taken into account in the design of market institutions and contractual arrangements at the time the sector is restructured. If they are not, the resulting inefficiencies and consumer burdens may ultimately lead to a second (or third) round of reforms.

A second set of problems arises with regard to the coordination of generation and transmission operations and transmission investments. This coordination historically took place within vertically integrated firms. Some of the coordination tasks that were handled through internal protocols are simply very difficult to decentralize effectively with market mechanisms. These coordination problems result from the difficulty of creating "enough" markets to support all important resource-allocation decisions, designing them to clear quickly enough to allocate fast-moving flows of electric power efficiently, temporary market power problems that arise from network congestion and related operating constraints, network externality problems, problems associated with lumpy transmission investments, and the difficulty of defining meaningful property rights for using the transmission network which do not degrade the efficiency of the system (Joskow and Tirole 2000). The implementation of electricity sector restructuring has sometimes ignored these problems, with unfortunate results.

A third related set of problems is associated with broader market power problems in competitive electricity markets. The objective of restructuring is not simply to create "unregulated markets," but to create reasonably *competitive* markets with good performance attributes. Electricity has unusual attributes that make spot electricity markets especially conducive to market power problems: non-storability, inelastic demand, and network congestion. Market power problems arose in the England and Wales wholesale market during the 1990s and have arisen in the United States. They have also plagued small developing countries which have restructured their electricity industries to rely on competitive wholesale markets.

Let me focus here on four specific types of problems that appear to be common across electricity sector reforms in developed countries.

6.1   Local market power problems

Under certain supply and demand conditions specific generating plants or small groups of generating plants located at specific locations on the network must be operated to maintain the physical integrity of the network. This is the case because legacy transmission networks have operating constraints that make it impossible to physically supply all demand at specific locations from remote generating plants under all supply and demand conditions.[24] After restructuring, the network operator typically runs one of more auction markets in which generators submit bids to supply energy or reserves in response to calls from the network operator to manage network congestion or other physical operating constraints at particular locations on the network. If generators know that they must be called by the system operator to run regardless of the price they charge, they are in a position to bid very high prices into the auction markets run by the network operator, at least until new investments in generating and transmission capacity are made to increase sufficiently the number of competing supply sources available under these conditions. That is, these generators have "local market power" under certain system conditions and can "hold up" the system operator and those who pay for its costs.

Industry restructuring initiatives have had problems identifying and dealing with these local market power problems. Some analysts have been surprised that these problems are so pervasive. They should not have been surprised. When transmission and generation were vertically integrated, investment and operating decisions involving generation and transmission assets were made jointly. When a vertically integrated electric utility considered investing more money in transmission import capability into an area it assumed that it would operate the transmission and generation facilities in an integrated fashion to minimize costs. It did not take "local market power" considerations into account when it made generation and transmission investments because it had no incentive to hold itself up. Restructured electricity sectors inherited the long-lived sunk transmission and generation investments of the past. However, with the separation of transmission and generation, unregulated generators located at such strategic locations on the network now had the incentive and ability to exercise local market power in the absence of mitigation mechanisms being introduced as part of the reform process.

Designing good local market power mitigation mechanisms has proven to be difficult and they have sometimes led to perverse results causing more costly problems than those they were supposed to fix.[25] One potential response would be simply to invest more in transmission capacity to remove the congestion and eliminate the opportunity to exercise local market power. This would properly be viewed as a cost of vertical restructuring to promote competition among power suppliers that is properly weighed against the potential benefits of these reforms. An alternative approach would be to rely on contractual mechanisms to mitigate local market power. For example, an option contract could be negotiated which specifies a competitive call price that the network operator pays if it must call on the generator out-of-bid-merit-order to meet local reliability constraints.[26] The terms of such a contract must be determined *ex ante* before restructuring is completed (or at least the basic contractual principles specified *ex ante*). Moreover, since there is small numbers bargaining both *ex ante* and *ex post*, the terms and conditions of such contracts are likely to have to be determined through a regulatory process.

When the new system covering England and Wales was created in 1990, essentially no consideration was given to local market power problems.[27] When local market power problems emerged the regulator was surprised and *ex post* price control mechanism were devised and applied.[28] The National Grid Company subsequently made additional transmission investments to reduce the network congestion that gives rise to local market power problems.

California also recognized the potential for local market power problems associated with generators at strategic locations on the grid and identified generators that would be designated "must run" before they were auctioned off. The California restructuring team also specified the terms and conditions of contracts to mitigate local market power while maintaining supplies from these units for local reliability purposes. Unfortunately, these contracts were poorly structured and had terrible incentive features, creating more problems than they solved.[29] Reforming them was a very contentious issue. The PJM restructuring[30] recognized local market power issues *ex ante* and built regulatory and contractual mechanisms into the restructuring program *ex ante*. These mechanisms were well designed and have performed well so far. New York recognized these potential local market power problems for New York City, but not for the rest of the state, as the restructuring process proceeded through the state. The New York City program relies on a set of mitigation rules that apply when imports into the city are constrained and the ownership of generating capacity within the city is highly concentrated. The local market power mitigation mechanisms for the rest of New York State were vague and remain controversial.

6.2   *Management of network congestion*

As supply and demand conditions on a transmission network change, equipment is forced out of service because it breaks down, or is taken out of service for maintenance, competing generators may attempt to schedule more supplies at particular points on the network than the network is capable of accommodating without creating an unacceptably high probability of system failure. That is, a transmission network can become congested at a large number of different locations under certain supply and demand conditions.[31] These supply and demand conditions, and the associated locations and magnitudes of network congestion, can change very quickly and the network operator must be prepared to manage any resulting congestion virtually instantly. This congestion management challenge arises in many situations other than those that are associated with the local market power problems discussed immediately above.

Some restructuring programs (e.g. PJM and New York in the United States) took the congestion management challenge very seriously and designed market mechanisms and network operating protocols around them.[32] They provide for prices of power to vary from one location to another. These market mechanisms effectively sought to replicate the way the system was operated when it was vertically integrated, replacing market-based bids for the marginal cost-based internal control signals historically utilized by vertically integrated forms. Other restructuring programs (e.g. New England and California) were built around the assumption that network congestion was not a serious issue and that the associated costs could be "socialized" (e.g. New England) or that congestion could be subsumed into a small number of large geographic zones (e.g. California). These latter restructuring initiatives are now being redesigned because network congestion has proven to be much more of a problem than had been assumed. These problems arise both because the incidence of network congestion is more frequent than had been assumed *and* because operating rules that ignored it create incentives for unregulated generators to behave strategically and to create congestion that would not otherwise exist.

When the industry was vertically integrated, utilities handled network congestion through their internal dispatching programs which generally took congestion into account internally when generators were scheduled and dispatched. They had no incentive to create congestion because there was no profit associated with doing so. Moreover, a great deal of potential congestion was not actually observed in the data because the congestion was anticipated by internal dispatch routines and it was not actually observed *ex post*. With vertical separation, the network operator must now always manage observed congestion, which makes its incidence more visible, and it must do so in a world where unregulated generators have an incentive to exploit any imperfections in the congestion management protocols to their advantage. Again, this is a legacy of long-lived investments in generating and transmission capacity made under different governance arrangements.

While decentralized mechanisms to manage congestion efficiently have been devised,[33] making them work well in practice has proven to be difficult. Their design has generally ignored transaction-cost considerations and implicitly assumes that all supplies are price-takers. The large number of congestion "markets" that must exist in theory to capture all of the rapidly changing network effects, the speed with which such markets would have to clear (simultaneously), and the presence of imperfect rather than perfect competition, all provide incentives that promote strategic behavior which seeks to exploit these imperfections under certain supply and demand conditions. We do not yet know how costly these imperfections are. However, I believe that they are likely to be large and that trying to fully remedy these problems with more and more complicated congestion market management mechanisms will be futile and probably counter-productive.

As a result of the interaction between congestion and the intensity of competition, as well as the challenges of managing a decentralized electric power network with a lot of congestion, it may very well make sense to "over-invest" in transmission capacity, compared to the investments that would have been made by a regulated vertically integrated monopoly, reducing congestion, simplifying the task of market-based congestion management, and enhancing competition in wholesale power markets. The additional transmission investments would be an additional cost of restructuring and deregulation. A cost that would then have to be compared against the expected benefits of competition in the supply of power.

6.3   Market power problems when supplies of generating capacity are tight

The demand for electricity varies widely from hour to hour and day to day. The demand on a system during the peak hours of a year may be three times the lowest hourly demand on the system. Demand may vary by a factor of 2 or more from peak to trough on a given day. However, the short-run elasticity of demand (day-ahead, hour-ahead, real-time) is very small (almost zero). The near-zero short-run demand elasticity reflects both the inherent willingness to pay for electricity, given sunk investments in appliances and equipment that use electricity, and the fact that few retail consumers (presently) actually can see and react to short-run price fluctuations because they do not have meters that give them these price signals[34] or the communications and control technology to react to them. The fact that real-time metering, communications and control technology had not diffused more widely under traditional industry structure and governance arrangements reflects both the costs of the associated equipment and the limited incentives regulated utilities may have had to invest in these technologies.[35]

The short-run competitive supply (marginal cost) curve for a typical thermal generation system rises very steeply as supply increases towards the capacity limits of the system. This reflects both the fact that electricity cannot be stored (ultimate in JIT manufacturing required) and the high marginal operating cost of the generating units that are called on (infrequently) when supply is very high.

Performance problems are frequently observed in wholesale spot power markets under conditions when demand is very high, supply is fairly inelastic (i.e. as less efficient capacity is turned on to meet high demand levels), and a large fraction of demand is served through the spot market. When these conditions coexist, even relatively small generators perceive that their bidding behavior in spot markets can influence the market price.[36] The result is a very serious market power problem that can lead to market clearing prices that are almost unbounded.[37]

This kind of problem was never observed when firms were vertically integrated monopolies. There were certainly situations when supply was very scarce and demand was very inelastic, but a regulated vertically integrated firm did not have the ability to exploit such market power opportunities in sales to its regulated retail customers because the prices these customers paid were fixed by regulation based on its supply costs. Vertically integrated utilities with excess capacity to sell to other utilities in the wholesale market may have had the incentive to charge high prices when supplies were tight, but these sales were subject to cost-based price caps and the vertically integrated utility buyers often could respond to high wholesale prices by running their own marginal generating capacity instead.[38] On the other hand, regulated vertically integrated electric utilities did not have incentives to use prices to ration scarce capacity efficiently and to install metering technology to facilitate rationing by price. Instead, non-price rationing (brownouts and rolling blackouts) was used to manage excess demand.

One of the potential benefits of competitive wholesale and retail electricity markets is that they will stimulate competing electricity suppliers to offer consumers who can respond to price volatility, price-sensitive contracts that provide the price signals, communications, and control systems which can facilitate consumer interaction with the wholesale spot market. Even a relatively small amount of price-sensitive demand can significantly reduce generator market power under these conditions. Again, however, restructured electricity sectors inherited the stocks of metering and communications equipment from the past and often operate with transition pricing policies that mute the incentives consumers have to choose price-responsive contracts. Accordingly, adaptations to respond to market power problems that arise during tight supply conditions have been slow to develop. This suggests in turn that it would be sensible to include as an important feature of restructured electricity sectors with wholesale and retail competition a substantial financial commitment to pay for installation of real-time metering, communications and control equipment *ex ante*, rather than waiting for "the market" to produce these investments. This is the case because even a relatively small investment in real-time metering and control can dampen market power and benefit all consumers, those with and those without real-time metering and control equipment.

Another factor that is important for reducing the incentive and ability suppliers have to inflate market prices under these conditions is the presence of forward contracts between generators and consumers (through marketing intermediaries) that commit the suppliers to supply predetermined quantities and predetermined prices to the network.[39] If a large fraction of demand is covered by forward contracts which specify prices and quantities *ex ante* this not only insulates consumers from price volatility but also reduces the incentives suppliers have to withhold output to drive up prices in the spot market. This is the case because most of their supply is already committed at a fixed price and suppliers get no benefit from higher spot prices on this "infra-marginal" supply. This in turn changes the strategic bidding calculus since the costs of failing to find a buyer for a supplier's remaining capacity now loom larger relative to the benefits of increasing market prices.[40]

The contracting strategy works best if the restructuring program can begin with a set of forward contracts that were specified administratively *ex ante* and which phase out gradually over time as the market evolves. New contracts can then be negotiated between retail suppliers and generators under competitive conditions. The restructuring reforms in England and Wales, Australia, New England, PJM and parts of New York took this approach. California did not and this is one reason for the California wholesale electricity market's meltdown in 2000.[41]

6.4   Coordination of transmission and generation investments

Most high-voltage transmission investments were undertaken by vertically integrated firms in conjunction with investments in new generating capacity to meet growing electricity demand and to replace antiquated generating equipment. That is, generating and transmission capacity enhancements were carefully coordinated by vertically integrated firms. Transmission and generation are both complements (some transmission investment is needed to accommodate production from a new generator) and substitutes (a generator located close to a demand center requires less transmission investment than one located in a remote area with little local demand). Transmission investments can also be lumpy and require longer planning, permitting, and construction times than new generating plants. The trade-offs between the location of new generating facilities and investments in new transmission facilities are complicated by the physical interdependencies of demand and supply at different locations on a transmission network. A vertically integrated firm which spanned a large enough geographic area could both coordinate generating and transmission investment and internalize potential network externalities.

In many countries that have implemented electricity sector reforms of this nature, it has proven to be difficult to stimulate adequate transmission investments in the right locations to accommodate the entry and exit of generators and to promote competition among existing generators over large geographic areas. That is, the design and implementation of decentralized mechanisms to coordinate the behavior of competing generators and a regulated independent transmission owner (or owners) has been a difficult challenge. The problems associated with stimulating appropriate transmission investments in turn undermine the performance of the competitive generation markets that rely on them.

7   Conclusions

During the 1990s, many countries reformed their electricity sectors to rely on competitive wholesale and retail markets to replace supply and marketing functions that were traditionally undertaken within regulated vertically integrated monopolies. While several of these programs achieved some of their goals for performance improvements, there have also been a number of common problems that have emerged. These problems have necessitated major *ex post* changes to market and/or regulatory institutions to mitigate them. Indeed, wholesale electricity market design appears to be a never-ending work in progress. The wholesale market institutions in England and Wales, for example, have been changed dramatically after a decade of experience with the original pool-based wholesale market framework. Moreover, numerous changes were made in these market arrangements during their initial ten-year run. Similarly, in the United States there have been serious market failures that have necessitated major market redesign efforts in California, New York, and New England only a few years after the initial restructuring and competition programs were put in place. It is fairly clear that short-run generator dispatch and congestion management in these new wholesale markets are less efficient than were vertically integrated utilities in performing these functions, while the longer-term benefits associated with new investments in generating capacity, new retail services, and continuing improvement in both are yet to be realized.

While extensive *ex post* market reforms have been necessary to deal with some market performance problems, they may also have a potential long-run cost. Suppliers of competitive services which acquired supply assets from the previous regulated monopolies or have made investments in new generating facilities, based their investment decisions on the rules of the game prevailing when the investments were made. The expectation that market rules may change considerably *ex post* will increase uncertainty and may increase the costs of or even deter new investments. Some *ex post* refinements are certainly likely to be necessary and should be factored into investment decisions. However, the magnitude of the *ex post* changes to market designs that have been required in several countries are not a necessary feature of restructuring regulated monopolies. Rather, they reflect in part the failure to apply TCE thinking and analytical techniques to evaluate alternative reform models and to design new market and regulatory institutions *ex ante* that reflect these considerations. At least some of the problems discussed here could have been avoided or their magnitude reduced if the reform process had proceeded from a TCE perspective.

Many policy-makers have been surprised by how difficult it has been to create competitive wholesale electricity markets that are not plagued by these and other problems. However, had policy-makers viewed the restructuring challenge through using a TCE framework, these potential problems are more likely to have been identified and mechanisms adopted *ex ante* to fix them. Instead, the restructuring programs have often gone forward (a) assuming that there were no economic efficiency reasons for why vertical integration between generation and transmission was the way electricity sectors evolved everywhere on earth, and (b) ignoring the configuration of long-lived sunk investments in the existing system and its implications for competitive market behavior in physical (spot) electricity wholesale markets. Had these factors played a more central role in the reform process, some of the most serious problems could have been avoided or their costs reduced.

The application of TCE analysis also leads to suggestions for improving performance with regard to local market power and congestion management issues, as well as related issues associated with the coordination of generation and transmission investment. Let me conclude with some observations about how the lens of TCE can be used to do a better job of reforming electricity supply industries to rely on competitive wholesale and retail markets for power:

1. The physical and economic attributes of electricity supply and demand make the creation of well-functioning competitive electricity markets a significant technical challenge. The legacy of historical sunk investments on the supply and demand sides of the market complicates the task even further than if we were creating a new set of governance arrangements from scratch. Successful reforms must recognize that it is difficult to create the necessary market and regulatory institutions to support well-functioning competitive electricity markets. The erroneous assumption that the traditional industry structures, in particular vertical integration between generation and transmission, emerged by accident or for some nefarious reason rather than as *relatively* efficient responses to important transactional attributes of electricity supply and demand inevitably leads to serious flaws in the reform program.

Successful reforms should begin with an understanding of the resource allocation tasks that have been performed by traditional governance arrangements, and how and why they were accomplished through internal organizational allocational mechanisms. Electricity markets and supporting regulatory arrangements do not design themselves. Basic market and regulatory institutions must be created by policy-makers from the system that they have inherited from the past. This task is best achieved by adopting a comparative institutional approach that carefully examines a full range of governance alternatives, drawing on international experience with electricity sector restructuring and market reform to choose the set of governance arrangements that is most likely to work well. By fully understanding the transaction-cost attributes of the key allocational tasks and the traditional mechanisms for undertaking them, policy-makers will be in a better position to design and evaluate alternative market and regulatory institutions. All of the resource-allocation tasks that were performed under traditional governance arrangements must be performed under new governance arrangements.

2. Electricity sector reforms necessarily must be built upon an infrastructure made up of long-lived historical sunk investments made over past decades. These investments were made within an institutional environment which did not contemplate the kinds of opportunism, coordination, and market power problems that can emerge in a decentralized system with many independent firms owning and operating different pieces of an industry. Market power problems, network congestion management, and coordination problems arising from restructuring of the existing configuration of assets should be expected and their existence carefully identified *ex ante* as an integral part of the design and implementation of liberalization reforms. Accordingly, electricity restructuring programs need to consciously and carefully include transition mechanisms to mitigate these problems until investments in new generating and transmission capacity can be made to move the system toward a new asset configuration that is less susceptible to them. These mechanisms will include contracts to deal with local market power problems, carefully structured congestion management protocols and rules for injecting and withdrawing power from the grid, and transitional contracts between generators and those entities responsible for procuring power for retail consumers that both protect consumers from exploitation and diminish incentives that generators may have to exercise market power. These transition mechanisms must be put in place at the outset of the restructuring program because they are difficult to implement *ex post*, after problems emerge, since

incumbent interests are likely to have a strong stake in preserving the status quo.

3. It is becoming increasingly clear that unregulated wholesale electricity markets work best when transmission congestion and constraints do not place significant limitations on the number of generators which can compete to serve demand and provide reliability to the network at specific locations. This suggests that the successful development of competitive wholesale electricity markets requires "over-investment" in transmission capacity compared to a governance structure that relies on vertically integrated monopolies subject to regulation. The cost of "over-investment" in transmission is a cost that must be paid to create competitive electricity markets that (we hope) will lead to lower-cost outcomes in other dimensions in the long run than did the institution of a vertically integrated monopoly.[42]

4. Many electricity sector reforms focus on the supply side and ignore the demand side of the equation. The emphasis on supply-side issues is appropriate. However, it is a mistake to avoid demand-side issues completely. A precondition for successful reform is the requirement that at least larger commercial and industrial consumers have real-time meters that require them to pay prices that reflect the fluctuating supply and demand conditions in the wholesale market and associated price volatility. This will provide these consumers with incentives to enter into hedging contracts, demand-management contracts, and to adjust their consumption to variations in wholesale market prices. Such demand-side initiatives will help to improve the performance of wholesale markets by encouraging forward contracting, reducing incentives generators may have to engage in strategic behavior to increase spot market prices, and increase the effective short-run elasticity of demand, further reducing market power problems.

NOTES

This chapter draws heavily on previous research and publications, in particular Joskow (1996, 1998, 2000).

1. See for example, Peltzman and Winston (2000).
2. Joskow (1991, pp. 76–8).
3. This includes both "structural separation," where one or more horizontal segments are organized into separate corporate entities and then sold to an unrelated entity or floated as a new company, as well as "functional separation," where activities in one or more vertical segments are operated separately both physically and financially from the rest of the firm. Meaningful functional separation implies that although the horizontal segments are owned by the same firm, they operate separately. That is, they must behave as if they are not vertically integrated.
4. See Joskow (1996) regarding the electricity sector.

5. See Joskow (1997) regarding the nature of the potential short-run costs and the potential long-term benefits associated with reforms in the electricity sector.
6. Joskow (1991, p. 77).
7. Joskow and Schmalensee (1983).
8. Joskow (1997, 2000). A longer version of the second paper can be found on my web page at http://web.mit.edu/pjoskow/www/.
9. Joskow (1998).
10. Joskow (2000) provides a detailed discussion and evaluation of electricity sector restructuring, competition and regulatory reforms in the United States. The California electricity crisis is discussed in Joskow (2001); see also chapter 25 in this volume.
11. Williamson (1985, 1996).
12. At considerable cost, metering, communications, and control equipment can be installed so that a specific set of generators can be dispatched to match a specific customer's demand and that demand curtailed if those generators do not perform. This is a very inefficient way to supply a customer with electricity. In addition to the metering, communications, and control costs, such an arrangement would sacrifice the network economies associated with a large electric power network.
13. Joskow (1996).
14. In all countries generation and transmission were vertically integrated. Separate distribution companies existed in many countries, but they typically purchased all of their power supply needs from neighboring vertically integrated generation and transmission (G&T) companies under long-term contracts.
15. Joskow and Schmalensee (1983); Joskow (1996).
16. The average rate of growth in electricity consumption was 2.9 percent per year over the 1973–94 period and 7.8 percent per year for the 1960–73 period for the OECD countries. See *Electricity Information 1995*, International Energy Agency, Paris, OECD, July 1996.
17. See for example Organización Latino Americana De Energía (1991).
18. In March 2001, major changes were made to the wholesale market institutions upon which this program was built. It is too early to evaluate the benefits and costs of these changes.
19. The discussion that follows draws heavily on Joskow (1998, 2000).
20. Joskow (1998).
21. This discussion focuses on countries which have large enough electricity supply systems, commercial and regulatory institutions that can support competitive power markets. This excludes many developing countries, especially small developing countries with small isolated electric power systems.
22. Rudnick (1996), Newbery and Pollitt (1996), for example.
23. Despite the recent supply problems in California, there is a huge amount of new merchant generating capacity in the construction pipeline in the United States. A tight supply situation today may become an excess supply situation in a couple of years.
24. Joskow (2000) contains a discussion of local market power problems in California.
25. Bushnell and Wolak (1999).

26. Joskow (1999).
27. Perhaps this is not surprising since little consideration was given to *any* market power problems when this system was created.
28. Office of Electricity Regulation (1992).
29. Bushnell and Wolak (1999); Joskow (1999).
30. "PJM" is the name for the Independent System Operator which is responsible for managing the transmission network and operating various short-term wholesale power markets in an area spanning Pennsylvania, New Jersey, Maryland (PJM), Deleaware, and Washington, DC. PJM was previously a consortium of utilities which has operated a "tight power pool" in this region since the 1920s, operating a centrally dispatched power pool for the vertically integrated utilities in these states.
31. Joskow and Tirole (2000).
32. Generally following concepts developed by Hogan (1992, 1993).
33. Hogan (1992).
34. Meters are typically read once a month and the consumer is billed based on a hypothetical load profile that allocates monthly consumption to specific hours during the previous month.
35. Though in the United States, traditional utilities in several states which have not restructured but continue to rely on regulated vertically integrated utilities rather than full-blown wholesale and retail competition (e.g. Wisconsin, Washington, Georgia) have made greater advances in real-time metering and control than have been made in states that have implemented radical restructuring programs.
36. To convince yourself that this is not a strange anomaly, write down a simple Cournot model with n symmetric firms producing a homogeneous product and a constant elasticity demand function for the product which has a very small demand elasticity (e.g. 0.1) You will see that price/cost margins can be quite high even with a relatively large number of generation suppliers. While electricity markets are probably not well described by a Cournot model, this exercise helps to make the point. See also Wolfram (1998) and Joskow and Kahn (2001).
37. Joskow (2001).
38. The derived demand for wholesale power by a vertically integrated firm is much more elastic than is the final demand of their retail customers since they can substitute their own (more expensive) internal supplies as wholesale market prices rise.
39. Green (1998), Newbery (1998), Wolak (2000). It is fairly clear that once contracts are in place, they change bidding incentives in spot markets and mitigate market power. However, when suppliers have market power it is not clear that they have incentives to enter into contracts that will undermine their market power.
40. Wolfram (1998).
41. Joskow (2001).
42. The potential long-run cost saving opportunities and other potential benefits of electricity sector restructuring are discussed in Joskow (1997).

Bibliography

Abreu, D. (1988). "On the Theory of Infinitely Repeated Games with Discounting," *Econometrica*, 56(2): 383–96

Adler, B.E. (1999). "The Questionable Assent of *Hadley* v. *Baxendale*," *Stanford Law Review*, 51: 1547–89

Aghion, P. and Bolton, P. (1992). "An Incomplete Contracts Approach to Financial Contracting," *Review of Economic Studies*, 59(3): 473–94

(1997). "A Theory of Trickle-Down Growth and Development," *Review of Economic Studies*, 64: 151–72

Aghion, P., Dewatripont, M. and Rey, P. (1994). "Renegotiation Design with Unverifiable Information," *Econometrica*, 6: 257–82

(1999). "Partial Contracting," mimeo

(2000). "Conceding Control to Induce Cooperation: A Partial Contracting Approach," mimeo

(2001). "Partial Contracting," *European Economic Review*, forthcoming

Aghion, P. and Tirole, J. (1997). "Formal and Real Authority in Organizations," *Journal of Political Economy*, 105: 1–29

Akerlof, G.A. (1970). "The Market for Lemons: Quality, Uncertainty and the Market Mechanism," *Quarterly Journal of Economics*, 84: 488–500

(1982). "Labor Contracts as Partial Gift Exchange," *Quarterly Journal of Economics*, 87: 543–69

(1984). "Labor Contracts as a Partial Gift Exchange," in G.A. Akerlof, *An Economist Theorist's Book of Tales*, Cambridge University Press: 145–74

Akerlof, G.A. and Yellen, J.L. (1986). *Efficiency Wage Models of the Labor Market*, Cambridge University Press

(1990). "The Fair Wage-Effort Hypotheses and Unemployment," *Quarterly Journal of Economics*, 105: 255–83

Aláez, R., Bilbao, J., Camino, V. and Longás, J. (1997). "Las relaciones interempresariales como estrategia de reducción de costes en el sector de la automoción: el caso del País Vasco y Navarra," *Economía Industrial*, 315: 85–100

Alchian, A.A. (1950). "Uncertainty, Evolution and Economic Theory," *Journal of Political Economy*, 58: 211–21

(1961). *Some Economics of Property Rights*, Rand Corporation, Santa Monica, California

(1998). "First Negotiation, First Refusal Rights," Personal correspondence, February 18

532   Bibliography

Alchian, A.A. and Demsetz, H. (1972). "Production, Information Costs, and Economic Organization," *American Economic Review*, 62(5): 777–95

Allam, D. and Le Gall, P. (1999). *La nature de la relation franchiseur-franchisé. Evolution, perspectives et incidences stratégiques, économiques, et juridiques*, Research Report, Université Paris I, Panthéon-Sorbonne

Allen, D.W., Lueck, D. (1992a). "Contract Choice in Modern Agriculture: Cropshare versus Cash Rent," *Journal of Law and Economics*, 35: 397–426

  (1992b). "The 'Back Forty' on a Handshake: Specific Assets, Reputation, and the Structure of Farmland Contracts," *Journal of Law, Economics and Organization*, 8: 366–76

  (1993). "Transaction Costs and the Design of Cropshare Contracts," *Rand Journal of Economics*, 24: 78–101

  (1995). "Risk Preference and the Economics of Contracts," *American Economic Review*, 85: 447–51

  (1998). "The Nature of the Farm," *Journal of Law and Economics*, 41: 343–86

  (1999). "The Role of Risk in Contract Choice," *Journal of Law, Economics, and Organization*, 15: 704–36

Alston, L.J., Libecap, G.D. and Mueller, B. (1999a). *Titles, Conflict, and Land Use: The Development of Property Rights and Land Reform on the Brazilian Amazon Frontier*, Ann Arbor, University of Michigan Press

  (1999b). "A Model of Rural Conflict: Violence and Land Reform Policy in Brazil," *Environment and Development Economics*, 4: 135–60

  (2000). "Land Reform Policies, the Sources of Violent Conflict and Implications for Deforestation in the Brazilian Amazon," *Journal of Environmental Economics and Management*, 39: 162–88

Alston, L.J., Libecap, G.D. and Schneider, R. (1996). "The Determinants and Impact of Property Rights: Land Titles on the Brazilian Frontier," *The Journal of Law, Economics and Organization*, 12(1): 25–61

Alt, J.E. and Shepsle, K.A. (1990). *Perspectives on Positive Political Economy*, Cambridge University Press

Amran, M. and Kulatilaka, N. (1999). *Real Options: Managing Strategic Investment in an Uncertain World*, Boston, Harvard Business School Press

Amendola, M. and Gaffard, J.L. (1998). *Out of equilibrium*, Oxford, Clarendon Press

Anand, B.N. and Khanna, T. (2000). "The Structure of Licensing Contracts," *Journal of Industrial Economics*, 48(1): 103–35

Ancel, V.P. (1999). "Force obligatoire et contenu obligationnel du contrat," *Revue Trimestrielle de Droit Civil*: 771

Anderhub, V., Gächter, S. and Königstein, M. (1999). "Efficient Contracting and Fair Play in a Simple Principal–Agent Experiment," *Working Paper*, July (forthcoming in *Experimental Economics*)

Anderlini, L. and Felli, L. (1994). "Incomplete Written Contracts, Undescribable States of Nature," *Quarterly Journal of Economics*, 109(439): 1085–124

  (1999). "Incomplete Contracts and Complexity Costs," *Theory and Decision*, 46: 23–50

Anderson, E. (1985). "The Salesperson as Outside Agent or Employee: A Transaction Cost Perspective," *Management Science*, 4: 234–54

Anderson, L. and Schmittlein, D.C. (1984). "Integration of the Sales Force: An Empirical Examination," *Rand Journal of Economics*, 15: 3–19

Anderson, L. and Hill, P.J. (1975). "The Evolution of Property Rights: A Study of the American West," *Journal of Law and Economics*, 18(1): 163–79

Anderson, T.L. and McChesney, F.S. (eds.) (2001). *The Law and Economics of Property Rights*, Palo Alto, Hoover Institution, monograph

Aoki, M. (1988). *Information, Incentives and Bargaining in the Japanese Economy*, Cambridge, Cambridge University Press

  (2001). *Toward a Comparative Institutional Analysis*, Cambridge, MA., MIT Press

Armstrong, C.M., Cowan, S.G.B. and Vickers, J.S. (1994). *Regulatory Reform – Economic Analysis and British Experience*, Cambridge, MA, MIT Press

  (1995). "Nonlinear Pricing and Average Revenue Regulation," *Journal of Public Economics*, 58: 33–55

Armstrong, C.M., Doyle, C. and Vickers, J.S. (1996). "The Access Pricing Problem: A Synthesis," *Journal of Industrial Economics*, 44(2): 131–50

Armstrong, C.M., Rees, R. and Vickers, J.S. (1995). "Optimal Regulatory Lag under Price Cap Regulation," *Revista Española de Economia*, Special issue: 93–116

Armstrong, C.M. and Vickers, J.S. (1991). "Welfare Effects of Price Discrimination by a Regulated Monopolist," *Rand Journal of Economics*, 22: 571–80

Arora, A. (1995). "Licensing Tacit Knowledge: Intellectual Property Rights and the Market for Know-How," *Economics of Innovation and New Technology*, 4: 41–59

  (1996). "Contracting for Tacit Knowledge: The Provision of Technical Services in Technology Licensing Contracts," *Journal of Development Economics*, 50: 233–56

  (1997). "Patent, Licensing and Market Structure in the Chemical Industry," *Research Policy*, 26: 391–403

Arora, A. and Fosfuri, A. (1999). "Licensing the Market for Technology," *CEPR Discussion Paper*, 2284, London

Arora, A., Fosfuri, A. and Gambardella, A. (2001). *Markets for Technology: The Economics of Innovation and Corporate Strategy*, Cambridge, MA, MIT Press

Arora, A. and Gambardella, A. (1994). "The Changing Technology of Technological Change: General and Abstract Knowledge and the Division of Innovative Labour," *Research Policy*, 23: 523–32

  (1998). "Evolution of Industry Structure in the Chemical Industry," in A. Arora, R. Landau and N. Rosenberg (eds.), *Chemicals and Long Term Economic Growth*, New York, John Wiley

Arora, A. and Merges, R.P. (2001). "Property Rights, Firm Boundaries, and R&D Inputs," Carnegie Mellon University, Pittsburgh, PA, unpublished manuscript

Arrow, K.J. (1962). "Comments on Case Studies," in R.R. Nelson (ed.), *The Rate and the Direction of Inventive Activity: Economic and Social Factors*, Princeton University Press

  (1971). *Essays in the Theory of Risk*, Amsterdam, North-Holland

  (1974). *The Limits of Organization*, New York, Norton

(1985). "The Economics of Agency," in J.W. Pratt and R.J. Zeckhauser, *Principals and Agents: The Structure of Business*, Boston, Harvard Business School Research College: 37–51

(1999). "Foreword," in G. Carroll and D. Teece (eds.), *Firms, Markets, and Hierarchies*, New York, Oxford University Press: vii–viii

Arrow, K.J. and Fisher, A. (1974). "Environmental Preservation, Uncertainty and Irreversibility," *Quarterly Journal of Economics*, 88: 312–19

Arrow, K.J. and Hahn, F.H. (1971). *General Competitive Analysis*, San Francisco, Holden-Day

Arruñada, B. (1996). "The Economics of Notaries," *European Journal of Law and Economics*, 3: 5–37

(1999a). *La lógica del aplazamiento de pago y la morosidad entre fabricantes y distribuidores*, Madrid, Marcial Pons

(1999b). *La directiva sobre morosidad: una mala solución para un falso problema*, Madrid, Marcial Pons

(1999c). *The Economics of Audit Quality: Private Incentives and the Regulation of Audit and Non-Audit Services*, Boston and Dordrecht, Kluwer

(2000). "Audit Quality: Attributes, Private Safeguards and the Role of Regulation," *European Accounting Review*, 9: 205–24

(2001). "The Role of Institutions in the Contractual Process," in T. Kirat and B. Deffains (eds.), *Law and Economics in Civil Law Countries*, Stamford, CT: JAI Press: 177–96

(2002). *Business Economics: A Contractual Approach*, Cambridge University Press, forthcoming

Arruñada, B., Garicano, L. and Vázquez, L. (2001). "Contractual Allocation of Decision Rights and Incentives: The Case of Automobile Distribution," *Journal of Law, Economics, and Organization*, 17: 256–83

Asanuma, B. (1989) "Manufacturer–Supplier Relationships in Japan and the Concept of Relation-Specific Skill," *Journal of Japanese and International Economies*, 3(1): 1–30

Athey, S. and Stern, S. (1998). "An Empirical Framework for Testing Theories about Complementarity in Organizational Design," *NBER Working Paper*, 6600

Audard, C. (1988). "Principes de justice et principes du libéralisme: la 'neutralité' de la théorie de Rawls," *Individu et Justice Sociale, Autour de John Rawls*, 172

Averch, H. and Johnson, L.L. (1962). "Behaviour of the Firm under Regulatory Constraint," *American Economic Review*, 52: 1052–69

Axelrod, R. (1981). "The Emergence of Cooperation Among Egoists," *American Journal of Political Science*, 75(2): 306–18

Ayres, I. and Gertner, R. (1989). "Filling Gaps in Incomplete Contracts: An Economic Theory of Default Rules," *Yale Law Journal*, 99(87): 87–130

Azariadis, C. (1975). "Implicit Contracts and Underemployment Equilibria," *Journal of Economic Theory*, 12(75): 1183–202

Baake, P. and Wichmann, T. (1999). "On the Economics of Internet Peering," *Netnomics*, 1: 89–105

Bai, C. and Tao, Z. (1999). "Contract Mixing in Franchising as a Mechanism for Public Good Provision," *Journal of Economics and Management Strategy*, 9(1): 85–113

Bain, J.S. (1947). *The Economics of the Pacific Coast Petroleum Industry*, part III, Berkeley, University of California Press

(1968). *Industrial Organization*, 2nd edn., New York, John Wiley

Bajari, P. and Tadelis, S. (1999). "Incentives versus Transaction Costs: A Theory of Procurement Contracts," unpublished paper

Baker, G, (1992). "Incentive Contracts and Performance Measurement," *Journal of Political Economy*, 100: 598–614

Baker, G., Gibbons, R. and Murphy, K.J. (1994). "Subjective Performance Measures in Optimal Incentive Contracts," *Quarterly Journal of Economics*, 109(439): 1125–56

(1997). "Implicit Contracts and the Theory of the Firm," *Technical Report*, 6177, National Bureau of Economic Research, September

(1999). "Relational Contracts and the Theory of the Firm," *Working Paper*, Harvard University

(2002). "Relational Contracts and the Theory of the Firm," *Quarterly Journal of Economics*, 107(1): 39–84

Baker, G. and Hubbard, T. (2000). "Contractibility and Asset Ownership: On-Board Computers and Governance in US Trucking," Harvard Business School, mimeo

Baker, G.P., Jensen, M.C. and Murphy, K.J. (1988). "Compensation and Incentives: Practice vs. Theory," *Journal of Finance*, 43(3): 593–616

Baldwin, C.Y. and Clark, K.B. (1992). "Capabilities and Capital Investment: New Perspectives on Capital Budgeting," *Journal of Applied Corporate Finance*, 5(2): 67–82

Baldwin, R. and McCrudden, C. (1987). *Regulation and Public Law*, London, Weidenfeld & Nicolson

Ball, P. (1994). *Designing the Molecular World: Chemistry at the Frontier*, Princeton University Press

Baranès, W. and Frison-Roche, M.A. (1994). "Foreword," in W. Baranès and M.A. Frison-Roche (eds.), *La Justice, l'Obligation Impossible*, Paris, Autrement, at 13

Barnard, C.I. (1938). *The Functions of the Executive*, Cambridge, MA, Harvard University Press (fifteenth printing, 1962)

Baron, D. (1985). "Regulation of Prices and Pollution under Incomplete Information," *Journal of Public Economics*, 28(2): 211–31

Baron, D. and Besanko, D. (1984). "Regulation and Information in a Continuing Relationship," *Information Economics and Policy*, 1: 267–330

(1992). "Information, Control and Organizational Structure," *Journal of Economics and Management Strategy*, 1: 237–75

Baron, D. and Myerson, R. (1982). "Regulating a Monopolist with Unknown Costs," *Econometrica*, 50: 911–30

Barro, R.J. (1997). "Economic Growth in a Cross Section of Countries," *The Economics of Productivity*, 2, Cheltenham, Edgar Elgar

Barron, J.M. and Umbeck, J.R. (1984). "The Effects of Different Contractual Arrangements: The Case of Retail Gasoline," *Journal of Law and Economics*, 27: 313–28

Barzel, Y. (1982). "Measurement Cost and the Organization of Markets," *Journal of Law and Economics*, 25: 27–48

(1989). *The Economics of Property Rights*, Cambridge University Press

Battigalli, P. and Maggi, G. (2000). "Contracting over Time when Writing is Costly," Princeton University, mimeo

Baumol, W. and Sidack, G. (1994). "The Pricing of Inputs Sold to Competitors," *Yale Journal of Regulation*, 11: 171–202

Bawa, V.S. and Sibley, D.S. (1980). "Dynamic Behaviour of a Firm Subject to Stochastic Regulatory Review," *International Economic Review*, 21: 627–42

Beales, H. and Muris, T.J. (1995). "The Foundation of Franchise Regulation: Issues and Evidence," *Journal of Corporate Finance: Contracting, Governance and Organization*, 2: 157–97

Beard, T., Kaserman, D. and Mayo, J. (1996). "Regulation, Vertical Integration, and Sabotage," mimeo

Beaudry, P. and Poitevin, M. (1993). "Signalling and Renegotiation in Contractual Relationships," *Econometrica*, 61: 745–82

Bebchuk, L.A. and Shavell, S. (1991). "Information and the Scope of Liability for Breach of Contract: The Rule of *Hadley* v. *Baxendale*," *Journal of Law, Economics and Organization*, 7(2): 284–312

(1999). "Reconsidering Contractual Liability and the Incentive to Reveal Information," *Stanford Law Review*, 51: 1615–27

Becker, G.S. (1975). *Human Capital: A Theoretical and Empirical Analysis with Special Reference to Education*, 2nd edn., New York, Columbia University Press

Beggs, A.W. (1992). "The Licensing of Patents Under Asymmetric Information," *International Journal of Industrial Organization*, 10: 171–91

Bénabent, A. (1992). "Rapport français, la bonne foi dans l'exécution du contrat," in *La Bonne Foi, Travaux de l'Association H. Capitant*: 291

Bercovitz, J.E.L. (1999). "An Analysis of the Contract Provisions in Business-Format Franchise Agreements," in J. Stanworth and D. Purdy (eds.), *Franchising Beyond the Millennium: Learning Lessons from the Past*, Proceedings of the 13th Conference of the Society of Franchising

Berg, J., Daley, L., Dickhaut, J. and O'Brien, J. (1992). "Moral Hazard and Risk Sharing: Experimental Evidence," *Research in Experimental Economics*, 5: 1–34

Berle, A.A. and Gardner, C. Means, Jr. (1932). *The Modern Corporation and Private Property*, New York, Macmillan

Bernanke, B.S. (1983). "Irreversibility, Uncertainty and Cyclical Investment," *Quarterly Journal of Economics*, 98: 85–106

Bernheim, B.D. and Whinston, M.D. (1998). "Incomplete Contracts and Strategic Ambiguity," *American Economic Review*, 88(4): 902–32

Bernstein, L. (1996). "Merchant Law in a Merchant Court: Rethinking the Code's Search for Immanent Business Norms," *Pennsylvania Law Review*, 144: 1766–1821

(1999). "The Questionable Basis of Article 2's Incorporation Strategy: A Preliminary Study," *University of Chicago Law School Law and Economics Working Paper* (2nd series): 74

Besanko, D., Dranove, D. and Shanley, M. (2000). *Economics of Strategy*, 2nd edn., New York, Wiley

Bessy, C. and Brousseau, E. (1998). "Technology Licensing Contracts: Features and Diversity," *International Review of Law and Economics*, 18: 451–89

Bessy, C., Brousseau, E. and Saussier, S. (2001). "Payment Schemes in Technology Licensing Agreements: A Transaction Cost Approach," University of Paris, mimeo, April

Bhattacharyya, S. and Lafontaine, F. (1995). "Double-Sided Moral Hazard and the Nature of Share Contracts," *Rand Journal of Economics*, 26: 761–81

Binmore, K., Shaked, A. and Sutton, J. (1988). "A Further Test of Noncooperative Bargaining Theory: Reply," *American Economic Review*, 75: 1178–80

Blair, R.D. and Kaserman, D.L. (1994). "A Note on Incentive Incompatibility under Franchising," *Review of Industrial Organization*, 9: 323–30

Blair, R.D. and Lafontaine, F. (1999). "Will *Khan* Foster or Hinder Franchising? An Economic Analysis of Maximum Resale Price Maintenance," *Journal of Public Policy in Marketing*, 18: 25–36

Blanchard, C. (1995). "Telecommunications Regulation in New Zealand: Light Handed Regulation and the Privy Council's Judgement," *Telecommunications Policy*, 19: 465–75

Boiteux, M. (1956). "Sur la gestion des monopoles publics astreints à l'équilibre budgétaire," *Econometrica*, 24: 22–40

Bolton, P. and Rajan, A. (2000). "The Employment Relation and the Theory of the Firm: Arm's Length Contracting vs. Authority," Princeton University, mimeo

Bonbright, J.C. (1961). *Principles of Public Utility Rates*, New York, Columbia University Press

Borenstein, S. and Bushnell, J. (2000). "Electricity Restructuring: Deregulation or Reregulation?," *Regulation*, 23(2): 46–52

Borenstein, S., Bushnell, J. and Wolak, F.A. (2000). "Diagnosing Market Power in California's Deregulated Wholesale Electricity Market," University of California Energy Institute, *Power Working Paper*, PWP-064r

Bradach, J.L. (1997). "Using the Plural Form in the Management of Restaurant Chains," *Administrative Science Quarterly*, 42: 276–303

Bradley, I. and Price, C. (1988a). "The Economic Regulation of Private Industries by Price Constraints," *Journal of Industrial Economic Studies*, 37: 99–106

(1988b). "The Regulation of British Telecom's Prices," University of Leicester, *Discussion Paper*, 72

Brainard, L. and Martimort, D. (1997). "Strategic Trade Policy with Incompletely Informed Policymakers," *Journal of International Economics*, 42: 33–65

Brickley, J.A. (1999). "Incentive Conflicts and Contractual Restraints: Evidence from Franchising," *Journal of Law and Economics*, 42: 745–74

(2001). "Evidence of Life-Cycle Pricing in Franchise Contracts," Simon School of Business, University of Rochester, mimeo

Brickley, J.A. and Dark, F.H. (1987). "The Choice of Organizational Form: The Case of Franchising," *Journal of Financial Economics*, 18: 401–20

Brickley, J.A., Dark, F.H. and Weisbach, M.S. (1991). "The Economic Effect of Franchise Termination Laws," *Journal of Law and Economics*, 24: 101–32

538   **Bibliography**

Brickley, J.A., Smith, C.W. and Zimmerman, J.L. (1997). *Managerial Economics and Organizational Architecture*, New York, Irwin/McGraw-Hill
Brousseau, E. (1993). *L'économie des contrats: technologies de l'information et coordination interentreprises*, Paris, PUF
    (1996). "Contrats et comportements coopératifs: le cas des relations interentreprises," in J.L. Ravix (ed.), *Coopération entre les Entreprises et Organisation Industrielle*, Paris, CNRS Editions
Brousseau, E. and Fares, M. (2000). "The Incomplete Contract Theory and the New-Institutional Economics Approaches to Contracts: Substitutes or Complements?" in C. Ménard (ed.), *Institutions, Contracts, Organizations, Perspectives from New-Institutional Economics*, Cheltenham, Edward Elgar
Brown, C. (1990). "Firms' Choice of Method of Pay," *Industrial and Labour Relations Review*, Special Issue, 43(3): 165S–82S
Brown, G.M. (2000). "Renewable Natural Resource Management and Use without Markets," *Journal of Economic Literature*, 38(4): 875–915
Brownsword, R. (1996). "From Co-Operative Contracting to Contract of Co-Operation," in D. Campbell and P. Vincent-Jones (eds.), *Contract and Economic Organisation, Socio-Legal Initiatives*, Aldershot, Dartmouth
Bull, C. (1987). "The Existence of Self-Enforcing Implicit Contracts," *Quarterly Journal of Economics*, 102: 147–59
Bushnell, J. and Wolak, F. (1999). "Regulation and the Leverage of Local Market Power in the California Electricity Market," paper presented to the 1999 NBER Summer Industrial Organization Workshop, July
Cadiet, L. (1987). "Interrogations sur le droit contemporain des contrats," in *Le Droit Contemporain des Contrats*, 9(10): 15–17
Caillaud, B. (1991). "Regulation, Competition and Asymmetric Information," *Journal of Economic Theory*, 52: 87–110
Cain, B.E., Ferejohn, J. and Fiorina, M. (1987). *The Personal Vote: Constituency Service and Electoral Independence*, Cambridge, MA, Harvard University Press
Carmichael, H.L. (1983). "The Agents-Agents Problem: Payment by Relative Output," *Journal of Labor Economics*, 1: 50–65
Carmichael, H.L. and MacLeod, W.B. (1997). "Gift Giving and the Evolution of Cooperation," *International Economic Review*, 38: 485–509
Carney, E.M. (1978). *Pricing Provisions in Coals Contracts*, Rocky Mountain Mineral Law Institute, New York/Matthew Bender: 197–230
Caves, R., Crookel, H. and Killing, J.P. (1983). "The Imperfect Market for Technology Licensing," *Oxford Bulletin of Economics and Statistics*, 45: 249–67
CEC, Commission of the European Communities (1997). *Report on Late Payments in Commercial Transactions*, Brussels, June 9, C(97) 2121
Champaud, C. (1962). "Le contrat de société existe-t-il encore ?," in *Le Droit Contemporain des Contrats*, 9(10): 125
Chandler, A.D. Jr. (1962). *Strategy and Structure*, Cambridge, MA: MIT Press
Charreaux, G. (1999). "La théorie positive de l'agence: lecture et relectures . . . ", in G. Koenig (ed.), *De Nouvelles Théories pour Gérer l'Entreprise du XXIè Siècle*, Paris, Economica, March: 61–141
Charreaux, G. (ed.), (1997). *Le Gouvernement des Entreprises: Corporate Governance, Théories et Faits*, Paris, Economica

Chaserant, C. (2000). *Rationalité et Gestion de l'Incomplétude dans les Relations Contractuelles*, Thèse pour le doctorat en sciences économiques, Université Paris X

Che, Y.-K. and Hausch, D.B. (1999). "Cooperative Investments and the Value of Contracting," *American Economic Review*, 89(1): 125–47

Cheung, S.N.S. (1970). "The Structure of a Contract and the Theory of a Non-Exclusive Resource," *Journal of Law and Economics*, 13(1): 49–70

Chirez, A. (1977). *De la Confiance en Droit Contractuel*, PhD Thesis, Nice

Chung, T. (1991). "Incomplete Contracts, Specific Investments, and Risk Sharing," *Review of Economic Studies*, 58: 1031–42

Church, J. and Gandal, N. (1992). "Network Effects, Software Provision and Standardization," *Journal of Industrial Economics*, 40: 85–103

Churchland, P.S. and Sejnowski, T.J. (1993). *The Computational Brain*, Cambridge, MA, MIT Press

Coase, R.H. (1937). "The Nature of the Firm," *Economica* NS, 4: 386–405, reprinted in O.E. Williamson and S. Winter (eds.), *The Nature of the Firm: Origins, Evolution, Development*, NewYork, Oxford University Press (1991): 18–33

(1960). "The Problem of Social Cost," *Journal of Law and Economics*, 2: 1–44

(1972). "Industrial Organization: A Proposal for Research," in V.R. Fuchs (ed.), *Policy Issues and Research Opportunities in Industrial Organization*, New York, National Bureau of Economic Research: 59–73

(1984). "The New Institutional Economics," *Journal of Institutional and Theoretical Economics*, 140: 229–31

(1988). "The Nature of the Firm: Origin, Meaning and Influence," *Journal of Law, Economics and Organization*, 4(1): 3–48

(1995). "My Evolution as an Economist," in W. Breit and R.W. Spencer (eds.), *Lives of the Laureates*, Cambridge, MA, MIT, Press: 227–49

Cockburn, I., Henderson, R. and Stern, S. (2000). "Balancing Incentives: The Tension Between Basic and Applied Research," MIT Sloan School, mimeo

Coeurderoy, R. and Quélin, B. (1997). "L'économie des coûts de transaction. Un bilan des études empiriques sur l'intégration verticale," *Revue d'Économie Politique*, 107: 145–81

Cohen, W., Nelson, R. and Walsh, J. (2000). "Protecting their Intellectual Assets: Appropriability Conditions and Why US Manufacturing Firms Patent (or not)," *NBER Working Paper*, 7552

Coipel, M. (1999). *Eléments de Théorie Générale des Contrats*, Preface by P. Van Ommeslaghe, Story Scientia

Collins, H. (1999). *Regulating Contracts*, London, Oxford University Press

Commons, J.R. (1932). "The Problem of Correlating Law, Economics, and Ethics," *Wisconsin Law Review*, 8: 3–26

(1934). *Institutional Economics: Its Place in Political Economy*, New York, Macmillan

Conlisk, J. (1988). "Optimization Cost," *Journal of Economic Behavior and Organization*, 9: 213–28

(1996). "Why Bounded Rationality?," *Journal of Economic Literature*, 34: 669–700

540   **Bibliography**

Conner, K.R. and Prahalad, C.K. (1996). "A Resource-Based Theory of the Firm: Knowledge Versus Opportunism," *Organization Science*, 7(5): 477–501

Conrad, J.M. (1980). "Quasi-Option Value and the Expected Value of Information," *Quarterly Journal of Economics*, 94: 813–20

Contractor, F.J. (1981). *International Technology Transfer*, Lexington MA, D.C. Heath

Cooper, R. and Ross, T.W. (1985). "Product Warranties and Double Moral Hazard," *Rand Journal of Economics*, 16: 103–13

Cornu, G. (1973). *La Protection du Consommateur et l'Exécution du Contrat en Droit Français, Travaux de l'Association H. Capitant*: 155

Cour des Comptes (1997). *La Gestion des Services Publics Locaux d'Eau et d'Assainissement*, Rapport Public, Paris, Editions du Journal Officiel

Courville, L. (1974). "Regulation and Efficiency in the Electric Utility Industry," *Bell Journal of Economics*, 5: 53–74

Cowan, S.G.B. (1997a). "Tight Average Revenue Regulation Can be Worse than No Regulation," *Journal of Industrial Economics*, 45: 75–88

(1997b). "Price Cap Regulation and Inefficiency in Relative Pricing," *Journal of Regulatory Economics*, 12: 53–70

Cox, G.W. (1987). *The Efficient Secret: The Cabinet and the Development of Political Parties in Victorian England*, Cambridge University Press

Cramton, P., Gibbons, R. and Klemperer, P. (1987). "Dissolving a Partnership Efficiently," *Econometrica*, 55: 615–32

Crémer, J. (1995). "Arm's Length Relationship," *Quarterly Journal of Economics*, 110: 275–96

Crew, M.A. and Kleindorfer, P.R. (1979). *Public Utility Economics*, New York, St. Martin's Press

(1996). "Price Caps and Revenue Caps: Incentives and Disincentives for Efficiency," in M.A. Crew (ed.), *Pricing and Regulatory Innovations under Increasing Competition*, London, Kluwer Academic

(1999). "Stranded Assets in Network Industries in Transition," in M.A. Crew (ed.), *Regulation under Increasing Competition*," London, Kluwer Academic

Crocker, K.J. (1983). "Vertical Integration and the Strategic Use of Private Information," *Bell Journal of Economics*, 14: 236–48

Crocker, K.J. and Masten, S.E. (1988). "Mitigating Contractual Hazard: Unilateral Options and Contract Length," *Rand Journal of Economics*, 19(3): 327–43

(1991). "Pretia ex Machina?: Prices and Process in Long Term Contracts," *Journal of Law and Economics*, 34: 64–9

(1996). "Regulation and Administered Contracts Revisited: Lessons from Transaction-Cost Economics for Public Utility Regulation," *Journal of Regulatory Economics*, 9(1): 5–39

Crocker, K.J. and Reynolds, K.J. (1993). "The Efficiency of Incomplete Contracts: An Empirical Analysis of Air Force Engine Procurement," *Rand Journal of Economics*, 24: 126–46

Crozier, M. (1963). *Le Phénomène Bureaucratique*, Paris, Editions du Seuil

Curien, N., Jullien, B. and Rey, P. (1998). "Pricing Regulation under Bypass Competition," *Rand Journal of Economics*, 29: 259–79

Cusumano, M. and Takeishi, A. (1991). "Supplier Relations and Management: A Survey of Japanese, Japanese-Transplant, and US Auto Plants," *Strategic Management*, 12: 563

Cyert, R. and March, J.G. (1963). *A Behavioral Theory of the Firm*, Englewood Cliffs, NJ, Prentice-Hall

Dalton, M. (1959). *Men who Manage*, New York, Wiley

Dang-Nguyen, G. and Pénard, T. (1999). "Interconnection between ISPs, Vertical Differentiation and Capacity Constraints," *Working Paper, ENST Bretagne*

Dasgupta, P., Hammond, P. and Maskin, E. (1979). "The Implementation of Social Choice Rules," *Review of Economic Studies*, 46: 185–216

Davis, L.E. and North, D.C. (1971). *Institutional Change and American Economic Growth*, Cambridge University Press

Dawkins, R. (1976). *The Selfish Gene*, New York, Oxford University Press

De Alessi, L. (1983). "Property Rights, Transaction Costs, and X-Efficiency: An Essay in Economic Theory," *American Economic Review*, 73: 64–81

De Fraja, G. and Waddams Price, C. (1999). "Regulation and Access Pricing," *Scottish Journal of Political Economy*, 46(1): 1–16

De Soto, H. (2000). *The Mystery of Capital. Why Capitalism Triumphs in the West and Fails Everywhere Else*, New York, Basic Books

De Vany, A. (1996). "Information, Chance, and Evolution: Alchian and the Economics of Self-Organization," *Economic Inquiry*, 34: 427–43

Deacon, R.T. (1999). "Deforestation and Ownership: Evidence from Historical Accounts and Contemporary Data," *Land Economics*, 75(3): 341–59

Deakin, S. and Michie, J. (eds.) (1997). *Contracts, Co-operation, and Competition; Studies in Economics, Management, and Law*, Oxford University Press

Debreu, G. (1959). "Theory of Value: An Axiomatic Analysis of Economic Equilibrium," *Cowles Foundation Monograph*, 17, Yale University Press

Dekel, E., Lipman, B.L. and Rustichini, A. (2001). "A Unique Subjective State Space for Unforeseen Contingencies," *Econometrica*, 69(4): 891–934

Demogue, R. (1934). *La Notion de Contrat*, in Randuv Jubilejni Pamatnik, Redigoval. Dr. Jan Krcmar: 38

Demsetz, H. (1967). "Toward a Theory of Property Rights," *American Economic Review*, 57(2): 347–59

(1968). "Why Regulate Utilities?," *Journal of Law and Economics*, 11: 55–65

(1983). "The Structure of Ownership and the Theory of the Firm," *Journal of Law and Economics*, 26: 375–90

(1988). "The Theory of the Firm Revisited," *Journal of Law, Economics, and Organization*, 4: 141–63

(1995). *The Economics of the Business Firm: Seven Critical Commentaries*, Cambridge University Press

(1998). "Dogs and Tails in the Economic Development Story," Second Annual conference of the International Society for the New Institutional Economics, Paris

Denning, A. (1979). *The Discipline of Law*, London, Butterworths

Derycke, P.-H. (1990). "Typologie des services publics locaux et choix d'un mode de gestion," in *Performances des Services Publics Locaux: Analyse Comparée des Modes de Gestion*, GREP-UNSPIC, Paris, Éd. Litec

Deschenaux, H. (1969). *Traité de Droit Civil Suisse, II, 1, Le Titre Préliminaire du Code Civil*, Editions Universitaires Fribourg

Desgorces, R. (1992). *La Bonne Foi dans le Droit des Contrats: Rôle Actuel et Perspectives*, PhD dissertation, Paris II

Despotopoulos, C. (1968). "La notion de synallagma chez Aristote," *Archives Philosophie du Droit*: 115

Dewatripont, M. (1988). "Commitment through Renegotiation-Proof Contracts with Third Party," *Review of Economic Studies*, 55: 377–89

(1989). "Renegotiation and Information Revelation over Time in Optimal Labor Contracts," *Quarterly Journal of Economy*, 104: 589–620

Dewatripont, M. and Maskin, E. (1995). "Contractual Contingencies and Renegotiation," *Rand Journal of Economics*, 26: 704–19

Dewatripont, M. and Tirole, J. (1994). "A Theory of Debt and Equity: Diversity of Security and Manager–Shareholder Congruence," *Quarterly Journal of Economics*, 109: 1027–54

Didier, P. (1999). "Brèves notes sur le contrat-organisation," *Mélanges Terré*: 633–7

Dixit, A. (1996). *The Making of Economic Policy: A Transaction Cost Politics Perspective*, Cambridge, MA, MIT Press

Dixit, A.K. and Pindyck, R.S. (1994). *Investment under Uncertainty*, Princeton University Press

Duesenberry, J. (1960). "An Economic Analysis of Fertility: Comment," in *Demographic and Economic Change in Developed Countries*, National Bureau of Economic Research/Princeton University Press

Durkheim, E. (1933). *La Division du Travail dans la Société*, Paris, PUF: 215–17

Dye, R.A. (1985). "Costly Contract Contingencies," *International Economic Review*, 26(1): 233–50

Economides, N. (1996). "The Economics of Networks," *International Journal of Industrial Organization*, 14: 673–99

(1998). "The Incentive for Non-Price Discrimination by an Input Monopolist," *International Journal of Industrial Organization*, 16: 271–84

(1999). "Quality Choice and Vertical Integration", *International Journal of Industrial Organization*, 17: 903–14

Economides, N. and Lehr, W. (1995). "The Quality of Complex Systems and Industry Structure, Quality and Reliability of Telecommunications Infrastructure," in W. Lehr (ed.), *Quality and Reliability of Telecommunications Infrastructure*, Mahwah, NJ and Hove, UK, Lawrence Erlbaum

Economides, N., Lopomo, G. and Woroch, G. (1996). "Regulatory Pricing Policies to Neutralize Network Dominance," *Industrial and Corporate Change*, 5: 1013–28

Economides, N. and Salop, S.C. (1992). "Competition and Integration Among Complements, and Network Market Structure," *Journal of Industrial Economics*, 40(1): 105–23

Economides, N. and White, L. (1995). "Access and Interconnection Pricing? How Efficient is the Efficient Component Pricing Rule?," *Antitrust Bulletin*, 40: 557–79

(1998). "The Inefficiency of the ECPR Yet again: A Reply to Larson," *Antitrust Bulletin*, 43: 429–44

Economides, N. and Woroch, G. (1992). "Benefits and Pitfalls of Network Interconnection," *Discussion Paper* EC–92.31, New York University

Edlin, A.S. and Reichelstein, S. (1996). "Holdups, Standard Breach Remedies, and Optimal Investment," *American Economic Review*, 86: 478–99

Eggertsson, T. (1990). *Economic Behavior and Institutions*, New York, Cambridge University Press

Encaoua, D., Michel, P. and Moreaux, M. (1992). "Network Compatibility: Joint Adoption versus Individual Decisions," *Annales d'Économie et de Statistique*, 25/26: 51–69

Epstein, S. (1992). "Testing Principal–Agent Theory: Experimental Evidence," *Research in Experimental Economics*, 5: 35–60

Epstein, D. and O'Halloran, S. (1994). "Administrative Procedures, Information, and Agency Discretion," *American Journal of Political Science*, 38: 697–722

(1996). "Divided Government and the Design of Administrative Procedures: A Formal Model and Empirical Test," *Journal of Politics*, 58: 373–97

Epstein, L. and Peters, M. (1996). "A Revelation Principle for Competing Mechanisms," Toronto, mimeo

Eswaran, M. and Kotwal, A. (1985). "A Theory of Contractual Structure in Agriculture," *American Economic Review*, 75: 352–67

Fama, E.F. (1980). "Agency Problems and the Theory of the Firm," *Journal of Political Economy*, 88: 288–307

Fama, E.F. and Jensen, M.C. (1983a). "Agency Problems and Residual Claims," *Journal of Law and Economics*, 26: 327–50

(1983b). "Separation of Ownership and Control," *Journal of Law and Economics*, 26: 301–26

Farnsworth, E.A. (1984). "On Trying to Keep One's Promises: The Duty of Best Efforts in Contract Law," *University of Pittsburgh Law Review*, 46: 1–20

(1990). *Contracts*, 2nd edn., Boston, Little, Brown

Faure-Grimaud, A., Laffont, J.J. and Martimort, D. (1999a). "The Transaction Costs of Delegated Supervision," IDEI Toulouse, mimeo

(1999b). "The Endogenous Transaction Costs of Delegated Auditing," *European Economic Review*, 43: 1039–48

Faure-Grimaud, A. and Martimort, D. (1999). "Political Stabilization by an Independent Bureaucracy," IDEI Toulouse, mimeo

(2000a). "Inside or Outside Regulation," IDEI Toulouse, mimeo

(2000b). "Regulatory Inertia," IDEI Toulouse, mimeo

Favereau, O. (1989). "Valeur d'option et flexibilité," in P. Cohendet and P. Llerena (eds.), *Flexibilité, Information et Décision*, Paris, Economica: 121–82

Feder, G. and Onchan, T. (1987). "Land Ownership Security and Farm Investment in Thailand", *American Journal of Agricultural Economics*, 69: 311–20

Fehr, E. and Gächter, S. (2000). "Fairness and Retaliation: The Economics of Reciprocity," *Journal of Economic Perspectives*, 14: 159–81

Fehr, E., Gächter, S. and Kirchsteiger, G. (1997). "Reciprocity as a Contract Enforcement Device: Experimental Evidence," *Econometrica*, 65: 833–60

Fehr, E., Kirchsteiger, G. and Riedl, A. (1993). "Does Fairness Prevent Market Clearing? An Experimental Investigation," *Quarterly Journal of Economics*, 108: 437–60

Flour, J. and Aubert, M. (1998). *Les Obligations*, I, 8th edn., nos. 110 *et seq.*, esp. nos. 128, 116, and 113

Foss, N.J. (1996). "On the Relations Between Evolutionary and Contractual Theories of the Firm," Department of Industrial Economics and Strategy, Copehagen Business School

Frank, R.H. (1988). *Passions within Reason*, New York, Norton

Freeman, C. (1968). "Chemical Process Plant: Innovation and the World Market," *National Institute Economic Review*, 45: 29–51

Freixas, X. and Laffont, J.J. (1984). "On the Irreversibility Effect," chapter 7 in M. Boyer and R.E. Kihlstrom (eds.), *Bayesian Models in Economic Theory*, Amsterdam, North-Holland, 105–14

French, K. and McCormick, R.E. (1984). "Sealed Bids, Sunk Costs, and the Process of Competition," *Journal of Business*, 57: 417

Frison-Roche, M.A. (1995). "Rapport de synthèse," in L'Échange des Consentements, *Revue de jurisprudence Communautaire*, 151, esp. (2)

Fudenberg, D. and Tirole, J. (1991). *Game Theory*, Cambridge, MA, MIT Press

Furubotn, E. (1976). "The Long-Run Analysis of the Labor-Managed Firm: An Alternative Interpretation," *American Economic Review*, 60: 104–23

  (1985). "Codetermination, Productivity Gains, and the Economics of the Firm," *Oxford Economic Papers*, 37: 22–39

  (1988). "Codetermination and the Modern Theory of the Firm: A Property-Rights Analysis," *Journal of Business*, 61: 165–81

  (1989). "Organizational Economics and the Analysis of Codetermination," *Annals of Public and Cooperative Economics*, 60: 463–74

  (1999). "Economic Efficiency in a World of Frictions," *European Journal of Law and Economics*, 8: 179–97

  (2001). "The New Institutional Economics and the Theory of the Firm," *Journal of Economic Behavior and Organization*, 45: 133–53

Furubotn, E. and Pejovich, S. (1974). *The Economics of Property Rights*, Cambridge, MA, Ballinger

Furubotn, E. and Richter, R. (1997). *Institutions and Economic Theory*, Ann Arbor, University of Michigan Press

Gabillon, E. and Martimort, D. (1999). "The Benefits of Central Bank's Independence," IDEI Toulouse, mimeo

Galanter, M. (1981). "Justice in Many Rooms: Courts, Private Ordering, and Indigenous Law," *Journal of Legal Pluralism*, 19: 1–47

Gallick, E.C. (1984). "Exclusive Dealing and Vertical Integration: The Efficiency of Contract in the Tuna Industry," Bureau of Economics Staff Report to the Federal Trade Commission; reprinted in S.E. Masten (ed.), *Case Studies in Contracting and Organization*, New York, Oxford University Press

Gallini, N. and Wright, B. (1990). "Technology Transfer Under Asymmetric Information," *Rand Journal of Economics*, 21(1): 147–60

Garey, M.R. and Johnson, D.S. (1979). *Computers and Intractability*, New York, W.H. Freeman

Gatty, J. (1998). *Quelles Concurrence pour les Services Publics d'Eau et d'Assainissement?*, Paris, Editions Agence de l'Eau Seine-Normandie

Gauthier, N. (1999). *La Bonne Foi dans Domat et Pothier et dans les Travaux Préparatoires du Code Civil*, Master's thesis at the DEA droit privé, Paris I

Gely, R. and Spiller, P.T. (1990). "A Rational Choice Theory of Supreme Court Statutory Decisions with Applications to the *State Farm* and *Grove City* Cases", *Journal of Law, Economics and Organization*, 6(2): 263–300

Ghestin, J. (1981). "L'utile et le juste dans les contrats," *Archives de Philosophie du Droit*, 26: 35

(1982). *L'Utile et le Juste dans les Contrats, Revue Dalloz, Chron.*: 1–10

(2002), "Les données positives du droit," *Revue Trimestrielle de Droit Civil*, 52: 11–30

Ghestin, J. (ed.), (1993). "La formation du contrat," in J. Ghestin (ed.), *Traité de Droit Civil*, 8, 10 Paris, Librairie Générale de Droit et de Jurisprudence

Ghestin, J. and Goubeaux, G. with the collaboration of Fabre Magnan (1994). "Introduction générale," in J. Ghestin (ed.), *Traité de Droit Civil*, 32, *et seq.* Paris, Librairie Générale de Droit et de Jurisprudence (trans.)

Gibbons, R. (1997). "Incentives and Careers in Organizations," in D.M. Kreps and K.F. Wallis (eds.), *Advances in Economics and Econometrics: Theory and Applications*, Cambridge University Press: 1–37

Gilbert, R.J. and Kahn, E.P. (eds.) (1996). *International Comparisons of Electricity Regulation*, Cambridge University Press

Gilbert, R.J., Riordan, M.H. (1995). "Regulating Complementary Products: A Comparative Institutional Analysis," *Rand Journal of Economics*, 26: 243–56

Gilson, R.J. (1984). "Value Creation by Business Lawyers: Legal Skills and Asset Pricing," *Yale Law Journal*, 94: 239

Giulietti, M. and Waddams Price, C. (2000). "Incentive Regulation and Efficient Pricing: Empirical Evidence," *Centre for Management under Regulation Research Paper*, 00/2, March

Glachant, J.M. (1998). "Le Pool d'électricité en Grande-Bretagne: un arrangement institutionnel hybride," *Revue d'Économie Politique*, 108(1): 87–107

(2002). "Why Regulate Deregulated Network Industries?" *Journal of Network Industries*, 3, forthcoming

Glachant, J.M. and Finon, D. (2000). "Why do the European Union's Electricity Industries Continue to Differ? A New-Institutional Analysis," in C. Ménard (ed.), *Institutions, Contracts, Organizations, Perspectives from New-Institutional Economics*, Cheltenham, Edward Elgar

Glais, M. (1996). "Les accords de coopération inter-entreprises: analyse typologique et panorama de la jurisprudence communautaire," *Revue d'Economie Industrielle*, 64(2): 82–94

Glais, M. and Gaffard, J.L. (1999). "Economie d'entreprise et gestion," in *Encyclopédie de Gestion et du Management*," Paris Ed. Dalloz: 568–77

Goetz, C.J. and Scott, R.E. (1981). "Principles of Relational Contracts," *Virginia Law Review*, 67: 1089–119

Goldberg, V.P. (1976a). "Regulation and Administered Contracts," *Bell Journal of Economics*, 7: 426–32

(1976b). "Towards an Expanded Economic Theory of Contracts," *Journal of Economic Issues*, 10: 45–61

(1985). "Price Adjustment in Long-Term Contracts," *Wisconsin Law Review*, 1985: 527–43

(1997). "The Gold Ring Problem," *University of Toronto Law Journal*, 47: 469

(1998). "Bloomer Girl Revisited or How to Frame an Unmade Picture," *Wisconsin Law Review*, 1051

(2000). "In Search of Best Efforts: Reinterpreting *Bloor* v. *Falstaff*," *St. Louis University Law Journal*, 45: 1465

(2002). "Discretion in Long-Term Open Quantity Contracts: Reining in Good Faith," *U.C. Davis Law Review*, 35: 319–385

Goldberg, V.P. and Erickson, J.E. (1987). "Quantity and Price Adjustment in Long Term Contracts: A Case Study of Petroleum Coke," *Journal of Law and Economics*, 30: 369–98

Gomaa, N.M.K. (1968). *Théorie des Sources de l'Obligation*, thesis, Paris, LGDJ, Preface by J. Carbonnier

Gordley, J. (1982). "Contract in Pre-Commercial Societies and in Western History," in *International Encyclopedia of Comparative Law*, VII, *Contracts in General*, chapter 2, Tübingen, JCB. Mohr Siekeck and Martinun Nijhoff: 3 *et seq.*

(1991). *The Philosophical Origin of Modern Contract Doctrine*, Oxford, Clarendon Press

(1995). "Enforcing Promises," *California Law Review*, 83(2): 547–614

Gordon, H.S. (1954). "The Economic Theory of a Common Property Resource: The Fishery," *Journal of Political Economy*, 62(2): 124–42

Gordon, R.A. and Howell, J.E. (1959). *Higher Education for Business*, New York, Columbia University Press

Göttinger, H. (1982). "Computational Costs and Bounded Rationality," in W. Stegmuller, W. Balzer and W. Spohn (eds.), *Studies in Contemporary Economics*, Berlin, Springer: 223–38

Gouldner, A. (1961). "The Norm of Reciprocity," *American Sociological Review*, 25: 161–79

Gounot, E. (1912). *Le Principe de l'Autonomie de la Volonté*, thesis, University of Paris: 358–9

Green, J. and Laffont, J.-J. (1977). "Characterization of Satisfactory Mechanisms for the Revelation of Preferences for Public Goods," *Econometrica*, 45: 427–38

(1979). *Incentives in Public Decision-Making*, Amsterdam, North-Holland

(1986). "Incentive Theory with Data Compressing," in W. Heller, R. Starr and R. Radner (eds.), *Uncertainty, Information and Communication*, Minneapolis, University of Minnesota Press: 239–53

Green, R. (1998). "The Electricity Contract Market in England and Wales," *Journal of Industrial Economics*, 47: 107–24

Green, R.J. and Newbery, D.M. (1992). "Competition in the British Electricity Spot Market," *Journal of Political Economy*, 100(5): 929–53

Green, R.J. and Waddams Price, C. (1995). "Liberalisation and Divesture in the UK Energy Sector," *Fiscal Studies*, 16(1): 75–89

Grindley, P. and Nickerson, J. (1996). "Licensing and Business Strategy in the Chemicals Industry," in R. Parr, and P. Sullivan (eds.), *Technology Licensing: Corporate Strategies for Maximizing Value*, New York, John Wiley

Grindley, P. and Teece, D.J. (1997). "Licensing and Cross-Licensing in Semiconductors and Electronics," *California Management Review*, 39(2): 8–41

Grossman, S.J. and Hart, O.D. (1983). "An Analysis of the Principal–Agent Problem," *Econometrica*, 51: 7–45

(1986). "The Costs and Benefits of Ownership: A Theory of Vertical and Lateral Integration," *Journal of Political Economy*, 94(4): 691–719

Grossman, G. and Helpman, E. (1999). "Incomplete Contracts and Industrial Organization," unpublished paper

Groves, T. and Ledyard, J.O. (1977). "Optimal Allocation of Public Goods: A Solution to the Free Rider Problem," *Econometrica*, 45: 783–809

Güth, W., Klose, W., Königstein, M. and Schwalbach, J. (1998). "An Experimental Study of a Dynamic Principal–Agent Relationship," *Managerial and Decision Economics*, 27: 327–41

Hagerman, J. (1990). "Regulation by Price Adjustment," *Rand Journal of Economics*, 21: 72–82

Hall, B.H. and Ham, R. (1999). "The Patent Paradox Revisited: Determinants of Patenting in the US Semiconductor Industry, 1980–1994," *NBER Working Paper*, 7062

Hall, R.L. and Hitch, C.J. (1939). "Price Theory and Business Behavior," *Oxford Economics Papers*, 2

Halonen, M. (2000). "Reputation and Allocation of Ownership," University of Bristol, mimeo

Hardin, G. (1968). "The Tragedy of the Commons," *Science*, 162: 1243–8

Harris, M. and Raviv, A. (1979). "Optimal Incentive Contracts with Imperfect Information," *Journal of Economic Theory*, 20: 231–59

Hart, O.D. (1990). "Is 'Bounded Rationality' an Important Element of a Theory of Institutions?," *Journal of Institutional and Theoretical Economics*, 14: 696–702

(1995). *Firms, Contracts, and Financial Structure*, Oxford University Press

Hart, O.D. and Holmström, B. (1987). "The Theory of Contracts," chapter 3 in T. Bewley (ed.), *Advances in Economic Theory: Fifth World Congress*, Cambridge University Press: 71–155

Hart, O.D. and Moore, J. (1988). "Incomplete Contracts and Renegotiation," *Econometrica*, 56: 755–86

(1990). "Property Rights and the Nature of the Firm," *Journal of Political Economy*, 98: 1119–58

(1999a). "Foundations of Incomplete Contracts," *Review of Economic Studies*, 66(1): 115–38

(1999b). "On the Design of Hierarchies: Coordination Versus Specialization," unpublished paper

Hart, O.D., Schleifer, A. and Vishny, R. (1997). "The Proper Scope of Government: Theory and an Application to Prisons," *Quarterly Journal of Economics*, 112: 1127–61

Hart, O.D. and Tirole, J. (1988). "Contract Renegotiation and Coasian Dynamics," *Review of Economic Studies*, 55: 509–40

Hauser, J. (1971). *Objectivisme et Subjectivisme dans l'Acte Juridique*, thesis, Paris, LGDJ, Preface by P. Raynaud, 90: 140

Hayek, F. (1945). "The Use of Knowledge in Society," *American Economic Review*, 35: 519–30

(1976a). *Law, Legislation and Liberty*, 2, "The Mirage of Social Justice," London, Routledge & Kegan Paul

(1976b). *Law, Legislation and Liberty*, 3, "The Political Order of a Free People," London, Routledge & Kegan Paul

Heckman, J.J. (1979). "Sample Selection Bias as a Specification Error," *Econometrica*, 47: 151–63

Hellwig, M. (1988). "Equity, Opportunism, and the Design of Contractual Relations: Comment," *Journal of Institutional and Theoretical Economics*, 144: 200–7

Helm, D. and Jenkinson, T. (1997). "The Assessment: Introducing Competition into Regulated Industries," *Oxford Review of Economic Policy*, 13(1): 1–14

Henderson, H.D. (1922). *Supply and Demand*. London: Nisbet

Henry, C. (1974a). "Irreversible Decisions under Uncertainty," *American Economic Review*, 64: 1006–12

(1974b). "Option Values in the Economics of Irreplaceable Assets," *Review of Economic Studies*, Symposium: 89–104

Hermalin, B.E. (1999). *Economics and Corporate Culture*, University of California, Berkeley, April

Hermalin, B.E. and Katz, M.I. (1993). "Judicial Modification of Contracts Between Sophisticated Parties: A More Complete View of Incomplete Contracts and Their Breach," *Journal of Law, Economics and Organization*, 9: 230–55

Hey, J.D. (1983). "Whither Uncertainty?," *Economic Journal*, Supplement: Conference Papers: 130–9

Hill, A. and Abdala, M.A. (1996). "Argentina: The Sequencing of Privatization and Regulation," in B. Levy and P.T. Spiller (eds.), *Regulation, Institutions and Commitment: Comparative Studies of Telecommunications*, Cambridge University Press

Hirshleifer, J. (1987). "The Emotions as Guarantors of Threats and Promises," in J. Dupré (ed.), *The Latest on the Best: Essays on Evolution and Optimality*, Cambridge, MA, MIT Press

Hodgson, G.M. (1998). "Competence and Contract in the Theory of the Firm," *Journal of Economic Behavior & Organization*, 35: 179–201

Hogan, W. (1992). "Contract Networks for Electric Power Transmission," *Journal of Regulatory Economics*, 4(3): 211–42

(1993). "Markets in Real Networks Require Reactive Prices," *Energy Journal*, 14(3): 171–200

Holburn, G.L.F. and Vanden Bergh, R. (2000). "Political Instability and Policy Insulation: The Diffusion of Utility Consumer Advocacy Legislation in the United States," Berkeley, University of California, mimeo

Holmström, B. (1978). *On Incentives and Control in Organizations*, PhD thesis, Stanford University

(1979). "Moral Hazard and Observability," *Bell Journal of Economics*, 10: 74–91

(1999). "The Firm as a Subeconomy," *Journal of Law, Economics, & Organization*, 15: 74–102

Holmström, B. and Milgrom, P. (1987). "Aggregation and Linearity in the Provision of Intertemporal Incentives," *Econometrica*, 55: 303–28

(1991). "Multi-Task Principal–Agent Analyses: Incentive Contracts, Asset Ownership, and Job Design," *Journal of Law, Economics and Organization*, 7: 24–52

(1994). "The Firm as an Incentive System," *American Economic Review*, 84: 972–91

Holmström, B. and Tirole, J. (1989). "The Theory of the Firm," in R. Schmalensee, and R.D. Willig (eds.), *Handbook of Industrial Economics*, New York, Elsevier Science: 61–133

Hubbard, R. and Weiner, R.J. (1986). "Regulation and Long-Term Contracting in US Natural Gas Markets," *Journal of Industrial Economics*, 35: 31–79

Ichniowski, C., Shaw, K.L. and Prennushi, G. (1997). "The Effects of Human Resource Management Practices on Productivity: Evidence from the Steel Industry," *American Economic Review*, 87: 291–313

International Energy Agency (IEA) (1996). *Electricity Information 1995*, Paris, OECD

(2000). *Energy Prices and Taxes – Quarterly Statistics*, Paris, OECD

Intrum Justitia (1997). *European Payment Habits Survey*, Amsterdam, Intrum Justitia

Iossa, E. (1999). "Informative Externalities and Pricing in Regulated Multiproduct Industries," *Journal of Industrial Economics*, 47(2): 195–219

Irrgang, W. (1972). *The Lincoln Incentive Management Program*, Technical Report, Arizona State University

Jackson, P.M. (1982). *The Political Economy of Bureaucracy*, Oxford, Phillip Allan

Jacobson, G. (1990). *The Electoral Origins of Divided Government*. Boulder, CO, Westview Press

Jamet-le Gac, S. (1998). *De l'Utilité de la Bonne Foi, une Analyse Economique de la Bonne Foi dans et pour l'Exécution des Contrats*, Master's thesis at the DEA Droit des Contrats, Lille II

Jensen, M.C. (1983). "Organization Theory and Methodology," *Accounting Review*, 58: 319–39

(1993). "The Modern Industrial Revolution, Exit, and the Failure of Internal Control Systems," *Journal of Finance*, 48(3): 831–80

(1994). "Self-Interest, Altruism, Incentives, and Agency Theory," *Journal of Applied Corporate Finance*, 7(2)

(1998). *Foundations of Organizational Strategy*, Cambridge, MA, Harvard University Press

Jensen, M.C., Fama, E.F., Long, J.B., Ruback, R.S., Schwert, G.W., Smith, C.W. and Warner, J. (1989). "Editorial: Clinical Papers and Their Role in the Development of Financial Economics," *Journal of Financial Economics*, 24: 3–6

Jensen, M.C. and Meckling, W. (1976). "Theory of the Firm: Managerial Behavior Agency Costs and Ownership Structure," *Journal of Financial Economics*, 3(1): 305 60

(1979). "Rights and Production Functions: An Application to Labor-Managed Firms and Codetermination," *Journal of Business*, 52(4): 469–506

(1992). "Specific and General Knowledge, and Organizational Structure," in L. Werin and H. Wijkander (eds.), *Contract Economics*, Oxford, Blackwell: 251–74

(1994). "The Nature of Man," *Journal of Applied Corporate Finance*, 7(2): 4–19

(1998). "Coordination, Control and the Management of Organizations: Course Notes," *Harvard Business School Working Paper*, 8-098

Jensen, M.C. and Murphy, K.J. (1990). "Performance Pay and Top Management Incentives," *Journal of Political Economy*, April: 225–65

John Paul II (1993). *Encyclique Veritatis Splendor*, August 6, Paris, Editions Mame/Plon, 35(59)

Johnson, R.N. and Libecap, G.D. (1982). "Contracting Problems and Regulation: The Case of the Fishery," *American Economic Review*, 72(5): 1005–22

Jones, F. (1983). *Input Prices under Rate of Return Regulation*, New York, Garland

Jones, R.A. and Ostroy, J.M. (1984). "Flexibility and Uncertainty," *Review of Economic Studies*, 51: 13–32

Joskow, P.L. (1985). "Vertical Integration in Long Term Contracts: The Case of Coal-Burning Electric Generating Plants," *Journal of Law, Economics & Organization*, 33: 33–80

(1987). "Contract Duration and Relationship-Specific Investment: Empirical Evidence from Coal Markets," *American Economic Review*, 77(1): 168–85

(1988a). "Asset Specificity and the Structure of Vertical Relationships: Empirical Evidence," *Journal of Law, Economics and Organization*, 4(1): 95–117

(1988b). "Price Adjustment in Long Term Contracts: The Case of Coal," *Journal of Law and Economics*, 31: 47–83

(1991). "The Role of Transaction Cost Economics in Antitrust and Public Utility Regulatory Policies," *Journal of Law, Economics & Organization*, 7(Special Issue): 53–83

(1996). "Introducing Competition into Regulated Network Industries: From Hierarchies to Markets in Electricity," *Industrial & Corporate Change*, 5(2): 341–82

(1997). "Restructuring, Competition, and Regulatory Reform in the US Electricity Sector," *Journal of Economic Perspectives*, Summer

(1998). "Electricity Sectors in Transition," *Energy Journal*, 19(2): 25–52

(1999). *Statement Concerning Settlement of Must-Run Contract Issues*, filed with the United States Federal Energy Regulatory Commission, docket nos. ER98-441-00, ER98-2550-000, Washington, DC, April

(2000). "Deregulation and Regulatory Reform in the US Electric Power Sector," in S. Peltzman and C. Winston (eds.), *Deregulation of Network Industries: The Next Steps*, Washington, DC, Brookings Institution Press

(2001). "California's Electricity Crisis," *Oxford Review of Economic Policy*, Autumn, 17(3): 365–388

Joskow, P.L. and Kahn, E. (2001). "A Quantitative Assessment of Prices in California's Wholesale Electricity Market During Summer 2000," *2001, NBER Working Paper*, 8157

Joskow, P.L. and Rose, N. (1985). "The Effects of Technological Change, Experience and Environmental Regulation on the Construction Costs of Coal-Burning," *Rand Journal of Economics*, 16(1): 1–27

Joskow, P.L. and Schmalensee, R. (1983). *Markets for Power. An Analysis of Electrical Utility Deregulation*, Cambridge, MA, MIT Press

(1986). "Incentive Regulation for Electric Utilities," *Yale Journal on Regulation*, 4(1): 1–49

(1987). "The Performance of Coal-Burning Electric Generating Units in the United States: 1960–1980," *Journal of Applied Econometrics*, 2(2): 85–109

Joskow, P.L. and Tirole, J. (2000). "Transmission Rights and Market Power," *Rand Journal of Economics*, 31(3): 450–87

Josserand, L. (1939). *De l'Esprit Des droits et de leur Relativité, Théorie Dite de l'Abus des Droits*, 2nd edn., Paris, Dalloz

Jourdain, P. (1992). "Rapport français, la bonne foi dans la formation du contrat," in *La Bonne Foi, Travaux de l'Association H Capitant*: 121

Jun Sunaga, (1985). "L'utile et le juste dans les contrats," *Revue Journal de l'Université Hosei*, 82(3–4)

Kalnins, A. and Lafontaine, F. (2001). "Multi-Unit Ownership in Franchising: Evidence from the Texan Fast-Food Industry," University of Michigan Business School, mimeo

Kamien, M. (1992). "Patent Licensing," in R.J. Aumann and S. Hart, (eds.), *Handbook of Game Theory with Economic Applications I*, Amsterdam, North-Holland: 331–54

Kandel, E. (1996). "The Right to Return," *Journal of Law and Economics*, 39: 329–56

Kandori, M. (1992). "Social Norms and Community Enforcement," *Review of Economic Studies*, 59(1): 63–80

Kandori, M. and Matsushima, H. (1998). "Private Observation, Communication and Collusion," *Econometrica*, 66(3): 627–52

Katz, M.L. and Shapiro, C. (1985a). "On the Licensing of Innovation," *Rand Journal of Economics*, 16(4): 504–20

(1985b). "Network Externalities, Competition, and Compatibility," *American Economic Review*, 75: 424–40

(1986). "Technology Adoption in the Presence of Network Externalities," *Journal of Political Economy*, 94: 822–41

Kaufmann, P.J. (1987). *Pizza Hut*, Harvard Business School Case

Kaufmann, P.J. and Lafontaine, F. (1994). "The Costs of Control: The Source of Economic Rents for McDonald's Franchisees," *Journal of Law and Economics*, 37: 417–43

Kenney, R.W. and Klein, B. (1983). "The Economics of Block Booking," *Journal of Law and Economics*, 26: 497–540

Kerr, S. (1975). "On the Folly of Rewarding A, While Hoping for B," *Academy of Management Journal*, 18(4): 769–83

Keser, C. and Willinger, M. (2000). " 'Principals' Principles and Hidden Actions: An Experimental Investigation," *International Journal of Industrial Economics*, 18: 163–85

(2001). "Theories of Behavior in Principal–Agent Relationships with Hidden Action," *Working Paper*

Keynes, J.M. (1922). "Introduction," in II.D. Henderson, *Supply and Demand*, London, Nisbet: v

Kirzner, I. (1973). *Competition and Entrepreneurship*, University of Chicago Press

Klein, B. (1980). "Transaction Costs Determinants of Unfair Contractual Arrangements," *American Economic Review*, 70: 356–62

(1988). "Vertical Integration as Organizational Ownership: The Fisher Body–General Motors Relationship Revisited," *Journal of Law, Economics and Organization*, 4(1): 199–213

(1992). "Contracts and Incentives: The Role of Contract Terms in Assuring Performance," in L. Werin and H. Wijkandere (eds.), *Contract Economics*, Cambridge, MA, Blackwell, 149–72

(1995). "The Economics of Franchise Contracts," *Journal of Corporate Finance*: *Contracting, Governance and Organization*, 2: 9–37

(1996). "Why Hold-Ups Occur: The Self-Enforcing Range of Contractual Relationships," *Economic Inquiry*, 34: 444–63

(1999). "Distribution Restrictions Operate by Creating Dealer Profits: Explaining the Use of Maximum Resale Price Maintenance in *State Oil* v. *Khan*," *Supreme Court Economic Review*, 9(1)

(2000). "Fisher-GM and the Nature of the Firm," *Journal of Law and Economics*, 43

Klein, B., Crawford, R.G. and Alchian, A. (1978). "Vertical Integration Appropriable Rents, and the Competitive Contracting Process," *Journal of Law and Economics*, 21(2): 297–326

Klein, B. and Leffler K.B. (1981). "The Role of Market Forces in Assuring Contractual Performance," *Journal of Political Economy*, 89: 615–41

Klein, B. and Murphy, K.M. (1988). "Vertical Restraints as Contract Enforcement Mechanisms," *Journal of Law and Economics*, 31(2): 265–97

(1997). "Vertical Integration as a Self-Enforcing Contractual Arrangement," *American Economic Review*, 87(2): 415–20

Klein, B. and Saft, L. (1985). "The Law and Economics of Franchise Tying Contracts," *Journal of Law and Economics*, 28: 345–61

Klein, P. (1999). "New Institutional Economics," in B. Bouckaert and G. De Geest (eds.), *Encyclopaedia of Law and Economics*, Cheltenham, Edward Elgar: 456–89

Klein, P. and Shelanski, H. (1995). "Empirical Research in Transaction Cost Economics: A Survey and Assessment," *Journal of Law, Economics and Organization*, 11(2): 335–62

Knight, F.H. (1921). *Risk, Uncertainty and Profit*, New York, Harper & Row

Koenig, G. (ed.) (1999). *De Nouvelles Théories pour Gérer l'Entreprise au XXIème Siècle*, Paris, Economica

Kranton, R. (1996). "Reciprocal Exchange: A Self-Sustaining System," *American Economic Review*, 86(4): 830–51

Krattenmaker, T.G. and Salop S. (1987). "Anticompetitive Exclusion: Raisin Rivals Costs to Achieve Power over Price," *Yale Law Journal*, 96. 209–93

Kreps, D.M. (1988). *Notes on the Theory of Choice*, Boulder, CO, Westview

(1990). "Corporate Culture and Economic Theory," in J.E. Alt and K.A. Shepsle (eds.), *Perspectives on Positive Political Economy*, New York, Cambridge University Press: 90–160

(1996). "Markets and Hierarchies and (Mathematical) Economic Theory," *Industrial and Corporate Change*, 5(2): 561–96; reprinted in G. Carroll and D. Teece (eds.), *Firms, Markets, and Hierarchies*, New York, Oxford University Press: 121–55 (1999)

Kreps, D., Milgrom, P., Roberts, J. and Wilson, R. (1982). "Rational Cooperation in the Finitely Repeated Prisoners' Dilemma," *Journal of Economic Theory*, 27: 245–52

Kuhn, T.S. (1970). *The Structure of Scientific Revolutions*, 2nd edn., Chicago University Press

Kumar, K.B., Rajan, R.G. and Zingales, L. (1999). "What Determines Firm Size?," University of Chicago, Graduate School of Business, mimeo

La Porta, R., Lopez-de-Silanes, F., Shleifer, A. and Vishny, R.W. (1997). "Trust in Large Organizations," *American Economic Review*, 87: 333–8

Laffont, J.J. (1995). "Industrial Policy and Politics," *International Journal of Industrial Organization*, 14: 1–27

Laffont, J.J. and Martimort, D. (1997). "Collusion under Asymmetric Information," *Econometrica*, 65: 875–911

(1998). "Collusion and Delegation," *Rand Journal of Economics*, 29: 280–305

(1999). "Separation of Regulators against Collusive Behavior," *Rand Journal of Economics*, 30: 232–63

(2000). "Mechanism Design under Collusion and Correlation," *Econometrica*, 68: 309–42

Laffont, J.J. and Maskin, E. (1982). "The Theory of Incentives: an Overview," in W. Hildenbrand (ed.), *Advances in Economic Theory*, Cambridge University Press

Laffont, J.J. and Meleu, M. (1997). "Reciprocal Supervision, Collusion and Organizational Design," *Scandinavian Journal of Economics*, 99: 519–40

Laffont, J.J., Rey, P. and Tirole, J. (1997). "Competition between Telecommunication Operators," *European Economic Review*, 41: 701–11

Laffont, J.J. and Tirole, J. (1990). "Optimal Bypass and Cream Skimming," *American Economic Review*, 80: 1042–61

(1993). *A Theory of Incentives in Procurement and Regulation*, Cambridge, MA, MIT Press

(1994). "Access Pricing and Competition," *European Economic Review*, 38: 1673–1710

(1996). "Creating Competition through Interconnection: Theory and Practice," *Journal of Regulatory Economics*, 10: 227–56

(1998a). "Network Competition I: Overview and Nondisciminatory Pricing," *Rand Journal of Economics*, 29: 1–37

(1998b). "Network Competition II: Disciminatory Pricing," *Rand Journal of Economics*, 29: 38–56

Lafontaine, F. (1992). "Agency Theory and Franchising: Some Empirical Results," *Rand Journal of Economics*, 23: 263–83

(2001). "Retail Pricing, Organizational Form, and the New Rule of Reason Approach to Maximum Resale Prices," University of Michigan Business School, mimeo

Lafontaine, F. and Shaw, K. (1999). "The Dynamic of Franchise Contracting: Evidence from Panel Data," *Journal of Political Economy*, 107: 1041–80

(2001). "Targeting Managerial Control: Evidence from Franchising," University of Michigan Business School, mimeo

Lafontaine, F. and Slade, M. (1997). "Retail Contracting: Theory and Practice," *Journal of Industrial Economics*, 45: 1–25

(2000). "Incentive Contracting and the Franchise Decision," in K. Chatterjee and W. Samuelson (eds.), *Game Theory and Business Applications*, Boston, Kluwer Academic Press

Lal, R. (1990). "Improving Channel Coordination through Franchising," *Marketing Science*, 9: 299–318

Landau, R. (1966). *The Chemical Plant: From Process Selection to Commercial Operation*, New York, Reinhold

Laurent, P. (1982). *Pufendorf et la Loi Naturelle*, Paris, Editions J. Vrin: 136
   (1993). "La politique Communautaire de la concurrence" Sirey, Ed. Dalloz
Law, P.J. (1995). "Tightes Average Regulation can Reduce Consumer Welfare,"
   Journal of Industrial Economics, 43(4): 399–404
Le Tourneau, P. (1995). "V° Bonne foi," in *Répertoire de Droit Civil*, Paris, Dalloz
Lee, S.H. and Hamilton, J.H. (1999). "Using Market Structure to Regulate a
   Vertically Integrated Monopolist," *Journal of Regulatory Economics*, 15(3):
   223–48
Leffler, K.B. and Rucker, R.R. (1991). "Transaction Costs and the Efficient
   Organization of Production: A Study of Timber Harvesting Contracts,"
   Journal of Political Economy, 99: 1060–87
Leibenstein, H. (1985). "On Relaxing the Maximization Postulate," *Journal of
   Behavioral Economics*, 14: 5–19
Lessius (1608). *De justicia et jure, ceterisque virtutibus cardinalis libri quatuor*, Paris,
   3rd edn., esp. Sectio tertia de contractibus, chapter XVII, *De contractibus in
   genere*
Levin, J. (1998). *Relational Incentive Contacts*, Department of Economics,
   Cambridge, MA, MIT, December
Levin, R.C., Klevorick, A.K., Nelson, R.R. and Winter, S.G. (1987).
   "Appropriating the Returns from Industrial R&D," *Brookings Papers on
   Economic Activity*, 14: 551–61
Levy, B. and Spiller, P.T. (1993). "Regulation, Institutions, and Commitment in
   Telecommunications – A Comparative Analysis of 5 Country Studies," *The
   World Bank Research Observer*: 215–66
   (1994). "The Institutional Foundations of Regulatory Commitment: A
   Comparative Analysis of Telecommunications Regulation," *Journal of Law,
   Economics and Organization*, 10(2): 201–46
   (1996). *Regulations, Institutions, and Commitment. Comparative Studies of
   Telecommunications*, Cambridge University Press
Lewin-Solomon, S.B. (1998). "The Plural Form in Franchising: A Synergism
   of Market and Hierarchy," Department of Economics, *Working Paper*, Iowa
   State University
Libecap, G.D. (1978). "Economic Variables and the Development of the Law:
   The Case of Western Mineral Rights," *Journal of Economic History*, 38(2):
   338–62
   (1989a). "Distributional Issues in Contracting for Property Rights," *Journal of
   Institutional and Theoretical Economics*, 145(1): 6–24
   (1989b). *Contracting for Property Rights*, New York, Cambridge University Press
   (1998a). "Common Property," in P. Newman (ed.), *The New Palgrave
   Dictionary of Economics and The Law*, 1, New York, Macmillan: 317–24
   (1998b). "Unitization," in P. Newman (ed.), *The New Palgrave Dictionary of
   Economics and the Law*, 3, New York, Macmillan: 641–3
   (2001). "Contracting for Property Rights," in T.L. Anderson and F.S.
   McChesney (eds.), *The Law and Economics of Property Rights*, Palo Alto,
   Hoover Institution, monograph
Libecap, G.D. and Smith, J.L. (1999). "The Self-Enforcing Provisions of Oil and
   Gas Unit Operating Agreements: Theory and Evidence," *Journal of Law,
   Economics, and Organization*, 15(2): 526–48

(2001). "Regulatory Remedies to the Common Pool: The Limits to Oil Field Unitization," *Energy Journal*, 22(1): 1–26

Libecap, G.D. and Wiggins, S.N. (1984). "Contractual Responses to the Common Pool: Prorationing of Crude Oil Production," *American Economic Review*, 74(1): 87–98

(1985). "The Influence of Private Contractual Failure on Regulation: The Case of Oil Field Unitization," *Journal of Political Economy*, 93(4): 690–714

Lindenberg, S. (1988). "Contractual Relations and Weak Solidarity: The Behavioral Basis of Restraints on Gain-Maximization," *Journal of Institutional and Theoretical Economics, Zeitschrift für die Gesamte Staatswissenschaft*, 144: 39–58

Littlechild, S. (1983). *Regulation of British Telecom Profitability*, London, HMSO

Llewellyn, K.N. (1931). "What Price Contract? An Essay in Perspective," *Yale Law Journal*, 40: 704–51

Loussouarn, Y. (1992). "Rapport de synthèse," in *La Bonne Foi, Travaux de l'Association H. Capitant*: 7

Lutz, N.A. (1995). "Ownership Rights and Incentives in Franchising," *Journal of Corporate Finance: Contracting, Governance and Organization*, 2: 103–30

Lyon-Caen, G. (1946). "De l'évolution de la notion de bonne foi," *Revue Trimestrielle de Droit Civil*: 75

Lyons, B.R. (1994). "Contract and Specific Investment: An Empirical Test of Transaction Cost Theory," *Journal of Economics and Management Strategy*, 3: 257–78

(1995). "Specific Investment, Economies of Scale, and the Make or Buy Decision: A Test of Transaction Cost Theory," *Journal of Economic Behavior and Organization*, 26: 431–43

(1996). "Empirical Relevance of Efficient Contract Theory: Inter-Firm Contracts," *Oxford Review of Economic Policy*, 12(4): 27–53

Macaulay, S. (1963). "Non-Contractual Relations in Business: A Preliminary Study," *American Sociological Review*, 28: 55–70

(1985). "An Empirical View of Contract," *Wisconsin Law Review*, 5(3): 465–82

Machlup, F. (1967). "Theories of the Firm: Marginalist, Behavioral, Managerial," *American Economic Review*, 57

Macho-Stadler, I.X., Martinez-Giralt, X. and Perez-Castrillo, D. (1996). "The Role of Information in Licensing Contract Design," *Research Policy*, 25(1): 25–41

Macho-Stadler, I.X. and Perez-Castrillo, D. (1991). "Contrats de licence et asymétrie d'information," *Annales d'Économie et de Statistique*, 24: 189–208

MacLeod, W.B. (2002). "Optimal Contracting with Subjective Evaluation," University of Southern California, mimeo, February

MacLeod, W.B. and Malcomson, J.M. (1988). "Reputation and Hierarchy in Dynamic Models of Employment," *Journal of Political Economy*, 96(4): 832–54

(1989). "Implicit Contracts, Incentive Compatibility, and Involuntary Unemployment," *Econometrica*, 57(2): 447–80

(1993). "Investments, Holdup, and the Form of Market Contracts," *American Economic Review*, 83(4): 811–37

MacLeod, W.B. and Parent, D. (1999). "Jobs Characteristics and the Form of Compensation," *Research in Labor Economics*, 18: 177–242

Macneil, I.R. (1974). "The Many Futures of Contracts," *Southern California Law Review*, 47(688): 691–816

(1980). *The New Social Contract: An Inquiry into Modern Contractual Relations*, New Haven, Yale University Press, 48

Maddala, G.S. (1983). *Limited Dependant and Qualitative Variables in Econometrics*, Cambridge University Press

Magill, M. and Quinzii, M. (1996). *Theory of Incomplete Markets*, Cambridge, MA, MIT Press

Magnusson, L. and Ottosson, J. (1996). "Transaction Costs and Institutional Change," in J. Groenewegen (ed.), *Transaction Costs Economics and Beyond*, Boston, Kluwer Academic

Malcomson, J.M. (1984). "Work Incentives, Hierarchy, and Internal Labor Markets," *Journal of Political Economy*, 92(3): 486–507

Mankiw, G. (1990). "A Quick Refresher Course in Macroeconomics," *Journal of Economic Literature*, December

Markou, E. and Parmar, M. (1999). "Pay and Performance under Price Cap Regulation: A Theoretical Framework," mimeo, May

Marsden, D. (1999), *A Theory of Employment Systems*, Oxford: Oxford University Press

Martimort, D. (1992). "Multi-principaux avec anti-sélection," *Annales d'Économie et de Statistique*, 28: 1–38

(1996a). "Exclusive Dealing, Common Agency and Multiprincipal Incentive Theory," *Rand Journal of Economics*, 27: 1–31

(1996b). "The Multiprincipal Nature of the Government," *European Economic Review*, 40: 673–85

(1997). "A Theory of Bureaucratization Based on Reciprocity and Collusive Behavior," *Scandinavian Journal of Economics*, 99: 555–79

(1998). "Multiprincipal Charter as a Safeguard against Opportunism," IDEI, University of Toulouse, mimeo

(1999a). "The Life Cycle of Regulatory Agencies: Dynamic Capture and Transaction Costs," *Review of Economic Studies*, 66: 929–48

(1999b). "Renegotiation Design with Multiple Regulators," *Journal of Economic Theory*, 88(2): 261–94

Martimort, D. and Rochet, J.C. (1999). "Le partage public-privé dans le financement de l'economie," *Revue Française d'Économie*, 14: 33–77

Martimort, D. and Stole, L. (1999a). "Contractual Externalities in Common Agency Equilibria," IDEI, mimeo

(1999b). "The Revelation and Taxation Principles in Common Agency Games," IDEI, mimeo

Marvel, H. and McCafferty S. (1984). "Resale Price Maintenance and Certification," *Rand Journal of Economics*, 15: 246–359

Maskin, E. and Tirole, J. (1999a). "Unforeseen Contingencies and Incomplete Contracts," *Review of Economic Studies*, 66(1): 83–114

(1999b). "Two Remarks on the Property-Rights Literature," *Review of Economic Studies*, 66(1): 139–49

Masten, S.E. (1982). *Transaction Costs, Institutional Choice and the Theory of the Firm*, unpublished PhD thesis

(1984). "The Organization of Production: Evidence from the Aerospace Industry," *Journal of Law and Economics*, 27: 403–17

(1988a). "Minimum Bill Contracts: Theory and Policy," *Journal of Industrial Economics*, 37: 85–97

(1988b). "Equity, Opportunism and the Design of Contractual Relations," *Journal of Institutional and Theoretical Economics*, 144: 180–95

(1988c). "A Legal Basis for the Firm," *Journal of Law, Economics and Organization*, 4: 181

Masten, S.E. (ed.), (1996). *Case Studies in Contracting and Organization*, New York, Oxford University Press

(1998). "Nominal Terms, Real Intentions, and Contract Interpretation," paper presented to the 2nd International Conference on New Institutional Economics, Paris, September

(2000). "Contractual Choice," in B. Boukaert and G. De Geest (eds.), *Encyclopedia of Law and Economics*, 3, *The Regulation of Contracts*, Cheltenham Edward Elgar Publishing and the University of Ghent: 25–45

Masten, S.E. and Crocker, K.J. (1985). "Efficient Adaptation in Long Term Contracts: Take-or-Pay Provisions for Natural Gas," *American Economic Review*, 75: 1083–93

Masten, S.E., Meehan, J.W. and Snyder, E.A., (1991). "Costs of Organization," *Journal of Law, Economics and Organization*, 7: 1–27

Masten, S.E. and Saussier, S. (2001). "Econometrics of Contracts: An Assessment of Developments in the Empirical Literature on Contracting," chapter 16 in this volume

Masten, S.E. and Snyder, E.A. (1991). "The Design and Duration of Contracts: Strategic and Efficiency Considerations," *Law and Contemporary Problems*, 52: 63–85

(1993). "*United States v. United Shoe Machinery Corporation*: On the Merits," *Journal of Law and Economics*, 36: 33–70

Mathewson, G.F. and Winter, R.A. (1985). "The Economics of Franchise Contracts," *Journal of Law and Economics*, 28: 503–26

Matutes, C. and Padilla, A.J. (1994). "Shared ATM Networks and Banking Competition," *European Economic Review*, 38: 1113–38

Maynard, J.T. and Peters, H.M. (1991). *Understanding Chemical Patents: A Guide for the Inventor*, American Chemical Society, Washington, DC

Mazeaud, D. (1999). "Loyauté, solidarité, fraternité, la nouvelle devise contractuelle," in *Mélanges Terré*: 603–34

Mazeaud, H.L.J. (1990). *Obligations*, 8th edn. by Fr. Chabas, Paris, Montchrestien, 2(1), no. 127

McAfee, P. and McMillan, J. (1995). "Organizational Diseconomies of Scope," *Journal of Economics and Management Strategy*, 4: 399–426

McCubbins, M.D. and Schwartz, A. (1984). "Congressional Oversight Overlooked: Police Patrols vs. Fire Alarms," *American Journal of Political Science*, 28(1): 165–79

McCubbins, M.D., Noll, R.G. and Weingast, B.R. (1987). "Administrative Procedures as Instruments of Political Control," *Journal of Law, Economics and Organization*, 3: 243–77

558   Bibliography

(1989). "Structure and Process, Politics and Policy: Administrative Arrangements and the Political Control of Agencies," *Virginia Law Review*, 75(2): 431–508

Meckling W. (1976). "Values and the Choice of the Model of the Individual in the Social Sciences," *Schweizerische Zeitschrift für Volkswirtschaft und Statistik*, December

Melumad, N., Mookherjee, D. and Reichelstein, S. (1995). "Hierarchical Decentralization of Incentive Contracts," *Rand Journal of Economics*, 26: 654–72

Ménard, C. (1995a). *L'Économie des Organisations*, Repères, Editions La Découverte

(1995b). "Comportement rationnel et coopération: le dilemme organisationnel," *Cahiers d'Economie Politique*, nos. 24–25: 185–207

(1996). "On Clusters, Hybrids, and Other Strange Forms: The Case of the French Poultry Industry," *Journal of Institutional and Theoretical Economics*, 152, March: 154–83

Ménard, C. (ed.), (2000). *Institutions, Contracts, Organizations, Perspectives from New-Institutional Economics*, Cheltenham, Edward Elgar

Ménard, C. and Shirley, M. (1999). *Reforming Contractual Arrangements: Lessons from Urban Water Systems in Six Developing Countries*, Washington DC, World Bank

Merges, R. (1998). "Property Rights, Transactions, and The Value of Intangible Assets," University of California at Berkeley, School of Law, mimeo

von Mehren, A. (1982). In *International Encyclopedia of Comparative Law*, 7, chapter 1, *A General View of Contract*, Tübingen, J.C.B Mohr Siebeck and Martium Nijhoff, 1, 25

Michael, S. and Moore, H. (1995). "Returns to Franchising," *Journal of Corporate Finance: Contracting, Governance and Organization*, 2: 133–55

Milkovich, G.T. and Newman, J.M. (1996). *Compensation*, New York: Irwin

Milkovich, G.T. and Wigdor, A.K. (1991). *Pay for Performance: Evaluating Performance and Appraisal Merit Pay*, Washington, DC, National Academy Press

Mill, J.S. (1961). *Utilitarianism*, Garden City, NY, Doubleday

Miller, G. (1992). *Managerial Dilemmas: The Political Economy of Hierarchy*, Cambridge University Press

Minsky, M.L. and Papert, S.A. (1988). *Perceptions*, 3rd edn., Cambridge, MA, MIT Press

Mirrlees, J. (1971). "An Exploration in the Theory of Optimum Income Taxation," *Review of Economic Studies*, 38: 175–208

(1999). "The Theory of Moral Hazard and Unobservable Behavior: Part I," *Review of Economic Studies*, 66: 3–22

Moe, T. (1984). "The New Economics of Organization," *American Journal of Political Sciences*, 28: 739–77

Molina (1614). *De justicia et jure tractatus*, Venice

Monopolies and Mergers Commission (MMC) (1982). *Contraceptive Sheaths*, Cmnd. 8689, London, HMSO

Monteverde, K. and Teece, D. (1982). "Supplier Switching Costs and Vertical Integration in the Automobile Industry," *Bell Journal of Economics*, 13: 206–13

Mookherjee, D. and Reichelstein, S. (1995). "Incentive and Coordination in Hierarchies," Boston University, mimeo

Moore, J. (1992). "Implementation, Contracts, and Renegotiation in Environments with Complete Information," in J.J. Laffont (ed.), *Advances in Economic Theory: Sixth World Congress*, I(5): 182–282, Cambridge University Press

Mueller, M. (1993). "Universal Service in Telephone History: A Reconstruction," *Telecommunications Policy*, 17(5): 352–69

Mulherin, J.H. (1986). "Complexity in Long Term Contracts: An Analysis of Natural Gas Contract Provisions," *Journal of Law, Economics & Organization*, 2: 105–17

Muto, S. (1993). "On Licensing Policies in Bertrand Competition," *Games and Economic Behavior*, 5: 257–67

Myerson, R. (1979). "Incentive Compatibility and the Bargaining Problem," *Econometrica*, 47: 61–74

(1982). "Optimal Coordination Mechanisms in Generalized Principal–Agent Problems," *Journal of Mathematical Economics*, June: 67–81

Myerson, R. and Satterthwaite, M. (1983). "Efficient Mechanisms for Bilateral Trading," *Journal of Economic Theory*, 28: 265–81

Neelin, J., Sonnenschein, H. and Spiegel, M. (1988). "A Further Test of Noncooperative Bargaining Theory: Comment," *American Economic Review*, 78: 824–37

Nelson, R. and Winter, S. (1982). *An Evolutionary Theory of Economic Change*, Cambridge, MA, Harvard University Press

Newbery, D.M. (1998). "Competition Contracts and Entry in the Electricity Market," *Rand Journal of Economics*, 29(4): 726–49

(1999). "Issues and Options for Restructuring the ESI," Department of Applied Economics, Cambridge University, mimeo

Newbery, D.M. and Green, R.J. (1996). "Regulation, Public Ownership and Privatisation of the English Electricity Industry," in R.J. Gilbert and E.P. Kahn (eds.), *International Comparisons of Electricity Regulation*, Cambridge University Press

Newbery, D.M. and Pollitt, M.G. (1997). "The Restructuring and Privatisation of Britain's CEGB – Was it Worth it?," *Journal of Industrial Economics*, 45(3): 269–303

Newell, A., Shaw, J.C. and Simon, H.A. (1995, originally published 1963). "Chess-Playing Programs and the Problem of Complexity," in E.A. Feigenbaum and J. Feldman (eds.), *Computers and Thought*, Menlo Park, CA, AAAI Press/MIT Press, 39–70

Nöldeke, G. and Schmidt, K. (1995). "Option Contracts and Renegotiation: A Solution to the Hold-Up Problem," *Rand Journal of Economics*, 26: 163–79

North, D.C. (1990). *Institutions, Institutional Change and Economic Performance*, Cambridge University Press

(1992). "Institutions," *Journal of Economic Perspectives*, 5(2): 97–112

OECD (1994). *Franchising Agreements*, OECD Report, Paris, OECD

(1995). *Research and Development Expenditure in Industry 1973–1992*, Paris, OECD

Office of Electricity Regulation (1992). *Report on Constrained-On Plant,* October
Office of Gas and Electricity Markets, UK (Ofgem) (1999a). *The New Electricity Trading Arrangements,* London, Ofgem
    (1999b). "The Social Action Plan: A Framework Document," London, Ofgem
    (2000). "Statement by Callum McCarthy, Director General of Ofgem Addressing the Scope for, and Experience of, the Abuse of Market Power by the Generators Under the Wholesale Electricity Pool in England and Wales," London, Ofgem
Oren, S. (2000). "Capacity Payments and Supply Adequacy in Competitive Electricity Markets," Berkeley, University of California, mimeo
Oren S. and Spiller, P.T. (2000). "Wild Prices Out West: What Can be Done?," *Public Utilities Fortnightly,* 138(20): 58–61
Organización Latino Americana De Energía (1991). "Proceeding of the Conference on Overcoming the Electric Power Sector Crisis in the Countries of Latin America and the Caribbean," September
Orléan, A. (ed.) (1994). *Analyse Économique des Conventions,* Paris, PUF
Ormaza, I. (1992). "Las relaciones producción alimentaria/distribución: el dominio de los fabricantes," *Distribución y Consumo,* 6: 10–25
Ornstein, S.I. (1985). "Resale Price Maintenance and Cartels," *Antitrust Bulletin,* Summer
Ostrom, E. (1990). *Governing the Commons: The Evolution of Institutions for Collective Action,* New York, Cambridge University Press
Padilla, J.L. (1996). "El pequeño comercio andaluz se une frente a los hipermercados," *Expansión,* June: 17
Palay, T.M. (1984). "Comparative Institutional Economics: The Governance of Rail Freight Contracting," *Journal of Legal Studies,* 13: 265–87
Pearce, D.G. (1992). "Repeated Games: Cooperation and Rationality," in J.-J. Laffont (ed.), *Advances in Economic Theory: Sixth World Congress,* I(4), Cambridge University Press: 132–74
Pearce, D.G. and Stacchetti, E. (1998). "The Interaction of Implicit and Explicit Contracts in Repeated Agency," *Games and Economic Behavior,* 23(1): 75–96
Peltzman, S. and Winston, C. (2000). *Deregulation of Network Industries: The Next Steps,* Washington, DC, Brookings Institution Press
Pénard, T. (1999). "Entry Strategy and Regulation of Telecommunications: A Judo Economics Approach," ENST Bretagne, mimeo
Perelman, Ch. (1968). *Droit, Morale et Philosophie,* LGDJ, Preface by M. Villey: 11–12
Parry, K. (1989). "Vertical Integration: Determinants and Effects," in chapter 4 in *Handbook of Industrial Organization,* Amsterdam, North-Holland: 183–255
Peters, M. (1999). "Common Agency and the Revelation Principle," Toronto, mimeo
Petersen, H. (1975). "An Empirical Test of Regulatory Effects," *Bell Journal of Economics,* 6(1): 11–26
Philippe, D. (1992). "Rapport belge, la bonne foi dans la formation du contrat," in *La Bonne Foi, Travaux de l'Association H.* Capitant: 61
Pingle, M. (1992). "Costly Optimization: An Experiment," *Journal of Economic Behavior and Organization,* 17: 3–30

Pipes, R. (1999). *Property and Freedom*, New York, Basic Books

Pirrong, C. (1993). "Contracting Practices in Bulk Shipping Markets: A Transactions Cost Explanation," *Journal of Law and Economics*, 36: 937–76

Poitevin, M. (1995). "Contract Renegotiation and Organizational Design," Montreal, Cirano, mimeo

Ponssard, J.P. (1975). "A Comment on the 'Irreversibility Effect'," Laboratoire d'Économétrie de l'École Polytechnique, mimeo, August

Portalis, V. (1844). *Discours Préliminaire*, Paris, minutes written by Locré, 88 (307)

Posner, R. (1976). *Antitrust Law: An Economic Perspective*, Chicago Universtiy Press

(1997). "Social Norms and the Law: An Economic Approach," *American Economic Review*, 87(2): 365–9

(1998). "The Parol Evidence Rule, The Plain Meaning Rule, and the Principles of Contractual Interpretation," *Pennsylvania Law Review*, 146: 533–77

Poughon, J.M. (1985). *L'Histoire Doctrinale de l'Échange et du Contrat*, thesis, Paris LGDJ, Preface by J.J. Baud, Foreword by J. Ghestin

Prendergast, C. (1999). "The Provision of Incentives in Firms," *Journal of Economic Literature*, 36(1): 7–63

Priest, G. (1981). "A Theory of the Consumer Product Warranty," *Yale Law Journal*, 90: 1297–1352

Rajan, R.G. and Zingales, L. (1998). "Power in a Theory of the Firm," *Quarterly Journal of Economics*, 113: 387–432

Ramsey, F.P. (1927). "A Contribution to the Theory of Taxation," *Economic Journal*, 37: 47–61

Ramstad, Y. (1994) "On the Nature of Economic Evolution," in L. Magnusson (ed.), *Evolutionary and Neo-Schumpeterian Approaches to Economics*, Boston, Kluwer Academic

Ranieri, F. (1998). "Bonne foi et exercice du droit dans la tradition du civil law," *Revue Internationale de Droit Comparé*: 1055

Rawls, J. (1955). "Two Concepts of Rules," *The Philosophical Review*, 64: 3–32

(1999). *The Theory of Justice*, New York, Belknap Press

Raynaud, E. and Valceschini, E. (1999). "Crédibilité d'un signal commun de qualité et structures de gouvernance," Centre ATOM, Université de Paris I, mimeo

Rees, R. (1984). "A Positive Theory of the Public Enterprise," in M. Marchand, P. Pestieau and P. Tulkens (eds.), *The Performance of Public Enterprises*, Amsterdam, North-Holland

Rey, P. and Tirole, J. (1986). "The Logic of Vertical Restraints," *American Economic Review*, 76: 921–39

Ricketts, M. (1994). *The Economics of Business Enterprise*, London, Harvester Wheatsheaf

Rindfleish, A. and Heide, J. (1997). "Transaction Cost Analysis: Past, Present, and Future Applications," *Journal of Marketing*, 61: 30–54

Riordan, M.H. and Sappington, D. (1987). "Awarding Monopoly Franchises," *American Economic Review*, 77(3): 375–87

Riordan, M. and Williamson, O. (1985). "Asset Specificity and Economic Organization," *International Journal of Industrial Organization*, 3: 365–78

Robbins, L. (1935). *An Essay on the Nature and Significance of Economic Science*, London, Macmillan

Robinson, J. (1933). *The Economics of Imperfect Competition*, London, Macmillan

Rock, E. and Wachter, M. (2001). "Islands of Conscious Power: Law, Norms and the Self Governing Corporation," 149 Symposium, Norms and Corporate Law, *University of Pennsylvania Law Review*: 1619

Rockett, K. (1990). "The Quality of Licensed Technology," *International Journal of Industrial Organization*, 8: 559–74

Romain, J.F. (1998). *Théorie Critique du Principe de la Bonne Foi en Droit Privé, des Atteintes à la Bonne Foi, en Général, et de la Fraude en Particulier ("Fraus omnia corrumpit")*, Brussels, Bruylant

Romer, P. (1991). "The New Keynesian Synthesis," *Journal of Economic Perspectives*, 7(1): 5–22

Rose, C.M. (2000). "Common Property, Regulatory Property, and Environmental Protection: Comparing Common Pool Resources to Tradable Environmental Allowances," *Working Paper*, New Haven, Yale Law School

Rose, J. (2000). "Price Spike Reality: Debunking the Myth of Failed Markets," *Public Utilities Fortnightly*, 138(20): 52–7

Rosen, S. (1985). "Implicit Contracts: A Survey," *Journal of Economic Literature*, 23: 1144–75

Ross, S. (1973). "Economic Theory of Agency: The Principal's Problem," *American Economic Review*, 63: 134–9

Roth, A. and Malouf, M. (1979). "Game-Theoretic Models and the Role of Information in Bargaining," *Psychological Review*, 86(6): 574–94

Rothschild, M. and Stiglitz, J.E. (1970). "Increasing Risk I: A Definition," *Journal of Economic Theory*, 2: 225–43

Rouhette, V.G. (1965). *Contribution à l'étude critique de la notion de contrat*, thesis, Paris

Rubin, P.H. (1978). "The Theory of the Firm and the Structure of the Franchise Contract," *Journal of Law and Economics*, 21: 223–33

Rudnick, H. (1996). "Pioneering Electricity Reform in South America," *IEEE Spectrum*, August: 38–45

Sacco, R. (1992). "Rapport italien, la bonne foi dans la formation du contrat," in *La Bonne Foi, Travaux de l'Association H. Capitant*: 131

(1999). *Dictionnaire, Contrat, Revue Européenne de Droit Privé*, Boston Kluwer Law International, 2: 237

Sako, M. and Helper, S. (1998). "Determinants of Trust in Supplier Relations: Evidence from the Automotive Industry in Japan and the United States," *Journal of Economic Behavior and Organization*, 34: 387–417

Salanié, B. (1994). *Théorie des Contrats*, Paris, Economica

(1997). *The Economics of Contracts: A Primer*, Cambridge, MA, MIT Press

(1999). "Développements récents en économétrie des contrats," *Revue Économique*, 50: 3611–20

Sappington, D. (1980). "Strategic Firm Behaviour under a Dynamic Regulatory Adjustment Process," *Bell Journal of Economics and Management Science*, 11: 360–72

(1983). "Limited Liability Contracts between Principal and Agent," *Journal of Economic Theory*, 29: 1–21

(1994). "Designing Incentive Regulation," *Review of Industrial Organisation*, 9(3): 245–72

Sappington, D. and Sibley, D. (1992). "Strategic Non-Linear Pricing under Price Cap Regulation," *Rand Jounal of Economics*, 23: 1–19

Sappington, D. and Stiglitz, J. (1987). "Privatization, Information and Incentives," *Journal of Policy Analysis and Management*, 6: 567–82

Sappington, D. and Weisman, D.L. (1996). "Seven Myths about Incentive Regulation," in M. A. Crew (ed.), *Pricing and Regulatory Innovations under Increasing Competition, Topics in Regulatory Economics and Policy Series*, Boston, Dordrecht and London, Kluwer Academic

Saussier, S. (1997). *Choix Contractuels et Coûts de Transaction*, PhD thesis, Université de Paris I-Panthéon-Sorbonne

(1998). "La durée des contrats interentreprises," *Économie et Prévision*, 135: 137–46

(1999). "Transaction Cost Economics and Contract Duration," *Louvain Economic Research*, 65(1): 3–21

(2000). "Contractual Completeness and Transaction Costs," *Journal of Economic Behavior and Organization*, 42: 189–206

Savage, L.J. (1954). *The Foundation of Statistics*, New York, Wiley

(1972). *The Foundations of Statistics*, New York, Dover

Schmalensee, R. (1987). "Competitive Advantage and Collusive Optima," *International Journal of Industrial Organization*, 5: 351–67

Schwartz, A. (1992a). "Legal Contract Theories and Incomplete Contracts," in L. Werin and H. Wijkander (eds.), *Contract Economics*, 7, Cambridge, MA and Oxford, Blackwell: 6–108

(1992b). "Relational Contracts in the Courts: An Analysis of Incomplete Contracts and Judicial Strategies," *Journal of Legal Studies*, 21: 271–318

(1994). "The Default Rule Paradigm and the Limits of Contract Law," *Southern California Interdisciplinary Law Review*, 3: 389–419

(1998). "Incomplete Contracts," in P. Newman (ed.), *The New Palgrave Dictionary of Economics and the Law*, 2, London, Macmillan: 277–83

Schwartz, P. (1999). *El grado de concentración de la distribución: "Peligra en España la competencia*," Madrid, Instituto de Estudios del Libre Comercio, IDELCO

Schwartz, P., Spiller, P.T. and Urbiztondo, S. (1993). "A Positive Theory of Legislative Intent," *Law and Contemporary Problems*, 57(1–2): 51–74

Schweizer, U. (2000). "An Elementary Approach to the Hold-Up Problem with Renegotiation," Department of Economics, Bonn University, mimeo, November

Scott, K. (1996). "The Evolving Roles of Contract Law," *Journal of Institutional and Theoretical Economics* (JITE), 152: 55–8

Scott, R.E. (2000a). "The Uniformity Norm in Commercial Law: A Comparative Analysis of Common Law and Code Methodologies," in J.S. Krause and S.D. Walt (eds.), *The Jurisprudential Foundations of Corporate and Commercial Law*, Cambridge University Press: 149–92

(2000b). "The Case for Formalism in Relational Contracts," *Northwestern University Law Review*, 94: 847–76

Searle, J. (1969). *Speech Acts*, Cambridge University Press

(1995). *The Construction of Social Reality*, New York, Simon & Schuster

Segal, I. (1999). "Complexity and Renegotiation: A Foundation for Incomplete Contracts," *Review of Economic Studies*, 66(1): 57–82

Selten, R. (1975). "Reexamination of the Perfectness Concept for Equilibrium Points in Extensive Games," *International Journal of Game Theory*, 4: 25–55

(1991). "Properties of a Measure of Predictive Success," *Mathematical and Social Sciences*, 21: 153–67

Selten, R., Sadrieh, A. and Abbink, K. (1999). "Money Does Not Induce Risk-Neutral Behavior, but Binary Lotteries Do Even Worse," *Theory and Decision*, 46: 213–52

Shackle, G.L.S. (1955). *Uncertainty in Economics and Other Reflections*, Cambridge University Press

Shapiro, C. (1983). "Premiums for High Quality Products as Returns to Reputations," *Quarterly Journal of Economics*, 98: 659–79

(1989). "Theories of Oligopoly Behaviour," in R. Schmalensee and R. Willig (eds.), *Handbook of Industrial Organization*, Amsterdam, North-Holland

Shapiro, C. and Stiglitz, J.E (1984). "Equilibrium Unemployment as a Worker Discipline Device," *American Economic Review*, 74(3): 433–44

Sharkey, W. (1982). *The Theory of Natural Monopoly*, Cambridge University Press

Shavell, S. (1984). "The Design of Contracts and Remedies for Breach," *Quarterly Journal of Economics*, 98: 121–48

Shelanski, H.A. and Klein, P. (1995). "Empirical Research in Transaction Cost Economics: A Review and Assessment," *Journal of Law, Economics and Organization*, 11(2): 335–61

Shepard, A. (1993). "Contractual Form, Retail Price, and Asset Characteristics," *Rand Journal of Economics*, 24: 58–77

Sherman, R. (1989). *The Regulation of Monopoly*, Cambridge University Press

Shirley, M. and Ménard, C. (2002). "Cities Awash: Reforming Urban Water Systems in Developing Countries," in M. Shirley (ed.), *Thirsting for Efficiency: The Economics and Politics of Urban Water Systems Reform*. Amsterdam and New York, Elsevier: 1–41

Shleifer, A. (1985). "A Theory of Yardstick Competition," *Rand Journal of Economics*, 20: 417–36

Shugart, M.S. and Carey, J.M. (1992). *Presidents and Assemblies: Constitutional Design and Electoral Dynamics*, Cambridge University Press

Simon, H.A. (1947). *Administrative Behavior: A Story of Decision Processes in Business Organization*, London, Macmillan

(1951). "A Formal Theory of the Employment Relationship," *Econometrica*, 19: 293–305; reprinted in H.A. Simon, *Models of Bounded Rationality*, II, Cambridge, MA, MIT Press (1982): 11–23

(1957). *Models of Man*, New York, John Wiley

(1961). *Administrative Behavior*, 2nd edn., New York, Macmillan (original publication, 1947)

(1976). "From Substantive to Procedural Rationality," in S. Latsis S. (ed.), *Methods and Appraisals in Economics*, Cambridge University Press: 129–48

(1978). "Rationality as Process and as Product of Thought," *American Economic Review*, 68: 1–16

(1985). "Human Nature in Politics: The Dialogue of Psychology with Political Science," *American Political Science Review*, 79: 293–304

Sinkondo, V.M.H. (1993). "La notion de contrat administratif: acte unilatéral à contenu contractuel ou contrat civil de l'administration?," *Revue Trimestrielle de Droit Civil*, 241

Smith, J.K. (1992). "National Goals, Industry Structure, and Corporate Strategies: Chemical Cartels between the Wars," in A. Kudo and T. Hara (eds.), *International Cartels in Business History*, Tokyo, University of Tokyo Press

Smith, J.L. (1987). "The Common Pool, Bargaining, and the Rule of Capture," *Economic Inquiry*, 25(4): 631–44

Soto (1553). *De justicia et jure libri decem*, Salamanca

Spengler, J. (1950). "Vertical Integration and Anti-trust Policy," *Journal of Political Economy*, 58: 347–52

Spitz, P.H. (1988). *Petrochemicals: The Rise of an Industry*, New York, John Wiley

Spiller, P.T. (1996). "Institutions and Commitment," *Industrial and Corporate Change*, 5: 421–52

(1999). "Restructuring Myths: On the Possibility of Competition in Small Power Sectors," Berkeley, University of California, mimeo

(2000). "An Analysis of the Wholesale Market and the General Electricity Act of El Salvador," LECG, September

Spiller, P.T. and Savedoff, W. (2000). "Government Opportunism and the Performance of Public Enterprise," in P.T. Spiller and W. Savedoff (eds.), *Spilled Water: Institutional Commitment in the Provision of Water Services*, InterAmerican Development Bank Series

Spiller, P.T. and Vanden Bergh, R. (1997). "Towards a Positive Theory of State Supreme Court Decision Making," Berkeley, University of California, mimeo

Spiller, P.T. and Vogelsang, I. (1993). "Notes on Public Utility Regulation in the UK: 1850–1950," Berkeley, University of California, mimeo

(1997). "Regulation without Commitment: Price Regulation of UK Utilities (With Special Emphasis on Telecommunications)," *Journal of Institutional and Theoretical Economics*, 153(4): 607–29

Spitz, P.H. (1988). *Petrochemicals: The Rise of an Industry*, New York, John Wiley

Spulber, D.F. and Sidak, G. (1996). "Network Access Pricing and Deregulation," *Industrial & Corporate Change*, 6(4): 757–82

Stallman, R. (1999). "The GNU Project, http://www.gnu.org/gnu/thegnuproject. html

Starck, Roland and Boyer (1998). *Obligations*, 2, 6th edn., 23(8), Paris, Litec

Stigler, G. (1939). "Production and Distribution in the Short Run," *Journal of Political Economy*, 47: 305–27

Stigler, G.J. and Becker, G.S. (1977). "De Gustibus Non Est Disputandum," *American Economic Review*, 67: 76–90

Stiglitz, J.E. (1974). "Incentives and Risk-Sharing in Sharecropping," *Review of Economic Studies*, 41: 219–55

(1977). "Monopoly Nonlinear Pricing and Imperfect Information: The Insurance Market," *Review of Economic Studies*, 44: 407–30

Stijns, S. (1990). "Abus, mais de quel(s) droit(s)?," *Journal des Tribunaux*, 20, January: 33–44

Stoffel-Munck, P. (1999). *L'Abus dans le Contrat, Essai d'une Théorie*, thesis, Aix-Marseille III; Paris, Librairie Général de Droit et de Jurisprudence (2000)

566   **Bibliography**

Stole, L. (1990). "Mechanism Design under Common Agency," MIT, mimeo
    (1991). "Mechanism Design under Common Agency," MIT, mimeo
Strambio, L., González, J. and Contreras, C. (1995). *La distribución alimentaria
    en España y su entorno europeo*, Madrid, Ronald Berger
Stuckey, J.A. (1983). *Vertical Integration and Joint Ventures in the Aluminum Indus-
    try*. Cambridge, MA, Harvard University Press
Supiot, A. (1994). *Critique du Droit du Travail*, 2ème partie, "La Subordination
    et la Liberté," Paris, PUF: 111–86
Taagepera, R. and Shugart, M.S. (1993). "Predicting the Number of Parties – A
    Quantitative Model of the Duverger Mechanical Effect," *American Political
    Science Review*, 87(2): 455–64
Tadelis, S. (1999). "What's in a Name? Reputation as a Tradeable Asset,"
    American Economic Review, 89: 548–63
Tallon, D. (1994). *Le Concept de Bonne Foi en Droit Français du Contrat*, Centro di
    studi e ricerche di diritto comparato e straniero, Saggi, conferenze e seminari,
    15, Rome
Tardiff, T.J. and Taylor, W.E. (1996). "Revising Price Caps: The Next Generation
    of Incentive Regulation Plans," in M.A. Crew (ed.), *Pricing and Regulatory
    Innovations under Increasing Competition. Topics in Regulatory Economics and
    Policy Series*, London, Kluwer Academic: 21–38
Taylor, L.D. and Weisman, D.L. (1996). "A Note on Price Cap Regulation and
    Competition," *Review of Industrial Organisation*, 11: 459–71
Teece, D.J. (1986). "Profiting from Technological Innovation," *Research Policy*,
    15(6): 285–305
    (1988). "Technological Change and the Nature of the Firm," in G. Dosi *et al.*
    (eds.), *Technological Change and Economic Theory*, London, Pinter
Terré, Fr. (1968). "Sociologie du contrat," *Archives de Philosophie du Droit*
Terré, Simler and Lequette, (1999). *Les Obligations*, 7th edn., no. 27
Thibierge-Gelfucci, C. (1997). "Libres propos sur la transformation du droit des
    contrats," *Revue Trimestrielle de Droit Civil*, 370
Tiller, E.H. (1998). "Controlling Policy by Controlling Process: Judicial influence
    on Regulatory Decision Making," *Journal of Law, Economics & Organization*,
    14(1): 114–35
Tiller, E.H. and Spiller, P.T. (1996). *Strategic Instruments: Politics and Decision
    Costs in Administrative and Judicial Process*, Center for Legal and Regulatory
    Studies, Graduate School of Business, University of Texas at Austin
Tirole J. (1985). *Concurrence Imparfaite*, Paris, Economica
    (1986). "Hierarchies and Bureaucracies: On the Role of Collusion in Organi-
    zations," *Journal of Law, Economics and Organization*, 2: 181–214
    (1992a). "Comments," in L. Werin and H. Wijkander (eds.), *Contract
    Economics*, Cambridge, MA and Oxford, Blackwell: 109–13
    (1992b). "Collusion and the Theory of Organizations," in J.J. Laffont (ed.),
    Advances in Economic Theory, 2, Cambridge University Press: 151–206
    (1994). "The Internal Organization of Government," *Oxford Economic Papers*,
    46: 1–29
    (1996). "A Theory of Collective Reputations (With Applications to the Persis-
    tence of Corruption and to Firm Quality)," *Review of Economic Studies*, 63:
    1–22

(1999). "Incomplete Contracts: Where Do we Stand?," *Econometrica*, 67(4): 741–82

Travis, A.S. (1993). *The Rainbow Makers: The Origins of the Synthetic Dyestuffs Industry in Western Europe*, London, Associated University Presses

Trigeaud, J.M. (1983). "Justice et fidélité dans les contrats," *Archives de Philosophie du Droit, Philosophie Pénale*, 28: 207

Truchet, D. (1987). "Le contrat administratif, qualification juridique d'un accord de volontés," in L. Cadiet (ed.), *Le Droit Contemporain des Contrats*, Paris, Economica: 186

Utilities Act (2000). chapter 27, London, Stationery Office

Van Ommeslaghe, P. (1992). "Rapport général, la bonne foi dans la formation du contrat," in *La Bonne Foi, Travaux de l'Association H. Capitant*: 25

Vanden Bergh, R. (1998). "The Evolutions of Institutions: Politics and Process in the American States," unpublished dissertation, University of California, Berkeley

Viandier, V.A. (1980). *La complaisance*, JCP, I. 2987, nos. 16 *et seq.*

Vickers, J. (1995). "Competition and Regulation in Vertically Related Markets," *Review of Economic Studies*, 62: 1–17

Vickers, J. and Yarrow, G. (1988). *Privatization: An Economic Analysis*, Cambridge, MA, MIT Press

Villey, M. (1969). *Seize Essais de Philosophie du Droit*, Paris, Dalloz

Vogelsang I. (1989). "Price Cap Regulation of Telecomm Services: A Long-Run Approach," in M.A. Crew (ed.), *Price Cap Regulation and Incentive Regulation in Telecommunications*, London, Kluwer Academic

Vogelsang, I. and Finsinger, J. (1979). "A Regulatory Adjustment Process for Optimal Pricing by Multiproduct Monopoly Firms," *Bell Journal of Economics*, 10(1): 151–71

Von Weisäcker, C.C. (1981). "A Welfare Analysis of Barriers to Entry," *Bell Journal of Economics*, 11: 399–420

Waddams Price, C. and Bennett, M. (1999). "New Gas in Old Pipes: Opening the UK Residential Gas Market to Competition," *Utilities Policy*, 8: 1–15

Waddams Price, C. and Hancock, R. (1998). "Distributional Effects of Liberalising UK Utility Markets," *Fiscal Studies*, 19(3): 295–320

Waterson, M. (1992). "A Comparative Analysis of Methods for Regulating Public Utilities," *Metroeconomica*, 43: 214–22

(1996). "Vertical Integration and Vertical Restraints," in T.J. Jenkinson (ed.), *Readings in Microeconomics*, Oxford University Press

Watts, R.L. and Zimmerman, J.L. (1906). *Positive Accounting Theory*, Englewood Cliffs, NJ, Prentice-Hall

Weill and Terré (1980). *Obligations*, nos. 24 and 49 *et seq.*

Weingast, B.R. (1995). "The Economic Role of Political Institutions – Market-Preserving Federalism and Economic Development", *Journal of Law, Economics and Organization*, 11(1): 1–31

Westgren, R.E. (1999). "Delivering Food Safety, Food Quality, and Sustainable Production Practices: The Label Rouge Poultry System in France," *American Journal of Agricultural Economics*, 81(5): 1107–11

Whinston, M.D. (2000). "On the Transaction Cost Determinants of Vertical Integration," January, mimeo

Wiggins, S.N. and Libecap, G.D. (1985). "Oil Field Unitization: Contractual Failure in the Presence of Imperfect Information," *American Economic Review*, 75(3): 376–85

Williams, D.L. (1996). "Incomplete Contracting and Ex-Post Opportunism: Evidence from Franchise Contract Terminations," UCLA, Department of Economics, mimeo

Williamson, O.E. (1971). "The Vertical Integration of Production: Market Failure Considerations," *American Economic Review*, 61: 112–23

(1975). *Markets and Hierarchies: Analysis and Antitrust Implications. A Study in the Economics of Internal Organization*, New York, Free Press

(1976). "Franchising Bidding for Natural Monopolies – In General and with Respect to CATV," *Bell Journal of Economics*, 7: 73–104

(1979). "Transaction-Cost Economics: The Governance of Contractual Relations," *Journal of Law and Economics*, 22(2): 233–61

(1981). "The Modern Corporation: Origins, Evolution and Attributes," *Journal of Economic Literature*, 19(4): 1537–68

(1983). "Credible Commitments: Using Hostages to Support Exchange," *American Economic Review*, 73: 519–40

(1985). *The Economic Institutions of Capitalism: Firms, Markets, Relational Contracting*, New York, Free Press

(1988a). "Corporate Finance and Corporate Governance," *Journal of Finance*, 43(3): 567–91

(1988b). "The Logic of Economic Organization," *Journal of Law, Economics and Organization*, 4: 65–93

(1991). "Comparative Economic Organization: The Analysis of Discrete Structural Alternatives," *Administrative Science Quarterly*, 36: 269–96

(1993). "Transaction Cost Economics and Organization Theory," *Industrial and Corporate Change*, 2: 102–56

(1995). "Introduction," in O.E. Williamson and S.E. Masten (eds.), *Transaction Cost Economics*, I, Brookfield, VT, Edward Elgar: xiii–xxvi

(1996). *The Mechanisms of Governance*, Oxford University Press

(1998). "Transaction Cost Economics: How it Works, Where it is Headed?," *De Economist*, 146: 23–58

(1999). "Public and Private Bureaucracies: A Transaction Cost Economics Perspective," *Journal of Law, Economics and Organization*, 15(1): 306–42

(2000). "The New Institutional Economics: Taking Stock, Looking Ahead," *Journal of Economic Literature*, 38: 595–613

Williamson, O.E. and Masten, S.E. (eds.) (1995). *Transaction Cost Economics*, Aldershot, Edward Elgar

Williamson, O.E, Wachter, M.L. and Harris, J.E. (1975). "Understanding the Employment Relation: The Analysis of Idiosyncratic Exchange," *Bell Journal of Economics*, 6(1): 250–78; reprinted in O.E. Williamson (1975), *Markets and Hierarchies*, New York, Free Press: 57–81

Wilson, J. (1989). *Bureaucracy: What Governement Agencies Do and Why They Do It*, New York, Basic Books

Wiseman, J. (1991). "The Black Box," *Economic Journal*, 101: 149–55

Wolak, F. (2000). "An Empirical Analysis of the Impact of Hedge Contracts on Bidding Behavior in a Competitive Electricity Market," *International Economic Journal*, 14(2): 1–40

Wolfram, C. (1999). "Measuring Duopoly Power in the British Electricity Spot Market", *American Economic Review*, 89: 805–26

Wolfram, K.D. (1998). "Strategic Bidding in a Multiunit Auction: An Empirical Analysis of Bids to Supply Electricity in England and Wales," *Rand Journal of Economics*, 29(4): 703–25

World Bank (Mary Shirley *et al.*) (1995). *Bureaucrats in Business. The Economics and Politics of Government Ownership*, New York, Oxford University Press

Wruck, K.H. and Jensen, M.C. (1994). "Specific Knowledge, and Total Quality Management," *Journal of Accounting and Economics*, 18: 247–87

Yellen, J. (1984). "Efficiency Wage Models of Unemployment," *American Economic Review*, 74(2): 526–38

Index of names

Abbink, K. 298
Abdala, M.A. 495n
Abreu, D. 239n
Adler, B.E. 123
AES 498n
Agences de l'Eau 443–5
Aghion, P. 11, 12, 38, 39, 193–4, 196, 202, 209, 210, 211n
Air Liquide 385
Air Products 385
Akerlof, G.A. 4, 6, 21, 128, 294, 295, 321
Aláez, R. 356n
Alaska Oil and Gas Conservation Commission 150
Alchian, A.A. 7, 16, 28, 56, 70n, 75, 84, 185, 223, 239n, 262, 274
Alkermes 377, 378
Allam, D. 335n
Allen, D.W. 279, 282, 284, 286, 291n
Alston, L.J. 142, 143, 145
Amendola, M. 400
American Uniform Commercial Code 125
Amoco 385
Anand, B.N. 389
Ancel, V.P. 103, 114n
Anderhub, V. 294, 295, 308, 310
Anderlini, L. 215, 230
Anderson, T.L. 155n, 288
Andonova, V. 355n
Aoki, M. 17, 29
ARCO 150
Argyris, C. 252
Armstrong, C.M. 362, 422, 425, 427, 428, 439n
Arora, A. 375–9, 386, 388, 389
Arrow, K. 4, 6, 24, 58n, 241, 242, 244, 245, 248–9, 374, 375
Arruñada, B. 18, 332, 356n, 357n
Asanuma, B. 71n
AT&T 358, 359, 367, 372n
Athey, S. 336n
Aubert, M. 104, 106–7, 114n, 115n

Automatic Generation Control 508
Averch, H. 419, 438n
Axelrod, R. 235
Ayres, I. 237
Azariadis, C. 20

Baake, P. 364
Bain, J.S. 51, 155n–156n
Bajari, P. 57
Baker, G. 70n, 186, 187–8, 189, 236, 239n, 267
Baldwin, C.Y. 270n
Baldwin, R. 481
Ball, P. 392n
Baranès, W. 115n
Barbeyrac, 111
Barnard, C.I. 7, 56, 241
Baron, D. 4, 19, 140, 170, 172, 429, 439n
Barro, R.J. 140
Barron, J.M. 324
Barzel, Y. 22, 155n, 274, 292n, 494n
BASF 385
Battigalli, P. 237
Baumol, W. 36
Bawa, V.S. 419
Beales, H. 322
Beard, T. 361
Bearnon, J.A. 497n
Beaudry, P. 178n
Bebchuk, L.A. 118, 237
Becker, G.S. 236, 284
Beggs, A.W. 375
Bell System 368
Bénabent, A. 112
Bennett, M. 19, 439n
Bercovitz, J.E.L. 281, 282, 285, 291n, 292n
Berg, J. 294, 296, 297, 298, 299, 305
Berle, A.A. 7, 52
Bernanke, B.S. 248, 249
Bernheim B.D. 71n, 237
Bernstein, L. 125n

Besanko, D. 19, 172, 420
Bessy, C. 18, 286, 376
Bhattacharya, S. 284, 319
Binmore, K. 296
Blair, R.D. 324, 335n
Blanchard, C. 363
Boeing 389
Boiteux, M. 417–8, 422
Bolton, P. 193, 194, 196, 202, 209, 210n, 236
Bonbright, J.C. 501n
Borenstein, S. 478, 483
Boyer 104
BP 387–8
Bradach, J.L. 320, 335n
Bradley, I. 427, 428
Brainard, L. 177n
Brickley, J.A. 28, 270n, 285, 292n, 322, 324, 334n, 336n
British Energy 498n
British Gas 430, 435, 439n
British Petroleum 150
British Rail 421
British Telecommunications 423, 430
Brousseau, D. 12, 18, 108, 109, 110, 286
Brousseau, E. 376, 391n
Brown, C. 234
Brown, G.M. 140, 141
Brownsword, R. 109, 110
Bull, C. 235, 236
Bürgerliches Gesetzbuch (BGB) 99
Bushnell, J. 478, 483, 529n, 530n

Cadiet, L. 103
Cahier des Charges 331
Caillaud, B. 434
Cain, B.E. 496n
California ISO Market Surveillance Committee 499n
California Power Exchange (PX) 482–3, 486, 488, 501n
California Public Utilities Commission (LPUC) 184, 487–8, 493, 499n
Canadian Radio-Television & Telecommunications 434
Carey, J.M. 496n, 497n
Carmichael, H.L. 236
Carney, E.M. 292n
Castillo, D. 355n
Caves, R. 374
Central Electricity Board 496n
Central Electricity Generating Board 480
Centrica 438n
Champaud, C. 103
Chandler, A.D. 7, 52, 103

Charreaux, G. 15–16, 270n
Che, Y.-K. 237
Chemical Age Project File 392n
Cheung, S. 45, 155n
Chirez, A. 107
Chung, T. 38
Church, J. 371
Churchland, P.S. 231, 239n
Clark, K.B. 270n
Coase, R.H. 6–7, 24, 29, 51, 56, 58n, 109, 164, 241, 248, 264, 289
Cockburn, I. 336n
Code Civil 101, 104, 106, 112
Coeurderoy, R. 25, 287, 461n
Cohen, W. 373
Coipel, M. 107, 114n
Collins, H. 124n
Comisión Ejecutiva Hidroeléctrica del Rió Lema (CEL) 489, 49–2, 501n
Commons, J.R. 45, 53, 54, 366, 367
Competition Commission 430, 481, 482
Computerland 415n
Conlisk, J. 88, 95n
Conner, K.B. 269
Conrad, J.M. 245
Contractor, F.J. 375, 376
Contreras, C. 343n
Cooper, R. 284
Cornu, G. 114n
Cour des Comptes 440
Courville, L. 438n
Cowan, S.G.B. 362, 422, 425, 428
Cox, G.N. 496n
Cramton, P. 177n
Crawford, R.G. 7, 16, 56, 70n, 185, 274
Crew, M.A. 420, 428, 439n
Crocker, K.J. 17, 26, 58n, 277, 280, 281, 282, 285, 286, 287, 288, 289, 291n, 292n, 461n
Crookel, H. 374
Crozier, M. 178n
Curien, N. 362, 432
Cusamano, M. 71n
Cyert, R. 7

Dalton, M. 178n
Dang-Nguyen, G. 364
Dark, F.H. 322, 324, 334n
Darwin, C. 47
Dasgupta, P. 177n
Davis, G. 485
Davis, L.E. 144
Dawkins, R. 53
De Alessi, L. 91, 368
De Fraja, G. 432

De Soto, H. 140, 143
De Vany, A. 76, 91
Deacon, R.T. 140
Deakin, S. 17
DeBeers 71n
Debreu, G. 241
Dekel, E. 239n
Demogue, R. 114n
Demsetz, H. 4, 7, 16, 45, 50, 51, 84, 141,
    142, 223, 257, 260, 261, 262, 264,
    368, 369, 426
Denning, A. 239n
Derycke, P.-H. 453, 461n
Deschenaux, H. 112
Desgorces, R. 112
Despotopoulos, C. 100
Dewatripont, M. 11, 38, 39, 175, 178n,
    196, 210, 211n
Didier, P. 109, 115n
Distillers 380
Dixit, A. 53, 58, 178n, 244, 248, 249
Dow Chemicals 384, 385, 386
Doyle, C. 362, 439n
Dranove, D. 420
Du Pont 379, 384, 385
Duesenberry, J. 50
Duke Energy International 489, 491–2,
    501n, 502n
Durkheim, 110
Duverger's Law 496n
Dye, R.A. 227, 237

Economides, N. 359, 361, 362, 372n
Edlin, A.S. 123
Eggertsson, T. 7, 141
Electricité de France 418
Encaoua, D. 364
Epstein, L. 178n
Epstein, S. 294, 296, 298, 299, 305, 500n
Erickson, J.E. 17, 283, 286, 289, 290,
    291n, 292n
Eswaran, M. 284, 319
Exxon 150, 384, 385

Falstaff brewers 133, 134, 136
Fama, E.F. 15, 252, 258–9
Fares, M. 8, 12
Farnsworth, E.A. 133, 239n
Farsi, M. 238n
Faure-Grimaud, A. 171, 172, 176, 191n
Favereau, O. 13, 244, 245
Feder, G. 143
Federal Communication Commission
    (FCC) 366, 369
Federal Communications Commission 429

Federal Energy Regulatory Commission
    (FERC) 484, 487, 496n, 499n, 501n
Fehr, E. 191n, 294, 295, 308
Felli, L. 215, 230
Ferejohn, J. 496n
Finon, D. 22
Finsinger, J. 422–3, 426, 427
Fiorina, M. 496n
Fisher, A. 242, 244, 245, 248–9
Fisher Body 16
Flour, J. 104, 106–7, 114n, 115n
Fosfuri, A. 18, 386, 388, 389
Foss, N.J. 81
France Telecom 358
Frank, R.H. 240n
Free Software Foundation 371
Freeman, C. 382
Freixas, X. 245
French, K. 138n
Frison-Roche, M.A. 103, 115n
Fudenberg, P. 177n, 191n
Furobotn, E. 7, 29, 141, 143, 291n

Gabillon, E. 176
Gächter, S. 191n, 294, 295, 308, 310
Gaffard, J.L. 400
Galanter, M. 52
Galland Act (1996) 355n, 356n
Gallick, E.C. 290
Gallini, N. 375
Gambardella, A. 377, 389, 391n
Gambrell, E. 386
Gandal, N. 371
Garey, M.R. 239n
Garicano, L. 355n, 356n
Gatty, J. 440
Gauthier, N. 112
Gely, R. 495n
Genentech 377, 378
General Electric 389
Gertner, R. 237
Ghestin, J. 27, 102, 103, 106, 114n
Gibbons, R. 70n, 177n, 186, 187–8, 189,
    218, 236
Gilbert, R.J. 431, 498n
Gilson, R.J. 128, 139n
Giulietti, M. 428
Glachant, J.M. 22
Glais, M. 20, 400
Glanchant, J.-M. 391n
Goetz, C.J. 216, 235
Goldberg, V.P. 17, 19, 20, 126, 128, 138n,
    139n, 274, 283, 286, 289, 290, 291n,
    292n, 494n, 495n
Gomaa, N.M.K. 100, 111

Gómez-Pomar, F. 355n
González, J. 343n
González, M. 355n
Gordley, J. 111
Gordon H.S. 155n
Gordon, R.A. 50
Göttinger, H. 75
Goubeaux, G. 102, 106
Gouldner, A. 178n
Gounot, E. 107, 111
Green, R. 177n, 178n, 239n, 438n, 494n,
    498n, 530n
Grindley 383, 384, 391n
Grossman, S.J. 10, 35, 37, 56, 57, 69, 70,
    71n, 176, 177n, 185, 192n, 193, 213,
    217, 220, 291n, 293, 377, 406
Güth, W. 294, 295, 305, 308

Hagerman, J. 422
Hahn, F.H. 241
Halcon/Scientific Design 383
Hall, B.H. 7, 391n
Halonen, M. 186, 187, 192n
Ham, R. 391n
Hamilton, J.H. 432
Hammond, P. 177n
Hancock, R. 436
Hardin, G. 140
Harris, J.E. 236
Harris, M. 177n
Hart, O. 11, 12, 35, 38, 39, 57, 71n, 175,
    176, 177n, 178n, 185, 191n, 192n,
    193, 213, 214, 217, 218, 220, 221,
    237, 239n, 274, 278, 283, 284, 289,
    291n, 292n, 293, 377, 406, 440, 445
Hausch, D.B. 237
Hauser, J. 105
Hayek, F. 56, 90, 107, 112, 113, 255
Heide, J. 58n
Hellwig, J.J. 82, 95n
Helm, D. 436
Helper, S. 71n
Helpman, E. 37
Henderson, H.D. 46
Henderson, R. 336n
Henry, C. 242, 244, 245, 248–9, 250n
Hercules 380
Hermalin, B.E. 122, 240n
Hey, J.D. 244
Hill, A. 495n
Hirshleifer 240n, 244
Hitch, C.J. 7
Hodgson, G.M. 269
Hoechst 385
Hogan, W. 530n

Holburn, G.L.F. 500n
Holmström, B. 46, 177n, 191n, 192n,
    211n, 214, 217, 218, 219, 274, 278,
    283, 284, 288, 291n, 292n, 293, 333
Howard, M. 391n
Howell, J.E. 50
Hubbard, R, 285
Hubbard, T. 186
Hviid, M. 438n

IBM 367, 389
Ichniowski, C. 336n
ICI 379, 385, 386
IFC 133–4
IG Farben 379
Intrum Justitia 343n, 348n
Iossa, E. 432
Irrgang, W. 239n
ITT 495n

Jackson, P.M. 418
Jacobson, G. 496n
Jamet-le-Gac, S. 113
Jenkinson, T. 436
Jensen, M.C. 15, 251–6, 258–65, 267–9,
    270n
John Paul II 115n
Johnson & Johnson 378
Johnson, D.S. 239n
Johnson, L.L. 419, 438n
Johnson, R.N. 140
Jones, F. 438n
Jones, R.A. 242, 248
Joskow, P.L. 17, 23, 54, 83, 277, 280, 282,
    288, 289, 290, 291n, 367, 461n, 478,
    499n, 503, 509, 511, 518, 528n,
    529n, 530n
Josserand, L. 112
Jourdain, P. 112
Jullien, B. 362, 432
Jun Sunaga 115n

Kahn, E.P. 498n, 530n
Kalnins, A. 335n
Kamien, M. 374
Kandel, E. 357n
Kandori, M. 236
Kaserman, D.L. 324, 361
Katz, M. 123, 364, 371, 375
Kaufman, P.J. 290, 322, 324, 334n
Kenney, R.W. 71n, 274
Kerr, S. 219, 229
Keser, C. 27, 294, 295, 299–304, 311
Kessides, I. 494n
Keynes, J.M. 46

Khanna, T. 389
Killing, J.P. 374
Kirchsteiger, G. 294, 295, 308
Kirzner, I. 412
Klein, B. 7, 16–17, 18, 56, 70n, 71n, 79,
    81, 156n, 185, 239n, 274, 283, 287,
    317, 321, 322, 323, 334n, 340, 357n
Klein, P. 25, 58n, 288, 461n
Kleindorfer, P.R. 420, 428, 439n
Klemperer, P. 177n
Knight, F.H. 8, 13
Koenig, G. 6
Königstein, M. 294, 295, 308, 310
Kotwal, A. 284, 319
Kranton, R. 236
Krattenmaker, T.G. 411
Kreps, D. 56–7, 191n, 192n, 236, 241,
    244
Krol, J. 385
Kuhn, T.S. 51
Kumar, J.B. 189

La Porta, R. 189
Laffont, J.J. 4, 19, 166, 171, 172, 175, 176,
    177n, 178n, 179n, 239n, 245, 362,
    364, 365, 426, 432, 433, 434, 445
Lafontaine, F. 18, 281, 282, 284, 285,
    287, 288, 290, 291n, 292n, 319, 322,
    324, 325, 333n
Lal, R. 284, 319
Landau, R. 380, 391n
Laurent, P.H. 399
Law, P.J. 428
Le Gall, P. 335n
Le Tourneau, P. 112
Lee, S.H. 432
Leffler, K.B. 56, 70n, 282, 284, 286, 317,
    321, 357n
Lehr, W. 361
Leibenstein, H. 81, 91
Leibsohn, D. 333n
Lequette 104, 107, 115n
Lessius, 111
Levin, J. 234, 236, 373, 390
Levy, B. 464, 467–8, 472, 494n, 495n
Lewin-Solomon, S.B. 324
Libecap, G.D. 22, 140, 142–6, 148–9,
    151, 155n, 156n
Lindenberg, S. 110
Lipman, B.L. 239n
Littlechild, S. 423, 424, 438
Littlechild Report 423
Llewellyn, K. 51–2, 55
Lonza 377
Lopomo, G. 372n

Loussouarn, Y. 112
Lueck, D. 279, 282, 284, 286, 291n
Lutz, N.A. 327, 334n
Lyon, T. 238n
Lyon-Caen, G. 112
Lyons, B. 58n, 277, 279, 281, 289

Macaulay, S. 59, 70n, 228, 339
Machlup, F. 7
Macho-Stadler, I.X. 375, 376
MacLeod, W.B. 221, 234, 235, 236
Macneil, I. 7, 55, 103, 109, 115n, 235
Maddala, G.S. 277, 462n
Maggi, G. 237
Magill, M. 239n
Magnusson, L. 368
Malcomson, J.M. 221, 235, 236
Malin, E.
Malouf, M. 297
Malthus, T. 47
Mankiw, G. 21
March, J.G. 7
Markou, E. 418
Mars 412
Martimort, D. 10, 166, 171, 172, 175,
    176, 178n, 179n
Martinez-Giralt, X. 376
Marvel, H. 410
Maskin, E. 123, 177n, 214, 221, 237,
    239n, 240n
Masten, S. 17, 19, 26, 58n, 72, 277,
    280–3, 285–90, 291n, 292n, 338,
    339, 340, 461n
Mathewson, G.F. 284, 317, 318, 323
Matsushima, H. 236
Matutes, C. 364
Maynard, J.T. 392n
Mayo, J. 361
Mazeaud, D. 110
Mazeaud, H.L.J. 104, 114n
McAfee, P. 172
McCafferty, S. 410
McCarthy, C. 498n
McChesney, F.S. 155n
McCormick, R. E. 138n
McCrudden, C. 481
McCubbins, M.D. 495n, 500n
McDonald's 290, 322, 323
McLeod, B. 28
McMillan, J. 172
Means, G. 7, 52
Meckling, W. 15, 251–3, 256, 260–5, 267,
    270n
Meehan, J.W. 291n
Meleu, M. 171, 178n

Ménard, C. 19, 20, 23, 108, 109, 290, 331, 440, 446, 448, 457, 461n
Merges, R.P. 377, 378, 391n
Michael, S. 322
Michel, P. 364
Michie, J. 17
Microsoft 290, 371
Milgrom, P. 214, 218, 219, 283, 288, 292n, 333
Milkovich, G.T. 229, 239n
Mill, J.S. 107
Miller, G. 81
Minsky, M.L. 230
Mirrlees, J. 177n, 214
Mitchell, W. 45
Mitsui Toatsu 385
Moe, T. 178n, 179n
Molina 111
Monopolies & Mergers Commission 422, 498n
Monsanto 384, 385, 386
Montevideo Gas Corporation 494n–495n
Mookherjee, D. 172
Moore, H. 322
Moore, J. 11, 35, 38, 39, 57, 177n, 185, 192n, 193, 221, 237, 239n, 377
Moreaux, M. 364
Mueller, B. 142, 145
Mueller, J.M. 368
Mulherin, J.H. 282, 285
Muris, T.J. 322
Murphy, K. 70n, 71n, 156n, 186, 187–8, 189, 236, 267, 340
Muto, S. 374
Myerson, R. 19, 177n, 239n, 291n, 439n

N'Guyen, G.D. 18
National Grid Company 519
National Power 480
Neelin 296
Nelson, R. 80, 81, 90
Nestlé 412
Newbery, D. 464, 473, 475, 494n, 498n, 529n, 530n
Newell, A. 239n
Newman, J.M. 239n
Nickerson, J. 383, 384
Nöldeke, G. 38
Noll, R.G. 495n, 500n
NOP Corporate 343n
North, D.C. 7, 14, 28, 141, 144, 254, 366, 494n

O'Halloran, S. 500n
Office of Electricity Regulation 499n, 530n

Office of Gas & Electricity Markets
The New Electricity Trading Arrangements (NETA) 482, 298n, 299n
Ofgas 438n
Ofgem 436, 479, 480–2, 498n, 499n
Oftel 369, 438n
Ofwat 461n
Onchan, T. 143
Oren, S. 483, 498n
Organización Latino Americana De Energía 529n
Orléan, A. 23
Ormaza, I. 356n
Ornstein, S.I. 410
Ostrom, E. 140, 142
Ostroy, J.M 242, 248
Ottosson, J. 368

Pacific Gas & Electric (PG&E) 484, 488, 501n
Padilla, A.J. 356n, 364
Palay, T.M. 290
Papert, S.A. 230
Parent, D. 234
Parmar, M. 418
Pearce, D.G. 236, 239n
Pejovich, S. 7
Peltzman, S. 528n
Pénard, T. 18, 361, 364
Perelman, C. 115n
Perez-Castrillo, D. 375, 376
Perora, A. 18
Perry, K. 406
Peters, H.M. 392n
Peters, M. 166, 178n
Petersen, H. 438n
Philippe, D. 112
Phillips 150, 385, 389
Pindyck, R.S. 244, 248, 249
Pingle, M. 81
Pipes, R. 140
Pirrong, C. 290
Poitevin, M. 175, 178n
Pollitt, M.G. 529n
Ponssard, J.P. 245
Portalis, V. 114n
Posner, R. 125n, 180, 240n
Poughon, J.M. 100, 101, 102
PowerGen 480
Prahalad, C.K. 269
Prendergast, C. 218, 230
Prennushi, G. 336n
Proctor & Gamble 389

Price, C. 427, 428
Priest, G. 284
Prudhoe Bay Unit 150, 152
Public Utility Commissions (PUCs) 470–1
Pufendorf, L. 111

Quélin, B. 25, 287, 461n
Quinzii, M. 239n

Rabin, M. 191n
Railtrack 421
Rajan, A. 236
Rajan, R.G. 189, 192n
Ramsey, F.P. 417–8, 422
Ramsey–Boiteux tariff 362
Ramstad, Y. 368
Ranieri, F. 112
Rasmusen, E. 238n
Raviv, A. 177n
Rawls, J. 112
Raynaud, E. 18, 331
Rees, R. 418, 427
Reichelstein, S. 123, 172
Rey, P. 11, 12, 38, 39, 196, 210, 211n,
    362, 364, 365, 410, 432
Reynolds, K.J. 282, 286
Rhône-Poulenc 385, 389
Richter, R. 87, 141, 143, 291n
Ricketts, M. 95n
Riedl, A. 294
Rindfleisch, A. 58n
Riordan, M.H. 40, 56, 426, 431
Robbins, L. 46
Robinson, J. 46
Robinson, S. 58n
Rochet, J.C. 178n
Rock, E. 190
Rockett, K. 374
Romain, J.F. 112
Romer, P. 21
Rose, C.M. 140, 155n, 471
Rose, N. 511
Rosen, S. 238n, 241
Ross, T.W. 214, 217, 284
Roth, A. 297, 310
Rouhette, V.G. 99, 111, 114n
Rubin, P.H. 317, 318, 319, 356n
Rucker, R.R. 282, 284, 286
Rudnick, H. 529n
Rustichini, A. 239n

Sacco, R. 99, 100, 112, 114n
Sadrieh, A. 298
Saft, L. 18, 321
Sako, M. 71n

Salanié, B. 10, 26, 241
Salop, S.C. 361, 411
San Diego Gas & Electric 499n–500n
Sappington, D. 160, 209, 422, 424, 426,
    427, 428, 434, 439n
Satterthwaite, M. 177n
Saussier, S. 19, 26, 281, 286, 289, 461n
Savage, L.J. 8, 15, 226
Savedoff, W. 494n, 497n
Schering-Plough 378
Schmalensee, R. 17, 146, 509, 511, 529n
Schmidt, K. 38
Schmittlein, D.C. 288
Schneider, R. 143
Schwartz, A. 23, 124n, 125n, 239n, 500n
Schwartz, P. 355n, 356n, 469n
Schweizer, U. 237
Scott, R.E. 120, 216, 235, 239n
Segal, I. 193, 221, 237
Sejnowski, T.J. 231, 239n
Selten, R. 298, 309, 302
SepraChem 377
Service Master 415n
Shackle, G.L.S. 13
Shaked, A. 296
Shanley, M. 420
Shapiro, C. 20, 236, 321, 357n, 364, 365,
    371, 375
Sharkey, W. 368
Shavell, S. 237, 292n
Shavell, V. 118
Shaw, J.C. 239n
Shaw, K.L. 333n, 335n, 336n
Shelanski, H. 25, 58n, 286, 288, 4641n
Shell 385, 386
Shepard, A. 324
Sherman, R. 419, 438n
Shirley, M. 440, 448, 461n
Shleifer, A. 191n, 439n, 440, 445
Shugart, M.S. 496n, 497n
Sibley, D.S. 419, 428, 434
Sidak, G. 362
Simler 104, 107, 115n
Simon, H. 7, 12, 13, 28, 53, 56, 213, 217,
    222, 223, 227, 229, 237, 238, 239n,
    241, 242, 246–50
Sinkondo, V.M.H. 99
Slade, M. 281, 284, 285, 287, 288, 291n,
    292n, 325, 333n, 334n, 336n
Slonim, 310
Smith, A. 3, 45, 47, 143, 148
Smith, C.W. 270n
Smith, J.K. 379
Smith, J.L. 151, 156n
Snyder, E.A. 282, 286, 290, 291n, 339, 340

Solvay 379
Sonnenschein, H. 296
Soto 111
Southern California Edison 484, 488
Spengler, J. 178n
Spiegel, M. 296
Spiller, P.T. 22, 23, 464, 467–8, 471, 472,
    483, 494n, 495n, 496n, 497n, 498n,
    500n, 501n
Spitz, P.H. 379, 380
Spulber, D.F. 362
Stacchetti, E. 236
Stallman, R. 371
Standard 379
Stark 104
Stern, S. 336n, 336n
Stigler, G. 284
Stiglitz, J.E. 4, 20, 26, 160, 236, 284,
    319, 321
Stijns, S. 112
Stoffel-Munck, P. 112
Stole, L. 166, 178n, 179n
Strambio, L. 343n
Stuckey, J. 54, 290, 292n
Supiot, A. 241
Sutton, J. 296

Taagepera, R. 496n
Tadelis, S. 57, 191
Takeishi, A. 71n
Tallon, D. 112
Tally, E. 238n
Tardiff, T.J. 439n
Taylor, L.D. 434
Taylor, W.E. 439n
Teece, D.J. 375, 386, 391n
TEL 379
Telecommunication Regulatory Authority
    (France) 358, 369
Terré, F. 104, 107, 115n
Texaco 385
Texas Instruments 389
Thibierge-Gelfucci, C. 111
Thompson, E. 239n
Tiller, E.H. 500n
Tirole, J. 12, 19, 46, 123, 124, 166, 170,
    175, 177n, 178n, 179n, 191n, 192n,
    193, 194, 210n, 214, 221, 237, 239n,
    240n, 278, 291, 292n, 362, 364, 365,
    410, 415n, 426, 432, 433, 434, 445,
    518, 530n
Transco 438n
Transmission Control Protocol/Internet
    Protocol 370
Travis, A.S. 389

Trigeaud, J.M. 110
Truchet, D. 99
Turner, D. 58n

Umbeck, J.R. 324
Uniform Commercial Code 123
Unilever, 412
Union Carbide 384, 385, 386, 388
Unión Telefónica del Rio de la Plata 495n
United Shoe Machinery Corporation 290
US Energy Information Administration
    497n

Vail, T. 358, 368
Valceschini, E. 351
Van Ommeslaghe, P. 112
Vanden Bergh, R. 470, 471, 500n
Vázquez, L. 355n, 356n
Viandier, V.A. 103
Vickers, J.S. 362, 422, 423, 424, 425, 427,
    428, 431, 439n
Villey, M. 100
Vishny, R. 440, 445
Vogelsang, I. 422–3, 426, 427, 496n,
    498n
von Mehren, A. 100
Von Weizsäcker, C.C. 412

Wachter, M. 190, 236
Waddams Price, C. 19, 428, 432, 436,
    438n, 439n
Waterson, M. 423, 424, 439n
Watts, R.L. 266
Weiner, R.J. 285
Weingast, B.R. 495n, 497n, 500n
Weisbach, M.S. 322, 324
Weisbrod 244
Weisman, D.L. 434, 439n
Westgren, R.E. 331
Whinston, M.D. 71n, 237, 292n
White, L. 362
Wichmann, T. 364
Wigdor, A.K. 229
Wiggins, S.N. 146, 149, 155n, 156n
Williams, D.L. 334n
Williamson, O. 4, 6–7, 10, 13, 19, 24–5,
    39, 40, 45, 54, 56, 71n, 72, 83, 87,
    89, 94n, 95n, 109, 141, 164, 165,
    170, 178, 185, 191n, 213, 214, 217,
    220, 226, 228, 236, 237, 238n, 239n,
    241, 250, 252, 253, 259, 261, 262–5,
    274, 283, 289, 315, 321, 339, 340,
    346, 366, 367, 369, 426, 437, 440,
    446, 447, 459, 461n, 494n, 495n,
    529n

Willinger, M. 27, 294–5, 299–304, 311
Wilson, J. 178n
Winston, C. 528n
Winter, R.A. 284, 317, 318, 323
Winter, S. 80, 81, 90
Wiseman, J. 89
Wolak, F.A. 483, 529n, 530n
Wolfram, C. 479, 480, 530n
World Bank 22, 440
Woroch, G. 361, 372n

Wright, B. 375
Wruck, K.H. 270n

Y. Rocher et Pronuptia 408, 415n
Yarrow, G. 423, 424
Yellen, J.L. 21, 294, 295, 321

Zimmerman, J.L. 266, 270n
Zingales, L. 189, 192n
Zylberszatajn, D. 355n

Subject index

access pricing 432–5
administration 347–8, 349
administrative controls 54–5
adverse selection 8–10, 21, 33–5
agency theory 213–14, 217–19
  contract design 282–3
  contract duration 277–9
  contracting decision 273, 274–5, 277–8
  incentives 285–6
  progress in 289–91
  vertical integration 287–8
alternating current networks 506–9
applicable law of contract 54–5
Assembly Bill (1966) AB 1890 483, 485,
  487
asymmetric interconnection and regulation
  360, 361–3
authority, role of 222–3
  in labor contract 241–2, 246–50

Ballantine beer 133–7, 139n
Bertrand competition 431, 434
best efforts clause 133, 134–7
biased principals 175–6
block clauses 396, 398
block exemption regulations 396–9
Bloor v. *Falstaff Brewing Corporation* 126–7,
  133–7
Bluefield case 501n
bounded rationality 20, 25, 28, 53, 57, 74,
  165, 181–2, 214, 219, 226, 237, 250,
  253, 259, 261, 292n

chemical process technology market 374,
  379–83, 389
chemicals industry structure 373–4
  licensing and innovation 384–91, 392n
Coase Theorem 160–1
codetermination 86–8
commitment constraints 13–14
communication, and incentive theory
  165–7, 172

Community Agreement Law 396
commutative justice principle 111–2
comparative contractual approach 50, 52,
  57
competition 20
  economies of scale 476–7
  telecoms networks 433
competition in utilities 421
  auctions 425–6, 431
  between generators 513–14
  networks 417, 433–4
  regulation 421, 424, 430, 432, 436
  unregulated firms 434–5
Competition Act 498n
Competition Transmission Charges 499n
competitive trading relationship 504
complete contracts 282–4, 287
conflict resolution 14, 20, 346–7
consensus agreement 399–401
contract theory 72–3
  models 6–8, 31–42
  role in economic analysis 16–20, 27–8,
    50–51, 57
  selection processes 28–9
contracts, budget-balancing requirement
  49, 50, 233, 235
  between firms and suppliers 16–17
  compliance with objective law 104–5, 113
  costs of enforcement 60–63
  costs of hold-up 62–3, 66–7, 70n
  definition 3–6
  duration 275–81
  economic organization 55–6
  exchange of value 101–2
  as framework 51–2, 55
  law 51, 55, 99–100
  meeting of minds 102–4, 106, 113
  renegotiation 174–5, 223, 237
  revision 337–8, 343–6
contractual
  efficiency 260–1
  freedom 105–6

contractual (*cont.*)
  incompleteness 13–14, 109
  procedure 112–3
  specification 61–2, 71n
control allocation
  participation constraints 205, 208
  wealth constraints 194–5, 197–8,
    201–10, 211n
Cooperation
  and efficiency 400–1
  principle 108–9, 110
  projects in EC 393
coordination 4, 5, 6, 14, 25, 251
  see also industrial organization, labor
    economics and efficiency wages, law
    and economics, organization design
corporate governance theory 266–7, 268
cost-plus contracts
  see General Motors-Fisher Body case
court enforcement of contract 60–3, 66,
    83, 124
cross-subsidization 433, 435–6, 437, 511

data networks 358–9
decision-making
  corporations 5, 81–2
  firms 73, 77, 79–83, 92–3
decision model 242–5, 247
decision rights 185, 257–9
default rules 117–18, 121–3
delivery delay 346–8
distribution
  agreements 17–18
  investment 477
double marginalization effect 172–3

earnouts 134–5, 138n, 139n
EC competition law exemptions 395–7
efficiency
  and contract revision 345, 347
  cost levels 418
  nationalized industries 418
  production 425
  property rights definitions 7, 37
  wages 20–1
  see also self-enforcement
  and wealth constraint 193–5, 200–1,
    202–5, 207–8, 211n
Efficient Component Pricing Rule (ECPR)
    362, 363
electricity 507
  demand 507–8, 510
  distribution 505, 508, 529n
  reform model 512–15
  retailing 506, 514
  transmission 506–8

electricity generation 476, 509
  consumption balance 507–8
  coordination 505–6, 517–18, 524–7
  privatization 463, 472–3
  reform model 512–15
  and transmission 473–5, 497n, 504,
    529n, 505, 524–5, 528
electricity reform
  problems with 504–5, 510, 517–25
Electricity Restructuring Act (1966) 499n
electricity supply, 473, 477, 506
  horizontal fragmentation 475, 477
  privatization 463, 472–3
  public ownership 475–6
  separation from generator 473, 475
  transportation costs 513–14
Electricity (Supply) Act (1926) 496n,
    498n
employment contract 246–9
energy crisis, California 483–5, 524, 529n
Energy Service Providers (ESPs) 512–13
enforcement 117, 118, 120, 121, 168
  see also self-enforcement
entrepreneurship in new institutional
    environment 75–6, 79–80, 89, 91,
    92–3
environment, law 140, 442
equality
  of benefits 111–13
  of parties 113–14
essential facilities
  access conditions 360–1
  regulation 361–3, 372
ex ante governance 227–9
exclusive territory arrangements 65–6
  see also franchising
explicit contracting 340–4
expropriation of sunk assets 466–7,
    495n

financial structure model 262, 265
firms 57, 73, 315
  black box theory 57–8
  boundaries and norms 185–6, 189
  decision-making 77, 79–83, 92–3
  nature of 47, 50
  profitability 76–7
  reputation of 190–1
  theory of 51, 72–3, 88–92
first-best solution 38–9
fixed-fee payments 374, 376, 381
flexibility 13, 242, 469–70
formal contracts 189–90
forward contracts 523–4
fossil-generated electricity costs 511,
    515

franchising 17–18, 284–5, 291n, 315, 317
  behavior of franchisee 322, 324–5,
    328–30
  contract terms 65, 321–2, 326–30,
    356n
  exclusive territories 322, 335n
  legal definition 316–17
  long-term contracts 328–9, 333n
  residual claims 315, 317–20
  royalty rates and advertizing fees
    317–19, 326, 335n
  sharing 318–20, 334n
  and territorial protection 408, 410,
    414n
  and transactions cost economics 281,
    292n
  of utilities 425–6, 431, 437
  vertical integration 322, 330
free will 103–5, 114n, 115n
full function
  see joint ventures

General Electricity Act (1966) 489, 491
General Motors v. Fisher Body 16–17, 61,
  63, 64, 66, 67–8, 70n, 71n
good faith 112–13, 127–8, 130–1,
  132–3, 138n
governance 49, 52–4, 55–6
  choice of mode 448–56, 460–1,
    504–5
  financial constraints 448, 450, 456
  and performance 457–9
  population size 449–50, 453, 456,
    4642n
  and transactions cost economics 76,
    83–4, 93
government subsidies 417–18

Herfindahl Hirschman index 411
hold-ups 185, 274
  ex post 213, 214, 223–4, 236, 238
  models 220–3, 236, 237
  role of human cognition 214–15
Hope Natural Gas case 501n
Horizon Corporation v. Weestcor Inc. 138n
human cognition 214–16, 221–2, 230–1,
  236, 238

implicit contracts
  between large retailers and suppliers
    344–6
  theory 20–1, ch. 11
incentive-based contracts 420, 422–4,
  434–5, 437
  distribution concerns 432, 435–6
  earnings-sharing plan 429–30

incentive compatibility constraints 159,
  166, 168, 177n
incentive constraints in positive agency
  theory 293, 296–8, 302, 311
incentive-insurance dilemma 6, 10
incentive intensity 54–5
incentive theory 3, 8–10, 12, 14–16, 21,
  24, 26, 27, 29, 31–5, 108, ch. 9
  in transactions cost economics 285–6
incomplete contract theory 3, 6, 8, 10–12,
  14–16, 24, 26, 29, 35–9, 51–3, 55–6,
  ch. 4
incomplete contracts 181, 185, 193, 213,
  237
  efficiency 193–5
  incentive theory 161–2, 176–7, 214
  non-verifiability of actions 194, 196
  property rights 213–14, 217, 220
  vertical intergration 282–3
independent regulation
  in electricity sector 476, 509–10
individual exemption regulation
  399–400–2
industrial organization 52
  theory of the firm 51, 57–8
infinitely repeated games 182–5, 187, 189,
  190, 192n
information
  costs 60–1, 377
  production and transfer 126–33
innovation, gestation period 400–1
institutional change and property rights
  141, 144–5, 146–7, 149
institutional environment 22, 29, 49, 56
institutions 7, 12, 14, 21–3, 47, 49
intangibles, trade in 18–19
intellectual property protection 373, 377,
  385
  see also patents and licensing contracts
interbrand competition 408–13
interconnection
  agreements 358, 359, 360, 361, 371
  tariffs 18–19
inter-firm contracts 4, 16–20, 55
internet networks 358, 359, 364, 370–2
interpretation of contract 117, 121
intra-brand competition 408–13
investment 467, 522
  and property rights 140, 142–3
  by suppliers 406–7
investment costs
  in developing countries' electricity sector
    516–17
  and transmission capacity 522
Irrelevance Theorem 160–1, 162, 172,
  174, 175, 176

joint ventures 399–401, 402–3, 414n
judicial institutions 468–71
just-in-time manufacturing 507, 514
justice, aim of contract 106–7, 110–14

Kirchoff's Laws 508
know-how transfer 375–7, 383
knowledge transfer costs 255–6

large retailers 345
    discipline mechanism 348–51
    opportunism 337, 342, 347, 349, 350, 351
    regulation and safeguards 350–4
Larwin-Southern Cal. Inc. v. J.G.B.
    Investment Company, Inc. 138n
law and economics 7, 19–20, 30, 51
Leclerc v. Commission 409
legislative and executive institutions 468–9,
    492, 485–8, 501n
Lewis v. Fletcher 138n
licensing
    see patents and licensing contracts
Lincoln Electric case 228–9
Locke v. Warner Bros. 138n
long-term cooperation agreements 4,
    17–18, 61, 63, 68–9
loss avoidance principle 304–5, 311

make-or-buy decision 49, 180, 185, 287–8,
    445–6, 453, 459, 460
managerial discretion framework 259–61
market
    economies 3, 20–1
    failure 417
    mechanism 520–1
    power: auction rules 479, 497n–498n; in
        electricity sector 465, 473, 475; in
        generation 478–80; local 518–20, 526;
        problems 517–8, 527; tight supplies
        522–4
    see also networks congestion, regulatory
        policy
Mattei v. Hoper case 126–33, 138n
measurement costs 60–1
modularization
    in data networks 370–1, 372
    governance structures 367–8, 370, 371
    in voice networks 367–70
moral hazard 8–10, 21, 31–2, 130, ch 17
multiprincipals 173–4

natural gas contracts 280–1, 285, 286
natural monopolies 416–17
    competition 421, 426, 430
    and transactions cost economics 503–4,
        526–8

neoclassicism 75, 78, 79
neoinstitutional environment 73
    contractual processes 76–8
    economic efficiency 88–92
    profit-seeking 74–5, 77
    theory 359–60, 365–71
net present value 244
networks 365, 358, 508, 513
    congestion 520–2, 526–7
    economics 359–65
    evolution 366–7
    technical and institutional change 359,
        367–8
New Institutional Economics 22, 45–8, 49,
    72–3, 141
non-active and passive competition clauses
    397–8
non-franchised systems 330–2
norms 180, 182–5, 191, 469, 481
nuclear generation 511, 515
null contract 353–7

oil and gas, property rights 141–2
Omni Group Inc. v. *Seattle First National*
    Bank 127
one-shot interaction experiment 295,
    299–305, 311
opportunism 71n, 405
    in electricity sector 464, 466–7, 469–72
    in retailing 337, 342, 347, 349, 350, 351
    of suppliers 505–6, 517
optimization 74, 77, 79, 91, 92–4
option value 244–5, 248, 249, 250
organization 5, 73
    market flexibility 249–50
    structure of electricity sector 464,
        474–8, 493
organizational architecture and positive
    agency theory 257–8, 260, 262, 267

Pain Avoidance Model 255, 261, 267
participation constraints 205, 208, 209,
    211n
    and wealth constraints 205–9
patents and licensing contracts 373–9,
    383, 390–1, 396, 470
payment
    delays 337–8, 347, 349, 352, 354
    period 337–8, 339, 341–3, 347, 351,
        355
peering agreements of internet providers
    359, 364, 371, 372
performance
    in electricity sector 512, 510–12,
        515–517
    evaluation 218–9, 229–34, 236, 238

political and social institutions 467–72, 480–1, 485–6, 492, 494, 496n, 500
positive agency theory 16, 251, 253, 256, 264
  and principal–agent theory 251, 256, 261, 262, 265, 269, 270n
  property rights 256–7
  social norms 253–5
  unit of analysis 262–3
price cap 422–8, 432–4, 437, 468, 481
price discrepancy 346–8, 349
pricing structure 285–7, 291n
principal–agent contracts 216–18, 231–4
  model 293, 294–9, 303, 311, 418, 420, 421, 423;
  residual claimancy rights 317, 332
  self-enforcement 59–60, 64, 70n
  sharing arrangements 319–20, 326
  see also positive agency theory
principle of independence 340, 395–6
private sector interest 463, 472
privatization
  electricity supply 472–3
  utilities 419, 420, 430
property rights 7, 10, 18, 22, 35–7, 57, 74, 140, 141, 185, 508
  definition 142, 143, 154–5
  in economic decision-making 140–4, 154–5
  enforcement costs 141, 145
  importance of 140, 142
  measurement problems 141, 144, 146–8
  network operators 359, 366, 367–8
  regulatory procedures 466, 470, 481
  resource use 140, 141, 143
  and transactions costs 83–8, 141, 144
  in transitional economies 140–1
  see also positive agency theory
PSI Energy v. Exxon Coal 291
public policy 16, 49, 51, 57–8
public utilities
  governance structure 440–1, 446, 447
  and transactions cost economics 447–8, 452–6, 457–60

quality assurance 341, 363–4

real-time metering and control 523, 528, 529n, 530n
reciprocity principle, in positive agency theory 295, 308, 312
regulation
  of contract process 119–23
  in electricity sector 464
  role of state 116–18, 124

regulatory
  governance 464, 467–72, 478–9, 493
  incentives 464, 472
  policy 479–82–94
relational contracts 235–6, 238, 239n
renegotiation game 196–7, 198
rent–efficiency trade-off 162–4, 169, 170, 172, 176
repeated interaction experiment 295, 305–10, 312
resource allocation
  in electricity sector 514, 527
Resource Management Company v. Weston Ranch and Livestock Company, Inc. 138n
Resourceful, Evaluative, Maximising Model (REMM) 253–5, 261, 267
revelation game 196, 198, 217
Revelation Principle 159, 160, 162–3, 164–8, 177, 178n, 239n
Rodriguez v. Barnett 138n
royalties 374–6, 381–2, 391n
RPI–X 423–4, 425, 438
  see also price cap

sales contract 246–9
sales price determination
  see inter-brand competition
Savage rationality 8, 10, 24, 25
self-enforcement 59–60, 62–4, 156n, 235–6, 339, 340
  complementarity 316, 323–5, 332, 336n
  contract terms 327–30
  in franchise contracts 315, 317, 320–3, 325
  in incomplete contracts 64–70
  non-franchised systems 330–2
  ongoing rent 317, 321
service regulation 419–20
side payments 144–5, 147–8, 151, 155
Siegel et al. v. Chicken Delight, Inc. 335n
simple contracts 38–9, 195–201
Skycom Corporation v. Telstar Corporation 139n
Smith v. Wheeler 138n
social utility
  aim of contract 106–11, 113–14
Southern California Edison v. Lynch 501n
Spanish Retailing Act (1966) 356n
Spanish Unfair Competition Act (1999) 356n
specialized process design
  engineering and construction firms (SEFs) 382, 388
  and technology licensing 383–7
spot auction markets 514, 518–19

state-contingent contracts 225–8, 230
state intervention, and property rights 23,
    51, 143
subsidies 468, 491, 493
sunk investment
    in electricity sector 465–6, 494n, 505–6,
        517, 526–7
supplier discounts 344–6, 355
surplus sharing 293–4, 302, 305
symmetric interconnection 363–5
System Marginal Price (SMP) 480

Taxation Principle 166
technology 18, 267–8
technology licensing 374–6
technology market 373, 380–1
technology-sharing agreements 377–8
technology-sharing cartels 379–80
technology transfer agreements 396–7
thefts of service 510, 516–17
trade 101–2, 142, 143
transaction 53–4, 73
transaction-cost economics (TCE) 72–4,
    76–80, 82, 165, 187
    contract duration 278–9
    contraction design 283–5
    incentives 285–6
transactions cost
    and contractual externalities 169–76
    and incentive theory ch. 10
    role of patents 376–8
transactions-cost theory (TCT) 3, 8,
    12–16, 20, 24–6, 29, 39–41, 49, 53–4,
    56–7, 251, 253–4, 259–66, 269,
    366–7
    agency costs 263–4
transactor's reputational capital 62–5,
    66–7, 68

unitization contracts 141, 143
    negotiations 149–54
    oil reservoirs 144–52, 155, 156n
Universal Service Obligation 435
utilities 491–3
    economies of scale 465–6, 476–7
    industry structure 430–2, 465
    pricing 465–8, 471, 480
    specific sunk investments 465–6
    widespread domestic consumption
        465–6

Utilities Act (2000) 436, 437, 482, 499n
utilities regulation
    in electricity sector 509–10, 527
    by government 465, 469, 480
    incentives 418–9, 420–1, 423, 426–9,
        437
    information problems 417, 421, 422,
        427, 430–7, 439n
    need for 420–1
    time-inconsistency 426–9

vertical contracts 404
    brand protection 405–6, 415n
    efficiency 404–7
    market share 411–13, 414n
    validation conditions 408–13
vertical integration 26, 51, 68–9, 70, 71n,
    170–2, 287–8, 361, 503, 505
    in electricity sector 464, 472–5, 508–9,
        526, 528n
    and franchising 322, 330
    and regulation 431–2, 434, 439n
vertical separation 503
    competition benefits 503–4
    congestion 521, 525
    costs 503–4
vocabulary of contract 117, 121

Wakefield v. *Telecom* 229, 239n
Walliser, B. 13
Walrasian market theory 3
    and ICT 10, 20
    problems 3–4, 8, 14–15
water quality standards 441, 445, 449,
    451, 453, 456, 457, 459
water sector (France) 441, 446
    delegated management 442–4, 453, 457,
        459
    direct management 42–4, 447–8, 453,
        457, 459, 460, 461
    franchising 442, 444, 445, 448, 453
    intermediary management 442–4, 453,
        456
    investment in supply 448–50, 453, 460
    privatization 443–4
wealth and bargaining power 194–5
    see also control allocation
welfare maximization 431–3, 435–7
    Ramsey–Boiteux pricing 417–8, 422
    RPI-X 424, 427–8